NORTH *by*

𝔖𝔥𝔞𝔨𝔢𝔰𝔭𝔢𝔞𝔯𝔢

ALSO BY MICHAEL BLANDING

The Map Thief: The Gripping Story of an Esteemed Rare-Map Dealer
Who Made Millions Stealing Priceless Maps

The Coke Machine: The Dirty Truth Behind the World's Favorite Soft Drink

NORTH *by*
Shakespeare

A Rogue Scholar's Quest for the Truth Behind the Bard's Work

MICHAEL BLANDING

BOOKS

NEW YORK

Hachette Books
Hachette Book Group
1290 Avenue of the Americas
New York, NY 10104
HachetteBooks.com
Twitter.com/HachetteBooks
Instagram.com/HachetteBooks

First Edition: March 2021

Published by Hachette Books, an imprint of Perseus Books, LLC, a subsidiary of Hachette Book Group, Inc. The Hachette Books name and logo is a trademark of the Hachette Book Group.

The Hachette Speakers Bureau provides a wide range of authors for speaking events.

To find out more, go to www.hachettespeakersbureau.com or call (866) 376-6591.

The publisher is not responsible for websites (or their content) that are not owned by the publisher.

Image Credits: Maps by Bier en Brood. *The Dial of Princes* photographs of signature and marginalia by Michael Blanding, reproduced by permission of Cambridge University Library. © Cambridge University Library. Photograph of Sir Thomas North's journal by Michael Blanding, courtesy of the British Library, London, UK © The British Library Board. Photograph of Dennis McCarthy by Cody O'Loughlin. Woodcut of *Arden of Faversham*, Private Collection/Bridgeman Images. Portrait of Edward 1st Baron North, courtesy of P. Pattenden/ The Master and Fellows of Peterhouse. Portrait of Roger 2nd Baron North, Private Collection, Photograph © Christie's Images/Bridgeman Images. Illustration of Kirtling Hall, courtesy of the British Library, London, UK © British Library Board, All Rights Reserved/Bridgeman Images. Photograph of Sir Thomas North's journal, describing his visit to Mantua, by Michael Blanding, courtesy of Lambeth Palace Library. Photographs of wax statues at Santuario Beata Vergine Maria delle Grazie, Curtatone, Italy, by Michael Blanding. Photographs of Giulio Romano, *Noble Banquet / Rustic Banquet,* Chamber of Cupid and Psyche, Palazzo Te, courtesy of Scala/Art Resource, NY. Portrait of Queen Elizabeth I, courtesy of the National Gallery, London, UK, Photo © Photo Josse/Bridgeman Images. Portrait of Robert Dudley, Earl of Leicester, courtesy of National Portrait Gallery, London, UK; Photo © Stefano Baldini/Bridgeman Images. Photograph of June Schlueter by Michael Blanding. Portrait of William Shakespeare, courtesy of National Portrait Gallery, London, UK/ Bridgeman Images. "The Ass Talks to the Mule" by Michael Blanding, courtesy of The Bodleian Library, University of Oxford. Portrait of Hercule-François Valois, Duke of Alençon, courtesy of Samuel H. Kress Collection, National Gallery of Art, USA. Portrait of Thomas Radcliffe, Earl of Sussex, courtesy of Anglesey Abbey, Cambridgeshire, UK, National Trust Photographic Library/Bridgeman Images. Illustration of Kenilworth Castle, courtesy of Kenilworth Castle, Warwickshire, UK © Historic England/Bridgeman Images. Photograph of Kenilworth Castle by Michael Blanding.

Print book interior design by Sean Ford.

Library of Congress Cataloging-in-Publication Data has been applied for.

ISBNs: 978-0-316-49324-6 (hardcover), 978-0-316-49328-4 (ebook)

Printed in the United States of America

LSC-C

Printing 1, 2021

To Rebecca, whom I cherish

CONTENTS

Contents

PROLOGUE

I t was the greatest party of Elizabeth's reign—nineteen days of gut-busting feasts, minstrel performances, bear-baiting, Italian acrobats, and jaw-dropping fireworks. All of it was designed for a single purpose: to woo a queen. When Robert Dudley, the Earl of Leicester, planned the festivities at his estate of Kenilworth Castle in July 1575, he was getting desperate. After fifteen years of vying for Queen Elizabeth's hand, he was no closer to a promise of marriage than when he'd begun.

The Kenilworth festival was his last-ditch attempt at winning the queen's affections, and Leicester spared no expense to impress her, spending lavishly on new gardens, gifts, and performances. As the party raged, nobles and gentry from across the realm—as well as commoners from the countryside—guzzled forty barrels of beer and sixteen barrels of wine a day as they pursued wanton encounters in the surrounding woods and fields. Leicester kept his eyes on the queen, anxiously watching for signs that she was enjoying the elaborate masques and other entertainments he had dreamed up in her honor.

On several nights, Leicester unleashed firework displays created by an Italian pyrotechnician over a man-made lake that lapped against the western wall of the castle. The spectacles lasted for hours, including dazzling dragons, fighting dogs and cats, and rockets that seemed to shoot out of the water itself. A contemporary observer described them as a "blaze of burning darts, flying to and fro, leams of stars coruscant, streams and hail of fiery sparks" of such intensity "that the heavens thundered, the waters surged, the earth shook."

Another night, the earl staged a giant water pageant as Elizabeth was making her way across a long bridge over the lake. An actor dressed as

I

the sea-god Triton rode across the water to her on a mechanical mermaid. Sounding a trumpet in the shape of a whelk, he commanded the seas to still, shouting: "You waters wild, suppress your waves and keep you calm and plain!" After his speech, another actor dressed as the fabled Greek musician Arion serenaded her from atop a twenty-four-foot-long mechanical dolphin. Music emanated eerily from the dolphin's belly, where an ensemble of musicians had been secreted inside.

There's no record of how the queen received the performance—whether she stood stony-faced, or smiled and clapped with joy, or felt a rise of love in her heart for the man who had gone to such extravagant lengths to please her. But the moment has been immortalized, after a fashion, in William Shakespeare's most beloved play, *A Midsummer Night's Dream*. In one scene, Oberon, King of the Fairies, reminisces to his underling Puck while in a jealous fit over the Fairy Queen Titania. "Thou rememb'rest since once I sat upon a promontory, and heard a mermaid on a dolphin's back uttering such dulcet and harmonious breath that the rude sea grew civil at her song, and certain stars shot madly from their spheres to hear the sea-maid's music?" he says to Puck. "That very time I saw, but thou couldst not, flying between the cold moon and the earth Cupid, all armed. A certain aim he took at a fair vestal thronèd by the west, and loosed his love shaft smartly from his bow as it should pierce a hundred thousand hearts."

For more than a century, those lines have been read as an allusion to Leicester, who shot a love arrow at his own vestal—England's famous "Virgin Queen" Elizabeth—at a pageant complete with dolphin, mermaid, and fireworks. It's less clear how Shakespeare, then a boy eleven years old, could have witnessed the spectacle; or why he would have included it in a play written around 1595, some twenty years after the event. In his book *Will in the World*, Harvard professor Stephen Greenblatt allows that "it is certainly conceivable" that Shakespeare's father may have taken him from their home in Stratford-upon-Avon, fourteen miles away, to see the display. If so, then perhaps Shakespeare stood with his father upon a promontory overlooking the lake to catch a glimpse of the entertainments, and perhaps the sight made such an impression on him that he remembered it for the next two decades, and perhaps he found a moment to work it into a play performed before the queen to remind her of her youthful wooing by her favorite courtier.

Those are a lot of "perhapses." It's not the only explanation, however, for how the Kenilworth water pageant could have inspired Shakespeare's comedy. The playwright could have heard a report from someone who attended, or read about it in a letter circulated after the event. Or there is another possibility: perhaps, another person wrote those lines—someone who attended the event as a guest and witnessed the pageant firsthand.

I FIRST HEARD the name Thomas North in October 2015. I had been invited to Lafayette College in Easton, Pennsylvania, to give a lecture about a book I'd written about a thief of rare maps. The weather was unseasonably warm, and the foliage was in full array, with a spectacular red maple lighting up the picture window of the library lecture hall. Afterward, the lecture's sponsors, English professor emerita June Schlueter and her husband, Paul, a literature scholar, took me to a dinner reception. Over a pasta buffet they introduced me to a scholar named Dennis McCarthy, a confident fifty-three-year-old who looked a decade younger than his age. McCarthy had attended my lecture with his adult daughter, Nicole Galovski, and only later did I learn that the two positioned themselves around the last remaining seats so that I would sit next to one of them.

McCarthy immediately pulled me into conversation, asking me about my book and telling me about his own research. "I bet you are the only other person here who knows where the words 'Hic Sunt Dracones' come from," he said. Of course, I replied—they're on the Hunt-Lenox Globe at the New York Public Library. Translated "Here Be Dragons," they are the words cartographers supposedly used to designate uncharted territory— but McCarthy had a different theory, speculating the words marked the location of giant lizards known as Komodo dragons. *Here Be Dragons* was also the name of his book on biogeography, he told me, and before long, we were spiritedly discussing maps and geography.

As the reception wound down, he invited me to continue talking over drinks with his daughter and her fiancé. It took me a half a second to decide. I was alone on a Thursday night in a small college town, and the thought of going back to my B&B was infinitely less appealing. I figured I could have a few drinks and continue an enjoyable conversation. I had no idea how this chance meeting would start me down a path to trace a literary mystery that I'd follow, along with McCarthy, for the next five years.

We headed to the College Hill Tavern, a bar with old sports memorabilia framed on the walls (GO LEOPARDS!) and students and locals drinking liquor from plastic cups. We sat at a chipped wooden high-top, straining to hear each other over the impromptu karaoke of nearby patrons. I don't know whose idea it was to order martinis, but amid conversation of maps and Galovski's impending wedding in the Azores, I was a bit foggy by the time McCarthy finally leaned across the table and told me he had a story for me.

"You know how Shakespeare used other sources to write his plays?" McCarthy asked over the din of amateur Bon Jovi. "Sure," I replied, trying to remember anything about Shakespeare's sources from my first-year college class. "Well, I found a source no one ever knew about before," he said. This unknown manuscript, he continued, was a treatise by a sixteenth-century courtier named George North. The work, he claimed, influenced some of Shakespeare's greatest plays, including *Richard III*, *Macbeth*, and *King Lear*.

But Shakespeare never even read the manuscript, McCarthy continued, as I struggled to follow his argument through a haze of classic rock and booze. Instead, George's relative, Sir Thomas North, had used it to write his own plays. Oh, he is one of *those*, I thought to myself—a conspiracy theorist who thought Shakespeare didn't write Shakespeare. But McCarthy hurriedly added that in fact he believed the Bard of Avon wrote every word attributed to him during his lifetime. He also believed, however, that Shakespeare had used these earlier plays by Thomas North for his ideas, his language, and even some of his most famous soliloquies. There was something about a murder involving North's sister, and an affair Queen Elizabeth may or may not have had with North's patron, the Earl of Leicester, and a tale of familial exile uncannily like Prospero's story in *The Tempest*.

I didn't believe any of it. Where are North's plays now? I asked. "Lost," McCarthy said—but so were most manuscripts written in the Elizabethan era. Why hadn't anyone discovered this before? "Because no one had the right tools to do so," he said, arguing excitedly that his computer-assisted techniques had the potential to finally solve the mystery of how— and why—Shakespeare's plays were written. I vaguely knew about the conspiracy theories that Shakespeare was a fraud, and the plays were really written by the Earl of Oxford or someone else. But this was something different. McCarthy's theory was more akin to saying Shakespeare plagiarized or collaborated with another writer. The theory seemed outlandish, but I liked McCarthy, and was somewhat amused by the lengths to which he'd gone to pitch me. I promised to look at whatever he sent me.

IN MORE THAN two decades as an investigative reporter, I've learned not to dismiss any story out of hand. Years ago, as a writer at *Boston Magazine*, I'd been contacted by a sixty-five-year-old man incarcerated for allegedly setting fire to his own store. The arson investigation turned out to be junk science, and he was freed after more than four years in prison. Soon after I wrote my article, the prosecution dropped attempts to retry him. More recently, I wrote an article for *The New York Times* about a rare copy of the first map to name America, which was expected to sell at Christie's auction house for $1 million. A map dealer came to me claiming it was fake, printed in the twentieth century on four-hundred-year-old paper. The giveaway was a spot where the map had been printed *over* the centuries-old glue that had bound the paper into a book. I contacted Christie's, which pulled the map from auction before my article even hit the newsstand.

So I wasn't opposed to considering McCarthy's theories—though I wasn't inclined to believe them, either. When I finally dug into the document he sent me six months later, I was surprised to find a persuasive amount of evidence pointing to the use of the manuscript as a source for nearly a dozen of Shakespeare's plays. I was intrigued enough to order McCarthy's self-published book about Thomas North, titled *North of Shakespeare*, and meet with him again—this time at a table by the water in Newburyport, Massachusetts. I listened as he spelled out his theories in a torrent of words, as if he couldn't get them all out fast enough.

McCarthy wasn't a trained academic scholar himself, he admitted; in fact, he hadn't even graduated from college. Yet, by that point he'd devoted more than a decade to his research on Shakespeare. Most of it was done at home through scouring the Internet and using open-source plagiarism software to compare the text of Shakespeare's plays with the works of Thomas North—an Elizabethan writer who'd translated *Plutarch's Lives*, a book well-known as the source for Shakespeare's Roman plays. But McCarthy saw something more in him—over an exceptional fifty-year literary career, he claimed, North had written dozens of plays, which Shakespeare had reworked to create the greatest canon of works in English literature. Many of them, he said, were written on behalf of his patron, the Earl of Leicester, as part of his never-ending quest to woo Queen Elizabeth.

Despite a decade of trying, however, McCarthy had only gotten one Shakespearean scholar to believe him—June Schlueter, my own patron for the Lafayette lecture. Interested enough, I told him that I would consider writing about him on two conditions—one, that he publish his research with a reputable publisher; and, two, that he get at least two more scholars to take his ideas seriously. Over the next three years, he met both those conditions. In 2018, he and Schlueter published the George North manuscript with the British Library as *A Brief Discourse of Rebellion and Rebels*, showing how Shakespeare borrowed from it, and winning endorsements from two prominent scholars. I wrote about that book for *The New York Times* in February 2018 under the headline: "Plagiarism Software Unveils a New Source for 11 of Shakespeare's Plays."

Both my article and McCarthy's book were well-received—though mostly by people sniggering about the fact that Shakespeare was a plagiarist. But this was only a small part of the story. McCarthy had yet to reveal his larger theory—that while Shakespeare used George North as a source for some of his plays, he relied on Thomas North as a source for nearly *all* of his works, and that he wasn't using prose works, but plays. As unorthodox as McCarthy's ideas were, I thought that they at least deserved an airing.

Then again, orthodox ideas become orthodox for a reason—they've been analyzed, challenged, and defended by generations of scholars and stood the test of time. A whole industry has been built around Shakespeare scholarship, with thousands of books, articles, classes, and professors all arguing on behalf of the authorship of the plays by William of Stratford-upon-Avon. What kind of new evidence would it take for a scholar who has built a career around *that* Shakespeare to consider an alternative point of view? And how would they treat the person who espouses it? As I watched McCarthy struggle to get anyone in the Shakespeare community to listen to him, I started conceiving of another project, a book that would investigate and test his theories, but also examine how knowledge gets created, and what it takes to change established ways of thinking.

WE MAY WANT to believe in the idea of Shakespeare as a solitary genius—the Bard of Avon, the Soul of the Age. While even mainstream scholars now believe he had at least some help in writing many of his plays, they've held fast to the belief that the bulk of the language and inspiration behind them was Shakespeare's and Shakespeare's alone. Yet for centuries, mysteries about William Shakespeare have gone unexplained, such as how a glover's son from Stratford could have had the intimate knowledge of Italy—a country he almost certainly never visited—or how he could have absorbed the experience of going to war, or used complex legal jargon, or read source material in French, Italian, Latin, and Greek.

Some of the reasons proposed to explain those mysteries are just as unsatisfying, relying on secret conspiracies in which an aristocrat such as the Earl of Oxford or Sir Francis Bacon actually wrote the plays, which Shakespeare then passed off under his own name. Besides the elitism implied by the idea that only a nobleman could have written such sublime works, such theories suffer from the obvious question of how, in the competitive world of Elizabethan theater, such a secret could have been held for so long. McCarthy's contention, that Shakespeare borrowed his material from Thomas North—a gentleman and scholar who moved in the uppermost levels of Queen Elizabeth's court—provides an intriguing and wholly original solution, in which the playwright could have legitimately put his own name on his rewritten plays, at the same time borrowing their essence from someone who fit all of the requirements for writing them. In addition to being a translator, North was a lawyer, soldier, diplomat, and courtier—a sixteenth-century Zelig who participated in some of the most crucial events of the age, and brushed shoulders with the brightest minds of the Renaissance. Understanding his inspirations and motivations, McCarthy contends, reveals hidden meanings and unfolds new depths of emotion in the familiar stories of Shakespeare's dramas. He even, I would come to find, developed an explanation for why Thomas North might have sold his plays to Shakespeare to adapt for the public stage. Over the next two years, I continued my conversation with McCarthy begun in that Pennsylvania bar. We traveled together through England, France, and Italy to retrace Thomas North's footsteps. Along the way, I began conducting my own research in overseas archives, teaching myself English secretary hand script to read old documents in an effort to prove or disprove McCarthy's audacious theories. As I considered how and why Thomas North might have written the plays that he did, I began to glimpse a new story that could answer age-old questions about Shakespeare and his works—if it could be believed.

Chapter One
THIS BLOOD CONDEMNS

(1551)

The more I sound his name the more he bleeds.
This blood condemns me, and in gushing forth
Speaks as it falls and asks me why I did it.
— *Arden of Faversham*

ennis McCarthy steps out of a car on a chilly November morning into the streets of a village in southeastern England. "We're in Faversham!" he says wonderingly, as if he can't quite believe it. He'd been reading about this town for the better part of a decade, focusing on a brutal incident that happened here more than 450 years ago—and yet he'd never been here before now. "Are you here about the murder?" a middle-aged woman with glasses asks, noticing us staring at a house across the street.

"Do you know about the murder?" McCarthy turns the question around, and she replies as if the killing happened last week, rather than in February 1551. "Oh yes, the blood was red and thick, and the snow was white as they dragged the body through the field." We're standing now outside of the scene of the crime—a white Tudor cottage with dark half-timber framing, filled in with white daub-and-wattle. Once, the home was attached to the gatehouse of the mighty Faversham Abbey. While that structure was already gone by the time of the murder, Abbey Street is still arguably the best-preserved medieval street in Britain, with England's oldest brewery at one end, and Arden's House, named after the town's most notorious former resident, at the other.

It was a messy killing. Thomas Arden, Faversham's one-time mayor, was sitting down to play at tables—a game similar to backgammon—with a tailor by the name of Thomas Mosby. The contest was fraught, since Arden was well aware that Mosby was having an affair with his wife. As they played, Mosby made a move and said, "Now, I may take you." At that signal, a man named "Black Will" suddenly burst out of a closet behind Arden and attempted to strangle him with a towel. When Arden failed to succumb, Mosby struck him on the side of the head with a fourteen-pound pressing iron, knocking him out.

Even that wasn't enough to do Arden in, however. As the murderers dragged him into a small office off the parlor, he began to groan again, and Black Will slashed him across the face with a dagger. Finally, he came out to tell Arden's wife, Alice, that the deed had been done. She rushed into the room with her own knife, furiously stabbing her husband seven or eight times in the chest as his blood gushed onto the floor.

The crime was an instant scandal. Not only had a woman risen up against her own husband, but Alice and Mosby had enlisted a crew of other townspeople, including Arden's own servants, in the killing. The betrayal was so great that twenty-five years later *Holinshed's Chronicles*, the definitive history of England, took a break from recounting the exploits of kings, queens, and nobles to detail the household crime for five full pages. Another fifteen years later, in 1592, the murder was immortalized in an anonymous play titled *The Lamentable and True Tragedie of M. Arden of Feversham in Kent*.

Commonly known as *Arden of Faversham*, the play is an early Elizabethan masterpiece, which kicked off a new genre of "domestic tragedy" concerned with workaday calamities rather than royal misfortunes. The author of that play, however, has always remained a mystery, with some scholars arguing fiercely for Thomas Kyd, author of later revenge tragedies, and others championing Christopher Marlowe, who grew up in nearby Canterbury. For the past half-century, however, many have increasingly believed it to be the first published play by the world's greatest dramatist: William Shakespeare.

It's that theory that's brought us here on this blustery day in 2018. Not only does McCarthy think that Shakespeare wrote the 1592 play, but he also believes it holds the key to a deeper secret about Shakespeare's works. Among Alice's relatives who would have been devastated by the crime was her fifteen-year-old half brother, Thomas North. He would later go on to become a translator and was famous in his lifetime for his translation of *Plutarch's Lives*, the Greek philosopher Plutarch's book of biographies and undoubted source for Shakespeare's *Julius Caesar* and *Antony and Cleopatra*. But McCarthy believes Shakespeare's debt to North is far greater—the translator, he contends, wrote a play about his own family's tragedy decades earlier, which Shakespeare later used to write his own play.

I FOLLOW MCCARTHY around the front of Arden's House, where a single red rose hangs off a trellis. He is sporting a white button-up shirt with the collar open and an olive-colored wool coat. At fifty-six years old, he has a square jaw and full head of dark hair, only slightly thinning in the corners. On his face is an almost permanent smirk, as if he is about to disprove, or at least question, anything at any moment.

Behind McCarthy follows his daughter, Nicole Galovski, a lanky thirty-two-year-old with blond corkscrew curls. A documentary filmmaker whose work has aired on Showtime, HBO, and Netflix, she is dressed the part in a black windbreaker and skinny jeans. With her is Bahareh Hosseini, a diminutive Iranian filmmaker carrying a heavy camera on her shoulder. For the past several years, Galovski and a rotating roster of camerapersons have been following her father around on his quixotic quest to prove Thomas North is the key to understanding Shakespeare's canon.

Even though the current tenants know we are coming, they don't know we're bringing a film crew. McCarthy seems anxious. "I'll just ask if they mind us filming them," he says. "No, Dad," Galovski breaks in, exasperated. "Don't ask them—let me handle it." Around the back of the house is a slick patio leading to an ancient-looking door with an iron knocker. McCarthy knocks, and the door opens to a cheerful woman in a fuchsia athletic top, who introduces herself as Irene Redman. "I'm just off to Pilates at the moment," she says, passing us off to her husband, Chris, a financial analyst whose white shirt bulges beneath a red tie and suspenders. "Do you mind if I film?" Galovski asks casually, as the camera rolls.

"No, no, that's all right," Redman says gamely as he invites us in. "Well, what I can do is show you around, and just sort of talk through the—" he pauses "—Arden story," saying the words as if not quite sure how to refer to the event. The house is divided into two parts, he explains, showing us a low-ceilinged kitchen with worm-eaten beams and exposed stone walls that were originally part of the abbey's gatehouse. The other part, he says, was built by Thomas Arden himself. There, the ceilings are higher and the walls covered in white plaster, some of which is original to the building. "After the Arden thing, this house fell into disrepair gradually," Redman says, leading into a foyer with a dining table and PlayStation controllers and soccer balls strewn around the floor. "In the 1950s, this whole street was going to be knocked down because it was a complete slum—and this was a brothel." Instead, local residents put together a plan to save the street, restoring the homes to their former Tudor glory.

To the left is an office with an Oriental rug and computer desk. "Is this where the murder took place?" McCarthy asks finally. "Well, I thought you were going to get round to that," Redman says with a laugh. Historians aren't exactly sure which room was the parlor where Arden and Mosby sat playing that night, he explains. But "people generally accept that it was probably this room," says Redman, motioning toward the office. We all gaze silently into it for a moment, imagining the violent events of nearly five centuries ago.

THE ERSTWHILE MAYOR lay on the floor, according to Holinshed's account, as Alice paid Black Will £10 ($6,300 in today's money) and he fled the scene. The remaining conspirators wiped up the blood, then threw the cloth and Alice's knife into a tub by the well. In those times, homeowners spread straw on the floor of their homes, and now the murderers carefully arranged the straw disturbed by the struggle back into place. Alice then bid her servants call two guests from London, along with Mosby's sister, and the five of them ate and drank while Alice played the innocent, wondering where her husband had gone. After their meal, Alice's twelve-year-old daughter played the virginals (a harpsichord-like instrument) while Alice danced with her guests and outside it started to snow. When they had gone, Alice sprang into action, enlisting Mosby and his sister—and even her own daughter—to drag Arden's stiffening body through the garden gate and into the meadow where the abbey once stood.

"His body would have been dragged this way," Redman says, leading us out into his backyard. We cross the lawn to a timeworn gate in a low stone wall, as a church bell tolls in the distance. "The body is found somewhere around here," Redman says, leading us around the wall to a small paved courtyard. Seeing it firsthand drives home just how intimate the whole affair was, with the body lying just a few hundred feet from the back of the house.

Snow was still falling as the murderers left the body, but it soon stopped, and a search party led by the town's current mayor came across Arden's body in the field. In one of history's earliest uses of forensic science, the mayor noticed straw from the house sticking in Arden's slippers, along with the partially covered tracks leading back through the gate. In the search of the house, they found the bloody cloth and knife in the tub. Faced with this evidence, Holinshed says, Alice confessed, crying out, "Oh, the blood of God help, for this blood have I shed."

The search party then went to the local inn where Mosby was staying and found blood on his clothes, leading him to confess as well. The ring of conspirators kept widening, eventually including Mosby's sister; two servants, Michael and Elizabeth; and three townspeople, including one who had helped hire Black Will to commit the murder. There was a good reason so many people were involved in the plot against Arden, says Redman. "He was absolutely hated."

THE ROOTS OF that hatred lay in the abbey that was no longer there. At 360 feet long, the cruciform structure once dominated the town, with an attached cloister that housed a thriving community of monks. All of it came literally crashing down when the abbey was demolished in 1538 under orders of King Henry VIII. Faversham Abbey's demise wasn't an isolated incident, but part of a grand scheme known as the Dissolution of the Monasteries, a cataclysmic reordering of English society that affected thousands of lives. Local residents blamed the abbey land's owner, Arden, for the destruction, but he was only a cog in a great wheel of bureaucracy that rode over England. One of those who set that wheel in motion was Thomas North's father.

Edward North was a prosperous lawyer when he married Alice Arden's mother (also named Alice) around 1528. They had four more children, two boys and two girls—including Thomas, who was born in 1535. "So Alice is Thomas's half sister," says McCarthy, standing in front of Arden's House after our tour. "She's fourteen years older than him." The family lived in Kirtling Hall, Edward's expansive estate in Cambridgeshire, sixty miles north of London, where Thomas grew up sheltered in a house filled with books, games, and servants. "He's born into Tudor luxury," says McCarthy. "He has archery, falconry. It's likely the family had a fool."

Eventually, Edward rose to become a clerk of Parliament, where he helped draft the legislation allowing the crown to seize the monasteries. He hired Arden as his secretary and he soon became Edward's right-hand man, writing his letters and helping draft laws. North rewarded him with an arranged marriage to his stepdaughter in 1537, when Alice was just sixteen years old. Arden followed North to a new post as treasurer of the Court of Augmentations—a ministry charged with selling the newly seized church lands. With an inside track on sales, Arden started buying and selling monastery lands, collecting fees on either end. Eventually, he began buying up properties in the town of Faversham, a port town with wharves teeming with sailors unloading sacks full of onions, barrels of salt, and casks of eels from Holland and France. Arden became customs collector, overseeing proceeds from that trade and skimming a little off the top.

Soon Edward North rose to become chancellor of augmentations, overseeing all the former monastery properties. That same year, Arden was allowed to buy the charter for the abbey lands for £117 ($116,000 today), including cottages and tenements he rented out to his fellow townsmen. "Thomas's father Edward was the one who was in charge of distributing all of these lands to various Englishmen," says McCarthy, "and Thomas Arden, his *son-in-law*, was the one who got all this abbey land." The townspeople watched as Arden tore down the abbey's outer gate and converted the guesthouse into his private residence, a U-shaped house curving around a great hall. On the window in the parlor, Arden apparently placed the North coat of arms—a crouching lion surrounded by three fleurs-de-lis, symbolizing strength and purity—as an homage to the man who had started him on his path to wealth.

THE ARDEN HOUSEHOLD had a secret, however, that threatened to destroy everything Thomas Arden had built. His wife, Alice, had begun an affair with Thomas Mosby, a tailor in Edward North's household. The liaison possibly began as far back as 1537—the year Arden married Alice. At some point, according to the Faversham Wardmote book—a journal of town records that includes a short account of the murder—Arden became aware of the situation and "willfully did permit and suffer the same." Another account, written by historian John Stow, upon which Holinshed's account is based, says there was a good reason for this: Edward North was fond of Mosby, and Arden was afraid of damaging his relationship with his patron by accusing North's favored servant of the affair.

As Mosby rose to become North's steward, he often visited Faversham, where, the Wardmote Book says, he also had a house, and treated Alice to "delicate meats and sumptuous apparel" in full view of the town. The histories don't say why Alice cuckolded her husband so flagrantly. But given the portrait of greed and ambition that emerges from them, it's not hard to see why Alice might have soured on him. In a six-year period, two-thirds of the lodgings Arden owned turned over to new tenants, implying he was raising rents. As a member of the town council, Stow says, Arden moved the town's annual St. Valentine's Day fair onto the old abbey grounds, earning him the rent at the expense of the town, "for the which deed he had many a curse." In another case, Holinshed says he "wrested" a piece of land from a man named Greene, and the two had come to blows over the situation—possibly a case of evicting him from a tenancy-at-will on former abbey lands.

Arden continued to enrich himself after becoming mayor in 1548, bankrupting the town with exorbitant salaries for himself and other officials, even as he apparently failed to pay his own taxes. In December 1549, angry town councilors stripped Arden of his privileges as a freeman, humiliating the man who'd so recently been mayor. Arden was suddenly surrounded by enemies and far removed from his patron, Edward North.

All of that made Alice confident that if Arden should disappear, he was so "evil beloved," in Stow's colorful turn of phrase, "that no man would make inquiry after his death."

As THE PLAY *Arden of Faversham* opens, Arden has just received deeds to the abbey lands, but is too distraught to celebrate, telling a confidant, Franklin, he has discovered love letters passing between Mosby and his wife. The play diverges from the historical record, however, in one crucial aspect: Mosby is not the steward for Edward North, but is employed by a fictional nobleman named Lord Clifford—an important clue in McCarthy's analysis.

After Arden confronts Alice, she implores Mosby to murder her husband, and he reluctantly agrees. In the play, Mosby is particularly villainous, painted as an uncouth social climber. Arden, meanwhile, comes across as a penny-pinching miser. When a sailor named Reede implores him to return the lease on a plot of land, Arden all but laughs in his face. Reede curses him, saying, "That plot of ground which thou detains from me, I speak it in agony of spirit—be ruinous and fatal unto thee!" The jilted landowner Greene also joins Alice and Mosby in their plot, helping enlist two scoundrels, Black Will and Shakebag, to carry out the deed.

What follows can only be described as black comedy, as the murderers try repeatedly to kill Arden without success. After failing to kill him at St. Paul's Cathedral in London, they convince Michael to let them into Arden's London house at night, but he gets cold feet and keeps the doors locked. They try to kill him on the road back to Faversham, but another lord arrives to invite Arden and Franklin to dinner on his estate. They try to ambush him on the way back, but get lost in the fog and fall into a ditch. "When was I so long killing a man?" Black Will sputters to Shakebag and Greene.

The play is no mere farce, however. As Alice and Mosby become more frustrated with their inability to kill Arden, they begin quarreling with each other. Mosby considers killing Alice and taking the land for himself. Alice, too, is having doubts, wondering whether to kill her husband at all, saying, "It is not love that loves to murder love." In an explosive scene, Mosby accuses Alice of bewitching him, while Alice alleges he only loves her for her husband's money. Finally, they fall, exhausted, back into each other's arms, resolving with a kiss to see their bloody deed through. The scene succeeds in humanizing both Mosby and Alice, even as their tragic fate is sealed.

When Black Will finally bursts out to strangle Arden in his parlor, the moment is played for maximum effect, with Arden looking from Mosby to Michael to Alice, imploring them for help, before realizing that they are all in on the conspiracy. Mosby slams the iron into Arden's head, before Alice deals the killing blow with her knife. Just as in the histories, the tracks in the snow betray the murderers. The play adds a macabre touch, however; as Alice is brought to see her husband's body lying in the field, his blood gushes forth as if in accusation, causing her to tearfully confess. The drama ends with an epilogue spoken by Franklin, who notes that Arden's body was found on the very plot of land the sailor Reede said would be his ruin. For two more years, the bloody print of Arden's body could be seen on the ground, where no grass would grow.

ARDEN IS A landmark of theater, the first surviving example of a tragedy involving ordinary people—rather than noble or mythological figures, as had been the case since Greek times. After it was first published in 1592, the play spawned many similar "domestic tragedies," but it was still rare in so intimately dramatizing real-life historical events. That not only includes the Arden murder, but also the social upheaval brought on by the Dissolution of the Monasteries, through which land—and the power that came with it—was suddenly up for grabs by anyone with the money and connections to seize it.

Given that *Arden of Faversham* was groundbreaking in creating a new dramatic form, scholars have long sought to determine the identity of its author. On April 3, 1592, printer Edward White recorded an entry for "The tragedie of Arden of Feversham & blackwill" into the Stationers' Register, the official record of London's publishing guild. Surviving today in just three copies, the play appeared in a quarto edition—a small format, half the size of a more formal folio edition—with no playwright's name on the cover page. That's not especially unusual for the time, when more plays were published anonymously than not. In fact, many quarto editions of Shakespeare's plays omitted his name. It was only seven years after his death, with the publication of the First Folio, that many of them were attributed to Shakespeare for the first time—making it entirely possible that another anonymous Elizabethan play could also have been his work.

The first person to make that claim was Edward Jacobs, an eighteenth-century Faversham historian who noted how many lines in *Arden* were similar to those in Shakespeare. A line by Mosby, "these eyes, that showed my heart a raven for a dove," for instance, sounds a lot like a line in *A Midsummer Night's Dream*, "Who will not change a raven for a dove?" Modern commentators have called out similarities in character and plot as well, comparing Mosby and Alice, for example, to Macbeth and Lady Macbeth. Shakespeare isn't the only authorship candidate, however. The geographic specificity in the play—down to the names of specific pubs and inns in Faversham—seems to point to someone intimately familiar with Kent, such as native son Christopher Marlowe. Victorian poet Algernon Charles Swinburne confidently attributed the play to either Shakespeare or Marlowe "unless there was some dramatist," he wrote, "who could rise to a height equal to theirs."

The turn of the twentieth century saw a new claimant arise—Thomas Kyd, a scrivener's son who was one of the most celebrated playwrights of his time before falling into obscurity after his death. In 1919, Henry Dugdale Sykes pointed out stylistic similarities between *Arden* and Kyd's masterwork, *The Spanish Tragedy*, also published anonymously by Edward White in 1592. Some critics split the difference, supposing the play to be coauthored by some combination of Shakespeare, Marlowe, and Kyd. That also wouldn't be unusual for the time, when many plays were written by multiple hands. In fact, far from the image we have today of Shakespeare as a singular genius, some scholars argue that a number of his plays are at least partly collaborations with other authors.

By far the biggest champion of Shakespeare's authorship of *Arden* has been MacDonald "Mac" Jackson, a professor at the University of Auckland in New Zealand, who has argued on the Bard's behalf since his 1963 university dissertation. In 2006, Jackson honed in on the intense "quarrel scene" between Alice and Mosby, subjecting it to computer analysis to determine the similarity of turns of phrase with more than a hundred plays written by Shakespeare and his contemporaries to see how many of them shared two-, three-, or four-word phrases with *Arden's* quarrel scene.

Of the twenty-eight plays with at least four phrases in common, the top eight were Shakespeare's, with another ten Shakespeare plays coming in hot behind them. Only two plays a piece by Kyd and Marlowe made the list, each with only a paltry four phrases each. The connections to Shakespeare, Jackson noted excitedly, were "not only numerous but of superior quality, including vivid and complex figurative modes of speech."

Kyd's defenders disputed that analysis—led by Sir Brian Vickers, a venerable British Shakespeare scholar who has authored dozens of books on the Bard. In an essay in the *Times Literary Supplement* in 2008, Vickers introduced a new digital scholarship technique, using Pl@giarism, an open-source software more commonly used to identify plagiarism in student term papers. Vickers employed it to compare the entire text of *Arden of Faversham* with Kyd's *The Spanish Tragedy* and *Soliman and Perseda*, finding sixty-eight common phrases of at least three words, and concluding "*Arden of Faversham* can now be attributed to Kyd with a high degree of probability."

Jackson countered by showing that Vickers's own techniques actually led to more three-word phrases in common with Shakespeare's *Henry VI, Part 2* and *The Taming of the Shrew* than with any of Kyd's plays. In a 2014 book, Jackson expanded upon his earlier analysis, concluding that Shakespeare wrote at least six of the play's seventeen scenes. The battle raged for a decade, with partisans for Kyd and Shakespeare continuing to fire broadsides (while Marlowe fell by the board). Australians Jack Elliott and Brett Greatley-Hirsch recently provided the most comprehensive analysis in the 2017 *New Oxford Shakespeare Authorship Companion*, slicing the play into thirty-five overlapping segments and applying new computer tests that, if anything, reveal an even closer association with Shakespeare, to whom they attribute nearly all of the segments. If the play was a collaboration, they conclude, Shakespeare was "responsible for the lion's share." Based on the analysis, the *New Oxford Shakespeare* named Shakespeare as an author of the play for the first time—officially attributing it to "Anonymous and William Shakespeare."

MCCARTHY WADED INTO this debate in 2013 with his own support of the Shakespearean side. In a paper published in the journal *Notes & Queries*, he used Vickers's techniques, employing a plagiarism detection software called WCopyfind, to compare *Arden* with all thirty-eight plays in Shakespeare's canon. His analysis resulted in dozens of multiword phrases in common. In addition to "a raven for a dove" in *A Midsummer Night's Dream*, other examples include "Thou know'st that we too" from *Julius Caesar*, and "I know he loves me well; but . . ." from *Richard III*. By themselves, many of the phrases don't seem particularly rare; but McCarthy performed an additional check, searching for them in Early English Books Online (EEBO), a massive database with the complete texts of some 125,000 published works between 1473 and 1700. For many of the phrases, he found only a handful of other uses in Shakespeare's time, whereas some were completely unique to *Arden* and Shakespeare. His analysis lent additional support for William Shakespeare as at least one of the authors of the 1592 play. That conclusion, however, was only a step toward his more radical theory that Shakespeare based the tragedy on an earlier play written by someone with firsthand knowledge of the crime: Thomas North.

"So I have WCopyfind right here on my desktop," McCarthy says to me on a Sunday afternoon a week before our trip to Faversham, sitting at the dining room table of his home, a neocolonial that backs up to a salt marsh on the New Hampshire coast. Three computer monitors stand amid a morass of open books, photocopies, and bric-a-brac as I nervously place my coffee cup on a sloping pile of books to one side. McCarthy fiddles with some settings in a busy dialogue box on the middle monitor. "I ignore punctuation, ignore numbers . . ." he says to himself as he checks and unchecks boxes. Finally, he settles on searching for strings of up to seven words, only allowing two imperfections—meaning at least five out of seven words in a row have to match. Then he pushes a button onscreen, and two columns of parallel texts open up on the right-hand monitor. On one side is *Arden of Faversham*; on the other, Thomas North's first work, *The Dial of Princes*, a sort of instruction manual for monarchs originally by Spanish Bishop Antonio de Guevara. North had translated and published it in 1557, just six years after Thomas Arden's murder.

Words common to both light up in red type. "These are all of the matches," McCarthy says, pointing to the sea of red words filling up the screen. "These are the lines in North, and these are the lines in *Arden of Faversham*." Most of them are familiar expressions or motivated by common circumstances, such as "he went to the house"—but not all. "Some of them really stand out," McCarthy says. One glaring example is *Arden's* subtitle, which reads, in part: "Wherein is showed the great malice and dissimulation of a wicked woman." He shows me that North's *Dial* has a chapter with the subtitle "Wherein is expressed the great malice and little patience of an evil woman"—a similar idea conveyed with a difference of only four words in thirteen. "It's impossible that that's a coincidence," McCarthy says, noting that no other work in EEBO has anything close. "And both are speaking about an evil woman," McCarthy emphasizes.

In all, McCarthy found more than two hundred phrases of four words or more shared by *Arden* and North, along with more than a thousand three-word phrases, swamping the number for Shakespeare or Kyd. Some of them are particularly compelling. One passage in *The Dial* about courtiers who "flatter" their way into the homes of "noblemen," for example, contains the phrases "jetting in his velvets and silks" and "the steward of the house." In a similar passage in the play, Arden complains that Mosby "crept into the service of a nobleman, and by his servile flattery" has "become the steward of the house" where he "bravely jets it in his silken gown."

One of McCarthy's most striking examples doesn't even have many words in common; but the similarity in sentiment is too uncanny to ignore. During the famous quarrel scene—the one that Mac Jackson praised as so Shakespearean—Alice laments that women can never seem to win. "If I be merry, you straightaways think me light," she says to Mosby. "If sad, you sayest the sullens trouble me; if well attired, thou thinks I will be gadding; if homely, I seem sluttish in thine eye." In *The Dial*, North makes the same point about a woman in almost the exact way: "If she laugh a little, they count her light; if she laugh not, they count her a hypocrite; if she go to the Church, they note her for a gadder." This kind of correspondence "isn't picked up on any plagiarism software," McCarthy says. "This is a full-on effort to rephrase."

Of course, one might logically conclude that Shakespeare (or whoever wrote *Arden of Faversham*) read North's *Dial of Princes* and reworked the phrases for the play. But McCarthy suggests it was actually North who was subtly plagiarizing himself while writing a fully formed play about his own family's tragedy—now lost—around the same time he translated *The Dial* in 1557. That theory, however, raises a new problem: scholars are united in believing the main source for *Arden of Faversham* to be the story in *Holinshed's Chronicles*, first published in 1577. So how could a play written in the 1550s have used a source from the 1570s? McCarthy answers that the chronology is backward: It wasn't Holinshed that inspired *Arden of Faversham*, but North's original *Arden* play that inspired Holinshed.

THE *CHRONICLES* IS actually a composite work, written by Raphael Holinshed, yes, but also by a number of historians he hired to help him. One of those assistants, John Stow, wrote a first draft of the Arden story, found among his papers after his death in 1605, thirteen years after *Arden of Faversham* was published. That manuscript, McCarthy says, contains many details lacking in the final published version of *Holinshed*, which nevertheless appear in the play—such as the fact that it stopped snowing early, and specific words in Reede's curse. That makes Shakespeare's reliance on *Holinshed* problematic. "You would have to argue that William Shakespeare has access not only to *Holinshed*, but also to Stow's manuscript," says McCarthy.

Given that the manuscript likely never circulated, however, he contends that both Shakespeare and Stow were relying on another source—North's play. "My claim, and I'm the one who's right," says McCarthy with a smirk, standing in front of Arden's house, "is that Thomas North wrote the original play, and that's how Stow is getting all this inside information." That would explain why both Stow and Holinshed contain snatches of dialogue, such as when Arden greets his wife with, "How now, Mistress Alice?" in the histories in the same place as he does in the play. "There's no reason to include that in a history," McCarthy contends, getting animated. "I mean, there's no point."

In fact, the publisher for *Arden of Faversham*, Edward White, registered publication of a now-lost play, *A Cruel Murder Done in Kent*, in 1577— just as Stow was writing his draft—that McCarthy believes may be

North's. In her definitive book on the historical Thomas Arden, historian Patricia Hyde further speculates Stow may have gotten the Arden story in part from Kentish historian William Lambarde, who happens to have been a schoolmate of Thomas North around 1557, the same time he was translating *The Dial of Princes.*

Then there's North's obvious personal connection with the historical characters of the play. Alice Arden would have been present at the North family estate in his earliest years; and after that, young Thomas would have seen her often at family gatherings during Christmas and other holidays. That intimate relationship could explain the richness of the portraits drawn of the play's characters, including Arden, Mosby, and especially Alice. One critic writes, Alice "emerges as the strongest and most active character," as well as the play's "most brilliant and troubling poet-rhetorician." He adds: "The best lines all are hers." North's devotion to his half sister, says McCarthy, could explain why Alice is treated so sympathetically despite the brutal act she commits. In addition, North would have also known Alice's daughter Margaret, who was twelve at the time of the murder, only three years younger than he was—and perhaps for her sake, he may have been unwilling to completely condemn her mother.

North's authorship could also clarify why the name of Mosby's employer in the play is not Edward North, but a fictional Lord Clifford. Multiple commentators have pointed out this substitution, surmising that whoever wrote the play may not have wanted to offend the North family. Strangely, however, the play doesn't use pseudonyms for other noblemen mentioned in the play, including some whose descendants were even more prominent. The substitution would make sense, however, if North was trying to somehow obscure his father's identity, conflicted over the role Edward played in the Dissolution—and in his sister's punishment.

Arden, as many scholars have noted, struggles to come to terms with the new social mobility of post-dissolution England, on the one hand, making Arden a tragic victim of betrayal, and on the other dwelling on his greed and ruthlessness in wringing out profit at others' expense. In the end, it is the land that rises up against Arden as much as his wife and servants—both in the jilted landowner Greene, who helps hire the murderers who kill him, and metaphorically through Reede's curse on the "plot of land" where his body is ultimately found.

It is almost as if, says critic Richard Helgerson, Alice didn't kill her husband, but "God himself, moved by 'the tears of the oppressed' has wrought 'vengeance' on Arden for the social and economic sin of preferring 'his private profit before common gain.'" Analyses like that one would become key for McCarthy in understanding the play's connection to Thomas North, who he says also seemed to blame the Dissolution—and his father—for his sister's crime.

THE TRIAL WAS brief. Alice and Mosby had already confessed to their crimes, and a commission of gentlemen from around Faversham quickly found all of the conspirators guilty. The case then went to the Privy Council, the king's innermost circle of advisers, to hand down punishment. By this time, that elite circle included Edward North, who decided the sentences along with the other lords.

Mosby and his sister were paraded in a cart through London before being hanged at Smithfield, the execution ground outside the city walls. The servants, Michael and Elizabeth, were executed in Faversham in front of their neighbors. Elizabeth burned at the stake, and Michael hanged, drawn, and quartered—a nasty form of execution in which a victim was hanged almost to death, his entrails ripped out and burned in front of him, before he was beheaded and his body chopped into pieces. Greene was hanged in chains, his dead body left to rot over Faversham's main square. Black Will fled to Flanders before authorities caught up with him there, also burning him to death.

Alice Arden was singled out for special attention for the egregiousness of her crime. The fact that Alice had betrayed her husband by committing adultery—especially with someone of a lower class—before murdering him was inconceivably wicked. Even her own stepfather, Edward North, showed her no mercy signing the orders condemning her to death. A particularly stomach-churning story claims that the night before she was to be executed, Alice's cell was left open for any man who wished to come and rape her. Whether or not that's true, her execution was carried out on March 14, 1551, the same day her lover, Mosby, was executed. While he was hanged in London, she was pulled in a cart to Canterbury, seat of the English church, and tied to a stake, where faggots of wood were heaped at her feet and set alight. A crowd of hundreds yelled and jeered as the flames licked up her legs to consume her.

It's hard to imagine what Edward North's son Thomas must have thought about her death. The fifteen-year-old may have had festive memories of Alice and her daughter from holiday visits. It's possible he had witnessed firsthand her coldness toward her husband, or her affections for his father's steward. It's possible, too, that he may have blamed his father in part for her death—both directly for signing the execution, and indirectly for his role in the Dissolution of the Monasteries. That anger could have fueled composition of a play that pins the guilt of the murder as much to Arden's greed as to Alice's lust, and seems to sympathize with a murderer. "Knowing North wrote the play helps us understand it in a way that we've never been able to before," McCarthy says.

One of the strongest pieces of evidence he points to for Thomas North's authorship comes from within the family itself. In 1658, Edward North's great-grandson, Dudley North, wrote a biography of his ancestor, drawing upon "perusal of the old and almost worn-out papers remaining at Kirtling." In it, he defends Edward's part in the Dissolution of the Monasteries, saying his "managing of that great trust were sincere." Nevertheless, he adds with obvious distaste, his role in the Dissolution "exposed him to the censure of some of his own posterity." He goes on to write cryptically that one of Edward's descendants blamed him for a "crime that had been the destruction of many families so raised, and would be the catastrophe of his." He thinks it presumptuous, however, to "apply the judgments of the Almighty with too much strictness to such and such a particular cause."

McCarthy takes all of this to be an allusion to Thomas North and his critical play, with the "crime" a reference to the Dissolution, and the "catastrophe," the Arden murder—even echoing the way the play seems to attribute Arden's murder to God's judgment. "That's exactly what Dudley North says, that one of his children wrote about this scandal in the house, and he ascribed it to divine retribution. So it was something the family knew about, and was irritated at Thomas North about 100 years later." A few pages later, Dudley calls out Thomas North directly for criticism, saying he "never had a steadiness" comparable to that of his brother Roger.

From all those clues, McCarthy concludes that while Thomas North may have removed his father's name from the play, his family was still upset a century later that it accused Edward of complicity in the death of his son-in-law and execution of his stepdaughter. In fact, North's authorship of *A Cruel Murder Done in Kent*, and the rift it created with his father, is key to McCarthy's larger theory about Thomas North. He believes that he didn't just write a play upon which *Arden of Faversham* was based, but that he also wrote other plays upon which Shakespeare based his work— in fact, nearly all of the plays in the canon.

The fallout from that familial conflict would ultimately explain why Thomas North wrote so many plays, and why he would eventually sell them to William Shakespeare to adapt. That understanding, however, would take McCarthy years to develop. His explorations into North's literary career didn't start with *Arden*, but more than a decade earlier, with a far more famous play.

Chapter Two
BUT THINKING MAKES IT SO

(2005–2009)

> ...there is
> nothing either good or bad, but thinking
> makes it so.
>
> *—Hamlet*

ennis McCarthy's eyes were swimming in his computer screen. What had he gotten himself into? Nothing he read was making any sense. "English Seneca read by candlelight." "A tiger's heart wrapped in a player's hide." Every line seemed to hold a half a dozen references he didn't understand, like the code of a secret club to which he didn't belong. Which, he supposed, is exactly what it was. His idea had been a simple one, if a bit naive. In the late fall of 2005, he had been working on some papers about the geography of evolution—looking at how changes to animals and plants move across the world. One day, he wondered if he could apply similar principles to ideas, tracing how a story moved from country to country, changing subtly along the way. Looking for a piece of literature to serve as an example, he figured why not use the greatest masterpiece in the English language: William Shakespeare's *Hamlet*.

So what if he didn't have any background in literature? He didn't have any training in evolutionary biology, either. In fact, he barely graduated from high school and dropped out of college without a degree, working as a freelance writer for most of his life. But if there was one thing he was good at, it was teaching himself a subject that interested him. After all, he'd wormed his way into the field of biology and written papers embraced by its practitioners. He was confident that with enough diligence he could crack the code of Shakespeare studies as well. Now, staring at his screen, he wasn't so sure. He'd put aside two weeks for this side project, and barely scratched the surface. Papers and books lay strewn around his dining room table, along with piles of loose change, used mugs, and pill bottles. "Empty desk, empty mind," he thought.

At forty-two years old, McCarthy liked challenging himself. *Hamlet* is a complicated masterpiece—a play in which the main character's defining action for the majority of the drama is deciding whether to act at all. *To be, or not to be?* He drives his girlfriend to suicide while deciding whether to avenge his father's death at the hands of his uncle, who has since married his mother. Along the way, he encounters a ghost and a dead jester, an overbearing would-be father-in-law, and two ridiculous schoolmates. Then there are the actors that Hamlet hires to perform a play-within-a-play to expose his uncle's guilt. When the play finally turns bloody in the last act, it does so with a vengeance, with almost everyone lying dead onstage by the curtain call. For sheer poetry, depth of feeling, and meditation on very existence, however, nothing in literature can rival it. For actors, Hamlet is the ultimate role, forcing them to dig deep into their craft as they alternately portray a coward, a genius, and a madman— or sometimes all three at once.

Where does such a story come from? The action, at least, takes place in Elsinore Castle in Denmark, and is based on an old Norse legend, but it seems to have made its way to England through a French version. Shakespeare's play first appears in 1603, in an edition known as the First Quarto, but that was clearly not the first English version of the tale. Scholars have identified another *Hamlet* before Shakespeare's, referenced as early as 1589. This so-called *Ur-Hamlet* no longer exists in any extant copies, but Shakespearean scholars believe that it was once performed in England and inspired William Shakespeare to write his masterpiece.

The question is: Who wrote it? That's what McCarthy was now trying to answer from his dining room table in New Hampshire. It didn't daunt him that more conventionally trained scholars had been asking that question for centuries. If there was one thing he'd learned from his forays into the history of science, it's that generations of people tend to look in the same place for answers. It takes a Darwin in the Galápagos to really change what we think we know—and make a new truth seem as though it had been obvious all along.

MCCARTHY STARTED SIMPLY, searching the web for "Ur-Hamlet" and seeing what came up. As the leaves fell outside his dining room window, he read about the different versions of *Hamlet*, and how the First Quarto of 1603 botches Hamlet's most famous speech. Instead of "To be, or not to be? That is the question," it reads: "To be, or not to be, ay, there's the point!" The speech takes on its familiar form by the Second Quarto, published in 1604 or 1605, and most famously in the First Folio version, published after Shakespeare's death in 1623. But all of those versions were attributed to Shakespeare.

McCarthy started digging deeper, looking for evidence of the *Ur-Hamlet*, written by another author before Shakespeare's play. He found the reference easily enough in the 1589 romance *Menaphon* by Robert Greene, written fourteen years before Shakespeare's First Quarto. Robert Greene was a sort of ringleader to a rowdy bunch of Elizabethan playwrights known as the University Wits who lurked about the Shoreditch public houses. The circle of writers was witty and vicious, and wittily vicious, as they competed for attention on the English stage. In the late 1580s, their antagonism broke out into brawl, fought with pens instead of swords. Instead of calling out one another directly, they used veiled allusions that would have been obvious to anyone within their circle, but opaque to outsiders—and are nearly incomprehensible today.

One of the literary combatants, Thomas Nashe, wrote a preface to Greene's work, in which he took jabs at his rivals, writing: "It is common practice now-a-days amongst a sort of shifting companions, that run through every art and thrive by none, to leave the trade of noverint whereto they were born"—McCarthy looked up *noverint* to find that it was a common Latin term beginning legal documents in Elizabethan times— "and busy themselves with the endeavors of art, that could scarcely Latinize their neck-verse if they should have need." *Neck-verse*, he found, referred to a sixteenth-century practice by which a condemned man could prevent his execution if he could recite certain psalms in Latin to prove he was a member of the clergy—thus transferring his case to ecclesiastical courts and literally saving his own neck.

Okay, McCarthy thought, so Nashe was criticizing lawyers turned writers who could barely write to save their lives. Then came the money passage: "yet English Seneca read by candlelight yields many good sentences, as Blood is a beggar, and so forth, and if you entreat him fair in a frosty morning, he will afford you whole *Hamlets*"—there it was!—"I should say, handfuls, of tragical speeches. But O grief! *Tempus edax rerum*, what's that will last always? The sea exhaled by drops will in continuance be dry, and Seneca, let blood line by line and page by page, at length must needs die to our stage."

What on earth did any of that mean? McCarthy began searching for the phrases one by one. Seneca, he found, was a Roman playwright known for writing bloodthirsty tragedies of revenge, particularly famous for the high body count they racked up. Senecan tragedy, he found, had had a revival in England starting in the 1560s, just as Elizabeth I was taking the throne, so "English Seneca" must have been a master of that genre. In fact, Shakespeare's *Hamlet* has been seen as a late Senecan tragedy—or at least one inspired by the form. McCarthy couldn't find anything online to decipher "Blood is a beggar," but *tempus edax rerum* was easy enough: it meant "time, devourer of all things" in Latin. So Nashe was taking a swipe at *Hamlet*, saying it was referencing an antiquated form, Senecan tragedy, that had outlived its usefulness on the stage, and so "must needs die."

And Nashe had a good motive to criticize the *Ur-Hamlet*, McCarthy discovered. Some lines recited within the play have been identified by scholars as a send-up of a play Nashe cowrote with Christopher Marlowe, *Dido, Queen of Carthage*, ridiculing its overwrought plot. So now Nashe was returning the favor, getting back at the author of the *Ur-Hamlet* by ridiculing *his* play as outmoded. But who was this "English Seneca" he was calling out? And could he be the author of the original *Hamlet*?

McCarthy began searching elsewhere in Nashe's preface for clues. In the sentence directly preceding the passage about *Hamlet* and English Seneca, Nashe wrote that he was returning to the topic of "trivial translators" he'd discussed earlier. As he waded his way through the dense set of allusions that begins the text, he came across a reference to other writers who "vaunt...Plutarch's plumes as their own."

Plutarch, McCarthy went on to learn, was another writer in Roman times, who'd written a set of biographies called *Lives of the Noble Greeks and Romans*, or simply, *Plutarch's Lives*. The most famous translator of the work into English was an Elizabethan writer by the name of Sir Thomas North. Another phrase in the same passage refers to catching "Boreas by the beard"—the Greek name for the north wind. Could Thomas North be "English Seneca"? McCarthy doubted it, but surprisingly, as soon as he searched for "Thomas North" and "Seneca," he found an immediate hit. This reference came from an even older work, a preface to Seneca's tragedy *Thyestes* written by Jasper Heywood in 1560. Appearing almost thirty years before Nashe's lament that Senecan tragedy was *over*, the form was then just on the verge of taking off in England.

Heywood makes an appeal to a group of writers at the Inns of Court— the early Tudor law schools—urging them to take up Senecan tragedy as a playwriting form. As the first name on his list of contenders, Heywood writes, "There shalt thou see the selfsame North, whose work his wit displays, and Dial doth of Princes paint, and preach abroad his praise." That, McCarthy further discovered, was a reference to *The Dial of Princes*, a kind of self-help manual for rulers that Thomas North had translated and published in 1557.

After weeks of painstakingly searching, McCarthy now had several arrows pointing in Thomas North's direction. When he searched for biographies of the English writer, however, he found little information. One biographer called him, encouragingly, "the first great master of English prose." Apart from that, almost every reference to North noted that Shakespeare used his translation of *Plutarch* to write his Roman tragedies, including *Julius Caesar, Coriolanus, Timon of Athens*, and especially *Antony and Cleopatra*—where whole passages of North's prose are taken almost verbatim by Shakespeare and turned into poetry.

In fact, after *Holinshed's Chronicles* and *Hall's Chronicle*, North's *Plutarch* was Shakespeare's greatest source for his plays, called by another writer "Shakespeare's storehouse of classical learning." While North is lauded as a translator, however, McCarthy found no indication that North was a poet or playwright, much less a gifted dramatist capable of writing something as profound as *Hamlet* (or even the *Ur-Hamlet*). If McCarthy was going to make such an audacious claim, he'd need to find more evidence.

McCarthy had always been good at figuring things out. He grew up in the 1960s in Amherst, New York, a few minutes outside of Buffalo, where he lived in an apartment complex in a working-class neighborhood. His father, an Irish American Korean War vet, worked in real estate, renting and flipping houses; his mother, who came from Irish and German descent, taught at the local elementary school. His father could be a strict disciplinarian at times—there was no mouthing off, ever—but both parents doted on him as their only child. "It was a fun neighborhood, with lots of kids playing Kick the Can at night," McCarthy tells me, sitting at the wooden table in his New Hampshire living room.

McCarthy was clearly bright as a child. According to his mother, Gloria, he was reading at a third-grade level by kindergarten, and a year later, he skipped a grade. By fourth grade, she remembers one of his teachers saying, "He's smarter than me, I can't answer his questions." Initially he did well at math and developed an early love for reading—consuming James Bond novels, Stephen King, even some classics like Mark Twain's *Huckleberry Finn*. But when it came to schoolwork, he was hopeless. "I didn't want to study anything that they gave me," he says. By middle school, he found himself virtually unable to concentrate in class. "My eyes would start at the top of a page, and I would get to the bottom and nothing would have gone through," he says. "I was formally ineducable."

He was still good at standardized tests, able to guess answers by the way the questions were asked and choices provided. While that might have cut it when he was younger, it wasn't good enough for Nichols School, the exclusive private academy where his parents sent him for high school. By tenth grade, he'd failed out and transferred to the town's public high school. His friend Michael Kizilbash remembers him as an awkward teenager—rail thin "with this thick puffy hair," he says. "I called him Q-tip for a while." He gained confidence playing sports, captaining the cross-country team and excelling at Ultimate Frisbee, playing on local club teams with Kizilbash.

More than anything, however, he excelled at missing classes. "When I was a senior, I was dating a girl who was wild and lovely, and it wasn't hard to talk me into skipping school," McCarthy says. "She'd say, Let's go to Niagara Falls, and I'd say, Okay." He skipped so many tests in Health, he wasn't sure he'd graduate. "They handed me the gown, and I sat there sick to my stomach not knowing if they were going to call my name." When they did, McCarthy says, his friends erupted in applause. "My parents thought I was really popular and all the kids loved me—they didn't know everyone was just relieved I graduated."

College didn't turn out much better. After high school, he drifted to the University at Buffalo, thinking he'd study computer science. In the mid-'80s, personal computers were changing from a novelty to a must-have, and the field seemed like it could only grow. He found himself unable to concentrate on debugging long lines of code, however. Coming home from school one weekend, he told his mother dejectedly, "I just don't see myself spending eight hours a day in front of a monitor." He started taking theater classes instead, scoring the lead in *One Flew Over the Cuckoo's Nest*, and even playing Tybalt in scenes from *Romeo and Juliet*. And he began writing, mostly horror stories in the vein of Stephen King.

As smart as he was, he couldn't seem to focus on a career. He saw friends go into premed, and while he respected them, he couldn't imagine becoming a doctor himself. "It just didn't seem exciting to me. I'd be pouring my life into this pursuit, and then die a doctor, and that would be on my tombstone—Dennis the doctor." He pauses. "I just think you've got one shot in life, you've got to go for something hugely big." Despite such lofty ambitions, he struggled to find himself, spending much of his time drinking, bartending part-time, playing Ultimate Frisbee, and dating. "I was kind of a serial monogamist," he says. "I always had a serious girlfriend in my life." One of those girlfriends—a waitress named Pauline Galovski, whom he dated for the better part of 1986—ended up pregnant. After they broke up, she gave birth to his baby, naming her Nicole, and McCarthy agreed to help support her.

After four years at college, he was a few credits shy of graduating when he decided to drop out and become a writer full-time, following his friend Kizilbash—and another girl—to Boston, where they moved in together on ritzy Beacon Hill. "Fortunately for me, she was doing well, and she supported my writing habit," he says sardonically. One novella he started featured a writer who inherited a haunted typewriter that started churning out short stories like a twisted mechanical Scheherazade, each one more horrific than the last. He never felt like his work was good enough to send out anywhere, however, and his manuscripts went unpublished.

He still read voraciously, plowing through five newspapers a day and going to the library to read books on popular science, physics, and astronomy. "I'd meet him at a bar, and he'd be with a group of girls, and say, 'Ask me absolutely any question about anything, and I'll answer it correctly,'" Kizilbash recalls. "And sure as hell, that's what he would do." After he and his girlfriend broke up, he fathered another child, Meagan, with a flight attendant he met while attending an Ultimate Frisbee tournament in Florida. "I had a bit of a wild period in my twenties," McCarthy admits. "I wasn't really rooted anywhere or doing anything—but eventually I got my act together."

JUST AS HIS Ultimate Frisbee team won the national championships—making it one of the best teams in the world—he lost interest in the party scene. "I was like, that's it, that phase is done," he says. He moved out of Boston to the North Shore of Massachusetts to get serious about writing, living in a procession of seaside towns with quaint New England names—Beverly Farms, Magnolia, Manchester-by-the-Sea. In addition to short stories, he began earning some money writing arts reviews for local newspapers, eventually graduating to features, such as one about how email had brought the love letter back.

One day in the mid-1990s, McCarthy received a phone call from his daughter Nicole, whom he'd seen when she was younger, but stopped after relations with her mother and new stepfather had become strained. Now seven years old, she called to ask him to come see her again. He drove the eight hours back to Buffalo the next day. After that, McCarthy began seeing his daughter every few months, easing into something like fatherhood.

In October 1997, McCarthy found himself at age thirty-four back in Buffalo. He had blown out his knee playing Ultimate Frisbee and was staying with his parents while seeing a doctor they'd recommended.

Limping into a local TGI Friday's on crutches, he began chatting up a twenty-nine-year-old brunette woman from Kalamazoo, Michigan, named Lori Seidl, who was sitting at the bar with her roommate. "I have a blown knee, no real job, no car, I'm living with my parents, and have two illegitimate children," McCarthy ticks off, amazed that she was willing to speak to him. Meanwhile, Seidl was on an upward career trajectory as a regional account manager for a pharmaceutical company. "So I was clearly punching above my weight here."

Lori remembers it differently. "I had my hair in a ponytail, no makeup, flannel shirt—so clearly he liked me for my mind," she says sarcastically. She was immediately attracted to his intelligence and sense of humor, as the two talked about everything from Mark Twain to obscure horror movies. "He was just laughing all the time," she says. "I think I fell in love with him for his laugh." They were dating by February. By June, they'd moved back to Massachusetts together; and by December, they were engaged to be married. They started living together in a house on a lake in a small town west of Boston.

After Lori McCarthy got a job working for biotech company Biogen in New Hampshire, they moved to their current colonial overlooking the woods and marsh on the seacoast outside Portsmouth. They had two children: Kennedy in 2000, and Griffin in 2004. Rather than McCarthy working at a newspaper and the couple paying for daycare, they decided he'd stay home and take care of the kids and continue writing freelance while Lori drove her territory around New Hampshire and Maine. "I would come home and he would have a Baby Björn with Kennedy sleeping on his chest, or a bouncy chair beside him so he could give her a bottle if she needed it," Lori remembers. "He always did a really good job at multitasking."

EVEN AS HE wrote for local papers, McCarthy continued reading popular science books by the likes of Carl Sagan, Richard Dawkins, and E. O. Wilson. Eventually, he started driving to Boston or Providence to slip into libraries at Harvard, Brandeis, and Brown to read science journals. "I would just walk straight in, and copy whatever articles I needed," he says. Sometimes he'd bring his children, striving to keep them from running through the stacks while he searched.

McCarthy became particularly interested in the science of biogeography—a hybrid field that explores how and why particular species of plants and animals exist where they do. "It's like the secret subject of geniuses," he says now, listing off the luminaries of the field— Charles Darwin and Alfred Wallace, co-fathers of evolution; taxonomist Carl Linnaeus; Alfred Wegener, who discovered continental drift; and Jared Diamond, author of *Guns, Germs, and Steel*. "It's one of the most significant subjects in the history of the world," he insists, "and very few people know about it." The more he surveyed findings in the field, the more he thought he might have something to contribute.

Looking at the Pacific Ocean, for example, he started identifying similar plants and animals—a flat oyster, a freshwater lizard, a flightless bird— found only on opposite sides of the Pacific, but not on any of the islands in between. He took this as evidence that the entire ocean had once been closed 200 million years ago, and these species had evolved from common ancestors as the continents drifted apart and the ocean opened. While he wasn't the first person to propose the idea, McCarthy thought he was able to show this phenomenon along the entire Pacific Rim, with matching species pairs in Japan–Canada, China–Mexico, Australia–Peru, and New Zealand–Patagonia, something he likened to a "zipper effect."

Of course, submitting a paper on the subject to an academic journal was a bold move for someone without a science degree—never mind someone who hadn't graduated from college. "I knew it was going to be difficult being the dreaded 'independent researcher,'" he tells me. But McCarthy didn't let his lack of credentials stop him. One of his favorite movie lines is from the 1997 film *The Edge*, written by David Mamet, in which Anthony Hopkins and Alec Baldwin are lost in the Alaskan wilderness. Needing to kill a Kodiak bear that is stalking them, Hopkins's character proposes they build a trap. When the other man protests they lack hunting experience, he yells, "What one man can do, another can do!" McCarthy may not have succeeded in school, but he believed he could do anything if he devoted enough time and energy to it.

He began by reaching out to some of the scientists he admired. One scientist from New Zealand, Michael Heads, had looked at distribution patterns of plants across the islands of New Zealand that could barely spread on their own, theorizing they had once been on opposite sides of continental plates that had spread apart over time. McCarthy wrote to Heads, praising his research, while sending him information on his own, asking him if it was something he thought he could publish. "I put it like, I am very interested in your work. I agree with it," he says. "And I think I've got something that reinforces it."

After a lively back-and-forth over email, Heads introduced McCarthy to editors at a peer-reviewed publication, the *Journal of Biogeography*, helping him submit his paper there. "The Trans-Pacific Zipper Effect: Disjunct Sister Taxa and Matching Geological Outlines That Link the Pacific Margins" appeared in October 2003. McCarthy followed that up with other papers, expanding on his theories about the Pacific while writing just a few miles from the Atlantic. A friend who worked at the Buffalo Museum of Science helped him get the unpaid position of research associate—a title at least—and the wife of another friend who taught at the University at Buffalo gave him access to electronic databases of scholarly journals. Now, he could find all of the academic research he needed without leaving his dining room table. As he continued his correspondence with Pacific-based biogeographers, one of them, a professor at the University of New South Wales in Australia named Malte Ebach, invited him to present at a biogeography conference in Cardiff, Wales, in August 2005.

"Like most sciences, biogeography is very much an echo chamber, where people are just carrying on the arguments that have been around for years, and there are no fresh ideas," Ebach tells me now over video chat from Australia. Paleontologists saw an event one way, whereas biologists saw it another, and geologists saw it still another. "It's like a family reunion, where students take on the rivalries of their supervisors." Without the baggage of a particular academic discipline, however, McCarthy was able to listen to different sides and mediate between them. "Everyone loved him, because he could speak their language," Ebach says.

After the conference, Ebach offered him a big break. He'd been trying to write a book about biogeography for Oxford University Press, he said, but had been having trouble adapting his scientific style for a more mainstream audience. He knew McCarthy had a background in journalism—would he like to give it a go? McCarthy jumped at the chance, writing up a proposal and a couple of chapters, and receiving a contract for the book. He titled it *Here Be Dragons*, after the cartography term *Hic sunt dracones*, which ancient mapmakers supposedly used to designate unknown or dangerous lands. In reality, he argues, the term referred to the location of Komodo dragons, those ten-foot-long lizards that inhabit remote islands of the Pacific. To explain how and why they developed where they did, McCarthy draws on research by Jared Diamond that suggests they likely evolved to their gargantuan size to eat pygmy mammoths—a fact that "invites a rather fantastic image, a lizard attacking and eating an elephant."

The book is full of entertaining anecdotes like that one, following in the footsteps of McCarthy's popular science heroes. In a chapter titled "The Bloody Fall of South America," McCarthy describes how a freak geological occurrence—the rise of the isthmus of Panama a few million years ago—led North American carnivores to go on a rampage in South America, wiping out the unique hoofed animals and marsupials that once lived there. Along the way, he describes how biogeography led to insights in other fields; for example, how the distribution of finches and iguanas on the Galápagos Islands gave Charles Darwin the epiphany that led to his theory of evolution. In a no less important example, the location of dinosaur fossils on different continents helped German scientist Alfred Wegener come up with the theory of continental drift, which he first published in 1915. Like Darwin, Wegener was attacked by his contemporaries, and he died without seeing his theories accepted. "Unfortunately, this is not that unusual a situation. Many scientists of the past who are acclaimed as revolutionary today were ignored or attacked by conventional scientists of their time and, like Wegener, died unknown," McCarthy wrote.

In fact, many of the examples in the book represent a common theme, which McCarthy can't help but point out: a struggle by determined outsiders to transform calcified scientific fields through facts and evidence, even when they are repeatedly ridiculed or ignored. "Established academics have much invested in the theories they have taught to others and written about in books and journals, and this can, at times, lead to unreflective antagonism toward daring and mutinous ideas," he wrote. "The result was intellectual stagnation" for half a century, he continued, "lost time on our scientific journey that can never be recaptured. But it was not the methods of science that had misled us, simply the frailties of humans. In the end, the scientific process triumphed."

WHEN OXFORD UNIVERSITY PRESS published McCarthy's book *Here Be Dragons* in December 2009, the book met with an enthusiastic reception. *Huffington Post*, for example, called it "a wonderful little book" and "a great pleasure" to read. Even more satisfying for an outsider crashing the gates of academia, *Science*, the gold standard of scientific journals, also gave it a positive review. McCarthy's book, it said, "delivers on its promise that we will never look at the world in the same way again."

By the time it appeared, however, McCarthy had long moved on. By now, McCarthy's two-week project to trace the origins of *Hamlet* had become an all-consuming passion. Once McCarthy had identified "English Seneca" as Thomas North in 2005, he began looking for any other references that might suggest North had written the *Ur-Hamlet*, or been at all connected to Shakespeare. The same way that dinosaur fossils or evolutionary ancestors left behind traces pointing to long-lost connections between continents, McCarthy figured that vestiges of North's prose must have found their way into Shakespeare's great tragedy. He had read almost all the way through the online text of North's first translation, *The Dial of Princes*, when he found himself drawn up short. In chapter forty-eight of the third book, North quotes a meditation on death by the Roman philosopher Secundus, who calls it a "kind of sleeping" and "a pilgrimage uncertain." In the very next paragraph, North quotes Seneca, who says, "For all those which are dead, none returned." McCarthy couldn't help but see an echo there of Hamlet's most famous soliloquy—and some of the most famous lines in the English language.

"To be, or not to be, that is the question," Hamlet says to himself, struggling with the pain of seeing his mother and usurping uncle together. He continues his meditation, asking "whether 'tis nobler in the mind to suffer the slings and arrows of outrageous fortune, or to take up arms against a sea of troubles, and by opposing end them." Later, he, too, compares death to sleeping, saying, "To die, to sleep; to sleep, perchance to dream. Ay, there's the rub, for in that sleep of death what dreams may come..." Then, in words that further resemble North's prose, he asks whether any of us would bear life's misfortunes if not for "the dread of something after death—the undiscovered country, from whose bourn no traveler returns."

The description of death as "a pilgrimage uncertain" and "an undiscovered country" seemed uncannily similar to McCarthy—and they weren't the only resemblances he found between Hamlet's speech and North's book. A few chapters after this, North quotes Panutius, secretary to Emperor Marcus Aurelius, musing, "Is it better that thou die and go with so many good; than that thou scape and live amongst so many evil?"—a phrase that, if you squint, could translate to: "To be, or not to be?" In the same passage, he continues, "What other thing is the grave, but a strong fort, wherein we shut ourselves from the assaults of life, and broils of fortune?"—a passage much like "slings and arrows of outrageous fortune." Elsewhere in the book, North refers to a "sea of troubles." And near the beginning of the work, McCarthy even found a passage combining forms of "perchance," "sleep," and "dream" into a single phrase, when North writes, "If perchance thou doest ask it, because sleeping has dreamed it."

Taken together, the chances that so many similar sentiments and specific phrases would be shared between Hamlet's soliloquy and North's earlier translation seemed vanishingly small to McCarthy. Even so, McCarthy knew from his work in biogeography that one couldn't take anything for granted. Although sometimes similar plants and animals appeared in different parts of the world because they shared a common evolutionary ancestor, sometimes they had evolved to become more similar because they shared a similar environment. Perhaps Shakespeare and North were both borrowing phrases from another writer; or maybe they were echoing common beliefs about death in the sixteenth century.

McCarthy found there was a way to check that—almost—using an online database called Early English Books Online (EEBO). The compendium then contained the full text of some 26,500 printed texts written between 1475 and 1640, identified by scholars as the most important works of early English prose. By searching in the database, someone could find out how many times a particular phrase had been used, and compare instances of words used in proximity to each other across volumes. Of course, the database only includes printed books, not manuscripts, and certainly not any books or manuscripts that had been lost over the centuries, but McCarthy figured it was the closest he'd be able to get to searching through all of Tudor-era prose.

When he started plugging in phrases, he found that, in fact, many of them were quite common. "A sea of troubles," for instance, appeared fifteen times in the EEBO dataset in works written before *Hamlet*. Other word groupings, however, were more unique. When McCarthy searched for the words "sleep," "perchance," and "dream" all within ten words of one another, *Hamlet* and *The Dial of Princes* were the only works that appeared. By themselves, none of these similarities proved that Thomas North wrote the *Ur-Hamlet*—after all, Shakespeare or another writer could have borrowed the phrases from *The Dial of Princes* directly. But together with the references he'd already found that seemingly pointed to North as the author, they added additional evidence to the case.

McCarthy also found other encouraging references showing North was much closer to English playwriting circles of the Elizabethan age. A play by Shakespeare's rival, Ben Jonson, lampoons a character named "John Daw"—a supposedly educated knight who turns out to be a buffoon. Some of the language in the play seemed to mimic North's own translation of *The Dial of Princes*, and in one passage, Jonson references not only Plutarch and Seneca, but also *The Moral Philosophy of Doni*, an obscure Italian book of fables that North also translated. Not for nothing, the name of that character could be seen as an allusion to the jackdaw or crow—a bird that feathers its nest with the feathers of others—an Elizabethan shorthand for a plagiarist. McCarthy wrote up the findings in a short paper, spelling out the traces of language he found in the passages that made him believe that John Daw was actually a reference to Thomas North.

Now that he was writing a book for Oxford University Press, he submitted the paper to *Notes & Queries*, a journal Oxford also publishes that contains short pieces on literary topics. McCarthy's paper on John Daw was accepted, appearing in the September 2007 issue. He followed it up with a paper naming *The Dial of Princes* as a source for Hamlet's soliloquy in *Notes & Queries* in March 2009. (McCarthy left out, for now, his larger suspicion of North as author of the *Ur-Hamlet*.) McCarthy was elated that he'd broken through with published scholarship in a new academic discipline, trumpeting on his website that he "may be the only researcher to have published papers in the leading journals of such disparate disciplines as geophysics, biogeography, and English literature."

As he continued pursuing the connections between Shakespeare and Thomas North, McCarthy often woke up at five in the morning, chasing a new find until dinner. "He almost had another place at the table," Lori McCarthy tells me. "You were setting a place for Shakespeare?" I ask. "No," she replies, "Thomas North." In fact, she says, she didn't realize how much the children were absorbing from his studies until one night when they were out for tacos, and some friends asked what he was writing. "My kids start going on and on about Shakespeare and all the plays," Lori says. "I was like 'Oh my God, your teachers are going to love you.' They knew more about Shakespeare than ninety percent of adults." Despite his growing obsession, McCarthy still found time to play with the kids in the yard after they got home from school, throwing the Frisbee with them and inventing a game called "poison ball" that became a hit with the neighborhood children. "I've known people whose spouses were so absorbed in their work that they're almost absentee," Lori says, "but he never makes us feel like we're not important."

Soon, McCarthy had more help for his project as well. In the decade since he reconnected with his daughter Nicole, the pair had become increasingly close. "They couldn't keep us apart, we were too similar," McCarthy says one night over dinner with Galovski and me in London. "We just had too much fun together." Starting when she was seventeen, Galovski says, they began carrying on long philosophical conversations over the phone and on weekend and summer visits. "We would talk for hours about the meaning of life and what we both wanted to do and what was most interesting in the world," she says. "I still consider my dad my best friend." Growing up in a religious household, Galovski decided to journey to Uganda at age nineteen to do aid work with a nonprofit organization. The trip didn't turn out as she had hoped, however, especially when her residence was broken into and some of her possessions stolen.

While in Africa, she went sightseeing with some friends to an area of the Congo that was then a flashpoint in the country's long civil war, writing a chatty blog post about the experience. When McCarthy read it, he was apoplectic. "I was angrier at her than I have ever been at anyone in my life," he says as Galovski picks up the story: "I said something like, 'Well, Mom supports me,' and he said, 'That's because your mom thinks when you die you'll be playing bocce with Saint Francis of Assisi on Cloud 9—while I *know* your blood will be soaking into the red African earth and you'll be buried in a box of your wasted potential.'" Galovski turns, smiling, to her dad, as McCarthy chuckles. "I swear that was off the cuff," he says. "I even thought to myself at the time, 'That's a good line.'"

A short while later, he convinced Galovski to move to New Hampshire, where she stayed in the basement and helped him with his Shakespeare research, tracking down papers and looking up references, while she planned her next steps. Eventually, she got a job as programming director for the New Hampshire Film Festival, which launched her documentary filmmaking career today. "The maddest my dad gets at me is if he thinks I'm not seeing reality clearly," Galovski says. "He's so focused on what's true—no matter what anyone else says. That's really inspired me now, obviously as a truth seeker through documentary film."

With Galovski's help, McCarthy delved deeper into the truth behind satires by Elizabethan playwrights. As he read through them, he began noticing other references to North, seeming to relate to other Shakespeare plays beyond just *Hamlet*, implying that perhaps North had a hand in writing more plays in the Shakespeare canon. "Everything just kept pointing to Thomas North, Thomas North," McCarthy says. In the same preface in which Nashe mocks "English Seneca," for example, he also refers to the "King of the Fairies," calling to mind Oberon in *A Midsummer Night's Dream*. In another work, Nashe seems to refer to the witches from *Macbeth* before complaining of a "dull, Northern clime." One work in particular seemed to go even further, describing a meeting between North and Shakespeare directly.

THE 1592 PAMPHLET *Greene's Groatsworth of Wit* purports to be the death-bed confession of writer Robert Greene—but it was almost certainly written by someone else. It's most famous now for containing a rare con-temporary reference to William Shakespeare, also invoking language of a crow feathering his nest with the plumage of other birds, to imply that he is a plagiarist. "There is an upstart crow," it says, "beautified with our feathers, that with his tiger's heart wrapped in a player's hide, supposes he is as well able to bombast out a blank verse as the best of you: and being an absolute *Johannes Factotum*, is in his own concept the only Shake-scene in a country." Not only is "Shake-scene" a clear reference to Shakespeare, but the association is cemented by the phrase "tiger's heart wrapped in a player's hide," a parody of the phrase "Oh, tiger's heart wrapped in a woman's hide," appearing in *Henry VI, Part 3*. "Johannes Factotum" is another word for jack-of-all-trades, which as an actor, playwright, and theater owner, Shakespeare certainly was; while "shake" was Elizabethan slang for "steal." Thus, as generations of scholars have concluded, at least one of Shakespeare's contemporaries accused him of stealing his scenes from other writers and passing them off as his own.

This one sentence has spurred centuries of speculation that Shakespeare didn't in fact pen the plays attributed to him, creating a cottage industry of conspiracy theories that the author of the canon is actually Francis Bacon; Edward de Vere, the Earl of Oxford; or another writer instead. Few scholars, however, have looked beyond that one reference to examine the rest of the pamphlet for clues. In fact, *Groatsworth* tells the story of a gentleman named Roberto, a scholar disowned by his family, who finds himself penniless. He meets an actor who promises to pay him for his plays. "Now famoused for an arch-playmaking-poet," the author writes, "his purse like the sea sometimes swelled; anon like the same sea fell to a low ebb. Yet seldom he wanted, his labors were so well-esteemed."

Those lines in *Groatsworth*, in fact, seem to imply an ongoing relation-ship in which the actor paid the "gentleman-scholar" for plays which he adapted for the stage over an extended period of time. Nothing, of course, in North's meager biography implied anything of the sort. *Groatsworth*, however, describes a fraught relationship between the gentleman-scholar and his father and brother, with whom he fell repeatedly into conflict. As McCarthy began researching the lives of Thomas North's own father and brother, he found uncanny similarities between them and the story described in *Groatsworth*. While Thomas's biography may have been sparse, the lives of his wealthier and more prominent family members were fleshed out in more detail. McCarthy now began to plumb them for clues that might explain how—and why—Thomas North might have begun writing plays.

Chapter Three

REMEMBERING THIS REALM

(1509–1555)

With profound sorrow, my heart is sore grieved,
Remembering this realm, my native country,
With manifold vices to be destroyed
& falling in decay.
　　　　—"The Ruin of a Realm," Edward North

Gold cloth and tapestries spilled from the windows of Cheapside on June 23, 1509, as crowds gathered along the streets below. The drinking had started early, with wine flowing freely from the conduits in place of the usual water, creating a festival-like atmosphere in the posh London neighborhood. Edward North, then an auburn-haired youth of about thirteen, was likely among the assembled throng straining to catch a glimpse of the future king as he rode triumphantly to his coronation in Westminster.

Following the priests in their long robes and then the line of noble lords on horseback, the prince finally emerged, dazzling in a doublet of gold and gemstones, the sun shining on hair the color of Edward's own. Behind him in a litter was his soon-to-be queen, the Spanish princess Katherine of Aragon. She had once been married to Prince Arthur, who had died of illness just five months after their wedding. So now she would marry his younger brother Henry, who would take the throne as Henry VIII.

Hopes were riding high for this robust youth, who at age eighteen was already six feet two inches tall and broad-chested. His father, Henry VII, had been young once, too, when he had ridden onto the battlefield of

Bosworth to depose the usurper Richard III, ending the Wars of the Roses and bringing peace to the kingdom. But the old king had grown dour and miserly with age. This new king seemed endlessly energetic, always engaging in athletic pursuits of archery, wrestling, and jousting. He was also studious, devoting himself to the philosophy of humanism, which taught that leaders of noble blood must put their learning into practice for the betterment of the realm.

Henry was taking over a capital city poised for prosperity. London stretched turtle-like along the Thames River for almost a mile, from the soaring spire of St. Paul's Cathedral to the ancient fortress of the Tower of London. The city was industrious and dirty, its wharves teeming with honey, wine, and pitch carried upriver on barges with the tide. Many of the best goods found their way to Cheapside, which overflowed with cloth and textiles and the world-renowned wares of gold- and silversmiths. With a population of over fifty thousand people, the city was already bursting out of its old Roman walls, and its streets were narrow and cramped, overhung with jetties from the upper stories. Rains could turn the ill-paved streets into a malodorous mud, mixed with bits of fish and animal droppings.

Yet there was an undeniable energy in the air, as new residents flocked from the countryside, among them Edward's father, Roger North, who came from a family of landed gentry near Nottingham. Drifting down to London before Edward's birth around 1496, he became a prosperous clothing merchant before dying at age sixty-one in 1509, the same year that the new king came to the throne. Before then, he provided Edward with a humanist education, enrolling him in St. Paul's School, newly founded by scholar John Colet to teach the classics to the future elite of English society, including lessons in Greek for the first time in England. Edward likely imbibed a skepticism for the church as well, as Colet and other reformers advocated a simpler form of religion, removed from the superstitious worship of relics and the gluttony of the priests.

He may have heard even stronger criticism of the church while continuing his studies at Peterhouse, the oldest college at Cambridge University. In the 1520s, Cambridge was abuzz with talk of religious reformation,

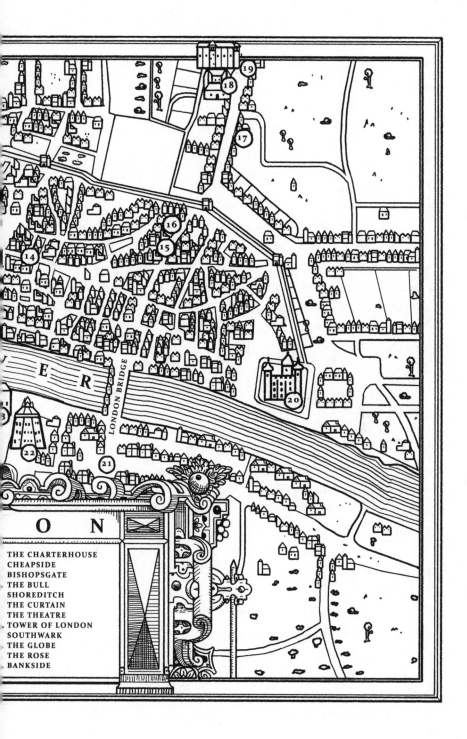

THE CHARTERHOUSE
CHEAPSIDE
BISHOPSGATE
THE BULL
SHOREDITCH
THE CURTAIN
THE THEATRE
TOWER OF LONDON
SOUTHWARK
THE GLOBE
THE ROSE
BANKSIDE

as the followers of German theologian Martin Luther met at the White Horse public house just outside Peterhouse's front gate. Among them was William Tyndale, who would defy the church by publishing the first English Bible, and Thomas Cranmer, who would soon play an even more significant role in England's religious reformation.

THE KING'S MARRIAGE to Katherine was by all accounts a happy one at first, with the vivacious queen more than equaling Henry's physical and intellectual appetites. After the previous century's wars had depleted the country's store of nobles, Henry created new ones with young courtiers drawn from the gentry and merchant classes that some bluebloods contemptuously termed "new men." Henry increasingly spent his time jousting, feasting, and playing at war with these new lords, leaving the business of running the country to others. Chief among them was Cardinal Thomas Wolsey, an adviser to Henry's father whom the king made lord chancellor, the highest office in the land, in 1515; three years later, the pope made him papal legate, his personal representative in England. From these lofty perches, Wolsey negotiated with the great powers of Europe and raised coin for Henry's ambitious endeavors.

After assuming the throne, Henry lost little time declaring war on England's ancient enemy, France. After a series of muddy skirmishes, he had little to show for it, succeeding in capturing a couple of French citadels while squandering most of the £1.25 million ($1.8 billion today) fortune his father had left him. New monarchs took the throne: Francis I of France; and Charles V of Spain, who also became Holy Roman Emperor, giving him control of a third of the Continent. Over the coming decades, the shifting wars and alliances of these three kings would dominate European politics, with Henry the most junior partner.

Wolsey steered the three rulers into an agreement of "universal peace" in 1520. Two years later, Edward North returned to London to study at Lincoln's Inn, one of the four prestigious Inns of Court that sprouted in the fields west of the city to prepare young men for the law and civil service. There he watched Wolsey parade his growing influence and wealth—the richest man in England after the king. For his daily journeys to Westminster, he rode on a mule covered in scarlet, with two silver crosses before him, accompanied by four footmen with poleaxes. He spent thousands of pounds on rich clothing, built himself the enormous palace of Hampton Court, and dined at the king's table on special meats reserved for him alone. When the highest-ranking noble, the Duke of Buckingham, grumbled privately, Wolsey personally oversaw his trial for treason and execution.

Resentments against Wolsey, however, continued to build. The peace the cardinal negotiated couldn't hold, and soon France and the Holy Roman Empire were at war, with England entering on the emperor's side. To fund the campaign, Wolsey pushed a new tax through Parliament, requiring every person in the realm to pay according to their means. As he studied law at Lincoln's Inn, Edward North channeled the anti-Wolsey sentiment sweeping the country into writing.

"With profound sorrow, my heart is sore grieved," the poem begins, "remembering this realm, my native country, with manifold vices to be destroyed & falling in decay." Titled "The Ruin of a Realm," the poem survives in two manuscript copies, both in the British Library in London. One of them is inserted into a sixteenth-century "commonplace book" of miscellaneous writings under the name "Northe." Just before the last three of the poem's thirty-seven stanzas is written: "The author," and following the first letter of each of the following lines spells out an acrostic, reading: "EDWARDE NORTH."

The poem laments the decay into which England has fallen due to the pernicious influence of both nobles and the clergy, especially one clergyman in particular. "For in gowns of silk and riding on their mules is their chief delight, and to bear a rule in great men's houses of high authority," North writes in a direct shot at Wolsey, "by reason of whose vices this realm is brought into great ruin." Perhaps North felt public sentiment was on his side, or perhaps he was just young and foolish, caught up in the fervor of the day. Whatever his intent, his literary rebellion was short-lived. In a cardboard box in Britain's National Archives is a sheaf of water-stained papers detailing in Latin the charges against Edward North of London and five other men for treason against the king, on January 27, 1524.

I found these documents myself, following a long trail of footnotes, as I, too, began researching the North family. For all of McCarthy's wizardry with computers, he is the first to admit he rarely sets foot into libraries or archives himself anymore. In our travels together in England, we stopped by Cambridge University Library to see a copy of *The Dial of Princes*, personally owned and annotated by Thomas North, and McCarthy seemed at sea signing up for a reader's card to visit the rare-books reading room. "The truth is, there is so much to find, I can spend my time more efficiently on the computer," he told me—just one more indication of how his approach radically differs from conventional scholars. And yet, as I paged through these and other documents in London archives, struggling to read Tudor secretary hand, they only seemed to bolster the story that McCarthy had been constructing about North's family history.

The ringleader of the plot against the king was a man named Francis Philipp, a schoolteacher at the court, who stood accused of calling for Henry VIII's "death and destruction." According to *Hall's Chronicle*, Philipp and his gang planned to ambush one of Wolsey's war tax collectors in Coventry before seizing nearby Kenilworth Castle as a base from which to make "battle against the king." Before they could, however, they were found out by a local cloth seller and taken to be imprisoned in the Tower of London. North doesn't seem to have taken part in the plot; however, according to the court documents, the rebels took him into their confidence, and he promised to keep their plans a secret. (Presumably it was his anti-Wolsey poem that caught their attention.) On February 4 and 5, 1524, the prisoners appeared at Westminster Hall for an inquest, where they were accused of lying and treason. North admitted his guilt, but the nine commissioners adjourned for Easter without a ruling.

Edward must have spent an anxious time in his cell, shivering in the raw cold of an English winter, while awaiting his fate. Weeks stretched into months without a verdict, until finally, on April 16, 1524, the commissioners returned to pronounce Philipp and his fellow conspirators guilty. Three of them were hauled out to Tyburn, the execution ground three miles west of the city, to be hanged, drawn, and quartered. North, meanwhile, was remanded back into custody, most likely to the Tower, where he sat again for months—alive, thank the Lord—but imprisoned. It's at this point, perhaps, he decided that criticizing Wolsey's decadence wasn't a cause worth dying for.

In another poem in the commonplace book, titled "The Complaint of North to the Cardinal Wolsey," he offers a full-throated apology to the cardinal. "Now being in prison, I am not able," it begins, "plainly to show his virtues innumerable." After all, he continues, "making was my joy, and is now my grievance"—most likely a reference to "making" his poetry, which North clearly blames for the trouble he is in. The rest of the poem relentlessly sings Wolsey's praises, including "his wit and goodly eloquence, very desirous of pure humanity, inflamed with virtue and goodly countenance," and other variations on the theme. "All of England for him is bound to pray!" he insists finally, before spelling out in an acrostic in the last lines of the poem: "GOD PRESERVE THOMAS LORD LEGATE AND CARDINALL." North ends the poem throwing himself on Wolsey's mercy as "a man troubled, trusting for grace, living in hope, all things to amend."

His sycophancy seems to have hit the mark. In another cardboard box in the National Archives is a long document in Latin calligraphy detailing the terms of a full pardon for North, releasing him for "any and all forms of insurrection, rebellion" and "misprision of treason." The pardon is dated January 24, 1525, almost a year to the day since charges were first brought against him. The long, uncertain days in prison must have taught North a lesson about what happens when you stick your neck out too boldly for a cause. When survival was at stake, he was quick to turn his writing around to flatter Wolsey—the object of his derision just a year before. There were plenty of martyrs who went to the scaffold rather than recant their religious or political beliefs. North, it seems, chose to play the long game, flattering his way out of prison while perhaps privately hoping for Wolsey's comeuppance. For that, at least, he would not have to wait long.

THEY CALLED IT the king's Great Matter. Queen Katherine became pregnant seven times, but only succeeded in giving birth to one child, the princess Mary, in 1516. Anxious for a male heir to the throne, Henry may have sincerely believed God was punishing him. But he also had a wandering eye, and by the time it fell on one of Katherine's ladies, Anne Boleyn, in the mid-1520s, he was ready to cast off his queen for a new one. With divorce virtually nonexistent in Tudor times, Henry set his mind to an annulment on the grounds that Katherine had previously consummated her marriage to Arthur (though he was sickly, and only fifteen when he died). He entrusted the job of securing the approval of the pope to Wolsey, who dispatched a messenger to Rome in 1527.

In the meantime, Edward's legal career recovered quickly from his brush with treason. Perhaps through the influence of his brother-in-law, an alderman, North became a counsel for the city of London. From that vantage, he watched Wolsey fail at his appointed task. By now, the Emperor Charles V had gained the upper hand in the continental wars, capturing the French king and driving deep into Italy to sack Rome and take Pope Clement VII prisoner. Since Charles V was Queen Katherine's nephew, there was little chance the pope would authorize the annulment now. Clement agreed only to an ecclesiastical court, which met in England in the upstairs hall at Blackfriars monastery.

Katherine fell at the king's feet. "I beseech you for all the loves that hath been between us, and for the love of God, let me have justice and right," she cried, claiming she'd never consummated her previous marriage. Wolsey did his best to argue the opposite, but the emperor's delegate demanded the case be recalled to Rome, and the pope acquiesced. Henry blamed Wolsey for the catastrophe, and Wolsey's enemies pounced, pressing charges against him of praemunire, the crime of putting the pope's interests over the king's.

Henry stripped Wolsey of his many posts and banished him to the north of England. The following year, the king accused him of treason for secretly conspiring with France and Spain, and soldiers brought Wolsey under guard on a slow march south to be placed in the Tower, where North had been locked up five years before. On the way, Wolsey's health gave out; he contracted dysentery and died.

EDWARD NORTH MUST have watched the fall of his old enemy with satisfaction—even as his own career was on an upswing. Around age thirty-one, he followed in his father's footsteps to become a freeman of the Mercers' Company, the first among the twelve livery companies that elected London's aldermen and mayor. The following year, he ended his long bachelorhood by finally settling down with Alice Squire, the rich widow of two marriages, who brought along her young daughter, the future Alice Arden. Their own daughter, Christian, was born in 1529, followed by a son, Roger, in February 1531. He was baptized in a parish in the bustling mercantile district between Cheapside and the wharves, attesting to the wealth North had achieved.

That same month, Edward North received his first official government appointment, as clerk of Parliament in Westminster. His biography in *The History of Parliament* suggests it was his poem "The Ruin of a Realm" that caught the attention of the clerk who helped North get the post. His anti-Wolsey screed, which had once almost caused his death, was now perfectly suited to the time. As Wolsey fell, the dam holding back the resentments against the church had burst; itinerant preachers began railing against the superstitious worship of relics, while in some villages, parishioners under the influence of radical Protestants destroyed statues of saints.

Following Wolsey's demise, Henry's new lord chancellor, the humanist scholar Thomas More, tried to hold the line against such iconoclasm. He publicly burned books of Martin Luther and William Tyndale, and was soon burning religious heretics as well. They stood atop wooden platforms in the Smithfield livestock market, just outside London's northwestern gate, as an executioner set the wood alight at their feet with a flaming torch. If the day was damp, it could take agonizing minutes for the wet wood to catch, slowly roasting victims alive, until the liquefying fat cracking from beneath their skin stoked the flames into a white-hot blaze.

By now, however, Henry's patience with the pope had run out, and he turned to a team of scholars, led by theologian Thomas Cranmer, to search for a loophole that would allow him to marry Anne Boleyn. They found it in a first-century text that declared the king of England to be God's representative within his own realm. As Henry declared himself "supreme head of the English church and clergy," More resigned his post out of conscience. The power vacuum was filled by another "new man," Thomas Cromwell, a former secretary of Wolsey who managed to skirt the long knives after his master's downfall to become a privy councilor and top adviser to the king. As Cromwell made the case for the king's new authority to Parliament, Henry married Boleyn secretly in 1533. Cranmer, now archbishop of Canterbury, formally approved the marriage, declaring Henry's marriage to Katherine void. Henry had won his fight against the pope—but the attack on the church was just beginning.

As EDWARD NORTH took on greater responsibilities for drafting legislation in Parliament, "his Sun began to ascend very fast to its zenith," as his great-grandson Dudley North later wrote in his biography. He now used some of the wealth from his new wife to make the most significant purchase of his life: Kirtling Hall, an estate twenty miles west of Cambridge that instantly gave him entrée into the upper levels of gentility.

North tore down a five-hundred-year-old medieval castle to construct a magnificent new manor with a profusion of chimneys springing from nearly sixty hearths, making it the largest house in the county. Visitors arrived through a great stone gatehouse with octagonal towers, crossing a flagstone courtyard to enter the great hall, which boasted an immense oak table with room for fifty people. Other rooms included a minstrel's gallery, a library, a private family chapel with a resplendent stained-glass window, and the so-called oyster room, "perhaps named for inlaid oyster-shell decoration." Nearly five hundred acres of grounds included wide lawns for bowling and tennis, a park stocked with deer, and fields worked by more than fifty tenant farmers.

In short, it was a home fit for the important courtier North was becoming. In his long stretches in London, he increasingly worked with Cromwell on a series of legislative acts to consolidate the king's power over the church. Katherine's daughter, Mary, was stripped of her right of succession, which was granted instead to the children of Anne Boleyn, including her newly born daughter, Elizabeth. Another law required an oath from every citizen declaring Henry supreme head of the Church of England and acknowledging his new marriage. By 1535, North joined an informal network of agents throughout the country confidentially reporting any acts of support for the papacy to Cromwell. On May 28 of that year, Edward and his wife gave birth to a second son, naming him Thomas.

The new baby entered the world in a dangerous time, when a man's beliefs on the matters of religion could spell his death. While I am in London in January 2019, I stop by the Charterhouse, another home Edward North acquired during those tempestuous years. Now a museum, the mansion sits in the heart of the city, but was just outside the wall during North's time. A guided tour leads into a great hall with dark oak wood paneling and tiered windows eight feet high overlooking a grassy courtyard. "This would have been Lord North's main reception room," says the tour guide, a white-haired British man named Neil. While some of the paneling was destroyed in 1941 during the Blitz, most of it is original, he says. "It would have looked pretty much as it does now." Upstairs is a great room hung with tapestries that, when North lived here, depicted the story of David and Goliath. He filled other chambers with Turkish carpets and chairs covered in gold cloth and black velvet from Venice and Bruges.

The building wasn't always a mansion, however. Out in the courtyard, Neil points out heavy gray stones that were once a part of a Carthusian monastery on the site. For centuries, the monks inside had devoted themselves to lives of silent asceticism in their cloister just north of the Smithfield cattle market. When Cromwell's agents knocked on the door, their prior, John Houghton, refused to sign the oath recognizing Henry's supremacy. He and several other monks were dragged three miles through the streets of London, to Tyburn, to be hanged, drawn, and quartered. Houghton's still-beating heart was cut out and rubbed in his face; afterward he was decapitated and the hand with which he had refused to sign nailed to the Charterhouse door.

Watching Houghton dragged through the streets was Thomas More, who was himself imprisoned in the Tower for refusing to sign the oath. Another protégé of Cromwell, Richard Rich, questioned him and said More denied Henry's supremacy—though More claimed Rich fabricated the declaration. Nevertheless, More was convicted based on Rich's testimony and taken to Tower Hill, where he was beheaded, his head hung on London Bridge as a warning to those who might defy the king. With reformers like Cromwell and Cranmer in charge, it was now Catholics who were burned at the stake, with the ashes of more than three hundred of them carried on the wind over Smithfield.

Cromwell didn't stop at executions, however, but rather saw an opportunity in England's wealthy monasteries by which, as historian Peter Ackroyd put it, "his master could grow rich as well as powerful." He began surveying church property, which then accounted for between a sixth and a third of all the property in the kingdom, cataloging silver candlesticks and golden chalices. At the same time, he sent "visitations" to suss out evidence of wickedness of abbots and monks, who were accused of drinking, whoring, sodomy, and embezzlement. As clerk, Edward North helped draft the legislation by which hundreds of religious houses were closed, their property sold. Richard Rich was made head of the new Court of Augmentations to handle the rent and sale of the properties.

By this point, the king was discontented with his new bride. In the spring of 1536, Anne Boleyn was arrested on suspicion of having affairs with other men at court. Gallons of ink have been spilled speculating on whether or not Boleyn was actually unfaithful, and why the king really turned on his second queen. Some blame her failure to produce a male heir; others, the influence of Cromwell; still others point to Henry's infatuation with a new mistress, Jane Seymour. Recent theories place the blame on a jousting accident that caused brain damage and constant leg pain that turned the once golden king into a sadistic monster. Whatever the truth, the charges against Anne were at the very least greatly exaggerated, including that she had engaged in incest with her brother and father. Nonetheless, she was found guilty, hauled out onto Tower Green, and beheaded by sword. Just eleven days later, Henry married Seymour, his third wife.

Cromwell, meanwhile, stepped up the pace of the Dissolution, moving onto the larger monasteries, including the great Charterhouse of London, which was torn down and converted into storage space for the king's tents, as well as a casino, with pits for wrestling matches and altars used as gaming tables. The newly acquired lands were dispensed as gifts to the king's favorites or sold off at fire-sale prices. Cromwell appropriated a half-dozen of the best properties, and others went to nobles and new men who consolidated their status with great new houses.

As North rose steadily in Cromwell's favor, he became treasurer of the Court of Augmentations in 1540 under Rich. Now he began acquiring new properties throughout the English Midlands—and continued thriving even as his mentor fell. Henry's third wife, Jane, finally gave him the male heir he longed for, with the birth of his son, Edward. She died a few days later, however, most likely due to an infection from the delivery. Seeing an opportunity to push forward church reforms, Cromwell helped engineer a new marriage, sight unseen, between Henry and the German Protestant Anne of Cleves.

Apparently, however, Henry found his new bride unattractive, divorcing her six months later. Cromwell got the blame, and now he was accused of treason, found guilty without a trial, and beheaded on Tower Hill. The same day, Henry married his fifth wife, the young Catherine Howard. She didn't last long, either. Accused of adultery—probably accurately this time—she was beheaded after only a year and a half of marriage.

THROUGHOUT ALL THIS turmoil, Edward North continued to rise, acquiring more and more properties, along with a knighthood from a grateful king in 1542. Henry used his new wealth to finance grand palaces of his own, along with more wars against Scotland and France, the king's enduring obsession. He married his sixth and final wife, Katherine Parr, in 1543, and the next year captured the French city of Boulogne-sur-Mer. North took on an even larger role in the plunder the following year, when he was promoted to chancellor of augmentations.

It was then that the king rewarded him with the plum grant of the Charterhouse for the bargain price of £50 ($42,500) a year. "The man put in charge of the disposal of monastic property by Henry VIII, surprise, surprise, ends up with the most valuable site," says Neil, the Charterhouse tour guide. North demolished the church and cloister, using their stones to construct a grand new home. Behind the mansion, he built stables filled with a dozen horses and converted one of the cloister's long passages into a bowling alley. "Above all," Neil tells our group, "Edward North was a great survivor."

By this time, North had survived and prospered in the king's administration for fifteen years, even as other courtiers had fallen victim to Henry's capricious temper. One morning in 1546, however, he was summoned to appear before the king. He arrived at court to find Henry walking in the courtyard with a serious expression, and North walked next to him in silence for several anxious minutes, before the king rounded on him, angrily saying, "We are informed that you have cheated us out of certain lands." North demurred, saying it wasn't true, after which Henry asked, "How was it then, did we give those lands to you?" North responded quickly, "Yes, sir, your majesty, and you were pleased to do so."

The king softened, according to the servant who witnessed the exchange, and the two then conferred in private for a long time, until they both emerged, with the king apparently satisfied. In another version of the story, the king summoned North to him after learning of a shortfall of some £3,000 ($2.4 million) in the accounts of the Court of Augmentations—but North was able to mollify the king by giving up some of his landholdings. Whatever happened, he clearly escaped punishment, trusting again to his power with language to survive—and profit—in a dangerous court.

North suffered no lasting consequences from the dustup; in fact, when the king became ill just before Christmas, he added North's name to a new Privy Council, alongside those of fifteen prominent courtiers and clergymen who would serve as the king's executors upon his death and form a council of regency that would rule the kingdom until Henry's son and heir, Edward, came of age. North was to receive a generous stipend of £300 ($237,300) for his services. Two days after signing his new will, Henry developed a fever, and a month after that, in the early morning of January 28, 1547, he died.

In the forty years of his rule, the once-shining prince had turned into a corpulent tyrant—but he had also overturned a calcified church and opened up new roads for advancement for ambitious men, completing England's transformation from a medieval kingdom to an early modern state. Now his absence left England in a precarious state, with a fragile heir too young to rule.

GOLD CLOTH AND tapestries once again hung from the windows of Cheapside to mark the coronation of nine-year-old Edward VI, resplendent in a jerkin of white velvet and rubies. This time, Edward North was riding in the procession with him, wearing a crimson robe and black velvet hat as he gazed out contentedly on the assembled crowds. They most likely included his own eleven-year-old son Thomas, who must have thrilled to the excitement of a coronation of a new king younger than himself. Little did he know how short the new king's reign would last.

Though Henry's will decreed the members of the council would rule jointly, it quickly split into factions. The king's uncle Edward Seymour, Duke of Somerset, declared himself Lord Protector, taking over rule of the realm. His chief antagonist was John Dudley, a protégé of Cromwell whom Somerset had replaced as lord admiral. Edward North had his own reasons for resenting Somerset, who pushed him out of his position at the Court of Augmentations in favor of one of his cronies. He threw his weight behind Dudley, the future Duke of Northumberland, and once again, he chose well.

Under Edward VI's fervent Protestant leadership, Archbishop Cranmer led a campaign of radical reformation, outlawing religious icons and tearing up the Latin mass to replace it with a new English prayer book. The changes were too much too soon for many in the countryside, who took up their pitchforks in 1549 in what became known as the Prayer Book Rebellion. When Somerset did little to quell the unrest, Northumberland led an assault against the rebel camp near Norwich in East Anglia, massacring as many as four thousand men. Seeing an opening amidst the chaos, Northumberland now led a coup d'etat against Somerset, and Edward North was among the first councilors to answer his call. Somerset was imprisoned, found guilty of treason, and executed, as Northumberland became regent over the king. North's influence on the Privy Council increased; not even the scandalous murder of his clerk, Thomas Arden, by his stepdaughter Alice Arden in 1551 could shake his new position close to the center of power.

In early 1553, Edward VI took to bed with a mysterious illness, and it was soon clear he was dying. As a devout evangelical, Edward ruled out his Catholic sister Mary as his heir. Under Northumberland's influence, he decreed instead that the line of succession would travel through his first cousin once-removed, Jane Grey, who happened to be married to Northumberland's son Guildford Dudley. When Edward VI died, the sixteen-year-old Jane ascended to the throne, even as Northumberland sent his son Robert Dudley to capture Mary as she fled northward toward Norwich, which still harbored bitter memories of Northumberland's massacre there. Robert was forced to call off pursuit, however, when word came that Mary was assembling an army.

The situation grew more hopeless by the day, as thousands of soldiers and East Anglian nobles rallied to Mary's side, and Northumberland rode out to meet them in battle. By this time, North had survived the falls of Wolsey, Cromwell, and Somerset; so he knew a losing cause when he saw one. Despite his friendship with Northumberland, he joined the other councilors in switching sides to support Mary's claim; Jane stepped down, forever after known as the "Nine-Day-Queen." Northumberland was sent to the Tower, desperately proclaiming his conversion to the "true Catholic faith," before he was beheaded on Tower Hill. He wasn't alone in suddenly recanting his beliefs, however. Suddenly, many who'd zealously followed Edward's Protestant revolution discovered they were actually Catholics after all.

FROM THE MOMENT Mary rode triumphantly into London, church masses were once again conducted in Latin, and the populace hauled out their statues and images of the Virgin Mary and other saints to put on display. Edward North declared his loyalty to Rome along with everyone else, receiving a full pardon from the new Queen Mary, a document that exists in stiff parchment in the National Archives, alongside the one from her father from thirty years earlier. North must have seemed too close to Northumberland for Mary to reappoint him to the Privy Council; but he quickly ingratiated himself back into her good graces with a speed that mirrors his earlier about-face to Wolsey. By 1554, she elevated him to a hereditary peerage as a baron, the lowest rank on the scale of English nobility, giving him permanent status in the House of Lords.

While the people initially accepted their new Catholic queen, that sentiment changed when she announced her choice of husband: Philip II, the emperor's son and king of Naples and Sicily. Many Englishmen were incensed over the idea of a foreigner as their king. In January 1554, schoolchildren pelted the Spanish ambassadors with snowballs. A more serious uprising occurred the following month, as Thomas Wyatt led several thousand men in an attempt to put Mary's Protestant half sister Elizabeth on the throne. After the failed rebellion, Mary executed the unfortunate Jane Grey and her husband, Guildford Dudley, sending Elizabeth to the Tower for a time alongside Northumberland's remaining sons, including Robert.

Edward North stayed loyal, however, appearing among eight English nobles who received Philip II when he disembarked in Southampton for the royal wedding that July. As the English people reacted despondently to the news of their new king, Mary pushed new laws through Parliament in 1555 to continue her counter-reformation, prohibiting heresy against the Catholic Church, punishable by death by burning. The platforms at Smithfield were once again pressed into service as radical preachers and bishops were set alight. No one was above suspicion; in the early days of her purge, Mary burned a butcher, barber, farmer, and upholsterer among the seventy-five people executed in London alone.

As the heresy trials spread they were overseen by North's ally Richard Rich, who had once led the Dissolution of the Monasteries, and now sentenced dozens of Protestants to death. Rather than cowing the public, however, the executions often had the opposite effect, engendering sympathy for the Protestant martyrs, even as Mary ordered more burnings. Edward, meanwhile, held aloft the sword of state at a ceremony to officially welcome the pope's new representative and acknowledge England's return to Catholicism. His appearances at court, however, became fewer as he spent more time at Kirtling. Increasingly, his thoughts turned to his children.

His elder son, Roger, was well on his way to assuming his duties as a lord, sitting in the House of Commons as a senior knight of the shire in 1555. It was not immediately clear, however, where his younger son, Thomas, would fit in. Now nineteen years old, he was immersed in study of books and languages, endeavors that may have positioned him for a career in the Church if he had showed any interest. Looking for a path to secure his son's advancement, Edward soon found the perfect opportunity—one that would make use of Thomas's skills while proving his loyalty to the new queen. He would become a secretary for a lord on an important mission—and he would take notes.

Chapter Four

UNDREAMED SHORES

(1555)

To unpathed waters, undreamed shores
—*The Winter's Tale*

The Alps come seemingly out of nowhere. One minute, we are cruising through the French countryside, past agricultural fields and stands of birch trees with their leaves just starting to appear; the next, we're staring at a wall of chiseled gray mountains emerging from the skyline ahead. It's April 2019, a few months after our trip to England, and a driver is taking us up these Alpine foothills in a boxy van. McCarthy is sitting next to me in a blue Oxford shirt, studying a laptop balanced on his knees while Galovski sits cheerfully behind us in a puffy black jacket. Turned around and filming us from the passenger seat is Ian Wexler, a beardy cameraman from Brooklyn who does sketch comedy on the side.

"From Pont Beauvoisin to Chamberry, five long leagues, where we passed by Mount Aiguberte, a great mountain, and very dangerous," McCarthy reads. "Here Master White...taking a hold of his horse's head to pull him nearer the rockside to keep him from falling down the hill, his horse going back pulled his master after him, and both together tumbled down the hill a great way, and here stayed, and yet neither of them hurt."

The narrator of poor Master White's mishap was the nineteen-year-old Thomas North, who for six months kept a journal of a long and sometimes treacherous expedition from London to Rome. Virtually no other information about North's youth has survived—aside from some speculation that he, too, probably attended Peterhouse at Cambridge University like his father. Thomas's voice, however, suddenly emerges, full-throated, from his account of an all-important delegation sent by the Catholic Queen Mary in 1555 to reconcile England with the pope.

"Mary was the daughter of Katherine of Aragon," explains McCarthy as we climb toward the mountains, "and believes her mother was really a Catholic martyr, divorced and de-queened unjustly. Now she wants a counter-reformation to bring Catholicism back." To achieve that reunion, she sent out three ambassadors: the diplomat Edward Carne; the noble-man Anthony Browne, Viscount Montague; and the clergyman Thomas Thirlby, Bishop of Ely—a cathedral city just twenty miles from Kirtling Hall. That made North's father his most prominent parishioner, and no doubt Edward had persuaded Thirlby to take his son Thomas with him on the trip.

If so, it was a shrewd move. Thirlby was on his way up—a new member of Mary's Privy Council and, some were whispering, in line to become lord chancellor. But this was no charity case. Clearly, the teenaged Thomas already displayed a quick wit and facility for languages—not only the Greek and Latin of a humanist education, but French and Italian as well. Traveling for months through the Continent would deepen those skills, while giving him ample time to prove his worth to the Bishop. "It looks like everything is going Catholic now," McCarthy says. "The Bishop of Ely is becoming one of the most significant power players, and so North wants his son to be his right hand."

Whether required in his official duties or not, the journal Thomas kept describes each of the towns the delegation passed through, noting the relative strength of castles and illustrious personages met along the way. But it also overflows with wondrous images of holy relics, wild animals, exotic foods, and magnificent palaces. Overall, it creates the impression of a sensitive and intelligent young man eager to soak up the sights and sounds of new land. "He's an extremely observant person," says McCarthy, "who is very curious and fascinated by dramatic scenes and compelling stories." We are now on our way to retrace North's journey for a very specific reason: McCarthy believes that some of those scenes and stories inspired one of Shakespeare's most evocative and romantic plays: *The Winter's Tale*.

WE DRIVE NOW into Chambery, an achingly cute Alpine town of narrow medieval streets lined with potted palm trees and clothing boutiques. North's delegation visited the town, capital of the then-independent Duchy of Savoy, on March 29, just over a month after they'd crossed the English Channel at Calais. In the previous few weeks, the train of 160 horses, lords, and men-at-arms had slowly wended its way through northern France to Paris, where North saw a "griffin claw," a "unicorn horn," and a crown of the king of France, which contained "a ruby as big as a walnut."

Three days later, the delegation arrived at the French court in Fontainebleau to meet with King Henri II himself, whom North describes as "a goodly tall gentleman, well made in all the parts of his body, a very grim countenance, yet very gentle, meek, and well beloved of all his subjects." After the audience, the delegation went on to meet with Henri's queen, Catherine de Medici, along with a richly dressed twelve-year-old girl—Mary Queen of Scots, who was then betrothed to Henri's oldest son, Francis. The experience of meeting so many foreign royals must have been a heady one for the young North, who notes that the young princess graciously received the Scottish gentlemen in the procession "and said unto us, she was very glad to see us, calling us her countrymen."

For the next week and a half, the delegation followed the Loire River, passing through the city of Lyons, as North described more wondrous sights, such as orange, lemon, and pomegranate trees planted in barrels taken indoors in winter. His taste of spring was brief, however, as soon the delegation began climbing into rougher country along the river Arc, which fell from the mountain so loudly "that it is able to make a man so deaf." Our own springlike atmosphere quickly disappears as we start climbing the forested foothills. We, too, twist along the rushing river, as the mountains now rise so high around us that we have to crane our heads to see their tops. The delegation must have felt a deep sense of foreboding as they led their horses against the curving sides of the valley. North, clearly overcome by the stress, wrote of "being always in danger of some stone falling upon us, that it seemed rather a hell than a highway to pass in."

Finally, on March 31, the delegation stumbled, exhausted, into the tiny Alpine village of Saint-André. As the sun set that afternoon, North ventured into a church, where he came across a pitiful sight: "a young child lying dead upon a board," and an old woman burning a candle and presenting an offering of peas and beans to the image of the Virgin Mary. North asked in French what she was meaning to do. She explained that "the child was born dead, and that she looked for the life of it, or at least to burst out a bleeding in some place of the body." If the body bled, North wrote, then the baby would be christened and given a proper burial. "If not, then it is cast into the river." Born in Protestant England, North may never have seen such an intercession to a saint before, and the experience clearly moved him enough to capture it in his journal.

Now, in search of this church ourselves, we pull off the highway and climb up to Saint-André, a village clinging precariously to the mountainside. The air is cold and thin, but the sun warms the slopes, and birds twitter in flowering trees as we wander among pitched triangular roofs. Finally we come across a heavy stone church near the center of town called Eglise de Saint-André, Notre Dame de l'Assomption—"Our Lady of the Assumption." According to a historical marker, it was originally constructed in 1507, but destroyed in 1597; the current structure, dating from 1956, still has the ancient remains of an old stone doorway built into the wall.

The church is locked, but as we are standing outside, an elderly woman with short, white hair and a colorful scarf passes by on her way home from church services in a neighboring town. This church, she says, is no longer active, but after a few calls, she is able to obtain the keys. "Our Lady had pity on you and she sent me here for you," says the woman, Marine. The interior is simple, with a high ceiling and slatted walls curving in a semicircle on which hangs a simple stone crucifix saved from the original church.

Afterward, Marine lets us into a small chapel down the street that dates from the seventeenth century and provides a better idea of how North's church may have looked. She opens the door to a narrow nave with a vaulted blue ceiling covered in faded frescoes depicting the Virgin Mary, Joseph, and Jesus. An elaborate gold-painted altarpiece features two angels flanking a large painting of *pietà*, depicting Jesus's mother, Mary, cradling her dead son in her lap after he was taken down from the cross. It was an image like this, claims McCarthy, that inspired the final scene in one of the young Thomas North's first plays, which Shakespeare adapted many decades later.

THE WINTER'S TALE may be Shakespeare's strangest play, a fantasia of romantic elements that never quite come together. Set in the kingdoms of Sicily and Bohemia, the drama mixes Christian imagery and pagan mythology in a sweeping tale of jealousy, love, and divine intervention. It is most famous for a line not even spoken—the stage direction "Exit, pursued by a bear." And it's *infamous* for Shakespeare's gaffe of setting that bestial chase on the "coast" of Bohemia—despite the region, located in modern-day Germany and the Czech Republic, being landlocked.

The play starts nine months into a visit from Bohemia's king Polixenes to the court of his childhood friend Leontes, the king of Sicily. When Leontes's wife, Hermione, persuades Polixenes to extend his stay, Leontes becomes irrationally jealous, accusing her of infidelity and ordering his gentleman-in-waiting, Camillo, to kill Polixenes. Defying his orders, Camillo helps Polixenes escape, and Leontes throws Hermione in prison, where she gives birth to a daughter. Believing the child to be Polixenes's, the furious king sends the daughter into exile and puts Hermione on trial, sending two messengers to the Oracle of Delphi to determine her guilt. When the oracle finds Hermione innocent, Leontes stubbornly refuses to abide by the judgment.

At this point, the play takes a darker turn. First Leontes's son Mamillius dies of sorrow; then Hermione's friend Pauline tells the king that Hermione herself has died of heartbreak. Leontes falls into despair, mourning day and night at their tombs and swearing he will never marry again. Meanwhile, a servant named Antigonus, charged with taking the princess into exile, abandons her on Bohemia's imaginary shore before meeting his offstage ursine doom. Mercifully, however, a shepherd finds the daughter and raises her as his own, calling her Perdita—"the lost one" in Latin.

Sixteen years pass and Perdita coincidentally meets and falls in love with Polixenes's son Florizel in disguise. The two are wed in a rustic ceremony, full of pagan imagery, including country dancers dressed up as satyrs. Finally, the young lovers return to Sicily, with Polixenes close behind, to find Leontes, still heartbroken and consumed with regret. Perdita is revealed to be Leontes's lost daughter, just in time for a surprise happy ending: Paulina reveals that she has kept a statue of Hermione in a chapel in her home. She brings Leontes to see it, and he swears it looks alive. Paulina tells everyone to prepare themselves for a miracle, and the statue really does come back to life. Hermione and Leontes embrace, the kingdoms are reconciled, and all is forgiven.

For centuries, the play has beguiled scholars, who have struggled to find meaning in its complex soup of contradictory elements. In the modern Folger edition, editors Barbara Mowat and Paul Werstine call it "so full of improbabilities that the play occasionally seems amused by its own audacity." Through the years, critics have fallen into one of two camps. The first, common during the seventeenth and eighteenth centuries, pans the play for its "far-fetched or clumsy plotting," condemning the sudden fury of Leontes as unrealistic and the statue scene as particularly beggaring belief. "Many found the idea to be ludicrous that Hermione might play dead" for years, writes critic Harold Bloom, "finally emerging in a gimmicky, stage-managed event."

The second camp, emerging during the Romantic period in the nineteenth century, is more forgiving, praising the play as an imaginative fantasy that casts a spell with its beauty. For these critics, the geographical errors and religious anachronisms were meant to highlight the otherworldliness of the tale. Modern scholars generally split the difference, finding The Winter's Tale "a rambling, perhaps an untidy play" but dripping with symbolism and emotional power, especially in its final revelation. "The scene never fails!" enthuses renowned Shakespearean Roma Gill. "I have heard—felt—the breathless, expectant silence of the most sophisticated audiences at Stratford-upon-Avon, wondering at the mystery. Many in these audiences have been scholars, critics, and lecturers who know all about the play and who have read it and seen it, edited, criticized, and taught it—but all knowledge is forgotten, and all disbelief willingly suspended, before the legitimate magic of Shakespeare's theatre."

THE PLAY IS dated toward the end of the playwright's career, with its first recorded performance in May 1611. Detractors see that late date of composition as an indication of Shakespeare's declining powers, whereas fans see it as part of a bold late-career turn into more experimental forms. McCarthy has a different view: just as he believes the 1592 *Arden of Faversham* was based on an earlier play by North, he thinks that *The Winter's Tale* was based on another play North wrote early in his career, soon after his return from the delegation to Rome. Viewed in that light, he says, all the play's strange elements fall neatly into place—because the play is not meant to be taken literally. Rather, he says, it's an allegory for the most important story of its day—the reconciliation of England with Rome, the very quest that North was recording in his journal. "*The Winter's Tale* is a celebration of the return of Catholicism," says McCarthy. "It is a rehabilitation of Katherine of Aragon, who is Hermione; and her daughter Mary, who is Perdita, coming back to become queen."

We are sitting now in an Alpine restaurant in a ski town fifty kilometers up the road from Saint-André, hard against the Italian border. Galovski and Wexler have ordered a raclette, a half-wheel of gooey Swiss cheese that comes with its own heater. When the top layer of cheese melts, one of them tilts the wheel down to scrape it onto a plate with a wooden spatula to spread on bread, and it sizzles while we talk. "Hermione goes on trial for supposedly living in adultery for consummating a relationship, and so does Katherine," says McCarthy. King Leontes, meanwhile, is Henry VIII, who put his wife on trial for supposedly consummating her marriage to his brother, Arthur. "Leontes even says at one point, Polixenes is like a brother to me," McCarthy notes. The Oracle of Apollo at Delphi is the pope, to whom Henry sent messengers only to be told Katherine was innocent, and Henry rejected the verdict, just like Leontes did. Mamillius is Henry's heir Edward VI, who died young from illness, and Perdita is Mary herself, sent into symbolic exile after she was denied the throne. Even Florizel has an analogue in Philip of Spain, who was king of Naples and Sicily.

Of course, in the play, Florizel is prince of Bohemia, not Sicily. But McCarthy has an explanation for that. In North's original play, he contends, Leontes was king of Bohemia, and Polixenes king of Sicily—analogues for

England and Spain, respectively. By Shakespeare's time, however, England was again at war with Spain, and so it wouldn't have made sense to make the noble Polixenes and Florizel rulers of that country. Thus, the play switches the kingdoms from North's original, putting the "bad" king Leontes in Sicily, and the "good" king Polixenes and his son Florizel in Bohemia. That would explain the geographic error that has long haunted Shakespeare, the description of Bohemia as "a desert country near the sea," complete with its incongruous coastline.

In fact, the kingdoms *are* switched in another version of the tale, the novel *Pandosto*, written by playwright Robert Greene and published in 1588, which scholars universally recognize as the source for Shakespeare's play. As with *Arden of Faversham* and *Holinshed*, however, McCarthy argues they again have it backward—that, in fact, both *Pandosto* and *The Winter's Tale* were based on North's 1550s original version. For one, Shakespeare gets his names for several characters from North's *Plutarch's Lives*— Polixenes and two other names, in fact, come from the same page, which also describes a sea storm off the coast of Libya.

While Greene uses completely different names for his characters, he includes a description of a sea storm off the coast of Libya in his novel that draws specific language from that same page, McCarthy tells us. He opens his laptop on the restaurant table and displays a graphic of the page from *Plutarch's Lives*, with arrows showing the elements that both Greene and Shakespeare have taken independently. "So Greene and Shakespeare are writing 25 years apart, but seemingly borrowing elements from the same passage," McCarthy says. "It's crazy for Greene, who just happens to write a sea storm and says, Let me look at page 1039 in *Plutarch's Lives*. But then Shakespeare starts naming characters from this exact same page, because he knows that the sea storm is borrowed from there? But then he doesn't even include the sea storm in the play!"

The more likely explanation, says McCarthy, is that North used the passage in a revised version of the play after translating Plutarch in 1580, and included both the names of the characters and the sea storm, which Greene and Shakespeare then borrowed independently of each other. The giveaway is that both Greene and Shakespeare mix up the location of the Oracle of Delphi, placing it on the "Isle of Delphos" instead (an apparent elision with the Isle of Delos, Apollo's supposed birthplace). The first and only other place McCarthy found that mix-up was in North's *Dial of Princes*—implying North may have repeated the error in his play, from which both Greene and Shakespeare both borrowed.

"That's gin!" he says. When I ask him, puzzled, what that means, he explains that an older cousin was a big fan of the card game gin, in which you call out the word when you draw the right card to win. He started using the expression for any moment in which an outcome had been decided beyond all doubt, and McCarthy adopted the practice. "I don't often say gin," McCarthy says. "But that's gin."

THE MOST IMMEDIATE evidence linking North with an early version of the play, in McCarthy's mind, is the descriptions in North's journal from his trip to Rome, starting with the scene of the woman in the church praying to the statue of Mary in Saint-André. More than one scholar has noted how the final scene of Hermione's resurrection seems to reference the restoration of Catholicism under Queen Mary. "Her preservation and revelation as a statue after sixteen years suggests the way many parishioners who bought images, vestments, and other church property auctioned under Henry and Edward VI, preserved and restored them to churches in Mary Tudor's reign," writes Ruth Vanita, a religion professor at the University of Montana.

Another scholar notes how the image of Perdita kneeling in front of Hermione's statue even calls to mind the way supplicants kneel before a statue of the Virgin Mary, seeking her grace. Perdita even says as much, pleading, "Do not say 'tis superstition, that I kneel, and then implore her blessing." After Hermione's statue miraculously comes alive, Leontes exclaims, "If this be magic, let it be an art lawful as eating." In 1611, that image would have seemed a throwback to the Catholic reign of Mary Tudor nearly fifty years before. But for someone writing in the 1550s, the debate about the legitimacy of praying to statues for miracles was at the heart of religious debate. "It's about the decriminalization of Catholicism," says McCarthy.

If that's true, then North's chance meeting in the snowy Alpine village with a woman beseeching Mary to resurrect her dead child may have conjured this image of Catholic devotion. On the page in his journal, North wrote the words "a fond superstition" in the margin, using the same word Perdita does about her own prayers. Whether or not he personally believed such miracles could occur, North must have been struck by the pitiful image of the grieving mother and her desperate hope for resurrection—so much so, according to McCarthy, that he used the image in a play to represent the resurrection of the Catholic Church. "People try to argue that Hermione never really died," he says. "They find it so hard to believe that Shakespeare—or anyone—could have thought such a resurrection from the dead could occur. But North saw a woman who did."

STORIES OF STATUES coming to life through divine power didn't originate with *The Winter's Tale*. Some scholars, for example, point to the story of Pygmalion in Ovid's *Metamorphoses*—in which a sculptor falls in love with his own statue, which is brought to life by the goddess Aphrodite—as a possible source for Shakespeare's inspiration. The image of a woman praying before a statue for resurrection isn't the only passage McCarthy believes North took for the play from his 1555 journal, however. In fact, he contends that North appropriated images from multiple encounters during his next few weeks on the road.

The delegation received devastating news in Saint-André: the pope, Julius III, had died. The ambassadors made the decision to press on anyway to meet with his successor, whomever that might be. Now, the most dangerous part of the journey began: crossing over the pass of Mont Cenis, a twelve-thousand-foot-high massif on the border of France and Italy. Today, the pass is closed even in mid-April, when the entire mountain face is turned into a giant ski area; we watch skiers in facemasks and heavy parkas slalom down a series of switchbacks tracing the timeworn approach to the pass.

As the delegation set out to climb that pass on April 2, it started to snow, soon worsening to a full-on blizzard. An awestruck North wrote about a mix of rain and snow that tumbled in great waterfalls from more than one hundred feet above them. In fear or exhaustion, he hired a guide to lead his horse, while he held on to its tail "for fear of falling backwards, it was so steep to the top." Along the way, he saw a starving man nearly buried in snow "making round balls of snow, and eating of them for very hunger." Still, the delegation had to traverse miles of snowfields, where they had to be careful to stay on the packed trail, or else "drown" in the deep drifts on either side. North encountered a church called the "Chapel of the Dead," containing as many as a thousand skulls of travelers who didn't make it, collected by monks after the spring thaw. Mercifully, none of the party added their heads to the collection. "We all passed without dangers, thanks be to God," North wrote in relief.

All of this wintry imagery so impressed North that he put it into *The Winter's Tale*, McCarthy says. Paulina berates the king after Hermione's death, telling him there is nothing he could do to atone. "A thousand knees," she says, "ten thousand years together, naked, fasting, upon a barren mountain, and still winter in storm perpetual, could not move the gods"—a fair evocation of North's harrowing crossing.

Once over Mont Cenis, the party was still not out of danger. In Italy at last, they found themselves in the middle of a war zone, where the French armies of Henri II were ravaging the emperor's cities. Approaching the town of Asti, the first of the emperor's holdings, troops shot from the walls, and North wrote of himself in the third person, saying that "Mr. Thomas North was in danger of killing." Another member of the party galloped ahead to tell the town they were from England, which was nominally allied with the emperor, and the delegation entered to a celebration instead.

For the next few days, soldiers escorted them from town to town. In Pavia, North stayed in La Certosa, a vast Carthusian monastery topped with a riot of spires and cupolas that he declared "the goodliest and best house in all Europe." North must have thought of his own home in London—the Charterhouse his father had acquired after the Carthusian monks had been driven out—and noted, perhaps with some guilt, that "all the monks" of La Certosa "be nobly born and descended." From Pavia, the party detoured north to Milan to spend the Easter holiday, before doubling back southeast through Lombardy. "We rode as between gardens," North wrote, "and to speak truth, my eyes

THOMAS NORTH'S

ITALY

--- AMBASSADORS'
ROUTE 1555

never saw any soil comparable to it for beauty and profit." After the traumatic mountain crossing, the fertile fields must have seemed like paradise.

As WE DRIVE now through Lombardy, a warm spring sun brightens the landscape. "The weather would have been just like this, minus a few degrees for climate change," says McCarthy, now behind the wheel of a rental car, as we pass rich fields of dark soil and bright green alfalfa. In the distance, rows of blue hills topped with far-off spires and towers look like the background of an Italian Renaissance painting. On our left, we spot the Torrazo of Cremona, a 367-foot brick bell tower that North also noted as the delegation arrived in the city on April 22, 1555. The next few days, McCarthy claims, were crucial in his composition of the play that Shakespeare would later adapt as *The Winter's Tale*.

In Cremona, the lords attended a wedding hosted by one Siginor Camillo Stanga, whom North goes out of his way to describe as "a very honest gentleman." Stanga must have made a particular impression on North, who named Camillo in *The Winter's Tale* after him, McCarthy argues. Despite betraying Leontes to help Polixenes escape, Camillo is constantly described as "honest" by other characters; even Leontes in the end praises Camillo's "worth and honesty." "Five times he's called honest," says McCarthy, who notes some critics have compared Camillo to Sir Thomas More, who opposed Henry's divorce with Katherine, even to the point of his own death.

As the delegation drew close to the city of Mantua, it encountered another scene that seems to eerily echo the play. On the morning of April 25, the party arrived at a church in the village of Curtatone named Santuario Beata Vergine Maria delle Grazie—Sanctuary of the Blessed Virgin Mary of Grace. One of the foremost pilgrimage sites in Italy, the sanctuary had been built in 1399 on the edge of a long lake by Mantua's ruler, Francesco I Gonzaga, in thanks to the Virgin Mary for the end of a plague that had devastated the city.

McCarthy and I now cross a wide plaza to enter the cool darkness of the church. Inside the spacious interior, a line of wooden pews faces an image of the Virgin Mary above an altar dating from the fourteenth century.

Strangely hanging above us is a taxidermied crocodile, which local legend claims was caught in a nearby river through the Virgin Mary's miraculous intercession. (In reality, it probably came from Egypt.) But that's not the end of the church's peculiar sights. All of the walls and pillars are painted a deep red, and bizarrely covered in patterns of body parts—eyes, hands, hearts, and breasts—made from yellow wax. Amid them, two tiers of galleries along both sides of the church are filled with dozens of painted sculptures made of wax and papier-mâché.

For centuries, pilgrims made offerings to Mary of these "ex-votos," statues commissioned in their likeness to intercede with the Virgin on their behalf. In 1517, a Franciscan friar melted down many of the sculptures and pressed the wax into molds to make the thousands of repeating body parts. He kept the best statues and built the galleries to display them. They are incredibly lifelike, painted in realistic flesh tones with rosy cheeks, and dressed in period clothing depicting the full range of early modern society. The Holy Roman Emperor Charles V is here, as well as at least one pope. But there are also noblewomen in embroidered dresses, soldiers in armor, and condemned criminals whom Mary apparently saved from execution. One has a noose around his neck, and another is held in the stocks, with an executioner about to swing a hammer down upon his head.

Rita Severi, a retired professor from the University of Verona, writes that these ex-voto sculptures, "like so many figures from the museum of Madame Tussaud, transform the church into a spectacular, theatrical place." Arriving at the church that morning, a spellbound North was clearly taken in by offerings to the Virgin, commenting on the "pictures of men, which she preserved (as they say)" and "such wonderful works of wax, as I never saw the like again." For someone who had never seen such lifelike painted sculptures before, the overall effect must have been mesmerizing. In the margin of his journal, he wrote the word: "miracles."

At least twice now in the space of a few weeks, North had seen offerings to the Virgin Mary, requesting her intervention, both in situations reminiscent of *The Winter's Tale*'s dramatic denouement. McCarthy points up at one statue of a woman in long robes, hands clasped in front of her in prayer. "That statue is typical of how Hermione would stand in the play," he whispers, so as not to disturb parishioners kneeling in the pews. In *The Winter's Tale*, in fact, the characters seem obsessed with how lifelike Hermione's statue seems. Paulina contends the statue is "life as lively mocked as ever still sleep mocked death," while Leontes exclaims, "Oh, thus she stood, even with such life of majesty—warm life, as it now coldly stands." Two gentlemen elaborate further, with one contending it is the work of "that rare Italian master, Julio Romano, who, had he himself eternity, and could put breath into his work, would beguile Nature of her custom." (That is, if he could only make his statues breathe, he'd put nature herself out of business.)

For centuries, scholars have struggled to explain why, of all artists, Shakespeare would pick Giulio Romano as the sculptor of Hermione's statue; in fact, he is the only contemporary artist mentioned in all of the plays. Born in Rome as Giulio di Piero Pippi de' Iannuzzi, he was one of the greatest pupils of Renaissance master Raphael, but he ran afoul of the pope's censors for a series of erotic drawings. At the invitation of Duke Federico II Gonzaga, he came to Mantua in 1524, taking the name Romano after his native city. Still, Giulio was primarily known as a painter and not nearly as well-known in England as other Italian artists such as Michelangelo or Raphael, making him a strange pick for Shakespeare's sculptor. According to Severi, however, Giulio may have in fact worked in wax statues, such as the ones in the Grazie church, including a funerary sculpture for Federico II Gonzaga's tomb. In the Grazie sanctuary itself, he designed the tomb for Baldassare Castiglione, an Italian diplomat and author of *The Book of the Courtier*, which he topped with a marble statue of a newly resurrected Christ.

Severi speculates that perhaps Shakespeare visited Grazie and was inspired by the wax statues there, associating them with Giulio—though she hastens to add that there's no evidence to support Shakespeare ever traveling to Italy. Alternatively, the playwright could have heard or read about the statues from another English traveler. For McCarthy, the explanation is obvious: North used his memory of these lifelike statues and conflated them with his experience in Saint-André to create the miraculous statue scene. "Severi's trying to find a traveler who managed to get this information to Shakespeare," McCarthy says. "We've got the traveler. Only, North didn't whisper this information in Shakespeare's ear, he wrote it down in a play."

THE GRAZIE CHURCH wasn't the only place where North encountered Giulio Romano. That afternoon, the travelers arrived in Mantua, where North would have had ample opportunity to see Giulio's work. The current duke, seventeen-year-old Guglielmo Gonzaga, treated the delegation to supper in his palace, where he was fond of showing off the paintings by Giulio commissioned by his family. It's possible, too, North saw Giulio's own tomb, in the nearby Church of San Barnaba, which included an inscription in Latin, reading: "Jupiter saw sculpted and painted bodies breathe and the homes of mortals made equal to those in heaven through the skill of Giulio Romano"—words reminiscent of the gentleman's description of the artist in *The Winter's Tale*.

In fact, scholars searching for Shakespeare's source for Giulio point to this inscription, which was printed in Giorgio Vasari's *Lives of the Artists*, a compendium of biographies of Renaissance artists first published in Italian in 1550. No English translation, however, existed until 1622, six years after Shakespeare's death, and there's no evidence the playwright could read Italian.

Other scholars have attempted to locate Shakespeare's source on almost any scrap of paper with Giulio's name on it—including an Italian book of instruction for young women in Italy, translated in 1598, that recommends "Jules Romain" as a model for home decoration, and an architecture treatise published in 1611, seven months after *The Winter's Tale* was first performed at court (leaving scholars to speculate that he must have viewed it before publication). North, however, didn't need to read about Giulio, says McCarthy—he saw his work firsthand. The artist's greatest work, in fact, may have played a special role in *The Winter's Tale*, one that has gone unnoticed for centuries.

On the evening of the delegation's arrival in Mantua, its members "went to the court," as North wrote, to formally deliver letters from Queen Mary to the Gonzaga family. This was almost certainly Palazzo Te, a palace designed, built, and decorated by Giulio, where the Gonzagas entertained their most important guests. We approach the palace now, a large white villa surrounded by a park where residents ride bicycles and walk their dogs. Once, the area had been a small island "a crossbow shot" from the city's southern wall. In one of Giulio's first commissions for Federico, he built the magnificent palace out of brick and stucco, decorating its interiors with frescoes.

Inside the palace, a tour guide with shoulder-length silver hair named Cristina leads us into an apartment Federico supposedly commissioned for his mistress, Isabella Boschetti, a married Mantuan noblewoman with whom he'd fallen desperately in love. Cristina points to frescoes Giulio painted on the walls with motifs incorporating a boschetta (literally "a small wood") along with erotic depictions of satyrs and maenads from Ovid's *Metamorphoses*. "Room after room we have these references," she says. Despite the extravagance of the palace, there is no evidence Boschetti herself ever stayed at Palazzo Te, and after a few years Federico seems to have lost interest in the palace, using it mainly for ceremonial occasions, such as two state visits from the Emperor Charles V.

North's delegation would have proceeded through the palace courtyard to enter a hall on its northern side. On its walls were *trompe-l'oeil* horses modeled after the Gonzagas' own treasured steeds, painted in front of pillars to give the illusion they were standing out from the walls. "Here guests were welcomed and received," Cristina tells us as we enter the chamber. The lords and ladies meeting the English delegation that evening included the duke's grandmother, wife, aunt, and daughter—and one lady, Hippolita, that particularly caught the eye of young North, who called her "one of the fairest ladies in the world." After introductions and speeches, the party likely moved on to the main event, a banquet arranged for them in the palace's most opulent room, the *Sala Di Amore e Psyche*— the Chamber of Cupid and Psyche.

"Wow, this is spectacular," sighs McCarthy as we enter the room, a broad grin on his face as he turns around slowly to take in the sight. If Palazzo Te were a play, this room would be its showstopping scene. Frescoes cover every inch of the walls and ceiling, tracing the mythological love story of Cupid and Psyche, a mortal woman for whom the god of love fell passionately after pricking himself with his own arrow. To earn his love, Psyche persevered through a series of impossible tasks set by Cupid's jealous mother, Venus—a story that must have particularly appealed to Federico in his impossible love for his mistress, Isabella Boschetti.

From the moment North's party entered the room, their eyes would have been transfixed by the octagonal panels on the ceiling and semi-circular lunettes on the walls that unfold the story of Psyche's hardships and eventual triumph in a dizzying spiral. Larger panels on each wall tell other mythological stories of forbidden couplings: The queen Pasiphaë, cursed by Neptune to fall in love with a bull, climbs into a cow costume to mate with it, later giving birth to the Minotaur. A randy Jupiter, penis erect, transforms into a serpent to slither into the bed of Olympias while his loyal eagle blinds her husband with a thunderbolt. (If there was any doubt of the subtext, Giulio painted Federico's face on Jupiter, and Boschetti's on Olympias.) Even the giant cyclops Polyphemus is struck by desire for the sea-nymph Galatea, glowering down at her from a towering fresco atop the fireplace.

"The legend is, that's on Sicily," McCarthy says, pointing up at the monster. But that is not the only connection he makes between this room and *The Winter's Tale.* If Thomas North's banquet here followed the pattern of a similar event for Charles V, the entourage would have sat at a table positioned diagonally in the northeast corner of the room, facing the room's greatest work: a rustic banquet to celebrate the marriage of Cupid and Psyche, attended by half-naked gods and goddesses. The happy couple reclines on a couch where the two walls meet, while on the far end of the left wall, the god Apollo relaxes with shepherdesses. Next to him, the god of wine, Bacchus, arrives with a camel, elephant, and other exotic animals while farmers bring baskets and sacks of food to the table. On the adjoining wall, two Horae—goddesses of the seasons— distribute flowers over the long feasting table while a couple of satyrs leer at them.

As the guests sat with Gonzaga and his courtiers, they must have felt almost as if they were taking part in the mythological feast, an effect heightened by the exotic delicacies brought to the table, including "green almonds," as North remarks, "the first that ever I saw." As he sat listening to the lords' conversation, North would have had ample time to admire the lurid frescoes, so different from the dark tapestries covering the halls of England. As he did, McCarthy believes, he was imagining how he would use all of their exotic imagery in creating another rustic banquet.

AFTER THE HEARTBREAK of Hermione's death, the fourth act of *The Winter's Tale* veers wildly from tragedy to comedy in depicting the Bohemian prince Florizel's courtship of the Sicilian exile Perdita. It's a forbidden love just like Federico's, since Perdita, unaware of her noble birth, now appears a lowly shepherdess. As the act begins, a peasant is preparing for a sheep-shearing festival, laying out sugar, currants, rice, and exotic spices such as saffron, mace, and ginger. Perdita appears wearing flowers in her hair, and Florizel tells her she is "no shepherdess, but Flora," one of the Horae. Florizel, meanwhile, disguises himself as a humble "swain," a country youth, but he tells Perdita they are attending "as a meeting of the petty gods, and you the queen on't." As the guests arrive—including Polixenes and Camillo, disguised to spy on the young lovers—Perdita distributes flowers. The party gets going, and twelve county dancers dressed up as satyrs perform for the feastgoers.

North took all of these elements from Giulio's fantastical feast, McCarthy says, beginning to give a tour of his own. "You have the spice trade here, with camels and elephants bringing sacks of food to the table," he says, gesturing up at the exotic animals of Bacchus as our guide looks on and Galovski and Wexler surreptitiously film him with an iPhone. "And there's Flora handing out flowers, and there are the satyrs." The other frescoes find their way into the play, too, McCarthy says. As Perdita frets over the thought of King Polixenes seeing his son dressed down in country clothing, Florizel calms her. "The gods themselves have taken the shapes of beasts upon them," he says. "Jupiter became a bull, and bellowed; the green Neptune a ram, and bleated; and the fire-robed god, Golden Apollo, a poor humble swain, as I seem now."

Energetically moving around the room, McCarthy points out Apollo lounging with the shepherdesses, his robe half-open, as if a "humble swain" (a country peasant), along with the other stories of gods changing into beasts to woo women. True, some of the myths are different. Florizel talks of Jupiter turning into a bull, not a serpent; and Neptune becoming a ram, not his curse of Pasiphaë; but the two gods are the same. He even points to a lunette on the wall just to the right of the banquet depicting one of Psyche's tasks—to shear a piece of the famed golden fleece from a flock of sheep—a possible inspiration for the sheep-shearing festival itself.

Of course, there are so many gods in the room, it would be hard to find one that *isn't* included in Giulio's overenthusiastic pastiche. But the overall setting of a rustic banquet, and some details, such as Flora scattering flowers, the satyrs, and Apollo dressed as a "swain" seem too specific to be coincidental. Moreover, McCarthy has an explanation for *why* North might want to mix up all of these lascivious Greek divinities with the Marian imagery he's included elsewhere in the play. "All these women are impregnated by all of these gods, just like the Virgin Mary," he says, so excited he can barely contain himself. What better way to bring back Catholicism, with all of its superstitious cults, McCarthy says, than appealing to the classics.

"People think it's a crazy play, but Thomas North is trying to say that all of this Roman mythology is beautiful. People are praying to these gods who have also impregnated women and had kings as children, and that's exactly what happens with the Virgin Mary." If McCarthy is right, then that revelation may have occurred to North in Mantua. "The only place in the world where you get all these Virgin Mary miracles and all of this pagan mythology is right here," says McCarthy, veering into hyperbole. "And it all occurred on the same day: April 25, 1555."

AFTER OUR TOUR of the palazzo, we walk a short distance through the park to an outdoor cafe, where McCarthy summarizes the confusion over *The Winter's Tale*. "It's all over the place. You've got pagan mythology, you've got Catholic imagery, then you've got this reference to Giulio Romano that no one can explain," he says, gesturing with his hands like an Italian. All of it falls into place, however, he says, bringing his hands back to the table with his café Americano, "when it's turned back into the life of Queen Mary."

Why does any of this even matter? I ask him. "A lot of people are going to say, well, who cares," McCarthy allows—but it's impossible, he argues, to fully understand the play without knowing why it was originally written. "It's like not knowing that *Animal Farm* is an allegory for the Russian Revolution," he says about George Orwell's 1945 book. "When you take *The Winter's Tale* as an allegory of Queen Mary's life everything makes sense. The wonder still stays, but now you've got this historical background to it, which enables the lesson and magnifies its importance."

As compelling as his theories seem to me, it's clear that McCarthy has a tougher climb to convince mainstream scholars. After our trip, I call Ruth Vanita, the University of Montana religion professor who so strongly argued for the play as an allegory for Mary's life, expecting her to be intrigued at least by McCarthy's ideas about an *Ur-Winter's Tale* penned by Thomas North. Instead, she dismisses them out of hand. "He's just made up these plays out of thin air?" she asks. "If the plays don't exist, and there's no evidence this guy was even a playwright, it's ridiculous."

McCarthy sent an email a few years earlier to Rita Severi, the Italian Shakespearean who pointed out the lifelike statues in the Grazie sanctuary as a possible inspiration for Hermione's resurrection scene. He included information about the journal and his theories, asking if perhaps Thomas North could be the traveler upon whom Shakespeare relied for inspiration. Severi wrote back, politely saying that she had already known about the journal, sending him a copy of her 2013 paper on Shakespeare and Giulio Romano, which mentions the Grazie church. That paper, however, didn't mention the journal, nor did a follow-up essay in 2016 about Shakespeare and Mantua. After McCarthy contacted her, however, she published both essays in a new book, almost identical except for the addition in the latter of a long discussion of North's journal, including the visit to the Grazie sanctuary and Palazzo Te, identifying it as the only sixteenth-century account that described the sanctuary's interior.

McCarthy tried to contact her before our own trip, without a response. I get her number through her publisher, and give her a call now as we walk the narrow streets of Mantua, asking if she could meet us. Unfortunately, she can't, she says, as it's a week before Easter and she is hosting friends. But she knows all about McCarthy's theories about Thomas North, she says. When I ask her if his 1555 visit might have inspired him to write an early version of *The Winter's Tale*, she rejects the idea. "No, I don't really agree with this hypothesis, because I stand by William," she says, using Shakespeare's first name as if he is one of her visiting guests. "I believe in William from Stratford-upon-Avon."

When I tell McCarthy about her reply, he is visibly frustrated. "I find it extraordinarily coincidental that she knew about this journal but didn't write about it until I contacted her about it," he says. "And then she doesn't even want to consider my theory." He is used to dismissals like this, however; in all his years pursuing his theories about Thomas North, he's heard versions of it many times. "They don't want to discuss it," he sighs as we walk down the cobblestone streets. "They don't want to be challenged." Although he might have broken through to biogeographers, he was finding Shakespeareans much tougher to crack, resistant to any alternative theory about how Shakespeare wrote his plays.

As he continued to follow Thomas North's life, McCarthy found that the young writer faced his own challenges as he joined a literary circle of courtiers trying to curry favor with their new, Catholic queen. Just like his father before him, Thomas would soon find that in the changing religious politics of the Tudor court, he was backing the wrong horse.

Chapter Five
PRINCES' FAVORS

(1556–1558)

Oh, how wretched
Is that poor man that hangs on princes' favors!
— *Henry VIII*

The Honourable Society of Lincoln's Inn rises from the heart of London's West End, just a few minutes' walk from the tourist crush of Covent Garden. As we arrive in the early evening on our way back from visiting Faversham, antique gas lamps are just starting to illuminate the streetscape as the sky fades to dark. "This is where North first began writing his plays and having them produced," says McCarthy confidently, gesturing back toward the red brick Gothic and Tudor spires that rise behind an aging brick wall. Of course, there's no evidence that those plays existed, much less that they were ever performed here, but that fact hasn't stopped McCarthy from believing it. "No one even published plays at the time with their names on them," he insists, adding that taking credit for playwriting would have been a particularly distasteful act for a gentleman such as North. That fact would start to change over the next few decades, however, starting at the Tudor law schools known as the Inns of Court, where English drama got its true start—and where McCarthy began to uncover clues suggesting North may have been a playwright after all.

When Thomas North arrived at Lincoln's Inn fresh off the delegation to Rome in early 1556, his fortunes were on an upswing, and studying here was his surest means to continue his advancement. The oldest of the four Inns of Court—which include Gray's Inn, the Middle Temple, and the

Inner Temple—the society had its beginnings in the fourteenth century as a lodging house for provincial lawyers practicing at Westminster or London. Over time, the Inns grew from legal societies to de facto law schools of England. By the sixteenth century, the only way to practice in court was to "pass the bar" in one of their great halls and become a barrister.

As the son of a barrister who had also attended Lincoln's Inn, North was given "special admission," which entitled him to sit with the Masters at the upper end of the Great Hall, rather than with the Fellows at the common tables. With annual costs for students ranging from £40 to £50 ($21,525 to $26,905), North was now literally looking down on the elite of English society—the sons of nobles and gentlemen, along with the occasional yeoman farmer or merchant. Lodgings were spartan, lacking hearths, and education was rigorous, with required lectures by senior lawyers and "moots" three times a week, in which students performed elaborate arguments based on hypothetical legal questions.

All of that, however, was just the exterior trappings of the inns. In fact, most of the young men there had no intention of studying years to become a lawyer, any more than liberal arts students today plan on becoming academics. Their fathers sent them to learn the ways of the world, soak up some culture, and learn how to protect their property. Students saw the experience as an opportunity to live close to city and the court, where they could gamble, duel, and pursue ladies. The records of Lincoln's Inn are full of student fines—even expulsions—for lying, stealing, stabbing, and bringing women to chambers. A few months after North arrived, the Masters declared that there "shall be no more playing of dice in the Hall except in time of Christmas." Someone later scratched out "except in time of Christmas." Arrest records of the time show innsmen to be familiar with the Bankside brothels.

The overall impression is of an all-male society of libidinous students at odds with their aged chaperones. Or as Jessica Winston, author of *Lawyers at Play*, puts it, "Youth and age, lust and law, quarrels and debates, trysts and tête-à-têtes—these oppositions characterize the early modern Inns of Court." These were the sons of the "new men" of Henry VIII's time, eager to distinguish themselves from mere barristers, even as they drank and gambled and played at swords. While no doubt influenced by this anarchic environment, Thomas North seems to have kept himself apart from it, spending long hours in his cold cell devoting himself to literary pursuits instead. In that, he was not alone. As the Renaissance made its slow advance across the Continent from Italy, the sons of the first flowering of humanist education increasingly began writing literature of their own.

THE BOOK NORTH chose to write was not an original work, but a translation of a book he must have picked up in Europe: *El Relox de Principes* by Spanish bishop Antonio de Guevara, an adviser to Holy Roman Emperor Charles V. A favorite read of Charles's son, England's new king, Philip II, it was an inspired choice for a young man looking to ingratiate himself with the new Catholic powers in Westminster. North called his translation *The Dial of Princes*, a more romantic version of the Spanish title, which translates to "The Clock of Princes." As Guevara explained, the book was a "clock of life," which instead tells us "how we are to occupy ourselves every hour."

The work fits into a genre all the rage in sixteenth-century Europe, known as *speculum principis*, or "mirror for princes"—didactic instruction manuals for royalty and nobility. Along with other examples of the genre, such as Niccolò Machiavelli's *The Prince* and Baldassare Castiglione's *The Book of the Courtier*, in North's day Guevara's book was a bestseller on the Continent; according to one Renaissance scholar, in fact, it was "the most widely read book in sixteenth century Europe" after the Bible. Guevara claimed that the work was based on an autobiography of Stoic Roman Emperor Marcus Aurelius that he had translated from Greek—though because Guevara apparently didn't know Greek, the book is almost surely his own invention. (Marcus Aurelius's actual *Meditations* had yet to be rediscovered.) After critics blasted Guevara for an early version, *The Golden Book of Marcus Aurelius*, that they said venerated a pagan ruler, Guevara rushed out a new version, three times as long, that held up the Roman emperor as the ideal model for a *Christian* prince.

This is the book North translated—in truth, generally a downer of a read, claiming that for a virtuous ruler, the privileges of power are overshadowed by its cares. As North spent long hours deciphering Guevara's text (working primarily from a French version), he soaked up Guevara's philosophy, a mix of humanism and stoicism teaching that a true ruler thinks of himself as a servant to his people; at the same time, no matter how tyrannical a ruler becomes, his subjects are never justified in rebelling against him, as it will only cause him to become more cruel.

Other sections of *The Dial* are full of practical advice for any person, covering marriage, pregnancy, and childrearing. The last part expounds on princely virtues, as Marcus Aurelius carries on dialogues with his counselors, including an extended meditation on death. The book, says McCarthy, was a storehouse of knowledge and philosophy, to which North would return again and again as he worked through his ideas about kings and rulers, relationships between men and women, and even the nature of life and death itself—as McCarthy first found in Hamlet's famous "To be, or not to be" soliloquy.

EVEN AS NORTH was diligently studying what makes an ideal ruler, he had a close-up example of how not to rule: England's own Catholic queen. While Londoners continued to grumble about Mary's foreign king and his rude Spanish entourage, her only hope for restoring their favor was giving birth to an heir with English blood. Unfortunately, Mary seemed to have inherited her mother's difficulty in having children, with a false pregnancy in her first years of rule. Philip left to return to Spain in August 1555, and she began to believe that God was punishing her for not rooting out all of the heretics in the realm. Mary stepped up her persecutions, sending dozens to the fires every month, and finally leading the architect of the Reformation, Thomas Cranmer, to the stake in 1556.

As her fires of atonement raged in Smithfield—visible, perhaps, to Thomas from his cell in Lincoln's Inn, as they were to his father Edward across the fields in the Charterhouse—Mary received more bad news from abroad. After some forty years on the throne, Emperor Charles V announced his abdication to live out his last years in a monastery, making his brother, Ferdinand, the new Holy Roman Emperor, and his son Philip king of his Spanish kingdom, including the Netherlands, Naples, and Sicily. Now that he had a crown of his own, Philip lost interest in his

English queen. Rumors came to England's shores of Philip chasing women overseas, even as Mary pined for his return.

In the midst of this anxiety and doubt, the Inns of Court provided a refuge from the outside world, where a select group of students continued their literary endeavors, translating classical authors such as Cicero, Ovid, and Virgil. (One scholar writes, "A study of the Elizabethan translations is a study of the means by which the Renaissance came to England.") They weren't completely removed from the outside world, however, instead seeing themselves as an enlightened elite who could give advice for good ordering of the "commonweal." As Mary spiraled into depression and violence, they increasingly pursued a darker mirror image to their *speculum principis* treatises.

Known as *de casibus* literature (after Italian writer Boccaccio's 1358 work *De Casibus Virorum Illustrium—The Fall of Princes*), these new stories were concerned not with rosy advice for princes, but cautionary tales from history about rulers who'd fallen spectacularly from power. Soon writers from across the inns were collaborating on a compendium of tales illustrating the downfall of English princes, kings, lords, and rebels of the fourteenth and fifteenth centuries, from the deposition of Richard II to the usurpation of Richard III, with all the Henrys in between. A fellow at the Inner Temple, William Baldwin, served as secretary for the group, pulling together all of the stories and collating them into a book published as *The Mirror for Magistrates*.

To say the book was influential is putting it mildly. It was arguably the most important book published in England in the sixteenth century, spurring a conversation about ethics of governing that would last for the next fifty years—up to and including Shakespeare's history plays on the same subjects a generation later. The project was published by London printer John Wayland, the same printer who would also publish North's *Dial of Princes*. While North most likely had his hands full with his own project, it's not impossible that he contributed to the *Mirror* in some form. At any rate, he certainly was involved in conversations with his fellow innsmen about the stories it contained. Winston writes, "*The Mirror* imagines a space—perhaps John Wayland's shop—where a group of men can gather to discuss literary, intellectual, and political ideas, and to challenge each other on these issues and questions." Soon, some of these debates were playing out on a more public stage as well.

The great hall at Lincoln's Inn was many things: dining commons, law classroom, mock courthouse—and one of England's first theaters. The "revels" at the Inns of Court were just as much a part of the culture of the society as the moots, presided over by a master of revels responsible for entertainments at Christmas and a half dozen other festivals during the year. As students tried to outdo each other with elaborate costumes, hired minstrels, and mechanical apparatus—often at their parents' expense—they competed for literary acclaim as well. Out of these scrappy student productions eventually blossomed one of the greatest literary creations of all time: Elizabethan drama.

WHEN NORTH'S FATHER, Edward, attended Lincoln's Inn in the 1520s, he had served as Christmas Steward three years in a row. Now, Thomas was afforded an even higher honor. Just eight months after he was admitted, on November 1, 1556, the members voted him to become master of revels—sharing the post with three other students. Clearly they saw promise in his writing skills beyond mere translation of prose. For McCarthy, this discovery was the first indication that Thomas was involved in the production of theater. "They were the ones providing the entertainments," he tells me. "That shows his interest in playwriting."

Thumbing through a copy of Lincoln's Inn's record books at the British Library, however, I find reason to be skeptical. By the following February—just three months later—the Masters fined North 26 shillings, 8 pennies ($675) for "not exercising the office of Master of the Revels," seriously calling into doubt how seriously North took the honor. Unfortunately, there are few records of the entertainments that were performed at the Inns of Court in the 1550s and 1560s, so the extent of North's involvement remains a mystery.

If he did take part in theater, however briefly, he would have been immersed in a rich stew of influences from centuries of English entertainments, from lives of the saints popular since medieval times, to folk dramas depicting the daring exploits of Robin Hood, complete with stock villains and hammy performances. Starting at the turn of the sixteenth century, more refined audiences at court watched allegorical morality plays with sedate actors portraying virtues such as Pity, Mercy, and Charity triumphing over the scene-stealing vices of Mischief, Pride, Idleness, and Riot. As morality plays started becoming secularized in the 1520s, some took on a more overtly political bent. Even as Edward North was writing his poem attacking Cardinal Wolsey, Henry VIII's former tutor John Skelton produced the play *Magnificence* about a prince misled by evil counselors—a thinly veiled attack on Henry's wicked counselor Wolsey and one of the first examples of *speculum principis* literature making the stage. In the 1530s, Thomas Cromwell apparently backed a play, *King John*, warning of the dangers of Catholicism. In 1553, the anonymous Christmas play *Respublica* criticized the enclosure movement that privatized common land.

If Thomas North attended university at Cambridge, as is commonly surmised, he would have also been well acquainted with classical plays from Greece and Rome, which were increasingly the mainstay of a humanist education—especially the comedies of Roman playwright Terence, who, according to one scholar of early drama, "held the position as dramatist in sixteenth-century Europe that Shakespeare holds in the English-speaking world today." Terence established the five-act structure later adopted by English playwrights, using colloquial Latin to put his characters in amusing circumstances, often based on mistaken identity and bawdy sexual situations.

North's first plays at Lincoln's Inn, McCarthy contends, were those inspired by the journal of his European trip. An *Ur-Winter's Tale* would have been more than at home in the environment of the Inns of Court, with its classical references, Catholic imagery, and allegorical story, which fits into a traditional morality play. Just as Perdita means "lost," McCarthy surmises that in an original version of the play, perhaps all of the characters may have had allegorical names, which were changed to the classical names derived from Plutarch when North later revised the play. While today's critics puzzle at its strange romantic pastiche, the story would have been instantly recognizable in 1557 as an allegory for Henry, Katherine, Philip, and Mary. There's another Shakespeare play, however, that wouldn't even require audiences to guess about its intent.

HENRY VIII IS, simply put, a terrible play. There's good reason Shakespeare's final history play, first performed in 1613, is almost never staged today—the play is a mess, really three or four playlets strung together rather than any kind of coherent drama. The seventeenth-century diarist Samuel Pepys wrote that the play "is so simple a thing, made up of a great many patches, that, besides the shows and processions in it, there is nothing in the world good or well done." British literary critic Tony Tanner calls it "hardly a play, or 'drama' at all."

Subtitled *All Is True*, the play focuses first on the downfall of the Duke of Buckingham at the hands of Cardinal Thomas Wolsey, who is portrayed as an unmitigated villain. That's followed by a long and sympathetic portrayal of Queen Katherine of Aragon, who is cast aside by Henry but almost turned into a saint with an extended dream sequence in which she is carried to heaven in white robes. Wolsey then gets his just deserts as his treason with France is revealed. The play then shows the rise of Anne Boleyn, who is blasted as an unscrupulous opportunist. That portrayal is, awkwardly, followed by a coda in which Thomas Cranmer praises the future coming of Anne Boleyn's daughter, Queen Elizabeth, prophesying a long and glorious reign.

Scholars throw up their hands trying to explain why Shakespeare would even write such a disjointed jumble so late in his career. One critic comments that "the play's structure is built on an apparently arbitrary pattern of rises and falls." Other critics find in it a cautionary tale of the "wheel of fortune" that raises up one figure after another only to see them laid low. Other commentators, however, have found in it a throwback to the *de casibus* tradition laid out in *The Mirror for Magistrates*—a series of stories about the fall of great personages. In fact, the play's prologue includes a line seemingly taken straight out of *The Mirror*: "Think you see them great," the narrator says, "see how soon this mightiness meets misery."

Seeing the play as a later adaptation of a drama North wrote in the late 1550s, says McCarthy, clears up the mystery. If North was striving for a position at court, then what better way to do it than to praise the queen's mother—whom Mary herself venerated as a saint—and at the same time depicting the downfall of her enemies in moralistic terms. The pivotal scene in the middle of the play, in which Katherine falls asleep and envisions a troop of angelic visitors holding garlands over her head and inviting her to a banquet, seems ripped from a Catholic miracle play designed to enshrine Katherine in heaven.

Even the unsympathetic portrayal of Wolsey makes sense in an *Ur-All Is True* written by North. While Wolsey was universally excoriated as a symbol of decay of the priesthood, he would have been particularly held up as an object of contempt by the son of Edward North. Thomas would have known all about his father's literary endeavors criticizing Henry VIII's minister, leading to his anxious year in the Tower—as I'd discovered in the National Archives. What better way for Thomas North to enact a kind of literary revenge? (The final coda with Cranmer praising Elizabeth, McCarthy says, could be explained as a later addition by Shakespeare and his cowriter John Fletcher to update the drama for Jacobean times.)

MCCARTHY FINDS FURTHER evidence to support his theory in details in North's journal of his trip to Rome. After leaving Mantua, the delegation traveled along the spine of the Apennine Mountains, feted along the way in Ferrara and Bologna, where they arrived to a greeting of "trumpets and drums." Continuing on to the coast at Pesaro, they were treated to another banquet where they were invited to meet with the ladies of the court. "As many of us as could speak Italian, or French, went to entertain these Ladies and Gentlemen," North writes. Even those who didn't speak the language sat down among them to behold "their surpassing beauties." As they were admiring "this heavenly and angelic troop of Ladies," a group of musicians struck up a tune, and the delegation members were encouraged "to take out a Lady or Gentlewoman to dance withal, and so they did."

A similar scene takes place in *Henry VIII*, employing some of the same language, says McCarthy. A group of foreign entertainers shows up at court, arriving (according to stage directions) with the sound of "drum and trumpet" and the shot of cannon. When Cardinal Wolsey asks who it is, he is told by a servant that it is a "noble troop of strangers" coming "as great ambassadors from foreign princes." Wolsey tells the lord chamberlain to welcome them, since he "can speak the French tongue," and then bring them to the Cardinal, "where this heaven of beauty shall shine at full upon them." Later, the chamberlain returns. "Because they speak no English," he tells Wolsey, the ambassadors wish to meet the ladies of the court and "under your fair conduct crave leave to view these ladies, and entreat an hour of revels with 'em." The ambassadors then proceed to dance with the ladies and enjoy a great banquet.

As similar as the passages are, they aren't unique. Scholars have traced some elements to another passage, written by Wolsey's gentleman-usher, George Cavendish, in a manuscript titled *The Life and Death of Cardinal Wolsey*. In that manuscript, Cavendish writes about a banquet given by Anne Boleyn in which there were "a number of the fairest ladies and gentlewomen" that appeared to be "celestial angels descended from heaven." While no one has speculated how Shakespeare could have obtained the manuscript, unpublished until 1641, McCarthy notes that the document, written sometime between 1554 and 1556, was widely circulated among Catholics during Mary's reign, and North could have acquired it through Thirlby or another member of the delegation and incorporated its language into his writing during the trip or when copying the journal upon his return.

McCARTHY POINTS TO more similarities between another passage in *Henry VIII* and one North wrote in his journal a few weeks later. Along the way to Rome, the delegation learned that the new pope, Marcellus II, had died, replaced with yet another pope, Paul IV. Unfortunately, this new pope was hostile to the Spanish Habsburgs, England's allies, casting a pall on the end of the delegates' long journey. Nevertheless, he richly received the ambassadors with gifts, including great wheels of Parmesan cheese and bacon, and invited them to the Vatican.

By coincidence, McCarthy and I arrive in Rome on Good Friday just as workmen are closing off roads by the Roman Forum in order to prepare for a procession around the Coliseum, presided over by Pope Francis I. In the evening, thousands of people will encircle the monument holding candles in a procession with the pope looking down from a chair on a platform above. Thomas North encountered similar scenes in 1555 when he was led into the presence of the pope along with Thirlby and the other ambassadors. The delegates entered the pope's summer palace of San Marco, where "the Pope sat in a conclave...in a great high chair." After "conclave," North made a parenthetical insertion, "(or consistory)," noting that the cardinals were sitting around him, and "the bishops underneath."

Two days later, the delegation witnessed an elaborate procession of the pope and his cardinals, which North described in detail. First came the "officers of his household" in "scarlet gowns. After them followed two, carrying each of them a mitre, and two officers next them with silver rods in their hands. Then the cardinals having a cross borne before them, and every cardinal his several pillar borne next before himself."

Similar passages occur in Cavendish's manuscript. In one section, he describes Katherine's trial before the pope's representatives, in which they sat "in the manner of a consistory"—the same phrase North uses—with the judges on high chairs, and "under the judges feet sat the scribes." In a completely different scene, Cavendish describes a procession of Cardinal Wolsey, noting, among other details, a "sergeant of arms before him bearing a great mace of silver, and two gentlemen carrying of two great pillars of silver," followed by "two cross bearers."

McCarthy believes that North was using Cavendish's manuscript as a sort of field guide to illustrate what he was seeing when he witnessed the pope's procession. "It's like if you are a bird watcher, and you go to Sibley's *Guide to Birds* to help figure out what you are seeing," McCarthy says as we are sitting together in the backseat of a taxi on the way to the Rome airport. "Only, he's got this thing describing religious processions."

The stage directions in *Henry VIII* echo both scenes, inventing an elaborate religious procession featuring Wolsey and other leaders on their way to the court at Blackfriars for Katherine's trial. It is the most detailed set of stage directions in any of Shakespeare's plays, beginning: "Enter two Vergers, with short silver wands; next them, two Scribes, in the habit of doctors; after them, the Bishop of Canterbury alone," and so it goes, including "two Priests, bearing each a silver cross" and "a Sergeant at Arms bearing a silver mace; then two gentlemen bearing two great silver pillars." After that, the king and queen sit onstage while the "Bishops place themselves on each side the court, in manner of a consistory;"—that word again—"below them, the Scribes."

McCarthy contends that the play is putting together both of the scenes from Cavendish in order to create the stage directions. Those two scenes take place in wildly different parts of Cavendish's manuscript, however. The only reason that the play puts them together, McCarthy says, is that North first put them together on consecutive days in his journal. "He puts together the consistory scene with the Wolsey procession because that's exactly what happens when he saw it," McCarthy says.

Providing further evidence that North's journal led to the play, McCarthy points out the quirky adverbial phrases, "after them" followed by "next them with," which occurs once in the journal and twice in the play's stage directions. Balancing his computer on his lap, McCarthy does a search in Google for the two phrases within twenty words of each other, only coming up with *Henry VIII* and the printed copy of North's journal. "It's a peculiar way of listing things that could refer to anything in the world—flowers, animals at the zoo, boats—and in billions and billions of sources, it only comes up in *Henry VIII* and North," McCarthy says. "There's no way that's a coincidence."

NORTH WROTE ONE more Catholic-leaning play during his student years at Lincoln's Inn, McCarthy believes: his early version of *Arden of Faversham*. Given all the correspondences he identified between that play and North's *Dial of Princes*, McCarthy suggests North wrote that play after the other two, when he was already heavily at work on that translation. If North did write this play around 1557, it would be shockingly advanced for the time. Domestic tragedies involving real people and real crimes wouldn't appear in England for decades. Then again, it would certainly make sense for North to write the play soon after the time when the murder took place—and when he was getting monthly reminders of his half sister's fate in the burnings of heretics taking place across the fields in Smithfield.

There's a lot in the play, too, that seems to argue for an earlier date—the stage directions are antiquated, with the repetition of "Here enters..." rather than the more common "Enter...," and the characters of Black Will and Shakebag seem like devils from religious drama come to life, at times emerging from and disappearing into mists. Then there's the miracle that ends the play, with Arden's body spontaneously bleeding and leaving a print in the grass for years. Most of all, however, there is the theme of the play, in which Arden's murder seems tied to his part in the Dissolution of the Monasteries.

When Mary came to power, her first instinct was to restore the monks to their homes and undo the pillaging of the religious houses. She quickly realized, however, that such a feat was impossible. Many of the monasteries had already been torn down, their stones repurposed into the homes of the nobles and gentlemen she now needed on her side to rule the realm. That would explain why North might write a play recognizing his family's complicity in the Dissolution—signaling his desire to make amends. "He's showing that the North family is totally on the Catholic boat, and have realized their mistakes," claims McCarthy. "So he's using that to get into the good graces of the queen."

As implied by Dudley North's later biography of Edward, however, McCarthy believes Thomas underestimated the response of his father— who was so furious with his son for criticizing him that his descendant was still writing about it a century later. And surprisingly, McCarthy finds more evidence for this view in *Greene's Groatsworth of Wit*, the satire that first calls Shakespeare an "upstart crow" and seems to reference North selling plays to Shakespeare. In the beginning of that story, the author describes a "Gentleman" of "exceeding wealth" who "had good experience in *Noverint*"—a term McCarthy had already learned was a reference to the Latin of property law. "By the universal terms therein contained," it continues, he "had driven many a young gentleman to seek unknown countries." McCarthy sees that as a possible allusion to the Dissolution of the Monasteries, which drove many monks out of their homes; some even fled England to Catholic countries such as France and Spain.

This gentleman, he continues, had two sons, but "esteemed but one, that being as himself, brought up to be golds bondman, was therefore held heir apparent of his ill-gathered goods." The other son was "a Scholar," and a "fool" who criticized his father for the practice of usury, or lending to people with interest. While the passage doesn't exactly refer to the Dissolution, says McCarthy, it does imply some criticism by the son over the way his father made his money—which would be exactly the case here.

Of course, the irony is that in apologizing for the Dissolution on behalf of his family, Thomas would be doing exactly what Edward himself did so many times—swaying to the prevailing religious winds, perhaps (with the naiveté of youth) expecting his father might be pleased at the way he atoned for his father's sins. By this time, however, Edward had already found his own ways to show his loyalty to the crown. As a new baron, he was now the only hereditary peer in Cambridgeshire, with landholdings stretching all around London. On New Year's Day 1557, he gave Queen Mary £20 ($10,060) in a purse, a gift more suited to a bishop or an earl than a mere baron. That year, Mary named Edward lord lieutenant of Cambridgeshire, the queen's personal representative in the county. As an even greater honor, she appointed him to a commission for suppression of heresy, along with Bishop Thirlby—Thomas's former master—and other prominent Catholics. Their charges were to "search for and examine suspects for heresy," referring them for fines, imprisonment, and worse. The man who had once been jailed for criticizing Cardinal Wolsey, and actively helped dissolve the monasteries, was now in his last act persecuting Protestants.

DESPITE HER EFFORTS, God continued to punish Mary with bad harvests, even as England was once again dragged into Europe's interminable wars. The new pope, Paul IV, had turned more virulently against the Habsburg Empire, excommunicating Philip II and allying with France to make war against Spain. In need of allies, Philip returned to England and persuaded Mary to attack France on his behalf. As Thomas North continued to work diligently on his translation of *The Dial of Princes*, troops mobilized to cross the channel to Calais, by this point England's last holding in France. North finally finished the book on December 20, 1557, bringing it to John Wayland for printing. In a little over two years, Thomas had completed a massive work of over six hundred pages. "He's twenty-two," McCarthy says. "It's really a colossal, mind-blowing work to have written by that time." The book was an immediate success, not just as a translation but—as a twentieth-century editor remarked—"as literature" in its own right.

Hoping to capitalize on his accomplishment, North dedicated the book to "the most high and virtuous princess Mary," writing that any ruler who dedicated her study "to the profit of the weal public, should be correspondingly of the commonwealth entertained, preferred, and honored." Of course, the dedication also implied that North's own adherence to humanist wisdom earned him the right to be "entertained" at court. No doubt, he hoped for an advancement to government office, just as his father's poem had helped him secure his own position decades ago. In that desire, however, he was disappointed. After all North's work, his book release fell victim to terrible timing. That December, Mary and her ministers were preoccupied with lists of ships and funds to reinforce their holdings in France. By January 1558, however, it was too late. In a surprise move, the French unleashed an attack on Calais, capturing England's last city on the Continent.

The loss was a crushing psychological blow for England; once again, Mary blamed Protestants for God's punishment, redoubling her efforts to root out heretics. The people, however, were disgusted by the brutality of her public burnings, which have forever earned Mary Tudor her nickname, "Bloody Mary." Ironically, she had done more to turn people against Catholicism than anything Henry VIII or Edward VI ever did. Still, God's punishments continued, with an influenza outbreak during the summer of 1558, leading to an untold number of deaths that year— including Thomas North's own younger sister, Mary. Even the queen took ill with fevers, insomnia, and depression, worsening into the fall. When it became clear she might not recover, she frantically sent for her half sister, Elizabeth, to make her promise to uphold the Catholic religion as her successor. Before Elizabeth made it to court, however, on November 17, 1558, Mary Tudor died after receiving Holy Communion. The Elizabethan era had begun.

Chapter Six

BLOOD AND REVENGE

(1558–1564 / 2006–2011)

> Vengeance is in my heart, death in my hand,
> Blood and revenge are hammering in my head.
>
> —*Titus Andronicus*

According to legend, Elizabeth was sitting under an oak at Hatfield House, an estate north of London, when she got the news of her half sister Mary's death, and immediately fell to her knees to thank God. Just twenty-five years old, she'd outlasted her brother and her sister, and survived the fires of the Protestant purge. Now Londoners lit bonfires of celebration, while courtiers such as the Norths, who had embraced Mary's regime, waited nervously to discover whether she would punish or forgive them.

That afternoon, Elizabeth assembled a shadow cabinet that seemed to prize practicality over persecution. Her new secretary of state was thirty-eight-year-old William Cecil, a quintessential bureaucrat who had been a fervently Protestant privy councilor under King Edward, but also one of the first ministers to swear fealty to Mary. During her reign, he stayed close to Elizabeth, and she came to trust him above all others. Her other chief counselor was Cecil's opposite: Robert Dudley, who arrived at Hatfield on a white horse, a dashing courtier to Cecil's cold-blooded technocrat. The son of Edward North's former ally John Dudley, Robert would soon play an outsized role in the fortunes of the entire North family—especially, contends McCarthy, Thomas's.

Robert Dudley would later say that he'd known Elizabeth "better than any man alive since she was eight years old." Though it's unlikely he and

Elizabeth began a love affair while imprisoned together in the Tower—
as some have romantically speculated—they nevertheless forged a unique
bond in surviving the trauma of Mary's persecution. Elizabeth named him
her Master of Horse, and he was by her side as she set out triumphantly
with one thousand nobles, knights, and gentry in her train. Before
entering London, Elizabeth paused at a way stop before the city gates: the
Charterhouse. As he met her with an artillery salute, Edward North must
have been relieved to know his head wouldn't be rolling for his part in
persecuting Protestants. Residents poured out of the city to surround his
manor, and Elizabeth greeted them to accept their congratulations.

For five days, Elizabeth sat in council meetings in North's great
hall, and entertained foreign ambassadors, as he—and his sons—had a
front-row seat to the new queen's government. Thomas would have found
Elizabeth to be of average height for a woman, five feet four inches tall,
with a slender waist and red, curly hair. While she was no great beauty,
perhaps, she exuded an air of confidence and gaiety that commanded
the attention and devotion of those around her. In one of her first acts,
Elizabeth shrank Mary's Privy Council, replacing members with younger
and more devotedly Protestant ministers; but Edward remained a baron,
riding near the head of the coronation procession in January 1559.

Gold cloth and tapestries once again spilled out of the windows of
Cheapside as Elizabeth rode in a litter of satin pillows, wearing a gold and
silver robe with ermine and lace trim. Once again, hopes ran high that a
new monarch might usher England into a prosperous new age. Elizabeth
was in bright spirits, joking with the crowd as her favorite courtier,
Dudley, rode behind her on a tall horse. The next morning, she walked
to Westminster Abbey on a carpet of blue cloth that onlookers frantically
tore up for souvenirs as she passed. Hundreds of torches lit the ancient
church, and, as one onlooker exclaimed, "the whole court so sparkled with
jewels and gold collars."

The North family watched with the others as Elizabeth took the crown
and the gospel was read in English, signaling the resumption of the
Protestant faith. Edward's firstborn son, Roger, received a special honor,
dubbed along with ten other men a Knight of the Bath, a distinction
bestowed only at a royal coronation. Roger had spent all night at the

Tower, undergoing a special bathing ritual before receiving the elite rank. Now at the coronation, his brother Thomas must have watched him with a mix of pride and envy. His own efforts translating the work of a Catholic bishop would earn him nothing in the new Protestant regime, while his brother received special advancement just by virtue of his birth order. After the ceremony, the new Sir Roger performed the additional honor of carving the meat for the coronation banquet.

A month later, Edward and Roger North both filed into Westminster Hall for Queen Elizabeth's first Parliament—in the House of Lords and House of Commons, respectively. As the assembly considered reinstating Edward VI's prayer book and repealing Catholic doctrines, both father and son voted against the measures. At sixty-two years old, Edward, it seemed, had finally stopped spinning and turned conservative in his old age. As Virginia Rounding says about his friend Lord Rich, perhaps "he had not been merely playing a part when upholding Catholic doctrine." After all "the zeal he had put into bringing people to condemnation," she writes, "he could not in the end 'turn, turn, and turn again.'"

Elizabeth made little move to persecute those who voted against the acts, however, determined not to repeat Mary's mistakes. Edward continued in his position as the queen's lieutenant in Cambridgeshire, while Roger became a "gentleman of the queen's chamber," an official member of court, with meal privileges and a salary of £30 ($20,420) a year. The Norths, it seemed, would pass smoothly into a new political era.

As McCarthy sat at his dining room table researching the biographies of Thomas's father and brother, he found the same privilege that saw Edward and his firstborn, Roger, rise in the ranks of Tudor society unfortunately extended to the historical record—where Thomas often appears as only a supporting actor in his family's drama. That inconvenient truth often forced McCarthy to squint to catch glimpses of Thomas's silhouette in the shadowy backgrounds of palace halls and military battlefields—and, to a lesser extent, forced me as well to read between the lines as I followed in the wake of his research.

Thomas continued to study at Lincoln's Inn at least for the next several years, and he also got married, to a woman named Elizabeth Colville, soon after the new queen's coronation. If Thomas's life is little documented, however, then his new wife's is even less so—a fate sadly common to most Renaissance women. Records suggest only that she was the widow of one of Lord Rich's many sons, implying that the marriage was arranged to bolster that family alliance. As for Thomas's burgeoning writing career, he was forced to start anew after the shift in political winds occasioned by Elizabeth's accession to the throne. "He put all of his cards into Mary and the Catholic reign," McCarthy tells me at one point as we drive across the English countryside. That went not only for his Catholic *The Dial of Princes*, but for the plays as well, he argues. "All the works he's writing at the time—his versions of *The Winter's Tale*, *Henry VIII*, *Arden of Faversham*—are explicitly Catholic works, curtain to curtain." Needing to pivot, as his father had done so many times, Thomas would have to find new ways to advance in the Elizabethan court. He would do that, McCarthy contends, by picking a side in the political issue that dominated court politics—and North's own playwriting career—for the next three decades: the marriage question.

"Nothing can be more repugnant to the common good, than to see a princess, who by marriage may preserve the Commonwealth in peace, to lead a single life, like a Vestal Virgin," declared the Speaker of the Commons during Elizabeth's first Parliament. Until recently, England hadn't had a female head of state for four centuries; now it was crowning its third queen in less than a decade. The thought that the young queen wouldn't marry, and soon, was inconceivable. The men around her, however, remained split on the best choice. Some, including William Cecil and some of the highest nobles, urged her to marry a foreign ruler who could bring valuable wealth and alliances to the kingdom. Others, who had Mary's disastrous marriage to Philip II fresh in mind, hoped for a domestic match that could unite the people behind her. The only thing her ministers agreed on was that, as the Spanish ambassador wrote, "everything depends upon the husband this woman may take."

With Philip II of Spain a nonstarter, the Holy Roman Emperor Ferdinand put forward his son Charles, the future archduke of Austria, but Elizabeth was leery of his Catholic faith. Meanwhile, the Protestant Erik, crown prince of Sweden, sent his brother to woo her on his behalf. In truth, there were few dukes of Europe who weren't vying for Elizabeth's hand. On the domestic side, both the rich but "flighty" Earl of Arundel and the handsome diplomat Sir William Pickering put forward their suits, only to see them both quickly squelched. Hanging over court was the threat of what happened if Elizabeth died childless. Officially, her heir was Catherine Grey, sister to the unfortunate Jane; but Catholics insisted the rightful heir was Elizabeth's cousin Mary Stuart, Queen of Scots and consort to the crown prince of England's enemy, France.

Elizabeth, for her part, seemed maddeningly uninterested in marriage—perhaps rightly surmising that a king would diminish her power. Or perhaps she was falling madly in love with her bosom companion, Robert Dudley. From the first spring of her reign, she was constantly out riding with the dashing courtier, and carrying on a flirtatious repartee in the halls of court, where she called him her "bonny, sweet Robin," and he alone called her "Bess." As Master of Horse, Dudley was one of the few men allowed into her intimate life. Amidst the serious business of court, writes biographer Sarah Gristwood, "Robert alone appeared to her in the guise of an invitation to play." Other courtiers watched with lidded eyes, alarmed that the queen had fallen in with a seed from the tree of the "bad Duke" Northumberland.

Whispers inevitably circulated that Dudley came into her bedchamber at night, and even that she had decided to marry him. The Venetian ambassador called Lord Robert "the King that is to be," while the Spanish ambassador lamented Elizabeth "will marry none but the favored Robert." There was one insurmountable obstacle to that betrothal, however: Robert Dudley was already married. Even while he flirted with Elizabeth, his wife, Amy Robsart, stayed home in East Anglia. Still, Dudley rose steadily in Elizabeth's favor, as the court openly divided again into factions, with Cecil and the nobles openly hostile to Dudley, who cultivated his own entourage of younger gentlemen. Among them was likely Roger North, who had married the daughter of Lord Rich, Winnifred, the widow of Dudley's older brother Henry, securing their friendship for years to come.

Unlike his bookish brother Thomas, Roger had always been energetic and physical—taking part in jousts as a boy, and now pursuing hunting, tennis, and gambling. In 1559, he moved with the rest of the court up the Thames to the queen's summer palace of Greenwich, where Dudley organized tournaments and masques. At one jousting tournament, servants set up a grand banqueting house of fir poles, covered with birch branches and sprigs of lavender and marigold. That day, Roger North was chosen as one of three challengers, taking on defender after defender; it was at this joust, perhaps, that North earned a crimson ribbon, tied personally on his arm by the queen, that later adorned his portrait.

The end of the festivities, however, was interrupted by the arrival of a messenger to the French ambassador, announcing that the French king, Henri II, had been mortally wounded ten days earlier at a joust of his own, when a wooden fragment from a lance pierced his eye through his helmet and lodged itself in his brain. That very afternoon, he lay dying in Paris. Mary Stuart's husband, Francis, then fifteen years old, would now ascend to the throne, making her queen of both Scotland and France. Soon— with the backing of Francis's ambitious mother, Catherine de Medici— she began declaring herself rightful Queen of England as well. Finding Elizabeth a husband had never been more urgent.

EVEN AS ROGER NORTH played in the intrigues of court, his brother Thomas remained behind the cool stone of Lincoln's Inn, insulated from the politics of Greenwich and Westminster. It must have been a difficult time for the family; after the death of Thomas's sister in 1558, his mother died in 1560, when North was twenty-five. Inside the Inns of Court, however, a new wind of tolerance was blowing, fostering a rush of new classical translations—including a new genre that McCarthy believes Thomas North would soon adopt. Until now, classical plays performed in England were comedies by Roman playwrights such as Terence and Plautus. In the early 1560s, however, writers began translating the first works of tragedy, starting with first-century Roman moralist and drama-tist Lucius Annaeus Seneca.

Since McCarthy first encountered the term "Senecan tragedy" in his earliest research on *Hamlet*, he had read eagerly to understand the impact of the classical author. Seneca lived in a violent time at the dawn of the Roman Empire, as the steady reign of Caesar Augustus descended into the tyranny of Tiberius, Caligula, and the mad emperor Nero. As

Nero's tutor, Seneca had a close-up view of the barbarities, watching as the emperor poisoned his own stepbrother, assassinated his mother, and kicked his wife to death. The Stoic philosopher resigned himself to the vicissitudes of fate, urging dispassionate reason in the face of conflict. But the characters in his plays are anything but stoic, constantly struggling with overwhelming rage and passion, inevitably leading to tragic results. That's not a contradiction—after all, what better way to warn against the dark side of passion than show its results in excess.

For his stories, Seneca drew on Greek stories that had occurred hundreds of years earlier as a safe way to comment on the politics of his own day. Some modern commentators see the plays as a warning to Nero, others as a plea to depose the despot. Now, the translators of the Inns of Court used Seneca's Roman plays to comment on the political dilemmas of their own turbulent times. Steeped in the world of didactic *speculum principis* and cautionary *de casibus* literature, they saw Senecan tragedy as one more way to counsel the rulers and magistrates leading England into a new, uncertain era.

The first Senecan translator, as McCarthy had discovered, was Jasper Heywood, a young Catholic Oxford fellow who had been a schoolmate of Elizabeth's, and reflected the anxieties of many fellow Catholics over what kind of revenge the queen might take. His inaugural translation, *Troas*, focuses on the Trojan queen Hecuba, warning about the tragic results that come with pride. His next, *Thyestes*, published in 1560, doubles down on that theme, focusing on a vindictive ruler, Atreus, who enacts revenge on his brother Thyestes by baking his sons into a pie and serving it to him at a banquet. According to the play's chorus, Atreus fails the test of rulership, becoming a brutal and sadistic villain, and choosing ambition and retribution over mercy.

Heywood may have been writing out of concern for Elizabeth's potential to take revenge against Catholics. But he was also writing to get the attention of the budding literary circle at the Inns of Court. In the preface to *Thyestes*, which McCarthy had first discovered in the first weeks of this research, Heywood describes a dream in which Seneca urged him to translate more of his tragedies, but Heywood directed the work to the Inns instead. "Go where Minerva's men and finest wits do swarm," he writes, referring to the Roman goddess of wisdom. "In Lincoln's Inn and Temple's twain, Gray's Inn and other more." Helpfully, he refers to several of these writers by name, putting Thomas's name first on the list: "There you shall find that selfsame North," he says, "whose work his wit displays and *Dial of Princes* paint, and preach abroad his praise." If McCarthy is right, that promise would soon be fulfilled, writing in the service of his brother's ally Robert Dudley.

DUDLEY HAD RISEN steadily in the queen's favor during the first few years of her reign. After William Cecil botched an invasion of Scotland in early 1560, Elizabeth turned away from him as her chief minister, elevating Dudley instead. She spent the summer of 1560 hunting and feasting with him, seeming more than ever that she would marry him, his own marriage notwithstanding. At that moment, however, a tragedy occurred that changed everything. In early September 1560, news arrived at court that Dudley's wife, Amy, was found lying at the bottom of a set of stairs at her home with a broken neck—dead. Like the truth of Anne Boleyn's affairs, the death of Amy Dudley is one of Tudor England's great unsolved mysteries and a source of endless speculation by historians. Almost immediately, talk from court to the Continent turned to foul play—with speculation that Dudley had killed his wife to marry the queen.

Those rumors were seemingly stoked by Cecil, who considered the idea of a King Robert a disaster for the country—and himself—and used the scandal as a way to get back into Elizabeth's good graces. They've since echoed down through the ages, making Dudley the favored suspect for centuries, reaching a peak of speculation in the nineteenth century. More recent observers have tended to exonerate Dudley in favor of the idea that Amy just had an accident, potentially brought on by a creeping illness. It's possible that Amy killed herself—though the eternal damnation that greeted suicides in the Elizabethan era makes that unlikely—or even that Cecil had Amy killed out of desperation to frame Dudley and stay in power.

Whatever the truth, the damage had been done. Dudley watched with rising panic as other suitors vied again for the hand of his beloved Bess, knowing how suspicious it would look if he pursued her. Elizabeth's feelings are harder to ascertain. Although she clearly loved Dudley, it's not clear she wanted to marry anyone; and she may have found in Amy's death a convenient way to have her cake and eat it too—putting Dudley off while keeping him at her side. Buying her more time, the Scottish threat died down as Mary's husband, the French king Francis II, died suddenly in December 1560 of a virulent ear infection after only seventeen months on the throne. Mary returned home to Scotland as Catherine de Medici took over rulership of the country as regent for her ten-year-old son, Charles IX.

By the following summer, Dudley had resumed his courtship, throwing a party on the river for the queen, during which he joked to the Spanish ambassador, a bishop, that he could marry them right there. Elizabeth seemed to be encouraging the relationship again, secretly meeting with him to dine at a country estate; but at the same time, keeping her options open—entertaining a new proposal of marriage from Sweden's new king, Erik XIV. By all accounts intelligent, artistic, and wealthy, the Protestant king seemed a good match to many at court, including Cecil. They invited Erik's emissary to England, and supporters began optimistically circulating portraits of Elizabeth and Erik together. Any week now, Erik himself was expected to arrive to personally offer his hand. Unfortunately, word came in November that bad weather had scuttled his trip. He promised to come in the spring, giving Dudley and his allies only the few months to stop the betrothal.

That Christmas, Dudley rode at the head of a parade of a hundred men on horses with gold harnesses, laughing and singing. The procession made its way along the Thames to the Inner Temple, where Dudley had been made an honorary member and dubbed Lord of Misrule for the feast. Dudley took the seat of honor in the torchlit hall, surrounded by an illustrious audience, including members of Parliament and the Privy Council. After a feast served on silver dishes, they witnessed a carefully choreographed series of masques that Dudley had helped plan, including a symbolic wooing of Beauty and Desire, after which Dudley was pointedly dubbed prince of England—which some took as a symbolic reference to his courtship of the queen.

The main event was an original play, called *Gorboduc*, penned by two members of the Inner Temple, Thomas Norton and Thomas Sackville, who had both been called out as "Minerva's Men" in Heywood's preface to *Thyestes*. Their play didn't disappoint. Though the content was drawn from an ancient English chronicle, the form was a bloody Senecan tragedy. The play begins with the quasi-historical King Gorboduc abdicating his throne and dividing his kingdom between two sons, one of which, in true Senecan fashion, kills the other. The other is then killed by his mother, even as a foreigner from the north, Fergus, also invades. After defeating that threat, the king's councilors debate who should be the rightful successor to the throne, settling on "such one born within your native land," resolving they should "in no wise admit the heavy yoke of foreign governance."

Recognized as the first original English tragedy, the play has been interpreted as a commentary on the question of Elizabeth's succession. Audience members at the time would have seen the defeat of the Scottish-sounding Fergus as a strike against Mary Queen of Scots. But they also may have caught a pointed criticism against the marriage with the foreign King Erik of Sweden, in favor of the native-born Robert Dudley. One observer named Robert Beale wrote that "many things were handled of marriage," pointing to an allegorical moment in the play in which the king is given two cups of wine—one good wine served in a clear glass, the other poisoned wine served in a golden cup. He took that as a reference to Elizabeth's choice, between the known quantity (Dudley) and a seemingly better but actually fatal option (Erik).

Hearing about the production, Elizabeth ordered Dudley and the players to present *Gorboduc* again at court, where it was performed in January 1562 before the highest lords of the realm. Afterward, Dudley began growing increasingly hopeful, even boasting to the Spanish ambassador about his chances with the queen. It's at this moment, McCarthy believes, that Thomas North wrote his own Senecan tragedy, fulfilling Heywood's request just as Sackville and Norton had. Like *Gorboduc*, it was a play that warned against marriage to a foreign ruler—with even more catastrophic consequences. And as with North's other works, McCarthy believes that Shakespeare later adapted it into his own play: *Titus Andronicus*.

TITUS IS A BLOODBATH. Shakespeare's most violent tragedy by far (and arguably the most violent play every written), the play pounds audiences with an unrelenting ferocity. By the time it's over, it includes rape, murder, execution, and dismembered limbs and heads, all the way up to a shocking cannibalistic climax. The play begins with the triumphant return of the Roman general Titus from a war with the Goths, a Germanic tribe, leading the captured Queen Tamora; her loyal servant Aaron, an African moor; and her son Alarbus, whom Titus executes over Tamora's protests. The Roman people offer to make Titus emperor, but the aging general refuses in deference to his friend Saturninus, who offers to marry Titus's daughter Lavinia. After a confused melee in which one of Titus's sons is killed, however, Saturninus changes his mind and decides to marry the Goth queen Tamora, while his brother marries Lavinia. So much for Act One.

Following that violent prelude, everyone decides to go hunting, and in the forest the Goths get their revenge for Alarbus's execution. Led by the villainous Aaron, Tamora's two surviving sons rape Lavinia and cut off her tongue and both her hands so she can't identify her abusers. At the same time, Aaron murders Lavinia's new husband and frames two of Titus's sons for the crime. He then tells Titus that the emperor will spare their lives if Titus or one of his two sons cuts off their own hand. Titus promptly chops off his own hand, only to discover the emperor executed them anyway. In one of the play's most grotesque scenes, Titus picks up one of his sons' heads, and Lavinia carries his severed hand in her mouth as they go off to seek their own revenge.

After Lavinia reveals who raped her by using her stumps to write in the sand, Titus sends another son, Lucius, off to raise an army from his erstwhile enemies, the Goths. Then, half-mad, he murders Tamora's sons and bakes them into a pie to serve to their mother at a banquet. Tamora falls for the trick, discovering with horror that she's eaten her children before Titus kills her. Titus then kills Lavinia to put her out of her misery. Saturninus then kills Titus, and Lucius returns with his Goth army to kill Saturninus and nearly everyone else. After a defiant speech by Aaron, in which he says he would have done it all again, Lucius commands that he be buried up to his waist in the ground to starve to death, and Lucius takes over as the new emperor. Roll credits. The end.

Titus Andronicus never actually existed in history—though there was an emperor Titus, who, along with his son Vespasian, waged war on both the Goths and the Jews. Much of the action of Shakespeare's play comes from a mishmash of Greek sources, including Ovid's *Metamorphoses*, which provides the story of the rape in the woods. In essence, however, it plays like an over-the-top mash-up of Seneca's greatest hits, right down to the finale of the baking of the sons into a pie, a clear homage to *Thyestes*. As one scholar says, *"Titus Andronicus* is perhaps best understood as an attempt at Seneca by a man whose sympathies were still with Ovid."

For centuries, audiences and critics alike have struggled to make sense of a Shakespeare play dripping with such butchery. In 1687, English dramatist Edward Ravenscroft wrote that it was "the most incorrect and indigested piece in all his works; It seems rather a heap of rubbish than a structure." In fact, Ravenscroft doubted Shakespeare wrote it at all, saying, "I have been told by some anciently conversant with the Stage, that it was not originally his and he only gave some master-touches to one or two of the principal parts or characters." In the eighteenth century, Samuel Johnson said the play can "scarcely be tolerable to any audience." In the twentieth, T. S. Eliot called it "one of the stupidest and more uninspired plays ever written," and more recently, Harold Bloom declared it "an explosion of rancid irony carried well past the limits of parody."

As one of Shakespeare's first plays to be printed, in 1594, many critics have chalked it up as a piece of immature juvenilia, whereas others have tried to explain it away as a piece of black comedy, melodrama, or parody of Shakespeare's rivals Thomas Kyd and Christopher Marlowe. It wasn't until a revival of the play by the Royal Shakespeare Company in 1955—with Laurence Olivier famously playing the role of Titus—that audiences began to see the play's dramatic potential. Another stage performance with Brian Cox in 1987 and Julie Taymor's lurid film starring Anthony Hopkins in 1999 further rehabilitated its reputation, to the point where the play has now become something of a cult classic.

Even so, the ghost of Ravenscroft's assertion that Titus is at least partially the work of another playwright has never entirely gone away. Many scholars today believe that Shakespeare collaborated on the play with another writer, George Peele, a classically trained veteran of the theater, which would at least explain the profusion of classical references in the play. But McCarthy has a different theory: he believes *Titus* was the reworking of a play by the young Thomas North, who wrote a version called *Titus and Vespasian* to support Robert Dudley's marriage to Queen Elizabeth. Like *Gorboduc*, he says, the play warns of the dire consequences of marrying a foreign leader—in this case, Tamora, the queen of the Goths. If anything, the association is even more explicit. In addition to being king of Sweden, Erik XIV had another title: *Götes Konung*—King of the Goths.

WHEN MCCARTHY FIRST began researching the identity of "English Seneca" back in the fall of 2005, he logically began with *Titus*—that most Senecan of Shakespearean tragedies. He quickly discovered a reference to the lost play *Titus and Vespasian* in Philip Henslowe's *Diary*—a journal by a theater producer that is the best source we have for Elizabethan drama. That play was performed in 1592, just two years before the publication of Shakespeare's *Titus*. Scholars have considered that a coincidence, assuming the play focused on Roman emperors Titus and Vespasian, perhaps featuring their conquest of Jerusalem. After all, there is no one named Vespasian in Shakespeare's play.

For McCarthy, however, the facts point to an early version of *Titus Andronicus*, written by North in the winter of 1562. At the time, North was swimming in the literary world of the Inns of Court, where he'd served (at least temporarily) as master of revels and written a *speculum principis* translation, *The Dial of Princes*. He'd been singled out by Heywood as the writer most likely to pen a Senecan tragedy, and according to one editor was even friends with Thomas Norton, one of the authors of *Gorboduc*.

North's 1555 trip to Italy may have provided other fodder as well. In the Ducal Palace in Mantua, he would have seen a painting on canvas of *The Triumph of Titus and Vespasian*, painted by, who else, but that "rare Italian master" Giulio Romano. In addition, when North first arrived in Rome, his delegation stayed at a newly built palace for the late Pope

Julius III, which North described as the most impressive building he'd seen after the Charterhouse in Pavia. He was particularly taken by two ancient marble pillars "of such mixture of colours, white and black." They were so valuable, he wrote, that the late pope "would not have given" them "for one million of gold." Early on in *Titus Andronicus*, Aaron uses the same language—"would not for a million of gold"—in a speech in which he also references the "Emperor's palace." Looking up the phrase in EEBO, McCarthy found no other uses of it before *Titus*. "And *Titus Andronicus* has it right in juxtaposition with a palace," he says.

While McCarthy and I are in Rome, we head to this palace, which is now the National Etruscan Museum of Villa Giulia, full of Roman mosaics and Renaissance frescoes. We crunch our way along the gravel walkways, looking for the pillars that so impressed North. At first, all of the columns look the same, a dull gray or mauve color. "Oh, there they are," McCarthy says suddenly, pointing across the yard to a loggia overlooking the villa's sunken courtyard, where two pillars are delicately mottled black and white. We walk around to the loggia, where McCarthy puts his hand up to lean against one of the pillars. "So North is standing right here," he says meditatively, looking up its marble length.

McCarthy doesn't think North had *Titus* in mind while he was in Rome, but rather went back to his journal to find a description of a Roman palace, and came across the line, adding it to his play. As for why he wrote the tragedy, McCarthy imagines North was trying to get Dudley's attention, the same way he'd written *The Dial* to please Mary, hoping he might earn a place as an adviser to the man most likely to become king. "He wanted to be Seneca, who became a counselor to Nero," McCarthy claims, "an English Seneca."

Unfortunately, there are no records of plays performed at Lincoln's Inn in the 1560s, so McCarthy has no direct evidence *Titus and Vespasian* was staged thirty years before Henslowe's record. In fact, he says, the play may not have even been performed at the time, too savage even for the hyper-violent Tudor era. "There is no work in the English language that is more brutal and agonizing than *Titus Andronicus*," says McCarthy, shaking his head in the Roman sunshine. "North fucking overdoes it. People are writing plays about why you shouldn't marry a foreigner, and why you should stick with the home guy, Dudley, and he says—no, let me tell you why you shouldn't marry a Goth, and it's the most brutal thing imaginable."

SOON AFTER MCCARTHY discovered the lost play, *Titus and Vespasian*, he found further evidence linking it to Shakespeare's drama. After *Titus Andronicus* appeared in England, he learned, a German version appeared on the Continent that most Shakespearean scholars believe was adapted from Shakespeare's play. There are some major differences, however— among them, in the German play Titus's son is not named Lucius: he is named Vespasian.

Scholars explain that away as a coincidence resulting from a German translator naturally associating the emperors Titus and Vespasian and changing the name. But McCarthy has a different theory: that both *Titus Andronicus* and the German play were derived from North's play. The more he searched, the more evidence he found to support the idea. Just after performing *Titus and Vespasian*, the same theater company performed another anonymous play that references Titus making "a conquest on the Goths"—along with three references to Vespasian. As he searched the databases, McCarthy found three more English plays of the period that reference both Titus and Vespasian with details that seem to allude to the plot of *Titus Andronicus*.

The strongest evidence of North's lost play, however, wasn't literary but visual. In 1925, a historian uncovered an illustration in a collection of papers held at Longleat House in southwestern England that seemed to depict the opening scene of *Titus Andronicus*. It includes Titus in a toga, along with two armed soldiers, confronting Tamora, who kneels with arms raised, begging him to spare the lives of her two captured sons. Meanwhile, Aaron the Moor menacingly brandishes a sword with his mouth open. Below the illustration is the caption "Tamora pleading for her sons going to execution," along with several dozen lines from the play. At the bottom of the page is the signature of the writer and illustrator Henry Peacham, with a date in Latin abbreviation.

Scholars at the time excitedly realized they had found the only contemporaneous drawing of one of Shakespeare's plays. Their excitement quickly turned to bafflement, however, when they realized that the details were all wrong. In the play, Tamora only begs for the life of one son, but the picture shows two. Also, Aaron doesn't speak in that scene in Shakespeare, much less wield a weapon. The text is wrong, too—interpolating the scene in Act One with Aaron's speech from Act Five in which he swears revenge. In the decades since, scholars have devised numerous explanations for the so-called Longleat manuscript, arguing, for example, that Peacham was creating a composite scene from memory, and then someone else later filled in the text, combining different passages to make it work. But others have questioned those explanations—noting that the illustration fills up less than a third of the paper, with the signature all the way at the bottom. "Why would someone take the top of a paper, and leave the rest of the page blank, unless they were ready to fill it in with dialogue," says McCarthy. "That's ridiculous."

Casting about for another explanation, McCarthy discovered a 1999 paper by June Schlueter, an English professor at Lafayette College, a small liberal arts college in Pennsylvania. Published in *Shakespeare Quarterly*—one of the two leading journals of Shakespeare studies—she argues the illustration wasn't based on Shakespeare's play at all. In fact, Schlueter writes, the drawing perfectly corresponds with the staging of the German play, in which the seven characters onstage in the first act match the seven in the drawing. In that play, the Goth queen begs for the lives of two sons, not one. And rather than standing silently, Aaron the Moor has a long monologue at the end of the scene that mirrors his rebellious speech in Act Five of *Titus Andronicus*.

If Schlueter was correct, then scholars had gotten it wrong for decades. The central figure, whom they'd thought was Titus, was actually the emperor, Saturninus; and the two "soldiers" were actually Titus and his son Vespasian. In the same essay, Schlueter also speculates that the German play wasn't based on *Titus Andronicus* at all, but that both it and Shakespeare's play were based on the lost play *Titus and Vespasian*, referenced by Henslowe. McCarthy read the words excitedly, realizing that a recognized scholar writing in a prestigious journal had come to a similar conclusion he had. Only, he had another theory, one that would take her argument a step further. The illustration isn't a depiction of the

German play at all—but is itself a drawing of the lost *Titus and Vespasian*, complete with the original lines of the play—written not by Shakespeare, but by Thomas North. How much would it take to persuade her to take that additional step? he wondered. Just as he had previously reached out to scholars of biogeography he thought might be sympathetic to his theories, he decided to contact Schlueter to find out.

Every inch of wall space in June Schlueter's home in Easton, Pennsylvania, is covered in books. Floor-to-ceiling bookcases line the living room and office downstairs, and snake up the stairway, out of sight. Her husband, Paul, a wisecracking octogenarian and expert on the British novelist Doris Lessing, stopped counting them at fifty thousand, he tells me on a tour of the home where they've lived together for forty years. An overflowing cabinet in the living room holds books to which either June or Paul has contributed. Another shelf in the living room holds books on Shakespeare, including a complete bound set of *Shakespeare Bulletin*, the journal June edited for two decades.

With a short bob of light brown hair, Schlueter exudes a grandmotherly quality—twice she asks me if I want to comb through a box of cast-off DVDs—combined with a sly sense of humor. Sitting on a couch in a blue cowl-necked sweater in a solarium off the dining room, she peers out of the window behind her. "I hate to say this, but I think I have blue tits," she deadpans. As I do a mental double take, she explains that she observed blue titmice at her bird feeder, even though scientists are doubtful the species exists in North America.

Schlueter grew up in a working-class town in northern New Jersey where her father ran a fix-it shop, repairing televisions and radios while her mother fixed the small appliances. A straight-A student in high school, she got a job working as a full-time secretary at a pharmaceutical company after graduating in 1960. "Feeling intellectually restless" after a few years, she applied to Fairleigh Dickinson University in New Jersey, taking classes in economics and social psychology. It took Schlueter eight years to earn her bachelor's; in the meantime, she got married and divorced and moved to New York City, where she worked as a secretary in law offices. When one firm moved to London, the owner asked Schlueter if she would take care of his Upper East Side townhouse. She spent several months there with a friend, reading T. S. Eliot and falling in love with poetry, before deciding to go back to school for literature. "It never occurred to me to become an academic," she says. "I was just reading because I loved it."

But become an academic she did, earning a master's degree from Hunter College, and then a PhD from Columbia in 1977. By this point, she'd discovered Shakespeare, of course, but she concentrated in modern drama. After earning her degree, she received an offer to teach English at Lafayette. It wasn't until 1983 that she returned to Shakespeare, when a colleague asked if she'd like to start coediting a new publication, *Shakespeare Bulletin*. Unlike other journals collecting literary interpretations of the plays, it focused on Shakespeare performances—an underappreciated aspect of Shakespeare studies at the time. She brought the journal to Lafayette, commuting back and forth to New York for performances. "I must have seen a hundred plays a year," she says.

A decade later when Schlueter became provost, she gave up modern drama to focus exclusively on Shakespeare. Again, her approach was unorthodox. Instead of focusing on the text, she was more interested in combing archives to find new documents that might shed light on Shakespeare and his world. Among other issues, she weighed in on the portrait on Shakespeare's First Folio, finding evidence that the engraving wasn't made by the famous Flemish engraver Martin Droeshout, as some believe, but by his nephew of the same name. "I really love the excitement of discovering something, answering questions that haven't been answered yet," she says—especially those questions that "maybe looked like there was no answer, or we were never going to find it."

Coming to Shakespeare relatively late in her career, she thinks, gives her a different perspective than other scholars in the field. "You go to graduate school, and you hear the narrative of Shakespeare that everyone agrees to," she says. "You don't want to go too far in creating a little detour from that roadmap, or you might become a pariah." By contrast, Schlueter started off the map entirely. "I had to form my own ideas." Perhaps that's what opened her up to a new interpretation of the Longleat manuscript. Early in her career, she'd spent time on a Fulbright scholarship in Kassel,

Germany. Years later, reading a translation of the German *Titus* on her couch, she was struck by the similarities with the illustration.

The revelation led her to publish the idea in the 1999 *Shakespeare Quarterly* article, which the journal's editor, Gail Kern Paster, praised as "one of those rare moments in literary study where a real discovery has been made." The *Chronicle of Higher Education* featured the story on its front page, and Schlueter wrote another version of the paper for the British *Times Literary Supplement*. Others were less convinced, however. Acclaimed Shakespeare scholar Richard Levin wrote another article for *Shakespeare Quarterly* in 2002 that pointed out the drawing didn't exactly match the scene in the German play either. After all, Aaron doesn't speak until everyone else has left the stage, and the figure in the center that Schlueter identified as the emperor has a long beard, even though in the play the emperor is younger than Titus. "Unless some new evidence comes to light, these questions remain unanswerable," he wrote. Schlueter moved on to other projects, and didn't think much about *Titus* or the Longleat manuscript until she received McCarthy's email almost a decade later.

SCHLUETER WAS SITTING in her book-filled office on the evening of April 14, 2011, when McCarthy's email arrived. "I am very much a fan of your work, especially your Longleat paper," it began. The sender went on to identify himself as the author of *Here Be Dragons* and several articles on Shakespeare, before mentioning he'd written his own article on the Longleat manuscript. "I thought you might be interested in this paper because it so closely follows yours," he said. Schlueter smiled to herself— he sure knew how to lay on the praise, she thought. But she was also touched that he'd continued to work on the mystery of the drawing after all these years, and she couldn't resist opening the attached document.

In it, McCarthy picked up on her speculation that *Titus Andronicus* was based on the lost *Titus and Vespasian*—detailing the many contemporary references he'd found in other plays. He then spelled out his evidence that the illustration actually depicted the earlier play, predating both Shakespeare and the German play. For starters, there was the date, which Peacham had written in a strange code of Latin numerals: "Anno m°. q°. q. q^{to}." A cataloger had written "1595" on the document, but that didn't quite make sense. Scholars agree that the *m* represents *millesimo* (1000), the first *q* represents *quingentesimo* (500), and the last *q* represents either *quarto* (4) or *quinto* (5); but the middle *q* is a mystery. If the date really were 1594 or 1595, that letter shouldn't be a *q* at all, but an *n* for *nonogesimo* (90).

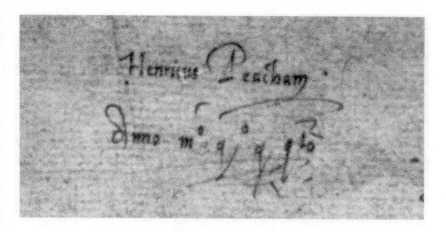

Longleat Manuscript, detail

Previously, Schlueter had consulted an expert on Elizabethan writing, who speculated that perhaps the middle *q* stands for *quinquaginta* (50) and the last *q* for *quadragintaquarto* (44), together adding up to 94. Scholar Jonathan Bate took a different tack, concluding that the third letter was not a *q* at all, but rather a *g* for *gentesimo*, an unconventional spelling for *centesimo* (100), and the date was actually 1604 or 1605. When McCarthy searched EEBO and Google, however, he couldn't find Latin dates that used any of these words. If the date really was 1605, it would be written *millesimo sexcentesimo quinto* (1000+600+5), not *millesimo quingentesimo centesimo quinto* (1000+500+100+5).

In an effort to solve the mystery, McCarthy enlarged the letter in Photoshop, comparing it with letters in other documents on EEBO. In fact, it did look more like a *g* than a *q*. Continuing to search for a better explanation, however, he discovered that Elizabethans had two ways of drawing the letter *s*, a short version and a long version. With a little imagination, perhaps, the Longleat letter could be a long *s*, standing for either *sexagesimo* (60) or *septuagesimo* (70), making the date 1564, 1565, 1574, or

1575. Of course, that explanation fit his hypothesis that Thomas wrote *Titus and Vespasian* in 1562. It created another problem, however: Henry Peacham wasn't born until 1578, so there is no way he could have made an illustration by then. With a little more research, however, McCarthy discovered the illustrator was actually known as Henry Peacham the Younger—and his father was Henry Peacham the Elder. Enlisting the help of a forensic document examiner, he compared signatures of both Peachams to the Longleat signature, concluding that it was that of the Elder, not the Younger.

Schlueter found herself nodding as she read through McCarthy's argument. Though not quite sure about the long *s* argument, everything else made total sense. She wrote back the next morning, effusing that "I found myself trembling with anticipation and delight as I moved through its pages." The next day, she responded with more detailed notes, suggesting other examples of both Peachams' signatures he could examine. McCarthy, in turn, responded that he was "awed and humbled at the depth of your analysis."

He and Schlueter went back and forth on revisions over the next week. McCarthy admitted that he'd already sent the article to a journal, the *Review of English Studies*—which Schlueter thought was a shame. If he really wanted to be taken seriously by Shakespeareans, he should send it to one of the two top journals in the field, *Shakespeare Survey* or *Shakespeare Quarterly*. "Shakespeareans are notoriously slow to accept new readings, even when the evidence is compelling, but it will get the conversation going and you will, finally, prevail," she predicted. Their emails over the next couple weeks read at times like an intellectual courtship. At one point, McCarthy frets, "I've noticed I've been starting my emails with 'Hi June,' while you have stayed with 'Dear Dennis.' I hope you don't mind my informality." In her next email, Schlueter teased him by opening it, "Dear Dennie," and signing off, "Junie."

One thing McCarthy didn't mention—in his paper, or to Schlueter—was Thomas North. Hesitant to reveal too much of his theory for fear of rejection, he limited himself to arguing about the play, not the author. At the last minute, however, he inserted three paragraphs at the end of the article spelling out the connection to *Gorboduc*, even speculating that the play had been written to support Dudley's campaign against the Swedish marriage. Schlueter enthusiastically embraced the addition, telling McCarthy that "it makes an already brilliant essay glow even more." Given their heightened expectations, McCarthy was crushed when he received a message from the editor of the *Review of English Studies* in June. "Thank you for offering your essay," it began. "I regret to say that it has not been selected for publication." The editor attached comments from an anonymous peer reviewer, who wrote, "I do not think it adds anything useful to our understanding of the Longleat MS: rather it makes the document even more puzzling than before." McCarthy wrote to Schlueter, "Ouch. Almost seems like I offended the reviewer in some way."

"I am stunned," she replied. "And here I was calling your work brilliant." Schlueter suggested they try again right away with one of the Shakespeare journals. McCarthy, however, was dispirited. By now, he'd spent nearly five years investigating Shakespeare's debt to Thomas North, and what did he have to show for it? He couldn't even get an essay published that didn't mention Thomas North's name at all. The thought of sending the article out again was demoralizing. Maybe he needed to consider more dramatic ways to get his ideas noticed.

In the winter of 1562, Robert Dudley's campaign to scuttle the Swedish proposal couldn't be going better. Soon after the players presented *Gorboduc* to the queen, Erik XIV's representative at court sighed in a missive back to Stockholm that "the Queen maketh so much of the L. Rob." By April, he had departed—ending Erik's proposal for good. Even some of Dudley's biggest enemies among the nobility now supported his cause, deciding that a King Robert would be better than no king at all.

In desperation, Cecil revealed that Dudley had been negotiating with Spain to support his marriage with Elizabeth, and that the Spanish ambassador was circulating rumors they were already secretly married. Furious, Elizabeth dismissed the ambassador from court and put any more marriage talk on hold. By the following year, Dudley's hopes revived when Elizabeth presented him with the castle of Kenilworth, a twelfth-century estate in the rolling hills of Warwickshire. They were quickly dashed again, however, when Elizabeth revealed a new plan—for him to marry Mary Queen of Scots.

"To Elizabeth at the time, it seemed like a political masterstroke," writes one biographer. She could go unchallenged in her sole rulership, while assuring a succession of royal blood and a child of her favorite, "sweet Robin," on the throne. The only person more horrified than Dudley at the prospect was the twenty-two-year-old Mary, who was disgusted by the thought of marrying Elizabeth's cast-off seconds. Her eye had already alighted on another suitor—her eighteen-year-old half cousin Henry Stuart, Lord Darnley.

As Elizabeth continued ahead with her plan, she decided to sweeten the pot by elevating Robert to the peerage, tickling his neck in view of the court while she fastened the ermine mantle around it. Dudley, however, had other ideas, secretly encouraging Darnley's overtures to Mary. In that endeavor, he found a surprising ally in Cecil, who saw a threat in Robert's potential marriage to Mary. With his blessing, Darnley traveled north to Scotland to court Mary. Elizabeth was angry of course when she found out, but Dudley was unfazed, choosing to believe ever afterward that she had never intended for him to marry her cousin; rather, the whole affair was a test of his devotion. Now he was free once more to pursue the queen, only now he was doing it as a member of the nobility: the newly created Earl of Leicester.

His advancement was also a promotion for the young men in his circle—including Roger, and perhaps Thomas North as well. For all of its brutality, *Titus Andronicus* ends on a hopeful note: "You sad-faced men, people and sons of Rome," says Titus's brother Marcus as the new emperor, Lucius, takes command. "Oh, let me teach you how to knit again this scattered corn into one mutual sheaf, these broken limbs again into one body." So must it have seemed to the brothers North, as both Erik XIV and Mary Queen of Scots cleared the field, and Elizabeth and Leicester's union was more or less inevitable.

At this moment, however, a personal tragedy marred the happiness of the North family. After leading a life of wealth and accomplishment for sixty-eight years, Edward North passed away at the Charterhouse on December 31, 1564. January dawned chill and cold—so frigid that the

Thames froze over with ice. In its cold light, the family journeyed north to Kirtling, where they laid their patriarch to rest in All Saints Church, next to the body of his first wife, Alice. They then retired to the warmth of Kirtling Hall, where his executors read out his last will.

As a loyal subject to the crown, Edward left a third of his lands to the queen, perhaps in thanks for her father's role in allowing him to acquire them. He left his second wife, Margaret, whom he married in 1561, all of his jewels, £500 ($276,775) in cash, and property in London, Southwark, and elsewhere. Other family members, friends, and even servants were also suitably rewarded, with property, cash, and proceeds from North's properties around London, Kent, and the Midlands. Almost everything else he left to his oldest son and heir, Roger. As his last act, on December 30, he even sold the Charterhouse to pay off Roger's substantial gambling debts, leaving him a smaller house in the Charterhouse yard.

Thomas North got almost nothing. Of all of his wealth, Edward left his second son the proceeds from just one parsonage in Suffolk—less than he gave one of his servants. It was not unusual at the time for lords to leave most of their wealth to their firstborn son, entailing it to his heirs in order to keep his estate together in perpetuity (fans of the television show *Downton Abbey* will recognize such an entail as the prime mover in the plot). Cutting out other children almost entirely, however, was extreme. To explain it, McCarthy once again cites Edward's lingering resentment over *Arden of Faversham*, finding more evidence in the allegorical tale of *Groatsworth of Wit*.

That pamphlet, in fact, takes its name from the very scene in which the patriarch Gorinius lies dying, telling his two sons that when he "first came to this city" his entire wealth was "an old groat"—a silver coin worth 4 pence. Now, he boasts, he has £60,000 in cash, and another £15,000 in jewels—all of which he is bequeathing to his son, Luciano. Turning to his other son, Roberto, he says, "I reserve for Roberto, thy well-read brother, an old groat...wherewith I wish him to buy a Groatsworth of wit: for he in my life has reproved my manner of life and therefore at my death, shall not be contaminated with corrupt gain." McCarthy sees a similar snub in Edward North's will. "It's like he was saying, 'You don't approve of the way I got all this wealth? Well, you are not going to get any of it.'"

Gorinius spends the rest of the scene counseling Luciano on the need to preserve his wealth, telling him not to "stand on conscience in causes of profit, but heap treasure upon treasure, for the time of need." Still, he adds, cynically, "seem to be devout, else shalt thou be held vile." He has no similar words of wisdom for Roberto. "Your books are your counselors, and therefore to them I bequeath you," he says. In much the same way, Thomas North had been effectively disinherited from his family's fortune, forced to rely on his brother's largesse or on his own writing to make a living.

If McCarthy is right, then the same year of his father's death, 1564, would see another event that would dramatically shape Thomas North's life in years to come: the birth, in Stratford-upon-Avon, of William Shakespeare.

Chapter Seven
BY ANY OTHER NAME

(1564–2014)

What's in a name? That which we call a rose
By any other name would smell as sweet.
                                              —*Romeo and Juliet*

hakespeare's face is on everything in Stratford-upon-Avon: Shake-speare scarves; Shakespeare T-shirts; Shakespeare mugs; Shakespeare fudge. Famous around the world as the birthplace of the Bard, Stratford is now an obstacle course of buses and tourists, all coming to pay homage to the greatest writer ever to live. On our way into town, McCarthy and I pass by a giant Victorian-era statue, a bronze Will Shakespeare heroically seated high atop a pedestal; surrounding him are smaller statues of some of his most iconic characters: Prince Hal, Falstaff, Lady Macbeth, and Hamlet. "That's North, that's North, that's North, that's North," McCarthy says, pointing at each one in turn. "So this is really the Thomas North memorial?" I ask. "Right!" McCarthy says.

"This is what you are taking on," muses Galovski, who has accompanied her father here into the heart of Shakespeare worship to capture visuals for her documentary. "I should get a shot of you walking against a sea of people coming the other way." We continue into a pedestrian-friendly walking district in the center of town, fighting our way through mobs of visitors and chattering school groups. The cameraperson Hosseini walks backward in front of McCarthy, capturing his bemused expression for the camera as he takes in the scene. "Dad, what do you think of this?" Galovski asks him. "Well, it's really amazing the amount of attention Shakespeare receives—and deservedly so," McCarthy says with a mischievous smile. "He was the *adapter* of the greatest works in literature, and without his industry and drive, a lot of these plays would have been lost."

Amidst a line of half-timbered Tudor buildings in various degrees of repair and authenticity, one stands out from the others—a picturesquely yellowed row house with a standing queue out front: Shakespeare's birthplace. Here, the faithful snake through a visitors center lined with vitrines of Shakespearean ephemera: a ceramic Shakespeare statue from the 1830s, a Shakespeare beer jug from the 1930s, a Shakespeare action figure from the 1990s. In a garden out back blooming with plants mentioned in the plays, actors perform Hamlet's soliloquy and Romeo's serenade on a loop.

"We like to say when you walk through this door, it's 1578," says a woman in a floral dress and bonnet, walking us into the house proper, "the year I started working here." She pauses for an imaginary snare hit before leading the tour through the house, complete with period crockery and plastic food artfully arranged on tables and vinyl patterned wallpaper Velcroed to the walls. "Upstairs," our tour guide says, "you will see the very room where Shakespeare was born." Visitors head up with anticipation, finally entering a small room where a slant of light falls upon a wooden bed with a red-and-green fabric canopy, with a small crib to one side. On the wall is written a line from *As You Like It*: "At first an infant, mewling and puking in his nurse's arms."

For all that the Shakespeare Birthplace Trust has done to keep the name of Shakespeare alive in his hometown, the actual room where Shakespeare was born is only a guess. Nor does any of the furniture or possessions in the house date from Shakespeare's time. Soon after his father died in 1601, a middle-aged William leased out the house as an inn, which it remained for the next 250 years. As we leave to head back downstairs, we pass a man playing Juliet, shouting out a window to his Romeo outside. "What's Montague?" he cries in falsetto, as tourists snap selfies and videos with their phones. "It is nor hand, nor foot, nor arm, nor face, nor any other part belonging to a man." He raises an eyebrow for comic effect. "Oh, be some other name! What's in a name? That which we call a rose by any other name would smell as sweet."

BESIDES HIS NAME, there's actually little left of Shakespeare in Stratford. In fact, for the most famous writer in English, historians know precious little about William Shakespeare's life. "Every biography of Shakespeare is maybe 80 percent the author's imagination," June Schlueter told me. It takes only flipping the pages of a few Shakespeare biographies to see what she means. Outside of vital records and a court case, few scraps of paper contain any facts about the man himself. "On only a handful of days in his life can we say with absolute certainty where he was," writes author Bill Bryson. In a half dozen signatures, his name is never spelled the same way twice—and not a single copy of any of his plays survives in his handwriting. That's not unusual. Elizabethans, on the whole, were not very good record keepers, especially when it came to the ephemeral art of drama. Scholars only know Thomas Kyd wrote *The Spanish Tragedy*— arguably the most popular play of the period—from an offhand comment in a pamphlet written two decades after he died.

We do know that William Shakespeare was baptized in Stratford on April 26, 1564, which means he was probably born around April 23, though even that date is speculative. Stratford was a prosperous market town in Warwickshire, three days' ride from London on bandit-infested roads. In Shakespeare's youth, the countryside was still raw from the whiplash back to Protestantism; images of saints in Stratford's church were whitewashed over the year of his birth. His father, John Shakespeare, was a glove maker, and some biographers see remnants of that art in allusions to glove making in Shakespeare's plays, such as a moment when Romeo's friend Mercutio compares his wit to soft goat kidskin known as chevril, "that stretches from an inch narrow to an ell broad."

"It is clear that he must have watched chevril being stretched by hand," says biographer Michael Wood. "No mere wearer of gloves would have known about this process." Much of Shakespeare's biography is similarly drawn from clues in his plays, retconned into the simulacrum of a life. In *Will in the World*—a Pulitzer finalist—Harvard professor Stephen Green-blatt makes an admirable attempt to piece together Shakespeare's earliest days, surmising that "Will almost certainly attended" the King's New School, a Stratford grammar school with a Latin-immersion curriculum. There, he may have "perhaps" read the Latin comedies of Terence and

Plautus. During his adolescence, he also "is likely to have seen" morality plays by passing theater companies, as well as the Hock Tuesday folk dramas in nearby Coventry.

Others see remnants of Shakespeare's country boyhood in references to the nearby Forest of Arden, which serves as the setting for *As You Like It*, and in fairytales about sprites and witches that presumably inspired *A Midsummer Night's Dream* and *Macbeth*. After those scant biographical facts, William Shakespeare disappears for two long stretches collectively called "the lost years," starting with 1578 to 1582, when Shakespeare was fourteen to eighteen. The "strong presence of legal situations" in the plays leads Greenblatt to speculate that he may have apprenticed with a small-town law clerk. Others surmise he worked as a country schoolteacher—or even traveled north to consort with Catholic freedom fighters.

Greenblatt finds evidence for that exciting theory in the will of an underground Lancashire Catholic named Alexander Houghton, who bequeathed theater costumes to his brother, and commended him to a "William Shakeshafte now dwelling with me." Houghton was tangentially related to Lord Strange's Men, one of the theater companies Shakespeare may have later joined, leading some writers to connect the dots. "All of Shakespeare's early history plays," Greenblatt writes, "were concerned with rebellion." Of course, "Shakespeare" is not "Shakeshafte," a common surname in Lancashire at the time. A critic of Greenblatt's book wrote in *The New York Review of Books* that "there seems to be no reason whatever to believe this except the pressure of a keen desire for it to be true."

William resurfaces in Stratford in November 1582 to marry Anne Hathaway, who was eight years his senior. In May 1583, his daughter Susanna was baptized—leading biographers to do the math and imagine a crossbow wedding. Across Stratford is another home, called Anne Hathaway's Cottage. Almost as soon as we file into the kitchen, however, the tour guide, a bald man in spectacles, tells us, "This was never a cottage, and it never belonged to Anne Hathaway." The thatched-roofed farmhouse was owned by Anne's father, and she did live there as a girl, but the original furnishings were sold long ago. Some have envisaged a loveless marriage, based on the depictions of difficult women in plays such as *The Taming of the Shrew* and William's later long stretches away in London.

In February 1585, William and Anne had two more children, the twins Hamnet and Judith—but no others, bucking the period's tendencies toward large families.

After that, Shakespeare disappears again for seven or so more "lost years," from 1585 to 1592, covering ages twenty-one to twenty-eight. Scholars have tried to stuff everything Shakespeare could possibly need for his plays into this period, conjecturing that he traveled in Italy, fought in wars in Flanders, or even sailed to America. Others imagine a more straightforward route to London with one of the traveling playing companies touring the provinces. It's anyone's guess which plays Shakespeare wrote first. Among the contenders are that Senecan tragedy, *Titus Andronicus*; Italian comedies such as *The Two Gentlemen of Verona* or *The Taming of the Shrew*; and early history plays such as *Henry VI, Parts 1, 2, and 3*—his first critical successes.

From there he pumped out one or two plays every year for the next two decades, mostly alternating between histories like *Richard III* and *Henry V* and comedies like *Much Ado About Nothing* and *As You Like It*. He borrowed their plots from English histories and Italian novellas, pastoral romances, and classics like North's *Plutarch*. The nineteenth-century playwright George Bernard Shaw, not a fan, called him an "'immortal' pilferer of other men's stories and ideas." Bryson somewhat more charitably dubs him "a wonderful teller of stories so long as someone else had told them first."

Starting in 1594, Shakespeare became part owner in the Lord Chamberlain's Men, for whom he then wrote and acted exclusively. In 1598, he also became part owner in the Globe Theater, which opened with the Roman tragedy *Julius Caesar*. There, he staged his four great tragedies—*Hamlet*, *King Lear*, *Othello*, and *Macbeth*—before ending his career with the whimper of the late romances, such as *The Winter's Tale*, and his last history, *Henry VIII*. In 1613, Shakespeare abruptly retired at the young age of forty-nine, returning to Stratford to live out the end of his days in the country with his wife in a home they called New Place.

Unfortunately, that home was torn down in 1759 in a fit of pique by a reverend who got sick of visiting tourists. The site is now an English garden, attractively laid out with flowers and hedges, and flags for each one of Shakespeare's plays, with the year it is thought to have been written. In the middle of the garden sits a wooden sculpture of a writing desk and chair. "We think that's where he would have written," a docent named Andrew, who wears black-rimmed glasses and a fedora, tells us. Recently, the site underwent a massive archaeological dig, which uncovered pottery shards, buttons, and bobkins, but nothing that could be definitively traced to William. "It was about what you'd expect from a rich family living in the country," Andrew says. "No copies of plays, I'm afraid."

THE SURVIVAL OF Shakespeare's plays was far from assured. In his lifetime, they appeared only in small quarto editions of varying quality; it took the intercession of two of his old theater companions to assemble the plays into a book in 1623. Known as the First Folio, it includes thirty-six plays, half of them published for the very first time. That haul is spectacular given the survival rates of the work of Shakespeare's contemporaries. Of the three thousand known plays from the Elizabethan and Jacobean periods, only about 230 texts—less than 10 percent—still exist today.

When the English Civil War broke out in 1642, dour Puritans banned public theater, burning scripts and tearing down the Globe for firewood. London stages went dark for twenty years, until the restoration of the monarchy. By that time, all of Shakespeare's fellow actors and playwrights were long dead, and a new generation of theater performers resurrected English theater from a collective amnesia. Audiences wanted witty and bawdy comedies, and the few Shakespeare plays that made it to the stage were heavily edited and adapted with new music, characters, and whole subplots—including a musical version of *Macbeth* "which featured flying witches, songs, dances, and a happy ending accompanied by a semi-operatic score." Poet John Dryden freely changed Shakespeare's texts in edited versions of the plays, complaining in 1679 that he "often obscures his meaning by his words, and sometimes makes it unintelligible"— words later echoed by generations of high school students.

The turnaround in Shakespeare's reputation, however, gathered speed in the eighteenth century, when tastemakers praised Shakespeare's "much greater sense of virtue than the present," and theaters staged *Henry V* as a rallying cry for yet another war with France. By the 1740s, a marble statue of the pensive playwright appeared in the Poet's Corner of Westminster Abbey, and within decades, says scholar Gary Taylor, "writers fell over one another in proclaiming Shakespeare the world's greatest dramatist and poet." At the head of the pack was Covent Garden theater impresario David Garrick, "the most famous man in Britain after the king," who built his career around Shakespeare. Audiences showed up two hours early to his Drury Lane Theatre to watch Garrick as King Lear rhapsodize wildly on the heath.

If a date could be assigned to Shakespeare's deification, it would be September 6, 1769, the first day of the Shakespeare Jubilee, a festival Garrick staged in Stratford-upon-Avon for hundreds of spectators. According to historian Andrew McConnell Stott, "not a single scene of Shakespeare was performed, let alone an entire play." Even so, it was a wild success, with spirited balls, ditties, odes, and parades performed in Shakespeare's honor that even days of pouring rain couldn't dampen. The highlight was an ode, performed by Garrick in a seven-hundred-foot-wide rotunda, in which he invoked English national pride to name Shakespeare a "demi-god" who "merits all our wonder, all our praise!" At Shakespeare's birthplace, Garrick hung a painting of a sun breaking through clouds in what he decided was Shakespeare's bedroom, which he said symbolized Shakespeare's lowly roots "from which his Strength of Genius rais'd him, to become Glory of his Country!" Meanwhile, hawkers sold souvenirs like holy relics, including an infinite number of tobacco stoppers, ink stands, and tea chests supposedly cut from the mulberry tree that once grew at New Place.

After the Jubilee, Shakespeare worship grew to such fervor that a 1775 German visitor commented that "English children know him before they have learnt their A.B.C. and creed." For the first time, scholars began to restore his works to their original text, as devotees continued to pour into Stratford. In the late Victorian period, Shaw coined the term "Bardolatry" to refer to the mad supplication at the altar of Stratford Will. It was only then, more than 150 years after Shakespeare's death, that scholars took the first steps to reconstruct Shakespeare's life and playwriting career. The effort crossed the Atlantic, where American critics and audiences discovered Shakespeare en masse for the first time, adding *Julius Caesar* and *The*

Merchant of Venice to high school students' curricula. In the United States, however, a significant backlash against Shakespeare also began, calling into question the very authorship of the plays.

THE FIRST RUMBLINGS started in the mid-1800s. Delia Bacon, a talented Connecticut schoolteacher and playwright who lectured to mixed audiences, set out on a trip to England in 1853 intending to write a series of magazine articles on Shakespeare. Instead, she came home doubting about whether someone with the author's limited education and life experience could have written the plays at all. In an essay published in *Putnam's Monthly*, she wrote that the author of the plays "carries the court perfume with him, unconsciously, wherever he goes"—with evidence of foreign travel and "the highest Parisian breeding." Shakespeare, by contrast, was nothing but a "stupid, ignorant, illiterate, third-rate play-actor," and an "old showman and hawker of plays." In a book the following year, she proposed an alternative author, who just happened to be her own namesake—Francis Bacon.

Her candidate was certainly one of the most impressive figures of his age, a true Renaissance man who wrote political tracts, philosophical essays, and utopian fiction. According to Delia, he was at the center of a group of frustrated nobles and writers, including Walter Raleigh and Edmund Spenser, who secretly wrote Shakespeare's *oeuvre* as a veiled critique of the monarchy. *The Tempest*, Delia claimed, was Francis Bacon's autobiography, alluding to his supposedly secret role in the founding of America. Despite her somewhat tortuous prose style, Delia's views were embraced by some of the greatest minds of her generation, including Ralph Waldo Emerson and Walt Whitman. Others ridiculed the book, calling her—with a twinge of sexism—crazy (even Emerson called her "a genius, but mad"). In her book, Delia promised to reveal a "cipher" that Bacon, who was known to write in code, used to hide the true philosophy of the plays. She died two years later, however; so it was left for others to take up that charge.

The hunt culminated in *The Great Cryptogram*, a one-thousand-page tome published in 1888 by Minnesota lawyer Ignatius Donnelly, who obsessively attempted to prove that Bacon hid secret messages throughout the plays. Using a complex method of counting words throughout the canon, Donnelly claimed to have discovered a confession by Bacon about political struggles among court factions, religious philosophy, and American colonization. The math behind the system, however, was malleable, conveniently adjusting to whatever Donnelly needed to spell out his narrative. "Nothing like it has appeared in cryptology before or since," comments one modern cryptologist. "And with good reason, for the system is no system at all."

Donnelly's revelations, however, led to a stampede of other writers sleuthing out increasingly more fantastical messages hidden in the plays. Detroit doctor Orville Ward Owen created a giant machine with two large reels, over which he stretched a one-thousand-foot length of cloth pasted with the text of Shakespeare and other writers. As he spun them, he revealed a sordid tale: Bacon was actually the son of Elizabeth and Robert Dudley and heir to the throne, but the queen was strangled to death by William Cecil's son Robert before she could reveal the truth.

Somewhat less luridly, William Stone Booth used the first and last letters of lines and pages in the First Folio to spell out acrostic signatures, finding, for example, FRANCISCO BACONO in the closing lines of *The Tempest*. The idea wasn't that far-fetched. As demonstrated by Edward North's acrostics in his Wolsey poems, the practice was an established fad among Elizabethan writers. Unfortunately, Booth had no consistent basis for choosing which letters he used to spell out his messages, taking them from the beginning, end, or even middle of lines as he saw fit.

His book, however, captivated deaf-blind activist Helen Keller, who wrote her thesis at Radcliffe College on playwright George Peele, and criticized the way Shakespeare's biographers turned him into an icon "whose godlike head is 'lost among the clouds.'" She, in turn, shared the book with author Mark Twain, who wrote his own book about Shakespearean authorship. Published in 1909, *Is Shakespeare Dead?* spells out many of the arguments that would be adopted by later doubters, peppered with Twain's trademark sarcasm.

As someone with an ear for dialect, Twain argued that Shakespeare could never have mastered the nuances of a lawyer, a courtier, and a soldier, if he had not been those things himself—anymore than others could master the argot of Twain's former profession of riverboat pilot. "The moment he departs, by even a shade, from a common trade-form, the reader who has served that trade will know the writer *hasn't*," he wrote. Warming to his subject, Twain compares Shakespeare biographers to paleontologists, who construct a skeleton of a Brontosaurus from "nine bones and six hundred barrels of plaster of paris."

While Twain didn't necessarily go along with the Baconites and their secret ciphers, he did agree with other doubters who postulated that many of Shakespeare's plays had earlier versions, "not by Shakespeare, whoever he was, and that these old plays were extensively reworked and 'transmuted' by Shakespeare." That author, he wrote, "not only had a very extensive and accurate knowledge of the law," but was also "well-acquainted with the manners and customs of the Inns of Court." By now, Francis Bacon was already falling out of favor as a ghost writer for Shakespeare. Despite his obvious talents, he had never been to Italy, wrote with a ponderous prose style, and was insanely busy with all of his other duties. Though some Baconites held strong into the 1930s, he was increasingly replaced by a new suspect.

THE FIRST PERSON to propose Edward de Vere, 17th Earl of Oxford, as the secret author of Shakespeare's plays was J. Thomas Looney, a school-teacher from Newcastle, England. Looney—whose name provides no end of amusement for Shakespeareans—could never square the message of *The Merchant of Venice* with the life of Shakespeare, a theater promoter who seemed to have more in common with the ruthless moneylender Shylock than the hapless merchant Antonio. Sometime in the 1910s, he drew up a list of attributes that the author of Shakespeare's plays *should* have, imagining him an educated poet and drama enthusiast; a lover of Italy, falconry, and music; a member of the aristocracy "in close proximity to royalty itself"; and a mysterious eccentric, with a somewhat conflicted attitude toward women. He searched through an Elizabethan poetry anthology, ticking off candidates one by one, until he came away with Edward de Vere.

Born in 1550, Oxford was educated at Cambridge and tutored by his uncle, Arthur Golding—the translator of one of Shakespeare's favorite books, Ovid's *Metamorphoses*. A ward of William Cecil, he studied law at Gray's Inn and became a favorite of Elizabeth at court, eventually marrying Cecil's daughter Anne. He also had a literary bent, apparently writing plays for his own group of players. From 1575 to 1576, Oxford traveled on the Continent, including months in Italy, with stops in Venice, Padua, and Florence—all locations featured in Shakespeare's plays. Oxford also led a dissolute life of violent duels, chronic debt, and sex with both genders. In short, says historian William Rubinstein, he "appears to have been both talented and violent, brave and erratic, bisexual, artistic and, despite his ancient title, perpetually in need of money."

As Looney delved further into Oxford's life, he came away with uncanny parallels with the plays. Like Lear, he had a conflicted relationship with his three daughters. Like Othello, he was convinced by an Iago-like friend that his wife had been unfaithful. The most obvious parallels, however, were with Hamlet. Cecil has oft been cited as a model for the officious minister Polonius. When Oxford was young, he stabbed and killed an unarmed man, just as Hamlet kills Polonius in the play; and Oxford rejected Cecil's daughter—his wife Anne—just as Hamlet rejects Polonius's daughter Ophelia. Looney hypothesized that a distraught Oxford began writing plays after Anne's death, releasing them under Shakespeare's name. The obvious problem with this theory is that Oxford died in 1604, a decade before Shakespeare's last play. Looney explained that away by claiming Oxford had written them before he died, after which they were adapted by other writers. Looney published a book on the topic in 1920, and Oxford immediately eclipsed Bacon as Shakespeare's suspected alter ego.

Even as traditional scholars derided Oxford's adherents as "Anti-Stratfordians," they lined up some high-profile disciples. Among them was psychologist Sigmund Freud, whose own thinking on the Oedipus complex had been influenced by *Hamlet*. Other writers began proposing increasingly Oedipal theories themselves, suggesting Oxford was Elizabeth's bastard son (again with Dudley) or her secret lover or—most adventurously—both. Those speculations were collectively known as the Prince Tudor theory. The Oxfordian cause died down after World War II, as new claimants continued to arise (including, most surprisingly, Christopher Marlowe, who died in 1593, before publication of *any* of Shakespeare's plays). It came roaring back, however, in 1984, with Charlton Ogburn Jr.'s nine-hundred-page tome *The Mysterious William Shakespeare*. The exhaustive account of Oxford's life included correspondences to the plays on every page. In 1573, for example, some of Oxford's men stood accused of robbing travelers on the road from Gravesend to Rochester; in *Henry IV, Part 1*, Prince Hal's associates, including Falstaff, also rob travelers on the same road.

In 1987, three United States Supreme Court justices considered the Oxford case in a mock trial before an audience in Washington, DC. They unanimously sided with Shakespeare, though not without doubts. Over the next few years, sympathetic coverage on PBS's *Frontline* and in *The Atlantic*, *Harper's*, and *The New York Times* continued to raise Oxford's profile—so much so that by the late 1990s, two of the three Supreme Court justices who'd presided over the mock trial reversed their positions. By 2007, the Shakespeare Oxford Fellowship included Shakespearean actors, such as Sir Derek Jacobi and Jeremy Irons—and even Sir Mark Rylance, former artistic director of Shakespeare's Globe theater in London. Oxford, it seemed, was poised for a breakthrough.

IN THE SUMMER OF 2011, McCarthy was still recovering from the rejection of the *Titus* paper when he saw something that made him feel much worse. At his computer one day, he came across an online trailer for a new film, called *Anonymous*. The two-minute preview opens with a dark and moody shot of Shakespearean actor Derek Jacobi standing alone on a New York stage. "We all know William Shakespeare, the most famous author of all time," he intones. "But what if I told you Shakespeare never wrote a single word?" The action shifts to an aerial shot of Elizabethan London—crowds at the Globe Theatre—quill taken to paper—cannon fire and an angry mob—an execution at the Tower—a curly, red-haired Queen Elizabeth, played by Vanessa Redgrave, carrying on an affair with a goateed playwright who is definitely not Shakespeare—ending with the tagline: "We've all been played."

McCarthy sat at his computer with his mouth agape. "I saw the coming attraction, and I almost had a friggin' heart attack," McCarthy says now in the car as we drive back from Stratford. The film, by Roland Emmerich, director of such popcorn flicks as *Independence Day* and *The Patriot*, was billed as a "historical thriller," going all-in on the most extreme Prince Tudor theories that Oxford was both Elizabeth's son and lover. After all his work on North, McCarthy feared the film was going to steal his thunder in a big way. "I was literally nauseous. I called Nicole and I started to cry," McCarthy admits. "He had a meltdown," agrees Galovski. With all of the attention that was sure to accompany the big-budget film, McCarthy was worried one of two things was going to happen—both of them potentially catastrophic.

The first possibility was that the movie would be so over-the-top, no one would believe it. "He was going to make any questioning of Shakespearean authorship seem absurd," McCarthy says. The other possibility was even worse—that the movie would be so convincing that it would bring out new amateur sleuths to explore the authorship question, and one of them would stumble upon North and take credit for the discovery. He'd be like Alfred Wallace, who wrote about natural selection before Charles Darwin—or Elisha Gray, who invented the telephone contemporaneously with Alexander Graham Bell. "They filed the patent on the same day," McCarthy says.

As the publicity for *Anonymous* mounted, so did McCarthy's panic. He began feverishly pulling together everything he had researched over the past five years, piling it into a book-length manuscript he called *North of Shakespeare*. It was big and bombastic—the literary equivalent, perhaps, of a Roland Emmerich film—beginning with a single declarative sentence: "Sir Thomas North wrote the masterpieces that Shakespeare adapted for the stage." McCarthy followed that line with everything he knew at the time about North's biography, his research on *Hamlet* and the satires, and his Longleat manuscript theories ripped from his failed paper with Schlueter. In a final chapter, he hastily pulled together autobiographical parallels he'd identified in several other plays, including *Love's Labour's Lost*, *As You Like It*, and *The Tempest*.

"I wanted to beat the movie out," McCarthy says, "and I thought if maybe people start buying my book and I could do a total end-run around scholarship—this was my wildest dream." He pauses. "It shows you how naive I was." At the time, Galovski was living at his family home in New

Hampshire, and she helped him format the pages and self-publish the book online. "Do you remember? It was like four in the morning, and we publish—" says Galovski. "We publish," McCarthy says, finishing her sentence, "and we're like, 'Our lives are about to change.'" "We broke out the champagne," says Galovski. "I was like, 'Refresh, refresh!'" says McCarthy. "We were like, 'How many hits? Is Thomas North trending right now?'" Galovski says, laughing.

McCarthy compares the moment now to the scene in the 2010 movie *The Social Network* in which Mark Zuckerberg puts Facebook live in his dorm room for the very first time. Only, instead of watching while the site racked up users, McCarthy received no response. He sold a few dozen copies in the first few months and garnered praise from Patrick Buckridge, an Australian Oxfordian and literature professor who congratulated him for solving the Shakespeare mystery at last—but mostly the book went unread.

Making matters worse, when *Anonymous* finally hit the theaters in October, the reviews were savage. Critics roasted it as "silly," "outlandish," "unintelligent," and, paradoxically, "not dumb enough." The film flopped at the box office, earning back only half of its $30 million budget worldwide, and failing entirely to create the splash McCarthy had feared. He now regrets publishing his book so quickly, before he was able to refine his ideas. "My life would be a lot easier in terms of getting published in journals now if I'd never published it," he says, "but then I run the risk of some guy saying, 'Oh, by the way, it's Thomas North,' and then I lose everything." Galovski nods. "You become Elisha Gray," she says. "Right, I become Elisha Gray, and no one knows who he is," says McCarthy. "I have some friggin' asterisk after my name."

Soon after publishing the book, McCarthy sent a sheepish email to Schlueter to tell her about it. "The bad news is, and I'm terrified to admit this to you," he wrote, "the work is very controversial, heretical even, and contends William Shakespeare wrote very close stage-adaptations of other people's works." He signed the email, "Your renegade student, Dennis." When Schlueter received a copy, she was disappointed—not so much by his unorthodox conclusions, as by his big-talking writing style.

She responded right away with a chiding note, saying, "You don't really expect a life-long conventional Shakespearean to give North a chance, do you?" In the same note, however, she again urged him to publish the *Titus* paper, offering to continue editing it.

McCarthy felt relieved. Finally, he'd told an established academic about Thomas North, and hadn't been totally rejected. A few months later, Schlueter sent him a more considered reply to the book, telling him that his was the first argument about Shakespeare authorship that she hadn't "dismissed out of hand" as a conspiracy theory—but that he wasn't doing himself any favors with his breathless tone. "Scholars typically adopt a more tentative, exploratory style," she counseled. "It's hard not to feel bullied when one reads your writing." By that time, McCarthy was getting bullied himself in online Shakespeare authorship forums by Stratfordians and anti-Stratfordians alike, who were disparaging his arguments, often with ad hominem attacks. McCarthy restrained himself in his replies, pushing back, but also correcting mistakes as he revised his work. "They are the most voracious fact-checkers imaginable," he says.

Around the same time, he stumbled across an article that completely transformed his research. Titled "Plagiarism Software Finds a New Shakespeare Play," the 2009 *Time* magazine piece described the work of British scholar Sir Brian Vickers—an owlish-looking professor at the University of London with big spectacles and wispy white hair. The article described how Vickers had analyzed the anonymous play *Edward III* using the novel technique of plagiarism software, concluding it was a collaboration between William Shakespeare and Thomas Kyd, the scrivener's son best known for *The Spanish Tragedy*. "With this method, we see the way authors use and reuse the same phrases and metaphors, like chunks of fabric in weave," Vickers told *Time*. "If you have enough of them, you can identify one fabric as Scottish tweed and another as plain gray cloth."

It was McCarthy's first introduction to using plagiarism software—a tool more typically used by professors to catch cheating students—to test authorship. He could barely contain his excitement. Here was an analysis that also questioned the orthodoxy of Shakespeare's canon—not by some bomb-throwing anti-Stratfordian, but by an established scholar who had been studying Shakespeare for forty years. Hell, he'd even been knighted.

The article suddenly gave McCarthy hope that with the right techniques, he, too, might be taken seriously.

Vickers was part of a quieter movement questioning authorship of the plays. Instead of replacing Shakespeare with someone else, it sought to recombine him with multiple "someones" with whom he'd cowritten the plays. In fact, they argued, in the theatrical world of Elizabethan England, collaboration was more often the rule than not. As drama first emerged into public theaters, companies fell over each other to produce up to a dozen new plays a year—enticing the cheering and jeering audiences to the playhouse. In that context, the "play's the thing" as Hamlet said— and publication an afterthought. "Plays were only rarely regarded as 'literature' in a sense recognizable today," says scholar Jonathan Hope. "They are better regarded as raw material fueling the profitable entertainment industry of early modern London, much as film scripts are the raw material of today's film industry."

Companies paid writers 40 shillings for an old play, and from £1 to £8 for a new one—and then, much like a modern-day screenwriter, the writer lost all control over how it was performed. As part owner of a company, Shakespeare would have had more control than most writers, but even he would have seen his plays adapted for different actors, or slashed to take on tour. In this inherently collaborative environment, companies employed syndicates of up to four writers to work on a single play, recombining them as writers moved between companies, season by season. By some estimates, says Heather Hirschfeld, "over half of the plays of the English Renaissance were scripted by more than one dramatist."

Publishing plays, on the other hand, often worked against the company's interest, since it invited other companies to pirate them. Playwrights were rarely credited, especially early on; from 1576 to 1597, only a quarter of title pages named authors. Scholars today debate how much Elizabethan playwrights even considered themselves literary figures as opposed to being jobbers for hire. While the idea of an individual "author" was alive and well in Greek and Roman times, it wasn't until the 1590s that authors' names began regularly appearing on English plays, and even then about half were still published anonymously, including Shakespeare's first eight plays. Writers such as Ben Jonson, Edmund Spenser, and Robert

Greene fiercely defended the authorship of their own works, but others seemed content to remain anonymous, or even see their work freely reworked by other writers. The word "plagiarism" (or "plagiary") didn't even enter the English language until 1598.

In light of those facts, Shakespeare would have been unique among his contemporaries if he *hadn't* written collaboratively with other playwrights. Thus to really understand Shakespeare as an author, Vickers and others argued, we first have to understand what he actually wrote. For them, the question wasn't whether Shakespeare wrote the plays, but how much Shakespeare there is in Shakespeare. "We cannot form any reliable impression of his work," wrote Vickers in his seminal 2002 work, *Shakespeare: Co-Author*, "unless we can identify those parts of collaborative plays that were written by him together with one or more fellow dramatists."

The available historical evidence, however, makes answering that question extremely difficult. Only six handwritten playhouse manuscripts survive *in total* from Shakespeare's time—none of them by the Bard, unless you count a fragment of the play *Sir Thomas More* that some believe contains Shakespeare's hand. While the First Folio only identifies Shakespeare as author of the plays, a quarto copy of *The Two Noble Kinsmen* lists both John Fletcher and Shakespeare as authors as early as 1634. Lacking any trustworthy external documents, Vickers and other scholars turned to the text itself for answers.

THE TECHNIQUE GOES back to at least the mid-nineteenth century, when earnest scholars pored over word choices and writing style to determine which parts of *The Two Noble Kinsmen* were written by John Fletcher, and which by Shakespeare. Soon they added *Henry VIII* to the list of plays in which Fletcher had a hand. In the 1920s, some argued that Shakespeare also collaborated with Peele on *Titus*; and with Thomas Middleton, an Oxford-educated son of a bricklayer, on *Timon of Athens*, one of Shakespeare's least popular plays. To make the claims, they pointed to passages in the works that closely mirrored passages in the coauthors' other plays, as well as "image clusters"—distinct combinations of words that seemed particular to each writer. Oftentimes, writers simply assigned coauthors to any passage they thought "unworthy of the Bard."

By the mid-twentieth century, scholars added Shakespeare's late romance *Pericles* and his three *Henry VI* plays to the list of cowritten plays—as well as arguing for Shakespeare's hand in a dozen anonymous plays of the period, including *Edward III*. A common theme emerged: the inferior plays were ripe for coauthorship, whereas the masterpieces were Shakespeare's alone. As New Zealand scholar MacDonald Jackson put it in 1979: "The more important the play or the proposed author, the greater the degree of skepticism a case of authorship will attract."

MacDonald, who had long argued for Shakespeare's authorship of *Arden of Faversham*, was an early user of computers for attribution studies. Along with Vickers and Gary Taylor, a ponytailed professor from Florida State University, he started in the 1980s using machine-readable databases, such as Early English Books Online (EEBO) or Literature Online (LiOn), to examine the most minute features of the plays—including the proclivity authors had for using alliteration or polysyllabic words, or even the rate of so-called function words, such as *and, or, then, over,* and *up.*

"Barely noticed by a reader," those words nevertheless make up "an individual's DNA, so to speak," write Hugh Craig and Arthur Kinney, two more recent entrants into the field from the University of Newcastle and the University of Massachusetts, respectively. They used the techniques to demonstrate that Shakespeare collaborated with Christopher Marlowe on *Henry VI, Parts 1 and 2.* At the same time, they warn that the method is "powerful but not infallible," since "the results of computational stylistics are always matters of probability, not of certainty."

As the major players in the field have come to different conclusions on authorship, they have often sniped at one another. "The fact that Taylor achieved such disappointing results" in one test, Vickers says, "may be due to his having designed it badly." Taylor counters, "The methodology by which Vickers investigated the Kyd canon was incapable of sustaining his conclusions." He compares it to a "one-horse race" in which the outcome was predetermined from the outset.

Other scholars have called the whole field into question, skeptical that computer analytics can succeed in analyzing literary forms. At the very least, the techniques are premised on a particular kind of collaboration in which multiple authors each wrote individual scenes bearing their own unique literary fingerprints. Crucially, the techniques also depend on having a control—a set of plays for each author written by him and him alone—in order to provide a reliable sample for determining linguistic style. If McCarthy is right, then that sample doesn't exist for Shakespeare, since all his plays use some combination of Shakespeare's and North's language, with other collaborators added into the mix as well. On the other hand, McCarthy thought, a control text of Thomas North's works did exist: his three translations, *The Dial of Princes*, *The Moral Philosophy of Doni*, and *Plutarch's Lives*. He could use them, along with Vickers's plagiarism techniques, to find common phrases in both North's translations and Shakespeare's plays.

MCCARTHY SETTLED ON WCopyfind, an open-source program developed by Lou Bloomfield, a physics professor at the University of Virginia. He started by downloading all of Shakespeare's plays into a master file of the canon—with around a million words in total. With the help of EEBO, he downloaded North's work as well, creating a control file of nearly nine hundred thousand words. Immediately, however, he recognized a problem. While the spelling in Shakespeare's plays has all been modernized, North's books are all written in Elizabethan English, in which spelling is creative at best. In order for the program to detect word matches, he would need to change it all.

He started on the first page of *The Dial*, changing "doth" to "does," correcting "vertue" to "virtue," and removing the final *e* from words like "wille" and "deathe." Eventually, he started using shortcuts to make global replacements. Even so, he spent six or seven hours the first day and only got through a few pages. When a quick test showed few results, he soldiered on for weeks, enlisting Galovski to help him as well. He waited until they were at least halfway through the file before running another test, customizing it to look for identical strings of up to six words with only one error. Then he took a deep breath, and pressed "Run."

The screen came alive with phrases in common, all marked in red on each side. "I couldn't believe it," he says now in the car as we drive back from Stratford. "It lights up all over the screen." As he scrolled through them, he says, he realized he was looking at thousands of phrases of three, four, five, and even six words. Some were iconic lines. The title *All's Well That Ends Well* appeared in *The Moral Philosophy of Doni* as "all is well that endeth well" and Lady Macbeth's "what is done cannot be undone" appears verbatim in *Plutarch's Lives*. Of course, the phrases could have both been borrowed from elsewhere, or just be commonplace coincidences. McCarthy plugged them one by one into EEBO to see if anyone else had used them by Shakespeare's time. While some did seem quite common, others, however, appeared only in North and Shakespeare. The five-word phrase "not of the blood royal," for instance, appeared only in *Plutarch* prior to *Henry IV, Part 1*. The eight-word phrase "word that might be to the prejudice of" appeared only in *The Dial* and *Henry VIII*.

Some passages even seemed to combine words and phrases from different texts. In *Richard II* a gardener compares the upkeep of the kingdom to tending a garden, using the phrases "noisome weeds," "wholesome flowers," "their fruits," and "superfluous branches." The first two phrases appear in the same sentence in *Plutarch*, while the second two phrases appear in the same sentence in *The Dial*—in a passage that also compares ruling a kingdom to gardening. "It's not just one line he's borrowing. He's borrowing an entire idea, an entire image," McCarthy says.

After weeks of research, he was eager to reveal his discovery to the world. Just as he had done with the biogeography scholars and June Schlueter, he sent his best forty examples to Brian Vickers, along with an email praising the British scholar's work. To his delight, Vickers replied with enthusiasm. "You've certainly opened up this topic, only partly glimpsed before, and this will be a valuable contribution to Shakespeare studies," he emailed. "I urge you to publish it!" He even proposed that McCarthy consider writing a book, and suggested a name for it: *Shakespeare's North*. (Not for the first time, McCarthy regretted rushing *North of Shakespeare* into print.)

McCarthy replied immediately, sidestepping the fact that he'd already self-published a book, and saying only that he'd prefer to publish an article. Vickers suggested he try the *Review for English Studies*—the same journal that had previously rejected his *Titus* paper. In May 2012, McCarthy sent in his paper with his forty examples, demonstrating that "North's influence on Shakespeare was far greater than anyone had previously realized." A month later, he received a reply from the editor, once again prominently featuring the words "regret," "disappointing news," and "not been selected for publication." He included a review from an anonymous peer reviewer who criticized the methodology as unproven at best. "Having run several of the searches on EEBO with slightly different parameters, forms, and spellings," the reviewer wrote, "I am not convinced that the method used is robust." All they proved is "what we already knew: that Shakespeare read North thoroughly."

Disappointed, McCarthy passed the email along to Vickers, who promised to write a reply to the editor. A few months later, he sent a 1,500-word email, with attachments, defending McCarthy's use of plagiarism software, and suggesting that the editor resubmit the paper to another peer reviewer who was more familiar with Shakespeare, North's *Plutarch*, and authorship studies. Vickers forwarded his response to McCarthy, promising to forward the editor's reply. The very next day, however, Vickers sent a very different email instead. "I'm glad that my intervention to *RES* made you happy," it started. "However, I don't go along with your wider agenda, as witnessed by your book."

Reading the email, McCarthy winced. "I'm afraid that a perfectly sound scholarly discovery will be drowned out by your ridiculous authorship theories," Vickers continued, adding it was a shame that now no one would publish the important parallels passages he'd discovered. "He completely changed his tune in 24 hours," McCarthy says. He can only guess what happened between the two emails, but he presumes that the editor had come across the listing for his book online, and forwarded it to Vickers, noting McCarthy's heresy. The same scholarship that was acceptable to show Shakespeare used North as a source was apparently impermissible to demonstrate North wrote source plays.

As WE CONTINUE our drive back from Stratford, Galovski takes over interviewing her father in the backseat, while Hosseini crams herself into the front seat to point her camera at them. "They know that these are important findings, but they know that these parallel passages help me," McCarthy says about his experience with the *Review of English Studies* and

Vickers. "They don't want to publish them, because they know what I'm going to argue with them."

Galovski asks him why after all of these years, he thinks it's been so hard to get people to take his theories seriously. "It's nearly impossible to convince someone who has become so identified with a particular idea—and this is particularly true with Shakespeare scholars," McCarthy responds. "Once they've formed an emotional attachment to their ideas, and written books about it and articles about it, their entire sense of self is wrapped up in their view of how Shakespeare worked and what he wrote. And they're just not going to surrender that." Eventually, however, he says the "truth will out"—to use a Shakespearean term—just as it did with Darwin and evolution, or Wegener and continental drift, as more and more people grow up without those emotional attachments. "Basically, I'm saying enough people have to die—which is an exact quote from Max Planck. He said, 'Knowledge progresses funeral by funeral.' "

Of course, I think to myself, it could be McCarthy who has developed the unhealthy emotional attachment, unwilling to give up on Thomas North after investing so many years of research—but his daughter beats me to the sentiment. "Do you think it's possible *you* die before people believe this?" Galovski asks bluntly. "No," McCarthy says immediately, as if unable to conceive of the idea. "No, at least a number of people will start believing it, and it will become bigger and bigger," McCarthy predicts as we pull off the highway into the parking lot of a roadside pub. "Then they'll start developing an emotional attachment to Thomas North," he jokes.

McCarthy wrote Vickers a conciliatory email, reassuring him that he wasn't an anti-Stratfordian, but the older scholar failed to reply. There was one academic who kept communicating with McCarthy, however: June Schlueter. The two met for dinner, and McCarthy continued to detail his theories about North's authorship of the plays. ("It was a pleasure to meet with you, North of Boston," Schlueter teased him later.) Over the next few months, McCarthy began sending results of his plagiarism research, gradually wearing down her skepticism, to the point where she started agreeing with him. "It kept repeating all of these parallels, and you reach a point where you can't resist any more," she told me in Easton. "It just seems so obvious."

The software bolstered their case for *Titus*, with dozens of shared phrases between the play and *The Dial*—the book North presumably just finished translating before writing *Titus and Vespasian* in 1562. Where *The Dial* has "I have been troubled in my mind," *Titus* has "I have been troubled in my sleep this night." Where *The Dial* has "God forbid that I should be so bold to say," *Titus* has "God forbid I should be so bold to press." Even the name Lavinia appears in North's book, in the story of a woman agonizing over the death of her husband on the battlefield. In a letter to the widow, the emperor Marcus Aurelius writes, "Lady Lavinia, most earnestly I desire thee, so vehemently not to pierce the heavens with thy so heavy sighs, nor yet, to wet the earth with thy so bitter tears." In *Titus Andronicus*, Titus similarly laments his daughter's rape with language combining heaven, earth, and tears. "When heaven doth weep, doth not the earth overflow?" he cries. "Then must my earth with her continual tears become a deluge."

McCarthy also analyzed two other versions of the Titus story, a prose history and a poetic ballad. Scholars always assumed both were derived from Shakespeare's play, but McCarthy found that both shared elements with *The Dial* that were not in Shakespeare—implying they had all borrowed from North. In the same story about Lavinia lamenting her husband, for example, North writes, "she scratched her face, she ruffled her hair, she tore her gown," while the prose history says Lavinia "tore her golden hair, shed floods of tears, and with her nails offered violence to that lovely face"— details absent in Shakespeare. "You would have to have the prose author and William Shakespeare both miraculously working from a 1557 work, and both borrowing elements from the same page," McCarthy says. "It's possible," he adds, cocking his head and smiling, "but I think it's unlikely."

McCarthy began revising his paper, sharing it with Schlueter in the fall of 2012. She edited it, taking out the information on the Longleat manuscript—her own baby—to streamline the argument to focus on the textual analysis. The following spring, she sent it out to the editor of the *Times Literary Supplement*, under the title "New Light on a Lost Elizabethan Play." Once again, however, the editor rejected it, saying that while he could concede that North's *Dial* was a source for *Titus Andronicus*, he didn't see why that meant North had written a play.

Even as they swallowed that rejection, however, Schlueter caught a notice requesting submissions for the summer 2014 issue of *Shakespeare Survey*, with the theme of "Shakespeare's Collaborative Plays." Though it seemed like a longshot, she persuaded McCarthy to let her send out the article as a joint contribution, under the title "A Shakespeare/North Collaboration." To his surprise, Schlueter received an email from the journal a few months later, beginning, "Delighted to accept the article..." Within a year, the paper appeared in an issue with some of the top names in the field: Gary Taylor wrote the introduction, and in a particularly sweet turn for McCarthy, their own paper was followed by Sir Brian Vickers's essay on "The Two Authors of *Edward III*."

Finally, after nearly ten years, McCarthy had succeeded in publishing a paper claiming Thomas North was a playwright. By the time the journal came out, however, he was already delving deeper into the digital techniques to find other connections between North's works and the canon. When he had started his work in 2005, he did it with only a vague inkling about when and why North had written his plays. As he started to analyze them one by one, however, he began noticing patterns. "It's an agonizing process, play by play," McCarthy says. "You dig up one fossil, then another, and you put it together." In particular, he noticed certain groupings of plays that seemed to borrow from each of North's works. Just as *The Winter's Tale* and *Henry VIII* seemed related to the journal, and *Arden of Faversham* and *Titus Andronicus* to *The Dial*, so, too, a group of plays seemed to borrow from North's next translation, *The Moral Philosophy of Doni*. These plays all had one thing in common: Italy.

Chapter Eight

WONDERS OF THE WORLD ABROAD

(1565–1570)

I would rather entreat thy company
To see the wonders of the world abroad,
Than, living dully sluggardized at home,
Wear out thy youth with shapeless idleness.
—*The Two Gentlemen of Verona*

At the beginning of Shakespeare's *The Taming of the Shrew*, a young gentleman disembarks in Padua, the great sixteenth-century Italian seat of learning. "Since for the great desire I had to see fair Padua, nursery of the arts, I am arrived fore fruitful Lombardy, the pleasant garden of great Italy," the scholar, Lucentio, says to his servant, Tranio. "Here let us breathe and haply institute a course of learning and ingenious studies." Nonplussed, his servant replies, "Let's be no stoics," urging him to pursue music, poetry, and food as well. "No profit grows where is no pleasure taken." Lucentio agrees, crying, "Gramercies, Tranio, well dost thou advise."

The exchange may as well have been Thomas North talking to himself, says McCarthy, as he arrived in Italy to continue his studies—and at the same time sample the bawdy delights of the late Italian Renaissance. When the plagiarism software first started revealing the verbal connections between Shakespeare's Italian comedies and North's *Moral Philosophy of Doni*, McCarthy felt as if a huge portion of North's life suddenly slid into place. After his father's death in 1564, Thomas North disappears from history for a decade—a period McCarthy considers his own "lost years." "This is still dark for me," he says. North surfaces only briefly in 1568, with a new edition of *The Dial of Princes*, which he signs from "my Lord North's house near London"—presumably his brother's house in Charterhouse yard. The same year, North received the "freedom of the city" of Cambridge, allowing him to own property there (an honor that also likely came on the coattails of his brother, a newly elected alderman of the city).

Political office, however, eluded Thomas; whatever skills he possessed as a writer, he apparently lacked the acumen to navigate court. His only other appearance in print that decade is with *Doni*, a book of moralistic animal fables originally by Italian writer Anton Francesco Doni, published in 1570. The book is dedicated to Robert Dudley, the Earl of Leicester, the same nobleman on whose behalf McCarthy believes North wrote *Titus and Vespasian*. At the time, McCarthy discovered, Leicester was obsessed with all things Italian—including art, music, literature, and theater. At the 1566 Christmas revels, George Gascoigne presented his play *Supposes*, a translation of an Italian work, Ludovico Ariosto's *I Suppositi*, which has been called the first prose English comedy. The performance sparked a new rage for Italianate entertainments at court that lasted well into the next decade.

Leicester led the way, often patronizing writers to translate Italian books, and sometimes imploring courtiers traveling to Padua and Venice to bring him back the latest texts. It would make sense if Thomas were among their number, traveling to Italy in 1569 or 1570 to acquire source material to curry the nobleman's favor. Just as North chose the Spanish *Dial* to appeal to the Catholic Queen Mary, he obviously picked this Italianate translation to appeal to Leicester's new love for the country. "He wanted to get into Leicester's good graces, and Leicester was very interested in these Italianate performances," McCarthy says.

In his dedication, North stressed his own relationship with the influential earl, saying he "heretofore tasted of your honor" (hinting at a prior patronage relationship, which McCarthy takes as a possible reference to *Titus and Vespasian*), and further reminding him of the connection to his father and his brother Roger, "whose bond to your lordship still increaseth with your large and friendly love to him." Finally, in a reference to the

Roman patron of arts, he declares, "I have made Your Lordship patron and my only Maecenas." McCarthy sees in that dedication a confirmation of his relationship with Leicester, possibly pointing to the fact that North traveled to Italy to find him books—and perhaps plays as well.

McCarthy found no hard evidence that he took such a trip, though a nineteenth-century editor of *Doni*, at least, speculates he must have made a "grand tour" of Europe to pick up the work. In addition, an Italian dedicatory poem in the beginning of the book, written by someone who only signs himself G. B., conveys Doni's own blessing on the work, saying, "If no person translated me before, North is the one who promotes me now." The poem implies that Doni had read North's translation and approved of it, says McCarthy. "Either North is sending the book to Italy and then the Italian is sending it back," he says, "or he is in Italy doing this, and the guy gives it to him right there."

A trip to Italy by North would also explain why McCarthy was finding so many links between *Doni* and Shakespearean plays with Italianate settings, including *The Taming of the Shrew*, *The Two Gentlemen of Verona*, *The Comedy of Errors*, and even his great tragedy, *Othello*. And it would also explain why Shakespeare set so many of his plays there, while so few of his contemporaries did. As McCarthy points out, an overwhelming number of those plays were based on Italian-language sources, most of them untranslated, and written in the 1560s, just around the time North would have visited.

THE LATE 1560s was a treacherous time in the English court, which was increasingly fractured by marital politics. Mary Queen of Scots did in fact marry her cousin Lord Darnley, and gave birth to a son, James, in 1566—posing a new threat to the English throne. Early the next year, however, an explosion ripped through the house where Darnley was staying, leaving him dead. Suspicion fell on Mary's supposed lover, the Earl of Bothwell, and Mary only confirmed it by marrying *him*. When Scotland's Protestant nobles rebelled, Mary fled into England, where Elizabeth welcomed her as a "guest," while holding her under indefinite house arrest. So long as Mary stayed there, however, she served as a rallying point for England's Catholics, putting new pressure on Elizabeth to find a husband.

Cecil still eyed a foreign match. When Elizabeth rejected France's King Charles IX as too young, he urged her to consider the Holy Roman Empire, now led by the Emperor Maximilian II, who offered marriage with his brother Charles, Archduke of Austria. Some powerful allies supported him, including Thomas Howard, the 4th Duke of Norfolk, the highest ranked peer in the realm. Conservative in religion, Howard bought the Charterhouse when Edward North was forced to sell it to pay for Roger's gambling debts—no doubt earning Roger's ill will as he looked at it from his smaller house in Charterhouse Yard. Joining Norfolk was his older cousin, the forty-year-old Thomas Radcliffe, Earl of Sussex, a veteran intriguer who had just returned from a stint as governor of Ireland. Both men desperately felt England needed a military alliance with Catholic France or the Holy Roman Empire to survive the century—and considered the idea of King Robert a disaster.

Tensions flared over the notorious tennis-court incident, when Leicester played against Norfolk at Whitehall. Leicester, "being very hot and sweating," grabbed a napkin out of the queen's hand and used it to wipe his face. The duke considered such behavior too "saucy" and threatened to smash his racket "upon his face." The queen rebuked Norfolk, humiliating him in front of the court, as he seethed at Leicester's cheek. Soon, the court was split into factions, Norfolk's men in yellow and Leicester's in purple, armed and brawling in the courtyards.

Leicester, of course, continued to push for his own marriage to the queen. The same month as the tennis-court fracas, he hired players from Gray's Inn to perform a masque at court in which the goddess Juno, representing marriage, triumphed over Diana, representing chastity. "This is all against me," the queen exclaimed. The next Christmas, a new play at Gray's Inn called *Jocasta* also seemed to advocate Elizabeth's marriage. Written by George Gascoigne and Francis Kinwelmersh, it included an epilogue from Christopher Yelverton, another of the "Minerva's Men" mentioned in Jasper Heywood's prologue. The only surviving manuscript of the play, now in the British Library, bears Roger North's signature, implying he was given it by the authors, and may have even had a hand in producing it.

It's difficult to determine exactly where Roger fell in the marriage debate. A letter from the Spanish ambassador identifies him with Norfolk's

faction—but that seems hard to believe given his family's ties to the Dudleys and his burgeoning friendship with Leicester. In the summer of 1567, Elizabeth sent a delegation to the Holy Roman Emperor in Vienna, officially to invest Maximilian with the prestigious Order of the Garter, and unofficially to negotiate the terms of her marriage to Archduke Charles. Led by Leicester's enemy, the Earl of Sussex, it also included Roger North, who, according to a nineteenth-century biographer, was possibly sent on Leicester's behalf to "discourage the suit."

The delegation sailed from Dover that June, cutting through the German petty states to arrive in the splendor of the emperor's court in Vienna six weeks later. Initial negotiations seemed promising, but they hit a snag over the Catholic archduke's desire to worship in public. Sussex negotiated a compromise whereby Charles could worship in private so long as he promised not to undermine the Church of England. Back in London, meanwhile, Leicester was actively sabotaging the marriage, spreading rumors about the Duke of Norfolk's Catholic sympathies, and encouraging preachers to rail against the marriage from the pulpit. When ambassadors returned to Vienna with the queen's reply on New Year's Eve 1568, Sussex could not have been more disappointed: she wouldn't allow the Archduke to practice Catholicism, even privately. Sussex wrote back desperately to Cecil, warning of "what great peril grows on all sides" if "the marriage were to fail." But Elizabeth wouldn't budge. The delegation took its time heading home, finally arriving back in London in May 1568.

It wasn't long before Sussex's warnings of danger came to pass. Secretly, Norfolk began plotting to marry Mary Queen of Scots and restore her to the Scottish throne, with him by her side. He included Sussex in his plotting, as well as Northern lords with Catholic sympathies, and even his enemy Leicester, who may have seen the scheme as a means to get rid of both Norfolk and Mary. Leicester had a change of heart, however, and confessed everything to Elizabeth. Furious, she brought Norfolk quickly to heel—but the spark he lit ended up kindling the so-called Northern Rebellion. The Northern lords raised an army of several thousand men in November 1569, setting out to liberate Mary from prison. The rebellion didn't last long. Elizabeth spirited Mary south and sent Sussex, along with Leicester's brother Ambrose, against the rebels, who were quickly routed and fled north to Scotland. Elizabeth vengefully ordered the execution of more than seven hundred captured rebels and commanded castles and villages burned to the ground, sending Norfolk to the Tower in disgrace. The sudden explosion of violence, however, showed just how fragile Elizabeth's reign remained.

IT WAS IN the midst of this troubled time that Thomas North released his new book of courtly advice, *The Moral Philosophy of Doni*. The book, by Anton Francesco Doni, originally appeared in Venice in 1552, and again there in a new quarto edition in 1567. At first glance, it fits into the *speculum principis* genre. But this philosophy book comes with a twist, dispensing its wisdom through exotic beast fables. In fact, Doni was only the latest interpreter of the collection of tales, which originated as far back as fourth- or fifth-century India, and came to Italy by way of Persia, Arabia, and Spain, gathering fables along the way. Even the original Sanskrit version, however, was conceived as a moral text, with an Indian sage called Bidpai instructing courtiers with "stories about animals that he claims even the most foolish of princes will understand," according to modern editors of the volume.

In his own prologue, North somewhat anxiously assures the reader that the book was no mere trifle, but rather "shall be a looking-glass" in which to more clearly discern "the most malignant effects of this, alas, our crooked age." Despite its moralizing framework, North's book employs a newly energetic, darkly funny, sometimes bawdy writing style. "*The Dial of Princes* and *Plutarch* are just straight histories with some humanist philosophy in them," says McCarthy. "But *Doni* has a darker edge—it's the most pessimistic and brutally dark of all Thomas North's work."

The book's forty-one tales wrap loosely around a central narrative of a duplicitous Mule that wheedles his way into court, bringing misery upon its king, a noble but overly trusting Lion. As that story unfolds, the various animals speak to each other through parables involving other animals, usually involving trickery, disguise, or betrayal. While North remains faithful to Doni's work, he frequently embellishes the tales with his own proverbs and spirited colloquialisms. In one tale about a bird, for example, Doni literally writes, "Kill it; what else would you want to do with this animal?" while North writes, "Out on her, whore! Kill her, ill-favored harlotry! What meanest thou to keep that foolish bird?"

North clearly has the most fun when translating the speeches of the Mule, which he often expands for dramatic effect. Despite being the ostensible villain of the story, the Mule jumps off the page much more fully formed than any of the other characters. He falls over himself with obsequiousness toward the Lion, filling his speech with flowery language even as he is deceiving him. His tone changes to a friendly persuasion to manipulate a dangerous Bull, and the story even has homoerotic overtones when he gives the animal a Judas kiss, saying the animals held hands and "kissed in the mouth"—which North embellishes as "kissed in the very mouth, even with their tongues."

To acquire the book, McCarthy believes, North traveled to Italy between publication of the new edition of *The Dial* in 1568 and *Doni* in 1570. "I imagine it is going to be a little like the 1555 trip, in that he's going to be hosted by some pretty important people, but he may have been traveling by himself as well," McCarthy says. "He's not going to be getting the embassy treatment." If North was as observant as he was on his earlier foray to Italy, however, then McCarthy imagines him delighting in the culture and entertainments so different from those in his native England.

CROSSING OVER THE Alps again from France, the first major city he would have come to was Milan—a place he knew already from the 1555 expedition. In his journal of that trip, he painted the picture of a powerful walled city with a castle "of such force, that none in all Europe is comparable to it." By the late 1560s, Milan had become even richer and more sophisticated—now the center of a powerful duchy ruled by Spain's Philip II (also nominal Duke of Milan). In Shakespeare's play, *The Two Gentlemen of Verona*, one of the title characters, Valentine, is also heading to Milan to seek his fortune, urging his best friend Proteus to join him. "I would rather entreat thy company to see the wonders of the world abroad, than—living dully sluggardized at home—wear out thy youth in idleness," he says. Like Lucentio in *The Taming of the Shrew*, the character could be a stand-in for North, says McCarthy. "Valentine is arguing that in order to be a truly enlightened person you have to travel, and that's what North does as well."

Eventually, Proteus follows Valentine to the city, where both men enter into the sophisticated court of the powerful Duke, and both fall in love with his beautiful daughter Silvia, creating the central conflict of the play. Scholars view *Two Gentlemen* as one of Shakespeare's first plays, written as far back as 1589. As such, it's full of the exuberance of youth, "offering his audiences," in the words of one scholar, "the vicarious experience of the excitement of foreign travel." They also agree, however, that Shakespeare didn't come up with the story himself—rather, he based it on a source play called *The History of Felix and Philomena*, acted at court by the Queen's Men in 1585. That play, in turn, was based on a popular Portuguese romance about the lovers Felix and Felismena, written by Jorge de Montemayor in 1559 and later translated into Spanish and French. "Shakespeare," writes Jonathan Bate, "is unlikely to have had enough Spanish or even French to have read it in published form, so his knowledge was probably based on a script or a viewing of the Queen's Men play, or even on having acted in it himself."

All of that is correct, McCarthy says, but misses one key fact: the Revels Accounts list an even earlier performance of a play at court with a similar name, *Philemon and Philecia*, performed in 1574 by Leicester's Men, the earl's own troupe of players. McCarthy believes North wrote the play for Leicester upon his return from Italy. Unlike Shakespeare, North would have been able to read the source story—and as it happens, another Spanish version of the tale was published in Venice in 1568 as part of the book *Diana Enamorada*, just before North's potential visit. That version includes an enchantress named Felicia. In the Spanish story, a woman disguises herself as a pageboy to follow her lover, and in Shakespeare's play, Proteus's lover Julia also dresses as a pageboy to follow him to Milan— further complicating the love triangle of Valentine, Proteus, and Silvia.

In its many lies, disguises, and mixed-up identities, the play seems to echo *Doni* as well. When McCarthy ran the play through his plagiarism software, he found dozens of phrases the two works had in common. Where *Doni* has "whoreson cankered mule," for example, the play has "thou whoreson ass"; where *Doni* has "fair, well favoured boy," the play has "fair, boy, as well favoured"; where *Doni* has "Dispatch, get thee hence," the play has "dispatch me hence."

Two Gentlemen also seems to contain some of the homoerotic subtext that North emphasized in the Italian work. The play ends in the wilderness outside Milan, where Proteus threatens to rape Silvia, before she is rescued by Valentine. Amazingly, however, Valentine then offers Silvia to Proteus in a gesture of friendship, saying, "That my love may appear plain and free, all that was mine in Silvia, I give to thee." It's a disturbing scene that turns many modern readers off. At least one critic, however, sees "the eagerness of Proteus and Valentine in *Two Gentlemen of Verona* to exalt male friendship above the feelings of men for women" as an example of the playwright's "understanding of homoerotic feeling." If anything, that understanding is only underscored when Proteus declines his friend's offer, having fallen in love with the pageboy, who is revealed to be Julia dressed as a man. Another critic notes, "Though the play has insistently staged friendship and cross-sex love as mutually exclusive alternatives, friendship between men is restored through (not at the cost of) marriage to women," showing "marriage and homoeroticism of male friendship can coexist."

McCarthy takes those references in both works to speculate that North had homoerotic inclinations as well—which he could finally express in the licentious atmosphere of Italy much more easily than in the repressed halls of England. "There are hints of bisexuality or homosexuality, especially in that trip," he tells me. "You can definitely see it in *Two Gentlemen of Verona*, where there's just extreme male bonding among these travelers." If that's the case, then it could provide a possible explanation to long-time speculation by some scholars that Shakespeare was gay or bisexual, especially considering the number of his plays that feature cross-dressing and swapping of gender roles as major elements of their plots.

ON OUR TRIP through Italy, we take a detour through Milan, eating lunch on the roof of La Rinascente department store, eye level with the magnificent Duomo, a cathedral covered with a forest of marble spires and statues. From there, we can see the mountains rising north of the city that are also mentioned in the play. In one scene, the Duke of Milan tells Proteus to meet him "upon the rising of the mountain foot that leads towards Mantua." At first, that seems to be an error, since Mantua is across flat fields to the east. At the time, however, those fields were often flooded, so travelers did take the road north toward the mountains before turning east—a fact that some observers have taken to show the playwright had firsthand knowledge of local geography.

For years, it was taken for granted that Shakespeare must have traveled to Italy at some point. However, the idea that Shakespeare took a grand tour of the Continent "has today been totally abandoned" in favor of "an intellectual journey of the mind, of memory and imagination," writes Michele Marrapodi, one of the foremost scholars of Shakespeare and Italy. The playwright, he and other scholars argue, soaked up Italian culture from books and conversations with Italian expats who frequented the Oliphant, a Bankside tavern near the Globe. If he couldn't read Italian perfectly, then Shakespeare read Italian sources alongside English or French translations that have since been lost. Of course, one of the reasons scholarly opinion has turned against the idea of an Italian jaunt for the

Bard is that it has become a favorite argument of anti-Stratfordians, who use it to prove that the Earl of Oxford was the true author of the plays.

Just as with the seacoast of Bohemia, critics have pointed out geographical howlers in *The Two Gentlemen of Verona* to show Shakespeare didn't know his Italy at all. The biggest gaffe is the fact Valentine and Proteus both travel from Verona to Milan by boat, despite both cities remaining landlocked in northern Italy. In an effort to show Shakespeare knew his geography after all, scholars as far back as the nineteenth century described a network of canals connecting the major cities of northern Italy. More recent critics have thrown cold water on the idea, with one calling the idea "strained and unconvincing to all but the most willing to believe."

In 2011, however, Richard Paul Roe, a California lawyer and Oxfordian, set out to prove critics wrong by traveling to Italy in search of the locations in the plays. In *The Shakespeare Guide to Italy*, Roe describes his discovery of old maps showing a canal connecting the Adige River in Verona and the Po River near Milan that could have made the gentlemen's trip possible. He even found vestiges of the old waterways, and plied a section of them by boat. Not only was boat travel the quickest route between the two cities, he argued, but it was also the safest and most comfortable method of journeying through land often beset by bandits. As an Oxfordian, Roe was careful throughout his book never to speculate on the identity of the author—referring to him simply as "the playwright." Of course that playwright, McCarthy thinks, wasn't Oxford or Shakespeare, but North.

We take Roe's book with us now as we head across the hilly country of northeastern Italy to one of the most popular destinations for English travelers in the sixteenth century: Padua. Home to a world-renowned university since the Middle Ages, the city was a magnet for a certain class of young, sophisticated English gentlemen sent by their fathers to supplement their humanist education. Private tutors and informal academies sprang up around the university itself, promoting not only study in mathematics and Italian, but also fencing, horsemanship, and music. Padua would have been a natural destination for North, where he could immerse himself in an atmosphere of culture and learning while he sought out sources for his plays.

We pass now through the city center, where the tall granite buildings of the university surround a winding pedestrian mall filled with students enjoying the sunshine at outdoor cafes. Following Roe, we navigate along one of Padua's many arrow-straight canals in search of the location where he placed the opening scene of *The Taming of the Shrew*. As soon as he arrives in Padua by boat, Lucentio almost immediately spies Bianca, the beautiful daughter of a Paduan merchant, Baptista Minola, and falls in love with her. He then goes to find a lodging house while planning how he will win her hand. If McCarthy is right in thinking the scene is at least partially autobiographical, then the spot might also be where North once stayed as well.

Roe set out to find that lodging house by seeking out St. Luke's Church, which is mentioned twice in the play. He located *Chiesa di San Luca Evangelista*, a small medieval church less than a half a mile south of the university. As it happens, an eighteenth-century map of Padua showed a boat landing on a canal just a minute's walk from the church. Next to it was the word *osteria*, an old Italian word for "inn" or "public house." We drive through increasingly narrow cobblestone streets lined with arched arcades, before locating the salmon-pink facade of the church. A short walk down along the canal, we find the boat landing Roe discovered on his map—now the only spot along the water where there isn't a building, just a stone wall overhung with a massive Italian stone pine.

Next to it, there is a large yellow building with arched windows and balustrades that could have been Baptista Minola's mansion. And across an ancient-looking bridge is the *osteria* Roe identified, a four-story structure with tall, arched windows. The building now houses part of the university's department of astronomy—though, coincidentally, a sign out front points out the way to Padua's youth hostel nearby. McCarthy and I stand on the bridge together looking up at the structure. I imagine a thirty-four-year-old Thomas North gazing back out the window over us, across the canal, perhaps catching sight of a beautiful young Italian woman, and imagining Lucentio and his servant disembarking at the landing and knocking on Baptista's door.

THE TAMING OF THE SHREW is one of Shakespeare's funniest plays, with a "battle of the sexes" plot that has inspired adaptations from the 1948 Broadway musical *Kiss Me Kate* to the 1999 teen rom-com *10 Things I Hate About You*. The conceit is simple: a Paduan merchant has two daughters, the delightful Bianca, who has multiple suitors vying for her hand, and her older sister, Katharina, the "shrew" who eats men for breakfast. Baptista vows not to wed his younger daughter before Katharina has also found a husband, leading to a search for a suitor who can "tame" the headstrong woman. Enter Petruchio, a gentleman from Verona spurred by the promise of a rich dowry to take on the challenge and match wits with "Kate" to force her to submit.

By today's standards, the play is unabashedly sexist, even cringeworthy, as Kate is "tamed" by denying her food, drink, and clothes, forced to debase herself before Petruchio and patriarchy. But the story is not without nuance; although Petruchio seems at first only interested in money, he becomes obviously attracted to her passionate spirit. And even while Kate submits herself without reservation—literally putting her hand beneath her husband's foot—her passion seems too hot to be held down for long. Depending on how the role is played, she can come across as truly submissive or merely playacting. Feminist interpretations of the play—such as a 2019 performance by the Royal Shakespeare Company in which the genders of all the characters were reversed—can turn the theme on its head.

The play is also considered one of Shakespeare's earliest, undoubtedly staged even before its first recorded performance in 1594. Complicating matters, an anonymous play titled *The Taming of a Shrew* appeared around the same time. Scholars long believed Shakespeare's *The Shrew* was an adaptation of *A Shrew*. More recently, however, some have theorized that both plays are adaptations of a longer, uncut version—a sort of *Ur-Shrew*. It's no surprise who McCarthy thinks authored that play: Thomas North.

From its opening scene, the language of the play is North's, he says. Lucentio's reference to "fruitful Lombardy, the pleasant garden of Italy" echoes language in North's journal while traveling through Lombardy, in which he writes, "We rode as between gardens." Later, another of Bianca's would-be suitors, the aged Gremio, boasts about his wealth, saying he has "a hundred milch-kine to the pail, sixscore fat oxen standing in my stalls." Sure enough, in the same entry in the journal, he notes that the delegation saw "one-hundred fat oxen in a stable." North also uses "milch kine to the pail"—a phrase meaning "dairy cows ready to milk"—in *Plutarch's Lives* when referring to an old man's wealth. "Nicole found that one," says McCarthy, who calls it an "exclusively Northern" phrase—meaning the Norths were the only ones who used it. Later, when examining Roger's account books for Kirtling, McCarthy once again came across the same phrase, "milch kine to the pail," suggesting it was a family expression.

Put together, the phrases "one-hundred fat oxen in a stable" and "four score milch kine to the pail" sound an awful lot like "a hundred milch-kine to the pail, sixscore fat oxen standing in my stalls." The similarities don't end there. In Gremio's speech from *Shrew*, he describes his luxurious home, which includes "plate and gold" and a bedroom with "canopies, fine linen, Turkish cushions." The corresponding passage in *Plutarch's Lives* also describes an exotic bedroom, complete with "gold & silver" and "a very rich bed" with "Persian chamberlains to make and dress it up." McCarthy sees the two houses as too similar to be coincidental. "They are both describing bedrooms, one is Persian, the other from Turkey," McCarthy says. "You have similar words—gold, rich—and here's the kicker, in each case after he compares bedroom furniture, they both start talking about cattle," even using that same rare expression, "milch kine to the pail."

As impressive as those matches are, however, McCarthy was unprepared for the sheer number of correspondences he would find with the plagiarism software between *Shrew* and *Doni*. The play shares more than fifty short phrases with North's translation, ranging from three to six words, including: "the love I bear," "unto the wished," "to pluck it out," "to see the end of this," "one half lunatic," and "skein of thread." Many of these phrases were relatively common at the time, but not all—"one half lunatic" appears in only one other work, and "skein of thread" in none except *Two Gentlemen of Verona*. All in all, the number of matches between the 111-page *Doni* and the 2,641-line *Shrew* struck him as remarkable.

One phrase particularly seemed to McCarthy to be a "smoking gun." In one of Doni's animal tales, the Ass tells the Mule about a magpie sent by "a merchant" to spy on his unfaithful wife. The wife, however, finds out about the scheme and tricks the bird by hanging its cage in a well. When the bird comes back, it complains to the merchant, beginning, "O Master, I have had an ill night today, there hath been such rain, tempest, and such noises." In *Shrew*, Lucentio similarly sends his servant boy Biondello on a stake-out, and the boy also comes back complaining about a rough night, saying: "Oh master, master, I have watched so long that I am dog-weary." He was successful, however, in his mission to find a man who can stand in as Lucentio's father in order to prove to Bianca that he is rich. That man, Biondello says, is a "mercante," using the Italian word for "merchant."

It's the only Italian word in the scene, and happens to be the very same word that *Doni* uses in the corresponding passage translated by North. McCarthy thinks North must have had the passage open while he was writing and used the Italian word by mistake. "There's no reason to do it," says McCarthy. "It's a translator's slip."

THE TAMING OF THE SHREW and Shakespeare's other early comedies are not only Italian in their setting, but they are also Italian in form—another clue that their author may have spent time in Italy. Starting in the sixteenth century, an entirely original new form of theater, called *commedia dell'arte all'improvviso*, exploded onto the streets and piazzas of cities throughout Northern Italy. It employed a troupe of performers portraying stock characters riffing on set-piece scenarios with improvised lines and slapstick comedy. While performers started forming companies as far back as 1545, it wasn't until the late 1560s that the form entered into its golden age, with troupes such as the Gelosi (the "Jealous") touring all the major towns between Venice and Milan, and eventually abroad as well.

Commedia dell'arte plots often center on the *innamorati*, the "lovers," naive young people kept apart through a variety of contrived circumstances. They are often thwarted or pursued by *vecchi*, the "oldsters," such as the doctor and pedant Gratiano, or the lascivious Pantalone, who tries to wile his way into the *innomorata*'s boudoir, before invariably getting his comedic comeuppance. Those just deserts often come at the hand of the *zanni*, the "clowns," servants or peasants who bait and trick the oldsters, or perform comedic bits of their own, eliciting belly laughs from the audience. They come in multiple varieties, including the roguish Brighella, the bumbling Pulcinella, and the prankish Arlecchino (in French Harlequin), who sows mischief in his diamond-patched bodysuit. Rounding out the cast is the *capitano*, a braggart modeled after foreign mercenaries, who often serves as the villain of the ensemble.

While the lovers and female actors performed with uncovered faces, the other characters all wore masks, requiring actors to use over-the-top vocalizations and physical gestures in their performances. The plays frequently employed quick wordplay, disguises, acrobatics, cross-dressing (by both men and women), mixed-up identities, and musical numbers to move their comedic plots along. "One of the most ancient plot lines," says one expert, "is the feigning of madness: often a character appears to be mad in order to manipulate and deceive others." A skilled troupe could perform the same scenario multiple ways to keep the material fresh.

Starting in the early twentieth century, Shakespearean scholars began recognizing *commedia* archetypes in the canon, especially in the early comedies. The servants of Valentine and Proteus in *The Two Gentlemen of Verona*, for example, are classic *zannis*: Valentine's servant Speed is clever and quick-witted, helping his feckless master pursue Silvia despite the difficulties presented by her father, the Duke. Proteus's servant Lance, meanwhile, is a slapstick buffoon. That's especially true in a long comedic scene that has been called "among the funniest scenes in Shakespeare," in which he pantomimes taking sad leave of his family, using his shoes as puppets and crying to his dog Crab (that was probably played by a real dog onstage).

The Taming of the Shrew is even more explicit in its elements of *commedia*, in both the witty repartee between Petruchio and Katharina, and the madcap disguises of the subplot. In one scene, the young lover Lucentio switches places with his servant, Tranio, disguising himself as a teacher in order to visit Bianca in her private chambers and so thwart the older, lecherous Gremio. "Disguised thus to get your love," he tells Bianca, "we might beguile the old Pantaloon"—a direct reference to the Pantalone of Italian *commedia*.

It's always been a mystery, however, where Shakespeare may have picked up the form. While Italian companies visited England as early as 1546, records of their visits stop around 1578, when Shakespeare was just fourteen. Even so, their influence seems to have lived on—with characters including Zany, Pantaloon, and Harlaken appearing in English plays through the end of the sixteenth century. Some scholars suppose he picked up influences from English plays employing Italian archetypes in London in the 1580s, or from English actors who had performed on the Continent, such as William Kemp, the celebrated fool of the Lord Chamberlain's Men, who played Lance, among other *zanni* roles.

McCarthy contends, rather, that Thomas North witnessed *commedia dell'arte* in Italy in 1570, and then worked it into his plays for years afterward. While *commedia*'s influence is most obvious in the Italian comedies, scholars today find it in a wide range of Shakespeare's plays, inspiring the Arclecchino-like Puck of *A Midsummer Night's Dream* and Ariel of *The Tempest*; the madness of Hamlet; and even the machinations of the villainous Iago in *Othello*—another play McCarthy believes was inspired by North's 1570 trip.

FROM PADUA, SIXTEENTH-CENTURY visitors inevitably traveled to Venice, the mythic capital of the Venetian Republic on the Adriatic Sea. Stories of the incomparable beauty and richness of *La Serenissima* had come to London along with the silks, glasswork, and metalwork that decorated upper-class Tudor homes. North would have found the empire at the height of its power, its magnificent churches and palazzi rising shimmering from its surrounding lagoon. "It was like New York City in the 1920s," says McCarthy. "And there's a geographical reason for that—it's right in the center of the Mediterranean, where all trade has to go through Venice." For humanists like North, Venice also stood as a political beacon—a free republic for more than one thousand years, where Italians, Germans, Greeks, Turks, and even Jews lived tolerantly side by side.

Despite that shining reputation, Venice also had a darker side in the eyes of some Englishmen, who saw it as a hotbed of mercantile greed, indulgence, and lust, where any sexual appetite could be fulfilled for a price. Courtesans paraded their services openly along the canals, and even respectable women only partially concealed their breasts beneath lace or white makeup. In his 1570 book *The Schoolmaster*, Elizabeth's former tutor, Roger Ascham, wrote that nine days in Venice contained "more liberty to sin than I ever heard tell of in our noble city of London in nine years." For those critics, an English traveler who went native in Italy became an *Inglese Italiano*—a pejorative epithet usually spat between the teeth. In McCarthy's imagination, however, the cultural melting pot of Venice would have held an irresistible fascination for North, with his cosmopolitan attitudes and possible sexual libertinism.

The year 1570 was an especially momentous one for the Republic. For centuries, Venice had lived in a wary truce with the Turks, even as the Ottoman Empire under Suleiman I "the Magnificent" had conquered Hungary and briefly besieged Habsburg Vienna. That March, however, Suleiman's son Selim II informed Venice it must surrender the strategic island of Cyprus, or face invasion. When Venice refused, the Turks made good on their promise, launching their attack on the island fortress of Nicosia in July.

It's on the eve of this historical invasion that the events of Shakespeare's *Othello* are set. As the story begins, the villainous Iago is furious that the Venetian general Othello, a black African Moor, has passed him over for promotion in favor of his lieutenant Cassio. In revenge, Iago and his henchman Roderigo create a disturbance in the street to wake up the nobleman Brabantio, telling him that Othello is sleeping with his daughter Desdemona. When they bring Othello before the Duke of Venice, however, Othello openly admits his love for Desdemona, and the Duke sanctions their marriage. At this very moment, the Venetians confirm that Turks have been sighted off Cyprus, and put Othello in charge of repelling the invasion.

More than any other Shakespeare play, *Othello* seems intimately tied to the tensions of a specific time and place. Cyprus was key to control of the Eastern Mediterranean; if Venetians lost the island, they could lose their access to the rich Eastern trade. Looking for scapegoats, the pluralistic society began lashing out at the foreigners in its midst, accusing not just the Turks, but also Africans and Jews of plotting against the Republic. As many scholars have noted, those anxieties over race and class—questions about who is a good Venetian and who is an outsider—pervade *Othello*, as well as Shakespeare's other Venetian play, *The Merchant of Venice*.

Interestingly, however, none of those tensions are present in *Othello*'s source, a book of Italian short stories published in Venice in 1565—years before the Turkish invasion—which McCarthy believes North picked up during his time in the Republic. Called the *Hecatommithi*, the book was written by Giraldi Cinthio and includes a story called "Disdemona and the Moor." Though the tale clearly inspired *Othello*, it also departs from it in key ways.

In Shakespeare's play, Iago works his revenge by stoking Othello's jealousy of his lieutenant Cassio, whom he implies has had an affair with Desdemona. Iago plants Desdemona's handkerchief on Cassio's bed, and in a fit of rage Othello strangles and kills his lover. In Cinthio's story, the nameless Iago character—called only "the Ensign"—also sets up the Cassio character, "the Captain," with the stolen handkerchief. But then the Ensign and the Moor conspire to kill Disdemona together. The Ensign strikes her with a sandbag, and both of them bring down the rafters upon her to make it seem like an accident.

The plot of Cinthio's story reads like a melodramatic cartoon compared with the emotional and psychological depth of *Othello*, in which Iago subtly plays on the Moor's insecurities, causing him to lash out in his final savage act of jealousy. Despite his single-minded savagery, Iago is by far the most intelligent character in the play, seducing generations of audiences with his dark humor and psychological control over the noble but naive Othello. Scholars have searched literature to find an apt antecedent to Iago's "motiveless malignity," as Samuel Taylor Coleridge famously described it. Some surmise the playwright took aspects of Iago's personality from the chivalric romance *Orlando Furioso*, an early-sixteenth-century work by Italian poet Ludovico Ariosto—but any attempt to find the exact combination of Iago's character traits has fallen short.

"Iago is one of the most complicated, fascinating, thrilling villains in history," says McCarthy. "He is in a sense the origin of evil—the evil that does not club you in the head, but whispers in your ear." We're sitting now at an outdoor cafe on the edge of Venice's Ghetto, the city's historically Jewish neighborhood, picking at a spread of caprese salad and charcuterie. McCarthy is relaxed in a pink dress shirt, with sunglasses hooked at his chest, drinking a Jack and diet Coke. Sunlight dapples the table through a bower of wisteria while motorboats and *vaporettos*—Venetian water taxis—rumble by us on the Grand Canal. There, McCarthy explains his surprising theory about the model for Iago's delicious evil: the Mule in North's *Doni*. "Cinthio provides a lot of the story," he says, "but the playwright transforms it, using the framing tale from *The Moral Philosophy of Doni*."

Just as the Mule manipulates the Lion into turning against his lieutenant, the Bull, so does Iago manipulate Othello into turning against his lieutenant Cassio, McCarthy says. In fact, the two works use some of the same language and imagery. Early in the story, for example, the Mule confides his ambition to his ally, the Ass. But the other animal shrugs, saying that, for him, "a great bundle of straw" is enough. Later, North writes, the Mule's "provender pricked him" as he considered the Bull's promotion—in other words, his coarse animal feed made him feel jealous—causing him to plot his revenge.

In the opening scene of *Othello*, Iago uses the same animal metaphor in convincing his henchman Roderigo to go along with his scheme to bring down Othello, telling him dismissively that some men are content to serve, "much like his master's ass, for naught but provender." The sentiment comes directly from *Doni*, McCarthy says. "It's almost confessing where he is getting this from," McCarthy says. "The Mule essentially says exactly that—I'm not going to be one of those guys who just enjoys his provender."

Iago goes on to say that he will only pretend to serve Othello while secretly serving his own ends, vowing that he won't "wear my heart upon my sleeve for daws to peck at." Similarly, the Mule tells the Ass that "the pen of his heart will not write all his thoughts in his forehead." Later, Roderigo confesses he loves Desdemona, saying, "It is not in my virtue to amend it," but Iago brushes him away. "Virtue? A fig," he says. "'Tis in ourselves that we are thus or thus." The Mule upbraids the Ass with almost the same words. "Tell me not of honesty or dishonesty," he says, "tut, a fig."

OF ALL OF his theories, McCarthy predicts, "one of the soonest to be accepted is that *Othello* is based on *Doni*." As the play progresses, he says, it reveals even more similarities with the story of the Lion and the Mule—as well as evidence that its author knew Venice. After our lunch, we climb aboard a *vaporetto* and set out down the Grand Canal, in search of traces of the play. Pastel-colored palazzi with tiers of arched windows rise from the shoreline on both sides. "It's pretty fucking magical," says Wexler as he points his camera, echoing centuries of tourists before him. While we zoom down the canal, people turn their heads to look at him filming McCarthy, no doubt thinking he must be a *paparazzo* following around an actor or film director.

We disembark at the Rialto Bridge, the iconic triangular bridge at the center of the island. The fact that the bridge isn't mentioned in either of Shakespeare's plays has been taken as evidence that the playwright *hadn't* visited Venice. The bridge, however, wasn't built until 1588—so if North wrote plays based on his visit to Venice in 1570, it would make sense that it wasn't included, explains McCarthy, walking beneath its span. We wind now through narrow passageways lined with ancient brick buildings, which occasionally open up into piazzas where foreigners at outdoor tables take their afternoon spritz. As we get closer to the city center of Piazza San Marco, the streets widen and the shops become fancier, with gondolas floating down the canals we cross. Tourists walk by with maps open on their smartphones, trying to navigate Venice's impossible maze of streets, as we look for more landmarks from the play.

After Iago raises the alarm that Othello is sleeping with Desdemona, he tells Roderigo to "lead to the Sagittary the raised search." Modern scholars have glossed the name as referring to a tavern with the sign of a centaur, Sagittarius (after the Latin word *sagitta*, meaning arrow). Roe, however, found a different explanation in some early-twentieth-century works, which associate the word *Sagittary* with the Italian equivalent, *Frezzeria*. During the Renaissance, Roe writes, the street was home to arrow makers. Whoever put Othello here, he speculates, did it intentionally as a nod to his martial prowess. "Here it is," McCarthy says, pointing up at a street sign above a fancy boutique. Indeed, the street seems like an ideal location for a distinguished general, with noticeably wider streets and buildings, only a few minutes' walk from the heart of the city: the columned piazza of San Marco, where the action of the play then moves.

We walk out into the broad piazza in the fading evening light, with the domes of the Basilica San Marco and the tall brick spire of the Campanile rising over it. Just beyond is the Doge's Palace, with its pink facade balanced delicately on spindly marble columns. We pay the entrance fee and walk into a spacious stone courtyard, surrounded on all sides by stories of arched arcades. Climbing up wide flights of marble stairs, we walk into huge halls hung with oversized canvasses by the late Renaissance master Tintoretto. If Thomas North did travel to Venice, he would have had the opportunity as a gentleman to enter the palace, just as Othello enters it in the play to plead his case before the Duke.

In Cinthio's tale, the Moor travels to Cyprus in a routine troop movement; the play heightens the tension by setting the expedition in the midst of the Turkish invasion. As the action moves to Cyprus, a storm decimates the Turkish fleet, even though the island remains under siege as Iago launches his "double knavery" to bring down both Cassio and Othello. Though *Othello* is a tragedy, numerous scholars have commented on how it mirrors many of the tropes of the Italian *commedia dell'arte*. Iago wears the mask of the *capitano*, as a braggart and a Spaniard who thwarts the *innamorati* Othello and Desdemona. But he also often acts like a Brighella in his humorous repartee with his crony Roderigo and his delight in sowing chaos and discord. The plot frequently turns on subterfuge and disguise, as Iago first gets Cassio drunk to discredit him in Othello's eyes, then approaches Cassio under the guise of friendship, suggesting he go to Desdemona to plead to get back into Othello's good graces. Meanwhile, again under the guise of concern, he plants doubts in Othello's mind about Desdemona's faithfulness, before finally planting her handkerchief on Cassio.

In North's *Doni*, the Mule pursues a similar strategy to drive a wedge between the Lion and the Bull, working what he calls a "double treason" to turn them against each other. He befriends the Bull, warning him that the Lion is displeased with him. If he sees the Lion look him in the eye and bend his ears, he says, then that means he may attack him, and he counsels the Bull to draw his weapons and look tough to dissuade him. Meanwhile, he warns the Lion that the Bull is intending to take over the kingdom. "He whispers into the ear of the king to make him suspicious of the Bull, telling him he is doing certain things to take over the kingdom, and then whispers into the ear of the Bull to get him to act in a suspicious manner," says McCarthy. Predictably, the Bull goes to court, where he sees the Lion acting in the way the Mule predicted, and prepares to fight him. Seeing that as a sign of aggression, the Lion attacks, savagely ripping him apart. "The King kills the Bull right in the middle of the court—it's vicious," McCarthy says.

Of course, in *Othello*, it's not Cassio whom Othello kills, but Desdemona. Giving in to his insecurities and believing Iago's lies about her unfaithfulness, he smothers her with a pillow, before realizing his error and killing himself. In Senecan fashion, the bodies pile up, as Iago kills Roderigo and his own wife, and wounds Cassio. In the end, both the Mule in *Doni* and Iago in *Othello* remain completely unrepentant about their crimes. After the Bull's death, the Mule says in a parody of Machiavelli, "All is well that endeth well." Even after his crimes are exposed, the Mule maintains his innocence, saying, "It is nothing true that is spoken," even as one animal after another testifies against him. As Iago's plot is likewise revealed by a letter found on Roderigo's body, he still refuses to confess. "What you know, you know," he says. "From this time forth I never will speak word"—his last lines in the play as he is dragged off to be tortured.

McCarthy believes North didn't write his source play for *Othello*, or *The Moor of Venice*, as the play is subtitled, until more than a decade later, in the late 1580s. But everything in it, he says, points back to a trip by North to Italy in 1570, in its debt to both Cinthio and *Doni*, and in its setting during the Turkish invasion. In actuality, the Turkish fleet that invaded Venice wasn't destroyed by a storm as it is in the play. After a long, bloody siege, Cyprus fell to the Turks in August 1571, its citizens massacred and sold into slavery. Christian Europe had at least one last battle left in it, however. In October 1571, a combined fleet of two hundred Venetian, Spanish, and papal ships sailed against the Turks from Messina, Sicily. Led by the charismatic Don John of Austria, the illegitimate son of Charles V and half brother of Philip II, the fleets met off the coast near Lepanto in southwestern Greece. In the halls of the Doge's Palace, a huge canvas by Andrea Vincentino depicts a chaotic tangle of oars, masts, and cannon fire as more than one hundred thousand men clash on hundreds of ships.

When the smoke cleared, the Christians had won their first major victory over the Turks at sea. Don John was a hero, and Venice was saved (at least for the time being). That was hardly good news for Leicester, however, as fresh from that victory, the dashing Austrian would become one of a number of new international suitors for Queen Elizabeth. That would pose a threat to the earl, says McCarthy, and to North as well, as his patron's fortunes became increasingly entwined with North's own.

Chapter Nine

TRUE LOVE NEVER DID RUN SMOOTH

(1571–1575)

Ay me! For aught that I could ever read,
Could ever hear by tale or history,
The course of true love never did run smooth.
—*A Midsummer Night's Dream*

The cry would go up—"The players are here!"—as a flourish of trumpets and drums sounded in the streets. In would ride a troupe of actors, some on horseback, others in a cart piled high with costumes, playbooks, and props. With the mayor's permission, they would set up boards upon barrel heads at the guildhall or churchyard, and strut across the stage as the crowds sighed, laughed, and cheered. Robert Dudley was one of the first lords in England to patronize his own theater troupe, which began touring the countryside as Lord Robert Dudley's Players as far back as 1559. When he became an earl, they rose as well, re-dubbed the Earl of Leicester's Men. Wearing the bear and ragged staff of his livery, they traveled from Plymouth to Newcastle, spreading his fame and goodwill across the land.

When Thomas North returned from the bright excitement of Italy, he became a house playwright for Leicester's Men, McCarthy contends, spinning out the Italianate comedies that delighted his patron and captivated the queen and court. As evidence, McCarthy points to *Philemon and Philecia*, the play performed at Hampton Court on Shrove Monday in 1574 that he insists was an early version of *The Two Gentlemen of Verona*. But McCarthy discovered other clues as well, suggesting a succession of more sophisticated comedies that North penned over the next few years as he grew ever closer to the earl and his quest to win the queen's hand.

Leicester's biggest rival in theater was also one of his biggest in politics: the Earl of Sussex, who along with chief minister William Cecil opposed his match with the queen. With the Duke of Norfolk now under house arrest at the Charterhouse, Sussex became the de facto leader of the conservatives at court, watching the queen's increasing favor for Leicester with alarm. He sponsored his own troupe, the Earl of Sussex's Men, and competed for the plum gigs at court during Christmastide and Shrovetide, before Lent. Those shows were particularly prized by acting companies, which received a set fee of £6 13s 4d (6 pounds, 13 shillings, and 4 pence), usually rounded up by a gift from the queen of £3 6s 8d to make an even £10 ($4,990). In 1572, Sussex became lord chamberlain, the chief officer of the royal household, putting him in charge of planning court entertainments. Even so, Leicester ultimately outdid him, performing nineteen times to Sussex's thirteen over the next decade.

A few months later, after the *Philemon* performance, Leicester did something unprecedented. Taking advantage of a moment when Sussex was ill, he applied for a royal patent from the queen to allow his company to perform their "comedies, tragedies, interludes, and stage plays" anywhere in the kingdom. The royal license lists his players, including their leader James Burbage, a joiner's apprentice from Kent known for his good looks and charm, along with John Perkin, John Lanham, William Johnson, and the clown, Robert Wilson. Historians count the move as one of the most important developments in the nascent English stage, granting a new status to players, who were previously seen as little more than vagabonds. Now, they had the queen's blessing to perform anywhere they wished, a right Leicester would soon use to advance his agenda across the kingdom.

ELIZABETH WAS NOW beset by enemies both at home and abroad. The unexpected violence of the Northern Rebellion had taken the bloom off Elizabeth's Tudor rose, betraying the Catholic discontent still seething in the countryside. Perhaps excited by the rebellion, the fanatical new pope, Pius V, excommunicated Elizabeth, forgiving any Catholic who assassinated her, and even floated the idea of an invasion of England led by the hero of Lepanto, Don John of Austria.

Ultimately, however, the true threat appeared closer to home. Cecil's agents rooted out a new scheme involving Norfolk to free Mary Queen of Scots and place her on the throne, masterminded by a Florentine banker named Roberto di Ridolfi. In January 1572, Roger North sat at Westminster Hall as one of the twenty-six peers presiding over Norfolk's trial, who unanimously sentenced him to death. As the realm's last remaining duke fell under the headman's axe, the undisputed leaders at court were now Leicester and Cecil, whom Elizabeth raised to a baron as Lord Burghley. The two settled into a truce: if not always agreeing, then at least defending and consoling each other from the tempers of their oft-difficult queen.

In Cambridgeshire, Roger North rose steadily in power as he took over the late duke's position as high steward of Cambridge, settling disputes with the university and overseeing musters of the militia. He gradually grew closer to Leicester as well, together embracing a militant new form of Protestantism known as Puritanism. Through a patronage network of local gentry, Roger soon commanded most of the local justices of the peace, extending his reach throughout the county at what one historian calls "unprecedented levels for a local magnate in the Tudor era."

At the Bodleian Libraries at Oxford, I page through Roger's account book from the period, detailing a prospering estate, with dozens of pounds spent each week on a rich diet of fish, lamb, veal, and capons. In his slanted scrawl, Roger recorded charges for bricklayers and tilers as he actively added on to his Kirtling manor. But he clearly hadn't totally mended his profligate ways, also recording large sums "lost at dice" or cards. Thomas, meanwhile, doesn't seem to have fared quite as well. His book of animal fables wasn't the bestseller that *The Dial of Princes* had been. A 1572 bill of sale at the National Archives records the sale of his property near Kirtling to a local innkeeper. He was now back to living off his brother's largesse, collecting an annuity of £40 ($24,475) from Roger while apparently living at his homes in Kirtling and London. Soon, however, both North brothers would join forces on a new mission on an international stage.

AFTER THE RIDOLFI PLOT, Burghley and Sussex grew even more anxious to marry Elizabeth off to a foreign ally. Following the collapse of negotiations with the Habsburgs, they turned their eyes toward Europe's other great power, France, where Catherine de Medici was always eager to marry off her wayward sons. She first proposed her third-born, the nineteen-year-old Henri, Duke of Anjou. When Elizabeth told the French ambassador, Bertrand de Salignac de La Mothe-Fénélon, she would consider the match, Catherine salivated, telling him, "What a kingdom for one of my children!" The obstinately Catholic Anjou, however, was less thrilled, turning up his nose at the thought of marrying the middle-aged Protestant queen, whom he privately called a *"putain publique"*—a "public whore."

Catherine quickly proposed her fourth son, Hercule-François, Duke of Alençon, whom she said "would make no scruple" over religion. He was even younger—just sixteen—and despite his heroic name, he was short and ugly, with a large nose and face badly scarred from childhood smallpox. But Elizabeth was running out of options. As a sign of goodwill, she sent a new envoy, Francis Walsingham, to negotiate a new peace treaty with France. A somber polyglot who spoke five languages and dressed in black, Walsingham is better known to history as Elizabeth's "spymaster," who would cultivate a network of informants in a fanatical defense of the queen and Puritanism in the coming years.

With his help, England and France agreed to a peace for the first time in decades, and Catherine eagerly followed it up with a formal marriage proposal. But now Elizabeth balked, saying that due to Alençon's age and appearance, "we cannot indeed bring our mind to like this offer." Catherine suggested a secret meeting on a ship to allay her fears. Elizabeth was on summer progress, hunting with Leicester at Kenilworth Castle, however, when a breathless messenger arrived. There had been a terrible massacre in Paris, he said, and no one yet knew how many had been killed.

The tale that emerged horrified all of England. Paris had been filled with revelers for the wedding of the French princess Marguerite of Valois to Henri of Navarre, the Protestant king of a mountainous kingdom on the border with Spain. The happy occasion, however, turned into a carnival of bloodshed after a failed assassination attempt on a French Huguenot leader. Fearing a reprisal, King Charles IX ordered a preemptive strike on all of the leading Protestants in the city. Just before dawn on St. Bartholomew's Day, August 24, soldiers of the king's guard broke into their homes, murdering them in their nightclothes and throwing their bodies into the street. As the sun rose, the sight touched off years of suppressed religious hatred, exploding into a frenzy of killing by Catholic soldiers and commoners alike. When the carnage was over, an estimated seventy thousand Huguenots had been slaughtered across France, in what became known as the St. Bartholomew's Day Massacre.

Elizabeth immediately returned to court, donning the black dress of mourning. Despite ambassador La Mothe's protestations of innocence, she and her ministers placed the blame for the mass slaughter squarely on the scheming Catherine de Medici. All thoughts of marriage vanished for the next two years, as Huguenots fled to their southern strongholds, and the French king's brother Henri lay siege to their seaside citadel of La Rochelle with an army of twenty-five thousand men. The siege ended in fiasco on both sides, as half of the Catholic soldiers died from dysentery, even as they inflicted heavy casualties with repeated artillery assaults. During a restive truce, the Catholics suffered another setback as France lost yet another young king: Charles IX died of tuberculosis, putting his flighty brother on the throne as Henri III.

In an effort to take the new king's measure, Elizabeth decided to tap a special ambassador to France. For the mission, she chose a diplomat who had served her well in Vienna: Roger North. This time, however, Roger wouldn't go alone, but would bring his French-speaking brother Thomas with him. The brothers North set sail with a delegation in October 1574, making quick work of the trip, thanks to fresh horses at every stage arranged by the French ambassador, La Mothe. Arriving at the French court, then in the southeastern city of Lyons, they found it riven by sectarian division. Henri of Navarre, whose wedding had run with so much blood, outwardly pretended St. Bartholomew's never happened and even helped lead the Catholics' assault on La Rochelle. Privately, however, he plotted with the Protestants alongside a surprising ally—the king's brother and Elizabeth's would-be suitor, Hercule-François, the Duke of Alençon.

Soon after their arrival at court, the Norths watched Alençon leading his sister onto the dance floor at a grand ball. The contrast between the shrunken, pockmarked young prince and the ethereal Marguerite could not have been greater, as Roger's eyes eagerly followed the princess across the floor. Seated next to him, the queen mother, Catherine de Medici, drew his gaze back to her son. "He is not so ugly nor so ill-favoured as they say; do you think so?" she asked. "No, Madam," Roger responded with a little bow. Apparently unsatisfied, Catherine replied, "It is from no fault on our part that the marriage with your mistress has not taken place."

Roger remained noncommittal, under strict instructions not to talk about any marriage with a French prince; officially, his charge was to congratulate the new king on his accession. Behind the scenes, however, he was also to gauge the king's appetite for war, and urge him to make peace with the Huguenots. It couldn't hurt, his instructions added, to find excuses to talk with the Spanish ambassador and drive a wedge between the two Catholic powers. Roger did as he was told—the "perfect courtier," as the resident English ambassador reported—impressing the queen mother with his Italian. (The Venetian ambassador had a different opinion, finding him pushy and antagonizing in his zeal to dissuade a Catholic alliance.) With his command of French, Thomas must have been invaluable to his brother in collecting intelligence, even as he sought out new foreign-language books and manuscripts himself. Perhaps, too, he enjoyed conversation with the French philosopher Michel de Montaigne, an adviser to the king; or admired a performance of *commedia dell'arte*, which Henri was fond of staging for his foreign guests.

Despite her Machiavellian reputation, Catherine de Medici was a great promoter of arts and culture, throwing legendary feasts of music and dance called "magnificences." Among other coups, she introduced the new art of ballet, cultivating the most beautiful young women of France in a whirling, erotic spectacle that an observer in 1573 compared to a "flock of cranes." Thomas must have sat captivated watching Catherine's troupe of angelic ladies-in-waiting, who became known as her "flying squadron"— an alluring battalion of thin-waisted beauties who swooped around court (and, it was said, in and out of the beds of courtiers) bandying wit and collecting morsels of intelligence to report back to the queen mother.

Thomas left early to return to London in mid-November, enthusing about the charms of the French court. According to La Mothe, he brought back reports of France's difficulties with the war, and desire for peace. According to McCarthy, however, he also brought back an idea for a new comedy based on his experiences abroad, a witty spectacle that would later become Shakespeare's play *Love's Labour's Lost*.

OF ALL OF Shakespeare's comedies, *Love's Labour's Lost* has the simplest plot. The king of Navarre entreats three courtiers—Berowne, Dumaine, and Longaville—to lock themselves away with him for three years of private, humanist study. The catch: no women allowed. Of course, almost immediately the Princess of France shows up along with three ladies-in-waiting, and one by one, the four men break their vows and fall to the ladies' wit and charm. Meanwhile, in the thinnest of subplots, a Spanish gentleman of the court, Don Armado, pursues a country dairymaid, writing her a letter that gets mixed up with one of the courtiers' letters, with predictably comic results. The quintessential braggart from *commedia dell'arte*, he presides over a cast of stock characters, including the pedant Holofernes, the country constable Dull, the buffoonish Costard, and the cheeky pageboy Moth. The play even has one of the earliest English uses of the word "zany," derived from the *commedia* term *zanni*.

One of Shakespeare's only plays without a recognizable source, the comedy is best known for its crackling dialogue—what Tony Tanner calls "a celebration of the energy and pleasure of language." The witty repartee of the lovers contrasts with the ludicrous malapropisms of the country characters—as Moth says, "They have been at a great feast of language, and stolen the scraps"—the whole linguistic festival brimming with puns, double meanings, and topical allusions that must have absolutely killed in the sixteenth-century court. The problem is, those same inside jokes make the play nearly impossible to perform today, with modern audiences left scratching their heads the same way an Elizabethan audience might throw up their hands at an episode of *Saturday Night Live*.

Scholars have tried in vain to unpack its many obscure references—starting with the names of the main characters. Obviously, the king of Navarre alludes to Henri of Navarre, who by Shakespeare's time had become Henri IV of France. Berowne, Dumaine, and Longaville also have real-life counterparts in three French noblemen: the Baron de Biron, the Duke de Mayenne, and the Duke de Longueville. As many have noted, however, during Shakespeare's heyday, these four men were on opposite sides of France's long civil war. Besides, by the time *Love's Labour's Lost* first appeared in 1598, Henri had converted to Catholicism, hardly making him a fit subject for the English stage. As twentieth-century scholar Frances Yates says, "If Shakespeare intended these names to represent contemporary French history, he carried out his intention in a singularly muddle-headed, or else willfully frivolous, manner."

That depends, however, on what you mean by "contemporary." As McCarthy found when he researched the names, all four of them took part on the Catholic side in the siege of La Rochelle, immediately predating North's delegation to Lyons in 1574. Henri of Navarre was one of the leaders of the seige; de Mayenne and Longueville fought alongside him; and Biron was appointed governor of the town. Had North turned the tables on the nobles—putting the besiegers under siege by the Princess of France and her beautiful ladies-in-waiting? Those ladies, he thought, must have been inspired in turn by the princess Marguerite and Catherine's "flying squadron" of mademoiselles.

Other scholars have proposed alternative scenarios—for example, that the play was inspired by a trip by Marguerite to Navarre in 1578 to visit her husband along with Catherine de Medici and her troupe of ladies— though none of the other three nobles were present. Most modern critics just assume Shakespeare chose French surnames that would be familiar to an English audience. Besides, other allusions in the play clearly point to events in the 1590s—so if North did write an early version of the play, it must have been substantially revised before its publication in 1598. McCarthy has an answer for that, too, right on the cover page of the quarto. The first play to bear Shakespeare's name, it reads: "Newly corrected and augmented by W. Shakespere." That's pretty much admitting it was revised from an earlier play, McCarthy says.

One character few scholars have tried to identify is the witty pageboy Moth. For McCarthy, however, his identity is obvious: La Mothe, the Norths' main go-between in their delegation to France. The boy is a master of elocution, who frequently shows up his master and the other country characters by twisting their words into howling puns. But he also gets his due when the country characters put on a "play-within-a-play," featuring the mythological hero Hercules, played by the diminutive pageboy Moth. "Great Hercules is presented by this imp," Holofernes says, "when he was a babe, a child, a shrimp." Besides being a joke at La Mothe's expense, McCarthy sees these quips as a reference to the famously short Hercule-François, the Duke of Alençon, whom La Mothe represented in his marriage negotiations with Elizabeth. Holofernes even makes a reference to the infant Hercules strangling a snake in his cradle, saying, "Thus did he strangle serpents in his manus [hand]"—a reference, perhaps, to Catherine de Medici, whom Alençon and his allies had taken in their plotting to calling "Madame de Serpente."

If so, says McCarthy, that reference would make sense as a sly dig by North on Leicester's behalf at Elizabeth's primary suitor—a more subtle version of his criticisms of Erik XIV in *Titus Andronicus*. But the Norths also had their own reasons to criticize La Mothe and the pit of vipers that was the French court. In public, Henri III and his mother were full of flattery for Elizabeth; behind closed doors, however, the king flouted the English queen, saying she was "not so dangerous a creature as she was deemed" and "not to be feared." It was even reported that two female dwarfs, dressed like Elizabeth, mimicked her in the queen mother's private chambers, to the evident delight of Catherine and her ladies. The crowning indignity came when the queen mother invited a jester into North's quarters, dressed in English-style clothing, to strut in front of Roger and his retinue. "It's just like the late King Henry of England!" Catherine cried mischievously. Roger responded coldly, "The tailors of France seem to have little idea how this great King dressed, considering he crossed the sea a few times and did some things worth talking about," referring to Henry's wars on the Continent.

When Roger arrived back in London to tell the queen about the insults, Elizabeth gave La Mothe a tongue-lashing as the ambassador anxiously insisted Roger must have misunderstood Catherine's French. Later, La Mothe got his revenge, telling Elizabeth that Roger had failed to raise the case of the two English merchants whose goods were confiscated at La Rochelle. Roger was so stung, he wrote a letter to the Privy Council, urging that La Mothe be called "to account for this shameless & manifest untruth." There's no record of what came of the fracas, but McCarthy sees in it a motive for Thomas to pen a play that mocked La Mothe along with Alençon. Whether or not the play was performed at court, the ill-treatment of her ambassadors once again cooled the queen to any thoughts of marriage to Alençon—at least for now.

WHEN MCCARTHY FIRST discovered the allusion to the four Frenchmen in *Love's Labour's Lost*, it was a revelation for him—his first indication that North might be basing his plays not only on his writings, but on his own life experiences as well. He knew, of course, that finding allegorical meaning in the canon was a slippery business. Others, after all, had found references to the lives of Bacon, Oxford, and Shakespeare himself in the plays—Stephen Greenblatt had written a whole book about it. It's possible he was just seeing what he wanted to see in the text—a phenomenon scientists call "confirmation bias." But what were the chances that not just two or three, but all four French names could be tied to Thomas's delegation? Or that the same play included a character named Moth and a seeming reference to Alençon? All doubt left his mind when he came across another play written around the same time that seemed to reference another of Elizabeth's marriage prospects.

The Revels Accounts lists the rehearsal of a play by Leicester's Men, "the matter of *Panecia*," on December 18, 1574, followed by two performances at Hampton Court on December 28 and New Year's Day 1575. While there is no surviving text for the play, a German play with a very similar name, *Die Schoene Phaenicia (The Beautiful Phaenicia)*, shares much of its plot in common with one of Shakespeare's most popular plays: *Much Ado About Nothing*. Both works, in turn, are based in part on a French story by François de Belleforest in *Histoires Tragiques*, published in Paris in 1569. Thomas could have easily acquired the French work on the delegation, coming back early to write and rehearse the play for Leicester in time for the Christmas revels. If so, contemporary audiences would not have missed the clear identity of the play's villain, Don John the Bastard.

By the time the Norths had returned from their French delegation, Burghley and Sussex had already pivoted back to the Habsburgs. After

England concluded a new treaty with Spain in late 1574, Philip II proposed a new candidate for Elizabeth to marry: his bastard half brother, Don John of Austria. The fact that Burghley and Sussex considered the match points to their desperation—Don John was a stalwart Catholic who had courted Mary Queen of Scots, and even considered invading England on behalf of the pope. For Puritans like Leicester and Roger North, the idea was a complete anathema. For that reason, McCarthy believes, Leicester took no chances, commissioning the play from Thomas North for the Christmas season of 1574, directly attacking Don John.

Much Ado was not only a success in Shakespeare's time, it has also remained popular ever since, soaring on the antics of its warring young lovers, Beatrice and Benedick. While all of Kate and Petruchio's banter leads to patriarchal submission, Beatrice and Benedick remain equals to the altar, arguably Shakespeare's most mature depiction of love. The play was David Garrick's favorite in the eighteenth century; in the twentieth, actor Kevin Kline called it an "indestructible crowd-pleaser." Its popularity has only grown after a lush film adaptation by Kenneth Branagh and Emma Thompson in 1993.

In fact, audiences love the "merry war" of wits by avowed women-hater Benedick and sworn spinster Beatrice so much that it's easy to forget that it's only the subplot of the play. The primary story concerns the wooing of Beatrice's cousin Hero by Benedick's friend and fellow soldier Claudio. In an effort to thwart him, Don John tricks Claudio into witnessing his servant making love to Hero's maidservant, whom Claudio mistakes for Hero, causing him to denounce her as unfaithful on their wedding day. In revenge, Beatrice asks Benedick to kill Claudio—setting up the main conflict of the play. "It's much like *Othello*, but a more pleasant, comedic version," says McCarthy. "And Don John is playing the part of Iago, of convincing someone that his lover is unfaithful."

Though the most immediate source of the tale was Belleforest's French version, this story too was originally Italian, told in 1554 by Bandello, who gave the heroine the name Fenicia and set the story in Messina, the port city of Sicily. None of those versions were translated into English in Shakespeare's lifetime, leading one critic to conjecture Shakespeare used "some source no longer known to us." McCarthy isn't the first to speculate that the source was the 1574 play *Panecia*; numerous other editions mention it as a possible inspiration for *Much Ado*, though, of course, none of them attribute it to North.

Like the source material, *Much Ado* is set in Messina, though it lacks the recognizable geography of other Italian plays. Messina does, however, happen to be the city from which the historical Don John of Austria disembarked for his triumphant battle of Lepanto. The playwright no doubt put the two facts together to place Don John in the story. Even more than Iago, Don John seems motiveless in his malice, acting with "pure evil," according to one critic. Another more lightly calls him "a comic villain who can hardly twirl his mustache without scratching his eye." The comedy plays up Don John's venality as characters continually harp on his status as a "bastard"—an insult just as much in Elizabethan times as now—and the play literally calls him "John the Bastard" in the stage directions.

"So there are three possible suitors to the queen—Erik XIV, King of the Goths; the Duke of Alençon; and Don John—and they are all attacked quite obviously in the plays," says McCarthy. The attack on Don John is particularly irrelevant after the 1570s, given that Don John didn't survive the decade, leading some scholars to wonder why Shakespeare would resurrect him decades later just to insult him. It would make perfect sense, however, in 1574, when he was one of the most fearsome generals in Europe. Ultimately, of course, Don John's plot is exposed—this is a comedy after all—by the intercession of the feckless night's watch and its comedic commander Dogberry, whose slapstick *zanni* antics are played like an Elizabethan version of Keystone Kops. In the end, both Hero and Claudio and Beatrice and Benedick ride off into the proverbial Mediterranean sunset, the latter couple bickering merrily away.

WHILE THOMAS NORTH'S relationship with his own wife is a mystery, he was clearly surrounded by strong women. His aunt Joan was a Protestant recusant who fled England during Mary's reign. His sister, Christian, left her husband, the Earl of Worcester, after his numerous affairs, and afterward the queen ordered him to pay her an annual pension. Meanwhile, North's own daughter Elizabeth was just entering adolescence—a time that leads many fathers to rethink their ideas about women. As North approached forty, he may have begun developing a more nuanced view of women that could explain the progression from Kate to Beatrice.

The complicated love life of his patron, the Earl of Leicester, on the other hand, has been obsessively documented. Now forty-two years old, Robert Dudley had spent his entire adult life chasing one lady: Queen Elizabeth. By 1575, that pursuit had benefited him with money, status, and power, but denied him a wife and an heir. He privately confided to his friend, Roger North, that "there was nothing in this life that he more desired than to be joined with some godly gentlewoman." But he knew if he married anyone other than Elizabeth, the jealous queen might banish him from court—costing him everything.

Into this complicated state of affairs walked Douglas Sheffield, a pretty widow ten years his junior (her masculine given name references the Scottish clan) who became infatuated with Leicester. The two had an affair, and afterward he tried to let her down easy, explaining in a letter that he couldn't become more serious "without mine utter overthrow," and callously suggesting he could help her find a husband. Sheffield, however, pushed for more; years later, she swore they were even secretly married.

In the summer of 1574, Sheffield gave birth to a son, whom Leicester recognized as his own, even giving him his own name: Robert Dudley. She lived in seclusion with the boy in his country house, even while Leicester remained at court. Elizabeth may have known about the relationship, but tolerated it so long as he remained by her side. Besides, she had her own flirtations, especially with Christopher Hatton, a tall, handsome courtier who first caught her eye while dancing in the masque of *Gorboduc*. When, in the spring of 1575, Hatton hinted that he wanted to buy the London mansion of the Bishop of Ely, Elizabeth called on Roger North to reason with his Cambridgeshire neighbor. North wrote a letter threatening an investigation into Ely's use of church lands if he didn't give up the residence, and the bishop relented, selling it to Hatton.

As Elizabeth set out on her annual summer progress that year, she was in a celebratory mood. The kingdom was at peace with both France and Spain, and newly prosperous after resumed trade with the Netherlands. Leicester, however, was consumed with anxiety. The queen was nearing the end of her childbearing years, and time was running out for any hope of marriage. As Elizabeth set out with a movable household of four hundred courtiers, cooks, and servants, he decided to throw everything into one last gambit for marriage at Kenilworth.

Since the queen's last visit, he'd feverishly upgraded the castle, building a new gatehouse and towers, and filling a grand apartment building with dark wood, tapestries, and satin-covered furniture. Knowing Elizabeth's love for gardens, he created a new Italianate enclosure filled with strawberry beds, and pear and cherry trees bursting with ripe fruit. In the center, he placed a white marble fountain decorated with aquatic scenes from Ovid's *Metamorphoses*, and along the castle wall built an aviary covered with golden mesh and filled with twittering birds.

Outside, Leicester expanded a hunting chase across the castle's 111-acre artificial lake, connecting it with a 600-foot-long bridge. The wooded grounds were landscaped with bowers, arbors, and seats, and stocked with red deer and other game. In all, Leicester was said to have spent more than £60,000 ($17.5 million) on the project—an expense from which his finances never fully recovered. Now, as the queen's entourage lumbered across the countryside, he set out to bring the castle to life, preparing a festival the likes of which England had never seen before—and would never see again.

In addition to hiring minstrels, dancers, and acrobats for entertainment, Leicester tapped playwright George Gascoigne to design a series of masques he hoped would touch the queen's heart. As Nottingham professor Janette Dillon says, it's as if "the estate as a whole became one great theatre waiting to receive the Queen as chief spectator, and in a sense also chief performer." It's unclear whether Leicester's Men took part in the entertainments, but since their performance records show a gap that month, scholars believe they likely also attended to support their lord patron.

As Leicester looked down on the colorful tents being pitched in the castle yard, he must have thought about the legions of guests about to descend on his palace—including Burghley, Sussex, Walsingham, and all of the kingdom's other most distinguished peers, knights, and councilors. His young nephew Philip Sidney, just back from a grand tour, would attend, as would his great friend Roger North. (One noble conspicuously absent was the Earl of Oxford, who was still traveling in Italy.) Just before riding out to escort the queen to the castle, he ordered the clock stopped at two o'clock—the dinner hour, and also, perhaps, a symbol of the union of Leicester and the queen. There it would remain throughout the festivities, as if time itself had stopped.

KENILWORTH STILL STANDS today, a historic ruin often bundled into package tours with Stratford-upon-Avon and the Cotswolds. As we approach it on a chilly November morning, a stiff wind blows off the surrounding fields where the artificial lake once stood, and the romantically crumbling walls of the castle stand out against the sky overhead. The pink sandstone edifice, however, still hints at the grandeur that greeted Elizabeth on the night of July 9, 1575, when, one historian writes, "the castle, twinkling with the light from thousands of candles and torches, looked like a fairy palace rising from the lake."

As we pass by the visitors center, I try to imagine the sultry July of 1575, when thousands of gay revelers descended upon the palace, pregnant with the hope or dread that Leicester would succeed in his wooing. "This was the Earl of Leicester's last chance to marry the queen and become King of England, which he desperately wanted," says McCarthy as we walk along the wide gravel approach, "and which Thomas North was hoping for as well." Unlike with Roger, there's no proof Thomas attended the festival—as an ordinary gentleman, he would have been too insignificant for chroniclers to note. It's not unlikely, however, that he accompanied his brother to the event. The North family's early-twentieth-century biographer Frances Bushby certainly places him there; like many writers, she also speculates an eleven-year-old William Shakespeare also attended from nearby Stratford and that "the poet may all have unwittingly rubbed shoulders with Sir Thomas."

For two centuries, Shakespeareans have been gamely placing the young Bard at Kenilworth, given the uncanny similarities between the festival and his magical fairytale of young lovers lost in the woods, *A Midsummer Night's Dream*. McCarthy doesn't rule out the idea that Shakespeare may have attended—most of the entertainments were performed in the open air, with locals allowed on the grounds at night—but he also thinks it more likely a gentleman with connections to Leicester attended, rather than a glover's son from the countryside. "As with other plays, he is using a source play," McCarthy says, "and the person who wrote the source play was Thomas North, Leicester's playwright, who was witness to these events."

Likely the most performed of all Shakespeare's plays, *Dream* has delighted generations of audience members with its depictions of an otherworldly fairyland. Professional theater companies and high school productions constantly reinterpret its woodland spirits, wrapping actors, as Leicester did, in silk or moss, or covering them in tulle, feathers, Lycra, leather, or tie-dye. At times lyrical, lusty, and ludicrous, the play ultimately comes down to a commentary on love. "It proposes that love is a dream, or perhaps a vision; that it is absurd, irrational, a delusion, or, perhaps, on the other hand, a transfiguration," says literary critic Catherine Belsey, "and that it constitutes at the same time the proper foundation for a lifelong marriage."

Scholars believe Shakespeare wrote the play sometime around 1594 or 1595, often seeing in it the beginning of Shakespeare's maturation as a playwright. Its sources include a mash-up of Chaucer's *Canterbury Tales*, Ovid's *Metamorphoses*, the Roman comedies of Plautus and Terence, Italian novellas like Ariosto's *Orlando Furioso*, and a healthy dash of *commedia dell'arte*—with the rascally fairy Puck as the ultimate Arlecchino. Some scholars have also identified a splash of Senecan tragedy—one calls it "Light Seneca"—in its plunge into a sinister woodland full of darkness and witchcraft.

Kenilworth's own transformation into fairyland began as soon as Queen Elizabeth approached the first gate. There, a female figure dressed in white silk appeared—one of the Sibyls, oracles from Greek mythology. "All hail, all hail," she cried, prophesying a long reign for the queen. "You shall be called the prince of peace, and peace shall be your shield." As the queen made her way through the tiltyard and into the castle's base court, a movable island floated toward her across the artificial lake, brightly blazing with torches.

Another woman in silks stepped off and approached her, saying she was the Lady of the Lake—the mythical enchantress who made King Arthur monarch by giving him the magical sword Excalibur. By invoking the imagery of Camelot, say historians, Leicester was intentionally suggesting "that the lord of the castle was of royal English ancestry and particularly that he was Arthur's heir." The lady bowed low, saying, "The lake, the lodge, and the lord are yours to command." Elizabeth, however, was having none of it. "We had thought indeed the lake had been ours, and do you call it yours now?" she said with a smirk, reminding Leicester who really owned the castle. "Well, we will herein commune more with you hereafter."

WE WALK NOW, as Elizabeth did, across the castle yard, where the ruins of Leicester's apartments loom over us with pointed arches and crumbling bay windows. A placard there displays an image of the earl, resplendent in a red satin tunic, white ruff framing his confident, goateed face. Leicester brought Elizabeth now to the castle keep, up a bridge lined with gifts from the Greek gods—songbirds, fruit, trays of fish, and a fountain of wine, complete with two glasses. For the next two weeks, each day came with new surprises—musicians in boats, bear-baiting, Italian contortionists, and nightly fireworks, which showered the sky above the castle with sparks and shook the earth with thunder. "It was like Disney World," McCarthy says as we walk among the ruins. We climb up a stone staircase carved with centuries of graffiti to stand now atop the ruined wall, where a fierce wind blows off the surrounding hills. Sheep graze far below us where the lake once stood, but I can still imagine it, stretching out, glittering in the sun, the long bridge crossing to the hunting chase beyond.

As the queen returned from hunting by torchlight one night, she was surprised by Gascoigne himself, who burst out of the trees as a "savage man" covered in moss and ivy, an uprooted oak sapling in his hand. He began by shouting for forest spirits—fawns, satyrs, and nymphs—before addressing the queen with a verse regaling Dudley's "true love." The poem, says McCarthy, is reminiscent of one of the opening scenes of *A Midsummer Night's Dream*, as the fairies and sprites of the forest welcome the Fairy Queen Titania. "He refers to dryads, and the people of the forest welcoming the queen," McCarthy says. "And *A Midsummer Night's Dream* has the exact atmosphere, the exact imagery." The name Titania is even used in Ovid's *Metamorphoses* as another name for the goddess Diana—who is often associated with Queen Elizabeth.

Not all of Leicester's performances ran smoothly, however. In one, Leicester himself was to rescue the Lady of the Lake, who had been kidnapped by an evil knight, and then implore Queen Elizabeth to revive her. The symbolism was clear—together, Leicester and Elizabeth could revive England. The players rigged up floating islands to make it look like the combatants were fighting on the water, but for some reason the show was called off, due to technical difficulties, or bad weather—or perhaps because the queen and her censors had nixed it.

The players hastily recast the performance two nights later, planning for King Triton on his mechanical mermaid to come directly to Elizabeth as she was crossing the bridge, and allow her to rescue the Lady of the Lake all by herself. As a reward, the queen received a song from a musician on a dolphin's back, a local singer named Harry Goldingham, playing the Greek god Arion. Singing poorly that night, however, Goldingham pulled off his mask in the midst of the song, exclaiming he "was none of Arion, not he, but honest Harry Goldingham." The queen nevertheless clapped with delight, saying it was her favorite part of the show.

It's this entertainment, says McCarthy, that some scholars point to as inspiration for Oberon's vision in *A Midsummer Night's Dream*, in which the fairy king tells the mischievous Puck that "once I sat upon a promontory, and heard a mermaid on a dolphin's back," who sang so beautifully that the stars shot from the sky. Oberon went on to witness Cupid aim his "love shaft" at a "fair vestal thronèd by the West," launching it "as it should pierce a hundred thousand hearts"—a fair representation of the elaborate lengths to which Leicester went to capture the affections of the Virgin Queen. An early-nineteenth-century scholar was the first to associate the scene with the Kenilworth entertainments, but the theory has since been embraced by numerous others, including Shakespeare biographer Stephen Greenblatt.

When McCarthy first read about it, he immediately saw it as another case in which Thomas North was re-creating one of the most important moments of his life in the plays. No one who attended Kenilworth would have been able to forget its magical sights. But knowing the stakes behind Leicester's proposal, North must have seen the scene as especially critical, not just for the earl but for himself—but as his last chance to become an adviser to the king of England. The image is so specific, McCarthy insists, that North must have sat there "upon a promontory" that very night watching the water pageant unfold. McCarthy looks now over the fields, using an illustration in the visitors guide to determine where the bridge would have crossed the shallow valley, and to locate where North must have sat. He points to a slight rise in the terrain, near a country road cutting across the field. "It's that hill, right there," McCarthy says. "That's where he watched this extraordinary performance."

Not everyone agrees that *A Midsummer Night's Dream* is based on the Kenilworth entertainments. Scholars point to other sources that describe similar scenes; a passage in Seneca's *Phaedra*, for example, mentions Cupid, a dolphin, and "love's power over the sea and stars." Other entertainments also used similar images, such as a four-day festival the queen attended in 1591 at Elvetham, featuring a masque with a fairy queen and a water pageant with Triton (though no dolphin). Even if Kenilworth *was* the source, some argue, the playwright wouldn't have had to attend the festivities to write about them. Two contemporary accounts—one by Gascoigne, and another by an attendee named Robert Langham—describe the entertainments in detail.

As he studied Thomas North's works, however, McCarthy identified another connection with Oberon's vision that had gone potentially unnoticed for centuries. Cupid's arrow misses the mark—"quenched in the chaste beams of the wat'ry moon," and instead lands on a "little western flower, before, milk-white, now purple with love's wound," which he calls "love-in-idleness," a folk name for wild pansy. If the juice of that flower is rubbed on a person's "sleeping eyelids," he tells Puck, that person will wake up to fall in love with the first person they see. "Fetch me this herb," he commands, intending to play a trick on Titania. Of course, Puck does, and sows mischief among four young lovers—Hermia, Lysander, Helena, and Demetrius—lost in the woods who, through the fairy's chemical intercessions, fall hilariously in and out of love with each other.

For being such an important element in the plot, no scholar has identified a source for the magical love juice behind all the trouble. In North's *Dial of Princes*, however, McCarthy noticed a reference to an "herb called Ilabia," which grows in Cyprus. When cut, North writes, it "droppeth blood," and if that blood is rubbed on a person while it's hot, they will fall in love with the person who does it; if rubbed cold, they will hate the person. Reading the passage, McCarthy realized that this could be the inspiration for Oberon's flower. In North's own copy of *The Dial of Princes*, now at Cambridge University, in fact, North specifically calls out the plant in his handwritten marginalia. "The blood-juice of this plant," McCarthy concludes, "is the bleeding herb from *A Midsummer Night's Dream*."

IN THE END, love is restored, and the couples take part in a group wedding to end the play. Just as in *Love's Labour's Lost*, they are entertained by a comical country cast performing a play-within-a-play (Puck dubs them "rude mechanicals") in the same way Leicester entertained his guests at his own castle. "This green plot shall be our stage, this hawthorn brake our tiring-house," the group's long-suffering director, Peter Quince, tells his cast—Bottom, Snout, Flute, Snug, and Starveling—just as Leicester's players must have used similar arrangements to change their costumes behind bushes and trees in the deer chase. In another potential homage to Kenilworth, an actor playing the part of a lion at one point rips off his mask to assure the audience that he's only Snug the Joiner, just like Goldingham did on his dolphin.

In an epilogue, Puck apologizes for his mischief, saying, "Give me your hands, if we be friends, and Robin shall restore amends." While Shakespeare's play may have ended in harmony, however, the queen's own "Sweet Robin" found himself unable to sway her with his dreamlike entertainments. The centerpiece of Leicester's productions was to be a masque by Gascoigne, featuring Diana (representing chastity) and Juno (representing marriage) fighting over a lost nymph named Zabeta, a stand-in for Elizabeth. Of course Juno wins, promising that "now in princely port"—Kenilworth—"a world of wealth at will, you henceforth shall enjoy, in wedded state."

Leicester's men never got to perform it, however. Though they were ready and in costume "two or three times" during her stay, Gascoigne reports the performance was canceled due to "lack of opportunity and weather." Some historians, however, believe the weather was just fine; rather, the queen caught wind of the masque's theme from her censors (perhaps even her lord chamberlain, Sussex) and refused to attend. Certainly *something* happened to upset Elizabeth, causing her to announce an abrupt early departure. Elizabeth's biographers have speculated that she might have gotten angry over Leicester's flirtations with her cousin Lettice Knollys, Countess of Essex, with whom the earl would soon become romantically involved. (Some even identify Knollys with that "little western flower" where Cupid's arrow falls.) It could be, however, that Elizabeth was just tired of being wooed so publicly by a man she never had any intention of marrying.

As she made preparations to depart, a panicked Leicester implored Gascoigne to write a new performance. The playwright hastily donned his "wild man" costume and ran after the queen on foot. When she wryly asked if she should stop her horse so he could catch his breath, he protested he could run another twenty miles by her side. Along the way, he told a story about a courtier named Deep Desire, whom the nymph Zabeta had cruelly turned into a holly bush. Ahead, the queen heard music and came across an actual holly bush, from which an actor suddenly spoke. "Stay, stay your hasty steps, O queen without compare," it moaned, telling her how the gods wept to see her go. "Live here, good Queen, live here, you are amongst your friends." Gascoigne assured the queen that it was within her power to release Deep Desire from his prison. But there's no record of Elizabeth's response; his account merely ends with the word "Finis."

It's a fitting epitaph to Leicester's two decades attempting to persuade the queen to be his wife. After Kenilworth, Leicester would still try to win Elizabeth's affections—or at least to prevent anyone else from winning them—but never with the same intensity. As his eyes increasingly turned to another woman, his thoughts turned to battlefield pursuits to champion the Puritan cause. Thomas North moved on, too, McCarthy believes, giving up on his dream to become "English Seneca" to Leicester's Nero. He continued to support his patron, however, and years later, McCarthy believes, he immortalized his wooing of the queen in an homage to a midsummer night. Meanwhile, Thomas sought out new ways to influence the rulers of England, as he began to embark now on the great work of his life.

Chapter Ten

IT WAS GREEK TO ME

(1576–1577 / 2013–2016)

Those that understood him smiled at
one another and shook their heads; but, for mine own
part, it was Greek to me.

—*Julius Caesar*

Largo di Torre Argentina, a ruined plaza in the heart of Rome, is literally crawling with cats. Tabbies and gingers lounge on arches and
broken pillars, sunbathing in the sunken ruins of the plaza. So many have
invaded the site that the Eternal City has left a sign amid the ruins warning against leaving cat food on this "important archaeological site." But
not a single monument acknowledges its historical importance: it was
here, on March 15, 44 BCE, that Julius Caesar was assassinated.

On that day, a cabal of Roman senators, fearing he was about to become
a dictator, stabbed him to death. Today, however, those events are most
familiar to audiences through Shakespeare's play *Julius Caesar*, which has
seared so many aspects of the killing onto our collective imagination.
Many of the play's most memorable details, in turn, come from another
source: "The Life of Julius Caesar," translated by Thomas North in his
book *Plutarch's Lives*. "Passage after passage and image after image is taken
for the play," McCarthy says, wearing a black collared shirt as he leans
against a low wall above the ruins. "People don't realize how many quotes
are taken directly from it."

There's the soothsayer who warns Caesar against the "Ides of March,"
the day he will be killed, for example. Then there's the scene after

the killing, where Caesar's friend Marc Antony waves his bloody shirt in the Forum, as Plutarch recounts in his "Life of Antony," and which Shakespeare turns into the famous line, "Friends, Romans, countrymen, lend me your ears. I come to bury Caesar, not to praise him." Eventually, Antony bands together with Caesar's nephew Octavian to defeat Brutus and the other murderers—a story North recounts in Plutarch's "Life of Brutus"—spawning the dictatorship that became the Roman Empire, which dominated the Mediterranean for the next four hundred years.

Scholars have long recognized North's translation as the source for Shakespeare's three Roman plays, *Julius Caesar*, *Antony and Cleopatra*, and *Coriolanus* (as well as the Greek *Timon of Athens*). Unlike other Shakespearean sources, which provide only the outlines of plot, however, North's *Plutarch* practically offers a script, which Shakespeare faithfully follows, scene after scene. "Shakespeare does not follow his other sources like this, where he's borrowing whole speeches," McCarthy says. "So clearly *whoever* the playwright was thought of North as different, and felt that this writing needed no improvement." Of course, McCarthy has a reason for that: Shakespeare wasn't copying North, but North himself was transforming his own prose translations into his own plays.

In *Plutarch*, for example, North writes that Caesar's wife, Calpurnia, had a nightmare that he would be killed and "prayed him if it were possible, not to go out of the doors that day." In the play, Calpurnia also has bad dreams and urges him: "Think you to walk forth? You shall not stir out of your house today." Caesar's response in both cases is the same—making fun of Calpurnia's demand; in the play, for example, he asks sarcastically if he should adjourn the Senate until "Caesar's wife shall meet with better dreams." McCarthy appreciates that moment of gallows humor in the tragedy. "It's kind of an edgy comment for the 16th century," he says, "and that's straight out of North."

While scholars acknowledge Shakespeare's debt to North, however, they tend to downplay it, McCarthy says as buses and scooters whiz by us in the busy square. "There is an effort to glorify Shakespeare all the time," McCarthy says. "Oh, he's making it much more beautiful—or what's really great here are the parts he adds, or takes out." For example, they point to Caesar's dramatic final response to Calpurnia, when he decides finally to go to the Senate. "Cowards die many times before their deaths; the valiant never taste of death but once," he says, in arguably the most famous lines from the play. "It seems to me most strange that men should fear," he continues, "seeing that death, a necessary end, will come when it will come."

That sentiment is only hinted at in *Plutarch*, in a line in which Caesar says, "It was better to die once, than always to be afraid of death." Scholars see Shakespeare's expansion of the thought as an indication of his superior genius. But McCarthy contends they just aren't looking in the right place. Using his plagiarism software, he discovered the same sentiments in another passage in North's *Dial of Princes*, in which he writes, "The cowardly heart falleth before he is beaten down, but the stout and valiant stomach, in greatest peril, recovereth most strength." A few lines later, he says men only "owest one death to the gods." And earlier in the same passage, he writes, "I know not why men fear so much to die," and try to escape "the voyage of death that is necessary." Put together, the passage contains all the essential elements of Caesar's quote, McCarthy argues: "coward–valiant–one death" and "fear–death–necessary." A few lines later, he even uses the phrase "Come that that may come."

"North sees an idea that Plutarch mentions," says McCarthy, "and then he goes to *Dial of Princes*, where there are all these speeches on death." As he began performing more searches, McCarthy not only began discovering more connections between the Roman plays and North's other works, he also began finding connections between North's *Plutarch* and Shakespeare's other plays. In particular, McCarthy says, the book was a source for another group of plays North was writing at the time—not about the history of Rome, but of England.

THOMAS NORTH STARTED translating Plutarch when he returned from the embassy to Lyons, working from a French translation by Jacques Amyot. But he certainly knew of the book long before. Lucius Mestrius Plutarchus was born in the Greek countryside around 45 CE, the generation after Seneca. After studying philosophy and the priesthood, he began working and reworking his *The Lives of the Noble Greeks and Romans*. Also known as the *Parallel Lives*, the book consists of matched biographies of statesmen and military leaders—one Greek, one Roman—along with a comparison between the two.

On its surface, the book explores how "great men" can have an impact on history. But Plutarch is the first to say he is not writing "histories" but "lives." Often "a little matter like a saying or a joke hints at character more than battles where thousands die," he writes. That emphasis on character over action makes the book a kind of proto-*speculum* tome, through which he hoped to influence his audience of elite, educated statesmen—the kind of men who in another time and place may have gone to the Inns of Court.

Inevitably, Plutarch paints his Greek fellow citizens as more virtuous than their Roman counterparts. But even the worst figures are treated compassionately, and the best are offered up complete with all of their faults. As one Plutarch scholar puts it, his biographies are "never painted in malice, never caricatured; rather, they show each subject in the light of its own features, that the observer might see for himself." Moral lessons in the work are often ambiguous, or even contradictory.

More than anything, Plutarch is a storyteller, creating vivid scenes in which readers can "see" events happening before their own eyes. After he was rediscovered in *cinquecento* Italy, Plutarch became the most widely read classical author in Europe, thanks in part to the gorgeous French translation by Jacques Amyot in 1559. A tutor to King Charles IX, Amyot was a classics professor turned bishop and counselor to Henri III—a French Seneca, if you will. His combination of classical knowledge and court savvy made his translation a masterpiece of French prose. Even today, one commentator raves that it's "near as any production of its time to being that inconceivable thing, a perfect translation."

Thomas North most likely met Amyot at the French court, conversing in French about great men and sage advice. After returning to England, he worked over his own translation for the next five years. Compared with Amyot's masterpiece, North's *Plutarch* gets more mixed reviews. Often, North follows Amyot word-for-word rather than translating it into vernacular. He mixes up character names and muddles geography (confusing, for example, the Oracle of Delphi with the Isle of Delphos), mistranslates words, and sometimes translates the same word different ways. Overall, the translation creates the impression of a rush job made by someone more interested in getting it out than getting it right.

For all of its faults, however, North's *Plutarch* has been hailed as one of the first great English classics, making up for its sloppiness with its excitingly vigorous prose. "His use of words tends much more towards raciness than elegance," says one early twentieth-century editor, who calls it full of "fierce slangy idioms" with "all the color of the Elizabethan imagination." As with his translation of *Doni*, North constantly inserts colloquialisms of his own making to bring the narrative alive. So Cassius "rose up on his feet and gave him two good whirts on the ear," Cicero suffers from "the worm of ambition," and his wife "wears her husband's breeches."

In other words, North's translation of Plutarch had all of the elements of a work ready-made for transformation into drama: thrilling writing, nuanced characters, vivid scenes, and ambivalent plots. "Shakespeare was able to follow Plutarch almost step-by-step," says one critic, because North's work "is so tautly constructed, dramatic, and full of incident—almost, already, like a play."

TAKEN AS A WHOLE, Shakespeare's three Roman plays offer up one of the greatest tragedies in world history: the transformation of Rome from a republic to an empire. *Coriolanus* dramatizes the birth of the republic; *Julius Caesar*, its death throes; and *Antony and Cleopatra*, the final triumph of tyranny. Scholars traditionally spread the plays out in the second half of Shakespeare's career, with *Caesar* in 1600 and *Antony* and *Coriolanus* both around 1606. McCarthy, however, believes that North wrote his versions in a tight triad in the late 1570s.

Scholars have long seen the Roman plays as veiled commentary on Elizabethan politics, even drawing analogues to specific events in Shakespeare's time—for example, comparing the uprising of citizens in *Caesar* with the London riots of 1599. In truth, however, their themes of unrest and rebellion would have seemed just as relevant during the turmoil of the 1570s, asking questions about what makes a good ruler, and when deposing a bad one is justified. Those concerns, in fact, have continued through today, notably in Stephen Greenblatt's 2018 book *Tyrant*—which does everything but name the then-sitting president—

and a performance by the National Theatre (UK), in which Caesar wears a red baseball cap.

Shakespeare's play offers a particularly dark version of Caesar's story, drawn from Plutarch, who can't help but disapprove of Caesar's attempt to seize absolute power. His Caesar comes across as arrogant and over-confident in his ability to sway the Republic to his ends, sidelining his fellow aristocrats, and ultimately falling prey to his own overreaching ambitions. In his definitive study of the Roman plays, Paul Cantor argues *Caesar* offers a warning to "monarchs against trying to govern absolutely, without reference to the common good"—a concern, certainly, of Thomas North and his fellow humanists from the Inns of Court, who urged a greater role for Parliament in the ruling of the realm.

And yet, at the same time, the play can't justify murder of a monarch and hardly champions Brutus and his fellow conspirators for putting an end to Caesar's tyranny. After Caesar dies at the end of Act Two, the rest of the play follows Plutarch's "Life of Brutus," showing how he and his fellow conspirators lose their grip on power, as Brutus stoically tries to justify the senators' actions, rather than winning over the hearts and minds of the masses. That central conflict—whether Caesar was a grasping tyrant or a great man taken down by squabbling bureaucrats—has had a timeless ap-peal, polarizing audiences through the centuries, and making the play one of Shakespeare's few dramas to be performed unedited since his death.

AS POPULAR AS it has been over the centuries, however, *Julius Caesar* has never been admired by critics as much as *Antony and Cleopatra*, Shakespeare's great tragedy about Marc Antony's doomed romance with the Egyptian queen. In the nineteenth century, Samuel Taylor Coleridge put the play on par with the tragedies of *Hamlet*, *Macbeth*, and *King Lear*. As *Oxford English Dictionary* editor F. J. Furnivall put it, "Shakespeare has poured out the glory of his genius in profusion, and makes us stand by, saddened and distressed, as the noble Antony sinks to his ruin, under the gorgeous coloring of the Eastern sky." More recently, twentieth-century critic A. C. Bradley lumped in Cleopatra with Hamlet and Falstaff as Shakespeare's only "inexhaustible" characters.

In this play, Shakespeare doesn't disguise his borrowing from North.

Modern editor David Bevington compiled a list of a dozen passages in which the play parallels North's "Life of Antony," sometimes merely turning North's phrasings into verse. When Antony first meets Cleopatra, for example, North writes that she took "her barge on the river Cydnus, the poop whereof was gold, the sails of purple, and the oars of silver, which kept stroke in rowing after the sound of the music of flutes." In *Antony and Cleopatra*, the character Enobarbus narrates this same meeting to Caesar, mirroring North's language for a dozen lines. In "the barge she sat in," he says, "the poop was beaten gold; purple the sails, and so perfumèd that the winds were lovesick with them. The oars were silver, which to the tune of flutes kept stroke."

Following North's "Life of Antony," the play traces the division between Caesar's nephew Octavian and his ally Antony, who set himself up as a godlike ruler over the eastern half of the Empire, indulging in a decadent love affair with Cleopatra. The shrewd Octavian declares war on Antony, and when their galleys meet in battle off the Greek coast of Actium, Cleopatra flees with her fleet at a crucial moment, causing Antony to follow her and sealing his doom. While the story could lend itself to an easy moral about a weak Antony falling prey to the Egyptian temptress, Plutarch presents it as a tragic love story, in which the reader sympathizes with Antony as a once-noble figure consumed by his own appetites.

The same pathos imbues Shakespeare's play, contrasting the parallel lives of Octavian and Antony: one the cruel autocrat, the other the decadent egoist. The real star of the play, however, is Cleopatra, arguably the most complex female character in the canon. Even as Antony is torn between his Roman duty and Egyptian sensuality, she fights for her political life, using her sexuality to control both Antony and Octavian; at the same time she seems genuinely smitten by Antony's charms. Her moods and actions change from scene to scene, from voluptuously seductive one moment to cruelly manipulative the next, in a role that has tested the chops of great actors such as Tallulah Bankhead, Vivien Leigh, and Vanessa Redgrave.

CRITICS OVER THE years have made inevitable comparisons between Cleopatra, queen of Egypt, and Elizabeth, queen of England. At first blush, the great seductress of three great men—Pompey, Caesar, and Antony—

couldn't be more dissimilar to the Virgin Queen, who famously avoided sexual entanglements. And yet Elizabeth was also the ruler of a small kingdom with a big navy, surrounded by the might of a much larger and more powerful empire, and she, too, manipulated foreign leaders through the promise of her courtship.

As I read the play after our trip to Rome, I see it differently in the context of North's support of his patron Leicester. To North, Elizabeth would appear to be more like Antony—a brave leader undone by a decadent foreign liaison—as Leicester's circle no doubt saw her flirtation with the French Duke of Alençon. In September 1575, Catherine de Medici sent another formal proposal of marriage with her son, and this time, Elizabeth didn't immediately say no. In fact, she expressed her interest in meeting with the duke face to face. Just as Antony was seduced by a foreign culture given to exotic pleasures of food and sexuality, so, too, would Elizabeth seem to North to be in danger of falling prey to the seductions of Catholic France. Was *I* just seeing what I wanted to see now—seduced by McCarthy's theories into confirming his own biases in the text?

While I ponder this, a strange scene toward the end of the play particularly catches my attention. As Octavian's forces are closing in on Alexandria, two night watchmen hear a ghostly parade of music in the air, and one asks the other what it means. "'Tis the god Hercules, whom Antony loved," he says, "now leaves him." Remembering how McCarthy identified Hercules before as a reference to Hercule-François Alençon, I wonder if this could similarly be a reference to the French duke, presaging Elizabeth's ruin. In the play, Antony kills himself the following day— followed by Cleopatra's famous suicide with a poisonous asp. Looking up the "Life of Antony" in North's *Plutarch*, I find the same scene—only with one change. There, the Alexandrian citizens interpret the strange music as Bacchus, the god of wine to whom Antony had sworn devotion, leaving him. That would make more sense, after all, as Bacchus was notorious for feasts with music and dancing. For some reason, the playwright changed the name, subbing in Hercules instead.

McCarthy is intrigued when I tell him, confessing he'd never seen *Antony and Cleopatra* in such allegorical terms. Thinking out loud, however, he says that it's possible North chose to dramatize the story for its applicability to the queen's marriage game. He's especially interested by the fact that it diverges from the source, meaning North would have deliberately changed the story to fit the allegory. Again, I wonder how much I am reading an interpretation into the text, and how much this is an uncanny confirmation of McCarthy's theories.

A PLAY AT that time criticizing the French would certainly have pleased Thomas North's patron, Leicester. Following his last-ditch proposal at Kenilworth, Leicester was a changed man, filled with Puritan zealotry. He was particularly exercised over Spanish attempts to break a Protestant rebellion in the Netherlands, urging Elizabeth to intervene. Under the circumstances, any marriage with a Catholic suitor—even a sometime Protestant sympathizer like Alençon—would be a catastrophe.

In the midst of these events, Leicester's Men were developing a new venue to take their patron's message directly to the people. On April 13, 1576, Leicester's leading player, James Burbage, signed a twenty-one-year lease for a plot of land in the suburb of Shoreditch, a half-mile north of London's city wall. There he erected the first structure specifically built for public performances in England since Roman times—a playhouse called, simply, The Theatre. The location was perfect. Situated on a former priory owned by the crown since the Dissolution, it was close to London but still free from meddling from the mayor and aldermen, who had become increasingly hostile to performances within the city limits.

Before The Theatre, public theater in London had been performed in the yards of inns such as the Bel Savage on Ludgate Hill, and the Bull, the Bell, and the Cross Keys on Bishopsgate. As crowds got bigger and rowdier, however, the city started cracking down on shows, requiring inn-keepers to pay a deposit with the city, earmarked for hospital expenses for audience members injured in the fray. While Burbage partnered with his brother-in-law James Brayne to build The Theatre, scholars also assume he had Leicester's backing, to provide a home base for performances when Leicester's Men were in town. The playhouse sat among undeveloped fields, squeezed between a horse pond, cattle pens, and a ditch used as a common sewer. Despite such insalubrious environs, the venue was a huge step up for performers.

Some three thousand spectators could fit within its circular or poly-gonal structure, watching plays by natural light from its open roof; when it rained, actors and audiences alike got wet. For one penny, audience members could stand in the yard, while more pennies earned access to increasing levels of the galleries. The Theatre was an immediate success, spawning a competitor, the Curtain, next door, within a year. Performances at both venues were chaotic affairs, full of public fights and pickpockets, but they were also lucrative for theater companies, ensuring everyone paid for performances. In 1577, yet another theater joined London's burgeon-ing entertainment scene. Since the gentry couldn't very well traipse up to Shoreditch to mix with the rabble, they filed into a new private performance hall at Blackfriars to watch performances by candlelight.

With this glut of venues, there suddenly weren't enough plays to satisfy demand. While traveling companies could put on the same show day after day, they now constantly needed fresh stories to refresh their repertoire for these new, standing venues. In the beginning, troupes recycled religious dramas or crowd-pleasing romantic fantasies from the travel circuit. As the playhouses increasingly competed for audiences, however, they created a boom for more sophisticated drama that within two decades would bloom into a golden age of English drama.

IT'S IN THIS context, McCarthy believes, that Thomas North embarked upon a new set of plays in the 1570s to both excite audiences and impart moral lessons from history closer to home. Just as Plutarch compared ancient Greek leaders with more recent Roman figures, he contends, North now set out to relate Roman history to English events. "He's doing exactly what Plutarch is doing, comparing lives," says McCarthy as we continue to walk around the sunken ruins where Caesar was killed. Numerous essays have pointed out the explicit references to Julius Caesar in Shakespeare's most famous tragedy, *Hamlet*. "But it's most obvious in the early English histories."

Shakespeare's first historical tetralogy—which includes *Henry VI, Parts 1, 2, and 3*, and *Richard III*—is set during the contentious period in the fifteenth century now known as the Wars of the Roses. Supposedly written in the late 1580s, they cover a time of civil strife just out of living memory of Shakespeare's audiences, sort of like making a movie today about World War I. With the weak Henry VI on the throne, the kingdom breaks out into war between the rival houses of York and Lancaster, symbolized by white and red roses, respectively. Shakespeare's plays about the conflict are unpopular today, lost in a muddy confusion of geographically named nobles; when staged at all, they are usually condensed from three parts to two and presented as part of a cycle leading up to the more crowd-pleasing *Richard III*.

In Shakespeare's own time, however, the plays were a massive hit, dramatizing a national history with bloody battles and backstabbing nobles that was the *Game of Thrones* of its time (indeed, George R. R. Martin based his series in part on the Wars of the Roses, exchanging Stark for York and Lannister for Lancaster). *Part 1* focuses on the exploits of noble English soldier Lord Talbot, battling in vain against the French forces of Joan of Arc, but tragically undermined by growing civil strife at home. *Part 2* sees King Henry marry the sinister French queen Margaret of Anjou, who exacerbates tensions at court, leading to two rebellions—the darkly comical peasant uprising of Jack Cade and the more consequential revolt of Richard, Duke of York. *Part 3* dramatizes the outbreak of war, with a series of bloody revenges and reprisals in four separate battles, and a body count that would do Seneca proud. Ultimately, Margaret kills York, and his son takes the crown as Edward IV, while his other son, Richard, kills King Henry VI, before plotting his own treacherous usurpation of the crown in *Richard III*.

The plot mirrors the Roman plays, says McCarthy, showing how civil war, assassinations, and infighting can pave the way to tyranny. But North was even more explicit about drawing those comparisons, he discovered, as he analyzed the plays with his plagiarism software. Just as *Titus* seems to draw from *The Dial*, and the Italian plays from *Doni*, so, too, he argues, do the histories pull language from *Plutarch's Lives* to a degree scholars have never realized. Shaking down the plays for correspondences, he found obsessive references to Julius Caesar—mentioned twice in each of the *Henry VI* plays and three times in *Richard III*—invariably before a character dies. "If they compare themselves to Caesar, they are going to get stabbed," McCarthy says.

He's not wrong, I find, as I search through the text. In the opening of *Part 1*, Joan of Arc ironically refers to herself as Caesar, foreshadowing her doom by play's end; in *Part 2*, the scheming Duke of Somerset invokes "Brutus' bastard hand" that "stabbed Julius Caesar" just before he is killed by pirates. Of course, it's hard to find a character in these plays who doesn't die a brutal death. But some details seem uncannily Plutarchan as well, McCarthy says. In *Part 2*, Henry VI's protector, the good Duke Humphrey, has a dream of his own downfall, reminiscent of Calpurnia's dreams before Caesar's death, before he is summoned to court at Winchester. Eventually he is accused on trumped-up charges of treason and assassinated by Queen Margaret and the conniving Suffolk.

More explicitly, King Henry VI complains in *Part 3* of his loss of power after being deposed, in terms seemingly ripped from the Roman play. "No bending knee will call thee Caesar now," he says to himself, "no humble suitors press to speak for right; no, not a man comes for redress of thee." Those words are no accident, says McCarthy. In North's *Plutarch's Lives*, he writes that Caesar "would have been contented to have redressed" the senators' demands; but as one requests he read his "humble suit," others "pressed nearer to him." With that the senators kill him. "That exact image, of humble suitors pressing around Caesar, is the exact language used when Caesar is stabbed," says McCarthy, leaning against a gate that leads down into the ruins where the act itself occurred. "All through the plays you have these comparisons. He writes the Roman tragedies, and then he uses them for the English histories."

THERE'S GOOD REASON Shakespeare scholars have never noticed these comparisons: in the traditional chronology, the *Henry VI* plays were written in the late 1580s, and *Julius Caesar* in 1599, so there's no way that the histories could have borrowed from the Roman plays. As for *Plutarch's Lives*, they have focused on it almost exclusively as a source for the Roman plays alone. These borrowings weren't casual on North's part, however, McCarthy says. Once again, he argues, they were a part of his ongoing campaign on behalf of his patron, Leicester, to prevent a foreign marriage—especially a French one, like the one Elizabeth was contemplating with the Duke of Alençon. The trouble in the plays, after all, starts when Henry VI marries the villainous Margaret of Anjou. "He's making analogies between the current English circumstances with the Medieval circumstances," McCarthy says. "Marrying a person of French background leads to the fall of the kingdom."

Part 1 even features the Duke of Alençon as a villain of the play, just as *Much Ado* features Don John. This fifteenth-century Alençon is not even a worthy adversary, cowardly refusing man-to-man combat with the English hero Talbot. The real French leader, Joan of Arc, is meanwhile presented as the devil incarnate, keeping her country in thrall by witchcraft, an over-the-top embellishment on histories of the time. By contrast, the English hero Talbot is the flower of chivalry, living and even dying honorably in contrast to the other scheming nobles in the play. The history upon which the play is based, Edmund Hall's *Union of the Two Noble and Illustrous Families of Lancaster and York* (otherwise known as *Hall's Chronicle*), hardly singles Talbot out for special treatment, referring to him in only a few sentences, as one of the leaders during the war. McCarthy found a good explanation for the embellishment: Talbot was an ancestor of the Earl of Leicester. By exalting him in the play, North was able to flatter his patron while pitting him against Alençon, his virtual enemy.

Even Margaret of Anjou is an oblique reference to the Alençon, McCarthy claims, since Hercule-François also became Duke of Anjou in 1576 when his brother became king. She, too, is presented in far nastier colors than appear in the histories, secretly scheming to turn all of the nobles against one another. In *Part 3*, she sadistically tortures York before killing him, throwing him a napkin dipped in the blood of one of his sons. York berates her impotently, calling her "she-wolf of France," and saying she has a "tiger's heart wrapped in a woman's hide!"—the line eventually paraphrased in *Groatsworth of Wit*.

Elizabethan audiences watching the play would have been conscious of the civil war that could break out in their own time should their queen die without an heir, with Mary Queen of Scots waiting in the wings. But the *Henry VI* plays seem to be warning of something worse—total chaos and catastrophe that could ensue during Elizabeth's reign if she chose the wrong husband. "Shakespeare's interpretation of the Wars of the Roses offers few glimmers of national regeneration or optimistic sentiment," writes Randall Martin. "It is a historical tragedy dominated by archetypal human experience of violence, suffering, and grief." That dark vision transcends even the plays' main source, *Hall's Chronicle*, written in 1550.

Notably, McCarthy found in his research that the plays don't rely much, if at all, on *Holinshed*, the definitive history of England that first appeared in 1577, and would have been a much more current source for someone writing in the late 1580s. Once again, he says, Shakespeare seems uncannily focused on older sources, even when more modern sources are available—or rather, North was using those older sources to write his own plays in the 1570s. Soon, however, he discovered a new source for the history plays that tied them even more closely to the North family. Not only were scholars unaware Shakespeare used the source—they weren't even aware it existed.

EVEN AS McCARTHY and Schlueter prepared their *Titus Andronicus* paper for publication in *Shakespeare Survey* in 2013, McCarthy was pessimistic that much of anything would come of it. Now, eight years into his quixotic quest, McCarthy was getting used to being ignored—when he wasn't being outright attacked, as he had been for his self-published book. Still, he didn't let it faze him, as he sat down at his computer nearly every day to run his plagiarism analyses and comb through sources on Google Books and EEBO, stacking more clues to show that Thomas North wrote the source plays. Some days, he worked twelve or fourteen hours, only taking breaks during the day to shoot hoops or throw the Frisbee with Kennedy and Griffin, who were showing promise at Ultimate themselves. "One good thing about my work, is that my children always know where they can find their dad," he quips. "If I get up to go to the store and they can't find me in the dining room, they think something terrible must have happened."

Sometimes, his wife Lori would have to cajole him out of the room to watch a movie or play a board game with the family—but she always admired his determination. At times, she would hear him talking to himself in the other room, crying out, "Oh my God!" or "No way!" as he stumbled across a particularly juicy connection. Despite all the rejection he's faced over the years, she says, it hasn't seemed to diminish that excitement.

"He never focuses on the latest rejection past a day or two," agrees his daughter, Galovski. "He just has an incredible bounce-back rate. Watching that resiliency has super-shaped me as well." His longtime friend Kizilbash speculates there may also be some pride behind his resolve—a desire to show the PhDs of the world that a college dropout can be just as smart as they are. "Just the testicular fortitude it takes to say I'm going to debunk and disrupt all these ideas that have been conventional for hundreds of years," he says. "He's not only satisfying his own curiosity, you have all of these people who are motivated to brush him aside. I think it's become a brass ring for him."

McCarthy has a simpler explanation for what's kept him going all these years: "I just keep finding more and more spectacular things." For someone who enjoyed figuring out things on his own terms, here was the ultimate puzzle—something he could devote endless hours to putting together, and never get to the end. All he needed was a computer and a flat surface, and he could journey back through hundreds of years of historical and literary analysis, always with the hope that in the next moment, he'd discover a crucial piece of evidence to crack the mystery wide open. And along with it, prove that the work to which he'd devoted more than a decade of his life had value.

By now, he had a whirlwind of evidence tying Thomas North to Shakespeare's plays. By his own count, he'd already written a million words on the topic. In spite of all his efforts, however, the overall narrative of Thomas North's life still remained elusive—glimpsed through only a handful of references in letters and account books. "It had always annoyed me when I first started doing this, that there was no biography of Thomas North," McCarthy says. One day, sitting in his New Hampshire dining room, he opened up a blank computer document in order to try to consolidate all of his evidence into a definitive order in which Thomas North had written his plays. One by one, he cut and pasted the covers of Shakespeare's corresponding plays into the file, matching them to their sister works, known sources, or historical events.

He started with the cover of *Arden of Faversham*, with the bloody hands of Alice Arden. One by one, he added other images—*Titus Andronicus* with its grisly banquet scene, representing North's early flirtation with Senecan tragedy; the lush scenes of Italy in *The Two Gentlemen of Verona* and *The Taming of the Shrew*; the French court of *Love's Labour's Lost*. As he looked at the growing chronology, it suddenly hit him: he was not only looking at the images and storylines of Thomas North's plays, but also of his life. "I was like, this is the friggin' biography," McCarthy says. "That's gin." The woodland fairyland of *A Midsummer Night's Dream* was the Kenilworth festival; the murder of *Julius Caesar* was North's great work of *Plutarch's Lives*; the heroic Talbot on the cover of *Henry VI, Part 1* was his patron, Leicester. "It's like in *The Sixth Sense* or *The Usual Suspects*, where there's something in front of the guy's face the entire time, and you should be embarrassed it took you so long to figure it out." He started conceiving of a new project, which would take a chronological look at North's life, showing how each play fit into his biographical concerns. He would title it *The Earlier Playwright*.

DESPITE ALL OF the compelling bits of evidence he'd amassed, however, he still didn't have a smoking gun. To really convince the Stratfordian establishment, he thought, he needed to find a truly unique source—one so rare that Thomas North could have used it but Shakespeare couldn't have. If such a source did exist, he thought, it would most likely have been at Kirtling Hall, in the North family library. But Kirtling had been torn down in the eighteenth century. What happened to the books that had once resided there? he wondered. McCarthy now tried to find out. For years after Roger and Thomas had died, he discovered, Kirtling was home to successive generations of Norths, until the 5th Lord North became Baron Guilford and moved the family seat—including his library—to Wroxton Abbey in Oxfordshire. For a time the family prospered, but by 1825 it was in decline and Wroxton was liquidated, all of its contents sold in a series of auctions.

Not all evidence was lost, however. Old families often claim ownership of their books with bookplates, which auctioneers often mention in sales as proof of provenance. In May 2013, McCarthy began searching Google Books for any mention of North or Guilford bookplates, and after examining dozens of potential sources, he finally got a hit. A 1927 auction catalog from London rare-book dealer Myers & Co. listed an "original manuscript of an unknown and unpublished work" by an author named George North. The volume, titled *A Brief Discourse of Rebellion and Rebels*, contained a bookplate from the Guilford family library at Wroxton Abbey. Dated 1576, however, the manuscript was dedicated to Roger, 2nd Lord North. That dedication, McCarthy read with increasing excitement, also praised Thomas North, saying that of "writers in English... master T.N. your brother for copy, eloquence, and good method, may claim palm and place with the best."

That hardly prepared McCarthy for what he read next. Among the poems in the manuscript, the listing continued, was one on the rebel Jack Cade. It concluded with a note in all caps, reading "IT IS EX-TREMELY INTERESTING TO COMPARE" the manuscript "WITH SHAKESPEARE'S TREATMENT OF THE SAME SUBJECT" in *Henry VI, Part 2*. It was exactly what he was looking for: a virtually unknown source that connected Thomas North and William Shakespeare. McCarthy literally jumped out of his seat, he remembers. "I was pacing and talking to myself like a madman."

He immediately began writing an email to Schlueter. "Wow! If we can find a unique link between George North's manuscript and the works of Shakespeare," he wrote, "then this would be dramatic evidence." There was only one problem, he told her: "I can't find it anywhere!" He'd already searched the online catalogs for the British Library, Cambridge, and Oxford, and come up blank. Schlueter took up the search, trying online catalogs for other libraries in the UK, and even visiting some in person on her next trip to Europe. There was no trace of the manuscript, which seems to have just briefly bobbed up out of the vast ocean of knowledge, and then sunk again without a ripple.

In the meantime, Schlueter and McCarthy began researching the identity of George North. Like Thomas North, he was a translator, who wrote a kind of guidebook to Scandinavia in 1561, around the same time Elizabeth was negotiating to marry Erik of Sweden. He fought as a soldier during the siege of La Rochelle, and later wrote several other translations, but didn't show up anywhere in genealogical analyses of the North family.

They did find a clue, however, in the account books kept by Roger North, now at the British Library.

A pair of books in brown leather binding, they bear Roger's scrawled notes of virtually every shilling he spent on his estate between 1576 and 1589—one of the most complete surviving accounts of any Tudor noble. On one of the first pages is a payment Roger made to George North for £5 on January 9, 1576, with another on April 22. Around the same time, Roger records several payments to Thomas, implying they were on the estate at the same time. Based on those records, McCarthy and Schlueter reasonably concluded George was a cousin of Roger and Thomas, who stayed at Kirtling for at least three or four months in early 1576, when he likely presented the manuscript to Roger.

After a few months of searching off and on, Schlueter thought of another source to try—a professor of medieval manuscripts at the University of Kent named Tony Edwards, with whom she had taken a course on rare books over the summer. She reached out that September, explaining their predicament. Initially, he, too, came up short. But a few months later, in April 2014, Edwards emailed her back with some good news: the manuscript, in fact, had been at the British Library the whole time.

A few years after the Myers listing, in 1933, *A Brief Discourse* was bought by another aristocratic bibliophile, William Cavendish-Bentinck, 6th Duke of Portland. After he died, the manuscript came to the British Museum in 1949 as part of a loan in lieu of estate taxes, a common practice for cash-strapped estates. The museum's book collections, in turn, became the British Library in 1973, and the manuscript formally entered the collection in 1990. Like many of the library's manuscripts, however, it hadn't been entered into the online catalog under its own name. Instead, it was listed along with the rest of Cavendish-Bentinck's former collection as part of the "Portland Papers."

Thrilled to have located the manuscript after nearly a year, McCarthy requested digital scans, which arrived a few weeks later. McCarthy put Galovski on the task of transcribing the pages and standardizing the spelling so he could subject it to plagiarism software. Finally, McCarthy once again took a deep breath, and pressed "Run," and the columns of text came alive on his screen.

INITIALLY, THE RESULTS from George North's *Brief Discourse* weren't as dramatic as they had been with Thomas North's *Dial*, *Doni*, and *Plutarch*. While clearly it contained some parallels with Shakespeare's plays, the strings of words in common were shorter, and the passages containing them more scattered throughout the text. That made sense, McCarthy rationalized. If Thomas was using his cousin George's book as a source, then he would put it into his own words in his plays, diluting the source with every step. But the more McCarthy investigated, the more connections he found—particularly with the early history plays he'd already guessed Thomas was writing at the time.

George North's *Brief Discourse* takes a simple theme and repeats it over and over: all rebels and rebellions are bad. The essay of about one hundred pages pulls out countless examples from ancient times, the Bible, and English history to argue that insurrection is never justified, and rebels always get their just deserts in the end. It even includes several first-person poems by famous English rebels—including Welsh leader Owen Glendower; the "Black Smith" Michael Joseph; and the Kentish trades-man Jack Cade—who universally lament their decisions and describe the terrible consequences that befell them as a result. Surely, the essay was written to please Queen Elizabeth and her aristocratic supporters like Roger North, even if it was hypocritical at best in a family that had taken part in its fair share of seditious behavior, including Edward North's treasonous poem against Cardinal Wolsey; Roger North's support of the rebellion against Spain in the Netherlands; and George North's own support for the Huguenots in France. At first blush, the uncompromising stance also hardly seems to align with Shakespeare's plays, which take a more nuanced stance toward revolt. "Shakespeare's characters have a wide range of attitudes toward civil rebellion," says Schlueter. "I didn't think it was going to be a major source."

As she and McCarthy analyzed the passages about Jack Cade, however, they found numerous parallels with *Henry VI, Part 2*. Cade appears in the fourth act of that play, leading a darkly comic rebellion that promises a workman's paradise—with him firmly in command. The carnivalesque atmosphere of his rebellion turns into a reign of terror, however, when

Dennis McCarthy at his home in New Hampshire
(*Cody O'Loughlin*)

Seventeenth-century woodcut for *Arden of Faversham*
(*Private Collection/Bridgeman Images*)

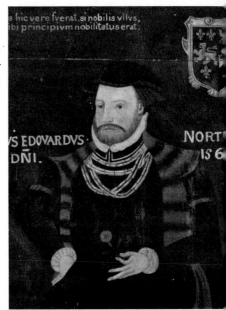

Edward North, 1st Baron North
(Courtesy of P. Pattenden/The Master and Fellows of Peterhouse)

Roger North, 2nd Baron North
(Private Collection, Photo © Christie's Images/ Bridgeman Images)

Watercolor illustration of Kirtling Hall
(British Library, London, UK © British Library Board. All Rights Reserved/Bridgeman Images)

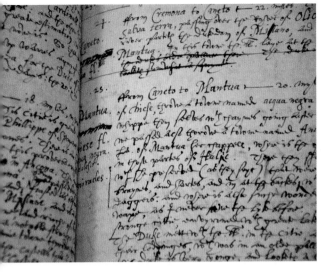

Page from North's journal, describing his visit to Mantua MS 5076 ff. 12v-13, {Thomas Thirlby} The Jorney of the Queene's Ambassadours unto Roome Anno 1555. The Reverend Father in God the Bishoppe of Ely, and Vicownt Montagu then Ambassadors.
(Image courtesy of Lambeth Palace Library)

Wax statues at Santuario Beata Vergine Maria delle Grazie, Curtatone, Italy
(Courtesy of author)

Giulio Romano, *Noble Banquet*, Chamber of Cupid and Psyche, Palazzo Te, south wall
(*Scala/Art Resource, NY*)

Giulio Romano, *Rustic Banquet*, Chamber of Cupid and Psyche, Palazzo Te, west wall
(*Scala/Art Resource, NY*)

Queen Elizabeth I
*(National Gallery, London, UK,
Photo © Photo Josse/Bridgeman Images)*

Robert Dudley, 1st Earl of Leicester
*(National Portrait Gallery, London, UK,
Photo © Stefano Baldini/Bridgeman Images)*

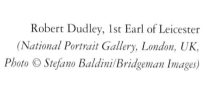

June Schlueter at her home in Easton,
Pennsylvania
(Courtesy of author)

The Longleat manuscript
(Public domain)

William Shakespeare
*(National Portrait Gallery,
London, UK/Bridgeman
Images)*

"The Ass Talks to the Mule," North's
Moral Philosophy of Doni, 1570
*(Douce S 195, p.30, The Bodleian Library,
University of Oxford)*

Hercule-François Valois,
Duke of Alençon
*(Samuel H. Kress Collection, National
Gallery of Art, Washington, DC)*

Thomas Radcliffe, 3rd Earl of Sussex
*(Anglesey Abbey, Cambridgeshire, UK,
National Trust Photographic Library/
Bridgeman Images)*

Illustration of Kenilworth Castle in the seventeenth century
(Kenilworth Castle, Warwickshire, UK © Historic England/Bridgeman Images)

Kenilworth
Castle today
*(Courtesy of
author)*

he starts ordering the massacre of anyone who can read and write. "The first thing we do, let's kill all the lawyers," says one of his henchmen, in an oft-quoted Shakespearean laugh line. "He's a fun figure, in that he's so evil," says McCarthy. "He has great lines—'Burn all the records of the realm. My mouth shall be the Parliament of England.' I mean, that's just really funny." By the end of the act, however, the fickle mob abandons Cade, and he flees London. In a later monologue, he describes how he spent five days as a fugitive, hiding in the woods in "hot weather" and so famished he had to "eat grass" and "sallet" (salad). As he sneaks into a garden, he is caught by its owner, Alexander Iden, who fights and kills Cade with a sword, vowing to drag his body "headlong by the heels, unto a dunghill, which shall be thy grave." There, Iden says, he'll cut off his head to present to the king, "leaving thy trunk for crows to feed upon."

Those oddly specific details of Cade's last days are nowhere to be found in any of the chronicles, including *Hall*, *Holinshed*, and *The Mirror for Magistrates*. Scholars have long thought Shakespeare simply invented them. When McCarthy and Schlueter read George North's essay, however, they spotted the similarities one after another—not just in the speech by Cade, but also in the one by Glendower, who hides in a cave, forced to "feed on moss, for famine great." Cade describes how his body was dragged "through London's streets, drawn like a mastie dog." Afterward, he says, it was left out in the sun "for carrion crows and worm's meat, to eat me flesh and fell."

In effect, McCarthy says, the play's Cade has become an all-purpose rebel, representing a composite of the punishments in George North's monograph. "You read the scenes of Jack Cade in *Henry VI, Part 2*, and you start realizing, 'This is why he's eaten by crows. This is why he's starving,'" he says. "If you are a rebel, this is what's going to happen to you." He pictures George North writing his anti-rebellion tract in the Kirtling Hall library, alongside his cousin Thomas, who was diligently translating *Plutarch's Lives*. And perhaps at the same time, around 1576, Thomas also began working on a series of anti-French plays for his patron, Leicester, working in details from his cousin's manuscript. "Everything lines up to exactly that moment," says McCarthy. "You've got the motivation, you've got the writings—and they were both written in the same friggin' library, maybe even at the same table."

The Jack Cade episode wasn't the only parallel with the manuscript, McCarthy realized as he continued to analyze it. Dozens of other phrases circled around the early histories—including one of the most famous speeches in all of Shakespeare.

"NOW IS THE winter of our discontent," cries the title character in the opening scene of *Richard III*, "made glorious summer by this son of York." After twenty years of devastating civil war, the Yorkist faction has emerged victorious, with King Edward IV firmly on the throne. No sooner has peace come, however, than his younger brother Richard begins plotting to take it for himself. One of the most delicious villains in the canon, Richard appears as a misshapen hunchback, with a lame leg and withered arm (despite the lack of historical evidence that he was at all deformed). Thus Richard reveals in diabolical soliloquy that instead of being happy that the wars have ended, he is miserable because he cannot enjoy peacetime.

"I, that am not shaped for sportive tricks, nor made to court an amorous looking glass," he says, "I, that am curtained of this fair proportion, cheated of feature by dissembling Nature, deformed, unfinished, sent before my time into this breathing world scarce half made up," has "no delight to pass away the time, unless to see my shadow in the sun and descant on mine own deformity." Finally, he reveals: "And therefore, since I cannot prove a lover to entertain these fair well-spoken days, I am determined to prove a villain."

For centuries, playgoers have been enthralled by the power of this un-repentant declaration of evil. "With a bold stroke," says David Bevington, "Richard takes over the stage in a way that has held audiences spellbound." As spectators revel in his gleeful amorality, he springs his plots against any-one ahead of him for the throne, including his own brothers; and Edward's two sons, the "princes in the Tower," whom he orders to be murdered. (When Richard leads them to the Tower, where they'll be assassinated, one of them asks, "Did Julius Caesar build that place, my lord?")

While the picture of Richard as a deformed monster didn't originate with Shakespeare's play—Sir Thomas More describes him as physically misshapen in his 1513 "History of Richard III," and *Hall's Chronicle* repeats the characterization—Shakespeare's play is the first work to explicitly blame Richard's evil proclivities on his misshapen body. (As one critic says about the play, "Richard, allegedly inspired by his own body, embraces deformity in all its lawless possibilities.")

George North doesn't mention Richard III in his *Brief Discourse*; in the introduction to his work, however, McCarthy found that he makes the same explicit connection between outward beauty and inward virtue, using some of the same words Richard does. It's up to us, North writes, "to view our own proportion in a glass, whose form and feature, if we find fair and worthy, to frame our affections accordingly." In other words, if we are good-looking, we should be good in our behavior as well. On the other hand, he continues, if nature has "deformed our outward appearance, and left us odible to the eye of the world," then "to cure, shadow, or salve the same" we must "moderate our inward man, as Nature herself may seem to be deceived in us." Put another way, if we are ugly, then we must fight against our outward appearance to prove nature wrong.

North's sentiment is the exact opposite of Richard's, McCarthy says. "In George North's argument, he is saying you should defy nature—if you are deformed, you should be virtuous, in order to give the lie to nature." Though the intent is different, however, both short passages use the same words to tie outward appearance and inward virtue: proportion, glass, fair, feature, deformed, nature, world, and shadow. "They're both using these eight peculiar terms, and they do it in almost the same order," says McCarthy. Beyond just identifying the source for an important Shakespearean scene, knowing its source sheds new light on the soliloquy. "Richard III is clearly not following a very important learning in humanism, that you maintain your virtue no matter your appearance," says McCarthy. "After all the horror he causes, he ends up getting killed."

ALL IN ALL, the discovery of the George North manuscript was a bombshell for McCarthy and Schlueter, injecting new life into their project just when they needed it. "Doors that had been closed just opened up widely," Schlueter told me. Eager to reveal it to the world, McCarthy and Schlueter began working on a paper about the parallels with the Jack Cade episode, sending it to *Shakespeare Quarterly* in the spring of 2015. The paper didn't mention Thomas North at all, only identifying the manuscript as a new source for Shakespeare. McCarthy was crestfallen, however, when the journal quickly rejected it—with an anonymous peer reviewer contending the similarities must be coincidental. McCarthy suspected that in reality he had been once more condemned for his heretical beliefs about Thomas North, which were easily found with an online search.

They had better luck with a conference on "Shakespeare and Scandinavia" to be held at Kingston University in Kingston upon Thames. Given George North's connection to Sweden, it seemed like the perfect opportunity to try, and Schlueter submitted their paper. To their delight, it was accepted for the conference's opening session. They both traveled to England in October, where they read the work to an appreciative group of scholars. "The only reason I got in was because of June," says McCarthy. The gathering, however, was just one small conference, and their presentation barely made a splash in the wider world of Shakespeare scholarship. As exciting as their discovery of the *Brief Discourse* seemed to be, they'd need to keep trying if they were going to get noticed.

No sooner had they returned than Schlueter saw another call for papers for the Shakespeare Association of America (SAA) conference the following spring. Among them was a seminar on *Arden of Faversham* coled by Gary Taylor, the authorship expert leading the publication of the *New Oxford Shakespeare*. As Schlueter submitted a proposal, McCarthy threw himself into writing a new paper about Thomas North as author of an Arden source play, demonstrating the correspondences with *The Dial of Princes* and the family connections to Alice and the Dissolution of the Monasteries. While North originally wrote his Arden play in the 1550s, McCarthy believes he revised it for publication in 1577 as *A Cruel Murder Done in Kent*—not long after his cousin George had penned his *Brief Discourse* at Kirtling.

Paper in hand, McCarthy headed down to New Orleans for the conference at the end of March 2016. Along with him went his daughter, Galovski, who had for the past few years been living in New York City following her father's example of an unconventional career path in pursuing a documentary film career despite her lack of film-school experience. By now, her tenacity had earned her an associate producer position at Fictionless, a company helmed by the Academy Award–winning director Ross Kauffman. As she watched her father continue to struggle to reveal his discoveries, she conceived of her own project on the side—one that would follow him around and capture the highs and lows of his quest. "It's going to be like a daughter's portrait of her father doing this amazing thing," she says, "kind of inviting people into one of our long talks over drinks until sunrise." There were only so many shots she could get of McCarthy typing away at his computer, however, so she was accompanying him to the conference, hoping to capture him facing off against other scholars.

The weather was warm and rainy as they checked into the Sheraton in downtown New Orleans. In the lobby, the organizers of the conference had set up a giant papier-mâché bust of the Bard—as if on a Mardi Gras float—and scholars from around the country lined up to take their pictures with it. Later, McCarthy led his entourage into a large, square conference room with a long rectangular table in the middle. At the end of the table sat Taylor, along with his wife, Terri Bourus, a professor of theater performance, who would colead the session.

McCarthy nervously eyed Taylor as he shuffled into the room. With a ponytail and goatee, the sixty-three-year-old Florida State professor stood out in a room full of gray-headed Shakespeareans. He'd made a name for himself by tilting against received wisdom, arguing in the late 1980s that Shakespeare's reputation was overblown, and that other Elizabethan playwrights were just as skilled as the Bard. It was Taylor, among others, who led the charge to use stylometric tools to prove Shakespeare collaborated on many of his plays with other writers. He'd earned his fair share of detractors, some of whom even accused him of hating Shakespeare. But Taylor seemed to revel in his status as *enfant terrible* of the Shakespearean academe, welcoming criticism and leveling withering broadsides against his colleagues with whom he disagreed. His wife and academic partner, Bourus, was a scholar in her own right, with several books on *Hamlet*. Short, with curly blond hair, she had a softer edge, displaying her theater background with her warm, welcoming personality.

Together, they now invited participants around the conference table, where fifteen spots had been reserved for participants who had written papers, while other chairs were arranged around the perimeter for spectators to observe in silence, as if watching a scholarly tennis match. Schlueter was supposed to sit "at table" with the participants, but at the last minute she gave up her seat, a spot near Taylor, to McCarthy. Before the meeting got under way, however, she says she asked Taylor if he could call on her first during the question-and-answer period, and she says he agreed. McCarthy took his place at the table, feeling self-conscious at the staring ring of spectators. ("It's the most bizarre thing," he told me later about sitting amidst the silent onlookers. "It's like *Eyes Wide Shut*, only with a discussion of *Arden of Faversham*.")

For all of his bravado when expounding on his theories in print, McCarthy was more deferential, even bashful, when faced with Shakespearean scholars in person. For the next two hours, Taylor and Bourus led the discussion about each of the papers in turn. Aside from McCarthy's paper and Taylor's own paper, which argued the play was cowritten by Shakespeare and poet Thomas Watson, none of the other papers addressed authorship, covering other literary or historical points instead. At one point, someone questioned why so many of the stage directions in *Arden* seemed so antiquated, and Taylor addressed McCarthy, mentioning his theory that the play was written in the 1550s. "But previously you said Shakespeare wrote the play, and now you are saying Thomas North wrote it," Taylor needled him.

"Well, I think North wrote it, and Shakespeare adapted it," McCarthy replied. That's all he got a chance to say, however, as the discussion moved on. As the moderators went around the table discussing papers, it seemed to Schlueter, watching from the outside, that they were intentionally avoiding discussing McCarthy's paper, as he sat awkwardly at the table in silence. "And you could tell he was doing it. What a scoundrel!" Schlueter tells me later. During the Q&A, Schlueter says, Taylor avoided calling on her until the very end, at which point she stood up and defended their paper, just as everyone was getting ready to leave.

Afterward, McCarthy, Schlueter, and Galovski met outside to debrief. McCarthy was downcast; here he'd come all the way to New Orleans to finally present his views to a room full of Shakespeare scholars, and he barely said three sentences. Schlueter was furious, feeling like Taylor had intentionally set them up—unwilling to allow McCarthy's unorthodox view of authorship into the discussion.

Later, I reach Taylor and Bourus in Florida, and they insist they didn't deliberately exclude McCarthy from the discussion. In an email, Taylor says he, too, has "often been frustrated" by the seminar format at conferences. "Time is limited, and everyone at the table considers their work and their opinion especially important," he says. "It is very easy to feel that the seminar leader is favoring one set of opinions over another." As for Schlueter, he couldn't show favoritism by calling on her over others in the audience. "I understand that she was unhappy not to get the first word; but I can assure you that other people were unhappy that they did not get the chance to speak publicly at all." (According to another participant, there were so many scholars at the table, no one got much of a chance to present their views.)

Whatever the explanation, once again McCarthy had failed to get a hearing on his discoveries. Even a scholar like Gary Taylor, who himself railed against the orthodox view of Shakespeare as solitary genius, seemed to him unwilling to take the further step—to see Shakespeare as an adapter of another writer's work. How could he get anyone to believe Thomas North used his cousin's manuscript to write *Richard III*, when he couldn't even get them to believe he wrote a play about his own sister? In order to truly explain how and why Thomas North wrote the plays, it seemed he'd need to put them into the context of his whole biography, overwhelming skeptics with the sheer number of connections. Turning back to his book project, *The Earlier Playwright*, he now set out to fill in the gaps in the chronology, play by painstaking Shakespeare play— including one that connected Thomas North to the queen herself.

Chapter Eleven
ALL THAT GLISTERS

(1578)

All that glisters is not gold—
Often have you heard that told.
Many a man his life hath sold
But my outside to behold.

— *The Merchant of Venice*

azing across his domain from atop Kirtling Hall's gatehouse in spring 1578, Roger Lord North was filled with mounting anxiety. The queen was coming to visit. In more than a decade ruling the estate, Roger had done his father's legacy proud. He could see dozens of workers tilling his fields, tending his fruit trees, and watching over herds of sheep and cattle. Everything pointed to the success of a proud country squire settling comfortably into middle age. Now, however, Roger was about to face the ultimate test, one that could make or break the reputation of a courtier. After all, this was not just any visit; Roger had just been informed that Elizabeth would be coming to Kirtling as part of her annual summer progress—a two-month jaunt that would take her clear up to East Anglia, as far as Norwich. On her return, Her Majesty would pass through Cambridgeshire, where she would be pleased to spend two nights at his estate.

Roger could hear the buzzing of handsaws and ringing of hammers as his workmen labored on a new banqueting house to accommodate the huge movable feast—equivalent to a large town picking up stakes and moving a dozen miles every night or two. In order to travel in comfort, Elizabeth brought her entire court, with all of its ushers, grooms, pages, cooks, ladies-in-waiting, maids, musicians, and over one hundred members of the Yeomen of the Guard. The queen's Privy Council conducted the business of state from country houses across the realm, and dozens of nobles and gentry tagged along for the traveling party. In all, the progress could include more than a thousand people, and even more horses.

The crown would provide the royal silver, and rich curtains embroidered with Elizabeth's insignia, but the rest of the preparations—and cost— would be Roger's responsibility. Great houses like Roger's engaged in a kind of "competitive opulence," in the words of one historian, spending hundreds of pounds a day on feasts and festivities. Some lords commissioned original songs, poetical orations, philosophical disputations, and masques full of Roman gods and fairies to amuse the queen and literally sing her praises. If Roger wanted to secure his future advancement at court, he would need to produce entertainments to be remembered. Thankfully, says McCarthy, he had someone in his own family whom he could call on to provide them: his playwright brother, Thomas. At the very moment Roger was surveying his domain, perhaps, Thomas was at work in the library on a new play specifically designed for the queen's visit: a darkly comic tale about a Jewish moneylender and a Venetian merchant.

IN CONTRAST TO the small towns we've visited so far, Kirtling is nothing more than a village. "And it's about to become Stratford-upon-Avon," McCarthy jokes to our driver, Mark, as we curve around country lanes through tunnels of yellowing trees on our own way to the former North family estate. "Start buying land in Kirtling now—you're welcome." According to official estimates, the population has remained steady at around three hundred people since the sixteenth century. Even after Kirtling Hall was pulled down, the gatehouse remained, now known as Kirtling Tower. Since World War II, it has been owned by the Fairhaven family, a British dynasty that made its fortunes in oil and railroads in America. As we drive, McCarthy tries to contact Lord and Lady Fairhaven, but the call goes to voicemail. He spoke to their assistant the day before, he tells us, and asked for permission to visit the property, but so far hasn't gotten a response.

He's particularly nervous given his last experience there. After he and Schlueter presented at Kingston upon Thames in 2015, he had arranged to meet a descendant of the North family, Mary Clow, at Kirtling, which he assumed was some kind of historic site or house museum. "There's a gate, but it's locked," he tells us. "Eventually, I just kind of jump over a fence and go in." He walked up to a large circular driveway with a lawn strangely filled with antique cars, and began knocking on doors. "I'm kind of looking in windows to see if I can see anyone," he continues, "and it starts to dawn on me that maybe I'm not supposed to be here." Just as he realized that the property was not a museum, he says, two black Range Rovers pulled up, disgorging the Fairhavens and their children.

"It looked like *Downton Abbey* getting out of one car, and a Ralph Lauren ad getting out of the other," McCarthy recounts. "They are all stunningly beautiful, and one woman is clearly in riding gear." To his surprise, he says, Lady Fairhaven immediately approached him and started talking. "Well, thank God, you're here, you've got to hear the story about this car," she said, in McCarthy's warming recollection. "George was here, and he said, 'That's a 1937 Bugatti,' and I said, 'How do you know?' and you won't believe what George did, he got right down on the ground and went underneath the car, looking at the engine." As she spoke, McCarthy gradually discerned there had been an antique auto show at the estate earlier that day, which explained all the cars on the lawn. "Lady Fairhaven, I'm very sorry to say I don't know what you are talking about," McCarthy said, telling her he was clearly in the wrong place. "I just wanted to say, however, that I do know that *Henry VI, Part 2* and *King Lear* were written on this property."

Lady Fairhaven, he says, didn't miss a beat. "Well that's even more interesting," she said, according to McCarthy, spending the next few minutes showing him around the grounds. "They were unbelievably kind and gracious," McCarthy concludes. "I went from thinking I'm going to jail to being escorted around the property." Even so, he's not excited now about arriving unannounced a second time. Mark pulls off onto a wooded driveway that GPS marks as the address of the estate. After a few dozen feet we come to a closed gate, with a sign reading NO ENTRY— CCTV IN OPERATION. McCarthy tries once again to call the Fairhavens' assistant, but the call again goes to voicemail. He and Galovski start arguing about whether to ring the buzzer and try to talk their way into the estate anyway.

After a few minutes, McCarthy's caution wins out over his daughter's spunk. "I can't believe you won't go up and talk to them—Grandma would," Galovski chides as Mark begins to reverse the car. "And you would, too," McCarthy replies to his daughter, not without pride. We drive for a half-mile up the road and pull onto a gravel road at the edge of the estate, which leads to All Saints Church, where McCarthy did eventually find Mary Clow that day. Emerging from the car, we see a squat medieval church, with a brick wall around a churchyard full of mossy tombstones. The air is chilly and raw, with a joint-seeping kind of cold, but despite the gloomy English weather, the scene is wonderfully pastoral. A path to the right leads to a gated wooden fence beside a wooded stream that wends its way to the former Kirtling Hall.

Thomas North would have walked the path on his way to celebrate services at his family church, I think to myself. "Do you ever feel sentimental, like this is hallowed ground?" Galovski asks McCarthy, as if reading my mind. "Not as much as you'd expect," McCarthy admits. "I don't know why. I am fascinated by it, but there is no spiritual moment of exaltation." On the other hand, he adds after a moment of thought, even after years of working on North and Shakespeare, he is still in awe of the writing. "The way he gets across ideas is absolutely spectacular," he says. "He is a masterpiece machine. And it's a mystery how anyone could come up with these masterpieces one after another, but by studying Thomas North, you start to see where the ideas come from." One of them, he contends, came all the way from Venice to Kirtling.

THE MERCHANT OF VENICE is technically a comedy, since it ends, like all comedies do, in marriage. But the play has a more sinister edge to it, which has made it simultaneously one of Shakespeare's most-performed and most-controversial plays. The story consists of two intertwined plots: Venetian merchant Antonio takes out a loan of three thousand ducats from the Jewish moneylender Shylock, who requires an unusual price if he forfeits: a pound of his flesh. Antonio takes out the loan to help his friend Bassanio woo the lady Portia, whose late father also set up an extraordinary wager: she can only marry a suitor who chooses correctly among three different caskets—small chests made of gold, silver, and lead—only one of which holds her portrait inside.

The play was originally entered into the Stationers' Register in 1598, as "a book of the Merchant of Venice, or otherwise called the Jew of Venice." But the story goes back much further, to yet another Italian book of stories, untranslated in Shakespeare's time—*Il Pecorone* by Giovanni Fiorentino. Published in Milan in 1558 and reprinted in Venice in 1560 and 1565, the book contains all the elements of the play—the merchant and the moneylender, the friend and the lady—in rich detail that leaves no doubt the playwright used it as his primary source. The only element missing is the casket contest, which comes from a Latin story collection called the *Gesta Romanorum*. That book, at least, was translated into English several times in the sixteenth century; Shakespeare source scholar Kenneth Muir pins *Merchant*'s source to a 1577 version by London printer Richard Robinson, based on the use of the rare word "insculpt."

That would make 1577 the earliest Thomas North could have written a source play, McCarthy deduced as he first started examining the play. He found a timeline boundary on the other side, too, in a 1579 pamphlet by poet and satirist Stephen Gosson, in which he rails against the evils of the theater. Gosson only dubs two plays "tolerable," both performed at the Bull. One called *The Jew*, he writes, concerns "the greediness of worldly choosers and the bloody minds of usurers." Since the nineteenth century, scholars have taken that description to be a tight summary of the twin plots of *The Merchant of Venice*—the casket plot and the flesh-bond plot, respectively—speculating that Gosson was describing an early source play for Shakespeare's comedy.

That was exactly right, McCarthy believes, imagining a play by North called *The Jew of Venice*—a companion to his other Venetian play, *The Moor of Venice*. "*The Jew* is one of the easiest plays to date in the canon," McCarthy tells me. "Everything about it says 1578." The plagiarism software supported the timing, too, with hit after hit from North's *Plutarch*, which Thomas was still writing at Kirtling at the time. "It's one of the most Plutarchan plays in the canon," McCarthy says. In one story in *Plutarch* about a man refusing to lend a relative money, for example, North uses the phrase "good round sums of money, many a time and oft." In the scene in which Shylock is deciding to lend money to Antonio, he says, "Three thousand ducats. 'Tis a good round sum," and then comments that Antonio has insulted him in the marketplace "many a time and oft." The name Portia, as well, comes straight out of the *Lives*, where she is the wife of Caesar's Brutus—a point Bassanio even mentions in *The Merchant of Venice*. In *Plutarch*, North describes Portia as "excellently well seen in philosophy, loving her husband well, and being of noble courage, as she was also wise"—an apt description of her character in *Merchant*.

The bigger question, however, was what inspired Thomas North to write that particular play at that moment in time. As with North's previous plays, McCarthy found the answer partially in the personal and political preoccupations of his patron, Leicester. But this time, he also found another motivation as well: his brother Roger's relationship with the queen.

WHILE IT'S NEVER easy to trace the blurry outlines of Thomas North's life, the late 1570s is a time in which it swims into slightly better focus, thanks to Roger North's account books, which include hundreds of entries for expenses, including for the queen's famous visit to Kirtling in 1578. When McCarthy first began exploring North's biography, he contacted the library to request scans of all seven hundred or so pages, reading between the lines of so many weekly orders of fish and capons to spy glimpses of Thomas's life. He found him entirely dependent on his brother, who paid Thomas a £10 quarterly pension on Lady's Day (March 25), Midsummer (June 24), Michaelmas (September 29), and Christmas (December 25). That adds up to £40 a year, or a modern-day sum of about $22,540—enough for Thomas to get by, especially considering his brother also took care of his room and board, but surely no princely salary. Roger sometimes recorded losing more at cards.

As the firstborn son, Roger was the indisputable family patriarch, doling out pensions of £25 a quarter to his own firstborn son, John, along with £10 each to his second son, Henry, and his sister Christian. Thomas seems often strapped for cash, since Roger often paid him a portion of allowance early, along with additional gifts and travel charges to London for him and his wife (whom he calls "Sister North"). He also gave small presents to Thomas's daughter, Elizabeth—Roger calls her "Bess"—for cloth to make a new gown or other apparel, and wages to Thomas's son, Edward, for work on the estate. And in December 1576, Roger recorded a payment of £46, 11 shillings, and 11 pence (more than $25,000) for "a lease of house and household stuff for Mr. Tho. North." Although there's no record of where that house might have stood, the North family's early-twentieth-century biographer Frances Bushby fancifully enthuses that there "we may picture him busily employed upon the great work by which he will be best remembered, his translation of *Plutarch's Lives*."

Even while Thomas was writing his great translation—and perhaps his Roman and early history plays as well—Roger was busily expanding his real estate empire, spending £309 ($160,490) in late May 1577 to purchase the nearby estate of Mildenhall, which his second son, Henry, would eventually inherit. Thomas's life outside Kirtling, however, seems to have been short-lived: by midsummer 1578, Roger recorded his residence back on the estate, along with his wife, daughter, and son. Overall, the account books give the impression of a satisfying, if predictable country lifestyle. Roger employed dozens of men, many of whom he refers to by first name in his accounts. He even adopted the son of one of his yeoman farmers as his "goodson," frequently giving him presents of cash and clothing. Several times a year, Roger hosted players to perform for the family during their tours of the countryside—including Leicester's Men in April 1576—and sometimes minstrels and Morris dancers as well. In March 1577, he even hired his own resident fool, paying for six yards of motley cloth to outfit him with hose, doublet, and coat. A few times a year, Roger traveled to London for a few weeks at a time to conduct business, but he seems to have dropped completely out of national politics. His only vice seems to have been gambling, recording losses of dozens of pounds per year at cards, dice, and bowls.

EVEN AS THE family lived on the estate, Roger paid the small fortune of £250 ($129,900) to send his son John on a trip to Italy, arranged through Leicester's Italian financier. John took after his father, cataloging his journey in an account book. Arriving in Padua in the fall of 1575, John took a room in town, as his uncle Thomas may have done five years earlier. There, the journal abruptly trails off, but it resumes again in late 1577 as he is leaving Venice to return to England—only with a notable difference: now he is writing in Italian. John North continued to keep his accounts in Italian even after he returned to London that November, committing wholeheartedly to the role of an *Inglese Italiano*.

The thin book, bound in a crusty, ivory-colored calfskin at Oxford's Bodleian Libraries, offers an intriguing window into the circles in which John and his uncle Thomas moved. Peeling apart its pages reveals a world of dinner parties set with Mediterranean foods—olives and salted lemons, capers and sweet Moscatello wine—Italian novellas, "singing books," and dancing lessons. John spent extravagantly on clothing—no doubt beyond his uncle's budget—dressing in boots of Spanish leather, doublets of Flanders silk, and aromatic perfumed gloves smelling of rosewater and ambergris. "The Italianate gentleman was a man changed not just inwardly, but in his words, his carriage, and even his odor," writes John Gallagher, a lecturer at Leeds University, who translated and studied the diary.

John seems to have had a special relationship with his uncle Thomas, inviting him to his dinner parties with cosmopolitan guest lists. Soon after his return to London, on February 21, 1578, he hosted Thomas, his wife Elizabeth, and their daughter Bess to a spread of meats, salmon, and eels in honor of the young Earl of Bath. Among the other guests were Italian fencing master Rocco Bonetti, who ran a school in Blackfriars; an unidentified Greek woman; and Richard Knollys, son of elder privy councilor Francis Knollys, one of Leicester's allies at council. The dinner was accompanied by paid musicians, and a month after that dinner, John purchased a lute from his uncle Thomas for 40 shillings, "a fashionable instrument with Italianate connotations" as Gallagher writes. Thomas's possession of such an instrument is an intriguing hint at his musical talents that would fit with his authorship of the plays, which often include songs and dancing as part of their plots.

Moreover, the Italianate circle in which Thomas lived in London would explain why he chose a Venetian story for the play he would present to the queen during her visit to his family's estate, McCarthy says—as well as the characterization of the play's most problematic character, the Jewish moneylender Shylock. That portrait leans heavily on anti-Semitic stereotypes of greed and vindictiveness, which continue to grate for modern audiences. Stephen Greenblatt, for one, calls the drama "a bone caught in the throat that can neither be coughed up nor comfortably swallowed." The depiction is open to interpretation, however. Just as some have tried to extract a feminist reading of *The Taming of the Shrew*, others have read *Merchant* as an exploration or even indictment of prejudice.

Shylock is hardly the monster seen in other plays of the time, such as Christopher Marlowe's *The Jew of Malta*, in which the titular villain is a caricature of homicidal avarice. Rather, the play takes care to show the harmful effects of the casual cruelty Antonio and other characters inflict upon Shylock, giving him a motive for his extreme collateral. In the most famous speech from the play, Shylock defends his own humanity, including the famous line: "If you prick us, do we not bleed?" which offers almost tragic depth to his character. A 2004 film version of the play starring Al Pacino, in fact, stripped much of the comedy out of the story to focus on the melancholy downfall of Shylock instead.

Considering Thomas North's potential trip to Italy adds new context to the play, argues McCarthy. Jews had been driven out of London in the thirteenth century, and outside of Spanish converts, Shakespeare had probably never even met one. North, on the other hand, could have encountered Jews in Venice in 1570, when xenophobia was at its peak on the eve of Lepanto. "The word Jew appears dozens of times in the canon, but almost every single time antisemitism occurs, it's a Northern Italian who's using it," McCarthy notes. North would have seen the discrimination against the Jews inflicted by Italians in Venice; at the same time, his own humanist education would have allowed him to at least sympathize with their plight. "He doesn't completely discount the stereotypes of the time," says McCarthy, "he was a bit of an elitist, who thought some people were better than others. But as a humanist you had to be merciful. He's always teaching that in the plays."

EVEN AS THOMAS and John were swirling around the edges of Leicester's Italianate circles, Roger was further deepening his friendship with the

Earl. In June 1577, Roger rode the hundred miles to Kenilworth to spend time as Leicester's guest, hunting and losing £50 at cards. As he rode through the deer chase with the other lords and ladies, Roger must have noticed the attention Leicester lavished on one guest in particular: Lettice Knollys, the Countess of Essex. A gentlewoman of thirty-five, Lettice was possessed of a vivacious personality and flowing red curls that, it must be said, gave her a passing resemblance to her cousin, Queen Elizabeth.

A regular hunting guest at Leicester's estate, Lettice was daughter to privy councilor Francis Knollys and the wife of Walter Devereux, Earl of Essex, a prestigious lord who had spent much of the early 1570s fighting Catholics in Northern Ireland. When Essex died soon after his return to Ireland in September 1576, an official inquest by Leicester's brother-in-law ruled out foul play (the cause was most likely dysentery); that didn't stop Leicester's enemies from claiming he poisoned him, adding to the long list of nefarious offenses laid at his feet since the death of his own wife. Some even whispered that Devereux's ten-year-old son, Robert, was actually Leicester's. Soon Leicester was courting Lettice more openly—risking the wrath of the queen if she found out.

Even as he pursued this new dalliance, Leicester's attentions turned to the Low Countries, which had become a giant chessboard in the never-ending game of religious wars and alliances between England, France, and Spain—that would eventually pull the North brothers into its mire. Leicester and his faction on the Privy Council urged Elizabeth to intervene on behalf of the northern United Provinces, now in open revolt against Spain under the charismatic William of Orange.

Elizabeth held off, worried about breaking her fragile truce with Philip, even as the conflict deepened. After unruly Spanish troops pillaged Antwerp, Spain sent in a new governor to restore peace: Elizabeth's one-time marriage prospect, Don John of Austria. Taking decisive control, Philip's bastard brother captured the citadel of Namur high in the Wallonian hills, pressing his advantage against William's troops. Around the same time, Elizabeth's spymaster Walsingham brought her a secret cache of letters written by Don John, begging his brother for permission to invade England.

Elizabeth was shocked out of her neutrality, promising a loan of

£100,000 ($56 million) to the Dutch States General, and even offering to send six thousand soldiers to fight. To lead them, she tapped her favorite courtier, Leicester, who jumped at a chance to strike a blow for Puritanism. Elizabeth suddenly thought better of the move, however, and sent an ambassador to negotiate peace instead. Leicester's disappointment turned to frustration at the news of a crushing defeat of the Dutch Protestant army at the hands of Don John in January 1578. In desperation, the States-General now turned to one of Elizabeth's other suitors, Hercule-François, the Duke of Alençon, promising him rulership of the Netherlands if only he let the Protestants worship freely under his protection.

Even as the pieces were moving on the chessboard of Holland, Leicester continued to play his own dangerous romantic game. In early 1578, he broke things off completely with his former mistress, Douglas Sheffield, meeting her in the gardens of Greenwich to offer her an astronomical annuity of £700 ($393,000) if she would only "disavow marriage" and give him custody of their son. Around the same time, Leicester received the not-unexpected news that Lettice was pregnant. He must have greeted the words with a combination of joy and dread. No matter that he honestly seemed to love her; there was no way he could risk offending the queen by openly marrying her cousin. At the same time, this was no Douglas whom he could string along forever. That spring, Leicester sent for a minister and married Lettice secretly at Kenilworth. He then purchased Wanstead, an estate twelve miles northeast of London, and set up his new wife there during her confinement.

Leicester couldn't have really thought his relationship would escape the queen's notice. According to later reports by the Spanish ambassador, Elizabeth visited him at his London home that spring and became extremely agitated. Afterward, Leicester disappeared from court for two months; historians have read between the lines to surmise that she had found out about his love affair with Lettice—though perhaps not about his secret marriage. Whatever her own feelings about marrying Leicester, she could hardly be expected to bear his affection for another. Like a wounded lover on a rebound, she promptly sent an ambassador to France to reopen marriage negotiations with Alençon.

As ELIZABETH started to prepare for her summer progress that May, she was in a foul mood, preoccupied by the stalemate in the Netherlands and the betrayal by her one constant friend. On top of everything, she developed a toothache, which shot dull shivers of pain through her face for months. Though the queen's doctors recommended the tooth be pulled, none of her councilors had the courage to tell her. In the midst of this distress, Elizabeth insisted on a mini-progress around London that May, as a prelude to her longer trip to East Anglia, stopping at Wanstead, among other houses.

Leicester wisely made himself scarce for the visit, instead sending his twenty-three-year-old nephew Philip Sidney, a gallant courtier and poet, to entertain her. For the occasion, he composed a long masque now known as "The Lady of May." In it, a lady asks a queen to choose for her between two suitors, a gamekeeper and a shepherd. The play has since been interpreted in various ways, arguing against marriage with Alençon, or in favor of intervention in the Netherlands. Either way, it was filled with praise for the queen and a conciliatory message from Leicester, as one of the actors presented Elizabeth with a necklace of agate beads. After the performance, Elizabeth was mollified enough to commit to sending £20,000 ($11.2 million) to support John Casimir, Count Palatine of Simmern, a German Protestant prince who had arrived in the Netherlands with a mercenary army to fight against Spain.

At the same time, another front broke out in Elizabeth and Philip's proxy war when Philip's nephew, Sebastian I, the king of Portugal, launched a crusade against the Sultan of Morocco, Abd al-Malik, who was supported by the Ottomans. The sultan sent envoys to Elizabeth to form an Anglo-Moroccan alliance against Spain, but once again, Elizabeth hesitated, sending munitions but officially holding fast to a position of neutrality.

Those concerns, too, tie into *The Merchant of Venice*, McCarthy found. The casket plot features two suitors, one from Morocco and one from Aragon, who both make the wrong choice in their attempts to woo Portia—gold and silver, respectively—before Bassanio wins in choosing lead. (The choice, in the context of the play, represents Bassanio's humility and lack of greed—or as a poem inside the golden casket famously reads, "All that glisters is not gold.") McCarthy sees the suitors as obvious stand-ins for the king of Morocco, Abd al-Malik, and the king of Portugal, Sebastian I, a member of the House of Aragon, who were both courting Elizabeth's support at the time that summer. "Portugal goes to war with Morocco, and both of them are sending envoys, and she stays neutral." By dramatizing that fact, McCarthy says, North could have been assuaging the worries of the French ambassadors and Spanish agents who accompanied the queen's progress and were worried Elizabeth might take sides. (Sebastian and Al-Malik both perished when their forces met in the Battle of Alcazar on August 4, 1578, though news of the fiasco didn't reach London until later in September.)

Those aren't the only suitors mentioned in the play. Among Portia's other failed courtiers is a "Neapolitan prince" whom she says "doth nothing but talk of his horse," so much that she thinks his mother "played false with a smith." As some have pointed out, that description fits Don John of Austria, who was based at the time in Naples, and renowned for his horsemanship and horse breeding—with an allusion, perhaps, to his bastard birth as well. Another suitor, the "County Palantine," could be German mercenary leader Count Palatine John Casimir (who had even tried briefly to court Elizabeth back in 1564). Meanwhile, Portia gives a "French lord, Monsieur Le Bon," special elaboration, as someone so full of himself he is "every man in no man" who "will fence with his own shadow." She adds, "If I should marry him, I should marry twenty husbands." That could be a dig at the flamboyant Duke of Alençon, notorious for playing every side of the conflicts in France and the Netherlands.

Most Shakespeare scholars see these suitors as just representing national stereotypes, rather than pointing to any specific individuals. As far back as the eighteenth century, however, Samuel Johnson noted in his edition of the play, "I am always inclined to believe, that Shakespeare has more allusions to particular facts and persons than his readers commonly suppose." Some scholars have tried, unconvincingly, to link these characters to personages in the 1590s; meanwhile, Don John, Casimir, and Alençon were all involved in the battles in the Netherlands, which consumed national politics in the summer of 1578.

THAT JUNE, ROGER NORTH joined Leicester in "taking the waters" in the thermal spa town of Buxton, north of Kenilworth—no doubt to prepare for the rigors of the summer progress. While they were there, Hatton sent a letter lamenting the queen was "found in continual and great melancholy," begging Leicester to intervene. Over the next few days, Leicester sent her several letters, which have since been lost to history. Whatever he said seems to have assuaged the queen's feelings. Hatton reported her mood had softened, and she was looking forward to his return. Popular historian Alison Weir writes, "Subtly, Elizabeth had set the tone for her future relationship with Leicester; in return for his behaving towards her as if nothing had happened and counting as her favorite, she was prepared to ignore his unfortunate marriage, as long as he put her needs first."

Amidst this unsettled mix of love and war, the queen set forth on her summer progress on July 11, 1578. In addition to escaping the city heat, the queen's summer progresses allowed her to both meet and impress her subjects, and nowhere was that more important than in East Anglia, late seat of the treacherous Duke of Norfolk. On her journey, Elizabeth rode in an open-sided carriage, her red curls visible to the crowds that hollered "God save the Queen!" as she passed. Leicester, too, set out from Buxton spa to meet with the entourage, eager to be reunited with the queen, and Roger North followed a few days later. The war in the Low Countries hung over the queen's first stop at Havering, as a messenger from William of Orange arrived with another request for aid, and Elizabeth gave him a royal harangue in front of Burghley. The next day, July 19, Leicester joined the court at last, brightening the queen's mood as the progress made its slow way across Essex.

On July 27, gentlemen from Cambridge University came to greet the queen with an oration, along with gifts of the New Testament with a red velvet binding, and perfumed embroidered gloves. Afterward, Elizabeth sat in on a philosophical dispute on "mercy versus severity in a prince," with, among others, Gabriel Harvey, a fellow at Pembroke College who would soon join Leicester's growing circle of writers—along with his friend, the budding poet Edmund Spenser. The next day, Roger North joined the party, with John dressed in a new wardrobe of clothes purchased in London. While John traveled back and forth between Kirtling and court over the next few weeks, there's no mention of Thomas North in either Roger's or John's accounts. Roger, however, did record Thomas's presence on his estate in July and September, so it's likely Thomas, too, accompanied the progress for part of its festivities—if he wasn't busy rehearsing for his play at Kirtling.

At the next stop at Melford Hall, another group joined the party— two ambassadors sent from the Alençon, who spent a long time in private conversation with the queen. There the old factionalism flared—this time directly involving Roger North. While dining with the French ambassadors, an edgy Elizabeth suddenly lashed out at her lord chamberlain, Sussex, reprehending him for the paltry spread of silver for her foreign guests. Stung by the attack, Sussex defended himself, saying he was sure the silver was as impressive as any progress he'd accompanied. Elizabeth silenced him and turned to Roger to ask him what he thought. Put on the spot, he agreed with Her Majesty that the spread was less than adequate. Sussex seethed at the affront, and later confronted North, furious that he hadn't taken his side. The bad blood continued for months, and Sussex even wrote Leicester, asking him to intervene; he became even angrier when the earl supported North instead.

Meanwhile, as the progress wended its way through Suffolk, Leicester and his fellow councilors tried in vain to get Elizabeth to act on the Netherlands. Elizabeth seemed more concerned with whether or not Alençon was sincere in his promises of marriage, writing Walsingham a desperate letter to demand to know the French duke's intentions. After years of skillfully manipulating the besotted princes of Europe, Elizabeth suddenly seemed sincerely interested in marriage—perhaps realizing this was her last serious chance, now that her doting Robin had moved on. The next day, seemingly panicked that Alençon was only toying with her, she finally promised the Dutch rebels a force of up to twelve thousand soldiers, accompanied by a £100,000 loan if they refused Alençon's rulership. But she had dawdled too long. The Dutch had already signed a treaty with Alençon, declaring him Defender of the Liberties of the Low Countries Against Spanish Tyranny, in exchange for a twelve-thousand-man army of his own.

By now, the queen had arrived in Norwich, where she was once again feted with orations and gifts, including a silver and gilt cup filled with

£100 of gold, golden spurs, and a velvet-lined casket with another £20 in gold. Sussex had commissioned six days of entertainments written by the poet Thomas Churchyard, who created a fantasia of gods and fairies, featuring the queen's favorite actor, Henry Goldingham. Even while Elizabeth was taking in all of these festivities, another group of French ambassadors joined the progress, assuring her in private that Alençon was indeed serious about his proposal for marriage. Elizabeth seemed giddy with the news, even giving one of the Frenchmen the gift of a gold chain, much to Leicester's consternation. The queen finally left Norwich on August 22, having achieved what she came for—a display of opulence and wealth that would be forever remembered in the city. As she left, Sussex begged leave to remove himself, all of the official entertainments having been performed.

Roger and John North also left the progress, hastening back to Kirtling to oversee final preparations for the queen's visit in ten days' time. As the queen's gentlemen ushers arrived to prepare the royal silver, Roger oversaw cartloads and hogsheads of food from London and the coast sent down into the larders. The court, meanwhile, lumbered through more great houses and their entertainments, including one show "featuring fairies," where the queen was presented with a "rich jewel" from her host. Finally, on the morning of September 1, 1578, the great mass of courtiers, horses, and servants came within sight of Kirtling at last.

WE MAKE OUR WAY to Kirtling, too, with a crow cawing in the chill as we push open the mossy gate leading to the Fairhaven estate. A bit of sun has crept through the clouds to illuminate a grassy field. Beyond a low stone wall flows a wide stream, which I realize suddenly is a moat around the estate, with a fountain at the far end spraying up water high into the air. Having abandoned our attempts to gain entry, we now follow a sign to a public footpath to get a better view, McCarthy and I walking together, and Galovski and Hosseini trailing behind. The landscape seems remarkably unchanged since Thomas North's time, with a cluster of stone barns in the middle distance and a fenced-in paddock up to our left.

We climb the slight rise, opening the gate into the paddock, where two horses graze farther up the hillside. We can now see Kirtling Tower behind the moat, next to a twentieth-century addition added by the Fairhaven family. "So the tallest part, which is clearly older, is the only part of Kirtling Hall that still exists from the Norths," McCarthy says. From our vantage, two handsome octagonal towers of red brick rise into the sky, with a crenelated gallery with three palladium windows between them. Back when the hall existed, it must have been an impressive sight, lording over the surrounding countryside with views in all directions.

Roger's guests arrived at this gatehouse, dusty from the road, in the early afternoon of September 1, 1578, marveling at the great gardens Roger had built, before riding inside to dismount in the courtyard. Once again, scholars from Cambridge were there to greet the queen with an oration and yet another gift—a "stately and fair cup," according to Churchyard. Servants unloaded the wagons, wearing tawny-colored livery with the North family crest—a crouching lion on an azure field with three fleurs-de-lis—on their arms, and gold chains to show off their patron's wealth. Meanwhile, famished courtiers descended on the banqueting house for the first of many feasts.

Roger had spent weeks gathering provisions, and now his guests devoured them, popping open hogsheads full of claret and beer and tucking into steaming plates of mutton, veal, lamb, and venison pasties, all overseen by a cook on loan from Leicester. "He spent an astronomical amount of money on the queen's visit," McCarthy says as we stand together in the horse paddock. "It was just ridiculous." Among other foodstuffs, Roger trucked in a cartload and two horse loads of oysters, slaughtered thirty-four pigs, and imported six cheeses from Holland. "They're serving every bird imaginable," McCarthy says, "not just geese and duck but swans, but everything." (Among other species, Roger's accounts list eighteen gulls, twenty-eight plovers, twenty-two partridges, and hundreds of pigeons.)

The following day, the queen no doubt hunted with the French ambassadors in the North family deer park, where Roger had built a new standing. That evening Roger treated the most distinguished guests to a private dinner in the manor house, with a menu of carp, sturgeon, beef, veal, lamb, and more birds, followed by dessert of apple, quince, and orange tarts and fritters. Instead of servants, gentlemen from the county humbly served as waiters. Following dinner, the queen sat in a corner of the hall talking with the ambassadors. A Spanish spy later reported that their voices dropped to a whisper as they began talking about the Alençon marriage. Later, the queen drew Leicester into a corner to talk as well, and as he left the chamber, he muttered in disgust to a fellow guest, "Suffice it that these Frenchmen want to marry the queen."

Despite the private drama, the visit was an overwhelming success for Roger, who acquitted himself well in his hospitality. "No whit behind any of the best," said Churchyard, "for a frank house, a noble heart, and well-ordered entertainment." Aside from the Cambridge oration, however, Churchyard doesn't elaborate on what that "entertainment" entailed. Nor does he mention Roger's own gift for the queen. Sometime before the festivities, Roger had secured a jewel for the cost of £120 ($67,285) to present to her during her visit to Kirtling. It would be strange if he didn't present it with some kind of grand entertainment—as Sidney had done with the necklace during "The Lady of May," and as other great houses had done with the various gilt cups, caskets, and jewels during their masques and fairy pageants. As he read about Roger's gift, McCarthy realized it was the last clue, cinching the performance of *The Merchant of Venice* at Kirtling.

IN ADDITION TO the casket and flesh-bond plots, *Merchant* has yet another subplot, about Antonio and Bassanio's friend, Lorenzo, who elopes with Shylock's daughter Jessica, taking with them a chest of her father's jewels. The abduction—based on another untranslated Italian tale, from Masuccio's 1550 *Il Novellino*—occurs at the same time Shylock is meeting the Christians for a dinner and a masque. The play builds toward the event for several scenes, and when Lorenzo finally arrives at Jessica's window, he tells her she has to dress in men's clothes to act as his torchbearer so her father doesn't recognize her.

Just as the couple is about to leave with Shylock's jewels in hand, however, Antonio suddenly arrives to tell them, "No masque tonight. The wind is come about." The change is so deflating, most scholars speculate that the masque scene did originally appear in the play; however, it was taken out in the adaptation that survives today. "It's a very Shakespearean scene, where a woman is dressed in disguise and has to fool her father," says McCarthy. "It's building towards this scene, and then they say 'No masque tonight'—it's the stupidest thing." The Al Pacino movie, in fact, stages the dinner anyway—heightening the contrast between the Jew and Christians together at the table—and makes sure to show Lorenzo opening the chest to display the jewels inside.

Placed in the context of the queen's progress, however, the scene suddenly makes sense. McCarthy realized excitedly that the original scene probably served the same purpose that masques did during other stops on Elizabeth's progress that year: to give a present to the queen—in this case, Roger North's £120 jewel. "It's like in Sidney's *Lady of May*, where a character gives a necklace to the queen, and a prop turns into the queen's gift," McCarthy says. What more dramatic a presentation than taking her gift out of a chest of jewels? In fact, more than any other Shakespeare play, *The Merchant of Venice* is obsessed with caskets and jewels—leading one critic to even suspect Shylock's whole character turns on a pun between Jew and jewel.

After Jessica escapes with Lorenzo, Shylock agonizes over a report that she sold a turquoise ring for a monkey. Later, Portia and her servant Nerissa both give rings to the men they plan to marry, as symbols of fidelity. After Antonio's ships predictably founder at sea, leaving him beholden to Shylock's bloody revenge, Portia, who is by far the smartest and most capable character, comes to the rescue. In the play's climax, she and Nerissa both cross-dress to disguise themselves as a lawyer and assistant at Antonio's trial, winning his freedom on a technicality: that Shylock can't take a pound of flesh without spilling a drop of blood, since that's not part of the deal.

The entire last act of the play turns on a conflict about the rings, which Portia and Nerissa trick their suitors into giving to them while they are disguised, before accusing them of infidelity once dressed as women again. By the end, the word "ring" has been mentioned thirty-five times in the play's last three scenes—perhaps a way of calling attention to Lord North's extravagant gift. And Queen Elizabeth would certainly have appreciated her stand-in Portia, wooed by multiple suitors, having one over on the men in the end.

In all, says McCarthy, *The Merchant of Venice* is one of the clearest examples of multiple streams of evidence all pointing in the same direction: toward a Thomas North play written for the queen's progress in 1578. It includes contemporary allusions, Plutarchan references, an Italian setting, a humanist message, and even a touch of Senecan revenge in Shylock's bloody scheme. "It's amazing how much it's a perfect match," he says. "I mean this is as rock solid as we can get."

THERE'S A NOTABLE GAP in McCarthy's analysis, however: nothing in Roger North's account book indicates he gave his brother money for a play that summer. In all, Roger paid the astronomical sum of £742 for the three-day event—more than $400,000 in today's money. The charges take up five pages, detailing vast quantities of food and drink, gifts for the queen's servants, and even 20 shillings for "keeping off wild fowl." But there are no payments for any players.

McCarthy speculates that perhaps Thomas wrote the play for Leicester's Men, instead. According to records of the company, however, the troupe performed in Maldon, forty miles south of Kirtling, on September 1. It's not inconceivable that the players could have traveled to Kirtling in a day in order to perform after supper on September 2—though for a company of players weighted down with theatrical equipment, that would have been quite a feat. They could have arrived, however, before the queen left Kirtling after dinner on September 3—performing their play that afternoon as a finale to her visit.

To explore that theory, I reach out to Laurie Johnson, a professor at the University of Southern Queensland in Australia, and an expert on Leicester's Men. After McCarthy shares some of his research on the play, Johnson writes back to say that he thinks it's "unlikely" that the troupe could have traveled to Kirtling that date. The distance seems too far to travel in so short a time—fifteen to twenty miles a day is more standard—and the itinerary is off the players' normal route. But "it is not impossible," he writes, saying he wouldn't reject the paper if it came to him for review. "I've noticed in the last couple of years an increasing number of reviewers who are inclined to reject submissions on the basis of only minor quibbles," he writes, adding that publication should be "in the interest of strengthening understanding rather than protecting orthodoxies or reputations." With that, he encourages McCarthy to push ahead to refine and publish his research.

Examining both Roger's and John's account books, McCarthy did find at least some evidence to connect Thomas with Leicester's Men that fall. In November, John accompanied his father, his uncle Thomas, and several other gentlemen to Mildenhall, Roger's newly acquired second estate. There, he reports, his father paid "the comedians of the earl of Leicester" 40 shillings for "making a comedy." Roger's household book confirms that payment "to my Lord of Leicester's players." The next day, Roger went back to Kirtling, while John and Thomas continued to a neighboring estate where they saw another comedy performed. Upon their return to Kirtling, Roger gave "my Lord of Leicester's players" another 40 shillings. Only on that occasion, he adds another payment: "my brother, 40 shillings." McCarthy doesn't think it's a coincidence that Roger gave Leicester's performers and Thomas the exact same amount on the same day. "Clearly, they were both performing a play together," he says.

Whatever the likelihood of an *Ur-Merchant* performed by Thomas North and Leicester's Men, Roger must have been elated at the success of his Kirtling entertainments as he continued to travel with the court back to London to finish out the queen's progress. Now that the French ambassadors had gone, the queen seemed back to her old self, sending a letter to Paris to say that while she'd received notice of Alençon's proposal of marriage, she would have to give it further thought before responding. Like a good Shakespearean comedy, however, the queen's progress did end in a marriage—though not one she would have condoned. Even as the queen made her way through the great houses of Essex, Leicester stole away to prepare his own home at Wanstead for the queen's arrival. Along with him, he took his friend Roger North, ostensibly to help with his preparations. The real reason for the trip, however, quickly became clear: Roger was to help witness yet another marriage, between Leicester and his secret wife, Lettice Knollys.

Apparently, Lettice's father wasn't happy with the clandestine Kenilworth nuptials, and had demanded they be married in public. That night, Roger and Leicester sat down to a dinner with Francis Knollys, Leicester's brother Ambrose, and Henry Herbert, the Earl of Pembroke. At seven the next morning, Roger met with Leicester's chaplain and walked with him to find the groom in a little gallery with a view of the gardens outside. There, the rest of the guests joined them, along with Lettice's brother Richard, to witness the simple ceremony. There was no time for a happy reception—that same day, the queen's advance servants arrived to prepare the house for her visit.

When Elizabeth arrived at Wanstead two days later, on September 23, the court celebrated the official end of the progress, with a feast thrown by Leicester in the queen's honor. None of Leicester's close friends and family, of course, mentioned the secret wedding that had taken place there just days before. Lettice likely even waited upon the queen before Elizabeth boarded her barge back to Greenwich that afternoon, none the wiser. Another successful summer progress was over. The queen's troubles with her neighbors abroad, however, were just beginning anew. When England did finally get drawn into war, however, it wasn't across the English Channel to the east, but across the Irish channel to the west. As McCarthy continued to research Thomas North's biography, he discovered it was a war North would directly take part in—fighting alongside one of the greatest poets of the age. And that poet, he found, may have had an even more personal connection with North.

Chapter Twelve

ONCE MORE UNTO THE BREACH

(1578–1582)

Once more unto the breach, dear friends, once more;
Or close the wall up with our English dead.

—*Henry V*

dmund Spenser, by all accounts, grew up the humble son of a London cloth merchant but showed early promise for letters, rising through the ranks at Cambridge's Pembroke College to earn a master's degree in 1576 at age twenty-four. There, he became friends with Gabriel Harvey, the young rhetoric professor who presented his poems to the queen during her 1578 progress. Spenser burst onto the literary scene a year later with the publication of *The Shepheardes Calender*, a collection of a dozen eclogues—short pastoral dialogues—published at Harvey's urging. One for each month of the year, the poems take the form of shepherds philosophizing on love and life, and sometimes real-life personages as well. The poem for April, for example, includes a flowery elegy to "fair Elisa" the "queen of the shepherds," an obvious stand-in for Queen Elizabeth, given by a shepherd named Hobbinol, who represents his friend Harvey.

The collection is best known, however, for its bookend verses, "January" and "December," which both feature a shepherd boy named Colin Clout—a thinly veiled version of the author himself—describing his unrequited love for a "country lass" named Rosalinde. "I love the lass (alas why do I love?)" Spenser writes, "She deigns not my good will, but doth reprove, and of my rural music holdeth scorn." A note included with the poem explains that Rosalinde is a "feigned name, which being well ordered, will bewray (reveal) the very name of his love and mistress."

For centuries, Spenser scholars worked to uncover the secret identity of Spenser's beloved by reordering the letters in the name. Over the years, they tried Rosa Lynde, Rose Daniel, and Rose Dinlei—the last after a family in Lancashire, based on a note in the "June" eclogue that says the poet wooed his Rosalind in the "North country" and the "North parts." Problem was, none of these imagined women were found to exist. In a 1908 essay, German scholar Percy Long demolishes the arguments one by one, lamenting that "in three-hundred years, no real person has been adduced by Spenser's Rosalind." After carefully considering all of the evidence, he then proposes his own surprising solution for the riddle of Spenser's beloved: Thomas North's daughter, Elizabeth North.

If you reorder the letters in Rosalinde, Long explains, they form Elisa Nord—the first name a shortened form of Elizabeth (which Spenser already used for the queen in the April eclogue), and the last the French word for "North." Seen that way, Long argues, the "North parts" is a punning reference to the North family manor at Kirtling. Elsewhere in the poem, Spenser says Rosalinde lives in a "neighbor-town" to Hobbinol's, in "the hills"—an accurate description of the relationship of Cambridge, which sits on flat land, to Kirtling, which oversees it from a high ridge.

In another note, Spenser admits that in spite of Colin's poetic license, Rosalinde isn't actually a simple country girl, but actually "a gentlewoman of no mean house, nor endowed with any vulgar and common gifts of nature and manners"—an apt portrayal of Elizabeth, who was raised in the cultured North family, and attended dinner parties in London with gentlemen and nobles. Percy Long stops there, with Spenser pining after Thomas North's daughter in the hills of Cambridgeshire. But when McCarthy first came across the reference, he immediately drew a connection to another Rosalind: the heroine of Shakespeare's *As You Like It*.

MOST SHAKESPEARE FANS would agree that *As You Like It* is not his finest comedy. With a rambling cast of characters carrying on languorous conversations against a woodland backdrop, the play is like a movie by Robert Altman or Richard Linklater, where plot takes a backseat to character and dialogue. What elevates the play above others—so much so that it's some Bardolaters' favorite—is its leading lady, Rosalind. From the moment she comes onstage, Rosalind takes over the play with sweet positivity and effervescent wit.

While other Shakespearean heroines like Portia and Beatrice hold court with intelligence and poise, only Rosalind makes her wit look effortless. "In Beatrice, it lays about us like lightning, dazzling but also alarming," says nineteenth-century critic Anna Jameson, "while the wit of Rosalind bubbles up and sparkles like a living fountain, refreshing all around." Rosalind has since been pegged as the prototype for later-day plucky heroines from Elizabeth Bennet to Jo March, remaining clear-eyed and idealistic even while carried away by her passions. If anything, her appeal has grown over the past century, among critics who continue to gush over her character with words like "enchanting," "empowering," "intelligent," "delightful," and "brave."

As the play begins, Rosalind's father, Duke Senior, has been banished by his younger brother, Duke Frederick, and now lives in the Forest of Arden with a Robin Hood–esque band of loyal followers. Meanwhile, the play's hero, Orlando, has also been denied his inheritance by his older brother Oliver, who sets him up to be killed at a wrestling match. Instead, Orlando wins, meets-cute with Rosalind, and the two fall in love. When the evil Frederick jealously banishes Rosalind, too, she heads off to Arden, disguised as a man, to search for her father.

Orlando similarly leaves home, pining after Rosalind, whom he meets in the forest, somehow not recognizing her and thinking she really is a man instead. When he confesses his lovesickness, she tells him the only cure is to woo her as if she were Rosalind. The rest of the play alternates between the strange flirtation between these lovers, and disputations about love, life, time, and nature among various shepherds, foresters, and other characters.

The play is loosely based on a story in Chaucer's *Canterbury Tales*, "The Tale of Gamelyn," which also features a younger son cheated by his brother, a wrestling match, and an exiled band of merry men. The main recognized source for the play, however, is a short novel published by Thomas Lodge in 1590 called, what else, *Rosalynde*. While many of the character names are different, the story contains all of the essential elements of *As You Like It*. The story even contains a remark in the Introduction, "If you like it, so," from which scholars believe Shakespeare took the name of his play, which first appeared in 1600. While Lodge's novel would seem to preclude an earlier source play by North, that doesn't stop McCarthy from surmising that, just like *Pandosto* and *The Winter's Tale*, *Rosalynde* and *As You Like It* could both be based on North's play.

In fact, *As You Like It* was one of McCarthy's earliest discoveries tying the plays to North's biography. When he first tried Googling "Thomas North" and "Shakespeare," all he got were endless pages about Shakespeare borrowing from *Plutarch's Lives*. He began trying names of other family members instead. When he plugged in "Elizabeth North," up popped Percy Long's one-hundred-year-old Spenser essay. The fact that a scholar had identified Thomas North's daughter as a Rosalinde was like a bolt of lightning—immediately associating Elizabeth North with one of the most beloved heroines of the canon.

"That's when I knew, okay, this was it," he says. "I hadn't read a word of *The Shepheardes Calender*. I was coming at it from a totally different angle." As McCarthy continued researching, however, he found multiple scholars speculating that Shakespeare used Spenser's poem collection as a source for *As You Like It*, with a heroine of the same name, and a similarly chatty cast of shepherds debating philosophy in a pastoral setting. If Rosalinde really was Elizabeth North, however, that would mean Spenser wooed Thomas North's daughter. What if, McCarthy thought, North had written his own play to memorialize the courtship? Only, instead of making Rosalinde an offstage heartbreaker, North made his Rosalind the central character—a witty and vivacious young woman who schools the hero on what it really means to love.

THE MORE MCCARTHY learned about Spenser, the more the theory made sense. The poet was a big fan of Chaucer, even putting him into *The Shepheardes Calender*, which helped explain why North would use the "Tale of Gamelyn" as a source for his play. And in a recent edition of *As You Like It*, McCarthy discovered, editor Juliet Dusinberre contended that another story in Chaucer, "The Wife of Bath's Tale," also influenced Shakespeare's play, even including the line, spoken by a strong-willed woman: "As you liketh, it suffices me." So maybe *Rosalynde* didn't inspire the title of Shakespeare's play, McCarthy thought—North got the line from Chaucer, and then Lodge included it as a clever nod to his source.

That wasn't the only literary allusion tying *As You Like It* back to Spenser. The poet was also a fan of Italian epic romances, such as Ariosto's *Orlando Furioso*, which would explain why North named Spencer's alter ego Orlando. And it would also explain a curious detail in the play, in which Orlando hangs poems on trees to sing his beloved's praises. "O Rosalind," he says, "these trees shall be my books, and in their bark my thoughts, I'll character, that every eye which in this forest looks shall see thy virtue." Scholars have noted the similarity to *Orlando Furioso*, in which the knight Orlando discovers the name of his beloved and *her* new lover carved together into trees, eventually causing him to go raging mad.

Spenser even copies that detail in *The Shepheardes Calender*, only it's Colin carving Rosalinde's name into the trees, saying, "I soon would learn these woods, to wail my woe, and teach the trees, their trickling tears to shed." In effect, says McCarthy, North is putting the *alter egos* of Spenser and his daughter into the same circumstances Spenser put Colin and Rosalinde into in his own poem, even mirroring Colin's language. In *As You Like It*, Rosalind is hardly impressed with Orlando's verses, which contain such clunkers as: "Sweetest nut hath sourest rind; such a nut is Rosalind." Telling her cousin about them, Rosalind deadpans, "Some of them had in them more feet than the verses would bear." That detail, too, fits with *The Shepheardes Calender*, in which Spenser's Rosalinde also "holdeth scorn" for Colin's "rural music"—his pastoral poetry.

At the end of his poem, Spenser melodramatically says goodbye to the world, writing, "After Winter cometh timely death," and asking his friend Hobbinol to "tell Rosalind that her Colin bids her adieu." In *As You Like It*, meanwhile, Orlando says something similar to Rosalind-in-disguise, telling her that if Rosalind doesn't want him, he will die. "Men have died from time to time," she responds cheekily, "and worms have eaten them, but not for love." McCarthy sees that as another swipe at Spenser's overly romantic verse. "It's a hysterical line," McCarthy says, "but you don't really get it unless you know that's what Spenser says—

that I would die for your love—and she's saying, that's the stupidest thing I've ever heard. It's showing that she likes him, and flirts with him, but she does mock his poetry."

McCarthy speculates that Thomas North, too, liked Spenser, who would have been twenty-six in 1578, and appreciated his attentions toward his eighteen-year-old daughter. Of all Shakespeare's heroes, Orlando is among the most noble, and only slightly less witty than Benedick and Petruchio. "He does tease his poetry, which Eliza North probably did as well," he says. "But he also thought he would have been a suitable match." In fact, McCarthy says, if Spenser did woo Elizabeth North, it's likely he met her during the queen's progress of 1578. McCarthy uncovered an anecdote told separately by two seventeenth-century historians, that Spenser, too, presented his poems to the queen during the progress, receiving from her a reward.

Searching for any other connection between Spenser and Kirtling, McCarthy found another clue: a reference to a receipt in Spenser's hand for the rental of a parsonage at Kirtling that November 1578 for a bishop for whom he was working at the time. And, amazingly, Spenser even seems to reference *The Jew of Venice* in a letter he wrote to Harvey the following year, signing off, "He that is found bound unto thee in more obligations than any merchant in Italy to any Jew there."

When I later read *The Shepheardes Calender*, I came across a clue of my own that seems to support McCarthy's theory. In his poem for the month of "July," Spenser says of Rosalind that "love then in lion's house did dwell." Percy Long speculates that's a reference to the Earl of Leicester, whom Spenser refers to as a lion in other works. That wouldn't match his identification of Elizabeth North with Rosalinde, however, unless she was living at Kenilworth, Wanstead, or Leicester House. I then remember the North's family crest, prominently displayed on the livery of Roger North's servants during the queen's summer progress: three fleurs-de-lis surrounding a crouching lion with his claws raised in the air.

As You Like It, in fact, contains a lion as well. In a hasty denouement to the play, Orlando's brother Oliver comes to the Forest of Arden, where Orlando saves him from a lion offstage. When he returns, Rosalind cries out, "How it grieves me to see thee wear thy heart in a scarf!" When

Orlando says it's only his arm, she says, "I thought thy heart had been wounded with the claws of a lion"—perhaps a chiding reference to the line in Spenser's poem comparing North's daughter to a lion.

In his plagiarism research, McCarthy had connected those lines with North's own writing, with "wounds of the claws of a lion" in *Plutarch's Lives*. The phrase even appears in a passage describing an Athenian king's infatuation with a courtesan, with whom he is so captivated that the other nobles refer to him as being wounded by a beast. That would make the line in the play a double pun, associating the "lion" in Spenser's poem with those in *As You Like It* and *Plutarch*. If so, it's one more piece of evidence tying the play to the Norths and Kirtling Hall. Once again, says McCarthy, multiple references, both literary and historical, point toward the same conclusion: that Spenser's wooing of Thomas North's daughter inspired *As You Like It*. "I mean, every play is part of North's biography," McCarthy says. "Anything that's big and important in his life finds its way into the plays."

If Spenser did ever woo Elizabeth North, he didn't ultimately succeed. The following October, he married another woman, Maccabaeus Childe, in Westminster. Elizabeth herself was married years later, in 1587, to Thomas Stuteville, a gentleman farmer from a neighboring estate. *As You Like It*, however, offers a happier ending to Rosalind and Orlando. After she has tutored him in the ways of love, Rosalind engineers a country wedding in which she marries Orlando alongside three other couples.

DESPITE THAT HAPPY ENDING, however, McCarthy reads between the lines to detect a budding conflict in the play—between Thomas North and his brother Roger. Analyses of *As You Like It* often include a discussion of the Elizabethan custom of primogeniture, whereby the firstborn son of a family receives the lion's share of wealth passed down from his father—and the second son is left with the scraps. The North family may have been an extreme example of the practice, with Edward North giving Thomas less than even the servants in his will, but many second sons were similarly disenfranchised.

"The psychological and socio-economic consequences of primogeniture for younger sons (and for daughters) seem to have been considerable," writes Louis Adrian Montrose, forcing them to live in a state of dependency upon their sibling just through an accident of birth. Numerous second sons wrote poems and pamphlets vehemently decrying the practice, as Thomas Wilson did in his *The State of England* in 1600: "My elder brother forsooth must be my master. He must have all, and all the rest that which the cat left on the malt heap, perhaps some small annuity during his life or what please our elder brother's worship to bestow upon us if we please him."

In other words, the younger son is at his brother's mercy, as Orlando is to Oliver in *As You Like It*, when he withholds his inheritance money. The reverse happens with the other sibling pair, as the younger Duke Frederick usurps the realm from his older brother, Duke Senior. The theme of brotherly conflict would recur repeatedly in Shakespeare's plays, including the English histories, *Hamlet*, *King Lear*, and *The Tempest*. Shakespeare, however, was the oldest of six children, with no known tension between them.

But conflict did occur in the lives of the North brothers, McCarthy contends, providing another link to the plays. He bases that speculation on the evidence in Roger North's household account book, in which he records wages of those living and working on the estate every quarter. In June 1576, Roger doesn't list his brother or family members on the estate. That December, Roger pays the £46 to lease his brother a "house and household stuff." While the North's biographer had seen in that a present from Roger to his brother, McCarthy sees the opposite—a sign Roger banished Thomas from the family home, sending him to another house instead. Thomas and his family are back on the estate as of midsummer 1578, through the following summer. But by September 1579, Thomas is once again absent, even though his family remains—the same situation as in *As You Like It*, in which Duke Senior is banished from the estate, while his daughter stays behind.

I'm not sure I agree. To me, the notations in Roger North's book seem far less clear, and far more fluid, than McCarthy's narrative would suggest. During the times Thomas isn't listed, he could just as well be living in London, pursuing his writing career, while his family stayed back on the Cambridgeshire estate. More tellingly, Roger continues to pay Thomas's annuity throughout this period—from the spring of 1576 all the way through December 1579. While the payments vary, they seem to average £30 to £40 annually, as well as numerous gifts for clothing and transport. Overall, the impression from Roger's accounts is of a generous lord—not some miserly Oliver or Duke Frederick.

Thomas North, however, didn't need to be physically banished from his brother's estates to feel the sting that comes from being a second son. Regardless of where he lived, it must have been humiliating for Thomas, at age forty-five, to beg loans from his brother, while Roger gambled away the equivalent of Thomas's entire annuity on a single night of cards; or to go hat in hand for shillings whenever he or his wife needed riding charges to London; or to see his son work in service, even while Roger spent hundreds of pounds sending his own son on a grand Italian tour.

That could be enough for North to cry, like Orlando does to Oliver: "The courtesy of nations allows you my better, in that you are the firstborn, but the same tradition takes not away my blood, were there twenty brothers betwixt us. I have as much of my father in me as you." And it could also be enough for him to concoct a revenge fantasy where he turns the table on his inherited familial order. By the end of their time in the forest, Orlando has rescued Oliver from the lion's claws, and his repentant older brother has restored his inheritance. Duke Senior also sees his lands restored, and by marrying Rosalind, Orlando becomes his heir—set to inherit a much vaster fortune than Oliver ever received.

"I must confess," Thomas Wilson writes in *The State of England*, being a second son "doth us good someways, for it makes us industrious to apply ourselves to letters or arms, whereby many time we become my master elder brothers' masters, or at least their betters in honor and reputation." Whatever his relationship with Roger, Thomas North must have also secretly harbored that hope.

IF CONFLICT DID EXIST between the two brothers, it could have started, once again, over *Arden of Faversham*. In 1577, London printer Edward White published *A Cruel Murder Done in Kent*, the play some scholars believe to be an earlier version of the Alice Arden story. If that's the case, then Roger couldn't have been too happy about seeing his family's dirty laundry aired for all to see—especially on the eve of his own triumph: hosting the queen on the progress the following summer. Either way, he must have been mortified to see the same story told in intimate detail in the publication that year of the two-volume *Chronicles of England, Scotland, and Ireland* by Raphael Holinshed.

At the same time, it must have pleased his enemies to see him embarrassed. After Sussex was publicly humiliated for his insufficient silverware during Elizabeth's 1578 progress, he continued to blame Roger North for shaming him in front of the queen and continued to speak ill about Roger at court. That October, Elizabeth stepped in, bringing Sussex into her audience chamber and imploring him to drop the feud. While he was conciliatory with the queen, he told others that he had to keep away from court lest he turn violent toward North, "which perhaps may offend her Majesty, whereof I would be very sorry, and yet my honor driveth me to it."

While there's no record of how the feud was resolved, a few months later, on March 3, 1579, Sussex's troupe of players acted out a masque called *The History of Murderous Michael* at Whitehall, "in the presence of the queen." I'm surprised to discover that E. K. Chambers, the early-twentieth-century historian who wrote the definitive history of the Elizabethan stage, speculates that perhaps this play, too, was an early version of *Arden of Faversham*—the title referring to Arden's servant Michael.

While Michael played only a bit part in the murder, amateur historian Richard Bradshaw writes in a recent essay, "Roger North's half-sister could hardly have been presented as the most murderous character in a play presented at Queen Elizabeth's court, where safety lay in subtlety." He speculates instead that perhaps the play was enacted by Sussex's company specifically "in an effort to subtly ridicule Roger North and the Earl of Leicester."

When I came across Bradshaw's essay in a book about Thomas Arden, I felt a bit like how McCarthy must have felt when he came across the essay by Percy Long. While researching a completely different tack, I neverthe-less found evidence to support McCarthy's argument that there was some kind of tension between Roger and Thomas North in 1579. Incredibly, Bradshaw further surmises that the playwright whom Sussex hired to write *Murderous Michael* was none other than Thomas Lodge, the son of a former mayor of London—who years later would go on to write the novel *Rosalynde*, about the brotherly feud at the heart of *As You Like It*.

Adding further credence to the theory, Bradshaw says that Leicester took quick revenge against the master of revels, Thomas Blagrave, summoning him to Leicester House for a private meeting with Sussex. A few months later, Blagrave was replaced as master of revels, forced to serve out the rest of his days as a clerk; Lodge's career, too, struggled for the next few years. Those facts are hardly conclusive—Blagrave was also guilty of financial mismanagement, which could also explain his demotion. But Bradshaw thinks perhaps Sussex had used his position to stage a masque dramatizing—or even parodying—the Arden murder before the queen, and Leicester had taken out his anger on the revels master for staging the play without his knowledge. Such a turn of events would justify Roger's anger toward Thomas, and perhaps explain why Thomas was living away from Kirtling that year.

THE THEORY WOULD also fit in with a wider conflict playing out between Leicester and Sussex—the return of Alençon as Elizabeth's suitor. By now, the duke had completely flubbed his Low Countries adventure, losing most of his army. Don John of Austria, meanwhile, caught camp fever in October 1578, passing the baton of office to his cousin, Alexander Farnese, the Duke of Parma, before taking to his bed and dying. Any relief the Protestants felt, however, disappeared when Parma proved an even more brilliant tactician, quickly driving the rebels north into Holland and Zeeland, known now as the United Provinces. As Alençon huddled with his ragtag army, Elizabeth feared his brother, the king of France, might intervene, igniting a conflict that could result in one of the two Catholic kingdoms gaining permanent control of the Netherlands.

At that moment, Elizabeth contacted Alençon, whom she nicknamed "Monsieur," telling him she was open to his proposal of marriage at last. It was a shrewd move; if Philip knew England was allied with Alençon, he would think twice about striking. But Elizabeth had personal considerations as well. Now forty-five, she had reached the end of her childbearing years, and Alençon was her last chance to marry. Alençon sent his personal representative, Jean de Simier, in January 1579 to woo Elizabeth on his behalf. His effect on Elizabeth was electric. She tittered like a schoolgirl as he poured sugared praises on her beauty, and daringly stole into her bedchamber to snatch a bedcap to send back to his master. In a play on his name, Elizabeth gave him the simian nickname "monkey," and carried a jewel-encrusted book from Alençon wherever she went.

Burghley and Sussex were thrilled, while Leicester and his allies turned their noses up in disgust—once again splitting the Privy Council into factions. The conflict spilled out into public, as preachers began giving sermons against the marriage, only to be quickly forbidden by Elizabeth. By June, Alençon proposed visiting England incognito to woo her in person, a move vehemently opposed by Leicester. It's at this point, many historians believe, that Simier struck back. Having heard the whispers about Leicester's private marriage with Lettice, Simier now told the queen, who was predictably furious. Even while Leicester was publicly advocating against her own marriage, he was enjoying his own— humiliatingly taking place just days before she herself was entertained at Wanstead. Elizabeth considered confining Leicester to the Tower, before sentencing him to house arrest at Greenwich instead. According to one story, she even "boxed Lettice's ears" in front of the whole court. As her fury relented, Leicester was let out of his rooms; Lettice was banned from court for a decade.

Simier's gambit had worked. Elizabeth now invited Alençon to visit, the duke arriving at Greenwich and moving into a tented pavilion on the grounds. Of course, the entire city knew he was there. John North wrote in his diary, simply, "Monsieur came to court this evening." Meeting him at last, the queen was pleasantly surprised: he was not nearly as ugly as she'd been told—and gracious and charming as well. "I have never in my life seen a creature more agreeable to me," she later declared. The couple enjoyed sunset dinners, walks in the gardens, and a court ball in which Elizabeth waved extravagantly to Alençon, hidden behind a curtain, while she showed off her dancing skills.

Impotent to sway the queen, Leicester was soon "cursing the French and greatly incensed against Sussex," according to the Spanish ambassador, "as are all of Leicester's dependents." He pleaded privately with Elizabeth, before leaving court in disgust as others fought on in his absence. One hot August day during Alençon's visit, Leicester's nephew Philip Sidney was playing tennis when Sussex protégé Edward de Vere, Earl of Oxford, tried to force his way onto the court. The two quarreled, with Oxford calling Sidney a "puppy," as the French delegation looked on from the gallery. Sidney returned the insult, then stormed off, waiting for Oxford to challenge him to a duel. Hearing of the incident, the queen called in Sidney to put a stop to it, scolding him about the respect he must show his social betters. Alençon left two days later, accompanied by great sighs from the queen.

McCarthy scoured the records to figure out where Thomas North was during all of this drama. On January 13, 1579, Roger North records a payment to Thomas of £8 for "going to London." On the same line, he records 2 shillings for "apparel to minstrels" and another 2 shillings "to player"—the second time he records a payment to his brother next to one for theater performers. Two months later, Thomas was apparently still in the city, as his nephew John records a supper in Westminster on March 25 "in the room of my uncle," implying Thomas had taken lodgings there. He also seems to be living beyond his means, as several times John lent his uncle money. That fall, Roger twice sent Thomas his pension through servants, again implying he was away from Kirtling.

There was good reason for Thomas to be spending so much time in London: after five years of work, he was finally readying his magnum opus, *Plutarch's Lives*, for publication. A notice in the Stationers' Register that April 6 announces that North licensed "a booke in English called Plutarks Lyves" to publisher Thomas Vautrollier, who had set up a press in Blackfriars. Preparing a tome as large as North's for publication would have taken many months of typesetting and proofing by his publisher.

While he was there, one of North's editors writes, North spent his time rubbing elbows with the literati at Leicester House, situated on the Strand between Westminster and Blackfriars. The house served as a sort of literary salon for Leicester's ever-changing stable of poets, essayists, artists, and foreign guests—including his sister Mary Sidney, her nephew Philip Sidney, the astrologist John Dee, and the young Italian linguist John Florio. Rounding out the group were Leicester's new poets, Gabriel Harvey and Edmund Spenser, who was finishing up *The Shepheardes Calender* and getting ready to embark upon his great new epic, *The Faerie Queene.*

All the while, Leicester's protégés continued to try to influence the queen. In August 1579, a Norfolk Puritan named John Stubbs published a pamphlet warning against attempts by the French, "the scum of Europe," to seduce Elizabeth as Satan tempted Eve. He even argued that Alençon must be up to nefarious purposes for wanting to marry an older woman. Elizabeth commanded Stubbs's right hand be cut off for writing such a "lewd, seditious book." One November morning, the crowd gasped as a cleaver was driven through his wrist with the whack of a heavy mallet. The now ironically named Stubbs managed to pull off his hat and croak, "God save the Queen!" before fainting. Elizabeth realized only too late the display was a blunder that—like her sister's burnings of Protestants years ago—only galvanized the public against her. But that wasn't the last anti-Alençon tract that emerged from Leicester's literary factory.

Around the same time, Spenser wrote an even more pointed allegory, circulated only in manuscript, called *Mother Hubberds Tale.* It told of an ape, aided by a crafty fox, who stole a crown from a sleeping lion and ruled his kingdom, filling it with foreign beasts. Most scholars agree this is a commentary on Alençon—represented by Elizabeth's "monkey," Simier—and aided by the foxlike Burghley, supplanting the lion-like Leicester in the queen's favor. (Some have also pointed out the similarities with North's *Doni*, which may have inspired the tale.)

No guesswork was needed for an open letter written to the queen by Philip Sidney that fall. It argued rationally, even elegantly, against the queen's marriage to "Monsieur" on the grounds that she would lose the support of her faithful Protestant citizens. The letter is a masterful essay, punctuated with examples of noble English monarchs like Henry V, and villainous ones like her own sister Mary. In spite of the sense it made—or perhaps because of it—the queen castigated the young courtier, forcing him away from London. Even so, the propaganda seemed to be working. When the Privy Council voted on the marriage, eight councilors sided against it, with only five for it. In November, she signed a marriage contract with Alençon anyway, formally giving her two months to persuade her subjects to go along with the deal.

WITH ALL HE HAD learned about Thomas North, McCarthy knew he *must* have lent his pen to Leicester's cause as well. Searching for clues, he found a listing in the Revels Accounts for a court performance by Leicester's Men of a play described only as "a history." It was canceled, however, because "her majesty could not come to hear it"—reminiscent of the canceled performances at Kenilworth. The company again performed a "history" on January 6, perhaps the same rescheduled play. While there's no evidence North wrote it, any number of plays from North's Plutarchan period could fit that description, McCarthy thought, including the *Henry VI* plays, which warned against a disastrous French marriage.

Whatever his involvement, the kingdom's mood turned away from the French marriage by early 1580. After Alençon and Simier departed, the spell over Elizabeth was lifted, and she began to see more clearly the division her flirtations were causing. Her two-month deadline passed without any action. Even so, she refused to forgive Leicester, perhaps hurting North's chances for recognition as he unveiled his greatest accomplishment. This time, North dedicated his great work to Queen Elizabeth herself. "For who is fitter to give countenance to so many great states than such an high and mighty Princess?" he wrote on January 16.

A week later, he added a postscript to his readers, urging them to appreciate the power of Plutarch's stories. "All other learning is private, fitter for universities than cities, fuller of contemplation than experience," North wrote. "Whereas stories are fit for every place, reach to all persons, service for all times," he added, "as it is better to see learning in noble men's lives than to read it in philosopher's writings." The book—more than one thousand pages long—was breathtaking in its scope, with twenty-eight paired histories of its Greek and Roman subjects. North's lively, readable style made it a popular success, attracting a broad cross-section of the literate public to its tales.

Once again, however, North's timing was off. With his patron, Leicester, out of favor, North couldn't expect to win the ears of Elizabeth and her counselors. At the same time, McCarthy began to speculate, North did something to further hurt his chances. Though Elizabeth had put the Alençon marriage on hold, she hadn't broken the betrothal contract.

That June, Elizabeth's counselors received terrifying news from overseas: Philip II was preparing to invade Portugal. It's hard to overstate just how much that would upset the balance of power in Europe—as Spain would now get access to Portugal's spice routes, and a launching pad to invade England as well. "It will be hard to withstand the King of Spain now," Elizabeth is purported to have said. She sent out fresh feelers to Alençon to renew their courtship, inviting him back to England once more.

On the very same day, Roger paid his brother the precise amount of £6 13s. 4d., equivalent to the archaic currency of 10 marks, the same amount paid for a play at court. "It's just a screwy amount of money," McCarthy says, "but that's the exact amount you give to someone who produces a play in court, down to the penny." A few weeks later, Roger followed that up with another payment for £3 6s. 7d., rounding the total amount to £10. "That's the reward that they get when the play is performed," McCarthy notes. And once again, on the same line that he records the payment, he separately records a payment of 40 shillings to Leicester's Men—the same amount he has paid them several times for performances at Kirtling.

Roger might have paid Thomas that money for other reasons—the most obvious being his £10 midsummer pension, though he had never broken it up into payments like that any other time. In McCarthy's mind, however, this was clear evidence that Roger paid Thomas to produce a play on behalf of his friend Leicester, to be performed by Leicester's Men at The Theatre. He even has a guess what the play might have been: *Henry VI, Part 1*—the most virulently anti-French play in the canon— which features the witch-like Joan of Arc and the mocking portrayal of the cowardly fifteenth-century Duke of Alençon.

"It's so anti-French, anti-Catholic, anti-Alençon that a lot of people thought that Shakespeare didn't write it," McCarthy says. "He wouldn't be this xenophobic and Francophobic and nasty, they said—but yes, he would, if Leicester or his brother were encouraging him to write that." Of course, that's also the play that lionizes Leicester's ancestor Talbot as the conquering hero of France, only to see him fall to the machinations of bickering royal counselors. A play stirring up the citizenry of London against the vile French, after all, could be just the thing to catch the conscience of the queen—and put the Alençon marriage back on ice. But it could also risk dramatic repercussions upon its author. "As North always does, it went far over the top of anything else," McCarthy says. "Queen Elizabeth just said, 'I've had enough.'"

As THE DRAMA OVER the Alençon marriage was playing out at home, a far more dangerous drama was unfolding overseas. After all of England's worries over a Catholic invasion, the attack finally happened in July 1579, when a disaffected Irish nobleman named James Fitzmaurice Fitzgerald landed a crew of some one hundred soldiers on Ireland's Dingle Bay. England had maintained a tenuous hold over its island neighbor since Henry VIII's time, but only truly dominated the Pale, a slice of territory surrounding Dublin. Supported by Spain and the pope, Fitzmaurice fortified the rocky outcropping of Smerwick and prepared to raise the country against English rule. Only a month later, he died in a raid; the spark he lit, however, was taken up by his cousin, Gerald Fitzgerald, Earl of Desmond, who launched what is now known as the Desmond Rebellion.

After initial attempts to quell the uprising failed, the Privy Council sent two thousand troops across the Irish Channel the following July under Lord Deputy Arthur Lord Grey. Accompanying him was a new secretary: Edmund Spenser. The poet's biographers agree Spenser didn't go to Ireland willingly—but was essentially banished by Elizabeth and Burghley over his caricatures in *Mother Hubberds Tale*. "Leicester, finding himself in a tight place, sacrificed his young admirer," writes Spenserian scholar Edwin Greenlaw, who speculates Leicester was more than willing to let Spenser go to Ireland if it took the heat off him.

A similar fate, McCarthy suspects, befell Thomas North as well. That August, Leicester wrote to Burghley about the Irish situation, and in the same letter added a postscript about Thomas North: "I am requested by my Lord North's brother to beseech your Lord for your favor towards him in his book he is to pass," presumably referring to *Plutarch's Lives*. "He is a very honest gentleman and hath many a good thing in him, which are drowned only by poverty." Burghey initially responded by commending North, "whom I think truly well of for many good parts in him," and saying he would advocate with the queen for a £10 annuity. A month later, however, Burghley and the Privy Council appointed Thomas captain of two hundred troops bound for Ireland. Perhaps it was North's choice to go to war, seeing military service as an opportunity to emerge from his brother's shadow. But reading between the lines of Leicester and Burghley's cordiality, McCarthy surmises that Thomas may not have gone on his own accord. "Leicester and Roger are getting him to write dangerous plays," he says. "Stubbs got his hand cut off, Sidney was banished from court, and Spenser and North were sent to Ireland."

For once, at least, North wasn't poor, as he led two hundred footmen from London to the port city of Chester, supported by £100 ($59,760) to feed and transport his men. Upon arrival in Ireland, he could look forward to a captain's salary of £36 ($21,510) a month—nearly as much as he received from his brother in a year. He arrived in Dublin on November 10—coincidentally one of the most momentous days of the war. A new force of more than six hundred Spanish and Italian mercenaries had landed at Smerwick to join with the Irish allies, and Grey and the still-loyal Irish lords raced across the island to meet them. Spenser most likely witnessed thousands of English troops surround and bombard the fort. According to some reports, Grey promised to let the defenders go free if they surrendered. When they did, however, English soldiers overran them, butchering indiscriminately. After the massacre, they hung any surviving Irish men and women on gibbets overlooking the sea. The assault was a shocking display of brutality, living in infamy as one of the worst abuses perpetrated by English soldiers in any war.

By the time North heard about the bloody business, he was already on the move to Dundalk, a seaside town on the northern edge of the English Pale. North never got a chance to try himself in battle, however. Returning to Dublin, Grey ordered the "cashing of some bands," including North's, to fill the ranks of the depleted units from battles in the south. On December 16, North and three other captains were honorably discharged—and their pay slashed. Barely a month into his Irish adventure, North was now a man without a band, with only a soldier's pension of £11 a month to support himself in an unknown land. North stayed in Dublin, where he began working in the service of the "governor"— presumably Grey himself. There, he would have seen Spenser, who was continuing work on *The Faerie Queene*, his epic allegory about Elizabeth Gloriana, the Virgin Queen. North, McCarthy thinks, also used the time to focus on literary pursuits—working on a new group of plays about England in a time of war.

SHAKESPEARE'S SECOND HISTORICAL tetralogy reaches even further back in time to the beginning of the fifteenth century. Also known as the Henriad for their focus on the rise of Henry V, the four plays start with England's last medieval king, the weak and ineffectual Richard II. Richard was deposed by his cousin Henry Bolingbroke, who became Henry IV; this was the "original sin" that sparked the Wars of the Roses a half-century later. The play *Richard II* explores that event—asking whether or not it's ever justified to depose a king. In the play, Richard is neurotic and solipsistic, vacillating between depression and extreme self-regard. When Bolingbroke arrives at his castle, Richard offers him the crown before Henry even asks—sparking endless debates on whether Richard "usurps himself" or just saw the writing on the wall.

The play is also one of Shakespeare's only plays to focus on Ireland, describing Richard's return from a disastrous Irish war, which he describes as the "Antipodes"—the ends of the earth. That's no accident, says McCarthy, as Thomas North set out for his own tour of duty there. In fact, the entire focus of the play is on banishment, McCarthy says, beginning with Richard's exile of Bolingbroke for a petty act. The play dwells on the injustice, including a scene between Bolingbroke and his father, in which his father urges him to tolerate the rough conditions of exile by living within his imagination. Bolingbroke retorts that one can't "wallow naked in December snow by thinking on fantastic summer's heat? Oh no, the apprehension of the good gives but the greater feeling to the worse." When he finally returns, Bolingbroke is still complaining about "eating the bitter bread of banishment," which left him "no sign, save men's opinions and my living blood, to show the world I am a gentleman."

Thomas North must have felt similarly abandoned in Ireland, says McCarthy, after he was stripped of his military commission and left to find solace in his imagination. The theme of banishment continues in the next history play, *Henry IV, Part 1*, which focuses not on its titular king, but on his son, Prince Hal, the future Henry V. As the king is beset by rebellions across the land, Hal is preoccupied with more carnal pursuits among the commoners of the Boar's Head Tavern. Over the course of this play, Hal gradually emerges from his self-imposed exile to take up the responsibilities of kingship. At the same time, McCarthy points out, it foreshadows the eventual abandonment of his tavern friends, in particular the jolly gourmand Falstaff. "No, my good lord," Falstaff jokes to Hal in one of the play's scenes. "Banish plump Jack, and banish all the world." Hal responds seriously: "I do, I will." The scene is only hinted at in Holinshed, who comments that Hal left his former drinking companions behind when he became king—a sure sign, says McCarthy, that North based the scene on his own experience instead.

The *Henry IV* plays are the only ones in the canon to give prominent roles to commoners, as Falstaff and his companions drink and carouse, commit highway robbery, and eventually go to war as footmen. Their buffoonish antics have led Shakespearean skeptics since Mark Twain to surmise that the playwright himself spent time among soldiers at war. North had ample time to observe his conscripts in close quarters on the road, aboard ship, and in camp, McCarthy says, and clearly warmed to the experience to paint the tavern denizens with affection and humor.

The anarchic Falstaff is contrasted with the play's primary villain—the rebel leader Henry Percy, otherwise known as Hotspur. As hot-headed as his moniker, Hotspur riles up the rebellious northerners to war against the crown, challenging Hal to single combat at the Battle of Shrewsbury. In the end, however, Hotspur emerges as an honorable and even admirable man—a throwback to the days of chivalry. After Hal kills Hotspur in battle, Falstaff sticks his sword into the body to claim credit for the kill. The humorous scene belies a darker symbolism about the death of honor at the hands of anarchy—a theme that would reach fruition in the second part of the play.

As HENRY IV DIES, the realm dies, too. *Henry IV, Part 2* opens with a world of gloom and disillusionment, with the king on his deathbed and a new wave of rebels fighting against the crown. "In every aspect of the play—in language, in honor, and in literal illness and crafty sickness—the theme of disease and decay predominates," says Harvard professor Marjorie Garber. Falstaff has clearly lost a step, holding court as bombastically as ever, but also suffering from gout and struggling to avoid his creditors. The play introduces a cast of unsavory new characters, including the prostitute Doll Tearsheet and Ancient Pistol, a *commedia dell'arte* braggart gone bad. The fight against the rebels, meanwhile, "is a much nastier, meaner business than the open fighting on the battlefield at Shrewsbury," writes Tony Tanner. "There is no honor, no chivalry, not even any honest combat."

The war in Ireland must have seemed similarly desperate to Thomas North, as the fighting turned even uglier after the Smerwick massacre. Grey led his forces in a campaign of scorched earth, laying waste to Desmond's plantations and destroying any cropland that could feed the rebels. As Spenser later wrote about the populace, from "woods and glens they came creeping forth upon their hands, for their legs could not bear them. They look like anatomies of death, they spoke like ghosts crying out of their graves." Still, the fighting raged on in rough woods and muddy bogs, as local chieftains settled old scores by accusing supposed conspirators, extracting confessions from them, and summarily executing the "guilty."

Henry IV, Part 2 ends with one of the most shocking moments in all of Shakespeare's plays. The rebels rounded up, Hal's brother Prince John offers them clemency, swearing "by the honor of my blood" that he will redress their wrongs if their leaders will surrender. Once the rebels disperse, however, he arrests the leaders, sentencing them to death, and commands his army to "pursue the scattered stray." In a 1961 essay, Paul Jorgensen calls the act "one of the most disturbingly dramatic, and least admired, scenes in Shakespeare." Even more bewildering is the fact that in *Holinshed*, the act isn't perpetrated by John, but by a minor character, and against only the rebel leaders. "Shakespeare alone is accountable for making the episode an important part of the political action by giving an estimable prince responsibility for the stratagem," says Jorgensen. Searching for an explanation for the betrayal, he points to the Irish wars, and specifically to Grey's Smerwick Massacre as possible inspiration for the scene.

Even if North didn't personally witness the massacre, it must have loomed large in his imagination, as he heard the details from his fellow captains and soldiers, and witnessed the brutal aftermath. While Spenser would eventually become an apologist for Grey's leadership in Ireland, North did the opposite, says McCarthy, turning away in disgust at the unprincipled and ignoble tactics of his fellow Englishmen. That emotion, he says, even colors North's depiction of one of England's greatest heroes, Henry V, as he takes a cynical view toward war in his namesake play.

HENRY IV'S DYING ADVICE to Hal is to "busy giddy minds with foreign quarrels"—that is, go to war against a foreign enemy to distract people from factional strife at home. In *Henry V*, the new king does that with a vengeance, invading France and winning a heroic English victory at Agincourt. The play is often seen as a crowd-pleaser, with audiences thrilling to Henry V's St. Crispin's Day speech, with its "band of brothers" standing up against seemingly insurmountable odds. Some critics, however, see the play as jingoistic in its fervent national enthusiasm, and Henry a caricature in his over-the-top machoism. Harold Bloom even suspects the playwright is in on the criticism. "*Henry V*, for all its exuberance," he says, "is essentially ironic."

The first cracks in Henry's armor occur offstage, as Falstaff dies unseen in the backroom of the tavern, while another character attributes his death to Henry's abandonment of him. They continue during the English siege of Harfleur. In a speech before the walls, Henry declares that if the citizens don't surrender, he will unleash his soldiers to rape and pillage the town—another chilling scene that finds little support in the historical record.

An even more horrifying episode occurs toward the end of the play when, in the midst of the battle, Henry orders the slaughter of captured French prisoners. He justifies the killings as a reprisal against a French attack on his own baggage train, after which one character sarcastically comments, "They have burned and carried away all that was in the King's tent, wherefore the King most worthily hath caused every soldier to cut his prisoner's throat. Oh 'tis a gallant king!" Taken together, the incidents, says David Bevington, "raise serious questions about the morality of war under the best of kings." But McCarthy sees in them something more—a commentary by the playwright on the immorality of the war in Ireland.

"He doesn't even try to hide it," McCarthy says. *Henry V* opens with an actor playing the chorus, who asks the audience to imagine the multitudes triumphantly welcoming Henry V returning like a "conquering Caesar" from the victorious fields of France—just as "were now the general of our gracious empress, as in good time he may, from Ireland coming, bringing rebellion broached the sword." It's the only time Shakespeare deliberately "breaks the fourth wall" to comment directly on current events, and since his *Henry V* appeared in 1599, scholars naturally assume the reference is to the Earl of Essex, the queen's general in Ireland during the Nine Years' War (between 1593 and 1603). But McCarthy believes it's a reference to Grey and the Desmond Rebellion.

What clinches it for him is the insertion of Shakespeare's only Irish character in any of the plays: a hard-swearing army captain named MacMorris, who is called in to help demolish Harfleur with mines placed in tunnels beneath the walls. That's a direct reference, he says, to James Fitzmaurice, the rebel who started the Irish war in which Thomas North took part. "Fitz" is the English version of "Mac," the Irish term for "son of," McCarthy points out, noting many documents of the time refer to him as "MacMorrice." Not only is the name shared, he says, but the character also shares several conspicuous traits with Fitzmaurice, who was known for swearing oaths, and famous for demolishing the city of Kilkenny. "He's a swaggering Irishman and an expert in the demolition of towns, which is exactly what Captain MacMorris is—I mean, it's over," McCarthy says. "Gin?" I ask, and he agrees: "Gin."

In the midst of the scene in which Henry orders the killing of the prisoners, the play stages a comic aside between two characters, in which they compare Henry with Alexander the Great in a direct parody of *Plutarch's Lives*. Referring to the birthplaces of the respective leaders, one says, "There is a river in Macedon, and there is moreover a river at Monmouth." He then goes on to say that, like Alexander, who killed his best friend while drunk, Henry also killed his best friend. "He never killed any of his friends," the other replies. But the first cuts him off, saying that he killed his friend Falstaff when he "turned away the fat knight with the great belly-doublet" who was "full of jests, and gipes, and knaveries, and mocks." The comment seems like a throwaway line in the heat of battle, but McCarthy sees in it something more—an attempt, à la Plutarch, to come to terms with the present by reckoning with the past.

Just as the figures in North's *Plutarch* are neither all good nor all bad, so are modern kings and heroes flawed, the play seems to say. How could the greatest king in English history commit acts of barbarity in war? The same way he could abandon his old friend when he took up the crown. And the same way men could murder and starve prisoners and civilians on the scorched fields of Ireland. As North wrote in his preface to *Plutarch*, "It is better to see learning in noble men's lives than to read it in philosopher's writings." By comparing Henry V to Caesar and Alexander, he could better understand England's war-hero king in all of his complexities and contradictions; and by comparing Lord Deputy Grey to Henry V, he could better make sense of his own experience in war, one of the most disturbing experiences of his life.

As THOMAS NORTH WATCHED the shores of the English Pale recede into the distance, he must have been filled with a combination of relief and disillusionment over his sixteen months abroad. In January 1582, a captain brought the head of John of Desmond, Gerald Fitzgerald's brother, to Dublin, where North must have seen it impaled on the gates of the castle. By now, Elizabeth had lost her taste for war, with its drain on her coffers. She began withholding supplies, forcing Grey to discharge soldiers en masse, to make their way unpaid and starving back across the Irish Sea. Before he disembarked, North obtained a letter to Burghley from the archbishop of Dublin, Adam Loftus, attesting to his many hours of service without pay. "His estate will be hard," Loftus wrote, urging the lord treasurer to assist him. "I am of the opinion you cannot secure a more honest and truthful gentleman."

North finally set sail from Dublin with two other captains, Thomas Maria Wingfield and writer Barnabe Rich, and with fair winds they arrived in Chester on Saturday, March 3. The next day, they attended a sermon at Chester Cathedral, which included a shocking exorcism of a fourteen-year-old girl who had claimed to have visions of the Virgin Mary. That night, the captains dined with the mayor and the preacher, who lent North £20, which he later claimed the "honest" North never repaid.

Once again, North was apparently destitute, with nothing to show for his military service. He was also a widower. While his daughter, Elizabeth, stayed on her uncle Roger's estate, the last reference to Thomas's wife occurs on November 22, 1580, meaning she must have died while he was away. There's no record that North received any compensation from Burghley, or that he returned to Kirtling to stay with this brother.

Alone and impoverished, North must have returned to London, where, McCarthy believes, he staged his new wartime plays. "Can this cockpit hold the vasty fields of France?" the chorus thunders in *Henry V*. "Or may we cram within this wooden O the very casques that did affright the air at Agincourt?" Scholars interpret that "wooden O" as a reference to the Globe Theatre, where Shakespeare performed his plays. But it could just as well be The Theatre, where Leicester's Men performed that summer. And that reference, McCarthy found, held another clue to pin down *Henry V* to the early 1580s, and connect Thomas North to another of Leicester's poets—Philip Sidney.

As McCarthy continued to search for references to Thomas North, he came across an early-twentieth-century paper written by Marguerite Hearsey, a professor at Hollins University, a women's liberal arts college in Virginia, arguing that Sidney had written one of his best-known works, *The Defence of Poesy*, in response to the opening preface of North's *Plutarch's Lives*. Sidney penned his work sometime around 1581 as a celebration of the power of poetry and its superiority to history or philosophy. Recognized as the first piece of English literary criticism, Sidney's work praises poetry's ability to break us free from reality with a "purifying of the wit" as opposed to the limitations of history, which is "tied, not to what should be but to what is."

Sidney goes on to deride historical plays as well, criticizing them for jumping around too much in time and space. "For where the stage should always represent but one place," he wrote, some "have Asia of the one side, and Afric of the other, and so many other under-kingdoms, that the player, when he comes in, must ever begin with telling where he is." He mocks plays about war in which "two armies fly in, represented with four swords and bucklers, and then what hard heart will not receive it for a pitched field?" Of course, that image calls to mind Shakespeare's history plays, in which battles involving thousands of men are often reduced to just four men with swords. And sure enough, some scholars have seen the chorus of *Henry V* as a response to Sidney's famous essay—apologizing (sarcastically) for stuffing the fields of France into the wooden O of the theater. "Where—oh for pity!" the chorus continues, "we shall much disgrace with four or five most vile and ragged foils, right ill-disposed in brawl ridiculous, the name of Agincourt." Even though Sidney's essay was written twenty years before the conventional date of *Henry V*, it wasn't published until 1595—making it reasonable for scholars to assume Shakespeare was mocking it in his 1599 play.

As McCarthy read through Sidney's essay, however, he felt the connection to both North and Shakespeare had to be more than a coincidence. In fact, the examples of plays Sidney mocked all had a familiar ring to them. That play with Asia on one side and Africa on the other sounded an awful lot like *Antony and Cleopatra*—in which several characters do indeed declare their location upon arrival. Another line criticizing plays "mingling clowns and kings" seemed a takedown of the Falstaff–Prince Hal relationship in the *Henry IV* plays. Another seemed to spell out the exact cast of characters in *Love's Labour's Lost*. From a conventional standpoint, in other words, Shakespeare's chorus responds to an essay that mocked his plays years before he'd written them.

Of course, McCarthy has a different explanation—that Sidney's essay derided North's source plays, and North added the chorus to clap back at his younger poetic rival. In fact, as McCarthy examined their relationship further, he came to believe that North hadn't only satirized Sidney in his great play about war—but also in his most famous play about love.

Chapter Thirteen

TO BE, OR NOT TO BE

(1582–1588 / 2016)

To be, or not to be, that is the question:
Whether 'tis nobler in the mind to suffer
The slings and arrows of outrageous fortune,
Or to take arms against a sea of troubles
And by opposing end them.

—Hamlet

When it comes to tourists, Stratford-upon-Avon has nothing on Verona. As we zoom into the northern Italian city on an April morning, I jockey past rental cars and dodge tour buses full of couples with love on the brain. Verona is synonymous with Shakespeare's tragically romantic play *Romeo and Juliet*—now the city's blessing and curse. You don't need to scratch its terra cotta roofs too hard to find the tackiness beneath. "Verona Sexy Shop!" blares a billboard we pass. "They know the Americans will be coming by here, that's why they have to put that in English," McCarthy jokes beside me in the passenger seat. "They're going to be all jazzed by the story of Romeo and Juliet and need to get busy," I add. "That's right," says Galovski from the backseat, affecting an Italian accent. "Sexy, sexy, sexy!"

All jokes aside, the juxtaposition is fitting for a play that includes the most lyrical poetry in the canon next to its bawdiest sexual punning. For every "But soft, what light through yonder window breaks?" there's an "Oh, that she were an open-arse, and thou a pop'ring pear." There's a reason for that, says McCarthy. The whole play is North's elaborate attack on the vision of starry-eyed romantic love presented by the courtier-poet Philip Sidney. "It's really more about the dangers of unconstrained, youthful passions," says McCarthy, before coining a mock Department of Tourism slogan: "Welcome to Verona, setting for the most famous anti-love story ever told."

Philip Sidney is best-known for *Astrophil and Stella*, a sequence of 108 sonnets dedicated to unrequited love. In Sidney's case, he had a real-life lady in mind: Leicester's stepdaughter, Penelope Devereux, Lettice's daughter by her first husband. Penelope did spurn Sidney's love, marrying Robert Rich. From the first lines of Sidney's poem—"Loving in truth, and fain in verse my love to show, that she (dear She) might take some pleasure of my pain"—the verses ache and groan with passion and self-flagellation. As every edition of *Romeo and Juliet* notes, the play's first lines are also a sonnet, written in the English rhyme-scheme used by Sidney. "Two households, both alike in dignity, in fair Verona, where we lay our scene," it begins, telling of the feuding Montague and Capulet families, and the "pair of star-crossed lovers," their children.

Romeo and Juliet's first meeting is a sonnet, too, recited in alternating lines between them, as they first meet at a ball thrown by Juliet's father and crashed by Romeo and his gang. From that moment, the two fall headlong in love, courting, marrying, and dying in the space of four days. Their love has made generations of readers swoon, as the story has been told and retold onstage and in film, from the lush 1968 version by Italian director Franco Zeffirelli to Baz Luhrmann's 1996 *Romeo + Juliet*, set in gritty "Verona Beach." Even the most casual viewer, however, can detect the irony in the beginning of the play, when Romeo is completely infatuated with another woman, Rosaline (itself perhaps a swipe at Spenser's *Shepheardes Calender*), only to glom immediately on to Juliet in the space of a few hours. "Romeo is in complete agony over Rosaline, and says he will never survive that loss, and then the instant he sees Juliet, it's all over," McCarthy says. "This is how North was parodying Sidney with his over-emotional love of Penelope Rich."

Now forty-seven years old, the translator of Stoic principles in *The Dial of Princes* would have been turned off by such an excessive display of emotion, McCarthy says. After the younger poet criticized North in

Defence of Poesy, he believes, North got back at him with a parody of his poems. Nowhere is that more apparent, he says, than in the most iconic scene from the play. After wedging our car into a parking space downtown, we follow the ubiquitous signs to "Casa di Giulietta." A graffiti-covered tunnel opens up into a small cobblestone courtyard, walls covered with hanging vines. There, jutting out from the medieval facade on the right, is *the balcony*. A carved platform of peach-colored stone, this is supposedly the spot where Juliet stood when the young lovers declared their love for each other.

Lovelorn visitors still drop letters addressed to Juliet into a mailbox, to be answered by the "Juliet Club," a volunteer squad of ladies who respond on the behalf of the famous Veronese maiden. In another corner, they pose with a bronze statue of Juliet herself, somewhat creepily cupping one of her breasts for luck. "She was only 13 in the play," McCarthy notes, shaking his head. Still, there's no denying the power of the scene in the play—with both lovers intoxicated by the very presence of the other. "With love's light wings did I o'erperch these walls, for stony limits cannot hold love out," Romeo calls up to Juliet. "My bounty is as boundless as the sea, my love as deep; the more I give to thee, the more I have, for both are infinite," Juliet exclaims.

After they agree to marry, Juliet returns to avian imagery, telling Romeo, "I would have thee gone—and yet no further than a wanton's bird, that lets it hop a little from his hand, like a poor prisoner in his twisted gyves"—in other words a child's pet bird on a string. "I would I were thy bird," Romeo eagerly replies. "Sweet, so would I," says Juliet, "yet I should kill thee with much cherishing." Numerous scholars have pointed out the similarities between the scene and the florid poetry of *Astrophil and Stella*, in which Astrophil envies Stella's pet bird for its proximity to his desired. Of course, Shakespeare, too, could have satirized Sidney's work, which was published 1595, just a few years before *Romeo and Juliet* first appeared, in 1597.

But it was North who had the motivation, McCarthy insists. "He shows that he can do it better than Sidney, at the same time he makes fun of it." Elsewhere, the play constantly undermines the young lovers' poetry with the coarse language of Juliet's nurse and Romeo's kinsman Mercutio, who deploys an endless store of sexual puns. In the same way, McCarthy says, North was having fun with Sidney, imitating his poetic style in one moment, before mocking it in the next.

BENEATH THE SURFACE, the Casa di Giulietta is actually a fraud. The balcony was added in the 1930s (the play only mentions a "window") and the bed in an upstairs exhibit is a prop from the Zefferelli film. The house never even belonged to the Capulet (or Cappelletti) family—it was an inn owned by the similar-sounding Da Cappello family, and only dubbed Juliet's house when the city bought it in 1905. The real story of the doomed lovers comes from Matteo Bandello's *Novelle*, published in Tuscany in 1554. That in turn led to the first English version in 1562, by Arthur Brooke, an Inns-of-Court man who wrote the three-thousand-line narrative poem *Romeus and Juliet*. Brooke's poem is universally acknowledged as Shakespeare's main—and perhaps only—source for the play. The poem is overtly moralistic, warning against the impetuousness of young love and sexual passion, which can only lead to ruin.

McCarthy naturally first thought that Brooke's poem was North's source as well. But as he examined it more closely, he developed a different theory: that Brooke actually based his poem on a play written by North in the early 1560s. The idea isn't totally off-the-wall—Brooke claims to base his work on Bandello, but in a preface writes, "I saw the same argument lately set forth on stage with more commendation than I can look for." While scholars have searched in vain for this staged version, McCarthy believes North could have written it for performance at Lincoln's Inn, based on a copy of *Novelle* he picked up during the 1555 delegation.

On the way back from Rome, North and the delegates traveled through a town North describes in his journal as "Villa Franca." Now known as Villafranca di Verona, it is only ten miles from Verona itself. As Richard Roe notes in his guide to Italy, *Romeo and Juliet*'s author seems to have a personal knowledge of the city, as there is a reference in the first scene of the play to "Old Free-town," the English translation of Villa Franca. One other name in the play clinches it for McCarthy. In Bandello's story, the names of the rival families are Montecchi and Capuleti. Although the latter is easy enough to derive from that source, Romeo's surname is less obvious. Thomas North, however, would have only had to look as far as one of the three lords leading his delegation to find it: Anthony Browne, 1st Viscount Montague. "North is traveling through this region with Montague," says McCarthy, "and then the name in Brooke's 1562 version is Montague."

Based on all the evidence, McCarthy contends that North wrote his original play in the 1560s, and then rewrote it twenty years later, changing its strictly moralizing tale to a more subtle criticism at Sidney. At the same time, he shows the tragic consequences of Romeo and Juliet's headlong passion, as both lovers end up killing themselves. "By the time he revised it, he really made it into the tragedy that it is today," McCarthy says as we walk the cobblestone streets of Verona. "This young poet Sidney had written this long essay about how poetry is better than historical facts," he continues. Whereas Sidney had criticized history for sticking to "what is" rather than "what should be," North was turning that criticism around to mock his overly sentimental verses. "It was an argument between poetry and truth," McCarthy says. "He's saying verse is okay, but it's best to stick to the reality of how things are."

Even when Thomas North was Sidney's age, after all, he was a relentless skeptic of unrealistic claims. As we leave Casa di Giulietta, we stop by the gift shop, a riot of hot pink and scarlet kitsch hocking rubber change purses and frosted shot glasses emblazoned with ROMEO GIULIETTA VERONA in a sketchy handwritten font. Among other items for sale is a key chain of Juliet's lucky bronze breast. As McCarthy picks one up, I comment on how supremely tacky it all is. "You are Thomas North. You're having the exact same reaction he did," McCarthy replies. During the 1555 delegation, he explains, North's party stopped several times at religious shrines purporting to contain saintly relics. "They could claim they had a nail from the cross of Christ, or some saint's finger," McCarthy says. At those times, North would express skepticism, saying, "They bore us in hand," an Elizabethan expression similar to "They pulled our leg."

How ironic, I say, that instead of talismans of religious significance, the gift shop here is now selling cheap keepsakes of over-idealized teenage love—possibly inspired by North's own play. "Now they are selling pieces of Juliet," McCarthy agrees. As I look around at the tourists scooping up magnets and wristbands, I imagine what North would have made of the scene. If McCarthy is right, then Sidney got the last laugh as his saccharine view of love won out in the end. Nowhere in the entire shop do I see anything with the name "Shakespeare," but I wonder, too, what the North of McCarthy's imaginings would have thought about yet one more shrine to Bardolatry—and the immortality that he missed.

By spring of 2016, McCarthy was doing what he could to give North that recognition, pulling together all of his writings into his new book project, *The Earlier Playwright*. It was a more focused and sober work compared with *North of Shakespeare*, laying out his arguments in a rational fashion that (mostly) avoided the bombast of his earlier work. By now, the draft amounted to more than two hundred thousand words—and he had only taken North's biography up to the early 1580s. Still, that would be enough, he thought, as he considered where to send it. He knew it would be fruitless to send it to Oxford University Press, which had published his first book, *Here Be Dragons*, but also has its own lucrative editions of Shakespeare's plays. "It'd be like trying to get the Koch brothers to buy an electric car," says McCarthy, referring to the conservative Texas oil family.

At the same conference where he'd sat in on the Arden seminar, Schlueter had introduced him to Michelle Houston, an editor from Edinburgh University Press, a respected academic publisher that also wasn't afraid to go outside the Stratfordian mainstream. In 2013, the press had published a book, *The Truth About William Shakespeare*, which took to task Shakespeare biographies, showing how they twisted the truth to fit their own ends. With McCarthy's blessing, Schlueter now sent Houston three chapters of his book. McCarthy and Schlueter were immediately encouraged by Houston's response, as she called the book "fascinating" and "really exciting work!"; though she also warned them she'd have to send the book out to peer reviewers for an outside opinion.

In May, Houston sent a short message to Schlueter with some bad news—of the two reviewers to whom she'd sent the manuscript, one of them wrote a negative review; the other refused to write a review at all. "Because of these factors, I am unfortunately unable to take this project any further," she wrote. She attached the anonymous review, which acknowledged that McCarthy's writing style was "perfectly clear and quite pleasant"—a recognition, at least, of all of the work he had done to tone down his overly boisterous prose. Unfortunately, that's where the compliments ended.

"I'm sorry to say that this work advances virtually no evidence for its central argument," it went on. "It is fundamentally unpublishable." It wasn't news that Shakespeare relied on Thomas North's prose for his plays, the reviewer continued, but McCarthy's idea that he relied on Thomas North plays instead was just fanciful. "None of this provides any evidence, or even any suggestion, of the phantom, now-lost intermediary texts that the author insistently imagines," the reviewer wrote. Perhaps McCarthy might publish a book about Shakespeare's use of the George North manuscript—so long as he didn't stray from the established documentary record. "The question of how Shakespeare may have been influenced by unpublished documents," the reviewer wrote, "is not answered by conjuring up additional phantom unpublished documents."

Schlueter was shocked. "In my many years of editing a Shakespeare journal and serving on the advisory board of a university press, I've never seen such an emphatic rejection—or heard of a reader refusing to do a report but advising you not to publish," she wrote to Houston. McCarthy was stung by the dismissive tone of the review. "You'd think that I had written a hate-filled screed, rather than arguing that Thomas North wrote *Philemon and Philecia* in 1574," he says.

He dashed off a 2,500-word reply to the reviewer, insisting that "the existence of Shakespeare's source plays is not a theory of mine but a conventionally accepted fact, referred to in all renowned books on Shakespeare sources." The only argument he was making is that one person wrote all of them. Even as he was writing the reply, however, he knew it was pointless, and never sent it. Once again, he'd been blocked by the academic gatekeepers. If anything, however, the rejection strengthened his resolve to see his project through to the end. After all, he was finally getting close to the moment in the 1580s when, he believes, Thomas North wrote his *Ur-Hamlet*, the play that had started McCarthy on his long quest in the first place. Now that he understood more about North's life and the political concerns of the time, he was finally on the verge of understanding why he wrote the play—and the inspiration behind Hamlet's famous soliloquy on life and death.

EVEN WHILE THOMAS NORTH was stuck on the muddy battlefields of Ireland, Elizabeth's flirtations with Alençon were reaching their denouement. As the French duke continued to bungle the war in the Netherlands, Elizabeth sent him a letter proposing a military alliance instead of marriage. She followed it up with £30,000 ($15.6 million) in support. Alençon decided instead to return to England, to press his suit for marriage—and more money. He arrived in London on November 1, 1581, and soon he and Elizabeth were again spending their days cuddling and whispering words of affection. By late November, the queen had seemingly made up her mind, kissing Alençon on the mouth in front of the court and telling the stunned assemblage that "the Duke of Alençon shall be my husband." Leicester and Hatton publicly begged her to change her mind, and the streets of London at once ignited with angry crowds at the news.

More than likely, that's exactly what Elizabeth had in mind to show the French that marriage was still an impossibility. Even as Sussex continued to press for marriage, Alençon settled instead for a payment of another £60,000 to finance his Netherlands adventures. When he finally set sail again in February 1582—a month before North's return from Ireland— Elizabeth made a big show over his departure, crying and saying she would give a million pounds to "see her frog again swimming in the Thames." Privately, however, she sent Leicester with a message to the Dutch to never allow Alençon to return. Leicester crowed to his friends that he'd left Alençon "an old husk, run ashore, high and dry."

He had a right to gloat. After everything, the queen wouldn't be marrying Alençon—or anyone else. Pushing fifty, Elizabeth's courting days were over; from that moment on, she embraced a new image of a Virgin Queen, married to the realm. Leicester, however, was only consolidating his victory. The following June, his longtime enemy, the Earl of Sussex, took fatally ill. On his deathbed, he continued to warn his supporters against Leicester, telling them, "You do not know the beast as well as I do." From then on, however, Leicester and his Puritan allies continually had the queen's ear. With no more marriage prospects to dangle before foreign rulers, Elizabeth was now on a collision course with the Catholic powers of Europe.

Sussex's death reverberated throughout the theater world as well. Even as he lay ill, the Privy Council created a new theater company under Elizabeth's direct patronage. Called the Queen's Men, it would be a super-company of the leading companies at court, including Leicester's, Sussex's, and Oxford's. Historians differ on the motivation behind the officially sanctioned crew, citing attempts to impose order after a riot at The Theatre in 1580, or attempts by the incoming lord chamberlain, Charles Howard, to prevent Leicester's total supremacy in the wake of Sussex's death.

Whatever the reasons, the Queen's Men instantly became the premier London company, dominating court performances. In addition to original plays, some of its performers brought their playbooks with them and reworked them for the new troupe. For New Year's 1585, the company performed *Felix and Philomena*, which McCarthy contends was a rewrite of North's original *Philemon and Philecia*, his source play for *The Two Gentlemen of Verona*. "There were a number of plays by the Queen's Men that are clearly takeoffs of Thomas North's plays," McCarthy says—citing *The Famous Victories of Henry V* and a comedy called *The Three Ladies of London*, which features an Italian debtor and a Jewish moneylender, suspiciously similar to *The Merchant of Venice*.

Even as the Privy Council raided the adult companies for their new theatrical supergroup, however, Edward de Vere, Earl of Oxford, swooped in to license a group of child actors as the Children of the Chapel Royal. He leased space at Blackfriars for their shows and hired playwright John Lyly to write plays. North, meanwhile, was continuing to write his own plays for Leicester's Men, says McCarthy, including his versions of *Twelfth Night* (based on a work by his traveling companion, Barnabe Rich) and *All's Well That Ends Well*. With Sussex gone, Oxford had taken the place of Leicester's chief rival in both politics and theater. North, McCarthy says, started inserting subtle digs against Oxford into his plays, including the highway robbery in *Henry IV, Part 1* (similar to the one committed by Oxford's servants) and more extensive biographical references in *All's Well*

That Ends Well, a comedy set in Florence that mimics key elements of Oxford's biography. Oxfordians point to these kinds of details, of course, to prove Oxford's authorship of the plays. What's really happening, however, says McCarthy, is that North inserted them to parody the rival lord.

Leicester's players were by now falling on hard times, squeezed out by the combined forces of the Queen's Men and the child players. The company increasingly relied on touring throughout the English countryside—and eventually farther afield as well. In the spring of 1583, Walsingham caught wind of yet another Catholic invasion plot against the queen led by Spain and the pope under the name *La Empresa de Inglaterra* ("the Enterprise of England"). Events became more dire the following June when Elizabeth received word that her longtime suitor, the Duke of Alençon, had caught fever in France and died. The queen went into mourning, weeping both over the loss of her "Monsieur" and the increased likelihood that England would be drawn into the Dutch war. That possibility became a certainty after a Catholic assassin murdered the Protestant leader William of Orange and Parma continued his relentless drive to take the great prize of Antwerp. By August 1585, she agreed to send six thousand soldiers, including one thousand cavalry, across the Channel. To lead them, she turned to her longtime companion, Leicester.

The earl was then suffering from the loss of his son and heir, who had caught a fever and died at Wanstead. Now, he began feverishly preparing for this new mission, commissioning shining new armor for his horses and fitting out a fleet of more than a hundred ships. He eventually set sail for Flushing in December 1585, with hundreds of troops, his own entourage of one hundred household retainers, and more than a dozen courtiers—including his loyal nephew, the newly knighted Sir Philip Sidney, and his right-hand man, Roger North.

LEICESTER'S CAMPAIGN IN the Netherlands became more of a royal progress than military tour, as he journeyed from city to city, each of which celebrated his arrival with fireworks, feasts, and performances. Leicester brought his own musicians and players as well, including Will Kemp, a clown renowned for musical performances and athletic tumbling, who would later become one of Shakespeare's most celebrated players. For now, he was the centerpiece of Leicester's lavish Christmas entertainments in honor of his hosts. High on the adulation, Leicester boldly accepted the title of Governor-General of the United Provinces, in strict defiance of Elizabeth's orders. Elizabeth dressed him down in letters, demanding he give up the title. Once again, Leicester and his supporters were on the outs—as Roger North grumbled in letters to Burghley that he was spending £26 a week of his own money in the "frost and cold" without reimbursement, even as he was passed over for governorship of a city.

Thomas North doesn't appear on any of the muster rolls for 1585 or 1586—but it's possible, says McCarthy, that he, too, accompanied Leicester to help stage his entertainments. In the summer of 1586, five of Leicester's players, including Kemp, made a goodwill tour of Northern Europe—including a three-month residency at the court of the king of Denmark, Frederick II, in the city of Helsingør. That location is better known as Elsinore, setting for Shakespeare's *Hamlet*. It's possible, says McCarthy, that North accompanied them there and was inspired by the ancient tale, while his brother continued fighting with Leicester in the Low Countries.

Even in the midst of the pomp and circumstance, fighting began that summer with a series of skirmishes near Utrecht in early May. By early August, Leicester had pushed his way up the river IJssel to threaten the strategic town of Zutphen. Along with his son-in-law, Robert Devereux, Earl of Essex, and his nephew Philip Sidney, he decided to set an ambush. Mist hugged the river valley in the early morning of September 22, 1586, as footmen lined the road, with cavalry in wait behind. It was so thick, in fact, that the English were surprised when the caravan of Spanish forces suddenly materialized through the fog. A frenzied battle broke out as the Spanish opened fire with their muskets and Essex led the horsemen into a courageous charge into their ranks.

Despite receiving wounds the day before, Roger rose out of his bed at camp and hastily joined the fray. Sidney, meanwhile, charged three times into the Spanish ranks; on the final sally, a Spanish musket ball shattered the bone just above his knee. Gallant as ever, he reportedly refused a drink of water in favor of a wounded fellow soldier, saying that his "necessity is greater than mine." After the victory, Leicester dubbed both Roger North and Essex knights banneret, the highest order of knighthood that could be received during battle. Sidney's wound festered, however, eventually turning gangrenous. Within three weeks, he had died, not yet thirty-two years old—and without a single line of his poetry yet published.

Leicester's circle was devastated by the death of his young nephew. "I have lost the comfort of my life," Leicester told Walsingham. He returned to England in November, accompanied by Essex and Lord North, while leaving his second-in-command, John Norris, with a weak and starving army. No sooner did Leicester leave, than the English captains manning the fort at Zutphen turned traitor, sacrificing the entire region Leicester had fought to conquer. He arrived just in time for a crucial debate in the hall of Westminster—the fate of Mary Queen of Scots. Walsingham's agents had uncovered yet another plot against Elizabeth, this one centering on a Catholic named Anthony Babington, who planned to personally assassinate the queen. This time, Mary was implicated through letters in the treason.

At the recommendation of her Parliament, Elizabeth agreed in December to execute her cousin. Leicester urged Elizabeth to be done with the task, but she procrastinated in giving the final order—worried about stirring up the hornet's nest of Catholic Europe, and setting the evil precedent of executing a duly appointed monarch. In the end, however, she gave in. As Mary was dragged out into the hall of Fotheringhay Castle, she cried out in Latin, "*In manus tuas, Domine, confide spiritum meum*" ("Into your hands, O Lord, I commend my spirit"), as the headsman took two blows of his axe to sever her head.

Condemnations poured in from France, Spain, and Scotland, as the queen turned with new urgency toward the war against the Catholics in the Low Countries. By now, however, lack of supplies had depleted her troops, who were so emaciated that 60 percent of the sick and wounded soldiers died. Leicester begged Walsingham to keep him from returning to the Low Countries, which seemed a lost cause without more investment from the queen. But Elizabeth would hear none of it, ordering Leicester back in June. Leicester never went "with a worse will to any journey or any place," he told Walsingham, as he boarded the ships with three thousand additional troops—and this time with both of the North brothers.

Thomas was appointed to lead 150 men from Cambridge and Ely, part of the new recruits Leicester called "the fairest and handsomest companies that ever I saw in my life." In reality, the new soldiers were green and inexperienced, and no match for Parma's veterans, who were now besieging the southeastern coastal town of Sluis. Rather than attack by sea, Leicester made a strategic blunder by sailing around to relieve the town by land. Thomas and Roger marched up the coastline with the rest of the army; however, the Spanish were dug in too deep, and the English troops watched helplessly as it fell—giving the Spanish access to the coast just sixty miles from England. As Leicester dispersed his army, Thomas was listed in September among the forces garrisoning in Flushing, with 130 of his original men, 14 of them sick. Some of them hadn't been paid in a year and were barely able to support themselves with food and clothing. Still, they fared better than some towns, where soldiers were forced to tear down houses for firewood.

As usual, says McCarthy, Thomas passed the time writing, finally finishing his version of *As You Like It*, inspired by Edmund Spenser's attempts to woo his daughter years ago. The miserable service Thomas and his brother spent in the Netherlands, McCarthy says, helps to explain one additional element in the play: the exile of Duke Senior and his band of men in the Forest of Arden. Scholars have often taken that location as a reference to the heavily wooded area of England by the same name nearby Shakespeare's hometown of Stratford-upon-Avon. *As You Like It*, however, is indubitably set in a French locale—as is Thomas Lodge's *Rosalynde*, in which the exiles are banished to the Ardennes Forest, on the border of northeastern France and the southeastern Belgium. The fact that Thomas North was stationed in the Low Countries, says McCarthy, explains why North would set his play in the Ardennes.

Like Duke Senior, McCarthy says, North really did seem to be exiled to the Low Countries, along with a few trusted lords. While the comedy doesn't seem to include any allusions to war, McCarthy does identify one scene that may obliquely refer to Leicester's army. When Orlando first arrives at the camp, he finds the men lamenting the death of a deer they have killed by a river. "It irks me the poor dappled fools, being native burghers of this desert city, should in their own confines with forkèd heads, have their round haunches gored," Duke Senior says.

Shakespeare's plays, says McCarthy, often use deer as a metaphor for slain soldiers—a point some other scholars have noted as well. "I myself must hunt this deer to death," says the future Richard III in *Henry VI, Part 2*, as he closes in on an enemy in battle. In *Julius Caesar*, Marc Antony uses the same language to refer to Caesar, saying, "How like a deer, strucken by many princes, dost thou here lie!" That line in turn references North's *Plutarch's Lives*, which describes Caesar as "hacked and mangled among them, as a wild beast taken of hunters." In *As You Like It*, McCarthy says, the reference to killing deer in their own "native dwelling place" might refer to North's disgust at destruction visited upon the Low Countries by the English and Spanish troops.

I'm skeptical at first of that connection—not least because North was stationed on the coast of Holland, more than fifty miles away from the Ardennes Forest. As I read through the English state papers, however, I came across a report that gives me pause. During a raid by Leicester's forces outside Antwerp, a group of several dozen soldiers surprised a wagon train of Parma's supplies, killing dozens of civilians, while more jumped into a river to escape. As the townspeople rose up against them, they fled into the surrounding forest where they had to hide in the woods "for four or five days without food." The details don't match exactly, but they are close enough to imagine that the incident might have inspired elements of the play—a band of troops exiled in the woods, civilian casualties by a river. Again I wonder if I am just reading into the documents to make the story fit, or finding another uncanny confirmation of McCarthy's theories.

After the loss of Sluis, Leicester's sickly bands languished in their garrisons as the army fell to infighting, Leicester casting particular blame at his subordinate commander John Norris. In truth, however, he had no one to blame but himself for his impotent strategies in the Low Countries, and the privy councilors were right to start pushing for his recall. As he and his followers made their way back home, however, they soon found another battle waiting on England's doorstep.

THEY CALLED IT the *Armada Invencible*, a giant navy that Spain was amassing in the port of Lisbon. After the English attack on the Low Countries and execution of Mary Queen of Scots, Philip II was finally ready to launch his great "Enterprise of England." Over the next few months, he assembled 130 ships, manned by 8,000 sailors, with another 18,000 troops onboard. The fleet's plan was to sail first to Holland, where it would meet up with an additional 18,000 troops under Parma, before crossing the Narrow Sea to attack.

Leicester returned home in late November in disgrace, relinquishing his position as Master of the Horse and slinking back to Wanstead. In early 1588, however, Elizabeth summoned him back to court, frantic at Spain's preparations, and urging him to lead the defense. The entire country, in fact, was in a panic due to a prophecy, by a fifteenth-century German mystic named Regiomontanus, that 1588 would spell disaster for England. Forebodingly, a solar eclipse in February was followed by a lunar eclipse in April, just after the queen's birthday—seeming to predict the worst. Letters went out to all of the maritime towns requesting ships to supplement the twenty-five warships of the queen's navy, commanded by Lord High Admiral Charles Lord Howard of Effingham and privateer Sir Francis Drake. Creaky seaport batteries were cleaned and repaired, arms and armor dragged out of the Tower, and beacons set up along the seacoasts to signal the first sighting of Spanish sails. Meanwhile, doubts remained about England's neighbor to the north and whether King James of Scotland would join in the attack in response to the execution of his mother.

Fortunately for England, strong headwinds and inadequate provisioning delayed the Invincible Armada's passage, forcing it into the Spanish port of A Coruña to retrofit, and giving the English a crucial extra month to prepare their forces. On paper, England had fifty thousand foot soldiers and ten thousand cavalry—though the number in fighting strength was far less. On June 24, Thomas North was put in charge of a band of three hundred men in the Isle of Ely, just north of Kirtling. A long ridge of dry land in the midst of the Cambridgeshire Fens, the area was often only accessible by causeway or boat. Though miles from the coast, Ely wasn't as safe a posting as it might seem. For years, Catholic recusants had been imprisoned in Wisbech Castle, north of the city. Now, several dozen of the most prominent were brought to the Bishop's Palace in Ely. When the Spanish army landed on England's shores, it was counting on an uprising of local Catholics to help depose the queen. As Thomas drilled his troops on the green, he must have cast a wary eye at the palace, knowing what would happen if the prisoners were freed to raise the local populace to arms.

After securing the prisoners in Ely, Roger led a force of footmen and horsemen south to Tilbury, near the head of the Thames Estuary, where Leicester had set up his camp. As the Spanish left A Coruña to sail up the Bay of Biscay at last, the earl assembled a force of twelve thousand men, "as gallant and willing men as ever were seen," and fortified the Thames with a boom of ships' masts linked with chains. Another six thousand troops protected Kent under Norris. Little did the English know, however, that the Spanish had a different target in mind. After the rendezvous with Parma, the Armada planned to land near Ipswich on the Suffolk coast. From there, it was an unimpeded fifty-mile march to North's posting guarding the Catholic recusants in Ely, with Kirtling caught in between.

Lookouts first sighted the sails of the Armada off the Lizard, the rocky peninsula on England's southwest tip, in the early morning of July 19, its ships of the line sailing in an imposing crescent-shape formation. As beacons flared to life along England's coastal hilltops, the English fleet set sail from Plymouth to meet them, counting on their longer guns and more maneuverable hulls to batter the Spanish from afar—lest the heavier Spanish ships grapple and board them for hand-to-hand combat. The tactics seemed to work, and the first battle went to the English, but Howard and Drake would have to come up with a more aggressive plan if they were to make a dent in the Invincible Armada as it beat its way up the coast.

Meanwhile, the countryside quaked with fears that the Catholics of the realm would seize the moment to rise up against their Protestant queen at last. "We are now in peril of goods, liberty, and life by our enemies the Spaniards," fretted a church pastor near Ipswich, "and at home, papists in multitudes ready to come upon us as usurpers." Standing atop Ely Cathedral and gazing out over the fens, Thomas North must have felt a similar sentiment. He was literally trapped on an island, surrounded by potential enemies on all sides—and not just foreign invaders, but also his own countrymen. Despite his service in two foreign wars, the real possibility of death must have never seemed so close. That realization, says McCarthy, gave rise to his greatest play.

THE SMELL OF DEAD leaves wafts from a soggy carpet in the churchyard of All Saints Church in Kirtling, where a haphazard scatter of gravestones stand covered with moss and lichen. "So this would have been the grave-yard?" Galovski asks her father as we approach. "Yes," McCarthy says. "Thomas North would have seen his fool buried here." In the sixteenth century, the Norths' servants would worship at their family church—and be buried there as well. "The gravediggers would have been here all the time," continues McCarthy. "He'd have heard them talk, and seen what they did." While he has no evidence, McCarthy imagines North watching Roger's motley fool get buried there, and the scene inspiring one of the most famous scenes in all of literature: the graveyard scene in *Hamlet*, in which the Prince of Denmark picks up the skull of his former fool, Yorick.

"Alas, poor Yorick! I knew him," Hamlet says, "a fellow of infinite jest, of most excellent fancy. He hath bore me on his back a thousand times, and now how abhorred in my imagination it is!" Turning sour, Hamlet cries, "Where be your gibes now? Your gambols, your songs, your flashes of merriment that were wont to set the table on a roar?" He then throws down the skull in disgust, before turning to his companion Horatio, and crying, "To what base uses we may return!" The scene has been acted, depicted, and parodied countless times, so much so that the image of a man with a skull is now shorthand for *Hamlet*, if not for Shakespeare, or for theater itself.

In fact, the play *Hamlet* is obsessed with death, from Yorick's skull in the graveyard to Hamlet's famous "To be, or not to be" soliloquy. Revisiting the play years after he first started working on it, McCarthy finally realized why: North wrote it while facing the possibility of death himself. He used that experience to turn a centuries-old Danish legend into a meditation on the nature of existence. "The play is obviously not autobiographical—*Hamlet* is an authentic legend—but he adds all sorts of autobiographical details and arguments, and patterns it after his life and experiences," McCarthy says. "He is Hamlet as much as, say, J. D. Salinger is Holden Caulfield."

For centuries, scholars have recognized *Hamlet* as one of Shakespeare's most personal plays, but outside the death of Shakespeare's son, Hamnet, a few years before it was first performed, around 1600, they've found little to connect the story to the playwright's life. By contrast, says McCarthy, North did more than just transport his own country churchyard to the chapel at Elsinore. The play reflects England's greatest moment of crisis—and North's own personal crisis as well, McCarthy says. "It's about Thomas North facing what he thinks is sure death during the Spanish Armada."

The play begins with Denmark on high alert, preparing for an invasion of a foreign enemy. The former king, Hamlet's father, had killed the king of Norway, and now his son, Fortinbras, is planning to attack Denmark in revenge. "They are building ships and gearing up for war," McCarthy says. "And there's been all these celestial phenomena—strange eclipses and disasters." Just as England's populace foresaw Elizabeth's demise in a prophecy and eclipses, so, too, does Horatio, watching from the walls of Elsinore, commenting that Julius Caesar met his death when the moon "was sick almost to doomsday with eclipse," as Denmark's moon has recently been as well.

In Fortinbras, McCarthy sees the threat of James VI of Scotland, who was likewise contemplating an invasion from the north at the same time the Armada attacked the south. "The thought was that James was going to join to avenge his mother," says McCarthy. Even the name of the avenging leader points to Scotland, he says. Translated from the French, *Fortinbras* literally means "strong-in-arm." Armstrong is the name of a clan of Scottish border reivers notorious for their attacks on England in the sixteenth century. Their leader, Kinmont Willie Armstrong, would almost certainly have helped James lead any attack.

None of those details—the celestial warnings, the foreign invasion, the avenging enemy king—exist in the original legend. All were added for the play, leading some scholars to speculate that they allude to a contemporary event, such as the invasion of another Spanish Armada in 1598. That attack, however, was a pale imitation of the original, fizzling out soon after it was declared, and had nothing to do with Scotland. "The truth of the matter is it wasn't that big of a deal," says McCarthy. "There wasn't all this massive shipbuilding or eclipses or anything like that, and everyone mocked it right afterwards."

On the eve of the invasion, Hamlet is confronted with a more personal conflict. The ghost of his dead father appears on the battlement of Elsinore telling him he was murdered by his brother—Hamlet's uncle, Claudius—who married Hamlet's mother, Gertrude, and took the crown himself. Even as Fortinbras is planning his invasion to avenge his father, Hamlet's father charges Hamlet with avenging his own. Meanwhile, says McCarthy, North was struggling with his own internal conflict over whether to stand and fight in the face of certain calamity. "They've got the Armada coming, the invasion from Scotland, and then all of these recusant Catholics that are going to rebel," says McCarthy. "The Spanish Armada alone is going to wipe them out, but fighting on all three fronts, they don't stand a chance."

HAMLET IS SO familiar to modern audiences, it almost seems like the story must have always existed. The play is full of quotable lines that have made their way into the English language: "Brevity is the soul of wit," "To thine own self be true," "Conscience does make cowards of us all"; so that most of us know the play in fragments before we even see it. From Laurence Olivier to Bart Simpson, the images of an actor, book in hand, reciting the famous "To be, or not to be" soliloquy are so ubiquitous that the play may be the closest thing the world has to a prolonged shared cultural experience.

As McCarthy learned when he first started researching the play, the outlines of the story stretch all the way back to the twelfth-century Danish legend of Prince Amleth, adapted into French by François de Belleforest for his *Histoires Tragiques*. That's the version scholars believe an unnamed playwright used to write the *Ur-Hamlet*, mentioned by Thomas Nashe in 1589 in the same essay that first turned McCarthy on to "English Seneca." Now, McCarthy further narrowed down the time in which a source play could have been written. One of its most significant sources is *Treatise of Melancholy*, a book written by Timothy Bright and printed in 1586 by Thomas Vautrollier, the same publisher who printed North's *Plutarch's Lives*. The book provides many of the descriptions of Hamlet's melancholy disposition. In one passage, for example, Bright recommends the best air for melancholics is "thin, pure, and subtle" and preferably from the "South and Southeast." That line, source scholar Kenneth Muir suggests, inspired Hamlet's famous confession that "I am but mad north-north-west. When the wind is southerly I know a hawk from a handsaw."

Another source dates the play even more precisely. When a group of traveling players arrives at Elsinore, Hamlet prevails upon them to recite a speech from a play in which the Trojan hero Aeneas addresses the African queen Dido. Hamlet damns the play with faint praise, saying it was acted "not above once" and "pleased not the million." One of the players then launches into a speech full of over-the-top bombast, with lines like "Out, out, thou strumpet Fortune!" For more than a century, scholars have seen that speech as a parody of Christopher Marlowe, a new playwright on the London theater scene who wrote his first play, *Dido, Queen of Carthage*, sometime around the spring of 1587. The play was probably cowritten with Thomas Nashe, explaining why he would get his own revenge by criticizing *Hamlet*'s author two years later.

"It's mocking Nashe and Marlowe's *Dido*—that's conventional," says McCarthy, noting that Marlowe was dead by the time Shakespeare's *Hamlet* was first performed around 1600, and Nashe died the following year. "Why Shakespeare wants to spoof a play written thirteen years before, we don't know." To him, the answer is simple: the parody was part of North's *Ur-Hamlet*, written sometime between *Dido*'s first performance in mid-1587 and the coming of the Spanish Armada a year later. North would have had good reason, then, to parody *Dido* as a pale imitation of his own *Antony and Cleopatra*. "*Hamlet* is necessarily dated in late 1587 to early 1588," McCarthy says now. "Every single important source is dated before that."

One source for the play, however, appears to call that date into question. In order to prove that Claudius murdered his father, Hamlet has the traveling players stage a performance of a play called *The Murder of Gonzago*, in which a duke named Gonzago is killed by his nephew, Lucianus, who pours poison in his ear as he is resting in his garden—the same method of murder, he tells Horatio, that Claudius used against his father. By asking Horatio to watch his uncle to see how he reacts, Hamlet says, "The play's the thing wherein I'll catch the conscience of the King."

Despite Hamlet's insistence that "the story is extant, and written in very choice Italian," scholars have searched in vain for a story of this murder in any language. They have surmised, however, that the play is based on the actual murder of Marchese Alfonso Gonzaga di Castelgoffredo, who was killed on orders of his nephew Marchese Rudolfo di Castiglione as he was resting in his own garden. Because that murder occurred in 1592, however, it couldn't have been included in a play North wrote in 1588.

SEARCHING FOR AN EXPLANATION, McCarthy came across an article by Shakespeare source scholar Geoffrey Bullough, who suggests the play-within-a-play could have been based on an alternate Italian murder. In 1538, the Duke of Urbino, Francesco Maria I della Rovere, was relaxing at his seaside villa in Pesaro when he was killed by a rival, Luigi Gonzaga, who poured poison in his ear while he was sleeping. In that case, the killing was not so much the Murder of Gonzago as the Murder by Gonzaga; but Della Rovere was also married to a Gonzaga—the Duchess Leonora—and the modus operandi was the same, so the playwright could have just switched the names.

Bullough found another element, too, that seemed to also hint at the murder as a source: a life-size portrait of Della Rovere painted by Titian. Now at the Uffizi Gallery in Florence, it matches key details of the description of the ghost of Hamlet's father, including a "grizzled" beard, a suit of armor, and an officer's baton or "truncheon" in his hand. "It's not fantastic to surmise," Bullough says, that a play based on Della Rovere's murder "contained an illustration or a description of the Duke based upon Titian's portrait, and that details of this were assimilated into the *Hamlet* play."

Reading this, McCarthy realized that he was looking at yet another connection to Thomas North. According to the journal of his 1555 trip to Rome, North and the delegation stopped in Pesaro and stayed at the

Della Roveres' villa, where they were hosted by Francesco Maria I's young grandson, Francesco Maria II. That meant that North could have seen the very Titian portrait that Bullough describes. Days before, in describing the dinner at Palazzo Te, North mentions meeting members of the family of the Duke of Mantua, Guglielmo Gonzaga, including "the Duke's grandmother, his mother's sister, the wife of Gonzago, and his daughter." The listing is the only time that the name appears in the journal, and North misspells it "Gonzago," just as it's spelled in *Hamlet*.

Furthermore, as McCarthy pieced through the genealogy, he realized that the Duke's "mother's sister" could refer to Leanora Gonzaga, who was still living and would have been sixty-two at the time. Thus, amazingly, North may have visited the scene of the crime, seen a portrait of the victim, and dined with the victim's wife, all within a few days. Years later, as he was looking for the reference in his journal, North could have come across the notation "wife of Gonzago" and mixed up the names. "North didn't have the name Della Rovere," McCarthy says, "so he is stuck with his own work, which has 'Gonzago.'"

Whatever the source of the play-within-a-play, McCarthy sees Hamlet's turn at dramaturgy as another key autobiographical detail. Just as Hamlet writes and directs a play for a theater troupe visiting Elsinore, so North was writing plays—maybe even *Hamlet* itself—for a theater troupe, Leicester's Men, that had just visited Elsinore. The two theater companies share some other key details. Hamlet's players had once performed in the city, but had fallen on hard times and were now forced to earn their living itinerantly instead—just like Leicester's Men, after losing many of its best players to the Queen's Men. Hamlet's schoolmate Rosencrantz further tells Hamlet that the players have been forced out of the city by "an aerie of children" that "berattle the common stages"—a reference perhaps to Oxford's chorister boys. (North's lingering resentments against Oxford's players would also explain why he parodied Oxford's life in Hamlet's relationship with Ophelia and her father, Polonius, whom Oxfordians believe is a caricature of Oxford's father-in-law, Burghley.)

Hamlet, meanwhile, has nothing but praise for the itinerant players, calling them "the abstract and brief chronicles of the time," and insisting it would be better to have a bad epitaph on your gravestone than "their ill report while you live." That, too, matches with North's experience, McCarthy says. Just as Hamlet's players were using theater to comment on the murder of the king, so, too, says McCarthy, had North written decades of plays about the queen's marriage and English politics. "Hamlet is taking an Italian legend and making it topical in order to comment on the current events in Denmark, and that is precisely what North is doing for Leicester's Men, commenting on England's situation with *Hamlet*."

JUST AFTER HAMLET makes his resolution to entrap Claudius with the performance of *The Murder of Gonzago*, he launches into the most famous soliloquy in the English language: "To be, or not to be, that is the question," he says. "Whether 'tis nobler in the mind to suffer the slings and arrows of outrageous fortune, or to take arms against a sea of troubles and by opposing end them." The speech has been endlessly interpreted and debated, with some contending that Hamlet, overcome with grief over his father's death, is contemplating suicide. Others see in the passage a struggle over whether to accept his uncle's usurpation or fight back—even if it means Hamlet's own death.

North's situation in writing his *Ur-Hamlet* could settle the question once and for all, McCarthy realized. He'd already identified the source of the soliloquy in *The Dial of Princes*, coming from a passage in which Marcus Aurelius is talking with his secretary Panutius on his deathbed. In that exchange, Aurelius contemplates whether it's better to live and contend with life's miseries, which he describes as "pikes and briars" and "assaults of life and broils of fortune," or to die and embark upon a "pilgrimage uncertain," not knowing whether an afterlife exists. In the play, McCarthy says, North transformed Aurelius's imagery into Hamlet's "slings and arrows of outrageous fortune," and "death, the undiscovered country."

Now, considering the passage as North would have written it on the eve of the Spanish invasion, McCarthy saw new meaning in the words. "If you read them as a man facing war, then it's obvious that the 'sea of troubles' is the Spanish Armada." As North awaited the inevitable onslaught of foreign troops and local Catholic rebels, McCarthy says, he turned for solace to *The Dial*, the book he'd translated thirty years before, looking for insight into what might await him if he didn't survive. "Even by age 22, he learned some of the most important ideas about confronting your own mortality," McCarthy says, "and they always stayed with him."

As he awaited the invasion, North's thoughts must have turned to his own future resting place at All Saints Church in Kirtling. After visiting the graveyard, we all enter the church together, our footsteps echoing off the cold stone of the entryway. Soft natural light filters in from rows of windows above as we make our way across ancient tiles to the far end, where, next to a simple altar, sits a tomb of black stone literally built into the wall. Carved with images of lions and cherubs, it carries an inscription in Latin, topped with the name "Edwardum Northum"—Thomas's father. Next to it is a larger and more garish memorial dedicated to Roger. Six stone pillars surround a life-size effigy of the lord, with a moustached face, lying in a full suit of armor with his helmet as a pillow. The tomb is capped by a riotous canopy full of griffons, cherubs, women, and ab-originals, but the paint is chipped and fading, and cobwebs grow among his clasped fingers. An inscription at his feet carries Roger's self-chosen motto: *Durum Pati* ("Endure the Hard Path").

From there, the monuments decline rapidly in glory. A pile of wooden chairs partially covers a simple black marble plaque on the floor dedicated to Roger's grandson Dudley, the 3rd Lord North—named after Robert Dudley, the Earl of Leicester. The 4th Lord North, also named Dudley, is memorialized on another plaque nearby, and so on through other members of the Norths and related families—all the way up to the 12th Baron and his mother, the last person entombed in the crypt here, in 1965. Thomas North's grave is not among them. But he must have imagined it here as he stood guard over the recusant Catholics in Ely in 1588. A part of him must have even wondered whether it would be better, if it came to it, to abandon his post and live rather than die fighting an intractable enemy.

That's the true meaning of Hamlet's speech, McCarthy says. "It's not about committing suicide," he says, leaning against the lectern in the empty church. "It's about whether or not to take on a suicidal fight." The turning point for Hamlet comes before the end of the play as he spies Fortinbras's army from afar, with twenty thousand men marching off to battle. Instead of invading Denmark, however, the Norwegian king changes his mind and decides to pass through on the way to attack Poland to "gain a little patch of ground that hath no profit in it but the name," according to one captain. Shamed by seeing men willing to "go to their graves like beds" for something so insignificant, Hamlet vows to challenge his uncle, crying, "From this time forth my thoughts be bloody or be nothing worth!"

For Hamlet, that decision doesn't go so well. Hamlet kills Claudius's counselor Polonius as he is spying on Hamlet behind a curtain, compelling his daughter Ophelia to drown herself, and his son Laertes to swear revenge. In the climactic duel between Hamlet and Laertes, confusion over a poisoned sword and a poisoned chalice leads to the death not only of Hamlet, but everyone else as well—including Laertes, Gertrude, and Claudius. In the end, Hamlet achieves his goal, even at the cost of his own life, using his dying breath to Horatio to make Fortinbras his heir. In the final scene of the play, Fortinbras arrives at last and commands a military funeral for Hamlet, letting "the soldiers' music and the rite of war speak loudly for him."

In the same way, McCarthy imagines, Thomas North made up his own mind, to stand and fight with his countrymen against Spain's "invincible" army, even if it meant his own death. Only, before he did, he would leave behind *Hamlet* as his legacy. "People say all the time, 'What does it really matter who wrote the plays?'" McCarthy says, bathed in natural light filtering in from the window above the altar. "Well, forget about giving credit, but it adds such an important dimension to the play to know that as he is writing it he actually believes he's going to die. He's literally trying to write his masterpiece, and make it as autobiographical as possible. It's about a man who is a playwright and poet, thinking about, 'Am I really going to take on this fight?'"

IN THE END, fortune's "slings and arrows" ended up striking the Spanish, rather than the English. As Howard and Drake continued to harry the Armada, the fleet anxiously awaited word of its rendezvous with Parma. Leicester had done one thing right, however; for all his bumbling in the Netherlands, he'd denied the Spanish a complete foothold on the coast. Unable to skirt the Dutch naval patrols, Parma was obliged to bring the bulk of his army south to France. As the Armada anchored off Calais to wait on the night of July 28, the English sent eight fire ships into the heart of the fleet, "the whole sea glittering and shining with the flame thereof." Panicking, the Spanish ships cut their cables, breaking formation as they fled, some stranding themselves on the Flemish sandbanks. As morning broke, the English navy descended upon the disheveled Armada at Gravelines, battering the ships with their long guns. While they gave chase over the next day, the wind changed, sending the Spanish into the North Sea as far as Scotland.

Collectively, the English held their breath waiting to see which side James VI would choose; finally, Elizabeth received a letter from him, written August 1, wishing her "all possible speed" in defeating the Spanish menace and offering his support and his troops. The next day, one of the realm's most prominent Catholics, Anthony Browne, Viscount Montague—the very noble whom North had accompanied on the delegation to Rome in 1555—volunteered to help personally defend Elizabeth against the Catholic invaders. England's worst fears of a Spanish-Scottish-recusant alliance failed to materialize. Prevented by the wind from returning south, the Armada resolved to round the British Isles, heading back to Spain for another try.

For another week, the troops at Tilbury stood in anxious worry that Parma might attempt to send his troops across the sea on barges without the Armada's support. On August 8, Elizabeth herself arrived to rally the troops, with a truncheon in her hand and Leicester by her side. Wearing a silver breastplate, she cried that she was "resolved, in the midst and heat of battle, to live or die amongst you all, to lay down for my god, for my kingdom, and my people." That very night, a warning rang out that Parma was attempting the crossing, but it turned out to be a false alarm. All told, only some one hundred English sailors died in all of the skirmishes with the Spanish. As the Armada battled storms around Scotland and Ireland, however, it lost dozens of ships; it finally struggled back into Spain with only half its fleet, and only eight thousand of its original twenty-eight thousand men; the rest had been killed or drowned.

Back in Westminster, Leicester stood with Elizabeth watching from an upper window at Whitehall while his stepson Essex led a triumphant military review in their honor. For several nights he dined alone with the queen as they relived old memories—truly reconciled at last. Still, all the stress of military life the past few weeks had taken its toll, and Leicester left with Lettice on August 26, to "take the waters" at Buxton, planning to stop by Kenilworth on the way. He never made it. He wrote the queen before stopping the next day at a hunting lodge near Woodstock, where he took sick to bed. His condition worsened over the next few days, and sometime around four o'clock in the morning on September 4, 1588, Robert Dudley, the Earl of Leicester, died.

Historians speculate he had long suffered from stomach cancer, perhaps worsened by a bout of malaria picked up on the Tilbury marshes. (Even in death, however, his enemies continued to snipe at him, spreading rumors that this time it was Leicester who'd been poisoned by Lettice.) When the queen heard the news, she shut herself inside her bedroom for days, supposedly refusing to open the door until her councilors broke it down. On his final missive, she wrote, "His last letter," keeping it in a box of treasures until her own death years later. If indeed Thomas North wrote *Hamlet*, then the irony would not have been lost on him that despite his fears, he had survived the threat of the Spanish Armada unscathed, while Leicester, his military commander and literary patron of so many years, had not. Nonetheless, he'd now need to find new means of support.

Chapter Fourteen
FULL OF SOUND AND FURY

(1588–1592 / 2015–2018)

Out, out, brief candle!
Life's but a walking shadow, a poor player
That struts and frets his hour upon the stage
And then is heard no more. It is a tale
Told by an idiot, full of sound and fury,
Signifying nothing.

—Macbeth

No one knows quite how or when William Shakespeare got himself to London. It's clear the glover's son from Stratford was cooling his heels in the provinces as late as May 1584, given the birth of his twin children nine months later. After that, it's anyone's guess. It's likely he joined a troupe of players traveling through the provinces in the mid-1580s—and there is no lack of candidates. Leicester's Men were regularly swinging through nearby Coventry, but so were Essex's, the Lord Admiral's, and Sussex's. Biographer Stephen Greenblatt and others romantically suppose he joined up with the Queen's Men, who passed through Stratford shorthanded in 1587 after one of the troupe's players was killed in a tavern fight.

However he came to the capital, Shakespeare arrived in a London theater scene poised on the verge of dramatic change. After a decade of public performances at the innyards and Shoreditch playhouses, a new theater opened in 1587 across the Thames on Bankside in Southwark: the Rose. A squalid district of brothels and alehouses outside the city's jurisdiction, Bankside would soon be transformed in the next decade into the world's premier entertainment district. Merchant-turned-theater impresario Philip Henslowe built the Rose as a fourteen-sided polygon with three tiers of galleries; at seventy-three feet across, it was smaller than James Burbage's The Theatre, but instantly its biggest competitor. With venues now on both sides of the river, companies jockeyed for audiences that had a sudden, insatiable appetite for plays.

When Leicester died in September 1588, his company of players died with him. The Queen's Men faltered that same month after the death of its lead player, Richard Tarlton, suddenly leaving a theatrical free-for-all. Many of Leicester's Men, including William Kemp, eventually ended up with Lord Strange's Men—a brand new company sponsored by Derby nobleman Ferdinando Stanley, Lord Strange (pronounced "Strang"). The company also included Richard Burbage, James's son, who was soon to be the greatest actor of his time. Most scholars believe Shakespeare also joined the company at some point, performing in the late 1580s at The Theatre and the Curtain.

There in the Shoreditch and Southwark public houses, he brushed elbows with a new generation of young playwrights, as hard-drinking as they were boastful. There was the wunderkind with a dangerous temper, Christopher Marlowe; the acerbic satirist Thomas Nashe; the mayor's son Thomas Lodge; the brawling poet Thomas Watson; the party boy George Peele; and—lording mirthfully over them all—Robert Greene, the self-proclaimed writer of his generation. Educated at Oxford or Cambridge, and ranging in age from twenty-one to thirty-three, the so-called University Wits ushered in a new age of theater, before fading as quickly as they came. Standing apart in education, but not influence, was the scrivener's son Thomas Kyd.

The opening salvo in this theatrical revolution was fired by Marlowe, whose overblown historical play *Tamburlaine the Great* had audiences swooning over the heady exploits of the titular Central Asian tyrant. Performed by the Admiral's Men—the company of Armada hero Charles Howard—at the Rose in 1587, the play was full of hyperbolic imagery, rousing swordfights, and grandiloquent speeches, proving so popular that Marlowe rushed out a sequel the following year. Around the same time, Kyd debuted *The Spanish Tragedy*, a bloodbath set against the Spanish-Portuguese war that singlehandedly revived Senecan revenge tragedy. With a ghost, a play-within-a-play, and high body count, the play is commonly compared with *Hamlet*—though it's hard to tell which influenced which.

Along with Peele's *The Battle of Alcazar* and Greene's *Orlando Furioso*, these new plays were bold, muscular, and bloody—the perfect accompaniment to the Armada era. According to Shakespearean scholars, they inspired the fresh-off-the-boat Stratford player to try his own hand at playwriting, penning the savage Senecan tragedy *Titus Andronicus* and the violent histories of *Henry VI, Parts 2 and 3*. In their estimation, Shakespeare was with the Wits but not of them, his Stratford grammar school education hardly able to compete with their university-bred repartee. More recently, scholars have speculated that Stratford Will worked more closely with the Wits than previously thought, collaborating with Peele on *Titus*, Marlowe on *Henry VI, Parts 2 and 3*, and Nashe on *Henry VI, Part 1*—as well as perhaps Kyd on *Arden of Faversham* and *Edward III*.

The record is complicated by the fact that many of Shakespeare's early plays seemed to already exist in other forms, such as the Queen's Men's plays *The Famous Victories of Henry V*, *King Leir*, and *The True Tragedy of Richard III*. Lord Strange's Men, meanwhile, played *Titus and Vespasian*, and the Admiral's Men performed a play called *Harey VI*. Scholars explain those "coincidences" in one of two ways, suggesting they were either early versions Shakespeare had written on the road or earlier plays by someone else that Shakespeare later reworked. McCarthy believes these plays to be scattered remnants of Thomas North's *oeuvre*, brought by the players to the companies where they landed, and reworked by them into knock-off productions. While a play, once sold, became property of the company that bought it, it's less clear what happened to scripts once a company disbanded. If North retained some of the playbooks he'd written for Leicester's Men, he could resell them again now. And at least some of them, McCarthy believes, North sold to Shakespeare.

After Leicester's death left him without a patron, North drifted down to London, where he might have met Shakespeare in any number of ways. *Plutarch's* publisher, Thomas Vautrollier, died in 1587, leaving his press to

Richard Field, a native of Stratford-upon-Avon who could have introduced them at his Blackfriars shop. Or they could have met through members of Leicester's Men, including William Kemp and Richard Burbage, who would both soon become Shakespeare's most important players.

Now in his mid-fifties, the down-on-his-luck older gentleman would have cut a curious figure among the upstarts pounding pints in Shoreditch. While they might have admired the writer of *Plutarch's Lives*, they may have also resented the old man with his pretentious stories about court life and nobles. One of them, says McCarthy, decided to express that disdain in print—including a possible reference to North's relationship with Shakespeare.

OF ALL THE WITS, the one with the wickedest sense of humor was Thomas Nashe, just twenty-one in 1588 but already employing his poison pen in a series of pamphlets attacking Puritanism. It's Nashe who first identified "English Seneca" in his 1589 preface to Robert Greene's *Menaphon*, mocking the unnamed playwright for creating outdated revenge tragedies. Three years later, in 1592, he waded into a "pamphlet war" between his mentor Greene and Leicester's protégé Gabriel Harvey that got so heated that Harvey came to London to confront him in person.

He was too late, as Greene had died that September. Although he gave up the ghost, he hadn't given up his invective. Later that year, the posthumous pamphlet titled *Greene's Groatsworth of Wit* appeared, claiming to be Greene's deathbed confession. In reality, scholars agree, it wasn't written by Greene at all—but by his printer, Henry Chettle, and, some believe, Nashe as well. "It is a memorably brilliant piece of writing," writes Oxford professor Katherine Duncan-Jones, "glancing, allusive, learned, and double-edged in a manner beyond the reach of the journeyman Chettle." This is the same work that McCarthy encountered early in his research as the source for the famous "upstart crow" passage that launched centuries of speculation about Shakespeare being a plagiarist.

McCarthy had already read into the pamphlet the story of Thomas North's disinheritance at the hands of his father—but there was more to the narrative. Later, the gentleman-scholar Roberto meets a country actor with an inflated sense of his own wit, and asks him for advice on how he might make money. "Why easily," the player says, "and greatly to your benefit: for men of my profession get by scholars their whole living." Confused, the gentleman asks, "But how do you mean to use me?" The actor replies, "Why, sir, in making plays, for which you shall be well paid, if you will take the pains."

Reading the passage, McCarthy realized he could be witnessing a satirical re-creation of the very moment that North met Shakespeare and agreed to sell him plays. The entire pamphlet, in fact, reads as a vicious parody of North's biography, he says. After Roberto is disinherited by his father, the story details his rivalry with his brother Luciano, who retains the family wealth. Roberto teams up with a woman, Lamilia, to trick Luciano into gambling away all his money to her and split the winnings. At this point in the story, Roberto and Lamilia face off with competing beast fables, just like in North's *Moral Philosophy of Doni*. Roberto's tale starts with a gentleman living "in the North parts" whose only heir is his daughter, and who is being wooed by a poor farmer—just as in Spenser's *The Shepheardes Calender*. The farmer is then fooled by another man who performs a "bed trick," in which a man sleeps with a woman who has been substituted in bed for his wife. The same scheme appears as a plot point in Shakespeare's *All's Well That Ends Well* and *Measure for Measure*. Of course, in 1592, those plays hadn't been written—at least not by Shakespeare—implying that Nashe was referring to North's earlier versions of the plays instead. "It's all a spoof on Thomas North's writing," McCarthy concludes.

He even thinks that he can identify the inspiration for Lamilia, the woman who comes between the two brothers. After Roger's wife died in 1578, he attempted to marry a rich daughter of a neighbor, but was rejected. In the late 1580s, however, he details numerous gifts and gambling debts paid to "Lady Rich"—that is, Penelope Rich, the daughter of Lettice Knollys, and the "Stella" to Sir Philip Sidney's "Astrophil." She was now in an unhappy marriage with Robert Rich and would later have an affair with another man. If *Groatsworth* can be believed, then Thomas somehow pushed her toward his brother, and it didn't end well.

Roger's account books end in 1589, so there's no way of reading between the lines to conjecture how such an affair might have ended, and whether it caused a rift between the brothers, as *Groatsworth* seemed to claim. What is clear, however, is that for some reason the pamphlet caused a stir at court, and within the year, Chettle issued an apology, in which he denied writing and regretted publishing it, saying one of the playwrights took offense at the story. He goes on to praise that person's "honesty" and "uprightness of dealing," saying that "diverse of worship" (meaning a variety of nobles) have defended him. With a lack of further evidence, scholars have variously speculated that the injured party was Shakespeare or Marlowe. But McCarthy has a different view: the person who had most cause to be offended was the "gentleman-scholar," Thomas North, and the only reason Chettle would have apologized is that in Nashe's effort to attack Thomas, he had hit too close to Roger—a rich baron with influence at court.

IF THOMAS NORTH and his brother had a falling out during this time, then it would explain why Thomas needed to sell his plays for money in the first place—having lost both the support of his patron, Leicester, and his pension from Roger. While North was selling his old plays to Shakespeare, however, McCarthy believes he was still continuing to write new ones—at this point composing his *Ur-Othello*, basing it on his own experiences in 1570s Venice—overlaid on the contemporary history of the Spanish Armada. (Just as the Turkish fleet is destroyed by storms on its way to Cyprus, so, too, were Philip's ships on their way to England.) And he also may have written another play about a ruler under attack from enemies both within and without: *King Lear*.

The story of the pre-Christian king of Britain has a long history, first appearing in Geoffrey Monmouth's twelfth-century chronicle of England. It was retold in *The Mirror for Magistrates* and *Holinshed's Chronicles*, and both Sidney and Spenser wrote their own versions in *Arcadia* and *The Faerie Queene*, respectively. Then there's the Queen's Men's *King Leir*, entered into the Stationers' Register in 1594. Scholars believe that play was written and performed as far back as 1590, variously attributing it to Thomas Kyd, Robert Greene, or one of the other University Wits. They are near united, however, in believing that the play was another source for Shakespeare's bleakest tragedy, of a king who gives away his kingdom, only to be betrayed by his own daughters. As McCarthy read the play in the context of Thomas North's life in London, however, he saw in it something else: the lament of a man drowning in poverty as he approached old age.

King Lear is Shakespeare's most challenging drama, as unrelenting in its tragedy as the storm that overwhelms its third act. "So great is the suffering depicted in Shakespeare's *King Lear*, that one has trouble finding the words to write about it," write editors Barbara Mowat and Paul Werstine. At the same time, the play has also been recognized as among the most sublime in the canon, an unflinching and honest exploration of what it means to be human, and an examination of whom we can and can't rely upon as we approach the end of life.

At the beginning of the play, the aging king divides his kingdom between his three daughters, telling them he'll give the most land to the one who expresses her love the most. As the older daughters, Goneril and Regan, gush with flattery, the youngest, Cordelia, stays silent, causing an enraged Lear to banish her to France and split her land between the other two. Once the kingdoms are separated, however, the older daughters spurn their father, sending him half-mad with grief into a storm out on the heath. Famously, Lear refuses to take responsibility for his state, declaring himself "more sinned against than sinning," even though he arguably brought the tragedy upon himself.

At the same time, another aging patriarch, the Duke of Gloucester, also fatally misjudges his children—making the sinister bastard son Edmund his heir over his legitimate son, the honest Edgar. Edmund betrays his father, too, setting him up to be arrested on trumped-up charges of treason. In one of Shakespeare's most gratuitous scenes, Gloucester's eyes are blinded onstage, sending him out into the storm as well. Scenes like that led generations of thespians to see the play as virtually unstageable, more allegorical than realistic in its sensibilities.

Yet the play has always fascinated readers, not only due to the sufferings of the mad King Lear, but also to the machinations of Edmund, the most vicious villain in Shakespeare, who "out-Iagos Iago" in Harold Bloom's words—and even out-Richards Richard III. Like those villains, he oozes charisma, especially in his famous soliloquy in which he rails, "Why bastard? Wherefore base? When my dimensions are as well compact, my mind as generous, and my shape as true, as honest madam's issue?" Strangely, Edmund adds primogeniture into his lament, rhetorically asking, "Wherefore should I stand in the plague of custom and permit the curiosity of nations to deprive me, for that I am some twelve or fourteen moonshines lag of a brother?"

Since Edmund is a bastard, the *order* of his birth wouldn't matter, but his complaint sounds remarkably similar to Orlando's in *As You Like It*, who decries the "custom of nations" for disinheriting him. That complaint also particularly troubled Thomas North as he entered the 1590s, McCarthy says. "It's clearly the darkest moment of his life," he says. "Leicester, who has paid him for plays throughout his life, has just died, Leicester's Men have disbanded, and now he no longer has his brother to support him either. He is literally facing poverty and hunger." Whatever part of himself North put into the bastard's complaint, however, McCarthy sees the true source for the character of Edmund in a real-life villain with whom North would have been intimately familiar.

When Thomas was posted to protect the Isle of Ely in 1588, the most notorious Catholic recusant under his guard was a Jesuit preacher by the name of William Weston, whose specialty was performing showy exorcisms to cast out devils—just as North had witnessed in Chester upon his return from Ireland. Imprisoned in Wisbech Castle during the Armada's invasion, Weston was in line to become Bishop of London had the Spanish succeeded in conquering England. The Catholic exorcist, however, didn't go by the name Weston—he called himself Father Edmunds, a nod to the famous recusant Edmund Campion. Numerous scholars have made the connection to the villain of Lear, contending the name of Gloucester's bastard would be instantly recognizable to audiences as a stand-in for the reviled Catholic.

After Lear and Gloucester flee into the storm, Gloucester's good son, Edgar, follows his father, appearing in the guise of Poor Tom O'Bedlam, a beggar possessed by demons. As often noted, the colorful names for the demons supposedly possessing Edgar—Obidictu, Hobbididence, Mahu, Modo, and Flibbertigibbet—appear in the 1603 book *A Declaration of Egregious Popish Impostures,* written by chaplain Samuel Harsnett about the exorcisms performed by Edmunds and other Catholics, leading them to believe that Shakespeare used the book as a source. McCarthy thinks it more likely that both North and Harsnett borrowed from a now-lost manuscript called "The Book of Miracles" that Edmunds himself is known to have written while imprisoned at Wisbech. Not only could North have had access to Edmunds's book as captain of the forces in Ely, but he might have had early access to Harsnett's manuscript as well. Harsnett's patron and mentor was Richard Bridgewater, a former Cambridge University orator who became vicar-general in Ely. When Bridgewater died in 1588, Thomas North married his widow, Judith. While she appears in the historical record as seldom as North's first wife, the connection could at least explain how North could have accessed the source.

MORE THAN AN ATTACK on a Catholic exorcist, however, *King Lear* presents an existential crisis for Lear himself, as the old man comes to terms with the loss of everything that matters. "The play's special understanding of old age explains in part why this most devastating of Shakespeare's tragedies is also perhaps his most moving," say Mowat and Werstine. The play, in fact, seems like a work written by an older man than Shakespeare, who was forty-two in 1606, the traditional date of the play's authorship. At age fifty-five in 1590, North was not only closer in age to Lear, but he had also weathered his own share of misfortunes. By now, he had failed in his attempts to find favor at court, or even financial security, says McCarthy. As he watched a younger generation of playwrights achieve success on the public stage, he poured some of himself into the disappointed Lear, McCarthy says.

To make sense of his condition, North did what he always did, he says, turned for solace to the philosophy that had sustained him for decades. "As *Hamlet* is about facing death, *King Lear* is about facing poverty," McCarthy says. "He went back to his teachings and tried to use that and face it in a stoic manner." The passage he chose was one from his *Moral Philosophy of Doni*: the fable of the river. One of the first tales in the book, it represents life as a raging river carrying treasures on its waves. Some people only wet their feet, living in servitude; others wade in up to their legs, working their whole lives and tasting only a little of life's pleasures; others swim into the current, grabbing the treasures, but eventually drowning—representing the lords and rulers who live large until "overtaken by some accident such as war, treason, poison, or man's force."

It's a bleak assessment of life—but aptly conveys Lear's experience in the storm, which often seems flood-like in its ferocity, McCarthy says. Using his plagiarism software, he found numerous parallels between the fable and Lear. As Lear is lost on the heath in "his little world of man," he "tears his white hair," which the winds "with eyeless rage catch in their fury and make nothing of." Similarly, the passage in *Doni* describes the "fury" and "raging" of the river, before comparing "the little world of our body" to the hairs cut off and thrown away by the barber that "cometh to nothing."

The sage of *Doni* isn't the only philosopher to whom North turned in describing Lear's despair, says McCarthy. In 1602, North published his last work, *Nepos's Lives*, an addendum to *Plutarch's Lives* with a dozen more biographies, starting with the "Life of Epaminondas," the philosopher-general of ancient Thebes. But McCarthy believes he had already written that first chapter by 1590, and used it now for *Lear*. When Gloucester first meets Lear in the storm, he urges him to come inside to shelter, but Lear brushes him off to talk to the disguised Edgar, whom he calls a "philosopher" and a "learned Theban," asking him nonsensically, "What is the cause of thunder?" That's a direct hit on North's translation, McCarthy says. At one point, Epaminondas marches his soldiers through a storm to attack an enemy, but seeing the storm as a bad omen, his lieutenants urge him to call off the attack. When they hear a crack of thunder, they ask him "what that thunder meant." Epaminondas tells them it's actually a bad omen for their enemies, meaning they will be destroyed in battle.

There is a reason that North might use this particular "Life" to make sense of the king's suffering, McCarthy says. In his chapter, North repeatedly stresses how Epaminondas "did love and embrace poverty," choosing to eat simply and cheerfully give away his money to the poor. In the same way, both Lear and Gloucester learn to embrace their fallen state. When one of Gloucester's former tenants tries to offer him shelter, Gloucester rejects it, saying, "Away, get thee away! Good friend, begone. Thy comforts can do me no good at all." Similarly, when a friend tries to bribe Epaminondas, he replies, "I have no need of money," adding, "I pardon thee, but get thee away."

Lear, too, finds redemption in the storm, at last taking responsibility for his downfall and repenting of his ill-treatment of his daughter Cordelia, as well as his selfish disregard for his own subjects. Realizing for the first time how the poor are left at the mercy of the elements, he vows to himself to "expose thyself to feel what wretches feel." Both Lear and Gloucester, McCarthy says, have learned the lesson of the river: "The people that go into the river—this stormy flood that is the centerpiece of this entire play—those are the ones that had the most, those are the ones that lose the most, but when they come out, they have a newfound spirit of charity."

Of course, neither life nor theater lends itself to such easy answers. By the last act of the play, Edmund has defeated Cordelia's invading army from France and taken her and her father prisoner. Goneril, meanwhile, murders Regan before killing herself. Finally, Edgar arrives to confront Edmund, telling him that their father, Gloucester, died. Suddenly overcome with grief, Edmund repents, but too late to rescind a secret order to murder Cordelia in her cell. In one of the most heartbreaking scenes in the canon, Lear arrives onstage holding the body of his dead daughter, before dying himself. As McCarthy explains his vision of the play, I find myself moved by this image of the aging North—a brilliant writer pouring his sadness into this tragic scene as he struggled to find meaning in his impoverishment. Giving in to McCarthy's theories for a moment, I imagine how North's life might have been different had he been recognized earlier for his talents; then again, perhaps if he had, we wouldn't have the poignant drama of *King Lear* today.

If there is any hope at the end of the play, it lies in Edgar, who is left to rule the kingdom alongside the Duke of Albany, the former husband of Goneril, who turned against her to side with Edgar. The ending—and indeed, the whole play—is conventionally seen as a symbol for the unification of Britain, showing the disastrous consequences when the kingdom is divided, and the hope when it is reunited under Edgar, representing England, and Albany, an ancient word for northern Britain, including Scotland. That reunification mirrors post-Armada Britain, after James of

Scotland sided with England over the Spanish invaders. With the death of his mother, Mary, James now increasingly seemed a compromise candidate for the English throne for both Catholics and Protestants. In his version of *Lear*, says McCarthy, North may have welcomed that succession, just as at the end of his *Hamlet*, he sympathetically portrayed James's stand-in, Fortinbras. Though he may have accepted his impoverished fate, that didn't mean it had to be permanent. Perhaps North thought a new monarch might give him the recognition and advancement he long sought.

EVEN AS MCCARTHY was sifting through the sources of *King Lear*, he stumbled across one more source that scholars had missed—because they didn't know it existed. When McCarthy and Schlueter first found George North's *A Brief Discourse of Rebellions and Rebels* hidden at the British Library, McCarthy subjected it to his plagiarism software, using the text of the entire Shakespeare canon. The *Henry VI* plays weren't the only hits he found. "It had *Lear* left and right," he tells me. "It was really surprising because they were written in two different times." Even more surprisingly, *Lear* seemed to use the same section of *Brief Discourse* as *Henry VI, Part 2*: the scenes about the rebel Jack Cade. When he is hunted and starving, Cade says his body will be left "for carrion crows and worm's meat to eat me flesh and fell." Lear uses the same phrase to describe his jailers as they are about to imprison him and his daughter, saying, "The good years shall devour them, flesh and fell, ere they shall make us weep. We'll see 'em starved first." McCarthy found only seven other instances of the phrase before *Lear* on EEBO, and none of them about eating—much less eating a human body. "It's right out of George North's view of Jack Cade," he says.

In another passage, the old king compares his ungrateful daughters to dogs, and Poor Tom replies with a nonsense list of dogs all running together. "Avaunt, you curs!" he cries. "Mastiff, greyhound, mongrel grim, hound or spaniel, branch or lym, bobtail tike or trundle-tail, Tom will make them weep or wail." The list, McCarthy found, echoes a canine inventory in Cade's monologue: "If trundle tail of currish kind with greyhound may compare," Cade declares, "or mastie made to hunt the hog with spaniel have his share, then worldly whelps account of me that durst presume to run." Cade's speech invokes a subversion of the social order, with dogs of all breeds mixed together, McCarthy says, the same way order has been inverted with Lear's downfall.

No character in the play represents that vision of a world turned upside down more than Lear's Fool, who accompanies him out onto the heath. The Fool is one of the strangest and most original characters in the Shakespeare canon—an anarchic sage quite unlike the stereotypical joking court jester. Even as Lear is raging against his state, the Fool constantly mocks and trivializes his suffering. Scholars, in fact, commonly interpret the character as an aspect of Lear himself, revealing the thoughts he would keep hidden. Once Lear admits his own foolishness for splitting his kingdom, the Fool disappears. But not before delivering a strange apocalyptic prophecy: "When priests are more in word than matter; when brewers mar their malt with water; when nobles are their tailors' tutors, no heretics burned but wenches' suitors, then shall the realm of Albion come to great confusion," he says, continuing in that dystopian vein for several lines before concluding, "Then comes the time, who lives to see't, that going shall be used with feet." The prognostication has long bewildered scholars, some of whom have surmised that it was added to Shakespeare's play by another writer.

Much, though not all, of the language clearly comes from a poem by Geoffrey Chaucer; the Fool, however, attributes it to the ancient wizard Merlin, saying, "This prophecy Merlin shall make, for I live before his time." (Lear lived in the eighth century BCE, three hundred years before Camelot.) The last line ("that going shall be used with feet") is particularly confusing. Some editors have interpreted it as a bizarre truism that—perhaps intentionally—undercuts the entire prophecy. In *A Brief Discourse*, however, McCarthy found an explanation for the quandary. In one passage, George North similarly warns of apocalyptic doom in which "drunkenness is taken for delight, robbery allowed purchase, lechery regarded solace, murder thought honest revenge, and rebellious treason esteemed." Those lines too match up with Chaucer's poem. North, however, attributes this vision to our "late Poet," who prophesied a "world and worldly causes turned top under tail" when "our mouth with milk and honey flows, but gall in heart doth bound."

When McCarthy looked up that combination of words, he found them in a seventeenth-century book called *British and Outlandish Prophesies*—attributed to Merlin. That couldn't be a coincidence, he thought, surmising that both the author of that book and George North must have been working from a now-lost source that conflated Chaucer and Merlin in the same prophetic passage. "There was some manuscript in Kirtling Hall that actually contained that, and attributed it to Merlin," he says. Even the last line, "that going shall be used with feet," made sense once he compared it with George North's list of role reversals, which ends with the result that "knaves ride and kings go on foot." In fact, that's exactly what happens to Lear in the play, in which he has given up his horses and is now wandering by foot. Taken together, he says, the manuscript offers an explanation for why the Fool would make the strange speech. "He quotes Merlin because *he* is a Merlin, a prophet of the upside-down," McCarthy contends. Far from being superfluous, as some scholars have speculated, he adds, the prophecy is essential to understanding the Fool's character—and adds new insight into one of Shakespeare's most iconic roles. "They thought the Merlin prophecy wasn't supposed to be in there, but it's actually one of the most important passages," McCarthy exults.

AFTER THE DEATH of her longtime favorite, Leicester, Queen Elizabeth's own world was turned upside down; but she soon righted it by latching on to a new object of affection—Leicester's twenty-two-year-old stepson Robert Devereux, the Earl of Essex. The dashing young courtier seemed like her Sweet Robin reincarnated. Tall, handsome, and auburn-haired, Essex was every bit his stepfather's heir, but beloved by the common people in a way that Leicester never had been. He slid easily into Leicester's place as Master of the Horse, moving into his apartments at court, and even taking over Leicester House, renaming it Essex House. But Essex could also be petulant and headstrong, making sudden demands of the queen, and then, when she denied him, sulkily withdrawing to the country.

Eager for revenge against the Spanish, Essex defied the queen's orders by joining an expedition led by Norris and Drake that raided A Coruña before assaulting Lisbon. Essex rode up to the gates of the city, challenging the governor to a duel, but the attack ultimately failed, leaving six thousand English dead from disease. The queen punished Essex by presenting a gold chain to a rival, Walter Raleigh, instead. True to form, Essex withdrew from court, bristling under the queen's tempers. At Essex House, he began secretly writing King James VI of Scotland, offering his service. His sister and confidante Penelope Rich even wrote him that her brother was "exceedingly weary, accounting it a thrall he now lives in." Any further attacks on the Spanish, however, were put on hold as England became embroiled in a new conflict on the Continent. That July, France lost yet another king when Henri III was assassinated by a radical Catholic. That technically made the Protestant Henri of Navarre king as Henri IV, but Catholics prevented him from taking up the crown. Driven from Paris, Henri frantically requested English aid. Starting in early 1591, Elizabeth reluctantly sent three thousand troops to Brittany, followed by four thousand soldiers to Normandy to assist in the siege of Rouen.

Essex literally begged on bended knee for the appointment to lead them, and Elizabeth relented. Among the troops sailing with him may have been Thomas North. Muster records show a "Captain North" appointed as lieutenant colonel, though don't include a first name. If he did accompany Essex, it was a short deployment. By the time Essex arrived, Henri IV was engaged in other battles, and English troops sat idly outside the city as the old enemy, disease, ravaged their ranks. Essex once again raised Elizabeth's ire by riding behind enemy lines to visit Henri and engaging in a pointless battle in which his own brother was killed. The queen angrily recalled him in January. Among her charges against him was that he had knighted dozens of his captains against her express orders, even some who didn't meet the minimum requirements for knighthood of owning land with an income of £40 a year. It's possible that one of those honored was North, who appears a month later in February 1592 as Sir Thomas North in a commission making him a justice of the peace in Cambridge—a public appointment at last, even if it was only a local honor.

Meanwhile, in France, the implacable Parma appeared before Rouen, forcing withdrawal of the remainder of the troops. After three years of fighting, Henri IV bowed to the inevitable and converted to Catholicism to enter Paris at last. All of the pointless fighting had depleted Elizabeth's treasury, forcing her to raise taxes over the grumbling of the populace.

Following the glorious victory over the Armada, a malaise settled over Elizabeth's twilight years. Hot summers followed by torrential rains caused harvests to fail and citizens to take to the streets. In June 1592, a riot in Southwark led to shutting down the Rose. A few weeks later, an outbreak of the plague shuttered all the London theaters throughout most of 1593.

Adding to the distress, Elizabeth's older councilors were dying one by one, including Walsingham and Hatton, until only Burghley remained. In their place jockeyed the headstrong Essex along with the studious Francis Bacon and the swashbuckling Walter Raleigh. By far the most capable courtier, however, was Burghley's son Robert Cecil, a hunchbacked bureaucrat skilled at handling—some might say manipulating—those around him. With fine speech and patient marshaling of details, he was every bit his father's heir. Essex, of course, hated him on principle, spawning a new generation of factionalism at court.

Even in the midst of this strife, Elizabeth couldn't bring herself to name an heir; even mentioning the topic could cause her to fly into a rage. Despite the clear claim of James VI of Scotland, there were actually multiple English contenders dangling from various branches of the Tudor family tree. As Essex continued his secret correspondence, Elizabeth quarreled moodily with James, accusing him of involvement in plots to overthrow her. In turn, she angered him by giving succor to one of his enemies—a Scottish lord whom James accused of trying to kill him with witchcraft.

IN THE EARLY 1590S, in fact, King James VI was obsessed with thoughts of witches. The creatures, in his estimation, had been wreaking havoc on Scotland with their dark feminine energy for years. When the twenty-four-year-old king's new queen, Anne of Denmark, disembarked for Scotland in 1589 and storms forced her to return, some blamed satanic influence. James went to Denmark himself to fetch her, and his journey, too, was beset by violent storms, sinking one of his ships. There, a Danish woman confessed to using witchcraft to hinder the queen's passage, and panic ensued, with James and his courtiers suspecting a much wider conspiracy. Eventually, under torture, a man and two women in North Berwick, Scotland, confessed to the sinister plot to kill the king—and pointed to James's cousin and rival, the Earl of Bothwell, as master of their coven.

Dozens of men and women were hanged or burned alive in the ensuing witch hunt, but Bothwell escaped in 1591, fleeing into exile in England under Elizabeth's protection two years later.

These dramatic events must have been in Thomas North's mind as he paged through *Holinshed's Chronicles* around that time, says McCarthy. They would become the backdrop for a new play he was writing in hopes of pleasing King James, about another witch-induced Scottish regicide—committed by an eleventh-century thane named Macbeth. The "Scottish play," as *Macbeth* is superstitiously known, is the darkest and most nihilistic in the canon, a gruesome and seductive tale of evil deeds. It's also often seen as Shakespeare's greatest play, his last tragedy, and his most satisfying to audiences—almost entirely due to the captivating couple at its center. Unlike Edmund or Richard III, who delight in their evil deeds, or Othello or Lear, who are oblivious to the pain they cause, Macbeth is both completely horrified by and completely aware of the consequences of his evil actions—and yet carries them out anyway. His wife, Lady Macbeth, is a willing accomplice, goading Macbeth into his crimes, and then shrinking from them even as he doubles down on his wickedness.

The story begins as Macbeth and his friend Banquo return from battle and meet three "Weird Sisters" who prophesy that Macbeth will be king—and Banquo's descendants will be kings thereafter. The prophecy seems to stir something Macbeth has already contemplated, and he and his wife plot to murder the king Duncan as he stays at their castle. After accomplishing the bloody deed, Macbeth becomes increasingly paranoid, murdering his friend Banquo and attempting to murder Banquo's son, who nevertheless escapes. As the forces of his enemies close around him, Macbeth murders the family of his rival Macduff, while Lady Macbeth sleepwalks around the castle at night, crying "Out, damned spot!" as she desperately tries to wash her hands of imagined blood.

In its gruesome depiction of the murder, the play takes liberties with history. In *Holinshed*, Duncan is a weak king, and Macbeth is justified in usurping the throne; the play, however, emphasizes Duncan's nobility, contrasting it with the evil nature of Macbeth's deeds. In the original tale, too, Banquo is also a coconspirator in the crime—a fact presenting special difficulties, as the historical Banquo was an ancestor of King James. Scholars see the change as an effort to appease James, by presenting his forefather in a more positive light. Other details in the play are plucked from two Latin histories of Scotland published in 1578 and 1582; a treatise on witchcraft from 1584; an account of the North Berwick trials called *News Out of Scotland*, published in 1591; and the Senecan tragedies of *Medea* and *Hercules Furens*, recently translated into English that same year.

Once again, McCarthy notes, all of the sources of the play would have been present for Thomas North to write an *Ur-Macbeth* around 1592—even though scholars believe Shakespeare didn't write it until more than a decade later, in 1606. The only suspected source not available was one James wrote himself, a book called *Demonology*, about his own investigations into witchcraft, published in 1597. In McCarthy's defense, however, most of the details in that book come from previous books on witchcraft, and some scholars believe James was already circulating it in manuscript form soon after the North Berwick trials in 1591.

The descriptions of the three Weird Sisters, who compel the death of the king, would have held a special macabre fascination for the superstitious James—confirming his own fears of dark powers plotting his own death. Just before Macbeth and Banquo meet with them for the first time, the audience finds them gleefully plotting the destruction of a sailor whose wife offended them. "Her husband's to Aleppo gone, master o' th' Tiger, but in a sieve I'll thither sail, and, like a rat without a tail, I'll do, I'll do, and I'll do," cackles the first witch, while the others offer to give her wind to speed her journey. The first witch continues to describe the miseries she'll inflict on him, saying she will "drain him dry as hay" as his ship is "tempest-tossed."

Researching the play, McCarthy was surprised to find there was a ship called the *Tiger* on which a merchant journeyed to Aleppo, then part of the Ottoman Empire, between 1583 and 1591. On his return journey, he ran into many misfortunes, including storms and extreme heat that caused him to almost die from thirst—all details matching the witches' incantation of the sailor's demise. For James, however, they would have sent a shiver down his spine as he recalled his own misfortunes at sea—which he was convinced had been caused by the dark powers of witchcraft.

"James holds a trial on three witches who he thinks tried to sink his ship," says McCarthy. "That's where these witches in *Macbeth* come from, and why they are able to control the weather." Once again, he contends, Thomas North is working current history into his play.

WHILE CONDUCTING MY own research in the archives to investigate McCarthy's theories, I make a discovery that sends a chill down my own spine. The rare-books room at Cambridge University Library holds Thomas North's own copy of *The Dial of Princes*, complete with his distinctive signature and a date of March 29, 1591. It's filled with underlined passages and marginal notes he made, presumably in preparation for a new edition of the book. McCarthy and I visited the library briefly to see it together in the fall of 2018, but he had never taken the time to look through it more fully. (Once again, it struck me how, in tying himself to his computer, McCarthy routinely failed to examine some of the simplest evidence available to him in person.)

North's signature and marginalia in his copy of The Dial of Princes

On a return trip to England the next summer, I flip through the pages in the library, where one of North's handwritten notes in the margins jumps out at me: "The condition of a wicked man, he is compared to a candle." It immediately calls to my mind Macbeth's final words, as his enemies are closing in and he learns his wife has killed herself. "Out, out, brief candle!" he says. "Life's but a walking shadow, a poor player that struts and frets his hour upon the stage and then is heard no more. It is a tale told by an idiot, full of sound and fury, signifying nothing." The

Table of contents of North's The Dial of Princes

text next to North's comment reads: "We may aptly compare an ill man to a candle, which after it is once light, it never leaveth burning 'til it have made an end to itself." It continues, "After he hath once begun to do evil, he never ceaseth daily to do worse." How likely a coincidence could it be that North had called out this passage in his book? I ask myself. Numerous commentators of the play have pointed out the way in which after Duncan's murder Macbeth seems compelled inexorably toward his doom. No sooner does Macbeth kill Banquo than he contemplates killing Macduff, saying, "I am in blood stepped so far that, should I wade no more, returning were as tedious as go o'er." Now, here was a passage about a wicked man that basically made the same point.

But that wasn't the only reference in North's marginalia that seemed relevant to *Macbeth*. In another marginal comment, he notes, "lewd women compared to hedge-hogs," and a few pages later writes about "strange meats dressed and eaten" next to a passage about "a horse roasted, a cat in jelly, little lizards with hot broth, frogs fried." As Macbeth journeys back to visit with the Weird Sisters again, they are famously stirring at their cauldron. "Thrice the brinded cat hath mewed," says the first, and the second answers, "Thrice, and once the hedgepig whined," before they drop their ingredients in the pot, including "eye of newt and toe of frog," and "lizard's leg and owlet's wing, for a charm of powerful trouble, like a hell-broth boil and bubble." Among the images in common between the two passages are cats, hedgehogs (or hedgepigs), frogs, lizards, and hot broth. Again, it strikes me as more than coincidental that North would call out these images in 1591, around the same time that McCarthy contends he wrote *Macbeth*.

Even more surprisingly, in the table of contents, North had underlined only one chapter heading: "Wherein is expressed the great malice and little patience of an evil woman," writing the words in the margin as well. That is the same thirteen-word string that McCarthy had previously called out as mirroring the subheading of *Arden of Faversham*, which was anonymously published in 1592: "Wherein is shewed the great malice and dissimulation of an evil woman." North could have consulted *The Dial* as he prepared his old play for publication for extra money in a plague year—picking out passages for both plays while he was at it. Editors of both plays have commented on Alice Arden's similarities to Lady Macbeth, in her attempts to pluck up Mosby's courage to murder her husband, for example, or in her inability to wash the blood from the floor. "With my nails I'll scrape away the blood. The more I strive the more the blood appears!" Alice cries, echoing Lady Macbeth's, "Out, damned spot!" and "What, will these hands ne'er be clean?" Some have even speculated that Shakespeare was inspired by *Arden* in writing his Scottish play. Here, now, was a source connecting both North and Shakespeare around the very time *Arden* was published.

I send McCarthy images of North's underlined passages and marginalia, and he throws himself into a frenzy, running them through his plagiarism software. Within a few days, he sends me even more connections between the book and both plays. At one point, for example, North writes in the margin, "women soothsayers, sorcerers, and enchanters," next to a passage about wet nurses who claim to "heal infants" and "wean them better than others," but actually poison them. In fact, many of the passages North marked in *The Dial* appear in a section concerned with breastfeeding, which, McCarthy tells me, *Macbeth* is weirdly obsessed with as well. Lady Macbeth chides her husband, telling him he is too "full o' th' milk of human kindness" to murder the king. "Come to my woman's breasts," she cries to summon evil spirits, "and take my milk for gall." Later, as Macbeth is preparing to renege on his promise to commit the deed, she swears she would take a nursing baby and "while it was smiling in my face, have plucked my nipple from his boneless gums, and dashed his brains out" had she promised him that she would. That disturbing image echoes one from *The Dial*, in which North describes the wet nurse of the wicked emperor Caligula, who in anger "tore in pieces a young child, and with the blood thereof anointed her breast," to make Caligula "suck together both blood and milk."

McCarthy agrees that the candle passage may have inspired Macbeth's soliloquy. However, he also found another passage that he believes North used to construct it: *Doni*'s parable of the river. In the midst of this nihilistic tragedy, he says, North once again turned to the bleak parable, which has this to say: "This worldly life representeth no more but the little world of our body, which carryeth a wonderful presence: and that little breath of ours once spent, it is then but a shadow, dust and smoke." It continues that "worldly favors" are like snow that with the sun "dissolveth and cometh to nothing." Putting the two passages together, McCarthy says, reveals Macbeth's self-defeating philosophy—a man is a candle that burns itself out, and life is but a shadow, ultimately signifying nothing.

As with *King Lear*, however, there is at least some hope at the end of the play. As Macbeth learns that the witches' prophecy has betrayed him, the forces of Macduff and Duncan's son, Malcolm, encircle his castle. Offering them assistance is an unnamed king of England. Even after Macbeth finally dies on the battlefield, Malcolm cries, "My thanes and kinsmen, henceforth be earls," once again symbolizing the union of Scotland and England that North might have desired.

ALSO AS WITH *LEAR*, McCarthy found a connection between *Macbeth* and George North's *Brief Discourse*—seemingly drawing, in fact, from one of the same passages. As Macbeth hires murderers to kill Banquo, he compares different classes of men to breeds of dogs, including "hounds and greyhounds, mongrels, spaniels, curs"—a list very similar to Cade's, and to Tom's in *Lear*. By now, McCarthy had teased out connections between George North's book and eleven different Shakespeare plays. At the same time he was trying to publish his book about Thomas North, *The Earlier Playwright*, he had also been working on a plan with Schlueter to publish George North's manuscript in its entirely. Together, they would write a commentary describing the correlations with Shakespeare's plays—without mentioning Thomas North at all.

This time, McCarthy contacted his former publisher at Oxford University Press, since the book would stay within Stratfordian orthodoxy by presenting George North simply as a Shakespearean source. When he reached out in the fall of 2015, the editor was enthusiastic, telling him she'd love to publish it—just so long as it passed peer review. McCarthy's heart sank. "Look," he told her, "this is what is going to happen— they're going to claim that it's coincidental, which is the most insane thing in the world. There are so many resemblances and parallels, it's crazy." Sure enough, when they sent out the manuscript in early 2016, the expected criticism came. "It is not impossible that a player could have read" the manuscript, the anonymous reviewer wrote. However, "I was not persuaded that a single one of the alleged parallels presented evidence Shakespeare had read the treatise."

As an example, the reviewer pointed to a passage in which McCarthy and Schlueter had identified eight words including "rebels," "death," "sword," and "rout." A search of those terms within thirty words of each other on EEBO yielded only Shakespeare's play *Henry IV, Part 2.* "This, like many of the proximity searches used, is so precise that it could have been carefully tailored to produce the outcomes the authors wanted to find," the reviewer said. Looking up "sword" within thirty words of "death," however, the reviewer found more than eight thousand hits. For that matter, the reviewer continued snarkily, searching for "Hey" within ninety-nine words of "Jude" revealed six hits in EEBO, though "I do not think that Paul McCartney is likely to have read any of them."

Reading the review, McCarthy was incensed—the reviewer had completely ignored the context of the passage. In *Discourse*, it occurs within a monologue by Owen Glendower, who led an uprising against Henry IV; the corresponding passage in *Henry IV, Part 2*, occurs within a speech about Glendower. "They are talking about the same rebellion with identical words," McCarthy says. "It's like finding 'To be, or not to be, that is the question,' and saying it's not a match because 'to be' is quite common." McCarthy worked himself up into writing a detailed response debating the review point by point. He even showed how searching for "golden slumbers" and "lullaby" in EEBO pulled up a 1603 comedy by Thomas Dekker upon which Paul McCartney had actually based his lyrics for the *Abbey Road* B-side song "Golden Slumbers"—along with an even older reference to the same lullaby in, of all places, *Titus Andronicus*. "This shows you the power of EEBO to trace the literary ancestry of English works—including even Beatles' songs," he concluded with satisfaction.

He stopped himself, however, before hitting "Send," feeling completely dejected. "I was ready to quit," he tells me one day over hamburgers at London's King Cross station. No matter how many times he sent his writings to the established journals and presses, it seemed they weren't letting him into the academic club. "They only allow in certain ideas, and are not going to allow in any other ideas they feel are heretical." After that, he was ready to just self-publish all of his findings on the Web. Schlueter was horrified when he informed her—telling him it would be the kiss of death, preventing any academic from ever taking him seriously. But she had another idea: a few years earlier, she had published a book with the British Library's own press about Elizabethan autograph albums. What if she reached out to her editor there? After all, it would be good publicity for the library to say it had a previously undiscovered source for Shakespeare in its archives.

A few weeks later, Schlueter wrote back with the good news—the British Library was interested. Given the expense of printing the manuscript, however, it wanted to coordinate with another publisher, recommending Boydell & Brewer, a small British press specializing in history and criticism. McCarthy winced when he heard the press insisted on sending out the manuscript for peer review, but at least they were open to suggestions on reviewers. Schlueter recommended David Bevington, one of the foremost Shakespeare scholars in the United States, whom she knew through American Shakespeare circles. If he gave the book his seal of approval, then it was as good as golden. In addition, she recommended Martin Meisel, a professor emeritus of dramatic literature at her alma mater, Columbia. Since he didn't specialize in Shakespeare, she hoped he might come to the review without the baggage of a Bardolater.

McCarthy settled in to wait, impatiently, as the press shared their manuscript with Schlueter's colleagues. Finally, just after the New Year in 2017, she forwarded Bevington's response. "Are you sitting down?"

she wrote. "CONGRATULATIONS!" The attached review was glowing. "New sources for Shakespeare do not turn up every day in the week," Bevington wrote. "This is a truly significant one, that has not heretofore been studied or published." The example of the *Richard III* soliloquy was "impressively convincing," he continued, as were the additional details on Jack Cade in *Henry VI, Part 2* and the Fool's prophecy in *Lear*. "The result is that this study is important not just because it shows so many convincing parallels and sources, but because the comparison then helps us understand some difficult passages," Bevington wrote, especially citing "the Fool's gnomic wisdom in *King Lear*, often in need of explication."

Meisel's review was similarly positive, calling the book an "impressively argued, ingeniously presented, and economically elaborated argument for North's *Discourse* as a source for Shakespeare's plays." He did have some "uneasiness," however, based on McCarthy and Schlueter's practice of sometimes including too many words within the same passage as evidence of uniqueness—citing the same example from *Henry IV, Part 2* as the other reviewer. "With the terms so commonplace, the larger the set, the less probative the uniqueness of the match," he wrote. That said, he concluded, "there is no question that the study and the document should be published." Finally, realized McCarthy, a book about his discoveries would be published—even if it was only a part of his theory.

BY THE TIME he received the news, I had been personally speaking with McCarthy about his theories for over a year. Since we first met during my book talk at Lafayette College, we'd spoken several times in person and over the phone. I told him I would consider writing a magazine article about his findings, provided he was able to publish his claims in a book and get two more scholars to buy into his ideas. He had now fulfilled both requirements, and so I crafted my own pitch, sending it to a dozen publications over the next few months. When I received rejections of my own, I started to get a sense of how McCarthy must have felt all those years; but finally, I succeeded with a pitch to *The New York Times* about a shorter story for the Arts section solely about the George North book, without getting into McCarthy's larger theories.

McCarthy, meanwhile, was becoming increasingly impatient about the slow pace of the publishing industry, as the publication date of the George North book continued to be pushed back from its original date that fall. Finally, Boydell & Brewer came back with a firm date: February 2018. I began making calls for my article, speaking with Bevington and Meisel, but also other Shakespeare scholars, such as Michael Witmore, director of the Folger Shakespeare Library in Washington, DC. After I sent him an advance copy of the book, Witmore wrote back positively, saying he found McCarthy and Schlueter's methods sound. "The claim for North's *Discourse* being a source of Shakespeare is as good as any other currently accepted argument for source study," he told me. "I think it will be accepted." While some studies cherry-picked phrases and then located them in Shakespeare, he continued, McCarthy and Schlueter had added statistical significance by searching for the same phrases in EEBO. "But I also think the statistical arguments are only icing on the cake," he added. "At its core, this remains a literary argument, not a statistical one."

Another scholar, Joseph Rudman, an expert in digital humanities from Carnegie Mellon University, gave a qualified approval for McCarthy's methods. By using an over-the-counter plagiarism software such as WCopyfind, it was impossible to really know how matches were made, he said—if McCarthy was really serious about his research, he would custom-design software and freely share its algorithms so other scholars could analyze and reproduce the techniques. One person who did not return my request to read the book was Brian Vickers, the British scholar who had pioneered the use of plagiarism software. "I can't undertake to read it for some time, being snowed under with uncompleted projects," he told me.

Before I finished writing, my partner Rebecca and I drove up to New Hampshire to have dinner with McCarthy and his family. Amidst chicken Caesar salad and vodka cocktails, we talked about Stephen King novels and his daughter Kennedy's success in sports—she was now playing for a nationally ranked Ultimate Frisbee club in Boston—as well as McCarthy's upcoming book. "I'm just so excited for him, it's unbelievably fascinating," said his wife, Lori. "And I keep telling him—when people ask, you were able to do this because of me." Everyone laughed, as McCarthy agreed.

I filed my story in late January, and then, just before it was published, my editor informed me that it was being considered for Page 1. There it appeared on February 8, 2018, under the headline "Book Points to Possible Source of Shakespeare's Inspiration." Among other quotes, I included one from Schlueter, who proudly called the self-taught McCarthy the "Steve Jobs of the Shakespeare community," and one from Witmore, who said, "If it proves to be what they say it is, it is a once-in-a-generation—or several generations—find."

More positive coverage for the book followed, including stories in *The Los Angeles Times*, *Smithsonian*, and *U.S. News & World Report*. The news even carried across the ocean to *The Times* of London, *The Telegraph*, and *The Guardian*, which, much to my chagrin, quoted Vickers. While he'd only read part of the book, he said, McCarthy "has made a good case for Shakespeare having read the work." He quickly followed that faint praise, however, by damning McCarthy's self-published book on Thomas North, "which claimed that North was the true author of Shakespeare's plays." He added, "Scholars are now rather skeptical of his work."

Vickers wasn't the only one who was skeptical. Despite the initial rush of positive publicity, a pair of reviews appearing almost a year later called McCarthy and Schlueter's conclusions into question. The more courteous of the two appeared in the London-based *Times Literary Supplement*, written by Laura Kolb, a Renaissance literature professor at City University of New York–Baruch. In it, she argues that the ideas in North's manuscript are hardly unique; many of them are well-worn ideas common to a number of literary sources from Cicero to the Bible. While she grants that some passages like Richard's monologue and Jack Cade's lament share common elements, that could still just be coincidence. When you put "proportion" and "glass" together, after all, "the likelihood that the author will select appearance words—like 'deformed' or 'fair'—increases," she writes. And even the context isn't quite the same in all cases: North's Cade, for example, is repentant of his crimes, whereas Shakespeare's remains defiant. "Slight but insistent manipulations of the evidence crop up everywhere," she says, "creating a kind of fog through which it is hard to see either Shakespeare or North clearly, let alone any possible relationship between them."

A more acid review appeared in *The Library*, a journal published by Oxford University Press, later in the year, written by Princeton literature professor Rhodri Lewis. He starts by mentioning McCarthy's self-published book on Thomas North, and the review goes downhill from there, ending by labeling McCarthy and Schlueter's work "an unusually bad book" that is "sustained by a deep ignorance of the cultural and intellectual worlds to which North and Shakespeare belonged." Far from unique, he argues, the phrases that McCarthy and Schlueter claim Shakespeare borrowed from North are all commonplaces found not only in English works of the sixteenth century, but also in Latin works widely read by educated audiences of the time.

The passage they cite as the source for *Richard III*'s opening monologue is drawn from a speech by Socrates in Apuleius's *Apologia*, he writes, and repeated in numerous Latin works, including Plutarch and Seneca— explaining why George North and Shakespeare would use the same words. The phrase the authors use to connect the Merlin prophecy to North— "our mouth with milk and honey flows, but gall in heart doth bound"— also comes from a common Latin proverb that North needn't have come across in a lost manuscript about Merlin. And it isn't just Latin sources. An exhaustive list of dogs—including greyhound, mastiff, curs, hounds, and even "trindle tail"—appears in English in a fifteenth-century hunting manual. "The points of contact between North and Shakespeare are strictly conventional, comprising readings and learning that were standard fare to those inhabiting the literary, educational, and social cultures of sixteenth-century England," Lewis concludes.

He ends the review with a taunting stab at McCarthy's real agenda that hits a little too close to the mark. "It can only be a matter of time before someone argues that as Stratford Will cannot have had access to a manuscript treatise as rarefied as the *Discourse*, and, as the *Discourse* had such a demonstrable impact on the genesis of the Shakespearean corpus, we must look elsewhere for the true author of the plays," he writes. "To, say, Thomas North." However McCarthy might protest, he couldn't deny that by not divulging his theory about Thomas North's source plays in the book, he failed to provide a feasible explanation for how George North's words might have ended up in Shakespeare, opening the possibility that both writers could have coincidentally drawn isolated elements from commonplace sources. On the other hand, if McCarthy revealed his master theory, he risked losing Shakespeareans who might otherwise be sympathetic to his discovery of a new source. Either way, the fact remained painfully obvious that no matter how much of a success his and Schlueter's book about the *Discourse* might be, he was still no closer to acceptance of his theory about Thomas North as the true author of the source plays.

Chapter Fifteen

OUR REVELS NOW ARE ENDED

(1592–1603)

> Our revels now are ended. These our actors,
> As I foretold you, were all spirits and
> Are melted into air, into thin air.
>
> —*The Tempest*

he University Wits burned out as quickly as they blazed onto the literary scene. Thomas Watson died in September 1592, likely due to plague, leaving behind two volumes of unpublished poems. The following May, Christopher Marlowe died at twenty-nine in a brawl supposedly over a tavern bill. Thomas Kyd died of unknown causes in 1594, and George Peele died, evidently of syphilis, in 1596. Of the Wits, only Thomas Nashe and Thomas Lodge would see the next century. And both of them, says McCarthy, continued to attack Thomas North.

In a 1594 pamphlet, *The Terrors of the Night*, Nashe seems to spoof North's tragedies. "Bondmen in Turkey or in Spain are not so ordinarily sold as witches sell familiars there," he writes in a digression. "Far cheaper may you buy a wind amongst them than you can buy wind or fair words in the court." McCarthy sees that as an allusion to North's witches in *Macbeth*, summoning winds to thwart the sailor from Aleppo—along with a knock on North's inability to secure a position at court. Nashe continues by discussing a "wizard" conjuring "hail, storm, and tempest"—which McCarthy takes as a reference to the Fool's prophecy in *King Lear*. He ends, asking, "How come I to digress to such a dull, Lenten Northern clime, where there is nothing but stock-fish, whetstones, and cods-heads?"

Besides the obvious pun on North's name, McCarthy says, those rare words all exist in the canon, with "Lenten" in *Hamlet*, "stock-fish" in *Henry IV, Part 1*, "whetstone" in *Macbeth*, and "cod's head" in *Othello*.

Thomas Lodge, meanwhile, takes up a similar vein of attack in his 1596 pamphlet *Wit's Misery*, in which he purports to reveal the "devils incarnate of his age." One of them he describes is a man who "wandered a while in France, Germany, and Italy to learn languages and fashions, and now of late days is stolen into England to deprave all good deserving." That description mirrors that of the gentleman-scholar in *Groatsworth*, says McCarthy—but his next line clinches the attack. "He walks for the most part in black under color of gravity," Lodge continues, "and looks as pale as the vizard of the ghost which cried so miserably at The Theatre like an oyster-wife, 'Hamlet, revenge!'" Besides being just really humorous, the phrase nods to *The Dial*, in which North describes a "prince, under the color of gravity"—as well as obviously to *Hamlet*. "The mischief is that by grave demeanor and news bearing, he hath got some credit with the greater sort," continues Lodge—a possible allusion, says McCarthy, to North's time as a diplomat and his connection with Leicester—"and many fools there be that because he can pen prettily hold it Gospel whatever he writes or speaks"—a possible backhanded attack on other writers like Shakespeare, who followed North's writings.

The world spawned by the Wits was changing rapidly, however. During the awful plague years of 1592 and 1593, companies struggled to survive. Pembroke's Men collapsed in the summer of 1593; Lord Strange's Men became Derby's Men, and then foundered after its patron died in 1594; Sussex's Men disappeared the same year, leaving only the Admiral's Men and the Queen's Men to struggle along. Scholars speculate Shakespeare jumped from company to company during this time as opportunities arrived, gradually rising up their ranks. When *Titus Andronicus* appeared in print in 1594, its title page professed that it had been performed by Derby's, Pembroke's, and Sussex's, perhaps tracing Shakespeare's peripatetic journey across the London theater scene.

Shakespeare found other ways to win acclaim as well during the plague years, publishing the narrative poem *Venus and Adonis*, an erotic narrative inspired by Ovid about a goddess's attempts to court a mortal man. While

Shakespeare's name didn't appear on the title page, he signed a dedication to Henry Wriothesley (pronounced "Risely"), the Earl of Southampton—the first time Shakespeare's name appeared in print. A confederate of the Earl of Essex, the twenty-year-old Southampton was a handsome fop with hair nearly down to his waist who was an avid lover of literature and theater. The poem was an instant hit, particularly among sighing schoolboys at Oxford and Cambridge, propelling Shakespeare's name into the limelight. He followed it up the next year with another classically inspired verse, *The Rape of Lucrece*.

By the time the theaters reopened in early 1594, the theater scene was transformed. After the chaos, the new lord chamberlain, Henry Carey, Lord Hunsdon, took the opportunity to create two officially sanctioned companies, one under his patronage and the other patronized by his uncle, the lord admiral. The Lord Chamberlain's Men, led by William Shakespeare and Richard Burbage, would perform at The Theatre, with the Lord Admiral's Men, led by Edward Alleyn, at the Rose. Playing at city inns would henceforth be forbidden. The situation created a state-sponsored duopoly with tight regulations—plays had to begin at two in the afternoon and end by five—but it also gave the crown's protection to theater in London, making players almost respectable.

The tidy arrangement didn't last long—a new theater, the Swan, soon opened next door to the Rose—but for years, the theater scene was defined by the competition between the two great companies. The golden age of theater in London now began, with dozens of different plays a month. New playwrights rushed to fill demand, including Thomas Dekker, George Chapman, and Thomas Heywood. The Lord Admiral's Men retained Marlowe's old repertoire, while the Lord Chamberlain's Men performed Shakespeare. Shakespeare's company also seemed to be especially close to Essex and Southampton, performing a special Christmas tribute to Essex at court at Christmas 1595.

ESSEX, MEANWHILE, REMAINED focused on winning his fame on the battlefield. In June 1596, he led a daring raid on the Spanish city of Cadiz, destroying several Spanish warships and looting the town. While London crowds welcomed him back as a conquering hero, his victory was ultimately tainted. In his rush to attack the town, he left a rich merchant fleet containing the eye-popping sum of 12 million ducats (£6 million, or $2.1 billion today) in the harbor, where the Spanish sank it—earning the ire of Queen Elizabeth for letting such a prize slip through his fingers. The raid also did little to dent Philip's efforts to prepare a second armada that summer, with more than 120 ships and 16,000 soldiers, sailing to join a new rebellion in Ireland. In early 1595, the chieftain Hugh O'Neill, the Earl of Tyrone, had rebelled in Ulster, and the old veteran John Norris was sent to pacify him. After some skirmishes, both sides agreed to an uneasy ceasefire.

In September 1596, however, Tyrone rose again in anticipation of the Spanish invasion. The Privy Council sent up an alarm to muster thousands of troops for battle. Among the councilors was a new member— Roger Lord North, who assumed duties as privy councilor and treasurer of the household that August. Roger retained his position as lieutenant of Cambridgeshire, and in that capacity, tapped his brother, Thomas, to lead one hundred troops from the county across the Irish Sea, with £250 ($87,895) to support himself and his troops. Thomas crossed to Dublin on October 11, bringing his son Edward along as his lieutenant, and joined the garrison of the city as it awaited word of the Spanish invasion. In the end, the threat never materialized, as storms once again scattered the Spanish fleet, sending the armada limping back to its ports.

Tyrone, however, continued the fight, inciting other chiefs to rebel as well. Sir Thomas North's main struggles, as always, were against lack of food and supplies. An unsigned memorandum at the time charged, "Of all the captains in Ireland, Sir Thomas North hath from the beginning kept a most miserable, unfurnished, naked, and hunger-starven band." Some of his soldiers died, while others' "feet and legs rotted off for want of shoes." Thomas left in December, no doubt in disgust, putting what remained of his band in the hands of his son, Edward.

After another failed ceasefire the following year, the younger North found himself in Carrickfergus, an English stronghold on the northeastern shoreline. When a band of several hundred Scottish soldiers approached the town, the governor came forward to parley with about two hundred men, including Edward and the other captains. Suddenly, the governor decided to charge—right into an enemy ambush. The Scots shot the governor in the head, killing him, as they tore through the English ranks with musket fire. In the ensuing melee, Edward's lieutenant dove into a river to escape, while Edward's horse was shot out from underneath him and he was forced to go on foot. Only a dozen men survived the battle, including Edward, who staggered back into the town around midnight, wounded but alive.

IF NORTH WAS distressed to hear about his son's brush with death, then he must have been heartbroken by news out of Flanders the same year. His favorite nephew, John, had been killed in battle, leaving behind his widow and two young sons. Between his own disastrous experience in Ireland, his family tragedy, and the general disquiet of Elizabeth's late reign, this was another low point in North's life, and he poured his grief, McCarthy says, into a rewrite of *Richard II*. The play was published anonymously in quarto form that August, noting only that it had been acted by the Lord Chamberlain's Men. No play in the canon focuses more on grief, McCarthy says, and all of the passages stem from one of North's works: "The Life of Seneca" in North's translation of *Nepos's Lives*, the supplement to *Plutarch's Lives* that he wouldn't publish until 1602.

While Richard II is in Ireland, his queen laments his absence, and her loyal counselor Bushy comforts her, telling her not to lose perspective. "For sorrow's eyes, glazèd with blinding tears, divides one thing entire to many objects," he says. That passage, says McCarthy, echoes a passage in North's "Seneca" in which the Stoic counselor says that "to remedy the griefs" of a "sorrowful life" requires that men understand the "error of their judgement—who see things as in water, and with a corrupt eye." In both cases, says McCarthy, a counselor is pointing out that distortions of vision cause grief, as if seeing objects through water. At that moment in the play, the queen receives news that Bolingbroke has landed back in England to seize the crown, and she gives way to despair, saying that hope is nothing but a "flatterer, a parasite, a keeper-back of death who gently would dissolve the bands of life which false hope lingers in extremity." In the same passage in Seneca, North uses similar words to describe a person putting "himself to death," saying he would "dissolve the bands of this life," when he distrusts "providence: the which would have us keep a steadfast hope and confidence."

The passages are too close to be coincidental, says McCarthy, each combining the words "hope," "keep," and "death," along with the long phrase "dissolve the bands of life." He found nothing remotely similar in EEBO. "It's indisputable that the queen's speech follows North," he says—adding that the borrowing is particularly problematic for Shakespeareans, since this passage wouldn't be published until five years after the quarto edition of the play. That means, at a minimum, the playwright would need to have had access to North's unpublished papers—though, of course, McCarthy believes that playwright was North himself, who then sold the resulting play to Shakespeare for his company.

Beyond private griefs, North might have also had another reason for revising *Richard II* at that time. The quarto version lacks the scene in which Richard gives up his crown, which would have been controversial to stage during Elizabeth's reign. Even so, Elizabeth took offense at the public performances of the play that year—worried some of her subjects might get ideas about the popular Essex making like Bolingbroke and trying to depose her. It's doubtful that North had such a revolution in mind, says McCarthy, but after venting his own grief about Elizabeth's disastrous military campaigns, he may have intended the play as a warning about abuse of power, referencing as it did Richard II's disastrous campaign in Ireland.

RICHARD II WASN'T THE ONLY play attacking the regime that summer. In July 1597, a newly reconstituted Pembroke's Men staged a satirical play at the Swan called *Isle of Dogs*. No sooner was it performed than Elizabeth and her Privy Council suppressed it as seditious, and seized all copies. Whatever it contained made them so angry that they canceled all productions for the summer and threatened to "pluck down" all of London's playhouses. Ultimately, the Swan was closed, Pembroke's Men folded, and Thomas Nashe, one of the coauthors, stopped writing plays entirely. The other author was thrown into prison for three months. Undaunted, however, this new playwright, Ben Jonson, continued writing, quickly becoming one of the most celebrated playwrights of his age.

The following October, Shakespeare acted in Jonson's play *Every Man in His Humour*, performed by the Lord Chamberlain's Men at the Curtain. Jonson's comedic playwriting style was wholly original—rather than complicated plots involving mistaken identities and romantic hijinks, he reduced characters to personality types, or "humours," which he then involved in simplified, classical plots. The form was wildly successful, immediately putting Jonson at the top of the theatrical world. His own "humour" was dark and melancholic. As the play was being performed, Jonson killed another actor in a duel in the marshy fields of Shoreditch. He was just as combative in print, vaunting his erudition with withering attacks on other playwrights—and making sure his name appeared on everything he published.

The Lord Chamberlain's Men were at the Curtain that fall because James Burbage's lease for The Theatre had expired and he was not able to come to terms on a renewal—nor were his sons after James's death. Shakespeare's fellow player Richard Burbage, however, found a loophole. While the lease covered the land, it didn't cover any structures built on it. Three days after Christmas 1598, Burbage showed up at The Theatre with a crew of workmen armed with swords, axes, and daggers. As snow fell, they dismantled the playhouse, loading its boards and timbers onto wagons, which they carted across the Thames to Bankside, where Burbage had secured a lease on a new plot of land for a new theater east of the Rose.

While they waited for it to be built, however, the Lord Chamberlain's Men fell on tough times, turning to publishing its plays to raise revenue. In addition to *Richard II*, it sold quartos of *Richard III*, *Henry IV, Part 1*, and *Love's Labour's Lost*—the last, published in spring 1598, newly "corrected and augmented" by "W. Shakspere." That description was accurate, McCarthy says, because the play was an expanded version of North's original; as time went on, and Shakespeare became more popular, the company dropped the qualifications, just referring to the plays as authored "by" Shakespeare.

Many of these quartos are today called Shakespeare's "bad quartos," inferior versions of his masterpieces. Most scholars speculate they were bastardized versions made by unscrupulous printers or actors trying to make a buck off Shakespeare's name. McCarthy notes, however, that in an otherwise litigious society, Shakespeare and his company never once sued to stop their publication. That's because, he says, they were not pirated copies at all, but officially sanctioned stage adaptations of North's plays. "Scholars would have you believe that there were all of these different printers and other people reworking the plays and selling them to make money on his name," says McCarthy wryly. "That's a conspiracy theory."

As for North, he says, he had no reason to object, either. Assuming Shakespeare had bought or otherwise acquired the plays legally, they were "Shakespeare's" works. And in a theatrical world in which copyright was fluid, and writers regularly edited, adapted, and rewrote each other's works, Shakespeare could put his name on the adaptations as being "his" plays. Despite his impoverished state, North was still a gentleman—and a knight at that. He could hardly advertise his association with the lowly trade of theater, no matter how respectable it was becoming. He considered his fame, such as it was, resting on his translations of classical works. That doesn't mean, however, that North's authorship of the plays wasn't advertised after a fashion, says McCarthy—if one knew where to look.

THE SUMMER OF 1599 saw arguably the most significant event in the history of theater—the opening in Bankside of a new London playhouse: the Globe. Crowds jostled for seats in the three tiers of galleries that wrapped around the polygonal space, or staked out standing room in the yard for its very first performance—most likely a production of *Julius Caesar* based on Thomas North's *Plutarch's Lives*. Shakespeare shared in the theater's profits along with four other actors, and rolled out hit after hit there for the next fourteen years. Crowds still pack into a full-scale replica that opened up in 1997, queuing up along the river hours before the show with 5 quid groundling tickets, still the best theatrical deal in London. Not to be outdone, more than a dozen other replicas exist around the world, including Globes in Italy, Argentina, Japan, New Zealand—and three in Texas alone.

The playhouse was so successful that the Lord Admiral's Men decamped from the Rose the following year to a new theater north of the city, the Fortune. But Shakespeare and his company weren't the only ones to open new theaters that summer. Ben Jonson began writing for a new children's company called the Children of the Chapel, performing indoors at Blackfriars. Around the same time, a Middle Temple innsman named John Marston began writing for the Children of Paul's. As they competed, the two playwrights began attacking each other in satirical allusions in a series of plays, finding they could get away with their bile more easily by putting it in the mouths of babes. The War of the Theaters had begun.

Also known as the Poetomachia, the yearslong literary quarrel mostly pitted Jonson against Marston and his fellow playwright Thomas Dekker—but Shakespeare's company was often sprayed with collateral damage. Some scholars believe, for example, that Dekker's 1601 play *Satiromastix* lampoons Shakespeare as Sir Adam Prickshaft, a lecherous balding poet who torments Jonson's stand-in, Horace. Others see in Jonson's 1600 play *Every Man Out of His Humour* a criticism of Shakespeare as a rank social-climber in the character of Sogliardo, who pursues a coat of arms with the facetious motto "Not Without Mustard"—a slam on Shakespeare's own quest for a coat of arms with the motto "Not Without Right."

In another 1600 play, *Cynthia's Revels*, Jonson sends up a similarly uncouth figure, named Asotus, a foolish dandy who dreams of being a courtier. He challenges a group of poets to a competition judged by Cynthia, another name for Diana—the virgin goddess who often represents Queen Elizabeth. The play, virtually unreadable today due to its dense thicket of satirical references, seems to caricature Shakespeare as Asotus, along with Jonson, Marston, and Dekker as other competitors in the poem-off. Another character becomes a mentor to Asotus in the ways of court manners and poetry—a poor Italian knight named Amorphus.

As McCarthy read through the play, he couldn't help but see once again a parody of the Shakespeare-North relationship. Amorphus bears all of the signifiers of previous caricatures of North, presented as a self-absorbed, multilingual courtier who has traveled to Padua and Venice, loves exotic foods, and speaks in beast metaphors. He boastingly describes himself as "an essence so sublimated and refined by travels" that he is now able "to speak the mere extraction of language." Nearly every word that comes out of his mouth, however, seems to mock a line from Shakespeare's plays. "Give me your ears," he says at one point, a seeming play on Marc Antony's "Lend me your ears" in *Caesar*. The uncouth Asotus, meanwhile, garbles his Latin just like the poet in *Groatsworth*, at one point misquoting Caesar's famous *"Veni, vidi, vici"* ("I came, I saw, I conquered") as *"Victus, victa, victum"* ("He's been conquered, she's been conquered, it's been conquered").

At the same time, Amorphus instructs Asotus in the art of poetry, telling him he must prove his genius. "If you find none," he continues, "you must hearken out a vein and buy; provided you pay for the silence as for the work, then you may securely call it your own." Once again, McCarthy reads in that a reference to Shakespeare buying plays from North. Amorphus then instructs Asotus in the art of making faces to reveal his inner thoughts, guiding him through "your merchant, your scholar, your soldier, your lawyer, courtier, etc." To his description of the courtier, Amorphus adds, apropos of nothing, a "somewhat a northerly face."

The references in *Cynthia's Revels* were only some of many McCarthy found to North in the various satires and counter-satires of the Poetomachia. "They were the newspapers of the time," he says. "Forget what some professor is saying in 2019—it's what the literary insiders were saying in 1599—they knew exactly what was going on." In another poem, "On Poet Ape," Jonson again seems to take a swipe at Shakespeare as an actor turned playwright "that would be thought our chief," who was nonetheless a "thief," saying he "would pick and glean, buy the reversion of old plays; now grown to a little wealth, and credit in the scene, he takes up all, makes each man's wit his own, and, told of this, he slights it."

In another play, *Epicene*, Jonson includes the character John Daw—the subject of McCarthy's first published piece on North in *Notes & Queries*—a pretentious knight who is associated with Seneca, Plutarch, and "an excellent book of moral philosophy...called *Doni's Philosophy*." In the quarto of Jonson's first work, *Every Man in His Humour*, published in 1601, he includes a subplot involving a jealous husband named Thorello—which McCarthy sees as a mash-up of Thomas Arden and Othello, mimicking certain lines from their respective plays. Those characters, in turn, are almost magically controlled by a character who, again, seems to caricature North—a scholarly gentleman with a wealthy older brother with an

Italianate name, Giuliano, who threatens him and cuts off his inheritance. North, McCarthy says, would soon take on that younger brother's name for a character in one of his own plays: Prospero.

EVEN AS THE POETS warred in the theaters, courtiers continued to battle for favor at court—and in actual wars abroad. After Spain's failed Irish armada, Essex led another counter-armada the following summer, but it was also scattered by storms, as well as an expedition to the Azores that missed capturing the Spanish treasure fleet by hours. In the midst of these defeats, his relationship with the queen became increasingly frayed. In July 1598, he had the effrontery to turn his back to her, and Elizabeth slapped him. Essex shockingly reached for his sword, leading to banishment from court. That summer was the end of an era. In August, the queen's loyal Lord Burghley died after forty years of service, attending Privy Council meetings to the last. The following month, England's most formidable enemy, Philip II, also died after a long illness.

Despite the passing of such giants, however, little changed, as their sons picked up where they left off—Robert Cecil dominating the English court, and Philip III continuing Spain's attempts to invade Ireland. The English position there had gone from bad to worse, after a surprise attack in which Tyrone massacred more than 1,200 English soldiers. Immediately, Essex volunteered to lead a new army against the uprising. Perhaps happy to see him gone, Elizabeth appointed him Lord Deputy of Ireland, with a massive army of 16,000 footmen and 1,300 horsemen—the largest fielded during Elizabeth's reign. After arriving in Ireland in April 1600, however, Essex wasted time fruitlessly chasing groups of rebels through the bogs, losing more than a half of his army to disease. He further incurred the queen's wrath by dubbing more knights against her orders. Elizabeth commanded him to march into Tyrone's stronghold of Ulster at once, despite Essex now being down to four thousand battle-ready soldiers, less than half the men in Tyrone's army. Finally heading north, Essex met to parley with Tyrone, sitting on horseback on one side of a river while Tyrone's horse stood in the water. During that conversation, they agreed to another truce—but Essex's enemies spread rumors that he had forged a secret deal with Tyrone to link up with Scotland and attack England. Elizabeth was once again furious, lamenting the mess her one-time favorite had made of the campaign.

Desperate to defend himself, Essex left Ireland to arrive suddenly at court, storming into Elizabeth's bedchamber still muddy from the road. The queen had finally had enough. Summoning several privy councilors, including Roger North, she put Essex under house arrest. The ensuing trial found him guilty on charges of disloyalty and squandering public funds. Adding to the injury, Elizabeth stripped all of the new knights he'd dubbed in Ireland of their titles, and took away a lucrative contract for revenues from imported wines, sending Essex into financial ruin.

Even as this drama played out at court, the North family suffered another blow. Roger North had never fully recovered from his wounds in the Netherlands. Despite numerous trips to Bath and Buxton to take the waters, his health continued to decline. Finally, on December 3, 1600, he died at his home near the Charterhouse at sixty-nine years old. Mourners filed into St. Paul's Cathedral for a state funeral for the long-time lieutenant of Cambridgeshire. No doubt, Thomas was among them, paying his respects to his brother.

When Roger's will was read, it followed the principles of primogeniture, passing Roger's title, along with Kirtling Hall and most of his other properties, to his grandson, John's son Dudley. But he also granted his younger son Henry £1,000 and the estate of Mildenhall, and generously doled out more than £1,000 to his various grandchildren. He gave money, clothing, and horses to various friends and household servants, and earmarked £4 for the poor of Kirtling. Only after all of the rest of his money and possessions had been distributed, did he include a line stating, "It is my will that out of the remainder with some portion my brother Sir Thomas North, his son Edward North, his daughter my niece Elizabeth be rewarded." No specific amount was noted, leaving it up to the discretion of his executors. Just as with his father's death, Thomas was essentially frozen out of the family estate, with not so much as even a parsonage this time.

EVEN AS THOMAS NORTH was reeling from that blow, he bore witness to— and may have even played a crucial part in—one of the most momentous events in London's history. Convinced Cecil and his other enemies at court were trying to destroy him, Essex reached out on Christmas Day to King James VI, assuring him of his support, and even proposing to replace Elizabeth with him early, "to relieve my poor country, which groans under her burden." Essex House became a nest of intrigue as he, Southampton, and a few trusted peers began fomenting plans to drive Cecil and his minions out of court. As part of their plan, some of Essex's men reached out to the Lord Chamberlain's Men and paid them 40 shillings atop their usual fee to stage a special performance of *Richard II*.

Historians speculate the performance that day, February 7, 1601, even included the scene depicting the deposition of the king—perhaps in hopes that it would inspire the people to revolt. According to the later testimony of one of the actors, the company initially refused to perform it, on the grounds that the play was "so old and so long out of use"—an odd protest for a play only five years old (bolstering McCarthy's belief it was based on an earlier play by North). Catching wind of the plot, Cecil sent men to demand Essex appear at court, but he refused. The next day, February 8, four privy councilors showed up at Essex House to take him into custody; Essex and his followers took them hostage instead. They then marched into the city with two hundred men, brandishing swords as they attempted to rally the populace with cries of "To the Court! To the Court!"

Essex was sweating and half-deranged as he made it to Cheapside, and soon his followers started abandoning him, until he had only about fifty left. They retreated back toward Essex House, outside the city walls, but found the gate blocked by a group of militia. After a brief skirmish, in which Essex's page was shot and killed, he and his followers raced to the river to board boats to return to Essex House by water instead. By now, the queen's forces had surrounded the residence, aiming two cannons from the Tower at the gate. Even Essex saw that his revolt was hopeless, surrendering along with his men.

A month after the aborted rebellion, the Privy Council recorded payments to eight men for defeating "the late attempts made by the Earl of Essex and his adherents." First on the list was Sir Thomas North, knight, who was rewarded £10—the highest amount out of any of the recipients. When McCarthy examined the catalogues of state papers on-line, however, he found no mention of Thomas North in any of the accounts of the rebellion, which name several other captains. In my own research examining the papers, I, too, could not find any record of North taking part. When I ask McCarthy about it, he proposes another theory: that given North's involvement in the theater, he caught wind of the performance at the Globe and warned the crown that the rebellion was coming. "They're performing *Richard II* the day before, and Shakespeare tells North about it, and then North informs the queen's men," McCarthy says. "So the next day they're prepared."

It's an audacious theory, to be sure, one that places North not only at the center of Shakespeare's canon, but also in the middle of a crucial historical event. There does seem to be some evidence to support it, however. After the rebellion, Cecil and the other councilors focused in on the performance of the play, interrogating all of the performers involved. In Essex's trial on February 12, Cecil held up the payment to Shakespeare's company as a key point of evidence, arguing that Essex figured himself another Bolingbroke, coming to depose the queen. Shakespeare and his company, however, weren't punished for the play's connection to the rebellion.

Thomas North, meanwhile, continued to receive rewards. On the same day as Essex's trial, the Privy Council appointed him to a new position as captain of the postern gate at the Tower of London, where he would watch over a little-used pedestrian gate in the corner of the city—a peaceful sinecure for the grizzled war veteran. Elizabeth signed Essex's death warrant for treason on February 23. The next day, the queen attended a court banquet where she watched one of Shakespeare's plays (though which one is lost to history). The following morning, Essex climbed the scaffold set up inside the Tower, where Anne Boleyn and Lady Jane Grey had been beheaded decades before. "My sins are more in number than the hairs of my head," he said in a loud voice before he commanded: "Executioner, strike home."

Elizabeth, too, seems to have taken the performance of *Richard II* seriously. In an audience with an antiquarian six months later to review historical records, she paused when they got to papers of Richard II. "I am Richard II, know ye not that?" she said suddenly. "This tragedy was forty times played in open houses and streets." Whatever role Thomas North played in putting down the Essex Rebellion—and whatever personal grievances he may have had against the queen—North remained loyal to the crown. For his service, the queen found a way to reward her long-suffering subject, with a pension of £40 a year. After all his years petitioning the court, he had finally received some small token of recognition. The following year, 1602, North published his last translation, *Nepos's Lives*, dedicating it to Queen Elizabeth and thanking her for "comforting and supporting my poor old decaying life." Whatever infirmity he was suffering, however, McCarthy believes North still had one last play to write.

"OUR REVELS NOW ARE ENDED," says the elderly magus Prospero toward the end of Shakespeare's romance-comedy, *The Tempest*. "These our actors, as I foretold you, were all spirits and are melted into the air," he continues, "the gorgeous palaces, the solemn temples, the great globe itself, yea, all which it inherit shall dissolve." When all's done, he says, "we are such stuff as dreams are made on, and our little life is rounded with a sleep." Besides a commentary on the transience of life—with Hamlet's terror over death transformed into a beneficent peace—this famous passage is often read as a meta-commentary on the stage. The play, about a bookish wizard who commands the elements on a deserted island, is often seen as an autobiographical elegy, the playwright saying goodbye to his art, as he contemplates the power and limitations of his craft.

There's a problem with that reading, however: none of the events of *The Tempest* match up, even symbolically, with any of the known events of Shakespeare's life. "Everyone says it seems to be the playwright's autobiography," McCarthy tells me, "but it has nothing to do with Shakespeare." When he began unpacking its many allusions, however, he found plenty to correspond with Thomas North's life—especially his final years.

The play begins with Prospero, the former Duke of Milan, exiled to a deserted island along with his daughter, Miranda. As Prospero tells his daughter, he was more devoted to his books than to ruling, and so was usurped and exiled by his power-hungry brother, who disinherited him from his kingdom. Of course, McCarthy reads those events as another commentary on Thomas and Roger North. "Both brothers are born to wealth, and one brother exiles the other from the family estate, and he has to live in poverty with his daughter," McCarthy says. In fact, he says, the play has virtually the same plot as *As You Like It*, with an exiled duke, a usurping brother, and a precocious daughter, only the setting is an island instead of a forest. *The Tempest*, however, represents something more, he says—North's attempt to reconcile himself with his brother as he approached the end of his life.

The titular storm shipwrecks a group of people onto the island, including Prospero's brother, Antonio; Alonso, the king of Naples; Alonso's brother, Sebastian; and the wise counselor Gonzalo. In a separate group is Alonso's son, Ferdinand, who meets Miranda and falls in love. In a third group is the comical jester Trinculo and the drunken butler Stephano, who team up with Prospero's half-human slave Caliban to try to take over the island. Antonio and Sebastian have their own plot in mind: to kill Alonso and make Sebastian king of Naples. The bare-bones plot, however, is little more than an excuse to showcase Prospero's magical skills, as with the help of the airy spirit Ariel, he manipulates all of the characters and plans his long-awaited revenge.

Traditionally dated to 1611, when it was played at Whitehall, the play is one of Shakespeare's few dramas without any recognizable source. Some have found in it references to a trio of pamphlets describing a shipwreck of English settlers on Bermuda in 1609—though the connection is admittedly tenuous. "The extent of the verbal echoes of these three pamphlets has, I think, been exaggerated," says source scholar Kenneth Muir, who points out that many of the details could apply to any shipwreck. Other elements have been sourced to a record of Magellan's circumnavigation from 1577, a collection of Spanish romances from 1586, and various plots from *commedia dell'arte*. The character of Prospero, meanwhile, seems inspired by a real-life Duke of Genoa, Prosper Adorno, who was deposed in 1561, and then returned to become deputy for the Duke of Milan in 1577. McCarthy sees a different origin for the name. North, he says, was inspired by Jonson's cheeky representation of him as a manipulator of the other characters in Jonson's *Every Man In*, and decided to use the name given to him, Prospero, for his own play. The name reminded him of the real-life story of Duke Adorno, giving him the Italian-in-exile plot.

Other details also seemed to McCarthy to match up with North's biography. In order to prove his love for Miranda, Prospero orders Ferdinand to perform manual labor by fetching logs—which McCarthy sees as a nod to his daughter's real-life husband, Thomas Stuteville. Unlike the poet Spenser, Stuteville was a gentleman farmer near Kirtling, whose name even appears in an early seventeenth-century book on horticulture. Even Stephano and Trinculo's bumbling attempted revolt—easily quelled by Prospero—seems reminiscent of Essex's ill-fated rebellion, which North played a part in putting down. But it's in Prospero's relationship with his brother, Antonio, that McCarthy sees the true relevance to North's life.

IN ADDITION TO an autobiographical swan song, *The Tempest* is also sometimes read as a political allegory for the colonization of the New World. As inspiration for that theme, scholars point to the essay "Of the Cannibals," by French humanist philosopher Michel de Montaigne. In it, he compares the so-called savages of the New World with "civilized" Europeans, arguing that if anything, Europeans are more brutal. As translated by John Florio in 1603, Montaigne wrote that nothing in America was "either barbarous or savage, unless men call that barbarism which is not common to them."

In *The Tempest*, the kindly counselor Gonzalo quotes Montaigne's essay practically verbatim as he enthuses about a kind of tropical utopia he could set up on the island—without laws, letters, wealth, or contracts. The Machiavellian courtiers Antonio and Sebastian immediately mock him, but the play at least partially endorses his worldview, as he and Ferdinand are the only admirable characters among the castaways. When McCarthy read about those similarities, he thought about North's own possible connection with Montaigne, who was a counselor at the French court during the North brothers' Lyons delegation in 1574. For most of his life, however, Montaigne lived in self-imposed exile, devoting himself to the study of books in the tower of his chateau outside Bordeaux—just like Prospero himself. Recent scholars have detected Montaigne's influence in many more passages in *The Tempest* than just Gonzalo's prelapsarian ode. And in his own research, McCarthy himself stumbled upon a startling connection to the play.

It's long been a mystery why exactly Shakespeare titled his play *The Tempest*, when the storm is over by the first scene (Harold Bloom suggests *Prospero* would have been a better title). As McCarthy researched Montaigne's life, however, he came across an indelible answer, never before considered. According to the editor of Montaigne's autobiography, the philosopher commissioned a painting above the doorway to his library of a ship wrecked on the rocks, with swimmers frantically fighting toward shore. The painting, only partially visible today due to years of weathering, was accompanied with a Latin inscription from the poet Horace, reading in part: "I have hung up my garments water-wet, unto that god whose power on seas is great."

The painting is seen as a symbol of Montaigne's renunciation of the world. North, says McCarthy, must have visited the chateau on his way home in 1574, or perhaps returning from Italy in 1571. Like Rosebud in *Citizen Kane*, he believes, the image holds the key to understanding *The Tempest*. As the firstborn son of a wealthy French lord, Montaigne was what Thomas North could have been, had he the money and leisure to devote himself to a life of humanist study, rather than being forced into a life of poverty. More than any other play in the canon, it's been noted, *The Tempest* is obsessed with the idea of memory, with some version of the word "remember" occurring more than twenty times. Amid all of the fantasy and slapstick humor, the play holds an undeniable wistfulness in Prospero's remembering the wrongs done to him—and the revenge he contemplates to redress them.

Now, nearing the end of his life and career, says McCarthy, Thomas North was doing the same thing with his play, turning as always to his philosophy for answers. Despite his image as a beneficent magician, Prospero is far from likable, coming across as cold and self-pitying, and even tyrannical in his domination of Caliban, Ariel, and his own daughter, Miranda. When, in the last act of the play, Ariel comes to tell Prospero that he has Antonio and the others trapped, however, he unexpectedly decides to show mercy. "Though with their high wrongs I am struck to th' quick, yet with my nobler reason 'gainst my fury do I take part," he says. "The rarer action is in virtue than in vengeance."

As Shakespeare scholar Eleanor Prosser first pointed out in 1965, the sentiment also stems from Montaigne. In his essay "Of Cruelty," the French philosopher says that it's "rare action" when someone naturally inclined to goodness forgives a wrong against him, but it's even more "noble" when someone "stung to the quick with any wrong or offense received should arm himself with reason against his furiously blind desire for revenge." With those words seemingly in mind, Prospero addresses the shipwrecked sailors one by one, exposing their wrongs, but also forgiving them. "For you, my most wicked sir, whom to call brother, would even infect my mouth," he says to Antonio, "I do forgive thy rankest fault— all of them." The play ends happily, with Ferdinand marrying Miranda, Prospero restored to his Dukedom, Ariel freed, and even Caliban pardoned for his attempted rebellion. In the same way, says McCarthy, the play also represents Thomas finally putting his anger and resentment toward his brother aside. "The whole play is about forgiveness," he says, "and in *The Tempest*, Thomas forgives Roger."

IN THE LAST act of *The Tempest*, Prospero vows to give up his "rough magic," breaking his staff and throwing his book in the ocean. At last, he comes onstage for a final speech. "Now my charms are all o'erthrown, and what strength I have 's mine own, which is most faint," he begins, appealing directly to the audience to save him with their applause. "As you from crimes would pardoned be, let your indulgence set me free." The speech is seen as the playwright's goodbye to his art—even though Shakespeare was only forty-seven years old at the time it was staged, and still had three more plays left to write. In McCarthy's estimation, however, *The Tempest* really was Thomas North's final play.

After Essex's execution, Robert Cecil was left as Elizabeth's uncontested chief minister, presiding over the last years of a dying queen. In the fall of 1601, the Spanish under Philip III finally succeeded in landing an armada of thirty-three ships in Ireland, disgorging more than three thousand men onto shore to aid Tyrone's rebellion. Despite that threat, Essex's successor in Ireland, Lord Mountjoy, brilliantly outmaneuvered Tyrone, winning a decisive battle at Kinsale. By 1602, Tyrone was a fugitive, and on March 30, 1603, he offered himself up for submission.

Elizabeth, however, did not live to see it. In her last years, the queen often sank into melancholy and depression, having outlived the counselors of her generation, and thinking about her one favorite who died prematurely, and the other who betrayed her. By 1601, she had told the French ambassador that she was "tired of life"—even as she still refused to name a successor. As she found the strength for a short summer progress north of London in 1602, Cecil had already begun a secret correspondence with James VI of Scotland, assuring him of his support.

Despite a high-spirited Christmas, Elizabeth's health declined rapidly at the start of 1603. She lived long enough to receive one last tribute from Thomas North that March, another dedication in a new edition of *Plutarch's Lives*. Soon afterward, however, she took to bed with what might have been tonsillitis or the flu, dying in the early morning hours of March 24. Elizabeth ended her life much like her father, her realm depleted by military misadventures, her coffers drained, and her citizens groaning under exorbitant taxes. In nearly a half century on the throne, however, she had presided over decades of relative peace and neutrality, brilliantly playing her enemies off one another, as her kingdom prospered in a great cultural flowering. The theaters built during her reign continued to ring with laughter and applause for decades.

Upon news of the queen's death, Cecil swung into action. By ten o'clock that morning, a rider was already on the way to Edinburgh to greet the Scottish ruler as James I, King of England, Scotland, and Ireland—all of Great Britain united at last. As bells rang and bonfires blazed throughout London, the queen's body was borne solemnly on the river to Whitehall in a barge lit by torches and draped in black velvet. Perhaps Thomas North was there to watch it floating down the Thames, contemplating how his own life and art were forever intertwined with Her Majesty's.

After the publication of his last edition of *Plutarch*, North seems to disappear from archival records. His biographers suppose he died soon after the queen, around seventy years old, never having achieved a position at court. McCarthy and Schlueter found one last record in their research—a lawsuit brought by a Sir Thomas North in 1607 over a family estate—that implies he lived at least a few years into the reign of the new King James. There is no will bequeathing any books or meager possessions, however, nor grave to mark where his body was buried. While his brother Roger reposes under his garish monument in Kirtling Church, Thomas seems to have vanished without a trace.

He did, however, leave behind three major translations of courtly wisdom—*The Dial of Princes*, *The Moral Philosophy of Doni*, and *Plutarch's Lives*—along with the minor work of *Nepos's Lives*. His biographies describe a life of variety and adventure, as a law student at the Inns of Court, a diplomat in France, a soldier in Ireland and the Netherlands, and a master of foreign languages and culture. To the extent his memory survives today, it's primarily as the source for Shakespeare's *Julius Caesar* and *Antony and Cleopatra*, with occasional mention of the masterful quality of his own prose. Is it possible, however, that all of this time, his greatest accomplishments have been hidden—that now, more than four hundred years after his death, he might be recognized as the true genius behind Shakespeare's plays?

Chapter Sixteen

SUCH STUFF AS DREAMS ARE MADE ON

(1603–1623 / 2018–2019)

We are such stuff
As dreams are made on, and our little life
Is rounded with a sleep.

—*The Tempest*

apers are strewn all over the kitchenette suite at the Marriott Residence Inn in Tallahassee, Florida, where McCarthy is pacing back and forth nervously in an untucked black button-up shirt and faded blue jeans. "Do you want to get coffee?" Galovski asks him. "I'm not sure," says McCarthy. "It's been a running debate all day," Galovski confides in me. "Maybe I'll have a sip," McCarthy finally allows. "I don't know, though, I'm feeling pretty relaxed."

It's March 2018, a month after my article about McCarthy and Schlueter's George North book in *The New York Times*, and McCarthy has invited me down to Florida for what he hopes will be the next stage in his journey to reveal Thomas North to the world—a private meeting with Gary Taylor, chair of the English Department at Florida State University, and coeditor of *The New Oxford Shakespeare*. Despite Taylor's rejection of his *Arden* paper two years earlier, McCarthy pitched him on his latest discovery, a journal by Thomas North that could be a source for *The Winter's Tale* and *Henry VIII*. Taylor agreed to meet him at three thirty that afternoon, for a half hour, to hear his case.

"It's two fifty-two," McCarthy says, "we need to go." Galovski rolls her eyes. "We're literally four minutes away," she says, snaking a microphone up under her father's shirt, as if he's going undercover to infiltrate the mob. "The problem is, I know it too well, I get bogged down in detail," McCarthy says to no one in particular, leaning against the cherry-veneered table. "Just be concise, make eye contact," suggests Galovski's camera-person for the day, Laura Hudock, a veteran director of photography who's worked for HBO and Showtime. "This is the only freaking thing happening in the world right now," McCarthy says, talking to himself in the car on the way to the university. "I have all the goods, I have all the goods, there's no reason to...I have all the goods."

Even though the journal is Thomas North's oldest extant piece of writing—and, McCarthy believes, inspired his oldest plays—it is one of the last things that McCarthy discovered. In the late summer of 2016, June Schlueter's husband, Paul, was doing some searches online and came across a listing for a nineteenth-century copy of a journal at the Huntington Library near Los Angeles, attributed to Thomas North. "We need that book!" McCarthy wrote when Schlueter sent him the listing. Unlike the George North manuscript, it was easy to find—a transcription had been made in the eighteenth century, and McCarthy located it immediately on Google Books, staying up all night to analyze it. By morning, he was already convinced North used it to write *The Winter's Tale* and *Henry VIII*.

A week later, Schlueter discovered a sixteenth-century manuscript copy of the journal, which had sold at Sotheby's in New York the previous December for $43,750. McCarthy tracked down the buyer, Lambeth Palace Library, and for a wild moment considered trying to buy it from them. "It will become one of the most valuable manuscripts in the world—and I can get it now for thousands!" he told Galovski enthusiastically. In the end, however, he settled for asking them for a digitized copy.

As he puzzled through the handwritten text, comparing it with other instances of North's writing, he started to believe it was North's original. Before now, he'd known little about North's life before his admission at Lincoln's Inn in 1556, and virtually nothing about those two plays, recognized as among the last Shakespeare wrote. Seeing them as plays sympathetic to the reign of Queen Mary, however, made sense. There was no way they could be performed during the Protestant reign of Queen

Elizabeth. However, King James was more moderate and sympathetic to Catholics, so if Thomas North had sold those plays to Shakespeare, the younger playwright could have adapted and staged them during James's reign.

He became increasingly excited as he teased out references to other plays, including the "garden of Lombardy" in *The Taming of the Shrew* and the "murder of Gonzago" in *Hamlet*. "It is like reading Darwin's journal after *On the Origin of Species*," McCarthy wrote to me shortly after the discovery. "I am bouncing off the walls." In order to connect the journal to the plays, however, McCarthy and Schlueter would have to definitively prove it was written by North. Aside from signatures, and the marginalia in *The Dial of Princes*, there is only one other extant example of North's handwriting, a legal document he wrote in 1591, strangely, about a case involving rights to sell beer in London. Comparing North's handwriting with that in the journal, McCarthy believed it matched—but handwriting analysis, as he'd learned from his work on *Titus Andronicus*, can be a shaky way of determining attribution.

Schlueter, meanwhile, traced the provenance of both the Huntington and Lambeth copies of the journal to the collection of nineteenth-century antiquarian Sir Thomas Phillipps, but there was no mention of Thomas North in the printed catalog of his collection. Schluter, however, located another, handwritten inventory of Phillipp's manuscripts, with copies at the Grolier Club in New York and at the Bodleian Libraries at Oxford. She got on a bus to the city, while I visited the Bodleian. Sure enough, both contained listings for the journal, with the notation "Sir Thos. Northe his travels." The catalog, however, was made hundreds of years after the journal. Where had the initial attribution come from?

While in London during the summer of 2019, I set myself to the hunt. The Phillipps listing included a parenthetical, reading "from Harl. Ms."—a reference to a third copy of the journal held in the Harleian collection at the British Library. That copy also dates from the sixteenth century, seemingly a copy of the journal now at Lambeth. In the library's catalog, however, there is no author listed, nor did I find any indication of one when I examined the document—bound into one of the library's heavy volumes of manuscripts. I contacted Tony Edwards, who originally helped McCarthy and Schlueter find the George North manuscript, to ask for advice. Within short order, he had traced the provenance of the manuscript back to Ralph Starkey, one of England's first archivists, who died in 1628, putting the manuscript tantalizingly within reach of North's life. I decided to take another look at the volume containing the manuscript, paging through every leaf in search of any clues.

After the journal, the next page in the volume is a one-page list of heraldry animals—an entirely different document. As I turned it, however, I saw the next page was blank except for a title in sixteenth-century script: "The booke and diare of the Ambassador's Jorney to Rome Sr Thomas North his travels."

This is where the attributions in the Huntington and Lambeth copies had come from, I realized. The page was apparently a cover to the journal, which had been folded over when it was bound into the manuscript volume, with another document mistakenly interpolated in between. I contacted the library's archivist, who confirmed the inscription matched the handwriting on the first page of the journal, which was transcribed in the late sixteenth century—when Thomas North was still alive. A contemporary of North's, at least, had identified him as the author.

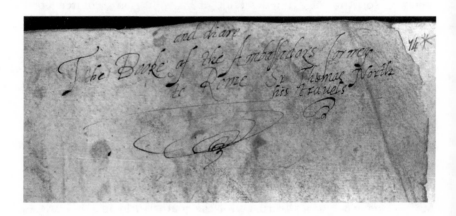

Title page of the British Library's copy of North's journal

MCCARTHY DOESN'T KNOW all of this yet on his way to talk to Gary Taylor in March 2018, but he already firmly believes in North's authorship of the journal. As we drive past palm trees and live oak draped with Spanish moss, he practices his opening to himself. "This isn't contradicting anything—we just have new information—we just have a new source—and North wrote it—and we know that because it has all of the same imagery, the same language." We park and take the elevator up to Taylor's office, where we are greeted by Taylor himself, who has a salt-and-pepper beard and wears his hair pulled back into a ponytail; like McCarthy, he is wearing an untucked black dress shirt.

Far from the gruff demeanor I'd expected, Taylor greets us warmly, ushering us into a conference room with a wall of windows through which the Florida sun streams. McCarthy makes apologetic small talk as Taylor introduces us to his wife, Terri Bourus, who is similarly wide-smiling and friendly. "You two are the first people I'm showing this to," McCarthy says as he opens up his laptop, launching into his rehearsed speech. "I do think it's a huge story, but it's not going to change what we know about Shakespeare. It only adds new information." Immediately, he becomes distracted by the fact that the remote control he brought to advance the slides isn't working, and attempts to fix it before beginning his presentation again in halting words. "The only thing this manuscript that I found, this journal that I found, is going to change, that I believe, in my opinion, it's going to change the story, the old story that he's buying, borrowing from Shakespeare in 1609 was North. North wrote an old play on *Winter's Tale* in the 1550s—don't scream about this, I'm going to get to this—and we know this because of the journal that we found."

He continues on in this muddled vein for a while, as Taylor and Bourus good-humoredly ask questions about the pages of the manuscript he's showing onscreen. "I'm moving quickly," McCarthy apologizes, "but this is kind of boring stuff. I'm gonna get to the good stuff in a second." Taylor deadpans, "I make a living off of boring." Finally, McCarthy starts showing the passages from *Pandosto* and *The Winter's Tale*, explaining why they are both borrowing from another earlier source. The tremor goes out of his voice as he relaxes into his main point, that the play is an allegory for Henry and Katherine of Aragon, before switching to another slide about the use of Cavendish's *The Life and Death of Cardinal Wolsey* in *Henry VIII*.

He's still talking so fast, however, that it's hard to keep up with his arguments. "Do you need some water or something?" Bourus asks kindly. "We just need to calm down here." Taylor agrees. "I know, it's intense." McCarthy is so determined to squeeze as much information as possible into thirty minutes, he doesn't even realize that the scholars are enjoying his findings. As Taylor goes to get a bottle of water for him, Bourus starts talking about restaurants. "Maybe we can grab dinner, we've got a nice place here near campus."

After that, McCarthy resumes at a slightly slower pace, taking them through the statues in the church at Curtatone and the frescoes of Palazzo Te, "honest Camillo," and "the Isle of Delphos." Bourus spends most of the conversation leaning forward and nodding, while Taylor leans back, arms crossed, his face a mask of concentration. When McCarthy finally finishes, it's nearly four thirty—he's been talking nonstop for almost an hour. "It's a lot to look at," Bourus says first. "What were you chasing down when you suddenly came on to this?" McCarthy carefully downplays his years of research. "I believe that North has written a few source plays for Shakespeare, so I've been looking for manuscripts of North," he says. "The problem is," he adds apologetically, "a long time ago I made ridiculous and wild claims, and now I'm trying to get serious."

Bourus smiles. "It happens to the best of us." Taylor adds, obviously joking, "Everything I've said has just been accepted immediately." Finally, he comments on McCarthy's presentation. Far from criticizing his findings, as McCarthy has been bracing himself for, he seems intensely curious in the manuscript, encouraging McCarthy to publish a transcription. "Clearly the journal is really important, and clearly Shakespeare is interested in North," Taylor says. The two talk for a few minutes as colleagues, discussing the difficulty and importance of Shakespeare source study, before we all make plans to meet for dinner later that evening. "It's a very compelling argument," says Bourus before we leave. "I'm looking forward to looking into it more."

After the meeting, McCarthy is elated about Taylor and Bourus's willingness to consider his work. "This is the second-best outcome possible," he says when we are back in the car. "The first would be for Gary Taylor to say, 'This proves everything.'" I can't help but ask him, however, if he's not being disingenuous by hiding the full extent of his theories about Thomas North and the source plays. "I have to downplay it," McCarthy insists. "If I say exactly what I think, I can't get in the door."

THE ENTIRE TIME I've followed McCarthy and his work, he's been adamant that there is no "conspiracy theory" behind Thomas North's contribution to the plays. Shakespeare really did write all of the plays attributed to him in his lifetime, McCarthy insists, even if they were rewritten or adapted from earlier plays by Thomas North. There's one aspect of his theory, however, that will be especially difficult for Shakespeare scholars to accept: he doesn't believe Shakespeare wrote all of the plays that we attribute to him *now*.

Shakespeare's company continued to stage plays at the Globe after James's accession, becoming the King's Men. And Shakespeare, McCarthy contends, continued to adapt the plays he had acquired from North even after the older writer's death, releasing them at the rate of one or two a year. Those plays, he says, included some of the greatest in the canon, such as *Macbeth*, *Antony and Cleopatra*, and *King Lear*, but also inferior work, such as *Timon of Athens*, explaining why Shakespeare's later output varies so much. (McCarthy thinks only two Shakespeare plays—*The Merry Wives of Windsor* and *The Two Noble Kinsmen*—have little or no North at all.)

In 1609, Shakespeare published more poetry in the form of his *Sonnets*, written over the previous two decades. Then in 1613, errant cannon fire during *Henry VIII* kindled on the thatch, causing the entire Globe to go up in flames, just as Prospero had predicted. That same year, William Shakespeare abruptly gave up the theater and returned home to Stratford at age fifty. In another three years, he had died. By that point, only about half of the thirty-eight plays or so we now think of as Shakespeare's canon had been published. The others may not exist at all today if it were not for the actions of two of his fellow King's Men, John Heminges and Henry Condell. In 1623, they assembled and published *Mr. William Shakespeares Comedies, Histories, & Tragedies* in a larger format than the quarto editions, a book now known as the First Folio. It included a eulogy by Ben Jonson, who, putting aside his previous animosity, was full of nothing but praise for the playwright, calling him the "Soul of the Age!" Still, he couldn't resist including a dig, saying, "Thou hadst small Latin, and less Greek"— the source of endless speculation on how much classical knowledge Shakespeare really had.

Beneath the title, in smaller type, a subheading assured readers that the plays were "Published according to the true original copies." However, no one knows exactly where or how Heminges and Condell acquired the scripts of the plays they published. For generations, scholars have pored over the texts, fighting over differences between the First Folio and earlier quartos in order to divine the author's true intent. Some of the plays, they've determined, are not the original versions at all. Discrepancies in characters and continuity in *Macbeth*, *Love's Labour's Lost*, *The Merchant of Venice*, and other plays have revealed them to likely be edited versions of the staged plays.

In other cases, they've determined that the plays in the First Folio are Shakespeare's originals, as opposed to the "bad quartos" that bastardized his work. McCarthy, however, believes the exact opposite—that those quartos are Shakespeare's staged adaptations, while the more literary versions in the First Folio are North's original plays, or at least closer adaptations of them. In that list, he includes *Hamlet*, *Richard III*, *Romeo and Juliet*, *Henry V*, and *Henry VI, Parts 2 and 3*. "They had a staged adaptation, and they had a masterpiece, and so for those plays, they went with the masterpiece," McCarthy speculates. "Those, I believe, are pretty much pure North."

McCarthy's still not alleging any conspiracy or deception—after all, North was some twenty years dead by that point, and Shakespeare seven— so Heminges and Condell may have thought they were truly publishing Shakespeare. That speculation, however, comes dangerously close to the anti-Stratfordian claim that "Shakespeare didn't write Shakespeare," at least for a half-dozen plays of the canon. McCarthy seems to realize that's a bridge too far, even for the sympathetic readers of his theories, and he hastens to add that it's not necessary to believe that North's plays are present in the First Folio in order to agree that Shakespeare rewrote North's source plays. Still, it's an enticing possibility to think that North's supposed plays may not be lost after all, but have been hiding in plain sight for nearly four hundred years.

SOME MONTHS AFTER our meeting with Taylor and Bourus, I reach back out to ask them about McCarthy's ideas. Over email, Taylor reiterates his interest, and his desire to see more. After all, he says, a major new trend in Elizabethan drama studies is the recognition that the vast majority of plays from the period have been lost. "We might think of them as 'invisible' planets or stars or black holes: something we cannot see, that nevertheless affects the gravitational field and movement of what we do see," he writes. "The danger is that the invisibility of the lost texts means that is very easy to speculate about them, and very hard to prove anything about them. Each case has to be judged on its own merits."

Nearly five years after McCarthy first told me his theories at a Lafayette student bar, it's fair to say I have thought about those theories more than anyone other than McCarthy himself. I've traveled with him to Kirtling, Faversham, Mantua, and Rome; spent hours discussing the finer points of *The Two Gentlemen of Verona* and *Henry VI, Part 2*; watched and read commentaries on twenty-seven Shakespeare plays; and spent days of my own in archives examining documents in London, Oxford, and Cambridge. Not once, in all that time, have I found anything to disprove the notion that Thomas North wrote source plays for all of the plays in Shakespeare's canon.

Nor, however, have I found anything that definitively proves it. Despite the First Folio, there are no surviving plays with Thomas North's name on them, or even any hard evidence North was a playwright. There are no references to his dramatic works in letters, theater registers, or revels records. There are no surviving documents that place him in Italy in 1570, or Kenilworth in 1575, or prove an angry queen sent him to Ireland in 1580. There are no coded messages in the plays, no acrostic spelling out I-A-M-T-H-O-M-A-S-N-O-R-T-H in the lines of Hamlet's soliloquy. In short, it's entirely possible McCarthy has devoted a decade and a half of his life to a fantasy—an imaginative and plausible one, to be sure, but a pipe dream, which may prove no less true than the notion that the Earl of Oxford or Sir Francis Bacon secretly penned all of Shakespeare's *oeuvre*.

What I am left with, however, is one indisputable thought: if Thomas North *didn't* write plays that Shakespeare adapted, then there are an awful lot of coincidences to suggest that he did. That his half sister Alice Arden was the subject of one of Shakespeare's likely plays. That the subtitle of *Arden of Faversham* almost exactly matches a chapter heading in North's *Dial of Princes*. That his father wrote poems criticizing Cardinal Wolsey, who is criticized in *Henry VIII*. That he visited Mantua and saw frescoes by Giulio Romano and lifelike statues like the one in *The Winter's Tale*. That he visited the home of the Duke of Urbino, subject of Hamlet's play-within-a-play, "The Murder of Gonzago," and even misspelled Gonzaga as Gonzago.

That he studied law at the Inns of Court, where he was urged to write Senecan dramas like *Titus Andronicus*. That his patron, the Earl of Leicester, was a fan of *commedia dell'arte* and Italian comedies like *The Taming of the Shrew*. That his second translation, *The Moral Philosophy of Doni*, features characters like those in *Othello*. That he visited France during a time when the four main characters in *Love's Labour's Lost* were besieging La Rochelle. That his brother, at least, attended the famous Kenilworth festival that seems to have inspired *A Midsummer Night's Dream*. That his *Plutarch's Lives* is the source for *Julius Caesar* and *Antony and Cleopatra*, from which Shakespeare alone took passages verbatim. That another relative wrote a manuscript that includes Jack Cade, like *Henry VI, Part 2*. That he went to war in Ireland against a MacMorris, who shares a name with the only Irish character in the canon. That his life story of poverty and familial conflict mirrors, at least in part, the plots of *As You Like It* and *The Tempest*.

And that doesn't even get into the thousands of verbal parallels that McCarthy has found with his plagiarism software between North's prose translations and the plays. Or the fact that so many of the plays seem to attack the queen's choice of suitors on Leicester's behalf—Erik XIV in *Titus Andronicus*, Don John of Austria in *Much Ado About Nothing*, and the Duke of Alençon in the *Henry VI* plays. Or that attacks by other playwrights in *Groatsworth of Wit* and *Cynthia's Revels* seem to point to Thomas North and call out his relationship with Shakespeare.

True, McCarthy has reversed the chronology of sources at times when it suits him, insisting *Pandosto* is based on *The Winter's Tale*, or *Rosalynde* on *As You Like It*, rather than the other way around—and argued that later references in the plays are a result of Shakespeare's revisions, enabling him to "have his cake and eat it too" when it comes to dating. Even in those cases, however, he provides plausible explanations for how and why his claims could be accurate. And there isn't a single *foreign-language* source of any of the plays that postdates McCarthy's chronology for North's playwriting career. McCarthy can line up nearly every play in the canon in terms of source, subject matter, and biography with the facts of Thomas North's life and writings. That body of evidence extends far beyond what any anti-Stratfordian has been able to amass for Edward de Vere, Francis Bacon, Mary Sidney, Henry Neville, Christopher Marlowe, Thomas Sackville, or any of the dozens of other authorship candidates.

"To say that Thomas North's life and the plays of the canon fit together like a jigsaw puzzle doesn't exactly do it justice," McCarthy enthuses to me. "These are like parallel cascades, where all the events, images, even the style and the setting, everything from the plays, matches, minute by minute, and detail by detail, for five decades. It's miraculous."

The bigger question may be: What does it matter? Does it really change the meaning, impact, or philosophy of any of the plays to know that Thomas North had at least a hand in writing them? Personally, I can say yes. Reading the plays with Thomas North's story in mind has dramatically altered the way I've read them—explaining why a statue comes alive in *The Winter's Tale*; why *Henry VI, Part 1* is so anti-French; why *The Merchant of Venice* is obsessed with jewels; and why *Romeo and Juliet* is as much a parody of young passion as a celebration of it.

Mostly, it's affected my readings of the tragedies and *The Tempest*. To think that Hamlet's soliloquy on death was written by someone facing his own imminent demise; or that King Lear's mad railing at the storm was written by someone undergoing his own impoverished dark night of the soul; or that Prospero's triumph over his brother was written by someone working out his own feelings of familial revenge, adds new depths of feeling to plays that already overflow with profound sentiment. For that reason alone, it seems to me, it's worth knowing how the plays were written and by whom.

FOR HIS PART, McCarthy argues that understanding who conceived of the plots and characters, language, and soliloquies of the canon is of utmost importance. Whether it's the Kenilworth festival, the Alençon marriage, or the Spanish Armada, you really can't truly appreciate the plays without understanding the impulses that helped create them, he says. "If you tell me an author, I can tell you why he is autobiographical," McCarthy challenges me in the car between Milan and Mantua. When I say Hemingway, he ticks off the facts of his life—that he was an ambulance driver in Italy in World War I; he goes to bullfights in Spain; covers the Spanish Civil War as a journalist; goes on safaris in Africa; and at the end of his life fishes for marlin in the Florida Keys. "That's *A Farewell to Arms*, *The Sun Also Rises*, *For Whom the Bell Tolls*, the short stories, and *The Old Man and the Sea*," McCarthy says.

You can do the same with F. Scott Fitzgerald, he says, who went to parties on Long Island and lived on the French Riviera, just as in *The Great Gatsby* and *Tender Is the Night*. *Moby Dick*'s Ishmael says, "A whale-ship was my Yale College and my Harvard," and Melville spent time on a whaler. "Agatha Christie rode on the Orient Express, Ian Fleming worked for British Intelligence, Stephen King lives in Maine, Joseph Conrad went to the Congo," McCarthy continues. "When you think about it, it would be really ridiculous to invent a complete story—write a book on a climate you've never been in, a town you've never seen, the types of people you've never met." Imagine switching two authors, he says. "You know, Dostoevsky writing about adventures on the Mississippi or Mark Twain writing about converting to Christianity in a Siberian prison camp. It doesn't work."

Of all major writers in English, he goes on, only Shakespeare seems exempt from such analysis. We take it for granted that he wrote on a wide array of subjects, according to what struck him in the moment—an Italian comedy one year, followed by an English history the next, followed by the greatest tragedies ever written. "If Shakespeare had originated the canon rather than adapted it, it would be about the people he met in Stratford, and contemporary London events, which there were plays on during the period," McCarthy says. Thomas North, on the other hand, "is one of the most autobiographical writers there is," he claims. "Starting out with his sister's murder, supporting Leicester, and then coming to Italy, both intellectually and experientially, the plays match North. What's he's studying and where he's traveling end up in the canon, year by year, decade by decade, and this lasts for 50 years."

While that fact seems so clear to him, McCarthy is well aware that convincing other Shakespeareans of that will be an uphill battle at best. "As humans, we didn't evolve to be objective realists, we evolved to form emotional attachments to ideas," he says, falling back on his first love, science. "There is no way that many people are going to believe it—they are just going to have one idea they are going to stick with their whole life. And they are going to be wrong."

IN AT LEAST one way, however, McCarthy has already changed some people's ideas about Shakespeare. While we are in London together, we stop by the British Library to see the George North manuscript that he and June Schlueter discovered. We enter a huge atrium, with a glass tower full of books that reaches up four stories high—the remnants of King George III's library. We make our way up to the Manuscripts Reading Room on the third floor, but are disappointed to find that the George North manuscript isn't available. The librarian tells us that it's on loan to an exhibit, but can't say where—it could be anywhere in the UK, or even abroad. "Is it possible it's somewhere in the building?" I ask. "It's possible," he says, though he doesn't seem hopeful.

We take the escalator back down through the atrium, where I spy the doorway to an exhibition with the sign above it reading TREASURES OF THE BRITISH LIBRARY. On a hunch, we enter the dim-lit gallery space, which includes artifacts ranging from papyrus fragments to Jane Austen's writing desk to draft skits for Monty Python. There, in the very first case by the entrance, is a label reading "Shakespeare." We walk up to it to find that the first two items in the case are an original copy of Shakespeare's First Folio and, next to it, George North's A Brief Discourse manuscript. "You've got to be kidding me," McCarthy says upon seeing it. The First Folio copy is open to the Jack Cade episode from Henry VI, Part 2, with a placard noting how Shakespeare used George North's manuscript as a source and describing some of the "unique details" that figure in both accounts. "They are literally quoting me," McCarthy says as he reads it. Neither his nor Schlueter's names, however, appear on the text.

"I have to take a picture of this to send to June," McCarthy says. Since photographs aren't allowed, I offer to stand on the other side of the case, my back to the guard desk, while McCarthy surreptitiously takes the shot with his phone. The irony is not lost on either of us that McCarthy is forced to use subterfuge to capture the item that wouldn't even be in the case were it not for him. Credit or no, McCarthy is ecstatic as we leave the exhibit and walk down the marble stairs toward the exit. "That is friggin' amazing," he says. "It's right there when you walk in—one and two, the First Folio and the manuscript."

Just before we leave the library, we pass—of course—a white marble statue of William Shakespeare, literally standing up on a pedestal, chin pensively in hand, and writing quill at the ready. The sculpture, I later learn, was commissioned by David Garrick, that great eighteenth-century promoter of Bardolatry, and is now literally the first thing visitors see when they enter the building. As we exit into the library's vast brick courtyard, I ask McCarthy how he's feeling, and he surprises me by telling me that as much as he's enjoyed studying Thomas North, he's honestly already thinking about moving on to other topics.

"What I need to do is, once I get all of the information out, I'm sure there will be lots of other people making further discoveries and I will be very happy for that," he says. I ask what's next. "I don't know, I'll return back to science," he says. "I think geophysicists may be wrong about the opening of the Pacific—it's something that interests me." As we cross the courtyard, we pass by another statue, a bronze sculpture of Sir Isaac Newton based on an illustration by the Romantic poet William Blake. The sculpture shows a seated Newton bending forward to measure the Earth with a pair of mathematical calipers. Around his back is a metal band that symbolically holds him to the ground.

Newton discovered his law of gravity in 1666—some sixty years after Thomas North's death—a fitting reminder that not everything we take for granted has always been known to be true. I joke that maybe McCarthy should try to disprove quantum mechanics next. "Well, ninety-nine percent of everything that people believe in science is correct," he says with a smirk. "There are just some little things on the margins—you've got to find those."

EPILOGUE

Exit, pursued by a bear.

—The Winter's Tale

As I looked through the images I took of North's *Dial of Princes* at the Cambridge University Library in the fall of 2019, I spotted one more intriguing bit of marginalia. On one page, Thomas North had written a comment: "Antigonus, a noble Roman, his wife, daughter banished." That caught my attention, knowing that in *The Winter's Tale*, King Leontes's noble counselor was also named Antigonus—and he was the one who had taken the king's daughter Perdita into her banishment on the mean shores of Bohemia (or, as McCarthy believes it to originally be, Sicily). Could there be some kind of connection?

As I looked through the surrounding pages, I found another comment in which North had noted, "the description of the Monster seen at Palermo." The page described a "huge monster" that had been supposedly spotted in "the realm of Scicil"—that is, Sicily. The creature, in North's translation, had two "horns like a goat," "hands like the feet of horses," and a face like a man's, "save that it had but one eye, which was in the middle of his forehead"—a cyclops, just like North had seen in the giant fresco at Palazzo Te. Furthermore, the description said, the monster rode on a chariot driven by four beasts—"two lions before, and two bears behind." At the word "bear," I started. Could this passage be the source of Antigonus's famous stage direction, "Exit, pursued by a bear"?

I sent the pages to McCarthy, asking if he had ever noticed this reference before, and he responded that he hadn't, but he was eager to check it out. Within forty-eight hours, he'd written back with several pages analyzing the passage. The Antigonus in *The Dial of Princes*, it seems, was a nobleman who had been banished to Sicily with his wife and daughter for some petty offenses. The monster, a punishment for piracy committed by the people of Sicily, arrived in Palermo while Antigonus was in exile, creating a storm with "a marvelous dark cloud, which seemed to darken the whole earth." Here, the text of *The Dial* again mentions "the lions with terrible voices roaring, the bears with no less fearful cries raging." Then a rain of fire killed thousands of people, including a group of pirates staying in the port city. Antigonus could hear their "doleful clamours and cries" and the storm even destroyed Antigonus's house and killed his daughter. In a letter to the emperor, Marcus Aurelius, Antigonus then complained his punishment was too harsh for his crime. The emperor responded sympathetically, saying, "Judges are so greedy to tear men's flesh, as if they were bears and man's flesh were anointed with honey."

In a tight array, says McCarthy, the passage contained numerous elements connecting it to the Antigonus subplot in *The Winter's Tale*. As the Antigonus of the play arrives in Bohemia with a group of sailors, one remarks that he "never saw the heavens so dim by day." At that point, a storm arrives that sinks the ship and kills the sailors aboard, at the same time that Antigonus, on shore, is chased offstage by the famous bear. Later, a clown appears, describing the scene he witnessed to the shepherd. "How the poor souls roared," he says, "and the sea mocked them, and how the poor gentleman roared and the bear mocked him, both roaring louder than the sea or weather."

In both cases, McCarthy notes, a dark storm is combined with a terrible beast, and the crying of the mariners is contrasted with bears' roaring. The Antigonus of *The Dial* is faced with the appearance of a huge, bear-like monster, while the Antigonus of *The Winter's Tale* is chased by an actual bear. As written by a young Thomas North, the passage in the play would have seemed like a long inside joke, as he cleverly inserted the classical allusions from the book he was transcribing into a totally different scene in a play. Or perhaps it was William Shakespeare who, at the end of his career fifty years later, came across the passage in North's work and decided to use it to shape the scene. Or perhaps the passage in the play has nothing to do with Thomas North, and Shakespeare just independently conjured up the name Antigonus, the shores of Sicily, the storm, the sailors, the lost daughter, and the bear—just another set of coincidences. But that doesn't seem likely. *Exit.*

APPENDIX A
TIMELINE OF THE PLAYS

The following chart includes Dennis McCarthy's estimated chronology of Thomas North's plays, versus the conventional chronology proposed by the Shakespeare Birthplace Trust.

Approx. date by Thomas North (revision)	Title (possible original title)	Approx. date by William Shakespeare
1555–1557	Henry VIII (All Is True)	1613
1555–1557	The Winter's Tale	1609–1610
1557–1558	Arden of Faversham (A Cruel Murder Done in Kent)	1592
1561	Titus Andronicus (Titus and Vespasian)	1592
1569–1571	The Two Gentlemen of Verona (Philemon and Philecia)	1589–1591
1569–1571 (rev. 1594)	The Comedy of Errors	1594
1570–1571	The Taming of the Shrew	1590–1591
1573–1575	Pericles	1607
1574	Much Abo About Nothing (Phaenicia)	1598–1599
1575 (rev. 1582)	Love's Labour's Lost	1594–1595
1575–1576	Julius Caesar	1599
1576–1577	Antony and Cleopatra	1606
1576–1577	Henry VI, Part 2	1590–1591
1576–1577	Henry VI, Part 3	1591
1576–1581	Coriolanus	1608
1577–1578	Richard III	1592–1593
1577–1584	Timon of Athens	1606

Approx. date by Thomas North (revision)	Title (possible original title)	Approx. date by William Shakespeare
1577–1584 (rev. 1594–1596)	Richard II	1594
1578	The Merchant of Venice (The Jew of Venice)	1596–1597
1580	Henry VI, Part 1	1592
1581	Henry IV, Parts 1 and 2	1596–1597 / 1597–1598
1581–1582	Henry V	1598–1599
1581–1588	A Midsummer Night's Dream	1595
1582	Romeo and Juliet	1595
1582–1583 (rev. 1601)	Twelfth Night (What You Will)	1601
1585–1587	All's Well That Ends Well	1606–1607
1587 (rev. 1600)	As You Like It	1599–1600
1587–1592	Measure for Measure	1603–1604
1588	Hamlet	1600–1601
1588–1590	King John	1596
1589	Othello (The Moor of Venice)	1603–1604
1590	King Lear	1605–1610
1592	Macbeth	1606
1596–1597	Cymbeline	1610–1611
1601–1602	Troilus and Cressida	1602
1603	The Tempest	1610–1611

Note: McCarthy believes that Shakespeare's *The Merry Wives of Windsor* (1596–1597) and *The Two Noble Kinsmen* (1613) contain little to no North.

APPENDIX B

EXAMPLES OF McCARTHY'S PLAGIARISM TECHNIQUES

The following examples, provided by Dennis McCarthy, illustrate his techniques for using plagiarism software to explore parallel passages between Thomas North's prose writings and William Shakespeare's plays.

NORTH'S *THE DIAL OF PRINCES*	*ARDEN OF FAVERSHAM*
They **flatter** the pages and servants…For the gorgeous Courtier…**jetting in his** velvets and silks, to beg and seek his dinner daily at every man's board, being **nobly** and honorably entertained of the prince, and able to bear his **countenance**… the **Noblemen** to whose **houses** they come to, are offended with them, **the Stewards of the house** murmur at them, the pages and **servants** mocks them **and laugh them to scorn** (619–620)	ARDEN: Crept into **service** of a **nobleman**, And by his **servile** flattery and fawning Is now become **the steward of his house**, And bravely **jets it in his silken** gown. FRANKLIN: No **nobleman will countenance** such a peasant (1.27–31) [Referring to the **servant** Michael] the white-livered peasant/Is gone to bed, **and laughs us both to scorn** (5.38–39)

North's *The Dial*	*Titus Andronicus*
Lady **Lavinia,** most earnestly I desire thee, so vehemently not to pierce the **heavens** with thy so heavy **sighs,** nor yet to wet the **earth** with thy so **bitter tears**... (488)	[About **Lavinia's** plight:] When **heaven** doth weep, doth not the **earth** o'erflow?... I am the sea; hark, how her **sighs** do blow! She is the weeping welkin, I the **earth:** Then must my sea be moved with her **sighs;** Then must my **earth** with her continual **tears** Become a deluge, overflow'd and drown'd (3.1.221–29)
but with many **<u>Tears shed on the earth</u>** (549)	And at thy feet I kneel, with **<u>tears of joy,</u> <u>Shed on the earth</u>,** for thy return to Rome (1.1.161–62)

NORTH'S *PLUTARCH'S LIVES*	*THE TAMING OF THE SHREW*
For he took not only **gold** & silver enough, as much as they would give him: but received a very **rich** bed also, & **Persian** chamberlains to make and dress it up, as if no Grecian servants of his could have served that turn. Moreover he received <u>four **score** milch kine to the pail</u> & **neat** herds to keep them… (325–26)	First, as you know, my house within the city Is **richly** furnishèd with plate and **gold**, Basins and ewers to lave her dainty hands; My hangings all of **Tyrian** tapestry; In ivory coffers I have stuffed my crowns; In **cypress** chests my arras counterpoints, Costly <u>apparel, tents, and canopies,</u> Fine linen, **Turkey** cushions bossed with pearl, <u>Valance of Venice **gold**</u> in needlework, Pewter and brass and all things that belongs To house or housekeeping. Then at my farm I have a <u>hundred **milch kine to the pail**</u>, <u>Six score</u> fat **oxen** standing in my stalls… (2.1.344–56)
[**gold, rich,** Persian, four s**core** milch kine to the pail, neat]	[**gold, richly,** Tyrian-Turkey, Six **score, milch kine to the pail,** oxen]

NORTH'S JOURNAL ENTRIES ON LOMBARDY (AND QUOTE FROM *PLUTARCH'S LIVES**)	*THE TAMING OF THE SHREW*
Lombardy…All the way betwixt Milan and Lodi, we rode as between **gardens**; and to speak truth, my eyes never saw <u>any soil comparable</u> to it for beauty and profit.…	I am arriv'd for fruitful **Lombardy**, The pleasant **garden** of great Italy,
Moreover, he received **four score milch kine to the pail**…*	Then at my farm, I have a **hundred milch-kine to the pail,**
We saw one **hundred fat oxen in** <u>a stable</u>	**Six score fat oxen** standing in <u>my stalls</u> (1.1; 2.1)

North's speeches on facing death in *The Dial*	*Julius Caesar* on facing death
The **cowardly** heart falleth **before** he is beaten down: but the stout and **valiant** stomach, in greatest peril, recovereth most strength. Thou art one man, and not two, **thou owest one death to the gods** [533]. **Men**...ought to **die but once**...[Yet] thinking to lead a sure life, **we taste a new death.** I know not why **men fear** so much **to die**...(why) fly the voyage of **death** which is **necessary** [526]. **Come** that that may **come** [559].	Caesar: **Cowards die** many times **before** their **deaths;** The **valiant** never **taste of death but once.** Of all the wonders that I yet have heard, It seems to me most strange that **men should fear,** Seeing that **death, a necessary** end, Will **come** when it will **come** (*Julius Caesar*, 2.2.32–37)
thou owest one **death** to the **gods** [533]	thou owest God a death (*Henry IV, Part 1*, 5.1.126)

Isolated Correspondences	
The Dial	*Julius Caesar*
coward(ly)-before-valiant	**coward-before-valiant**
Taste a new **death...die but once**	**taste of death but once**
I know not why **men fear**	It seems to me most strange that **men** should **fear**
death which is **necessary**	**death** a **necessary** end
Come that that may **come**	Will **come** when it will **come**

This exact deathbed discussion in *The Dial* was also the inspiration for the most famous soliloquy in history: *Hamlet*'s "To be, or not to be" speech (3.1.66–92).

NORTH'S *THE DIAL*	*HAMLET*
First, Hamlet and Panutius both ask whether it is better to endure the torments of fortune and evils of the world or to die and so escape the suffering. Directly following this question, Hamlet describes death as a way to escape "the slings and errors of outrageous fortune," while Panutius describes death as a way to escape "the assaults of life and broils of fortune": [* denotes echoes from other speeches on death in *The Dial*.]	
<u>Is it better that thou **die**</u>, and go with so many good; than that thou scape, and live amongst so many evil…? What other thing is the grave, but a strong fort, wherein we shut ourselves from <u>**the** assaults of life **and** broils **of** fortune</u>? (535)	To be, or not to be, that is the question, Whether 'tis nobler in the mind to suffer **The** <u>slings **and** arrows **of** outrageous **fortune**</u>…
plunge themselves so deep into **a sea of troubles**…and utterly perish (724)*	Or to take arms against **a sea of troubles,** And by opposing end them.
Death is an eternal **sleep**… <u>a pilgrimage **un**certain</u>…For, of all those which are dead, **none returned** (524)	To **die, to sleep**…/death <u>The **un**discover</u>'d coun<u>try</u>, from whose bourn No traveler returns

when we **sleep** the enticements of the **flesh** do not provoke us…we feel not the anguishes of the body, neither suffer the passion of the mind to come… **and a thousand calamities** which do torment their **hearts**… …**of so long life**… (132, 472, 15)*	To die, **to sleep** No more; and by **a sleep** to say we end The **heart**ache, and the **thousand** natural shocks That **flesh** is heir to… There's the respect That makes **calamity of so long life**.
Then, both Hamlet and Panutius, after listing life's miseries, answer their own question, noting that we should wish for death because it would bring a welcome end to these sufferings:	
Truly we ought **to be** more desirous of that we find in death (536)	'tis a consummation/ Devoutly **to be** wish't…
But Hamlet and Aurelius then point out a rub. Yes, death may indeed stop the suffering, but it still remains so uncertain that it also bring fear and dread:	
Life is so troublesome that it **weary**eth us: and <u>**Death** is so doubtful, that it feareth us</u>… I desire no more to **live**: but for that <u>I **know not**</u> whither I am carried by death… (558)	…who would fardels bear, To grunt and sweat under a **weary life**, But that the <u>dread of something after **death**</u>… And makes us rather bear those ills we have Than fly to others that <u>we know not</u> of

North's *Plutarch's Lives*	*Antony and Cleopatra*
The poop whereof **was of gold, the sails of purple,** and **the oars of silver,**	The poop **was** beaten **gold;** **Purple the sails**.../The oars were **silver,**
which kept stroke in rowing after the sound of the music **of the flutes...**	Which to the tune **of flutes kept stroke...**
For the **person of herself: she was laid** under a **pavilion of cloth-of-gold of tissue...**	**For** her own **person,** It beggared all description: **she** did **lie** In her **pavilion — cloth-of-gold of tissue —**
attired like the Goddess **Venus,** commonly drawn in **picture...** **On** either hand of **her,** **pretty** fair **boys** appareled as...**Cupid, with** little **fans** in their **hands...**	O'er**pictur**ing that **Venus** where we see The fancy outwork nature. **On** each side **her** Stood **pretty** dimpled **boys,** like smiling **Cupids,** With divers-colored **fans...**
Her ladies and **gentlewomen... like** the nymphs, **Nereides,** which are the **mermaids** of the waters... some **steering the helm,** others **tending the tackle** and ropes of **the barge,** out of the which there came a wonderful,	Her **gentlewomen, like the Nereides,** So many **mermaids, tended** her... At **the helm** A seeming **mermaid steers. The** silken **tackle** Swell with the touches of those flower-soft **hands...** From **the barge**
passing sweet savor of perfumes that **perfumed** the **wharf's** side (981)	A strange invisible **perfume** hits the sense Of the adjacent **wharfs** (2.2.202–23)

Glendower's and Cade's lament about their final hours in George North's *Brief Discourse*	Cade's lament about his final hours in *Henry VI, Part 2*, Act 4, scene 10
see **Jack Cade** and the Black Smith... shrined **with a halter**	[From prior scenes 4.9.8–4.9.9s.d:]... is the traitor **Cade** surpris'd?...Enter multitudes **with halters**...
Myself to **hide** in cave:	...**I hid me** in these woods...
...scorching heat...	...this hot weather.
Each bird, each bush a foe I deem	...durst not **peep** out, for all the country is laid for me [*Henry VI, Part 3*: **fear each bush an officer; bird**]
Pain bad me yield, shame willed me **stay** with **hungry** chops to fast: Which I endured, till double death constrained me at the last. **To feed on moss for famine great** [**stay, hungry, famine, feed on, moss**]	now am I so **hungry** that...I could **stay** no longer...I can eat **grass**... sallet... ...must serve me to **feed on**... **Famine** and no other hath slain me. [**stay, hungry, famine, feed on, grass**]
...**faltering limbs...feeble legs**	...**limb to limb,** and thou art far the lesser; Thy **leg** a stick...
...**through London streets, drawn like a mastie dog.**	Hence **will I drag thee headlong by the heels**
For Carrion Crows and worm's meat, ...**beasts**	Leaving thy trunk for **crows**... **carrion kites and crows; beast** (5.2.11–12)

GEORGE NORTH'S *BRIEF DISCOURSE*	*RICHARD III*
...to view our own **proportion in a glass,** whose **form and feature** if we find **fair** and worthy, to frame our affections accordingly; if otherwise **she** have (by skill or will) **deformed** our outward appearance and left us <u>odible to the eye of the **world**</u>, then (to cure, **shadow,** or salve the same) so to govern and guide our behavior, and so to moderate our inward man, as <u>**Nature** herself may seem to be **deceived**</u> in us. Whereunto no cunning can easier attain than by making our own minds true mirrors of all our actions (Dedication, 0v-1)	But I, that am not shaped for sportive tricks, Nor made to court an amorous **looking glass;** I, that am curtailed of this **fair proportion,** Cheated of **feature** by **dissembling Nature,** **Deformed,** unfinished, sent before my time Into this breathing **world** scarce half made up... Have no delight to pass away the time, Unless to see my **shadow** in the sun And descant on mine own **deformity.** And therefore, since I cannot prove a lover... I am determinèd to prove a villain... (1.1.14–21, 25–30)

NORTH'S *THE DIAL* AND *PLUTARCH'S LIVES*	*RICHARD II*
Alcibiades…was not altogether so corrupt, neither simply evil: but as they say of the **land** of Egypt, that for the **fatness** and lustiness **of the soil**, it bringeth <u>forth both</u> **wholesome herbs** <u>and also</u> **noisome weeds** (*Plutarch's Lives*, 584) [Margin: **Children** in their youth apt to entertain all vices.] Tutors and Master of Princes and great Lords…ought to know from what evils or wicked customs they ought to withdraw them: For when the **trees** are tender and young, it is more necessary to bow them and <u>**cut off**</u> the **superfluous branches** <u>with knives than to gather</u> **their fruits** with baskets (*The Dial*, 343–44)	Gardener: Go bind thou up yon dangling apricots Which, like unruly **children**, make their sire Stoop with oppression of their prodigal weight. Give some supportance to <u>the bending twigs</u>. Go thou, and like an executioner **Cut off** <u>the heads of too-fast-growing sprays</u> …I will go root away The **noisome weeds** <u>which without profit suck</u> **The soil's fertility** <u>from</u> **wholesome** flowers. Servant: …the whole **land**, Is full of **weeds**, her fairest flowers choked up, Her **fruit trees** all unpruned, her hedges ruined, Her knots disordered, and her **wholesome herbs** Swarming with caterpillars… Gardener: O, what pity is it That he had not so trimmed and dressed his **land** As we this garden!… Had he done so <u>to great and growing men</u>, They might have lived to bear and he to taste **Their fruits** of duty. **Superfluous branches** <u>We lop away</u>, that bearing boughs may live (3.4.29–39, 43–47, 55–57, 61–64)

NORTH'S *NEPOS'S LIVES*	*RICHARD II*
North on griefs of the inward soul, its cause being a lack of perspective, like looking in water, and the abandonment of *hope* by those *who would dissolve the bands of life*:	Queen–Bushy exchange on griefs of the inward soul, its cause being a lack of perspective, like looking in water, and the abandonment of *hope* by those *who would dissolve the bands of life*:
[Describing griefs that create a "**sorrowful** life":] Besides all this, there are the **griefs of the soul**...If the **grief** of the body affects the rest and contentment of the mind—much more doth <u>the **inward grief**</u> and anguish.	Queen [describing grief]: yet I know no cause Why I should welcome such a guest as **grief**... Some unborn **sorrow**, ripe in fortune's womb, Is coming towards me, and my **inward soul** With nothing trembles: at some thing it **grieves** More than with parting from my lord the king.

cont. on next page

[Stoic counsel:] to remedy the **griefs** before named… [Seneca] sheweth the wrong which men of understanding do, and <u>the error of their judgment</u>—who **see things** as in the water and **with** a corrupt **eye**…	Bushy [stoic counsel]: Each substance of a **grief** hath twenty shadows, Which shows like **grief** itself, but is not so; For sorrow's <u>eye, glazed with blinding tears,</u> <u>Divides one **thing** entire to many objects;</u> <u>Like perspectives,</u> which rightly gazed upon Show nothing but confusion, **eyed** awry Distinguish form: so your sweet majesty, Looking awry upon your lord's departure, Find shapes of **grief**, more than himself, to wail… /weep not: <u>more's not **seen**</u>; Or if it be, 'tis **with** false **sorrow's eye**, <u>Which for **things** true weeps **things imaginary**</u>.
[The *dissolve-the-bands-of-life* addendum:] **He would** have this wise man put himself to **death**, and of his authority and power **dissolve the bands of this life** without leave of the sovereign Captain and with a testimony of a strange cowardliness and distrust of the doctrine of the eternal Providence: the **which would** have us **keep** a steadfast **hope** and confidence, yea even when things seem to be most <u>desperate</u> (113–15)	Queen [*dissolve the bands-of-life* addendum]: Who shall **hinder** me? I will <u>despair</u>, and be at enmity With cozening **hope**. **He** is a flatterer, A parasite, a **keep**er-back of **death**, Who gently **would dissolve the bands of life** **Which** false **hope lingers** in extremity…(2.2.6–72)

NORTH'S *MORAL PHILOSOPHY OF DONI*	*KING LEAR*
And he that with **fury** (passing the rest) with an insatiable desire would needs go further, plunged his whole body in the **water**...it was most swift and **raging**, and they could not get out of the midst, but even as much as they could do in swimming to keep themselves **above water**... This worldly life representeth no more but <u>the **little world of** our body</u>... seem but as snow, which with the first beams of the Sun <u>dissolveth</u> **and** <u>cometh to</u> **nothing**. Lord, what cost do we bestow upon our **hairs**... which...are despised and thrown away (12r–13r)	Contending with the fretful elements; Bids the wind blow the earth into the <u>sea</u>, Or swell the curled **waters 'bove** the main, That things might change or cease; tears his white **hair**, Which the impetuous blasts, with eyeless **rage**, Catch in their **fury and** make **nothing** of; Strives in <u>his **little world** of man</u> to outscorn The to-and-fro-conflicting wind and rain (3.1.3–10)
ISOLATED CORRESPONDENCES	
above water, fury, raging, <u>this **little world of** our body,</u> <u>our **hairs**...despised and thrown away</u> And cometh to **nothing**	**waters 'bove, fury, rage,** his **little world of** man **hair**...catch in their fury **and** make **nothing** of

NORTH'S *THE DIAL* AND *MORAL PHILOSOPHY OF DONI*	*MACBETH*
after he hath once begun to do evil, he never ceaseth **daily** to do worse...we may aptly compare an *ill** man to a **candle**, which after it is once **light**, it never leaveth burning til it have made an end of itself (*The Dial*, 450v) This worldly **life**...carryeth a wonderful presence: and that little breath of ours **once** spent, it **is then but a shadow, dust,** and smoke. These worldly favours and temporal goods, in the judgment of the wise, seem but as snow, which with the first beams of the Sun dissolveth and cometh to **nothing**...A man should never trust this foolish life. It is but a fire kindled on the coals, which, consuming itself, giveth heat to others (12r–13r)	To-morrow, and to-morrow, and to-morrow, Creeps in this petty pace from **day to day** To the last syllable of recorded time, And all our yesterdays have **lighted fools** The way to **dusty** death. Out, out, brief **candle!** **Life's but a** walking **shadow**, a poor player That struts and frets his hour upon the stage And then is heard no more. **It is** a tale Told by an idiot, full of sound and fury, Signifying **nothing** (5.5.22–28)

ISOLATED CORRESPONDENCES	
Never ceaseth **daily**	Creeps...from **day to day**
Candle...light	Lighted...candle
dust, foolish, breath-spent, fire-smoke,	**dusty, fools,** candle-out
life...is but a shadow,	Life's but a walking **shadow,**
presence-heat, cometh to **nothing**	sound and fury, signifying **nothing.**

ACKNOWLEDGMENTS

If I've learned anything from this book, it is that good creative work is a collaboration—and this book is no exception. I have to thank my agent, Gillian MacKenzie, for believing in this idea from the beginning, and encouraging me to pursue it in as expansive a way as possible. I also have to thank Hachette Books for enthusiastically embracing this project, including Paul Whitlatch, who acquired it, and Brant Rumble, who took over as editor and jumped in with both feet, remaining endlessly supportive and patient throughout my long and sometimes tortuous writing "process."

I would like to thank everyone at the Hachette team who worked on the book in ways large and small, including assistant editor Mollie Weisenfeld, publisher Mary Ann Naples, associate publisher Michelle Aielli, marketing director Michael Barrs, publicity manager Michael Giarratano, art director Amanda Kain, production editor Amber Morris, copyeditor Mike McConnell, designer Sean Ford—and everyone else behind the scenes who has worked to make this book a success.

Many people have read this book at various stages of its creation and offered insightful comments and feedback that have vastly improved it at every stage of the process. They include Ann Blanding, Alex Marzano-Lesnevich, Dawn Oates, Katherine Ozment, Rebecca Uchill, and especially Jenn Mattson and Lara Rosenbaum, who offered more extensive comments in the final stretch. Writing a book that blends Shakespearean literary criticism, Elizabethan history, and modern-day travelogue isn't an easy lift, and so I greatly appreciated each and every one of you who plowed through my prose as I figured out the best form for this narrative.

While I've always been a fan of the Bard, writing this book was a deep dive into archival and historical research. I have to thank Tony Edwards for his expert manuscript sleuthing, as well as Ben Sanderson and Julian Harrison at the British Library, Giles Mandelbrote at Lambeth Palace Library, and all of the curators and librarians at the National Archives, the Bodleian's Weston Library, Cambridge University Library, Boston College Library, and Harvard's Widener Library, who helped me locate the books and documents that brought this book to life. Portions of this book were written in the reading rooms of the British Library, and I like to think that some of the magic of that special place infuses its pages.

As I attempted to teach myself secretary hand to decipher Tudor documents, I was helped immensely by others who were better equipped than I to read and interpret them. They include Linda Watson and Olin Moctezuma Burns who helped transcribe documents I couldn't, and John Gallagher, who generously sent me his transcription of John North's diary. I also have to thank Jelmer Noordeman and Koen Harmsma, who created the gorgeous maps that help to bring Thomas North's travels alive. In my own travels, I met many lovely people who helped me navigate and interpret locations that were key to the narrative, especially Irene and Chris Redman, who opened their home to us in Faversham.

I especially have to thank my family—most importantly, Rebecca Uchill for her inspiration and support that sustained me through long hours at the keyboard, her academic sensibility that kept me grounded in my explorations, and her vast patience for listening to recitations of the histories of Tudor royals at the dinner table. A big shout out as well to Zachary and Cleo Blanding for their tolerance during the times this book took me away from much more fun activities, and for their cheerful interest in William Shakespeare and Thomas North. Your English teachers can thank me later, and one day I *will* write you a fantasy novel.

The McCarthy family, including Lori, Kennedy, and Griffin, graciously let me into their home on numerous occasions, and I sincerely appreciate their hospitality and good humor. A special acknowledgement to Nicole Galovski, and her camera crew of Bahareh Hosseini, Ian Wexler, and Laura Hudock. You were all great traveling companions, and I appreciate your letting me make you characters in my work at the same time you made me a character in yours. This book literally would not exist without June and Paul Schlueter, who invited me to speak at Lafayette five years ago—which was not only a delightful opportunity to talk about my last book, but also set me on the path to my next. Thanks as well to Neil McElroy and Diane Shaw for hosting my visit there. And of course, June continued to be gracious in sharing her work with me throughout this project.

Last but not least, I have to extend a big appreciation to Dennis McCarthy for opening up his research to me and entrusting me with telling his story. I can only hope I've done it justice. It's been a long and fascinating ride so far, and I can't wait to see what you discover next.

BIBLIOGRAPHY

Ackeren, Marcel van, ed. *A Companion to Marcus Aurelius.* Wiley-Blackwell, 2012.

Ackroyd, Peter. *Shakespeare: The Biography.* Nan A. Talese, 2005.

———. *Tudors: The History of England from Henry VIII to Elizabeth I.* St. Martin's Griffin, 2014.

Adams, Simon. *Leicester and the Court: Essays on Elizabethan Politics.* Manchester University Press, 2002.

Alexander, Catherine M. S., ed. *The Cambridge Companion to Shakespeare's Last Plays.* Cambridge Companion to Authors. Cambridge University Press, 2009.

Appleford, Amy. *Learning to Die in London, 1380–1540.* University of Pennsylvania Press, 2015.

Armstrong, Edward Allworthy. *Shakespeare's Imagination, a Study of the Psychology of Association and Inspiration.* L. Drummond, 1946.

Artese, Charlotte. *Shakespeare's Folktale Sources.* University of Delaware Press, 2015.

Axton, Marie. *The Queen's Two Bodies: Drama and the Elizabethan Succession.* Royal Historical Society, 1977.

Barber, Bruno. *The London Charterhouse.* MoLAS Monograph, No. 10. Museum of London Archaeology Service, 2002.

Barber, C. L., Peter Erickson, and Coppélia Kahn, eds. *Shakespeare's "Rough Magic": Renaissance Essays in Honor of C. L. Barber.* University of Delaware Press, 1985.

Baretti, Joseph. *Dizionario Delle Lingue Italiana Ed Inglise.* J. Richardson, 1760.

Bartels, Emily C., and Emma Smith. *Christopher Marlowe in Context.* Cambridge University Press, 2013.

Bartlett, Kenneth R. *The English in Italy, 1525–1558: A Study in Culture and Politics.* Slatkine, 1991.

Bassi, Shaul. *Shakespeare's Italy & Italy's Shakespeare: Place, "Race," Politics.* Palgrave Macmillan, 2016.

Bassi, Shaul, and Alberto Toso Fei. *Shakespeare in Venice: Exploring the City with Shylock and Othello.* Elzeviro, 2007.

Bate, Jonathan. *Soul of the Age: A Biography of the Mind of William Shakespeare.* Random House, 2009.

———. *How the Classics Made Shakespeare.* E. H. Gombrich Lecture Series. Princeton University Press, 2019.

Bazzotti, Ugo, ed. *Palazzo Te Mantua.* Skira, 2007.

Beauclerk, Charles. *Shakespeare's Lost Kingdom: The True History of Shakespeare and Elizabeth.* Grove Press, 2010.

Beckingsale, B. W. *Thomas Cromwell: Tudor Minister.* Palgrave Macmillan, 1978.

Bednarz, James P. *Shakespeare & the Poets' War*. Columbia University Press, 2001.

Bellamy, John. *The Tudor Law of Treason: An Introduction*. Routledge, 2014.

Bevington, David. *Shakespeare and Biography*. Oxford University Press, 2010.

Black, Jeremy. *Mapping Shakespeare: An Exploration of Shakespeare's World through Maps*. Conway, 2018.

Blois, Lukas de. *The Statesman in Plutarch's Works: Proceedings of the Sixth International Conference of the International Plutarch Society*. Mnemosyne, Bibliotheca Classica Batava. Supplementum 250. Brill, 2004.

Bloom, Harold. *Rosalind*. Chelsea House Publishers, 1992.

———. *Shakespeare: The Invention of the Human*. Riverhead Books, 1998.

———. *Christopher Marlowe*. Infobase Publishing, 2009.

———. *Cleopatra: I Am Fire and Air*. Scribner, 2017.

Bourgeois, Eugene J. *The Ruling Elite of Cambridgeshire, England, c. 1520–1603*. Studies in British History. Vol. 74. Edwin Mellen Press, 2003.

Boyle, A. J. *Tragic Seneca*. Routledge, 2009.

Braden, Gordon. *Renaissance Tragedy and the Senecan Tradition: Anger's Privilege*. Yale University Press, 1985.

Bradley, A. C. *Oxford Lectures on Poetry*. Atlantic Publishers & Dist, 1999.

Bradley, Simon, and Nikolaus Pevsner. *Cambridgeshire*. Yale University Press, 2015.

Brigden, Susan. *New Worlds, Lost Worlds: The Rule of the Tudors, 1485–1603*. Penguin Books, 2002.

Briggs, Asa. *A Social History of England*. Penguin Books, 1999.

Brotton, Jerry. *The Sultan and the Queen: The Untold Story of Elizabeth and Islam*. Viking, 2016.

Bryson, Bill. *Shakespeare: The World as Stage*. Atlas Books/HarperCollins, 2007.

Budra, Paul. *A Mirror for Magistrates and the de casibus Tradition*. University of Toronto Press, 2000.

Bullough, Geoffrey. *Narrative and Dramatic Sources of Shakespeare*. Routledge and Paul; Columbia University Press, 1957.

Burrow, Colin. *Shakespeare and Classical Antiquity*. Oxford University Press, 2013.

Burrow, J. W. *A History of Histories: Epics, Chronicles, Romances, and Inquiries from Herodotus and Thucydides to the Twentieth Century*. Knopf, 2008.

Bush, M. L. *The Government Policy of Protector Somerset*. McGill-Queen's University Press, 1975.

Bushby, Frances. *Three Men of the Tudor Time (Classic Reprint)*. FB&C Limited, 2016.

Cantor, Paul A. *Shakespeare's Roman Trilogy: The Twilight of the Ancient World*. The University of Chicago Press, 2017.

Carroll, D. Allen, ed. *Greene's Groatsworth of Wit: Bought with a Million of Repentance (1592)*. Center for Medieval and Early Renaissance Studies, State University of New York at Binghamton, 1994.

Cavendish, George. *Life of Cardinal Wolsey*. Chiswick, from the Press of C. Whittingham, for Harding, Triphook, and Lepard, 1825.

Cecil, Evelyn. *Primogeniture; a Short History of Its Development in Various Countries and Its Practical Effects*. J. Murray, 1895.

Chambers, E. K. *The Elizabethan Stage*. Clarendon Press, 1923.

Charter-House, Its Foundation and History. Charterhouse, 1849.

Charterhouse in London. S&N, 2011.

Chernaik, Warren L. *The Myth of Rome in Shakespeare and His Contemporaries*. Cambridge University Press, 2011.

Cole, Mary Hill. *The Portable Queen: Elizabeth I and the Politics of Ceremony.* University of Massachusetts Press, 1999.

Cole, Michael W., and Rebecca Zorach, eds. *The Idol in the Age of Art: Objects, Devotions and the Early Modern World.* Routledge, 2009.

Cosmescu, Dragoș. *Venetian Renaissance Fortifications in the Mediterranean.* McFarland, 2015.

Convegno internazionale di studi su "Giulio Romano e l'espansione europea del Rinascimento." *Giulio Romano,* Mantova, Palazzo ducale, Teatro scientifico del Bibiena, 1–5 ottobre 1989. Accademia nazionale virgiliana, 1989.

Craig, Hugh, and Arthur F. Kinney. *Shakespeare, Computers, and the Mystery of Authorship.* Cambridge University Press, 2009.

Cunningham, Peter. *Extracts from the Accounts of the Revels at Court.* Shakespeare Society, 1842.

Dillon, Janette. *Performance and Spectacle in Hall's Chronicle.* The Society for Theatre Research, 2002.

Donaldson, Ian. *Ben Jonson: A Life.* Oxford University Press, 2012.

Doni, Anton Francesco. *The Earliest English Version of the Fables of Bidpai; The Moral Philosophy of Doni.* Trans. Thomas North. Ed. Joseph Jacobs. D. Nutt, 1888.

———. *Moral Philosophy of Doni Popularly Known As the Fables of Bidpai: Popularly Known As the Fables of Bidpai.* Trans. Thomas North. Ed. Donald Beecher, John A. Butler, and Carmine Di Biase. Dovehouse Editions, 2003.

Doran, Susan. *Monarchy and Matrimony: The Courtships of Elizabeth I.* Routledge, 1996.

———. *Elizabeth I and Her Circle.* Oxford University Press, 2015.

Dovey, Zillah. *An Elizabethan Progress: The Queen's Journey into East Anglia, 1578.* Fairleigh Dickinson University Press, 1996.

Dowling, Maria. *Humanism in the Age of Henry VIII.* Croom Helm, 1986.

Drake, Nathan. *Shakespeare and His Times.* T. Cadell and W. Davies, 1817.

Dryden, John, ed. *Troilus and Cressida ... to Which Is Prefix'd, a Preface Containing the Grounds of Criticism in Tragedy.* Able Swall and Jacob Tonson, 1679.

Duff, Tim. *Plutarch's Lives: Exploring Virtue and Vice.* Oxford University Press, 1999.

Duffy, Eamon. *The Stripping of the Altars: Traditional Religion in England, c.1400–c.1580.* Yale University Press, 2005.

———. *Fires of Faith: Catholic England under Mary Tudor.* Yale University Press, 2010.

Dugdale, William. *The Antiquities of Warwickshire.* E. J. Morten, 1973.

Duncan-Jones, Katherine. *Shakespeare: Upstart Crow to Sweet Swan, 1592–1623.* Arden Shakespeare Library. Arden, 2011.

———. *Shakespeare: An Ungentle Life.* A&C Black, 2014.

Dunton-Downer, Leslie, and Alan Riding. *Essential Shakespeare Handbook.* DK, 2013.

Dutton, Richard. *Shakespeare, Court Dramatist.* Oxford University Press, 2016.

Edward VI, King of England. *Literary Remains of King Edward the Sixth. Ed. from His Autograph Manuscripts, with Historical Notes and a Biographical Memoir.* Burt Franklin Research & Source Works Series, no. 51. Burt Franklin, 1963.

Edwards, John. *Mary I: England's Catholic Queen.* Yale University Press, 2011.

Elizabeth I, Queen of England, King of England James I. *Letters of Queen Elizabeth and King James VI. of Scotland.* Ed. John Bruce. Printed for the Camden Society, 1849.

Ellis, David. *The Truth About William Shakespeare: Fact, Fiction and Modern Biographies.* Edinburgh University Press, 2013.

Ellis, Herbert Alexander. *Shakespeare's Lusty Punning in* Love's Labour's Lost. Studies in English Literature. Vol. 81. Mouton, 1973.

Elton, G. R. *The Tudor Revolution in Government; Administrative Changes in the Reign of Henry VIII.* Cambridge University Press, 1953.

Erbesato, Gian Maria. *Guide to Palazzo Te.* Edizion Moretti, 1987.

Erne, Lukas. *Beyond* The Spanish Tragedy: *A Study of the Works of Thomas Kyd.* Manchester University Press, 2001.

Escobedo, Andrew, ed. *Edmund Spenser in Context.* Literature in Context. Cambridge University Press, 2017.

Falls, Cyril. *Elizabeth's Irish Wars: With Seven Illustrations and a Map.* Constable, 1996.

Forgeng, Jeffrey L., Jeffrey L. Singman, and Will McClean. *Daily Life in Elizabethan England.* Greenwood Press, 1995.

Fraser, George MacDonald. *The Steel Bonnets: The Story of the Anglo-Scottish Border Reivers.* Skyhorse Publishing, 2008.

Friedman, William F., and Elizebeth Friedman. *The Shakespearean Ciphers Examined: An Analysis of Cryptographic Systems Used as Evidence That Some Author Other Than William Shakespeare Wrote the Plays Commonly Attributed to Him.* Cambridge University Press, 1957.

Frost, Ulrich. *Das Commonplace Book von John Colyns: Untersuchung und Teiledition der Handschrift Harley 2252 der British Library in London.* P. Lang, 1988.

Frye, Roland Mushat. *The Renaissance Hamlet: Issues and Responses in 1600.* Princeton University Press, 2014.

Furnivall, Frederick James, W. R. Morfill, and Richard Williams. *Ballads from Manuscripts.* Vol. 1 and 2. AMS Press, 1968.

Garber, Marjorie. *Shakespeare After All.* Knopf Doubleday Publishing Group, 2008.

Gascoigne, George. *Gascoigne's Princely Pleasures, with the Masque: Intended to Have Been Presented Before Queen Elizabeth, at Kenilworth Castle in 1575.* J. H. Burn, 1821.

George, David J., and Christopher J. Gossip, eds. *Studies in the Commedia dell'Arte.* University of Wales Press, 1993.

Goody, Jack, Joan Thirsk, and E. P. Thompson. *Family and Inheritance: Rural Society in Western Europe, 1200–1800.* Cambridge University Press, 1976.

Goy-Blanquet, Dominique. *Shakespeare's Early History Plays: From Chronicle to Stage.* Oxford University Press, 2003.

Graham, Kenneth J. E., and Philip D. Collington, eds. *Shakespeare and Religious Change.* Early Modern Literature in History. Palgrave Macmillan, 2009.

Gray, Patrick. *Shakespeare and the Fall of the Roman Republic: Selfhood, Stoicism and Civil War.* Edinburgh Critical Studies in Shakespeare and Philosophy. Edinburgh University Press, 2019.

Greenblatt, Stephen. *Shakespearean Negotiations: The Circulation of Social Energy in Renaissance England.* University of California Press, 1989.

———. *Will in the World: How Shakespeare Became Shakespeare.* W. W. Norton & Co., 2004.

———. *Tyrant: Shakespeare on Politics.* W. W. Norton & Co., 2018.

Greene, Robert. *The Life and Complete Works in Prose and Verse of Robert Greene.* Ed. Alexander Balloch Grosart. The Huth Library. Printed for private circulation only, 1881.

Grey, Ernest. *Guevara, a Forgotten Renaissance Author.* 1973 edition. Springer, 2008.

Gristwood, Sarah. *Elizabeth and Leicester: The Truth about the Virgin Queen and the Man She Loved.* Penguin, 2008.

Guevara, Antonio de. *Archontorologion, or the Diall of Princes.* Trans. Thomas North. B. Alsop, 1619.

Gurr, Andrew. *The Shakespearian Playing Companies*. Clarendon Press; Oxford University Press, 1996.

———. *Playgoing in Shakespeare's London*. Cambridge University Press, 2004.

———. *The Shakespeare Company, 1594–1642*. Cambridge University Press, 2004.

Guy, John. *Tudor England*. Oxford University Press, 1988.

———. *Elizabeth: The Forgotten Years*. Penguin, 2016.

Hadfield, Andrew. *Edmund Spenser's Irish Experience: Wilde Fruit and Salvage Soyl*. Clarendon Press, 1997.

———. *Edmund Spenser: A Life*. Oxford University Press, 2014.

Hall, Edward. *Hall's Chronicle; Containing the History of England, During the Reign of Henry the Fourth, and the Succeeding Monarchs, to the End of the Reign of Henry the Eighth, in Which Are Particularly Described the Manners and Customs of Those Periods*. Printed for J. Johnson [etc.], 1809.

Halpin, N. J. *Oberon's Vision in the Midsummer Night's Dream, illustrated by a comparison with Lylie's Endymion*. Shakespeare Society, 1843.

Hamilton, Albert Charles. *The Spenser Encyclopedia*. University of Toronto Press, 1997.

Hardwicke, Philip Yorke, Earl of, ed. *Miscellaneous State Papers. From 1501 to 1726, etc*. W. Strahan & T. Cadell, 1778.

Harris, William O. *Skelton's Magnyfycence and the Cardinal Virtue Tradition*. University of North Carolina Press, 1965.

Hattaway, Michael. *The Cambridge Companion to Shakespeare's History Plays*. Cambridge University Press, 2002.

Hirschfeld, Heather Anne. *Joint Enterprises: Collaborative Drama and the Institutionalization of the English Renaissance Theater*. University of Massachusetts Press, 2004.

Hoak, D. E. *The King's Council in the Reign of Edward VI*. Cambridge University Press, 1976.

Hoenselaars, A. J. *The Cambridge Companion to Shakespeare and Contemporary Dramatists*. Cambridge University Press, 2012.

Holderness, Graham. *Shakespeare and Venice*. Ashgate, 2010.

Holdsworth, Angela. *A Portrait of Lincoln's Inn*. Third Millennium Pub., 2007.

Holinshed, Raphael, et al. *Holinshed's Chronicles of England, Scotland, and Ireland*. J. Johnson [etc.], 1807.

Holt, Mack P. *The French Wars of Religion, 1562–1629*. Cambridge University Press, 2005.

Homem, Rui Carvalho, and Fátima Vieira. *Gloriana's Rule: Literature, Religion and Power in the Age of Elizabeth*. Universidade do Porto, 2006.

Honourable Society of Lincoln's Inn. *Admissions Register Vol 1, 1420–1799*, 1896.

———. *Black Books Volume 1, 1422-1586*. 1897.

Hope, Jonathan. *The Authorship of Shakespeare's Plays: A Socio-Linguistic Study*. Cambridge University Press, 1994.

Hope, Warren, and Kim R. Holston. *The Shakespeare Controversy: An Analysis of the Claimants to Authorship, and Their Champions and Detractors*. McFarland, 1992.

Hume, Martin A. S. *The Courtships of Queen Elizabeth: A History of the Various Negotiations for Her Marriage*. Eveleigh Nash & Grayson, 1926.

Hurst, Gerald B. *A Short History of Lincoln's Inn*. Constable, 1946.

Hutchinson, Robert. *The Last Days of Henry VIII: Conspiracies, Treason and Heresy at the Court of the Dying Tyrant*. Weidenfeld & Nicolson, 2005.

———. *House of Treason: The Rise and Fall of a Tudor Dynasty*. Phoenix, 2009.

———. *The Spanish Armada: A History*. Thomas Dunne Books, 2014.

Hyde, Patricia. *Thomas Arden in Faversham: The Man Behind the Myth*. Faversham Society, 1996.

Jackson, MacDonald P. *Studies in Attribution, Middleton and Shakespeare*. Inst. f. Angelistik u. Amerikanistik, Univ. Salzburg, 1979.

———. *Determining the Shakespeare Canon: Arden of Faversham and a Lover's Complaint*. Oxford University Press, 2014.

Jacob, Edward. *The History of the Town and Port of Faversham: In the County of Kent*. Author, 1774.

Jacobs, Susan G., ed. *Plutarch's Pragmatic Biographies: Lessons for Statesmen and Generals in the Parallel Lives*. Columbia Studies in the Classical Tradition. Vol. 43. Brill, 2018.

James, Brenda, and W. D. Rubinstein. *The Truth Will Out: Unmasking the Real Shakespeare*. Regan, 2006.

Jamoussi, Zouheir. *Primogeniture and Entail in England: A Survey of Their History and Representation in Literature*. Tunis: Centre de publication universitaire, 1999.

Jenkins, Elizabeth. *Elizabeth and Leicester*. Coward-McCann, 1962.

Jepson, Tim. *National Geographic Traveler: Italy*. National Geographic Books, 2012.

Jones, Hunter S. *Sexuality and Its Impact on History: The British Stripped Bare*. Casemate Publishers, 2018.

Jones, Joseph Ramon. *Antonio de Guevara*. Twayne, 1975.

Jonson, Ben. *Ben Jonson's Plays*. Vol. 1. Ed. Felix Emmanuel Schelling. Dutton, 1910.

Kastan, David Scott. *A Will to Believe: Shakespeare and Religion*. Oxford Wells Shakespeare Lectures. Oxford University Press, 2014.

Keenan, Siobhan. *Travelling Players in Shakespeare's England*. Springer, 2002.

Kelley, Donald R., and David Harris Sacks, eds. *The Historical Imagination in Early Modern Britain: History, Rhetoric, and Fiction, 1500–1800*. Cambridge University Press, 1997.

Kells, Stuart. *Shakespeare's Library: Unlocking the Greatest Mystery in Literature*. Counterpoint, 2019.

Kerrigan, John. *Shakespeare's Binding Language*. Oxford University Press, 2016.

Kidnie, Margaret Jane, and Sonia Massai. *Shakespeare and Textual Studies*. Cambridge University Press, 2015.

Klein, Holger Michael, and Michele Marrapodi. *Shakespeare and Italy*. Edwin Mellen Press, 1999.

Knecht, Robert Jean. *Catherine de' Medici*. Longman, 1998.

———. *The French Religious Wars 1562–1598*. Osprey Publishing, 2002.

Knutson, Roslyn Lander. *The Repertory of Shakespeare's Company, 1594–1613*. University of Arkansas Press, 1991.

———. *Playing Companies and Commerce in Shakespeare's Time*. Cambridge University Press, 2001.

Kohn, Thomas. *The Dramaturgy of Senecan Tragedy*. University of Michigan Press, 2013.

Kurland, Michael. *Irrefutable Evidence: Adventures in the History of Forensic Science*. Rowman & Littlefield, 2009.

La Mothe Fénélon, Bertrand de Salignac. *Correspondance Diplomatique de Bertrand de Salignac de La Mothe Fénélon*. Paris, 1840.

Lake, Peter. *How Shakespeare Put Politics on the Stage: Power and Succession in the History Plays*. Yale University Press, 2016.

Langham, Robert. *A Letter, Wherein Part of the Entertainment Untoo the Queenz Majesty, at Killingwoorth Castl in Warwick Sheer, in This Soomerz Progrest 1575, Iz Signified*. J. Sharp, 1784.

Lawner, Lynne. *Harlequin on the Moon: Commedia Dell'arte and the Visual Arts*. Harry N. Abrams, 1998.

Lea, Kathleen M. *Italian Popular Comedy: A Study in the Commedia Dell'arte, 1560–1620, with Special Reference to the English Stage*. Russell & Russell, 1962.

Leggatt, Alexander. *Shakespeare's Tragedies: Violation and Identity*. Cambridge University Press, 2005.

Leicester, Robert Dudley, Earl of. *Correspondence of Robert Dudley, Earl of Leycester, during His Government of the Low Countries, in the Years 1585 and 1586*. Ed. John Bruce. Printed for the Camden Society by J. B. Nichols and Son, 1844.

Levin, Carole, Anna Riehl Bertolet, and Jo Eldridge Carney, eds. *A Biographical Encyclopedia of Early Modern Englishwomen: Exemplary Lives and Memorable Acts, 1500–1650*. Taylor & Francis, 2016.

Levith, Murray J. *Shakespeare's Italian Settings and Plays*. St. Martin's Press, 1989.

Lewis, Christopher Piers. *A History of Kirtling and Upend: Landowners and People in a Cambridgeshire Parish, 1000–2000*. Magazine Lane Press, 2000.

Lipscomb, Suzannah. *The King Is Dead: The Last Will and Testament of Henry VIII*. Pegasus Books, 2016.

Loach, Jennifer. *Edward VI*. Eds. George Bernard and Penry Williams. Yale University Press, 1999.

Loades, David. *Mary Tudor: A Life*. Wiley, 1992.

———. *Henry VIII: Church, Court and Conflict*. A&C Black Business Information and Development, 2007.

Lodge, Thomas. *Wit's Misery, 1596*. Scolar Press, 1971.

Looney, J. Thomas. *"Shakespeare" Identified in Edward de Vere, the Seventeenth Earl of Oxford*. Frederick A. Stokes Company, 1920.

Luke, Mary M. *The Nine Days Queen: A Portrait of Lady Jane Grey*. W. Morrow, 1986.

MacCulloch, Diarmaid. *The Boy King: Edward VI and the Protestant Reformation*. University of California Press, 2002.

———. *Thomas Cromwell: A Revolutionary Life*. Viking, 2018.

Madden, Thomas F. *Venice: A New History*. Penguin Books, 2013.

Mahon, Ellen M. and John W. Mahon. *The Merchant of Venice: Critical Essays*. Routledge, 2002.

Marrapodi, Michele. *Shakespeare's Italy: Functions of Italian Locations in Renaissance Drama*. Manchester University Press, 1997.

———. *Shakespeare, Italy, and Intertextuality*. Manchester University Press, 2004.

———. *Italian Culture in the Drama of Shakespeare & His Contemporaries: Rewriting, Remaking, Refashioning*. Anglo-Italian Renaissance Studies Series. Ashgate, 2007.

———. *Shakespeare and the Italian Renaissance: Appropriation, Transformation, Opposition*. Routledge, 2016.

Martyn, Trea. *Queen Elizabeth in the Garden: A Story of Love, Rivalry, and Spectacular Gardens*. BlueBridge, 2012.

Masten, Jeffrey. *Textual Intercourse: Collaboration, Authorship, and Sexualities in Renaissance Drama*. Cambridge University Press, 1997.

Matthiessen, F. O. *Translation*. Harvard University Press, 2014.

Mattingly, Garrett. *The Armada*. Houghton Mifflin Harcourt, 2005.

Matusiak, John. *Wolsey: The Life of King Henry VIII's Cardinal*. The History Press, 2014.

Maxwell, William Stirling. *Don John of Austria*. Longmans Green & Co., 1883.

Mays, Andrea. *The Millionaire and the Bard: Henry Folger's Obsessive Hunt for Shakespeare's First Folio*. Simon & Schuster, 2016.

McCarthy, Dennis. *Here Be Dragons: How the Study of Animal and Plant Distributions Revolutionized Our Views of Life and Earth*. Oxford University Press, 2009.

———. *North of Shakespeare: The True Story of the Secret Genius Who Wrote the World's Greatest Body of Literature*. CreateSpace Independent Publishing Platform, 2011.

McCarthy, Dennis, and June Schlueter. *"A Brief Discourse of Rebellion and Rebels" by George North: A Newly Uncovered Manuscript Source for Shakespeare's Plays.* D. S. Brewer, 2018.

McCrea, Scott. *The Case for Shakespeare: The End of the Authorship Question.* Praeger, 2005.

McDonnell, Michael. *The Registers of St Paul's School, 1509–1748.* The School; distributed by the Gavin Press, 1977.

McLane, Paul E. *Spenser's Shepheardes Calender; a Study in Elizabethan Allegory.* Notre Dame, Ind., 1961.

McPherson, David C. *Shakespeare, Jonson, and the Myth of Venice.* University of Delaware Press; Associated University Presses, 1991.

Meyer, G. J. *The Tudors: The Complete Story of England's Most Notorious Dynasty.* Bantam, 2011.

Miola, Robert S. *Shakespeare and Classical Tragedy: The Influence of Seneca.* Clarendon Press, 1992.

Montaigne, Michel de. John Florio, ed. *The Essays.* Edward Blount, 1603.

———. *The Autobiography of Michel de Montaigne.* Ed. Martin Lowenthal. Vintage, 1956.

More, Sir Thomas. *More's History of King Richard III.* University Press, 1883.

Morris, F. O. *A Series of Picturesque Views of Seats of the Noblemen and Gentlemen of Great Britain and Ireland: With Descriptive and Historical Letterpress.* W. Mackenzie, 1860.

Mortimer, Ian. *The Time Traveler's Guide to Elizabethan England.* Penguin Books, 2014.

Mosley, Charles, ed. *Burke's Peerage, Baronetage and Knightage.* 107th edition. Burke's Peerage, 2003.

Muir, Kenneth. *Shakespeare as Collaborator.* 1960. Reprint Psychology Press, 2005.

———. *The Sources of Shakespeare's Plays.* 1977. Reprint Psychology Press, 2005.

Murray, John Tucker. *English Dramatic Companies, 1558–1642.* Constable and Company Limited, 1910.

Nashe, Thomas. *The Terrors of the Night or, A discourse of apparitions.* John Danter for William Jones, 1594.

Neill, Michael, and David Schalkwyk, eds. *The Oxford Handbook of Shakespearean Tragedy.* Oxford Handbooks. Oxford University Press, 2016.

Nelson, Alan H., and John R. Elliott, Jr, eds. *Records of Early English Drama: Inns of Court.* 3 vols. D.S. Brewer, 2011.

Nepos, Cornelius; Thomas North, trans. *The liues of Epaminondas, of Philip of Macedon, of Dionysius the Elder, and of Octavius Caesar Augustus…* Richard Field, 1602.

Nichols, John. *John Nichols's* The Progresses and Public Processions of Queen Elizabeth I: *A New Edition of the Early Modern Sources.* Eds. Elizabeth Goldring, Faith Eales, Elizabeth Clarke, and Jayne Elisabeth Archer. Oxford University Press, 2014.

Norland, Howard B. *Drama in Early Tudor Britain, 1485–1558.* University of Nebraska Press, 1995.

———. *Neoclassical Tragedy in Elizabethan England.* Associated University Press, 2009.

Normand, Lawrence, and Gareth Roberts. *Witchcraft in Early Modern Scotland: James VI's Demonology and the North Berwick Witches.* University of Exeter Press, 2000.

North, Dudley. *Some Notes Concerning the Life of Edward Lord North, Baron of Kirtling.* s.n., 1658.

Norton, Thomas, and Thomas Sackville. *Gorboduc; or, Ferrex and Porrex.* Regents Renaissance Drama Series. Ed. Irby B. Cauthen. University of Nebraska, 1970.

O'Dell, Leslie. *Shakespearean Scholarship: A Guide for Actors and Students.* Greenwood, 2001.

Ogburn, Charlton. *The Mysterious William Shakespeare: The Myth & the Reality.* EPM Publications, 1992.

Oliver, Jennifer H. *Shipwreck in French Renaissance Writing.* Oxford University Press, 2019.

O'Neill, James. *The Nine Years War, 1593–1603: O'Neill, Mountjoy and the Military Revolution.* Four Courts Press, 2018.

Orlin, Lena Cowen. *Private Matters and Public Culture in Post-Reformation England.* Cornell University Press, 1994.

Palfrey, Simon, and Tiffany Stern. *Shakespeare in Parts.* Oxford University Press, 2007.

Palmer, William. *The Problem of Ireland in Tudor Foreign Policy, 1485–1603.* Boydell & Brewer, 1994.

Parker, Barbara L. *Plato's Republic and Shakespeare's Rome: A Political Study of the Roman Works.* University of Delaware Press, 2004.

Parker, David Reed. *The Commonplace Book in Tudor London: An Examination of BL MSS Egerton 1995, Harley 2252, Lansdowne 762, and Oxford Balliol College MS 354.* University Press of America, 1998.

Pearce, Joseph. *The Quest for Shakespeare.* Ignatius Press, 2008.

Pelling, C. B. R. *Plutarch and History: Eighteen Studies.* Classical Press of Wales and Duckworth, 2002.

Pendergast, John S. Love's Labour's Lost: *A Guide to the Play.* Greenwood Press, 2002.

Penniman, Josiah Harmar. *The War of the Theatres.* Series in Philology, Literature and Archaeology. Vol. 4, no. 3. Publications of the University of Pennsylvania. Ginn, 1897.

Pepys, Samuel. Eds. Richard Griffin Braybrooke and Henry Benjamin Wheatley. Trans. Mynors Bright. *The Diary of Samuel Pepys.* George Bell & Sons, 1893.

Perkins, Jocelyn. *The Most Honourable Order of the Bath: A Descriptive and Historical Account.* Faith Press, 1920.

Peterhouse. *A Biographical Register of Peterhouse Men and Some of Their Neighbours from the Earliest Days (1284) to the Commencement (1616) of the First Admission Book of the College.* The University Press, 1927.

Petersen, Lene B. *Shakespeare's Errant Texts: Textual Form and Linguistic Style in Shakespearean "Bad" Quartos and Co-Authored Plays.* Cambridge University Press, 2010.

Phythian-Adams, Charles. *Desolation of a City: Coventry and the Urban Crisis of the Late Middle Ages.* Cambridge University Press, 2002.

Pincombe, Michael, and Cathy Shrank, eds. *The Oxford Handbook of Tudor Literature: 1485–1603.* Oxford University Press, 2009.

Plat, Sir Hugh. *Floraes Paradise.* H. L[ownes], 1608.

Plutarch, Lucius Mestrius. *The Lives of the Noble Grecians and Romanes.* Trans. Thomas North. Thomas Vautroullier and John Wight, 1579.

———. *Shakespeare's Plutarch.* Trans. Thomas North. Ed. Tucker Brooke.

———. *The Lives of the Noble Grecians and Romans Compared Together By That Grave, Learned Philosopher and Historiographer Plutarke of Chaeronea.* 2 vols. Trans. Thomas North. Ed. Roland Orvil Baughman. Heritage Press, 1941.

———. *Selected Lives from the Lives of the Noble Grecians and Romans.* Trans. Thomas North. Ed. Paul Turner. Southern Illinois University Press, 1963.

———. *Shakespeare's Plutarch: The Lives of Julius Caesar, Brutus, Marcus Antonius, and Coriolanus in the Translation of Sir Thomas North.* Trans. Thomas North. Ed. T. J. B. Spencer. Peregrine Books. Penguin Books, 1964.

_____. *Plutarch's Lives.* Alan Wardman, ed. Elek, 1974.

Pogue, Kate Emery. *Shakespeare's Family.* Greenwood Publishing Group, 2008.

Pollard, A. F. *Wolsey.* Longmans, Green & Co., 1953.

Porter, Stephen. *Everyday Life in Tudor London: Life in the City of Thomas Cromwell, William Shakespeare & Anne Boleyn.* Stroud, Amberley Publishing, 2016.

Potter, Lois. *The Life of William Shakespeare: A Critical Biography.* Blackwell Critical Biographies. Wiley-Blackwell, 2012.

Preeshl, Artemis. *Shakespeare and Commedia dell'Arte: Play by Play.* Routledge, 2017.

Prendergast, Maria Teresa Micaela. *Railing, Reviling, and Invective in English Literary Culture, 1588–1617: The Anti-Poetics of Theater and Print.* Routledge, 2016.

Prest, Wilfrid R. *The Inns of Court Under Elizabeth I and the Early Stuarts, 1590–1640.* Rowman and Littlefield, 1972.

Price, Diana. *Shakespeare's Unorthodox Biography: New Evidence of an Authorship Problem.* Contributions in Drama and Theatre Studies, no. 94. Greenwood Press, 2001.

Purchas, Samuel. *Hakluytus Posthumus, Or Purchas His Pilgrimes.* J. MacLehose and Sons, 1905.

Redmond, Michael J. *Shakespeare, Politics, and Italy: Intertextuality on the Jacobean Stage.* Anglo-Italian Renaissance Studies Series. Ashgate, 2009.

Richardson, Catherine. *Domestic Life and Domestic Tragedy in Early Modern England: The Material Life of the Household.* Manchester University Press, 2007.

Riggs, David. *Ben Jonson: A Life.* Harvard University Press, 1989.

Ringler, William A. *Bibliography and Index of English Verse in Manuscript, 1501–1558.* Mansell, 1992.

Ringrose, Hyacinthe. *The Inns of Court: An Historical Description of the Inns of Court and Chancery of England.* R. L. Williams, 1909.

Risk, James Charles. *The History of the Order of the Bath and Its Insignia.* Spink, 1972.

Roberts, Jane, and Hans Holbein. *Drawings by Holbein from the Court of Henry VIII: Fifty Drawings from the Collection of Her Majesty Queen Elizabeth II, Windsor Castle; Catalogue.* Harcourt Brace Jovanovich: Johnson Reprint Corp, 1987.

Roe, Richard Paul. *The Shakespeare Guide to Italy: Retracing the Bard's Unknown Travels.* Harper Perennial, 2011.

Rosenberg, Eleanor. *Leicester, Patron of Letters.* Columbia University Press, 1955.

Roth, Mitchel P. *Historical Dictionary of Law Enforcement.* Greenwood Publishing Group, 2001.

Rounding, Virginia. *The Burning Time: Henry VIII, Bloody Mary, and the Protestant Martyrs of London.* St. Martin's Press, 2017.

Rouse, Mike. *A View into Cambridgeshire.* T. Dalton, 1974.

Rudlin, John, and Olly Crick. *Commedia dell'Arte: A Handbook for Troupes.* Routledge, 2001.

Salzman, L. F. *The Victoria History of the County of Cambridgeshire and the Isle of Ely.* Oxford University Press, 1938.

Scardigli, Barbara. *Essays on Plutarch's Lives.* Clarendon Press; Oxford University Press, 1995.

Scarisbrick, J. J. *Henry VIII.* University of California Press, 1968.

Schelling, Felix Emmanuel. *Elizabethan Drama, 1558–1642: A History of the Drama in England from the Accession of Queen Elizabeth to the Closing of the Theaters.* Houghton Mifflin, 1908.

Schoenbaum, Samuel. *Shakespeare's Lives.* Oxford University Press, 1991.

Schoone-Jongen, Terence G. *Shakespeare's Companies: William Shakespeare's Early Career and the Acting Companies, 1577–1594.* Routledge, 2016.

Scott, Franklin Daniel. *Sweden, the Nation's History.* Southern Illinois University Press, 1988.

Segall, Barbara. *Secret Gardens of East Anglia: A Private Tour of 22 Gardens.* Frances Lincoln, 2017.

Seneca, Lucius Annaeus. *Seneca.* Ed. David R. Slavitt. Complete Roman Drama in Translation. Johns Hopkins University Press, 1992.

———. *Thyestes.* Ed. Caryl Churchill. Nick Hern Books, 1995.

————. *Seneca: Thyestes.* Ed. Peter Davis. Duckworth, 2003.

————. *Seneca: Thyestes: Edited with Introduction, Translation, and Commentary.* Ed. A. J. Boyle. Oxford University Press, 2017.

————. *Seneca: Tragedies, Volume I: Hercules. Trojan Women. Phoenician Women. Medea. Phaedra.* Trans. John G. Fitch. Bilingual edition. Reprint. Harvard University Press, 2018.

————. *Seneca: Tragedies, Volume II: Oedipus. Agamemnon. Thyestes. Hercules on Oeta. Octavia.* Trans. John G. Fitch. Bilingual edition. Reprint. Harvard University Press, 2018.

Severi, Rita. *Art in Shakespeare and Other Essays.* Pàtron editore, 2018.

Shapiro, James. *A Year in the Life of William Shakespeare: 1599.* Harper Collins, 2005.

————. *Contested Will: Who Wrote Shakespeare?* Simon and Schuster, 2010.

————. *Shakespeare and the Jews.* Columbia University Press, 2016.

Shaw, William Arthur. *The Knights of England: A Complete Record from the Earliest Time to the Present Day of the Knights of All the Orders of Chivalry in England, Scotland, and Ireland, and of Knights Bachelors. Incorporating a Complete List of Knights Bachelors Dubbed in Ireland.* Genealogical Publishing Co., 1970.

Shirley, Timothy Francis. *Thomas Thirlby: Tudor Bishop.* Published for the Church Historical Society by SPCK, 1964.

Sidgwick, Frank. *The Sources and Analogues of* A Midsummer-Night's Dream. Shakespeare Classics. Vol. 9. AMS Press, 1973.

Simons, Jay. *Jonson, the Poetomachia, and the Reformation of Renaissance Satire: Purging Satire.* Taylor & Francis, 2018.

Skidmore, Chris. *Edward VI: The Lost King of England.* St. Martin's Press, 2007.

————. *Death and the Virgin: Elizabeth, Dudley and the Mysterious Fate of Amy Robsart.* Phoenix, 2011.

Skinner, Quentin. *The Foundations of Modern Political Thought. Vol. 1 The Renaissance.* Cambridge University Press, 1979.

Slaney, Helen. *The Senecan Aesthetic: A Performance History.* Oxford University Press, 2016.

Slocombe, George. *Don John of Austria, the Victor of Lepanto (1547–1578).* Nicholson and Watson, 1935.

Small, Roscoe Addison. *The Stage-Quarrel Between Ben Jonson and the So-Called Poetasters.* Forschungen Zur Englischen Sprache Und Litteratur, Hft. 1. M&H Marcus, 1899.

Smith, Winifred. *The Commedia dell'Arte.* B. Blom, 1964.

Smyth, Charles. *Cranmer & the Reformation Under Edward VI.* Greenwood Press, 1970.

Sobran, Joseph. *Alias Shakespeare: Solving the Greatest Literary Mystery of All Time.* Free Press, 1997.

Sohmer, Steve. *Shakespeare's Mystery Play: The Opening of the Globe Theatre 1599.* Manchester University Press, 1999.

Somerset, Anne. *Elizabeth I.* Anchor, 2010.

Spenser, Edmund. *The Shepheardes Calender; the Original Edition of 1579 in Photographic Facsimile.* Ed. Heinrich Oskar Sommer. J. C. Nimmo, 1890.

Stadter, Philip A. *Plutarch and the Historical Tradition.* Routledge, 1992.

Staley, Gregory A. *Seneca and the Idea of Tragedy.* Oxford University Press, 2009.

Starkey, David. *The Reign of Henry VIII: Personalities and Politics.* F. Watts, 1986.

Stationers' Company (London, England), Edward Arber, and Charles Robert Rivington. *A Transcript of the Registers of the Company of Stationers of London; 1554–1640, A. D.* Private print, 1875.

Stillinger, Jack. *Multiple Authorship and the Myth of Solitary Genius.* Oxford University Press, 1991.

Stewart, Alan. *Philip Sidney: A Double Life*. Random House, 2011.

Stewart, Derek James. *The Armstrongs: The History of a Riding Family, 1040–1650*. American Academic Press, 2017.

Stone, Lawrence. *The Family, Sex and Marriage in England 1500–1800*. Weidenfeld & Nicolson, 1977.

Stott, Andrew McConnell. *What Blest Genius? The Jubilee That Made Shakespeare*. W. W. Norton & Co., 2019.

Suitner, Gianna, and Chiara Tellini Perina. *Palazzo Te in Mantova*. Edizioni Electa, 1990.

Survey of London. *The Charterhouse: Survey of London*. Paul Mellon Centre for Studies in British Art, 2010.

Swinburne, Algernon Charles. *A Study of Shakespeare*. Chatto and Windus, 1880.

Sykes, Henry Dugdale. *Sidelights on Shakespeare: Being Studies of The Two Noble Kinsmen. Henry VIII. Arden of Feversham. A Yorkshire Tragedy. The Troublesome Reign of King John. King Leir. Pericles Prince of Tyre*. The Shakespeare Head Press, 1919.

Tallis, Nicola. *Crown of Blood: The Deadly Inheritance of Lady Jane Grey*. Pegasus Books, 2016.

———. *Elizabeth's Rival*. Simon and Schuster, 2018.

Tanner, Tony. *Prefaces to Shakespeare*. Harvard University Press, 2012.

Tassi, Marguerite A. *Women and Revenge in Shakespeare: Gender, Genre, and Ethics*. Susquehanna University Press, 2011.

Taylor, Gary. *Reinventing Shakespeare: A Cultural History from the Restoration to the Present*. Vintage, 1991.

Taylor, Gary, and Gabriel Egan. *The New Oxford Shakespeare: Authorship Companion*. Oxford University Press, 2017.

Taylor, Marion Ansel. *Bottom, Thou Art Translated. Political Allegory in* A Midsummer Night's Dream *and Related Literature*. Keizersgracht 302–304 Rodopi, 1973.

Temple, Philip. *The Charterhouse*. Yale University Press, 2010.

Thirlwell, Angela. *Rosalind: Shakespeare's Immortal Heroine*. Pegasus Books, 2017.

Thomas, Christopher, Bruno Barber, and Alfred Thomas. *The London Charterhouse*. MOLA, 2002.

Thomas, Vivian. *Shakespeare's Roman Worlds*. Routledge, 1989.

Ticknor, George. *History of Spanish Literature*. Harper and Brothers, 1854.

Tomarken, Edward. *As You Like It from 1600 to the Present: Critical Essays*. Garland, 1997.

Tosi, Laura, and Shaul Bassi. *Visions of Venice in Shakespeare*. Anglo-Italian Renaissance Studies Series. Ashgate, 2011.

Twain, Mark. *Is Shakespeare Dead?: From My Autobiography*. Harper & Brothers, 1909.

University of California. Department of English. *Essays Critical and Historical Dedicated to Lily B. Campbell, by Members of the Departments of English, University of California*. University of California Press, 1950.

Vickers, Brian. *Shakespeare, Co-Author: A Historical Study of Five Collaborative Plays*. Oxford University Press, 2002.

Vieira, Rui Carvalho Homem e Fátima. *Gloriana's Rule: Literature, Religion and Power in the Age of Elizabeth*. Universidade do Porto, 2006.

Vince, Ronald W. *Renaissance Theatre: A Historiographical Handbook*. Greenwood Press, 1984.

Wadsworth, Frank W. *The Poacher from Stratford: A Partial Account of the Controversy over the Authorship of Shakespeare's Plays*. University of California Press, 1958.

Waldman, Milton. *Elizabeth and Leicester*. Collins, 1946.

Walker, Greg. *The Politics of Performance in Early Renaissance Drama*. Cambridge University Press, 1998.

Wall, Wendy. *Staging Domesticity: Household Work and English Identity in Early Modern Drama*. Cambridge University Press, 2002.

Walsh, William Shepard. *Handy-Book of Literary Curiosities*. J. B. Lippincott Company, 1892.

Watson, Andrew G., and D'Ewes Library. *The Library of Sir Simonds D'Ewes*. Trustees of the British Museum, 1966.

Watt, R. J. C. *Shakespeare's History Plays*. Longman, 2002.

Weir, Alison. *The Children of Henry VIII*. Ballantine Books, 1997.

———. *The Life of Elizabeth I*. Ballantine Books, 1999.

———. *Henry VIII: The King and His Court*. Ballantine Books, 2002.

Wells, Stanley. *Shakespeare's Tragedies: A Very Short Introduction*. Oxford University Press, 2017.

Whigham, Frank. *Seizures of the Will in Early Modern English Drama*. Cambridge Studies in Renaissance Literature and Culture 11. Cambridge University Press, 1996.

White, Martin, ed. *Arden of Faversham*. Methuen Drama, 2007.

White, Paul Whitfield, and Suzanne R. Westfall. *Shakespeare and Theatrical Patronage in Early Modern England*. Cambridge University Press, 2002.

Whitelock, Anna. *The Queen's Bed: An Intimate History of Elizabeth's Court*. Macmillan, 2014.

———. *Mary Tudor: England's First Queen*. Penguin Books, 2016.

Wickham, Glynne, Herbert Berry, and William Ingram. *English Professional Theatre, 1530–1660*. Cambridge University Press, 2009.

Wiggins, Martin, and Catherine Richardson. *British Drama 1533–1642: A Catalogue*. Vol. 2, *1567–1589*. Oxford University Press, 2012.

Wiles, David. *Shakespeare's Clown: Actor and Text in the Elizabethan Playhouse*. Cambridge University Press, 1987.

Williams, Leslie Winfield. *Emblem of Faith Untouched: A Short Life of Thomas Cranmer*. Eerdmans, 2016.

Williams, Neville. *Henry VIII and His Court*. Macmillan, 1971.

Williams, Neville, and Antonia Fraser. *The Tudors*. Royal History of England. University of California Press, 2000.

Williams, Robin. *Sweet Swan of Avon: Did a Woman Write Shakespeare?* Wilton Circle Press, 2006.

Wilson, Derek. *Sweet Robin: A Biography of Robert Dudley, Earl of Leicester*. H. Hamilton, 1981.

———. *In the Lion's Court: Power, Ambition and Sudden Death in the Reign of Henry VIII*. Hutchinson, 2001.

———. *The Uncrowned Kings of England*. Constable & Robinson, 2005.

Wilson, Michael I. *A Family of the Stuart Age: The Norths of Kirtling*. Barbon Books, 2016.

Winston, Jessica. *Lawyers at Play: Literature, Law, and Politics at the Early Modern Inns of Court, 1558–1581*. Oxford University Press, 2016.

Wood, Michael. *Shakespeare*. Basic Books, 2003.

Woolfson, Jonathan. *Padua and the Tudors: English Students in Italy, 1485–1603*. University of Toronto Press, 1998.

Yates, Frances A. *A Study of Love's Labour's Lost*. Norwood Editions, 1976.

Zander, Horst. *Julius Caesar: New Critical Essays*. Routledge, 2005.

SHAKESPEARE EDITIONS CONSULTED

Bevington, David M. *The Complete Works of Shakespeare*. Pearson, 2014.

Collier, John Payne. *The Works of Shakespeare*. Redfield, 1853.

Evans, G. Blakemore. *The Riverside Shakespeare*. Houghton Mifflin, 1974.

Antony and Cleopatra: Bloom, Harold, and Neil Heims. *Bloom's Shakespeare Through the Ages*. Chelsea House, 2008; Loomba, Ania. Norton Critical Editions. W. W. Norton & Co., 2011; Mowat, Barbara A., and Paul Werstine. Folger Shakespeare Library. Simon and Schuster, 2010.

Arden of Faversham: White, Martin. New Mermaids. Bloomsbury, 2017.

As You Like It: Bate, Jonathan, and Eric Rasmussen. RSC Shakespeare. Modern Library, 2010; Bloom, Harold, and Pamela Loos. *Bloom's Shakespeare Through the Ages*. Chelsea House, 2008; Brown, Pamela Allen, and Jean E. Howard. *Texts and Contexts*. Bedford/St. Martin's, 2014; Dolan, Frances E. Pelican Shakespeare. Penguin Books, 2017; Dusinberre, Juliet. Arden Shakespeare. Cengage Learning EMEA, 2006; Marcus, Leah. Norton Critical Editions. W. W. Norton & Co., 2012; Mowat, Barbara A., and Paul Werstine. Folger Shakespeare Library. Simon and Schuster, 2009.

The Comedy of Errors: Bevington, David M. Bantam Books, 1988; Foakes, R. A. Arden Shakespeare. Arden, 2000.

Hamlet: Bate, Jonathan, and Eric Rasmussen. RSC Shakespeare. Modern Library, 2008; Thompson, Ann, and Neil Taylor. Arden Shakespeare. Bloomsbury Publishing, 2016.

Henry V: Cottegnies, Line, and Karen Britland. Arden Critical Reader. Arden, 2016; Craik, T. W. Arden Shakespeare. Thomas Nelson, 1998.

Henry VI, Part One: Mowat, Barbara A., and Paul Werstine. Folger Shakespeare Library. Washington Square Press, 2008; Taylor, Michael. Oxford Shakespeare. Oxford University Press, 2003.

Henry VI, Part Two: Mowat, Barbara A., and Paul Werstine. Folger Shakespeare Library. Washington Square Press, 2008; Warren, Roger. Oxford Shakespeare. Oxford University Press, 2002.

Henry VI, Part Three: Martin, Randall. Oxford Shakespeare. Oxford University Press, 2001; Mowat, Barbara A., and Paul Werstine. Folger Shakespeare Library. Simon and Schuster, 2009.

Henry VI, Parts I, II and III: Bate, Jonathan, and Eric Rasmussen. RSC Shakespeare. Modern Library, 2012.

Henry VIII: Crewe, Jonathan V. Pelican Shakespeare. Penguin Books, 2018; McMullan, Gordon. Arden Shakespeare. Arden, 2000; Mowat, Barbara A., and Paul Werstine. Folger Shakespeare Library. Simon and Schuster, 2011.

Julius Caesar: Bate, Jonathan, and Eric Rasmussen. RSC Shakespeare. Modern Library, 2011; Mowat, Barbara A., and Paul Werstine. Folger Shakespeare Library. Simon and Schuster, 2011; Raffel, Burton, and Harold Bloom. Yale University Press, 2006.

King John and Henry VIII: Bate, Jonathan, and Eric Rasmussen. RSC Shakespeare. Modern Library, 2012.

King Lear: Mowat, Barbara A., and Paul Werstine. Folger Shakespeare Library. Simon and Schuster, 2015.

Love's Labour's Lost: Bate, Jonathan, and Eric Rasmussen. RSC Shakespeare. Modern Library, 2008; Furness, Horace Howard. New Variorum Edition. American Scholar Publications,

1966; Hibbard, George Richard. Oxford Shakespeare. Oxford University Press, 1994; Holland, Peter. Pelican Shakespeare. Penguin Books, 2018; Mowat, Barbara A., and Paul Werstine. Folger Shakespeare Library. Simon and Schuster, 2009.

Macbeth: Braunmuller, A. R. New Cambridge Shakespeare. Cambridge University Press, 2008; Clark, Sandra, and Pamela Mason. Arden Shakespeare. Bloomsbury, 2015; Mowat, Barbara A., and Paul Werstine. Folger Shakespeare Library. Simon and Schuster, 2013.

The Merchant of Venice: Bate, Jonathan, and Eric Rasmussen. RSC Shakespeare. Modern Library, 2010; Braunmuller, A. R. Pelican Shakespeare. Penguin Books, 2017; Clarke, Helen Archibald, and Charlotte Endymion Porter. Crowell, 1904; Drakakis, John. Arden Shakespeare. Bloomsbury, 2010; Kaplan, M. Lindsay. *Texts and Contexts*. Bedford/St. Martin's, 2002; Mahood, M. M. New Cambridge Shakespeare. Cambridge University Press, 2018; Mowat, Barbara A., and Paul Werstine. Folger Shakespeare Library. Simon and Schuster, 2011.

A Midsummer Night's Dream: Griffith, Trevor. Shakespeare in Production. Cambridge University Press, 1996; Ioppolo, Grace. Norton Critical Editions. W. W. Norton & Co., 2018; McDonald, Russ. Pelican Shakespeare. Penguin Books, 2016; Mowat, Barbara A., and Paul Werstine. Folger Shakespeare Library. Simon and Schuster, 2009.

Much Ado About Nothing: Bate, Jonathan, and Eric Rasmussen. RSC Shakespeare. Modern Library, 2009; Cox, John F. Shakespeare in Production. Cambridge University Press, 1997; Humphreys, A. R. Arden Shakespeare. Arden, 1981; Klein, Holger. New Critical Edition. Institut für Anglistik und Amerikanistik, Universität Salzburg, 1992; Mares, Francis Hugh. New Cambridge Shakespeare. Cambridge University Press, 1988; Mowat, Barbara A., and Paul Werstine. Folger Shakespeare Library. Simon and Schuster, 2018; Quiller-Couch, Arthur, and John Dover Wilson. Cambridge University Press, 1923. *Much Ado About Nothing and Taming of the Shrew*. Wynne-Davies, Marion. New Casebooks. Palgrave, 2001.

Othello: Mowat, Barbara A., and Paul Werstine. Folger Shakespeare Library. Simon and Schuster, 2009.

Richard III: Holland, Peter. Pelican Shakespeare. Penguin Books, 2017; Mowat, Barbara A., and Paul Werstine. Folger Shakespeare Library. Washington Square Press, 2004.

Romeo and Juliet: Bate, Jonathan, and Eric Rasmussen. RSC Shakespeare. Modern Library, 2009; Mowat, Barbara. A., and Paul Werstine. Folger Shakespeare Library. Simon and Schuster, 2011; Watts, Cedric. Wordsworth Editions, 2000; Weis, René. Arden Shakespeare. Bloomsbury, 2015.

The Taming of the Shrew: Bate, Jonathan, and Eric Rasmussen. RSC Shakespeare. Modern Library, 2010; Mowat, Barbara A., and Paul Werstine. Folger Shakespeare Library. Simon and Schuster, 2014; Orgel, Stephen. Pelican Shakespeare. Penguin Books, 2016.

The Tempest: Bate, Jonathan, and Eric Rasmussen. RSC Shakespeare. Modern Library, 2008; Mowat, Barbara A., and Paul Werstine. Folger Shakespeare Library. Washington Square Press, 2004; Tiffany, Grace. Evans Shakespeare Edition. Cengage Learning, 2011; Vaughn, Alden T., and Virginia Mason Vaughn. Arden Critical Reader. Bloomsbury, 2014.

Titus Andronicus: Bate, Jonathan. Arden Shakespeare. Arden, 2005; McDonald, Russ. Pelican Shakespeare. Penguin Books, 2017; Mowat, Barbara A., and Paul Werstine. Folger Shakespeare Library. Simon and Schuster, 2010; Waith, Eugene M. Oxford Shakespeare. Oxford University Press, 1984. *Titus Andronicus and Timon of Athens*. Bate, Jonathan, and Eric Rasmussen. RSC Shakespeare. Modern Library, 2011.

The Two Gentlemen of Verona: Bate, Jonathan, and Eric Rasmussen. RSC Shakespeare. Modern

Library, 2011; Mowat, Barbara A., and Paul Werstine. Folger Shakespeare Library. Simon and Schuster, 2009.

The Winter's Tale: Bloom, Harold, and Paul Gleed. *Bloom's Shakespeare Through the Ages*. Chelsea House, 2010; Dolan, Frances E. Pelican Shakespeare. Penguin Books, 2017; Gill, Roma. Oxford School Shakespeare. Oxford University Press, 2013; Mowat, Barbara A., and Paul Werstine. Folger Shakespeare Library. Simon and Schuster, 2009; Pitcher, John. Arden Shakespeare. Arden, 2010.

NOTES

Abbreviations

APC: Acts of the Privy Council

BL: British Library

Bodl.: Bodleian Libraries, Oxford University

CSP: Calendar of State Papers

CUL: Cambridge University Library

Harl.: Harleian Manuscripts (British Library)

LP: Letters and Papers of Henry VIII

JND: John North Diary

NPQ: *Nichols's Progresses of the Queen*

ODNB: *Oxford Dictionary of National Biography*

RNHB: Roger North Household Book

SP: State Papers

TNA: The National Archives

General notes: All quotations from Shakespeare's plays are from David Bevington, *The Complete Works of Shakespeare*, 7th edition. Quotations from Thomas North's *The Dial of Princes* are from the 1619 edition. Quotations from North's *The Moral Philosophy of Doni* are from the 2003 edition edited by Donald Beecher, et al. Quotations from North's *Plutarch's Lives* and *Nepos's Lives* are from the original editions of 1579 and 1602.

Nobles are referred to by their title as of the date it was conferred; thus, for example, Robert Dudley, Earl of Leicester, is referred to as Dudley before 1564 and Leicester thereafter; William Cecil, Lord Burghley, is referred to as Cecil until 1571 and Burghley thereafter.

All currency comparisons throughout this book are made with the Bank of England's inflation calendar, www.bankofengland.co.uk/monetary-policy/inflation/inflation-calculator. Amounts in pounds are multiplied by 1.3 to calculate approximate amounts in dollars.

Regarding dates: The year in Tudor England officially began on Lady's Day, March 25; however, this book follows the convention of starting the appropriate year as of January 1. In addition, after 1582, England retained the Julian calendar, while Roman Catholic countries adopted the Gregorian calendar, creating a difference of about ten days. For sake of clarity, this book follows the "old style" dating used by Elizabethan England at the time.

PROLOGUE

Quotations from *A Midsummer Night's Dream* (*AMND*) in this chapter are as follows: "Thou rememb'rest...sea-maid's music": *AMND* 2.1.148–154; "That very time...thousand hearts": *AMND* 2.1.155–160.

1 greatest party of Elizabeth's reign: Sarah Gristwood, *Elizabeth and Leicester*, 239–248; Elizabeth Jenkins, *Elizabeth and Leicester*, 236–245; Trea Martyn, *Queen Elizabeth in the Garden*, 73–89; Stephen Greenblatt, *Will in the World*, 43–47; Andy McSmith, "The great Kenilworth booze-up: How to party like it's 1575," *The Independent*, December 17, 2007; Sabrina Feldman, "Thomas Sackville, Shakespeare, and the 1575 Kenilworth Festivities," Humanities Lit Authors Shakespeare, Google group, https://humanities.lit.authors.shakespeare.narkive.com/dvcrQp3V/thomas -sackville-shakespeare-and-the-1575-kenilworth-festivities.

1 "blaze of burning darts": Robert Langham, *A Letter, Wherein Part of the Entertainment unto the Queen's Majesty at Kenilworth Castle, NPQ,* 249.

1 giant water pageant: Langham, 260–263; George Gascoigne, *Princely Pleasures at the Court of Kenilworth, NPQ,* 304–308; William Dugdale, *Antiquities of Warwickshire,* I., 249; N. J. Halpin, *Oberon's Vision in the Midsummer Night's Dream,* 18–20; Martyn, 84–85; Jenkins, 240–241.

2 Triton...on a mechanical mermaid: The three contemporary sources, Langham, Gascoyne, and Dugdale, disagree on some of the details of the water pageant; for example, Langham and Dugdale have Triton swimming on the mermaid, while Gascoyne has him "in the likeness of a mermaid." For the sake of the narrative, I split the difference between the three narrators and describe what I think to be the most likely scene.

2 For more than a century: Halpin credits James Boaden with being the first person to suggest this, in his *Essay on the Sonnets of Shakespeare* (1837).

2 less clear how Shakespeare: Halpin, 20–25; Nathan Drake, *Shakespeare and His Times,* I., 37–39.

2 "it is certainly conceivable": Greenblatt, 43.

5 contacted by a sixty-five-year-old man: Michael Blanding, "Up in Smoke," *Boston Magazine*, April 2011.

5 wrote an article: Michael Blanding, "Why Experts Don't Believe This Is a Rare First Map of America," *The New York Times*, December 10, 2017.

6 wrote about that book: Michael Blanding, "Plagiarism Software Unveils a New Source for 11 of Shakespeare's Plays," *The New York Times*, February 7, 2018.

CHAPTER ONE: THIS BLOOD CONDEMNS

Quotations from *Arden of Faversham* (*Arden*) are from the New Mermaids edition, edited by Martin White, as follows: "The more I sound his name": *Arden* 14.4–6; "That plot of ground": *Arden* 13.32–34; "When was I so long": *Arden* 14.1; "It is not love that loves": *Arden* 8.59; "these eyes, that showed": *Arden* 8.87; "Wherein is showed": *Arden*, subtitle; "crept into the service": *Arden* 1.27–31; "If I be merry": *Arden* 13.108–11.

Quotations from Shakespeare's (other) plays are as follows: "Who will not change": *A Midsummer Night's Dream* 2.2.120; "Thou know'st that we too": *Julius Caesar* 5.5.26; "I know he loves me well; but": *Richard III* 3.4.15.

Quotations from Thomas North's *The Dial of Princes* (*Dial*) are as follows: "Wherein is expressed...": *Dial*, The Table; courtiers who "flatter": *Dial* 619–620.

9 best-preserved medieval street: "Spotlight on: Faversham," *Kent Life*, August 28, 2015; Tom Dyckhoff, "Let's Move to Faversham, Kent," *The Guardian*, October 24, 2014.

10 It was a messy killing: Patricia Hyde, *Thomas Arden in Faversham*, 84–85; *Holinshed's Chronicles*, Second Edition, 1587, vol. 3, 1062–1066, reprinted in Martin White, ed., *Arden of Faversham*, 119; Stowe's Historical and Other Collections, vol. VI, BL Harl, MS 542. Plut XLVIII B, reprinted in Hyde, 121; Faversham Wardmote Book, reprinted in Edward Jacob, *The History of the Town and Port of Faversham: In the County of Kent*, 198–199.

10 took a break from recounting...five full pages: Richard Helgerson, "Murder in Faversham: Holinshed's impertinent history," in Donald R. Kelley and David Harris Sacks, eds., *The Historical Imagination in Early Modern Britain*, 133–136.

10 new genre of "domestic tragedy": Lena Cowen Orlin, *Private Matters and Public Culture in Post-Reformation England*, 8–9, 76; Wendy Wall, *Staging Domesticity*, 215; Helgerson, 137–139; Frederick Kaj Olof Bengtsson, "True and Home-Born: Domestic Tragedy on the Early Modern English Stage," Columbia University dissertation, 2014.

12 "fell into disrepair...a brothel": interview with Harold Goodwin and Michael Frohnsdorff, Faversham Society; "Abbey Street," Faversham.org, www.faversham.org/history/places/abbey-street.

12 "generally accept that it was probably this room": Goodwin and Frohnsdorff; Nigel Morgan, "The Outer Gatehouse and Guest House," Faversham Papers, no. 114.

12 The erstwhile mayor lay: This account follows *Holinshed's Chronicles*. The accounts in Stow and the Wardmote book contain subtle differences, but in general the narrative is the same.

13 earliest uses of forensic science: Michael Kurland, *Irrefutable Evidence: Adventures in the History of Forensic Science*, 24–27; Kristy Baxter, *Detectives by the Decade* (podcast), "Episode 1: The murder of Thomas Arden and how the ensuing investigation made forensic history."

14 Edward North was a prosperous lawyer: Hyde, 28–29; P. R. N. Carter, "North, Edward, first Baron North," *ODNB*; A. D. K. Hawkyard, "North, Edward"; *The History of Parliament*.

14 who was born in 1535: P. S. Allen, "The Birth of Sir Thomas North," *The English Historical Review*, Volume XXXVII, Issue CXLVIII, October 1922, pp. 565–566.

14 Arden as his secretary: Hyde, 18–26.

14 inside track on sales...North coat of arms: Orlin, 24–30; Hyde 28, 39–47, 60.

15 as far back as 1537...North's favored servant of the affair: Orlin, 45–46; Hyde, 62–65.

15 "willfully did permit": Wardmote, 199.

15 "delicate meats and sumptuous apparel": Wardmote, 198.

15 "for which deed he had many a curse": Stow, 122.

15 "wrested" a piece of land: *Holinshed*, 114; Stow, 118.

16 so "evil beloved...after his death": Stow, 120.

16 Lord Clifford: *Arden* 1.32.

17 first surviving example: Orlin, 76.

17 Dissolution of the Monasteries...seize it: Randall L. Martin, "'Arden winketh at his wife's lewdness, & why!': A Patrilineal Crisis in Arden of Faversham," *Early Theatre* vol. 4 (2001), 13–33, 15; Frank Whigham, *Seizures of the Will in Early Modern English Drama*, 67, 77.

17 recorded an entry: Lionel Cust, "Arden of Faversham," *Archaeologia Cantiana,* vol. 34 (1920), 101–138, 124.

18 first person to make that claim: Peter Kirwan, "Arden of Faversham," Shakespeare Documented (website), Folger Shakespeare Library.

18 Mosby and Alice...to Macbeth and Lady Macbeth: Whigham, 108; Cust, 123.

18 intimately familiar with Kent: MacDonald Jackson, *Determining the Shakespeare Canon,* 100–111.

18 Swinburne..."equal to theirs": Cust, 125; Jackson, *Determining,* 254, quoting Algernon Charles Swinburne, *A Study of Shakespeare,* 1880.

18 new claimant: Henry Dugdale Sykes, *Sidelights on Shakespeare,* 48–76; Brian Vickers, "Thomas Kyd, the Secret Sharer," *Times Literary Supplement,* 2008; expanded version published on Brian Vickers website, www.brianvickers.uk/wp-content/uploads/2016/05/Vickers-Thomas-Kyd-The-Secret-Sharer.pdf.

18 split the difference: Cust, 126.

18 biggest champion: Darren Freebury-Jones, "In Defence of Kyd: Evaluating the Claim for Shakespeare's Part Authorship of *Arden of Faversham," Authorship,* vol. 7, no. 2 (2018), 1; Tom Lockwood, "Introduction," in White, *Arden of Faversham,* xxix.

18 In 2006, Jackson honed in: Jackson, "Shakespeare and the Quarrel Scene in 'Arden of Faversham,'" *Shakespeare Quarterly,* vol. 57, no. 3 (Autumn 2006), 249–293.

19 twenty-eight plays with..."modes of speech": Jackson, "Quarrel Scene," 259–260.

19 In an essay..."degree of probability": Vickers, "Thomas Kyd, the Secret Sharer."

19 more three-word phrases: Jackson, *Determining,* 113–114.

19 at least six: Jackson, *Determining,* 122–126 (Scenes 4–9).

19 partisans for Kyd and Shakespeare: Freebury-Jones (2018); Marina Tarlinskaja, "Shakespeare in *Arden of Faversham* and the Additions to *The Spanish Tragedy*: Versification Analysis," *Journal of Early Modern Studies,* no. 5 (2016), 175–200; Hugh Craig and Arthur F. Kinney, *Shakespeare, Computers, and the Mystery of Authorship.*

19 most comprehensive analysis: Marcus Strom, "Australian Data Sleuths Link Shakespeare to Anonymous 16th-Century Play," *The Sydney Morning Herald,* November 11, 2016.

19 "responsible for the lion's share": Jack Elliott and Brett Greatley-Hirsch, "*Arden of Faversham* and the 'Print of Many,'" in Gary Taylor and Garbriel Egan, eds., *The New Oxford Shakespeare: Authorship Companion,* 139–181.

20 with his own support: Dennis McCarthy, "Shakespeare and Arden of Faversham," *Notes & Queries,* vol. 60, no. 3 (September 2013), 391–397.

20 plagiarism detection software called WCopyfind: "WCopyfind," The Plagiarism Resource Site, https://plagiarism.bloomfieldmedia.com/software/wcopyfind.

20 Early English Books Online: "About EBOO," Early English Books Online, https://eebo.chadwyck.com/marketing/about.htm.

22 scholars are united: Jackson, "Quarrel Scene," 255; Lockwood, xxvii.

22 "How now, Mistress Alice?": Stow, 120.

22 same place as he does: *Arden* 14.269.

23 Kentish historian William Lambarde: Hyde, 13.

23 "emerges as the strongest...best lines are all hers": Helgerson, 140.

23 known Alice's daughter: As evidence of this theory, when Margaret sold the remainder of the abbey property in 1568, she kept one small piece of it named Almery Croft—the very field where Arden's body was discovered lying in the snow seventeen years earlier—and gave it to her cousin, Thomas North. Cust, 103.

23 Multiple commentators have pointed out: Whigham, 67; Helgerson, 143; Cust, 114.

24 Alice didn't kill her husband…"before common gain": Helgerson, 143. See also Ian McAdam, "Protestant Manliness in Arden of Faversham," *Texas Studies in Literature and Language*, vol. 45, no. 1 (Spring 2003), 42–72, 65.

24 trial was brief…to consume her: Hyde, 92–99; Orlin, 79–84.

24 inconceivably wicked: Catherine Belsey, "Alice Arden's Crime," *Renaissance Drama*, New Series, vol. 13 (1982), 83–102, 94–96; Hunter S. Jones, *Sexuality and Its Impact on History*, 73.

25 wrote a biography of his ancestor: Dudley North, *Some Notes Concerning the Life of Edward Lord North, Baron of Kirtling, 1658*; "perusal of the old": *Some Notes*, 2; "managing of that great trust…catastrophe of his": *Some Notes*, 8; "apply the judgment of the Almighty": *Some Notes*, 9; "never had a steadiness": *Some Notes*, 31.

CHAPTER TWO: BUT THINKING MAKES IT SO

Quotations from *Hamlet* and other plays in this chapter are as follows: "To be, or not to be…": *Hamlet* 3.1.57–67; "tiger's heart wrapped": *Henry VI, Part 2* 1.4.137.

Quotations from Thomas North's *The Dial of Princes* (*Dial*) are as follows: "kind of sleeping…none returned": *Dial* 524; "Is it better…broils of fortune": *Dial* 535–536; "sea of troubles": *Dial* 724; "if perchance thou": *Dial* 129.

28 Hamlet is the ultimate role: Susannah Clapp, "Genius, coward…or madman? Why Hamlet gives actors the ultimate test," *The Observer*, August 9, 2015; Jonathan Bate and Eric Rasmussen, eds., *Hamlet* (RSC), 172–179.

28 old Norse legend…French version: Ann Thompson and Neil Taylor, eds., *Hamlet* (Arden), 65–71.

28 known as the First Quarto: Thompson, 8; Bate, 25.

28 as early as 1589…write his masterpiece: Thompson, 45–46, 71–72; Bate, 5.

29 different versions of *Hamlet*…attributed to Shakespeare: Thompson, 18–19; Bate, 10–11.

29 "It is common practice…": Thomas Nashe, preface to Robert Greene, *Menaphon*, in *The Life and Complete Works in Prose and Verse of Robert Greene*, 15.

31 "Plutarch's plumes…Boreas by the beard": *Menaphon*, 11, 10.

31 "There shalt thou see": Jessica Winston, *Lawyers at Play*, 46.

31 "first great master of English prose": Sidney Lee, "North, Sir Thomas," *ODNB*, 1895, 179; Richard Chambers, "Sir Thomas North," *Chambers' Cyclopaedia of English Literature*, 1901, 258; "Sir Thomas North," *Encyclopedia Britannica*, 1911, vol. 19, 760.

31 "storehouse of classical learning": "North, Sir Thomas," *ODNB*.

32 "grew up in the 1960s…good job at multitasking": Interviews with Dennis McCarthy, Nicole Galovski, Pauline Hawkins, Michael Kizilbash, Gloria McCarthy, Lori McCarthy, and Yvonne Pickard.

34 how email had brought the love letter back: Dennis McCarthy, "The History of the Love Letter," *North Shore Magazine*, February 8, 1996, 3–5.

36 he likened to a "zipper effect": Dennis McCarthy, "The Trans-Pacific Zipper Effect: Disjunct Sister Taxa and Matching Geological Outlines That Link the Pacific Margins," *Journal of Biogeography*, vol. 30, no. 10 (October 2003), 1545–1561.

36 distribution patterns of plants: Michael Heads, "Biogeographic Disjunction Along the

Alpine Fault, New Zealand," *Biological Journal of the Linnean Society*, vol. 63, no. 2 (February 1998), 161–176.

37 invited him to present: Interview with Malte Ebach; "The Fourth Revolt/The Cardiff Presentation," http://www.4threvolt.com/Cardiff2.html.

38 Komodo dragons.... "eating an elephant": Dennis McCarthy, *Here Be Dragons*, 67–68.

38 "The Bloody Fall"... once lived there: McCarthy, *Dragons*, 106–117.

38 gave Charles Darwin the epiphany: McCarthy, *Dragons*, 1–19.

38 Alfred Wegener... "died unknown": McCarthy, *Dragons*, 23–39.

39 in December 2009: "Here Be Dragons," Amazon.com.

39 "wonderful little book": Dan Agin, "Book Review: *Here Be Dragons*," *Huffington Post*, March 18, 2010.

39 gave it a positive review: Devorah Bennu, "Asking Why Who Is Where," *Science*, vol. 328, no. 5986 (June 25, 2010), 1637.

39 echo there of Hamlet's most famous soliloquy: Dennis McCarthy, "A 'Sea of Troubles' and a 'Pilgrimage Uncertain' / *Dial of Princes* as the Source for Hamlet's Soliloquy," *Notes & Queries*, vol. 56, no. 1 (March 2009), 57–60.

41 "John Daw": Dennis McCarthy, "Sir Thomas North as Sir John Daw," *Notes & Queries*, vol. 54, no. 3 (September 2007), 321–324.

41 followed it up with a paper: McCarthy, "A 'Sea of Troubles.'"

42 trumpeting on his website: "Dennis McCarthy / Author Bio," The 4th Revolt, www.4threvolt.com/AuthorBio.

44 "There is an upstart crow...": D. Allen Carroll, ed., *Greene's Groatsworth of Wit*, 84–85.

44 "shake" was Elizabethan slang for "steal": *Oxford English Dictionary*, "Shake" 16 a-b; Peter Bereck, "The 'Upstart Crow,' Aesop's Crow, and Shakespeare as a Reviser," *Shakespeare Quarterly*, vol. 35, no. 2 (Summer 1984), 205–207; H. J. Oliver, "Shakespeare the Shake-Scene," *Notes & Queries*, NS 26 (1979), 115.

44 "Now famoused for an arch-playmaking-poet": *Groatsworth*, 76.

CHAPTER THREE: REMEMBERING THIS REALM

In addition to sources below, secondary historical sources consulted for this chapter include: Peter Ackroyd, *Tudors*; Susan Brigden, *New Worlds, Lost Worlds*; David Loades, *Henry VIII*; John Matusiak, *Wolsey*; Diarmaid MacCulloch, *Thomas Cromwell* and *The Boy King*; G. J. Meyer, *The Tudors*; A. F. Pollard, *Wolsey*; Alison Weir, *Henry VIII* and *The Children of Henry VIII*; Neville Williams, *Henry VIII and his Court*; Derek Wilson, *In the Lion's Court*.

46 triumphantly to his coronation: *Hall's Chronicle*, 507–509.

47 to the philosophy of humanism: David Crowther, "New Learning: England's First Humanists," The History of England, https://thehistoryofengland.co.uk /resource/new-learning-englands-first-humanists/; David Crowther, "Mountjoy, Henry VIII's Humanist Mentor," https://thehistoryofengland.co.uk/resource/mountjoy-henry -viiis-humanist-mentor/; "The Early English Humanists," *Encyclopedia Britannica*, www.britannica.com/topic/education/The-early-English-humanists.

47 London stretched: "A Map of Tudor London," The London Topographical Society (The Historic Towns Trust, 2018).

47 over fifty thousand people: Stephen Porter, *Everyday Life in Tudor London*, 10.

47 Edward's birth around 1496: P. R. N. Carter, "North, Edward, first Baron North,"

ODNB; A. D. K. Hawkyard, "North, Edward," *The History of Parliament*, www.history ofparliamentonline.org/volume/1509-1558/member/north-edward-1504-64; Frances Bushby, *Three Men of the Tudor Time.*

47 prosperous clothing merchant: Charles Mosely, ed., *Burke's Peerage*. www.thepeerage.com /p21133.htm i211329.

47 in St. Paul's School: "About St. Paul's," St. Paul's School (website), www.stpaulsschool .org.uk/about.

47 scholar John Colet: David Crowther, "John Colet and the Convocation of 1512," The History of England, https://thehistoryofengland.co.uk/resource/john-colet-and-the -convocation-of-1512/; Jonathan Arnold, "John Colet, Preaching and Reform at St. Paul's Cathedral, 1505–19," *Historical Research*, vol. 76, no. 194 (November 2003), 450–468.

47 future elite of English society: Among Paulines of the time were Thomas Wriothesley, future Lord Chancellor; Anthony Denny, future gentleman of the privy chamber and one of Henry's closest friends; William Paget, future privy councilor and one of Henry's top diplomats; and John Leland, "father of English local history."

47 continuing his studies at Peterhouse: *History of Parliament*; Peterhouse, *A Biographical Register of Peterhouse Men*, 236; email to author from Dr. Roger Lovatt, archivist at Peterhouse, Cambridge, who wrote: "I think it is certain that Edward, 1st Baron North, attended Peterhouse, probably around 1515, but unfortunately the Admissions Registers for these years have not survived." Later in life, North made a large bequest to the college.

50 Martin Luther...religious reformation: Virginia Rounding, *The Burning Time*, 4– 5, 10, 17.

50 study at Lincoln's Inn: "North, Edward," *ODNB*; *History of Parliament.*

51 "With profound sorrow...falling in decay": Edward North, "The Ruyn' of a Ream'," BL, Harl. 2252, 25–28, lines 1–4; printed in Frederick James Furnivall, W. R. Morfill, and Richard Williams, *Ballads from Manuscripts*, 1.152–166.

51 survives in two manuscript copies: The first is inserted, awkwardly, into a book of heraldic devices, BL Landsdowne 858. See also William Ringler, *Bibliography and Index of English Verse in Manuscript, 1501–1558*, TM 2006.

51 sixteenth-century "commonplace book": This book was compiled by John Colyn, a member of the Mercers' company, a clothiers guild to which North's father also belonged. BL Harl. 2252, no. 33, back. See also Ringler, TM 1425; Ulrich Frost, *Das Commonplace Book von John Colyns*, 203–205; David Parker, *The Commonplace Book in Tudor London*, 102–106; Robert Kinsman, "Skelton's *Colyn Cloute*: The Mask of *Vox Populi*," in University of California Department of English, *Essays Critical and Historical Dedicated to Lily B. Campbell*, 17, 260.

51 first letter of each of the following lines: North, "Ruin," 239–250.

51 "For in gowns of silk": North, "Ruin," 141; "by reason of whose vices": "Ruin," 146.

51 sheaf of water-stained papers: TNA, KB 9/492/2.

52 ringleader of the plot against the king: *Hall's Chronicle*, ff. 222–223; *Holinshed's Chronicles*, 882. See also Ben Parsons, "That Which Stains a New Pot: Schoolteachers on Trial in the Fifteenth and Sixteen," lecture delivered on November 18, 2013, reprinted in *Transactions of the Leicester Literary and Philosophical Society*; Charles Phythian-Adams, *Desolation of a City*, 149–157; Amy Appleford, *Learning to Die in London, 1380– 1540*, 213.

52 found out by a local cloth seller: "Receipt by William Umpton, of Coventry, draper...as

reward for discovering the insurrection intended to have been made by Francis Philippe and his adherents," LP, February 14, 1524 R.O.

52   promised to keep their plans a secret: TNA, KB 9/492/2, Enrollment, lines 7–9.

52   appeared at Westminster Hall: National Archives, "Court of King's Bench," http://www.nationalarchives.gov.uk/help-with-your-research/research-guides/court -kings-bench-crown-side-1675-1875.

53   another poem in the commonplace book: Edward North, "The Complaynte of Northe to the Cardnall Wolsey," BL Harl, MS 2252, leaf 33b, printed in *Ballads from Manu-scripts*, ed. Frederick J. Furnivall, 1.336–9. See also Frost, 211–213; Ringler, TM 1094, TM 606.

53   "Now being in prison": North, "Complaint," 1; "making was my joy": "Complaint," 7; "his wit and goodly eloquence": "Complaint," 44; "All of England for him is bound to pray": "Complaint," 77; acrostic in the last lines: "Complaint," 36–73.

53   full pardon for North: LP Jan 1525, 24 (January 24, 1525); TNA C82/554.

53   "misprision of treason": P. R. Glazebrook, "Misprision of Felony—Shadow or Phantom?" *The American Journal of Legal History*, vol. 8, no. 3 (July 1964), 189–208; John Bellamy, *The Tudor Law of Treason*.

54   counsel for the city: *History of Parliament*; "North, Edward," *ODNB*.

54   "I beseech you for all the loves": George Cavendish, *Life of Cardinal Wolsey*, 149–150.

55   freeman of the Mercer's Company: *History of Parliament*.

55   settling down with Alice Squire: Patricia Hyde, *Thomas Arden in Faversham*, 38; "North, Edward," *ODNB*.

55   widow of two marriages: Hyde, 34–36; "North, Edward," *ODNB*.

55   the future Alice Arden: According to Hyde's math, she was thirty at the time of the murder in 1551, making her seven in 1528 when Edward North married her mother.

55   daughter, Christian, was born . . . February 1531: P. S. Allen, "The Birth of Sir Thomas North," *The English Historical Review*, vol. 37, no. 148 (October 1922), 565–566. Roger's birth year is indicated as "mdxxx," but the author lists it as 1530/31. By regnal year calculations, February of that year would be officially 1530 but actually 1531.

55   clerk of Parliament: *History of Parliament*; LP v. Feb 1531 38; xvi. Sept. 1540, R.O.

55   suggests it was his poem: *History of Parliament*.

55   destroyed statues of saints: Eamon Duffy, *The Stripping of the Altars,* 380–381.

55   stood atop wooden platforms . . . white-hot blaze: Rounding 7, 26–27, 115–116.

56   drafting legislation in Parliament: The Clerk of the Parliaments: Role and Functions, www.parliament.uk/about/faqs/house-of-lords-faqs/lords-cofp/; *History of Parliament*; P. R. N. Carter, "Sir Brian Tuke," *ODNB*.

56   "his Sun began to ascend": Dudley North, *Some Notes Concerning the Life of Edward Lord North, Baron of Kirtling, 1658,* 7.

56   Kirtling Hall: Christopher Piers Lewis, *A History of Kirtling and Upend*, 1–2, 6, 9–10; Bushby, 10.

56   medieval castle . . . "oyster-shell decoration": Lewis, 13, 22–23; Michael Wilson, *A Family of the Stuart Age*, 13–14.

56   five hundred acres of grounds . . . fifty tenant farmers: Lewis, 28; Wilson, *A Family,* 15.

57   agents throughout the country: B.W. Beckingsale, *Thomas Cromwell: Tudor Minister*, 99.

57   May 28 of that year: Allen, "The Birth of Sir Thomas North."

57   Now a museum: The Charterhouse (website), www.thecharterhouse.org.

57   great room . . . Venice and Bruges: North house inventory, 1565, Bodl. North MS b.12, ff.15–47, 97–101, reprinted in *The Charterhouse: Survey of London*, 198–251.

58   "his master could grow rich": Ackroyd, 84.

58   surveying church property: Duffy, *Stripping*, 383.

58   jousting accident: Michael McCarthy, "The Jousting Accident That Turned Henry VIII into a Tyrant," *The Independent*, April 18, 2009.

58   storage space for the king's tents: *Survey of London*, 36–38.

59   chancellor of augmentations: Bushby, 12; *History of Parliament*; "North, Edward," *ODNB*.

59   plum grant of the Charterhouse: LP xx, April 14, 1545, 33. Charterhouse, *Charter-House, Its Foundation and History*, 11.

59   demolished . . . grand new home: Christopher Thomas, Bruno Barber, and Alfred Thomas, *The London Charterhouse*, 71–82.

60   summoned to appear before the king: North, *Some Notes*, 10–11.

60   another version of the story: *History of Parliament*.

60   added North's name: Suzannah Lipscomb, *The King Is Dead: The Last Will and Testament of Henry VIII*; D. E. Hoak, *The King's Council in the Reign of Edward VI*.

61   crimson robe and black velvet hat: College of Arms MS I. 7 ff 32–38v.

61   pushed him out: "North, Edward," *ODNB*; *History of Parliament*; Bushby, 18.

61   threw his weight behind Dudley: Bushby, 19.

61   future Duke of Northumberland: Dudley was Earl of Warwick starting in 1547, and not officially Duke of Northumberland until 1550. For the sake of simplicity, however, this chapter refers to him as Northumberland from the beginning.

61   among the first councilors to answer his call: *History of Parliament*.

62   hauled out their statues: Duffy, *Stripping*, 490–491.

63   among eight English nobles: Bushby, 21–22; John Edwards, *Mary I*, 183; Anna Whitelock, *The Queen's Bed*, 250; Loades, 223.

63   platforms at Smithfield: Eamon Duffy, *Fires of Faith*, 97–99; Rounding, 257.

63   butcher, barber, farmer: Ackroyd, 268; Whitelock, 283.

63   upholsterer: Rounding, 275; Duffy, *Fires*, 90.

63   now sentenced dozens: Duffy, *Fires*, 119–120, 128; Rounding, 304, 334–336.

63   engendering sympathy . . . more burnings: Duffy, *Fires*, 114; Rounding, 342–343.

63   ceremony to officially . . . became fewer: Bushby, 22; Eugene Bourgeois, *The Ruling Elite of Cambridgeshire*, 157.

63   senior knight of the shire: Bourgeois, 169.

CHAPTER FOUR: UNDREAMED SHORES

This chapter assumes that Thomas North is the author of the 1555 journal describing the ambassadors' trip to Rome, the discovery and provenance of which will be discussed more thoroughly in chapter 16.

Quotations from *The Winter's Tale* (*TWT*) are as follows: "unpathed waters": *TWT* 4.4.570; "Exit, pursued by a bear": *TWT* 3.3.57; "Do not say 'tis superstition": *TWT* 5.3.43–44; "If this be magic": *TWT* 5.3.137–138; "A thousand knees": *TWT* 3.2.210–213; "worth and honesty": *TWT* 5.3.146; "life as lively mocked": *TWT* 5.3.19–20; "Oh, thus she stood": *TWT* 5.3.34–36; "that rare Italian master": *TWT* 5.2.98–100; "no shepherdess, but Flora": *TWT* 4.4.2; "swain": *TWT* 4.4.30; "as a meeting of the petty gods": *TWT* 4.4.4–5; "The gods themselves have taken": *TWT* 4.4.25–31.

Unless otherwise noted, all quotations and descriptions of North's trip are taken from "The Journey of the Queen's Ambassadors unto Rome, anno 1555," printed in Philip Yorke, Earl of Hardwicke, ed., *Miscellaneous State Papers. From 1501 to 1726*, 62–102. The text is printed from the British Library's copy, BL Harl, MS. All dates for the delegation's journey are taken from the copy at Lambeth Palace Library, MS 5076.

Quotations from Thomas North's Journal (*TNJ*), from Hardwicke, are as follows: "From Pont Beauvoisin to Chamberry...neither of them hurt": *TNJ* 72; "griffin claw...as a walnut": *TNJ* 66; "and said unto us": *TNJ* 68; "able to make a man so deaf": *TNJ* 73; "rather a hell than a highway": *TNJ* 73; "young child lying dead": *TNJ* 73; "child was born dead": *TNJ* 73; "so steep to the top": *TNJ* 74; "making round balls of snow...drown": *TNJ* 74; "Chapel of the Dead...thanks be to God": *TNJ* 74–75; "in danger of killing": *TNJ* 77; "goodliest and best house": *TNJ* 80; "all the monks...be nobly born": *TNJ* 80; "We rode as between gardens": *TNJ* 82; "a very honest gentleman": *TNJ* 84; "pictures of men...miracles": *TNJ* 85; "went to the court": *TNJ* 85; "green almonds": *TNJ* 85.

65   probably attended Peterhouse: Tom Lockwood, "North, Sir Thomas," *ODNB*.

67   train of 160 horses: "The Last National Embassy to Rome," *The Month*, vol. 116 (1912), 46–55.

70   "so full of improbabilities": Barbara Mowat and Paul Werstine, eds., *The Winter's Tale* (Folger), xiii.

70   fallen into one of two camps...split the difference: Harold Bloom, *Bloom's Shakespeare Through the Ages: The Winter's Tale*, 57.

70   "found the idea to be ludicrous": Bloom, 17.

70   "rambling, perhaps an untidy play": Gordon Wilson Knight, *The Crown of Life: Essays in Interpretation of Shakespeare's Final Plays*, in Bloom, 117.

70   "The scene never fails!": Roma Gill, *The Winter's Tale* (Oxford), xxvii.

72   source for Shakespeare's play: Kenneth Muir, *The Sources of Shakespeare's Plays*, 266.

72   gets his names for several characters: *Plutarch's Lives*, 1039. Of course, North's *Plutarch* wasn't published until 1580, so North couldn't have used the names in the original version of the play. McCarthy speculates that North used different names in the original version, but changed them in a revision to the play after Greene's novel in 1588, but before Shakespeare's play in 1609–1610.

73   "Her preservation and revelation...Mary Tudor's reign": Ruth Vanita, "Mariological Memory in *The Winter's Tale* and *Henry VIII*," *Studies in English Literature, 1500–1900*, vol. 40, no. 2, *Tudor and Stuart Drama* (Spring 2000), 311–337, 320.

73   image of Perdita kneeling: Darryll Grantley, "*The Winter's Tale* and Early Religious Drama," *Comparative Drama*, vol. 20, no. 1 (Spring 1986), 17–37, 34.

74   story of Pygmalion: Leonard Barkan, "'Living Sculptures': Ovid, Michelangelo and *The Winter's Tale*," *ELH*, vol. 48, no. 4 (Winter 1981), 639–667. Another suggested inspiration for the statue scene is Euripides's play *Alcestis*, which features a wife resurrected through the intercession of the demigod Hercules. While it's been famously said that Shakespeare knew "small Latin and less Greek," he could have read Ovid in English, or a Latin translation of Euripides's play. Sarah Dewar-Watson, "The Alcestis and the Statue Scene in the *Winter's Tale*," *Shakespeare Quarterly*, vol. 60, no. 1 (Spring 2009), 73–80.

75   "Mr. Thomas North was in danger of killing": The British Library version has "my Lord North's younger son was in danger of killing." In the Lambeth Palace Library version, someone, presumably North himself, has crossed out that appellation and written "Mr. Thomas North" instead.

77   compared Camillo to Sir Thomas More: Thomas Merriam, "Did Shakespeare Model Camillo in *The Winter's Tale* on Sir Thomas More?," *Moreana*, vol. 19, no. 75/6 (1982),

91–101; Peter Milward, "The Morean Counsellor in Shakspeare's Last Plays," *Moreana*, vol. 27, no. 103 (1990), 25–32; Leslie O'Dell, *Shakespearean Scholarship: A Guide for Actors and Students*, 100.

77 Santuario Beata Vergine...wax and papier-mâché: *Citta di Curtatone* (guidebook), Provincia di Mantova, Uffici del Comune di Curtatone, 15; Attilo Zanca, "The Crocodile of Santuario of Saint Mary of Grazie," www.fermimn.edu/grazie/inglese/s4.html.

78 Franciscan friar...upon his head: Jennifer Adams, Il Libro dei Miracoli: *Intersections of Gender, Class, and Portraiture in Italian Multimedia Votive Sculpture, 1450–1630*, unpublished dissertation, Arizona State University, 2012; Michael W. Cole and Rebecca Zorach, eds., *The Idol in the Age of Art*, 180.

78 "like so many figures": Rita Severi, *Art in Shakespeare and Other Essays*, 35.

79 Shakespeare would pick Giulio Romano: Georgianna Ziegler, "Parents, Daughters, and 'That Rare Italian Master': A New Source for *The Winter's Tale*," *Shakespeare Quarterly*, vol. 36, no. 2 (Summer 1985), 204–212; Barkan, 655.

79 Born Giulio...native city: Gian Maria Erbesato, *Guide to Palazzo Te*, 3–5; Gianna Suitner and Chiara Tellini Perina, *Palazzo Te in Mantua*, 8–10.

79 Giulio may have in fact worked: Severi, *Art in Shakespeare*, 74; Rita Severi, "What's in a Name. La Fortuna di Giulio Romano Nel Periodo Shakespeariano," Convegno internazionale di studi su "Giulio Romano e l'espansione europea del Rinascimento," *Giulio Romano*, 405.

79 newly resurrected Christ: Myron Laskin, Jr., "Giulio Romano and Baldassare Castiglione," *The Burlington Magazine*, vol. 109, no. 770 (May 1967), 300, 302–303.

79 from another English traveler: One such possibility is Thomas Hoby, an English diplomat who translated Castiglione's work in 1561 and wrote an unpublished travelogue of his time in Italy in 1564. But Hoby never mentions the sanctuary in his writings and died in 1566, when Shakespeare was two years old.

80 inscription in Latin...could read Italian: Barkan, 656–657.

80 No English translation: Ziegler, 205.

80 attempted to locate Shakespeare's source: Ziegler; Tom Rutter, "Shakespeare, Serlio, and Giulio Romano," *English Literary Renaissance,* Vol. 49, No. 2 (Spring 2019), 248–272.

80 Palazzo Te, a palace: Ugo Bazzotti, ed., *Palazzo Te Mantua*, Skira Guides, 2007–2011, 8–9, 12, 37–45, back cover; Erbesato, 9, 11–12, 16–29; Suitner, 11–20, 50, 53–77.

81 "Room after room": Dott. Cristina Barozzi, Mantova, Guida Turistica Abilitata.

CHAPTER FIVE: PRINCES' FAVORS

Quotations from *Henry VIII* (*H8*) are as follows: "Oh, how wretched": *H8* 3.2.367–368; "Think you see them great": *H8* Prologue 27–30; "drum and trumpet...full upon them": *H8* 1.4.50–61; "Because they speak...hour of revels with 'em": *H8* 1.4.66–73; "Enter two Vergers...below them, the Scribes": *H8* 2.4.

Quotations from Thomas North's Journal (*TNJ*) are as follows: "the Pope sat in a conclave": *TNJ* 96; "officers of his household...before himself": *TNJ* 98.

Secondary historical sources for this chapter include: Peter Ackroyd, *Tudors*; John Edwards, *Mary I: England's Catholic Queen*; David Loades, *Mary Tudor: A Life*; G. J. Meyer, *The Tudors*; Alison Weir, *The Children of Henry VIII*; Anna Whitelock, *Mary Tudor: England's First Queen*.

87 Lincoln's Inn: Angela Holdsworth, *A Portrait of Lincoln's Inn*, 10, 25–28; Gerald Hurst, *A Short History of Lincoln's Inn*, 5–6; Agas Map of Early Modern London (c. 1561), https://mapoflondon.uvic.ca/agas.htm.

87 in early 1556: Lincoln's Inn, *The Records of the Honourable Society of Lincoln's Inn. The Black Books,* vol. 1, 1897, 62.

88 beginnings in the fourteenth century...become a barrister: Holdsworth, 12; Hurst, 3–5; Jessica Winston, *Lawyers at Play*, 24; Hyacinthe Ringrose, *The Inns of Court*, 3–5; Phyllis Allen Richmond, "Early English Law Schools: The Inns of Court," *American Bar Association Journal*, vol. 48, no. 3 (March 1962), 254–259.

88 "special admission": *Black Books,* vol. 1, vii; xi–xii; Richmond, 256.

88 £40 to £50: Winston, 34, quoting Wilfrid R. Prest, *The Inns of Court Under Elizabeth I*, 27–28.

88 elite of English society: Asa Briggs, *A Social History of England*, 122.

88 "moots" three times a week: Winston, 33.

88 no intention of studying years: Richmond, 258; Winston, 3–12.

88 records of Lincoln's Inn...Bankside brothels: Richmond, 258; Winston, 40.

88 "no more playing of dice": *Black Books*, 318 (November 13, 1556).

88 "Youth and age, lust and law": Winston, 23.

89 Antonio de Guevara: "Antonio de Guevara," Britannica Academic, *Encyclopedia Britannica*, April 8, 2019.

89 adviser to...Charles's son: Carolyn Nadeau, "Blood Mother/Milk Mother: Breastfeeding, the Family, and the State in Antonio de Guevara's *Relox de Principes* (*Dial of Princes*)," *Hispanic Review*, vol. 69 (Spring 2001), 153–174, 155.

89 bestseller on the Continent: Joseph Ramon Jones, *Antonio de Guevara*, 54.

89 "most widely read book": Quentin Skinner, *The Renaissance*, 215.

89 translated from Greek: Jones, 27–28; A. E. Waite, *"The Dial of Princes"* (review), *The Bookman*, 1920.

89 blasted Guevara...*Christian* prince: Marcel van Ackeren, ed., *A Companion to Marcus Aurelius*, 499; Jones, 60.

89 privileges of power are overshadowed: Jones, 53; A. R. Bossert III, "The Golden Chain: Royal Slavery, Sovereignty, and Servitude in Early Modern English Literature, 1550–1688," Thesis, University of Maryland, 2006, 141.

90 servant to his people: Jones, 56; Bossert, 141.

90 never justified in rebelling: Bossert, 57.

90 Other sections...meditation on death: Jones, 57–59.

91 refuge from the outside...Virgil: Winston, 106.

91 "A study of the Elizabethan translations": F. O. Matthiessen, *Translation*, 3.

91 *The Mirror for Magistrates*: Winston, 127–148.

91 *"The Mirror* imagines a space": Winston, 148.

92 great hall...first theaters: Hurst, 13.

92 half dozen other festivals: *Black Books*, xxxiii.

92 students tried ...parents' expense: Ringrose, 73–74.

92 served as Christmas Steward: *Black Books*, 218, 222, 224.

92 become master of revels: *Black Books*, 318; Alan H. Nelson and John R. Elliott, Jr, eds., *Records of Early English Drama: Inns of Court*, vol. 1, 80.

92 Masters fined North: Nelson, 81.

92 lives of the saints...sexual situations: Howard Norland, *Drama in Early Tudor Britain*, 5–15, 37–47, 50–60, 65–83.

94   "so simple a thing": Samuel Pepys, *The Diary of Samuel Pepys*, January 1, 1663/64.

94   "hardly a play, or 'drama' at all": Tony Tanner, *Prefaces to Shakespeare*, 469.

94   "arbitrary pattern of rises and falls": Jonathan Bate and Eric Rasmussen, eds., *King John and Henry VIII* (RSC), xiv.

94   "wheel of fortune": Lee Bliss, "The Wheel of Fortune and the Maiden Phoenix of Shakespeare's *King Henry the Eighth*," *English Literary History*, vol. 42 (1975), 1–25.

94   taken straight out of *The Mirror*: Paul Budra, A Mirror for Magistrates *and the* de casibus *Tradition*, 83.

96   procession around the Coliseum: Laura Serrano-Conde, "Pope Leads Way of the Cross Procession Dedicated to Migrants," *Agence EFE*, April 20, 2019; "Pope Francis Leads Via Crucis at Rome's Colosseum on Good Friday," *Vatican News*, April 19, 2019; "Pope Leads Good Friday Procession," *CBC News*, April 19, 2019.

97   most detailed set of stage directions: Gordon McMullan, ed., *Henry VIII* (Arden), 2.

99   "Gentleman" of "exceeding wealth"…people with interest: D. Allen Carroll, ed., *Greene's Groatsworth of Wit*, 43–46.

100   only hereditary peer: Eugene Bourgeois, *The Ruling Elite of Cambridgeshire*, 99.

100   gave Queen Mary £20: Loades, 360.

100   commission for suppression of heresy: Eamon Duffy, *Fires of Faith*, 93.

101   "as literature" in its own right: Ernest Gray, *Guevara, a Forgotten Renaissance Author*, 101–103.

101   ministers were preoccupied: *CSP Domestic: Edward VI, Mary, and Elizabeth, 1547–80*, vol. 11, 65–67, 71–72.

CHAPTER SIX: BLOOD AND REVENGE

Quotations from *Titus Andronicus* (*TA*) are as follows: "Vengeance is in my heart": *TA* 2.3.38–39; "would not for a million of gold": *TA* 2.1.49; "Emperor's palace": *TA* 2.1.46; "You sad-faced men": *TA* 5.3.67–72.

Quotations from Thomas North's Journal (*TNJ*) are as follows: "of such mixture of colours": *TNJ* 95.

Secondary historical sources for this chapter include: Sarah Gristwood, *Elizabeth and Leicester*; Chris Skidmore, *Death and the Virgin*; Anne Somerset, *Elizabeth I*; Alison Weir, *The Life of Elizabeth I*; Anna Whitelock, *The Queen's Bed*; Derek Wilson, *Sweet Robin* and *The Uncrowned Kings of England*.

103   with an artillery salute…congratulations: Marion Colthorpe, "The Elizabethan Court Day by Day: 1558," Folgerpedia, https://folgerpedia.folger.edu/The_Elizabethan _Court_Day_by_Day.

103   near the head: Elizabeth I's coronation procession, BL Egerton MS 3320.

103   Knight of the Bath: William Arthur Shaw, *The Knights of England*, 153; Clive Aslet, "By Order of the Queen, Chivalry Is not Dead," *The Telegraph*, May 9, 2014; Jocelyn Perkins, *The Most Honourable Order of the Bath*; James Charles Risk, *The History of the Order of the Bath*, 5–14.

104   carving the meat: C. G. Bayne, "The First House of Commons of Queen Elizabeth," *The English Historical Review*, vol. 23, no. 92 (October 1908), 643–682.

104   "he had not been merely playing a part": Virginia Rounding, *The Burning Time*, 372–373.

107   Seneca lived in a violent time: Jessica Winston, *Lawyers at Play*, 155; A. J. Boyle, *Tragic*

Seneca, 211–212; Gordon Braden, *Renaissance Tragedy and the Senecan Tradition*, 8; David Slavitt, *Seneca*, xi-xiv.

107 mad emperor Nero: "Nero (37 AD–68 AD)," BBC History, www.bbc.co.uk/history /historic_figures/nero.shtml.

108 urging dispassionate reason...results in excess: Braden, 1–30, 39; Helen Slaney, *The Senecan Aesthetic*, 21–24; Boyle, 24–34; Gregory Staley, *Seneca and the Idea of Tragedy*, 66–70, 93–95.

108 drew on Greek stories: William Calder, "Seneca: Tragedian of Imperial Rome," *Classical Journal*, vol. 72 (1976), 1–11, 9, quoted by Winston, 157.

108 warning to Nero...new, uncertain era: Winston, 157–160; Staley, 70–72; Boyle, 211–212.

108 Jasper Heywood: Howard Norland, *Neoclassical Tragedy in Elizabethan England*, 47.

108 *Troas*: Winston, 160–164; Boyle, 67–73; Thomas Kohn, *The Dramaturgy of Senecan Tragedy*, 110–114; Lucius Annaeus Seneca, John Fitch, ed., *Seneca: Tragedies, Volume 1*, 163–169.

108 *Thyestes*: Winston, 155–157; Boyle, 43–56; Kohn, 124–132; Seneca, John Fitch, ed., *Seneca: Tragedies, Volume 2*, 217–227; Seneca, Caryl Churchill, ed., *Thyestes*, xii; Seneca, P. J. Davis, ed. *Seneca: Thyestes*, 37–63.

110 new proposal of marriage...courtship of the queen: Henry James and Greg Walker, "The Marital Politics of Gorboduc," *The English Historical Review*, vol. 110, no. 435 (February 1995), 109–121; Greg Walker, *The Politics of Performance in Early Renaissance Drama*, 199–200, 208–209; Marie Axton, *The Queen's Two Bodies*, 40.

111 *Gorboduc*: "Gorboduc," *The Concise Oxford Companion to English Literature*, ed. Dinah Birch and Katy Hooper, 289; Marie Axton, "Robert Dudley and the Inner Temple Revels," *The Historical Journal*, vol. 13, no. 3 (September 1970), 365–378; Axton, *Two Bodies*, 45–48; Norland, 71–81; Walker, 201–204; Thomas Norton and Thomas Sackville, *Gorboduc*.

111 form was a bloody Senecan tragedy: Norton, xvi-xvii; Norland, 74.

111 "such one born within your native land": Norton, 5.2.170–173.

111 first original English tragedy: Norton, xiii; Norland, 74.

111 commentary on...Elizabeth's succession: Norton, xxiii-xxviii.

111 strike against Mary Queen of Scots...fatal option (Erik): Walker, 205–207, 213–215.

111 Elizabeth ordered Dudley: Norton, xiii.

113 mashup of Seneca's greatest hits: Robert Miola, *Shakespeare and Classical Tragedy*, 16–32.

113 "*Titus Andronicus* is perhaps best understood": R. J. Kaufmann, "The Seneca Perspective and the Shakespearean Poetic," *Comparative Drama*, vol. 1, no. 3 (Fall 1967), 182–198.

113 "the most incorrect...than a structure": Quoted in Russ McDonald, ed., *Titus Andronicus* (Pelican), xxix; Jonathan Bate, ed., *Titus Andronicus* (Arden), 78.

113 "scarcely be tolerable": quoted in Leslie Dunton-Downer and Alan Riding, *Essential Shakespeare Handbook*, 302.

113 "one of the stupidest": quoted in McDonald, xxx.

113 "explosion of rancid irony": Harold Bloom, *Shakespeare: The Invention of the Human*, 83.

113 immature juvenilia: McDonald, xxix; Bate, 3.

113 black comedy, melodrama: Tony Tanner, *Prefaces to Shakespeare*, 588.

113 or parody: Marjorie Garber, *Shakespeare After All*, 84; Bloom, 78.

113 revival of the play...Brian Cox: Bate, 1, 11.

113 Julie Taymor's: Thomas Cartelli, "Taymor's 'Titus' in Time and Space: Surrogation

and Interpolation," *Renaissance Drama*, New Series, vol. 34, *Media, Technology, and Performance* (2005), 163–184.

114 never entirely gone away: McDonald, xxx; Bate, 3.

114 most Senecan of Shakespearean tragedies: Miola, 13; Stanley Wells, *Shakespeare's Tragedies*, 15.

114 *Titus and Vespasian*: Eleanor Grace Clark, *"Titus and Vespasian,"* *Modern Language Notes*, vol. 41, no. 8 (December 1926), 523–527; Howard DeW. Fuller, "The Sources of *Titus Andronicus*," *PMLA*, vol. 16, no. 1 (1901), 1–65; Dennis McCarthy and June Schlueter, "A Shakespeare/North Collaboration: *Titus Andronicus* and *Titus and Vespasian*," *Shakespeare Survey*, vol. 67 (2014), 85–101; Terence G. Schoone-Jongen, *Shakespeare's Companies*, 151–155.

114 King of the Goths: McCarthy and Schlueter, 88; Franklin Daniel Scott, *Sweden, the Nation's History*, 66; Sydney Charleston, *Historical and Statistical Handbook, by Order of the Swedish Government* (US Government Printing Office, 1914), 188. The Goths, a nomadic Germanic people, originally hailed from Götaland, in what is now southern Sweden.

114 friends with Thomas Norton: Anton Francesco Doni, Donald Beecher, John A. Butler, and Carmine Di Biase, eds., *The Moral Philosophy of Doni*, 204.

114 other fodder as well: During North's trip to Rome, the delegation also passed through the Italian city of Ferrara, where the duke's private secretary, the Italian playwright Cinthio, was an early adopter of Senecan tragedies—the most famous of which even includes a scene in which the main character carries the dismembered head and hands of a family member. As Tempera remarks (237), "Much of what we call Renaissance Senecanism is really Italian Senecanism: *Titus Andronicus* is more like a play of [Cinthio] than a play of Seneca." Boyle, 150–151; Charlton, 65–66, 79–94; Mariangela Tempera, "'Horror…is the sinews of fable': Giraldi Cinthio's Works and Elizabethan Tragedy," *Actes du Congrès de la Société Française Shakespeare*, no. 22 (2005), 235–247; Miola, 4, 12.

114 painted by, who else: *"The Triumph of Titus and Vespasian,"* Louvre Museum Official Website, http://cartelen.louvre.fr/cartelen/visite?srv=car_not_frame&idNotice=13889&langue=en.

116 German version: *"Tito Andronico,"* Early Modern German Shakespeare, http://www.unige.ch/emgs/plays/tito-andronico-und-der-hoffertigen-kayserin-tito-andronico-and-haughty-empress.

116 "a conquest on the Goths": Anonymous, *A Knack to Know a Knave*, quoted in McCarthy and Schlueter, 98.

116 historian uncovered an illustration: Bate, 38–41.

117 she argues the illustration: June Schlueter, "Rereading the Peacham Drawing," *Shakespeare Quarterly*, vol. 50, no. 2 (Summer 1999), 171–184.

119 new publication, *Shakespeare Bulletin*: "Shakespeare Bulletin Records, 1982–2003," Skillman Library, Lafayette College, https://archives.lafayette.edu/wp-content/uploads/2013/06/shakespearebulletin_0.pdf.

120 Gail Kern Paster…its front page: Scott Heller, "A Fresh Look at a Cryptic Drawing Puts 'Titus Andronicus' in a New Light," *Chronicle of Higher Education*, June 4, 1999.

120 another version of the paper: June Schlueter, "A Tragic Misunderstanding," *Times Literary Supplement*, February 19, 1999, 16.

120 Richard Levin wrote another article: Richard Levin, "The Longleat Manuscript and *Titus Andronicus*," *Shakespeare Quarterly*, vol. 53, no. 3 (Autumn 2002), 323–340.

120 there was the date…1574, or 1575: Dennis McCarthy, *North of Shakespeare*, 133–139.

121 Scholars agree…1605: Bate, 39. Bate further speculates that the last letter could also

stand for *quartodecimo* (14) or *quintodecimo* (15), making the date 1614 or 1615. This would be in keeping with his hypothesis that the text in the Longleat manuscript comes not from Quarto 1 of Titus, published in 1595, but from Quarto 2, published in 1600, or Quarto 3, published in 1611.

122   Henry Peacham wasn't born...the Younger: McCarthy, *North*, 139–141.

125   Edward left a third: Will of Edward North, 1564, TNA PROB 11/48/64. Transcribed by Nina Green, 2018, Oxford Shakespeare website, www.oxford-shakespeare.com.

125   not unusual...however, was extreme: Zouheir Jamoussi, *Primogeniture and Entail in England*, 32–75; Lawrence Stone, *The Family, Sex, and Marriage*, 87–90; Joan Thirsk, "The European Debate on Customs of Inheritance, 1500–1700," in Jack Goody, Joan Thirsk, and E. P. Thompson, eds., *Family and Inheritance*, 177–191; Joan Thirsk, "Younger Sons in the Seventeenth Century," *History*, vol. 54, no. 182 (October 1969), 358–377; Linda Pollock, "Younger Sons in Tudor and Stuart England," *History Today*, vol. 39, issue 6 (June 1989), 23–29.

125   "first came to this city"..."bequeath you": D. Allen Carroll, ed., *Greene's Groatsworth of Wit*, 46–47.

CHAPTER SEVEN: BY ANY OTHER NAME

Quotations from Shakespeare's plays in this chapter are as follows: "that stretches from an inch": *Romeo and Juliet* 2.4.82–83; "not of the blood royal": *Henry IV, Part 1* 1.2.137–138; "word that might be to the prejudice of": *Henry VIII* 2.4.151–152; "noisome weeds...superfluous branches": *Richard II* 3.4.29–66.

Quotations from *Titus Andronicus (TA)* in this chapter are as follows: "I have been troubled in my sleep": *TA* 2.2.9; "God forbid I should be so bold to press": *TA* 4.3.91; "When heaven doth weep": *TA* 3.1.221–29.

Quotations from Thomas North's *The Dial of Princes (Dial)* in this chapter are as follows: "I have been troubled": *Dial* 543; "God forbid that I should be": *Dial* xi; "Lady Lavinia...become a deluge": *Dial* 448; "she scratched her face": *Dial* 489.

Secondary historical and biographical sources for this chapter include: Peter Ackroyd, *Shakespeare: The Biography*; Jonathan Bate, *The Soul of the Age*; David Bevington, *Shakespeare and Biography*; Bill Bryson, *Shakespeare*; Stephen Greenblatt, *Will in the World*; Lois Potter, *The Life of William Shakespeare*; Samuel Schoenbaum, *Shakespeare's Lives*; Michael Wood, *Shakespeare*.

129   "80 percent the author's imagination": Bryson, 16; Bevington, *Shakespeare and Biography*, 1.

129   "On only a handful"...single copy: Bryson, 9. The possible exception is three pages of a play called *Sir Thomas More* that some scholars believe Shakespeare helped write.

129   Scholars only know...after he died: Bryson, 18; Lukas Erne, *Beyond The Spanish Tragedy: A Study of the Works of Thomas Kyd*, 6.

129   "Will almost certainly attended": Greenblatt, 26.

130   "is likely to have seen": Greenblatt, 31.

130   "All of Shakespeare's early history plays": Greenblatt, 113.

131   It's anyone's guess: According to Bryson, "depending on whose authority you favor, Shakespeare's debut written offering might be any of at least eight works: *Comedy of Errors, Two Gentlemen of Verona, Taming of the Shrew, Titus Andronicus, King John, Henry VI 1, 2, 3*—hardly any two lists are the same."

131   fit of pique: Denise Winterman, "The Man Who Demolished Shakespeare's House,"
      BBC News Magazine, March 7, 2013, www.bbc.com/news/magazine-21587468;
      Ackroyd, 326; Andrew McConnell Stott, *What Blest Genius?*, 32; Schoenbaum,
      108–109.

132   half of them published: Bryson, 162; Schoenbaum, 30.

132   less than 10 percent—still exist: Bryson, 18–19.

132   Puritans banned public theater...whole subplots: Stott, xv-xvii; Gary Taylor, *Reinventing Shakespeare*, 7, 11–12.

132   "which featured flying witches": Stott, xvii.

132   "often obscures his meaning: John Dryden, *Troilus and Cressida*, Preface (1679).

132   gathered speed...wildly on the heath: Taylor, 66, 121; Stott, xviii, 26–29, 39–40.

133   "writers fell over one another": Taylor, 121.

133   "most famous man": Stott, xviii.

133   Shakespeare Jubilee: Stott, xix, 77, 87–88, 129–132, 135.

133   souvenirs...mulberry tree: Stott, 129–132; James Shapiro, *Contested Will*, 28–29.

133   "English children know him": Stott, 177.

133   reconstruct Shakespeare's life: Taylor, 169–173.

133   American critics and audiences: Taylor, 199–204.

134   Delia Bacon: Warren Hope and Kim R. Holston, *The Shakespeare Controversy*, 1–5;
      Shapiro, 84–87.

134   critique of the monarchy: Hope, 16–21.

134   Ralph Waldo Emerson and Walt Whitman: Hope, 29.

134   reveal a "cipher": Frank W. Wadsworth, *The Poacher from Stratford*, 42–43.

134   Ignatius Donnelly...spell out his narrative: William Friedman and Elizebeth Friedman,
      The Shakespearean Ciphers Examined, 27, 37–44; Shapiro, 121; Wadsworth, 55.

135   "Nothing like it has appeared": Hope, 54.

135   Orville Ward Owen: Wadsworth, 63.

135   William Stone Booth: Friedman, 116–146.

135   established fad: William Shepard Walsh, *Handy-Book of Literary Curiosities*, 12.

135   Helen Keller..."whose godlike head": Shapiro, 116.

135   Mark Twain...Twain argued: Hope, 38.

136   "The moment he departs": Mark Twain, *Is Shakespeare Dead?*, 14–17.

136   "not by Shakespeare": Hope, 70.

136   already falling out of favor: Brenda James and W. D. Rubinstein, *The Truth Will Out*,
      116–119.

136   held strong into the 1930s: Wadsworth, 67–93.

136   with the ruthless moneylender Shylock: J. Thomas Looney, *"Shakespeare" Identified in
      Edward de Vere, the Seventeenth Earl of Oxford*, 2.

136   drew up a list of attributes...searched anthology: Looney, 84–104, 108; Hope, 100–
      102; Shapiro, 172–173.

136   Edward De Vere: James, 71–73; Hope 103, 106; Joseph Sobran, *Alias: Shakespeare*,
      108–142.

137   "both talented and violent": James, 73.

137   officious minister Polonius...under Shakespeare's name: Looney, 214–227; Sobran, 111.

137   problem with this theory: Hope, 108–111.

137   Looney explained that away: Looney, 345–368

137   psychologist Sigmund Freud: Shapiro, 153–164, 182–189; Hope, 123.

137   most surprisingly, Christopher Marlowe: Shapiro, 7; Hope, 85–86.

138 Charlton Ogburn Jr's....same road: Charles Ogburn, *The Mysterious William Shakespeare*, 528–529.

138 Supreme Court justices considered...reversed their positions: Tyler Fo, "Justice Stevens's Dissenting Shakespeare Theory," *The New Yorker*, July 29, 2019.

138 PBS's...*New York Times*: Chris Jones, "The Great Shakespearean Debate," *Chicago Tribune*, October 20, 2002.

138 Derek Jacobi ...Mark Rylance: "List of notable signatories," The Shakespeare Authorship Coalition, https://doubtaboutwill.org/signatories/notable.

138 came across an online trailer: "*Anonymous*—Trailer," Sony Pictures Entertainment, April 7, 2011, YouTube, http://www.youtube.com/watch?v=uBmnkk0QW3Q.

138 film, by Roland Emmerich: "*Anonymous* (2011)," Internet Movie Database, http://www.imdb.com/title/tt1521197.

139 autobiographical parallels: These elements are addressed in this book in chapters 9, 12, and 15, respectively.

140 scene in the 2010 movie: "*The Social Network* (2010): Facebook Creating Scene," IlluminaTV World, YouTube, http://www.youtube.com/watch?v=aMuBngVO6QE.

140 "silly...not dumb enough": "Critics Reviews for *Anonymous*," Rotten Tomatoes (website), www.rottentomatoes.com/m/anonymous_2011.

140 only half of its $30 million: "*Anonymous* (2011)," IMDB.

141 across an article...and Thomas Kyd: Gaëlle Faure, "Plagiarism Software Finds a New Shakespeare Play," *Time*, October 20, 2009.

141 he'd even been knighted: "Professor Brian Vickers Awarded Knighthood" (press release), School of Advanced Studies, University of London, January 7, 2008, www.sas.ac.uk/about-us/news/professor-brian-vickers-awarded-knighthood.

142 up to a dozen new plays a year: Roslyn Lander Knutson, *Playing Companies and Commerce in Shakespeare's Time*, 40–41.

142 "Plays were only rarely regarded": Jonathan Hope, *The Authorship of Shakespeare's Plays*, 3; the analogy is also made by Lene Petersen, *Shakespeare's Errant Texts*, 15.

142 40 shillings...£1 to £8: Knutson, 35–36, 50.

142 up to four writers: Knutson, 50–51; Heather Anne Hirschfeld, *Joint Enterprises*, 17.

142 "over half of the plays": Hirschfeld, 1.

142 against the company's interest: Jonathan Hope, 3–4.

142 from 1576 to 1597...first eight plays: Petersen, 15.

142 Ben Jonson...freely reworked: Petersen, 11–16.

143 didn't even enter the English language: Brian Vickers, *Shakespeare, Co-Author*, 523; "plagiary, 1. a" and "plagiarism 1," *Oxford English Dictionary*.

143 "cannot form any reliable impression": Vickers, 1.

143 six original handwritten play manuscripts: James Purkis, "Shakespeare's Straying Manuscripts," in Margaret Jane Kidnie and Sonia Massai, *Shakespeare and Textual Studies*, 39.

143 turned to the text itself: Potter, 18–27; Plutarch, Paul Turner, ed., *Selected Lives*, 3–6.

143 *Two Noble Kinsmen...Timon of Athens*: Vickers, 333–432, 244–290.

143 "image clusters": Potter, 24. This phenomenon was explored most thoroughly by Edward Allworthy Armstrong in *Shakespeare's Imagination* (1946), and Kenneth Muir, *Shakespeare as Collaborator* (1960).

143 "unworthy of the Bard": Vickers, viii–ix.

144 added Shakespeare's late romance...*Henry VI* plays: most notably Cyrus Hoy with Fletcher and Beaumont, and David Lake.

144   *Edward III*: Folger Shakespeare Library, "The Raigne of King Edward the Third, 1596," Shakespeare Documented, https://shakespearedocumented.folger.edu.

144   "The more important the play": Vickers, quoting MacDonald Jackson, in Jackson, *Studies in Attribution*, 161.

144   alliteration or polysyllabic words: Hugh Craig and Arthur F. Kinney, *Shakespeare, Computers, and the Mystery of Authorship*, 10–11; Vickers, ix.

144   "an individual's DNA": Craig, 4–5.

144   "powerful but not infallible": Craig, 24.

144   "having designed it badly": Vickers, 95.

144   "methodology by which Vickers investigated": Gary Taylor and Gabriel Egan, eds., *The New Oxford Shakespeare: Authorship Companion*, 49.

144   whole field into question: Vickers, 101.

145   depend on having a control: Jeffrey Masten, *Textual Intercourse*, 19.

145   WCopyfind: "About This Site," The Plagiarism Resource Site, https://plagiarism .bloomfieldmedia.com/sample-page.

147   sent a very different email: Sir Brian Vickers declined an interview for this book.

148   exact quote from Max Planck: Pierre Azoulay, et al., "Does Science Advance One Funeral at a Time?," *American Economic Review*, vol. 109, no. 8 (2019), 2889–2920, 2889. The actual quote, by the originator of quantum physics, is: "A new scientific truth does not triumph by convincing its opponents and making them see the light, but rather because its opponents eventually die, and a new generation grows up that is familiar with it." But it's often paraphrased as McCarthy does.

149   "tore her golden hair": "Prose history of *Titus Andronicus*," 41–42, in Eugene M. Waith, ed., *Titus Andronicus* (Oxford), Appendix A.

150   Within a year, the paper appeared: Dennis McCarthy and June Schlueter, "A Shakespeare/North Collaboration: *Titus Andronicus* and *Titus and Vespasian*," *Shakespeare Survey*, vol. 67 (2014), 85–101.

CHAPTER EIGHT: WONDERS OF THE WORLD ABROAD

Quotations from *The Two Gentlemen of Verona* (*2GV*), *The Taming of the Shrew* (*TOTS*), and *Othello* (*O*) in this chapter are as follows: "I would rather entreat": *2GV* 1.1.5–8; "Since for the great desire": *TOTS* 1.1.1–9; "Let's be no stoics…well dost thou advise": *TOTS* 1.1.31–41; "thou whoreson ass": *2GV* 2.5.41; "fair, boy, as well favoured": *2GV* 2.1.47; "dispatch me hence": *2GV* 2.7.88; "That my love may appear": *2GV* 5.4.82; "upon the rising": *2GV* 5.2.49; "a hundred milch kine to the pail": *TOTS* 2.1.355–356; "plate and gold…Turkish cushions": *TOTS* 2.1.344–354; "master, I have watched": *TOTS* 4.2.60–64; "Disguised thus to get your love": *TOTS* 3.1.33; "much like his master's ass": *O* 1.1.49–50; "wear my heart upon my sleeve": *O* 1.1.66–67; "Virtue? A fig": *O* 1.3.322–323; "lead to the Sagittary": *O* 1.1.162; "double knavery": *O* 1.3.395; "What you know": *O* 5.2.310.

Quotations from Thomas North's Journal (*TNJ*), *The Moral Philosophy of Doni* (*Doni*), and *Plutarch's Lives* (*PL*) are as follows: "heretofore tasted…only Maecenas": *Doni* Epistle; "shall be a looking-glass": *Doni* Prologue; "kissed in the very mouth": *Doni* 38–39; "whoreson cankered mule": *Doni* 99; "fair, well favoured boy": *Doni* 88; "Dispatch, get thee hence": *Doni* 69; "We rode as between gardens": *TNJ* 82; "milch kine to the pail…make and dress it up": *PL* 325–326; "O Master, I have had an ill night": *Doni* 81; "a great bundle of straw": *Doni* 29–30; "provender pricked him": *Doni* 41; "pen of his heart": *Doni* 60; "Tell me not of honesty":

Doni 52; "double treason": *Doni* 75; "All is well that endeth well": *Doni* 96; "It is nothing true": *Doni* 109.

Secondary historical sources for this chapter include: Sarah Gristwood, *Elizabeth and Leicester*; Anne Somerset, *Elizabeth I*; Alison Weir, *The Life of Elizabeth I*; Anna Whitelock, *The Queen's Bed*; Derek Wilson, *Sweet Robin* and *The Uncrowned Kings of England*.

152   "freedom of the city": Tom Lockwood, "North, Sir Thomas," *ODNB*; Ian Mortimer, *The Time Traveler's Guide to Elizabethan England*, 40; Stephen Porter, *Everyday Life in Tudor London*, 29.

152   newly elected alderman: John Craig, "North, Roger, second Baron North," *ODNB*; Frances Bushby, *Three Men of the Tudor Time*, 51.

152   dedicated to Robert Dudley: Anton Francesco Doni, Donald Beecher, John A. Butler, and Carmine Di Biase, eds., *The Moral Philosophy of Doni*, 97.

152   *Supposes*: Jessica Winston, *Lawyers at Play*, 202–204.

153   must have made a "grand tour": Anton Francesco Doni, Joseph Jacobs, ed., *The Earliest English Version of the Fables of Bidpai; Moral Philosophy*, lii.

154   Juno, representing marriage: Winston, 197–198; Diego Guzmán da Silva to King Philip II of Spain, March 12, 1565, *CSP Simancas (Spain)*.

154   *Jocasta*: Winston, 205–208.

154   only surviving manuscript: *Jocasta*, BL Add MS 34063.

154   letter from the Spanish ambassador: da Silva to the King, May 11, 1566, *CSP Simancas (Spain)*.

155   burgeoning friendship with Leicester: "North, Roger," *ODNB*, states the two were "close friends from the late 1560s." See also Roger Lord North to Leicester, March 29, 1566, *CSP Domestic*, in which Roger asks Leicester to "continue his friendship towards his sister."

155   "discourage the suit": Bushby, 52.

155   cutting through the German petty states: "Papers relating to the proposed marriage of Queen Elizabeth...," *Archaeologia*, vol. 35 (1853), 202–212.

156   queen's reply on New Year's Eve: Earl of Sussex to William Cecil, January 3, 1568, *CSP Foreign*.

156   "what great peril grows": Sussex to Cecil, January 10, 1568, *CSP Foreign*.

156   appeared in Venice...fables along the way: Doni, *Moral Philosophy*, 18–27; Doni, *English Version*, viii; Maria Grazia Bellorini, "Thomas North traduttore di Anton Francesco Doni," *Aevum*: Rassegna di Scienze, Storiche, Linguistiche e Filologiche, vol. 38 (1964), 84–103; "Tracce di cultura italiana nella Formazione di Thomas North," *Aevum*, vol. 41 (1967), 333–338.

157   "stories about animals": Doni, *Moral Philosophy*, 16.

157   "embellishes the tales...foolish bird?": Doni, *Moral Philosophy*, 50–55.

158   "the vicarious experience": Michele Marrapodi, *Shakespeare and the Italian Renaissance*, 8.

158   based it on a source play: Jonathan Bate and Eric Rasmussen, eds., *Two Gentlemen of Verona* (RSC), viii; Lois Potter, *The Life of William Shakespeare*, 149–150.

158   "is unlikely to have had": Bate, *Two Gentlemen of Verona*, viii.

159   *Philemon and Philecia*: Martin Wiggins and Catherine Richardson, *British Drama 1533–1642*, 109 (558).

159   Spanish version: George Ticknor, *History of Spanish Literature*, vol. 3, 97.

159   a disturbing scene: Jeffrey Masten, "*The Two Gentlemen of Verona*: A Modern Perspective," in Barbara Mowat and Paul Werstine, eds., *Two Gentlemen of Verona* (Folger), 200; Janet

Adelman, "Male Bonding in Shakespeare's Comedies," in C. L. Barber, Peter Erickson, and Coppélia Kahn, eds., *Shakespeare's "Rough Magic,"* 76–79.

159   "the eagerness of Proteus": Kate Emery Pogue, *Shakespeare's Family*, 46

159   only underscored: Bate, *Two Gentlemen of Verona*, xiii–xiv.

159   "play has insistently staged": Masten, *Textual Intercourse*, 199–221.

160   "intellectual journey of the mind": Marrapodi, *Renaissance*, 2.

160   soaked up Italian culture: Murray Levith, *Shakespeare's Italian Settings and Plays*, 90; Laura Tosi and Shaul Bassi, *Visions of Venice in Shakespeare*, 4–5.

161   "strained and unconvincing": Levith, 89.

161   discovery of old maps: Richard Paul Roe, *The Shakespeare Guide to Italy*, 35–62.

161   magnet for a certain class: Kenneth Bartlett, *The English in Italy*, 139.

162   old Italian word for "inn": *Dizionario delle linque Italiana ed Inglise*, 1760; Tim Jepson, *National Geographic Traveler: Italy*, 350.

163   unabashedly sexist: Stephen Orgel, ed., *The Taming of the Shrew* (Pelican), xxix–xxxi.

163   attracted to her passionate spirit: David Bevington, *The Complete Works of Shakespeare*, 110; Orgel, xxxvi–xxxvii.

163   truly submissive or merely playacting: Jonathan Bate and Eric Rasmussen, eds., *Taming of the Shrew* (RSC), xi–xix.

163   Royal Shakespeare Company: "The Taming of the Shrew," Royal Shakespeare Company (website), 2019, www.rsc.org.uk/the-taming-of-the-shrew.

163   one of Shakespeare's earliest: Bate, *Taming of the Shrew*, 114.

163   Scholars long believed: Barbara Mowat and Paul Werstine, eds., *Taming of the Shrew* (Folger), 233; Bate, *Taming of the Shrew*, ix.

163   a sort of *Ur-Shrew*: Michael J. Redmond, *Shakespeare, Politics, and Italy*, 125.

163   "pleasant garden of Italy": North isn't the only English writer to refer to Lombardy as a garden—the same reference is made by expat Italian John Florio in 1591, who says, "Lombardy is the garden of the world," and in a popular 1611 travelogue by Thomas Coryat, who writes, "As Italy is the garden of the World, so is Lombardy the garden of Italy." But both postdate North's journal by thirty years. See Levith, 43.

165   stock characters…scenarios: Winifred Smith, *The Commedia dell'Arte*, 1–14; Lynne Lawner, *Harlequin on the Moon*, 16–23.

165   as far back…abroad as well: Lawner, 11; John Rudlin and Olly Crick, *Commedia dell'Arte: A Handbook for Troupes*, 6, 14–24, 57–59.

165   *innomorati…zanni*: Lawner, 35–58.

166   Arlecchino: Lawner, 39; David J. George and Christopher J. Gossip, eds., *Studies in the Commedia dell'Arte*, 3.

166   *capitano*: Lawner, 59–60; Rudlin, 8.

166   quick wordplay…musical numbers: Smith, 18.

166   "feigning of madness": Lawner, 25.

166   *commedia* archetypes in the canon: Artemis Preeshl, *Shakespeare and Commedia dell'Arte*, xiv; Andrew Grewar, "Shakespeare and the Actors of the Commedia dell'Arte," in George, 14.

166   classic *zannis*: Preeshl, 111–112.

166   "among the funniest scenes": Mowat, *Two Gentlemen*, xiv.

166   even more explicit: Grewar, in George, 31–23.

166   direct reference to the Pantalone: Preeshl, 145–147, 153–154; Grewar, in George, 18–19.

166   As early as 1546…stop around 1578: Kathleen M. Lea, *Italian Popular Comedy*, 352–354; Grewar, in George, 15–16.

167   English plays employing Italian archetypes: Michele Marrapodi, "Shakespeare's Romantic Italy: Novelistic, Theatrical, and Cultural Transactions in the Comedies," *Italian Culture in the Drama of Shakespeare*, 52–53.

167   mythic capital: Graham Holderness, *Shakespeare and Venice*, 27–32.

167   political beacon...tolerantly side by side: Tosi, 68–70; John Drakakis, ed., *The Merchant of Venice* (Arden); Holderness, 32–38.

167   darker side: Tosi, 72; Holderness, 38–43.

167   Courtesans paraded...white makeup: Shaul Bassi and Alberto Toso Fei, *Shakespeare in Venice*, 117; Holderness, 43–46.

168   "more liberty to sin": Levith, 6; Marrapodi, *Renaissance*, 258.

168   a wary truce...or face invasion: Thomas Madden, *Venice: A New History*, 324–328.

168   launching their attack: Roe, 175; Dragoş Cosmescu, *Venetian Renaissance Fortifications in the Mediterranean*, 174.

168   Shakespeare's *Othello* are set: Tosi, 21, 48.

168   tied to the tensions: Bassi, 172.

169   *Othello*'s source: Kenneth Muir, *The Sources of Shakespeare's Plays*, 182

169   it also departs from it: Tosi, 60; Karen Zych Galbraith, "Tracing a Villain: Typological Intertexuality in the Works of Pinter, Webster, Cinthio, and Shakespeare," in Marrapodi, *Renaissance,* 107, 117; Muir, 191–192.

169   melodramatic cartoon: Tosi, 47.

169   "motiveless malignity": Bassi, 35; Levith, 35.

169   from the chivalric romance: Jason Lawrence, "'The story is extant, and writ in very choice Italian': Shakespeare's dramatizations of Cinthio," in Michele Marrapodi, *Shakespeare, Italy, and Intertextuality,* 100.

171   Sagitary: Roe, 163–164; Bassi, 85.

171   different explanation...arrow makers: Roe, 166–167.

172   routine troop movement: Tosi, 44; David McPherson, *Shakespeare, Jonson, and the Myth of Venice,* 77; Muir, 186.

172   mirrors many of the tropes: Pamela Allen Brown, "Othello italicized: Xenophobia and the erosion of tragedy," in Marrapodi, *Intertextuality,* 145.

173   bloody siege...Turks at sea: Madden, 331–334.

CHAPTER NINE: TRUE LOVE NEVER DID RUN SMOOTH

Quotations from *Love's Labour's Lost* (LLL) and *A Midsummer Night's Dream* (AMND) are as follows: "true love never did run smooth": *AMND* 1.1.132–134; "Great Hercules is presented...in his manus": *LLL* 5.2.584–587; "once I sat upon a promontory...Fetch me this herb": *AMND* 2.1.149–174; "This green plot shall be": *AMND* 3.1.3–4; "Give me your hands": *AMND* 5.1.432–433.

Secondary historical sources for this chapter include: Stephen Greenblatt, *Will in the World*; Sarah Gristwood, *Elizabeth and Leicester*; Elizabeth Jenkins, *Elizabeth and Leicester*; Trea Martyn, *Queen Elizabeth in the Garden*; Anne Somerset, *Elizabeth I*; Nicola Tallis, *Elizabeth's Rival*; Alison Weir, *The Life of Elizabeth I*; Anna Whitelock, *The Queen's Bed*; Derek Wilson, *Sweet Robin* and *The Uncrowned Kings of England*.

175   one of the first lords...across the land: Sally Beth MacLean, "Tracking Leicester's Men: the Patronage of a Performance Troupe," in Paul Whitfield White and Suzanne

R. Westfall, eds., *Shakespeare and Theatrical Patronage*, 250–252; John Tucker Murray, *English Dramatic Companies 1558–1642*, vol. 1, no. 26; Richard Dutton, *Shakespeare, Court Dramatist*, 14–15.

176   received a set fee: Dutton, 13.

176   chief officer of the royal household: Alison Weir, *Henry VIII*, 58; Andrew Gurr, *The Shakespearean Playing Companies*, 61.

176   ultimately outdid him: Gurr, 167, 182, 193.

176   royal patent from the queen: Maclean, 260; Murray, 27–28; E. K. Chambers, *The Elizabethan Stage*, ii.87.

176   new status to players: Gurr, 36–37; Wilson, *Uncrowned Kings,* 297.

177   Roger North sat: Frances Bushby, *Three Men of the Tudor Time*, 57.

177   "unprecedented levels": Eugene Bourgeois, *The Ruling Elite of Cambridgeshire*, 210–211.

177   account book from the period: "Account of personal, household, and estate expenditure of Roger from July 1572 to Sept 1573," Bodl., North b.12, ff. 49–54v.

177   1572 bill of sale: Thomas North to Leonard Beall, TNA E211/536.

177   collecting an annuity: The "anuete" is listed in Roger's account book as "my sister North her husband's anuete." Since Roger's younger sister had died, and his older sister was now Lady Worcester, this must be Thomas's wife, Elizabeth. In the next entry, Roger lists charges for riding "sister North" to London.

179   St. Bartholomew's Day Massacre: Robert Jean Knecht, *The French Religious Wars*, 163–169; Robert Jean Knecht, *Catherine de' Medici*, 158–163; Mack Holt, *The French Wars of Religion*, 84–95; Dana Schwartz, "The Wedding Ended in Blood," *Noble Blood* (podcast), November 26, 2019.

179   lay siege to their seaside citadel: Knecht, *Wars*, 170–178.

179   ended in fiasco: Knecht, *Wars*, 178–185.

179   Norths watched Alençon…"has not taken place": Martin Hume, *The Courtships of Queen Elizabeth*, 181; Bushby, 66–67.

180   congratulate the new king: "Instructions to Lord North, in special embassage to the French King," September 5, 1574, *CSP Foreign*.

180   urge him to make peace: "Private Memorial to Lord North touching his Charge," October 5, 1574, *CSP Foreign*.

180   the "perfect courtier": Valentine Dale to Francis Walsingham, November 4, 1574, *CSP Foreign*.

180   had a different opinion: Giovanni Francesco Morosini to the Signory, November 2, 1574, *CSP Venice*.

180   performance of *commedia dell'arte*: John Rudlin and Olly Crick, *Commedia dell'Arte: A Handbook for Troupes*, 17.

180   ballet…"flying squadron": Ewa Kociszewska, "War and Seduction in Cybele's Garden: Contextualizing the Ballet des Polonais," *Renaissance Quarterly*, vol. 65, no. 3 (Fall 2012), 809–863; see also Knecht, *Catherine*, 235.

180   Thomas left early: La Mothe-Fénélon to Henri III, November 18, 1574, in Bertrand de Salignac Fénélon, *Correspondance diplomatique de Bertrand de Salignac de la Mothe Fénélon*, vi, 292.

181   he brought back reports: La Mothe-Fénélon to Henri III, November 20, 1574, *Correspondance*, vi, 295–296.

181   simplest plot: George Richard Hibbard, ed., *Love's Labour's Lost* (Oxford), 12–13.

181   quintessential braggart…term *zanni*: Murray Levith, *Shakespeare's Italian Settings and Plays,* 3; Andrew Grewar, "Shakespeare and the Actors of the *Commedia dell'Arte*,"

in David George and Christopher Gossip, eds., *Studies in the Commedia dell'Arte*, 35–39.

181   without a recognizable source: John Pendergast, Love's Labour's Lost: *A Guide to the Play*, 29.

181   "celebration of the energy": Tony Tanner, *Prefaces to Shakespeare*, 76.

181   linguistic festival…topical allusions: Pendergast, xix, 118; Herbert Alexander Ellis, *Shakespeare's Lusty Punning in* Love's Labour's Lost; Joseph Sobran, *Alias: Shakespeare*, 185.

181   killed in the sixteenth-century court: William C. Carroll, *"Love's Labour's Lost:* A Modern Perspective," in Barbara Mowat and Paul Werstine, eds., *Love's Labour's Lost* (Folger), 255; Jonathan Bate and Eric Rasmussen, eds., *Love's Labour's Lost* (RSC), vii.

181   nearly impossible to perform: Hibbard, 4.

181   tried in vain to unpack: Hibbard, 49–51; Bate, xiv–xv; Sobran, 185; Geoffrey Bullough, *Narrative and Dramatic Sources of Shakespeare*, vol. 8, 428–429; Pendergast, 5.

182   on opposite sides…a fit subject: Pendergast, 5.

182   "singularly muddle-headed, or else willfully frivolous, manner": Frances A. Yates, *A Study of* Love's Labour's Lost, 3.

182   trip by Marguerite to Navarre: Peter Holland, ed., *Love's Labour's Lost* (Pelican), xxxviii.

182   first play to bear: Pendergast, 1–3; Yates, 1.

182   witty pageboy Moth: Bate, xi.

183   "not so dangerous a creature": Thomas Wilkes to Francis Walsingham, November 8, 1574, *CSP Foreign*; Bushby, 69.

183   two female dwarfs: La Mothe to Catherine de Medici, December 28, 1574, *Correspondance*, vi, 330–335; Bushby, 70.

183   jester into North's quarters…wars on the Continent: La Mothe to Henri III, December 28, 1574, *Correspondance*, vi, 325–326; Bushby, 70–71.

183   arrived back in London: La Mothe to Henri III, December 12, *Correspondance*, vi, 316.

183   to tell the queen: La Mothe to Catherine de Medici, December 18, *Correspondance*, vi, 320–321; Marion E. Colthorpe, ECDbD, 1574, 45.

183   gave La Mothe a tongue-lashing: La Mothe to Henri III, *Correspondance*, vi, 329–335; Colthorpe, 46; Bushby 75.

183   so stung, he wrote: "Letter from the Lord Northe, to the Lords of the Counsell, 1574 touching the French Ambasadors untrue report of him," December 11, 1574; BL MS 1579, no. 24.

184   "the matter of *Panecia*": Chambers, i.223.

184   *Die Schoene Phaenicia*: Allison Gaw, "Is Shakespeare's *Much Ado* a Revised Earlier Play?," *PMLA* vol. 50, no. 3 (September 1935), 715–738; Felix Emmanuel Schelling, *Elizabethan Drama, 1558–1642*, vol. 2, 490.

184   based in part on a French story: Bullough, 65–67; as discussed in chapter 13, Belleforest's *Histoires Tragiques* is also the main source for *Hamlet*.

184   would not have missed…Don John: Artemis Preeshl, *Shakespeare in the Commedia dell'Arte*, 192.

185   considered the match: William Stirling Maxwell, *Don John of Austria*, vol. 2, 287.

185   considered invading England: Stirling Maxwell, 22; George Slocombe, *Don John of Austria*, 228–229.

185   Garrick's favorite: John Cox, ed., *Much Ado About Nothing (MAAN)* (Shakespeare in Production), 11.

185   "indestructible crowd-pleaser": John Andrews, ed., *MAAN* (Everyman), xiii.

185   "some source no longer known to us": Francis Hugh Mares, ed., *MAAN* (New Cambridge), 1.

185   isn't the first to speculate: Holger Klein, ed., *MAAN* (New Critical); A. R. Humphreys, ed., *MAAN* (Arden); Arthur Quiller-Couch and John Dover Wilson, eds., *MAAN*, 102.

186   lacks the recognizable geography: Levith, 78, 82.

186   no doubt put the two facts together: "Don John of Austria, bastard son of Charles V," British Library (website), www.bl.uk/collection-items/don-john-of-austria-bastard-son-of-charles-v.

186   motiveless in his malice: Barbara Mowat and Paul Werstine, eds., *MAAN* (Folger), xiii.

186   "pure evil": Michele Marrapodi, *Shakespeare and the Italian Renaissance*, 68.

186   "a comic villain": Henry Berger, Jr. "Against the Sink-a-Pace: Sexual and Family Politics in *Much Ado About Nothing*," in Marion Wynne-Davies, ed., *MAAN* (Palgrave), 26.

186   harp on his status: Richard Paul Roe, *The Shakespeare Guide to Italy*, 232; *MAAN* 4.1.187 and 5.1.180.

186   *zanni* antics...Keystone Kops: Preeshl, 193–194; Mitchel Roth, *Historical Dictionary of Law Enforcement*, 96–97.

186   His aunt Joan: Kathy Lynn Emerson, "A Who's Who of Tudor Women," http://www.tudorwomen.com.

186   His sister, Christian: "Christian North Somerset," Carole Levin, Anna Riehl Bertolet, and Jo Eldridge Carney, eds., *A Biographical Encyclopedia of Early Modern Englishwomen*, 179–180. Note this article wrongly states that Christian died in 1564, when she was noted in Roger's Kirtling accounts through late 1580s.

187   "joined with some godly gentlewoman": SP 12/148, ff. 55–75, quoted by Tallis, 182, and Gristwood, 229 (as "goodly gentlewoman").

187   "without mine utter overthrow": Wilson, *Uncrowned Kings*, 309; Gristwood, 227–228; Anna Whitelock, 152.

188   upgraded the castle: William Dugdale, *Antiquities of Warwickshire*, 249.

188   Italianate enclosure: Janette Dillon, "Pageants and Propaganda: Robert Langham's Letter and George Gascoigne's Princely Pleasures," in Michael Pincombe and Cathy Shank, eds., *The Oxford Handbook of Tudor Literature: 1485 to 1603*, 627.

188   hunting chase...other game: Robert Langham, *A Letter, Wherein Part of the Entertainment unto the Queen's Majesty at Kenilworth Castle*, NPQ, 241–242.

188   "The estate...became one great theatre": Dillon, 627.

188   Leicester's Men took part: Dillon, 629.

188   legions of guests: For a complete list of all known to be present at the Kenilworth Festival, see *NPQ*, 298.

188   his great friend Roger North: Kenilworth "game book," Kent History and Library Centre, De L'Isle U1475 E93, f. 6-6v. Consulted by kind permission of the Viscount De L'Isle from his private collection.

189   clock stopped at two: Langham, *NPQ*, 280.

189   "looked like a fairy palace": Wilson, *Uncrowned Kings*, 311.

189   certainly places him there..."with Sir Thomas": Bushby, 91.

190   most performed: Peter Holland, ed., *A Midsummer Night's Dream (AMND)* (Oxford), 1; Trevor Griffith, ed., *AMND* (Shakespeare in Production), 1.

190   tulle...tie-dye: Holland, *AMND*, 24–29; Grace Ioppolo, ed., *AMND* (Norton), xvi–xxii; Griffith, 1–80.

190 "It proposes that love is a dream": Catherine Belsey, "*A Midsummer Night's Dream*: A Modern Perspective," in Barbara Mowat and Paul Werstine, eds., *AMND* (Folger), 182.

190 maturation as a playwright: Russ McDonald, ed., *AMND* (Pelican), xxix-xxxi.

190 sources include a mash-up: Ioppolo, 73–109.

190 dash of *commedia dell'arte*: Preeshl, 58–61.

190 "Light Seneca": Robert Miola, *Shakespeare and Classical Tragedy*, 179–187.

190 one of the Sibyls..."with you hereafter": Langham, *NPQ*, 244–245; George Gascoigne, *Princely Pleasures at the Court of Kenilworth, NPQ*, 290–295; Charles Read Baskervill, "The Genesis of Spenser's Queen of Faerie," *Modern Philology*, vol. 18, no. 1 (May 1920), 50; Elizabeth Sterrantino, "Authorized Discourse at the Kenilworth Entertainments," *Early English Studies*, vol. 1 (2008), 7–9.

191 up a bridge...with thunder: Langham, *NPQ*, 245–253; Gascoigne, *NPQ*, 295–297.

191 "savage man": Langham, *NPQ*, 250; Gascoigne, *NPQ*, 297–304.

191 Titania is even used: Holland, *AMND,* 32.

192 Leicester himself was to rescue...nixed it: Gascoigne, *NPQ*, 308; Sterrantino, 9–10; Dillon, 632–633.

192 recast the performance: Langham, *NPQ*, 260–263; Gascoigne, *NPQ*, 304–308; Sterrantino, 10.

192 pulled off his mask: Dillon, 629, quoting from Harley MS 6395.

192 early-nineteenth-century scholar: N. J. Halpin, *Oberon's Vision*, 17–29.

193 Not everyone agrees: Frank Sidgwick, *The Sources and Analogues of* A Midsummer Night's Dream, 66–68.

193 passage in Seneca's *Phaedra*: Miola, 179

193 festival...at Elvetham: Holland, *AMND*, 29; Marion Ansel Taylor, *Bottom, Thou Art Translated*, 82–86.

193 folk name for wild pansy: David Derbyshire, "Midsummer Night Love Potion Proves a Work of Fiction," *The Telegraph*, February 14, 2002, http://www.telegraph.co.uk/news/uknews/1384809/Midsummer-night-love-potion-proves-a-work-of-fiction.html.

193 "herb called Ilabia"..."droppeth blood": *Dial*, 383.

194 North's own copy: *The Dial of Princes*, CUL, Adv.d.14.4, "The Table" (f. 238); see Kelly Quinn, "Sir Thomas North's Marginalia in His *"Dial of Princes*," *The Papers of the Bibliographical Society of America*, vol. 94, no. 2 (June 2000), 283–287.

194 centerpiece of Leicester's productions: Gascoigne, *NPQ*, 309–322.

194 weather was just fine: Whitelock, 161; Dillon, 634; Baskervill, 51; Sterrantino, 13–14.

195 abrupt early departure: Gascoigne, *NPQ*, 322.

CHAPTER TEN: IT WAS GREEK TO ME

Quotations from *Julius Caesar (JC)*, *Antony and Cleopatra (A&C)*, *Henry VI, Part 1 (1H6)*, *Henry VI, Part 2 (2H6)*, *Henry VI, Part 3 (3H6)*, and *Richard III (R3)* are as follows: "It was Greek to me": *JC* 1.2.282–284; "Ides of March," *JC* 1.2.17; "Friends, Romans, countrymen": *JC* 3.2.75–76; "Think you to walk forth?": *JC* 2.2.8–9; "meet with better dreams": *JC* 2.2.99; "Cowards die many times...it will come": *JC* 2.2.32–37; "the barge she sat in...flutes kept stroke": *A&C* 2.2.205; "'Tis the god Hercules": *A&C* 4.3.21–22; "Brutus' bastard hand": *2H6* 4.1.138; "No bending knee": *3H6* 3.1.18–20; "she-wolf of France": *3H6* 1.4.111; "tiger's heart": *3H6* 1.4.137; "The first thing we do": *2H6* 4.2.74; "'Burn all the records": *2H6*

4.7.12–14; "hot weather...sallet": *2H6* 4.10.1–15; "headlong by the heels...to feed upon": *2H6* 4.10.79–83; "Now is the winter...prove a villain": *R3* 1.1.1–41; "Did Julius Caesar build": *R3* 3.1.69.

Quotations from Thomas North's *The Dial of Princes* (*Dial*) and *Plutarch's Lives* (*PL*) are as follows: "prayed him if it were possible": *PL* 793; "better to die once": *PL* 790; "cowardly heart falleth...that may come": *Dial* 533; "contented to have redressed": *PL* 787; "humble suit": *PL* 1062; "pressed nearer to him": *PL* 794.

197   acknowledge Shakespeare's debt: Vivian Thomas, *Shakespeare's Roman Worlds*, 93–99.

198   After studying philosophy: Susan Jacobs, *Plutarch's Pragmatic Biographies*, 13; Tim Duff, *Plutarch's Lives: Exploring Virtue and Vice*, 1–2; Emil Ludwig in Plutarch, Ronald Baughman, ed., *The Lives of the Noble Greeks and Romans*, xiii.

199   "great men"...not writing "histories": Duff, 15, quoting North's "Life of Alexander," 1–3; see also Ludwig, xiv; Plutarch, T. J. B. Spencer, ed., *Shakespeare's Plutarch*, 7–8.

199   elite, educated statesmen: Jacobs, 6–8, 25.

199   paints his Greek fellow citizens: Plutarch, Spencer, ed., *Shakespeare's Plutarch*, 8.

199   "never painted in malice": Ludwig, xiii.

199   ambiguous, or even contradictory: Jacobs, 1–5; Duff, 9.

199   "see" events happening: Duff, 42; Ludwig, xiv; Lukas de Blois, *The Statesman in Plutarch's Works*, 2.

199   most widely read: U. Von Wilamowitz-Moellendorf, "Plutarch as Biographer," in Barbara Scardigli, ed., *Essays on Plutarch's Lives*, 47; Plutarch, Spencer, ed., *Shakespeare's Plutarch*, 7; Plutarch, Paul Turner, ed., *Selected Lives*, vii.

199   tutor to King Charles IX: Robert Jean Knecht, *The French Religious Wars*, 157.

199   masterpiece of French prose: Plutarch, Spencer, ed., *Shakespeare's Plutarch*, 9; Plutarch, Turner, ed., *Selected Lives*, xi.

199   "near as any production": Plutarch, Turner, ed., *Selected Lives*, xi.

199   more mixed reviews: Plutarch, Spencer, ed., *Shakespeare's Plutarch*, 9; Plutarch, Turner, ed., *Selected Lives*, xii; Plutarch, Tucker Brooke, ed., *Shakespeare's Plutarch*, xv-xvii.

200   first great English classics: Plutarch, Baughman, ed., *Noble Greeks*, vi.

200   excitingly vigorous prose: Plutarch, Turner, ed., *Selected Lives*, xiii.

200   "use of words tends": Plutarch, Brooke, ed., *Shakespeare's Plutarch*, xvii.

200   "worm of ambition": Plutarch, Turner, ed., *Selected Lives*, xiii.

200   "Shakespeare was able to follow": J. W. Burrow, *A History of Histories*, 112–113; Alessandro Serpieri, "Shakespeare and Plutarch: Intertextuality in action," in Michele Marrapodi, *Shakespaere, Italy, and Intertextuality*, 45–58.

200   greatest tragedies in world history: Paul Cantor, *Shakespeare's Roman Trilogy*, 23; Barbara Parker, *Plato's Republic and Shakespeare's Rome*, 113–117.

200   commentary on Elizabethan politics: Colin Burrow, *Shakespeare and Classical Antiquity*, 213–214.

200   London riots: Burrow, *Classical Antiquity*, 205.

200   deposing a bad one: Duff, 4; Robert S. Miola, "Julius Caesar and the Tyrannicide Debate," *Renaissance Quarterly*, vol. 38, no. 2, (1985), 271–289; Patrick Gray, *Shakespeare and the Fall of the Roman Republic*, 22–23; Jonathan Bate and Eric Rasmussen, eds., *Julius Caesar* (RSC).

201   National Theatre...red baseball cap: "National Theatre Live: *Julius Caesar* (2018)," Internet Movie Database, https://www.imdb.com/title/tt7122324/.

201   disapproves of Caesar's: Plutarch, Spencer, ed., *Shakespeare's Plutarch*, 14; Plutarch,

Brooke, ed., *Shakespeare's Plutarch,* xix; Burton Raffel, ed., *Julius Caesar* (Annotated Shakespeare), xix.

201 overreaching ambitions: Clifford Ronan, "Caesar On and Off the Renaissance's English Stage," 74–84; Martin Jehne, "History's Alternative Caesar's: Julius Caesar and Current Historiography," 63–66. Both essays in Horst Zander, ed., *Julius Caesar: New Critical Essays.*

201 "monarchs against trying": Cantor, 25.

201 follows Plutarch's "Life of Brutus": Plutarch, Brooke, ed., *Shakespeare's Plutarch,* xxiv.

201 Brutus stoically tries to justify: Coppelia Kahn, *"Julius Caesar: A Modern Perspective,"* in Barbara Mowat and Paul Werstine, eds., *Julius Caesar* (Folger), 220; Gray, 61; Cantor, 47.

201 to be performed unedited: Zander, 12–22; Bate, *Julius Caesar,* xiii.

201 never been admired: Zander, 1; Ania Loomba, ed., *Antony and Cleopatra* (Norton), 167–178.

201 Coleridge put the play on par: Loomba, 167; Harold Bloom, *Cleopatra,* 59.

201 "Shakespeare has poured out": Loomba, 171.

201 "inexhaustible" characters: Loomba, 178; A. C. Bradley, "Shakespeare's *Antony and Cleopatra," Oxford Lectures on Poetry,* 1999.

202 list of a dozen passages: Bloom, 47–48.

202 reader sympathizes with Antony: Duff, 69.

202 real star of the play: Cynthia Marshall, *"Antony and Cleopatra: A Modern Perspective,"* in Barbara Mowat and Paul Werstine, eds., *Antony and Cleopatra* (Folger), 304; Bloom, xi.

202 inevitable comparisons: Keith Rinehart, "Shakespeare's Cleopatra and England's Elizabeth," *Shakespeare Quarterly,* vol. 23, no. 1 (Winter 1972), 81–86.

203 Elizabeth didn't immediately say no: Susan Doran, *Monarchy and Matrimony,* 144–145.

203 I find the same scene: North, *Plutarch's Lives,* vol. 2, 1754; see also Bloom, 4.

204 twenty-one-year lease: Glynne Wickham, Herbert Berry, and William Ingram, *English Professional Theatre,* 287; Andrew Gurr, *Playgoing in Shakespeare's London,* 11; Richard Dutton, *Shakespeare, Court Dramatist,* 18; Simon Adams, *Leicester and the Court,* 37; Derek Wilson, *Uncrowned Kings,* 296–297.

204 free from meddling: Wickham, 287.

204 city started cracking down: Dutton, 17.

204 partnered with his brother-in-law: Gurr, 15; Adams, 39.

204 had Leicester's backing: E. K. Chambers, *Elizabethan Stage,* vol. 2, 88.

204 performances when Leicester's Men: Dutton, 18.

204 undeveloped fields…common sewer: Adams, 29–33.

205 three thousand spectators…levels of the galleries: Dutton, 18; Wickham, 287–288.

205 the Curtain, next door: Adams, 75.

205 chaotic affairs…everyone paid: Gurr, 69, 11.

205 troupes recycled: Gurr, 145–146.

206 usually condensed: Jonathan Bate and Eric Rasmussen, eds., *Henry VI, Parts I, II, and III* (RSC), x; Phyllis Rackin, *"Henry VI, Part 1: A Modern Perspective,"* in Barbara Mowat and Paul Werstine, eds., *Henry VI Part 1* (Folger), 257.

206 massive hit: Michael Hattaway, *Cambridge Companion to Shakespeare's History Plays,* 7.

207 refers to herself as Caesar: *1H6,* 2.1.39.

208 the villainous Margaret: Roger Warren, ed., *Henry VI, Part 2* (Oxford), 58. Margaret of Anjou, surprisingly, is even to blame for the events of *Richard III,* stalking characters

from the wings and leveling curses against them, despite the fact that the historical Margaret was dead by the time Richard came to power. Phyllis Rackin, *"Richard III*: A Modern Perspective," in Barbara Mowat and Paul Werstine, eds., *Richard III* (Folger), 347; Peter Holland, ed., *Richard III* (Pelican), xxxviii–xxxix.

208   the flower of chivalry: Dominique Goy-Blanquet, *Shakespeare's Early History Plays*, 35, 45.

208   ancestor of the Earl: Christine Hartweg, "Robert Dudley's Noble Ancestors," *All Things Robert Dudley*, March 25, 2018, https://allthingsrobertdudley.wordpress.com/2018/03 /25/robert-dudleys-noble-ancestors.

208   "Shakespeare's interpretation": Randall Martin, *"Henry VI, Part 3:* A Modern Perspective," in Barbara Mowat and Paul Werstine, eds., *Henry VI, Part 3* (Folger), 277.

209   don't rely much, if at all, on *Holinshed*: Goy-Blanquet, 41, 96, 131–132.

212   1927 auction catalog… *Henry VI, Part 2*: Myers & Co, *An Illustrated Catalog of Fine and Rare Books* (London: Myers & Co., 1927), Item 205, 47.

213   pair of books in brown leather binding: Lord North's Household Account Book, British Library, Stowe 774; some extracts are provided in William Stevenson, "The Booke of howshold Charges and other…" *Archaeologia: or Miscellaneous Tracts Relating to Antiquity* (January 1821), 19, 283–301. Hereafter, Roger North Household Book (RNHB).

213   payment Roger made to George North: RNHB vol. 1, f. 5v.

213   several payments to Thomas: RNHB 1, ff. 6, 16, 18.

213   bought by another aristocratic bibliophile: I reconstructed this timeline with the help of Julian Harrison, lead curator, Medieval Historical and Literary, at the British Library, who consulted British Library records.

214   George North's *Brief Discourse*: Dennis McCarthy and June Schlueter, *"A Brief Discourse of Rebellion and Rebels."*

215   nowhere to be found in any of the chronicles: *Brief Discourse*, 28–33.

216   "With a bold stroke… audiences spellbound": David Bevington, *The Complete Works of Shakespeare*, 644.

217   repeats the characterization: Brain Walsh, "New Directions: Audience Engagement and the Genres of *Richard III*," in Annaliese Connolly, *Richard III: A Critical Reader*, 96.

217   "Richard, allegedly inspired": Rebecca Lemon, "'Streams of Blood': Treason, Tyranny and the Tudor State in Shakespeare's *Richard III*," in Connolly, 112.

217   "to view our own proportion in a glass": 0v, in *Brief Discourse*, 100.

218   writing a new paper: June Schlueter and Dennis McCarthy, "A Cruel Murder Done in Kent: Revisiting *Arden of Faversham*," unpublished paper presented at the Shakespeare Association of America conference, March 26, 2016.

221   no one got much of a chance: Interview with Catherine Richardson.

CHAPTER ELEVEN: ALL THAT GLISTERS

Quotations from *The Merchant of Venice* (MV) include: "All that glisters": *MV* 2.7.65–66; "Three thousand ducats": *MV* 1.3.101; "many a time and oft": *MV* 1.3.104; "Neapolitan prince… twenty husbands": *MV* 1.2.38–61; "No masque tonight": *MV* 2.6.65.

Quotations from North's *Plutarch's Lives* (PL) include: "good round sums": *PL* 370–371.

Secondary historical sources for this chapter include: Sarah Gristwood, *Elizabeth and Leicester*; Anne Somerset, *Elizabeth I*; Nicola Tallis, *Elizabeth's Rival*; Alison Weir, *The Life of Elizabeth I*; Anna Whitelock, *The Queen's Bed*; Derek Wilson, *Sweet Robin* and *The Uncrowned Kings of England*.

222   make or break the reputation: Zillah Dovey, *An Elizabethan Progress*, 6.

222   dozen miles: Sian Ellis, "Elizabeth I Slept Here," *British Heritage*, July 13, 2016.

222   Elizabeth brought her entire court: Dovey, 21; Karen Lyon, "How Queen Elizabeth I Spent Her Summer Vacation," *Folger Magazine*, 2007, https://shakespeareandbeyond .folger.edu.

223   Privy Council...thousand people: Dovey, 2–3.

223   "Competitive opulence"...hundreds of pounds a day: Mary Hill Cole, *The Portable Queen*, 75.

223   commissioned original songs...sing her praises: Lyon.

223   has remained steady: *A History of the Country of Cambridge and the Isle of Ely,* Volume 10, *Chevely, Flendish, Staine, and Staploe Hundreds*, Victoria County History, London, 2002, 57–63, accessed through British History Online.

223   the Fairhaven family: "The Fairhaven Family," National Trust (UK), http://nationaltrust .org.uk.

224   George was here: McCarthy isn't sure the name was "George," and a spokesperson for Lady Fairhaven says she doesn't recall who it was who went beneath the car.

225   All Saints Church: "A Short Guide to All Saints Church Kirtling, with some local history," E.G.M. Mann & Son, Fordham, Ely, 1979, Cambridgeshire Archives, P101/25/14.

225   sinister edge to it: Jonathan Bate and Eric Rasmussen, eds., *Merchant of Venice* (RSC), viii.

225   most-performed: M. M. Mahood, ed., *Merchant of Venice* (NCS), 61.

225   most-controversial: John Drakakis, ed., *Merchant of Venice* (Arden), 1.

225   two intertwined plots: A. R. Braunmuller, ed., *Merchant of Venice* (Pelican), xxix.

226   entered into the Stationers' Register: Drakakis, 2; Bate, vii.

226   untranslated in Shakespeare's time: Mahood, 2.

226   no doubt the playwright used it: Drakakis, 37–38; Mahood, 5; Braunmuller, xxix.

226   only element missing: Braunmuller, xxix-xxx; Drakakis, 39.

226   rare word "insculpt": Kenneth Muir, *The Sources of Shakespeare's Plays*, 89.

226   1579 pamphlet: Stephen Gosson, *The Schoole of Abuse*, Renascene Editions, transcribed by Risa Bear, 2000, from the Arber edition of 1895, http://www.luminarium.org /renascence-editions/gosson1.html.

227   Portia, as well, comes: Drakakis, 163.

227   £10 quarterly pension: RNHB v. 1, ff. 16, 18, 24v, 28v, 39, 54, etc.

228   calls "Sister North": RNHB 1, f. 52v, 54.

228   presents to Thomas's daughter: RNHB 1, ff.51, 51v.

228   "lease of house": RNHB 1, f. 29.

228   "we may picture him": Frances Bushby, *Three Men of the Tudor Time*, 184.

228   nearby estate of Mildenhall: RNHB 1, f. 42.

228   one of his yeoman farmers: RNHB v. 2, f. 2.

228   players: Leicester's Men RNHB 1 f. 15; Essex's Men RNHB 1 f. 16v; Howard's Men RNHB 1 f. 55v.

228   minstrels and Morris dancers: RNHB 1 ff. 24v, 65v.

228   hired his own resident fool: RNHB 1, f. 37.

228   a trip to Italy: John Gallagher, "The Italian London of John North: Cultural Contact and Linguistic Encounter in Early Modern England," *Renaissance Quarterly,* vol. 70 (2017), 88–131, 98.

229   took a room in town: Gallagher, 90; John North Diary (JND), Bodl., MS Add C 193, 16.

229   leaving Venice to return: Gallagher, 91; JND, 88v.

229   Mediterranean foods: Gallagher, 99–100.

229 perfumed gloves... "even his odor": Gallagher, 108.

229 inviting him to his dinner parties: JND, 29.

229 purchased a lute... "with Italianate connotations": Gallagher, 103–104.

230 anti-Semitic stereotypes: Brandon Ambrosino, "Four Hundred Years Later, Scholars Still Debate Whether Shakespeare's 'Merchant of Venice' Is Anti-Semitic," *Smithsonian*, April 21, 2016.

230 "a bone caught in the throat": "Shylock on Stage and Page," Letters, *New York Review of Books*, December 9, 2010.

230 2004 film... Al Pacino: "*Merchant of Venice*—2004," Internet Movie Database (IMDB); Mahood, 61–62.

231 rode the hundred miles to Kenilworth: RNHB 1, f. 44v.

231 rode through the deer chase: Kenilworth Game Book: Kent History and Library Centre, De L'Isle U1475 E93 ff. 22–23. Consulted by kind permission of the Viscount De L'Isle from his private collection.

231 A regular hunting guest: Kenilworth Game Book, ff. 6, 7, 8, 9v, 10, 14, 14v.

232 purchased Wanstead: *NPQ*, 547.

233 doctors recommended the tooth be pulled: Dovey, 7

233 stopping at Wanstead... "Lady of May": Dovey, 14; *NPQ*, 547.

233 launched a crusade: Jerry Brotton, *The Sultan and the Queen: The Untold Story of Elizabeth and Islam*, 70–76.

234 didn't reach London until later: Brotton, 82.

234 dig at the flamboyant... "readers commonly suppose": Some Oxfordians have recognized these allusions; see, e.g., "Dating Shakespeare's Plays: The Merchant of Venice," http://datingshakespeare.co.uk; Michael Delahoyde, "The Merchant of Venice," Washington State University, https://public.wsu.edu/~delahoyd.

235 "Elizabeth had set the tone": Weir, 314.

235 meet and impress her subjects: Nancy Schmid, "Elizabethan Progresses, 1559–1603," Dissertation, University of Wisconsin, 1971, 2–4.

235 than in East Anglia: David Loades, "Foreword," in Dovey, xii.

235 Roger North followed a few days later: RNHB 1, f. 66v.

235 Leicester joined the court: Dovey, 26–27.

235 along with gifts: *NPQ*, 572.

235 Gabriel Harvey: *NPQ*, 574, 578; Dovey, 34.

235 John traveled back and forth: Dovey, 36, 41; JND, 39.

236 Thomas's presence on his estate: RNHB 1 ff.67, 75v.

236 group joined the party: Dovey, 37.

236 private conversation with the queen: Dovey, 43.

236 lashed out at... Sussex: Dovey, 45.

236 writing Walsingham a desperate letter: Dovey, 49.

236 orations and gifts: Dovey, 63–72.

237 six days of entertainments: *NPQ*, 720–721.

237 serious about his proposal: Dovey, 78–81; Susan Doran, *Monarchy and Matrimony*, 149.

237 much to Leicester's consternation: Dovey, 80.

237 Sussex begged leave: Dovey, 94.

237 Roger and John North also left the progress: Dovey, 97.

237 prepare the royal silver: Wendy Barnes, "Queen Elizabeth Slept here; Gloriana's East Anglian Progress 1578," February 8, 2016, public talk at Colchester Archaeological Group, report by Mary Coe, http://caguk.net.

237   more great houses: Dovey, 95, 97, 99, 104.

237   queen was presented with a "rich jewel": Dovey, 107.

238   Roger's guests arrived...own gift for the queen: Dovey, 115–116; *NPQ*, 751–752; William Stevenson, "The Booke of howshold Charges and other..." *Archaeologia: or Miscellaneous Tracts Relating to Antiquity* (January 1821) 19, 286–290, 298; RNHB 1, ff. 72–74v; Bushby, 121, 148.

239   "No whit behind any of the best": *NPQ*, 751.

239   cost of £120: RNHB 1, f. 75; *Archaeologia*, 290.

239   based on another untranslated Italian tale: Drakakis, 39.

240   pun between Jew and jewel: Drakakis, 92.

241   detailing vast quantities: RNHB 1 ff. 72–75; *Archaeologia*, 287–290; *NPQ*, 834–840.

241   performed in Maldon: Maps and Touring Itineraries for Leicester's Men, online supplement to *Shakespeare and Theatrical Patronage*, https://web.ics.purdue.edu/~pwhite/patronage /leicesterappendix.html; Jeffrey Forgeng, Jeffrey L. Singman, and Will McClean, *Daily Life in Elizabethan England*, estimates horses could travel thirty to forty-five miles a day; email correspondence with Sally-Beth MacLean and Laurie Johnson.

242   for "making a comedy": JND f. 45.

242   confirms that payment: RNHB 1, f. 79v.

242   John and Thomas continued to a neighboring estate: JND ff. 45.

242   another 40 shillings..."my brother, 40 shillings": RNHB 1, f. 80.

242   give it further thought: Dovey, 122. Much to Leicester's annoyance, she also continued to hold out sending more aid to the States General in the Netherlands.

242   yet another marriage: Dovey, 148; Tallis, 169–170.

CHAPTER TWELVE: ONCE MORE UNTO THE BREACH

Quotations from *As You Like It (AYLI)*; *Richard II (R2)*; *Henry IV, Part 1 (1H4)*; *Henry IV, Part 2 (2H4)*; and *Henry V (H5)* in this chapter are as follows: "Once more unto the breach": *H5* 3.1.1; "Sweetest nut hath sourest rind": *AYLI* 2.3.107–108; "Some of them had in them": *AYLI* 3.2.163–164; "Men have died": *AYLI* 4.1.101–102; "How it grieves me...claws of a lion": *AYLI* 5.2.19–23; "The courtesy of nations": *AYLI* 1.1.44–47; "Antipodes": *R2* 3.2.49; "wallow naked in December": *R2* 1.3.298–301; "eating the bitter bread...I am a gentleman": *R2* 3.1.21–27; "No, my good lord...I will": *1H4* 2.4.468–476; "by the honor of my blood": *2H4* 4.2.55; "pursue the scattered stray": *2H4* 4.2.120; "busy giddy minds": *2H4* 4.5.212–213; "band of brothers": *H5* 4.3.60; "they have burned and carried away": *H5* 4.7.7–10; "There is a river in Macedon...knaveries, and mocks": *H5* 4.7.26–48; "Can this cockpit hold...Agincourt": *H5* Prologue 11–14; "Where–oh for pity!": *H5* 4.0.49–52.

Quotations from Thomas North's *Plutarch's Lives (PL)* are as follows: "wounds of the claws": *PL* 954; "For who is fitter": *PL* xxiii; "All other learning is private": *PL* xxvii.

Secondary historical sources for this chapter include: Sarah Gristwood, *Elizabeth and Leicester*; Anne Somerset, *Elizabeth I*; Nicola Tallis, *Elizabeth's Rival*; Alison Weir, *The Life of Elizabeth I*; Anna Whitelock, *The Queen's Bed*; Derek Wilson, *Sweet Robin* and *The Uncrowned Kings of England*.

244   Edmund Spenser...at age twenty-four: Andrew Hadfield, "Spenser, Edmund," *ODNB*; Andrew Hadfield, *Edmund Spenser: A Life*, 17–82.

244   during her 1578 progress: *NPQ*, 575–708.

244 *The Shepheardes Calender* . . . personages as well: Andrew Hadfield, *Spenser: A Life,* 119–140.

244 "fair Elisa . . . queen of the shepherds": Edmund Spenser, *The Shepheardes Calender: The Original Edition of 1579 in Photographic Facsimile,* H. Oskar Sommer, ed., "April," f. 12.

244 represents his friend Harvey: Jason Scott-Warren, "Harvey, Gabriel," *ODNB.*

244 "country lass": *Calender,* "January," f. 1; "I love the lass . . . holdeth scorn": f. 2; "feigned name . . . love and mistress": f. 2v.

245 For centuries . . . from a high ridge: Percy Long, "Spenser's Rosalind 'In honour of a private personage unknowne,'" *Anglia: Zeitschrift fur englische Philogie,* vol. 31 (January 1908), 72–104, 31; see also Hadfield, *Spenser: A Life,* 143–146; N. J. Halpin, "On Certain Passages in the Life of Edmund Spenser," *Proceedings of the Royal Irish Academy (1836–1869),* vol. 4 *1847–1850,* 445–451; Richard Mallette, "Rosalind," in A. C. Hamilton, ed., *The Spenser Encyclopedia,* 622.

245 "North country" and the "North parts": *Calender,* "June," f. 25; "neighbor-town": "January," f. 2; "the hills": "June," f. 23; "gentlewoman of no mean house": "April," f. 14v.

245 not his finest comedy: Harold Bloom, *Rosalind,* 65.

245 plot takes a backseat: Bloom, *As You Like It (AYLI),* 47; Barbara Mowat and Paul Werstine, eds., *AYLI* (Folger), 233.

246 "In Beatrice, it lays about us": Leah Marcus, ed., *AYLI* (Norton) 241; Bloom, *AYLI,* 51.

246 Elizabeth Bennett to Jo March: Angela Thirlwell, *Rosalind,* 186–187, 192.

246 carried away by her passions: Bloom, *AYLI,* 79.

246 disputations about love . . . other characters: Jonathan Bate and Eric Rasmussen, *AYLI* (RSC), xv-xvi; Marcus, 237; Bloom, *AYLI,* 48.

246 main recognized source: Kenneth Muir, *The Sources of Shakespeare's Plays,* 125–127.

247 "Wife of Bath's Tale": Juliet Dusinberre, *AYLI* (Arden), 2.

248 Italian epic romances: Orlando Furioso was based, in turn, on the French *Song of Roland.* As another nod to this derivation, Orlando's late father in *As You Like It* is named Roland.

248 carved together into trees: Leah Knight, "Writing on Early Modern Trees," *English Literary Renaissance,* vol. 41, no. 3 (Autumn 2011), 462–484; Miranda Johnson-Haddad, "Englishing Ariosto: *Orlando Furioso* at the Court of Elizabeth I," *Comparative Literature Studies,* vol. 31, no. 4 (1994), 323–350; Michele Marrapodi, *Shakespeare, Italy, and Intertextuality,* 97–100.

248 "I soon would learn these woods": *Calender,* "June," f. 24; "after Winter cometh timely death": *Calender,* "December," f. 51.

249 Spenser, too, presented his poems: Thomas Fuller, *Histories of the Worthies of England,* 1662, quoted in Hadfield, *Spenser: A Life,* 82; John Manningham, *Diary,* quoted in John Payne Collier, *The Works of Shakespeare,* vol. 1 (1853), xcix.

249 receipt in Spenser's hand: John Roffens, bill of receipt, November 23, 1578, North Family Papers, University of Kansas, MS 240A:1024.

249 "He that is found bound": Quoted in Helen A. Clarke and Charlotte Porter eds., *The Merchant of Venice* (Crowell), 104. See also James Shapiro, *Shakespeare and the Jews,* 98.

249 "love then in lion's house": *Calender,* "December," 49v.

250 he married: Hadfield, *Spenser: A Life,* 140.

250 to Thomas Stuteville: Peterhouse, *A Biographical Register of Peterhouse Men,* 19.

250 discussion of the Elizabethan custom: See, for example, Pamela Allen Brown and Jean E. Howard, eds., *AYLI* (Bedford), 165–167; Mowat, xiv-xv.

250 "The psychological and socio-economic": Louis Adrian Montrose, "'The Place of a

Brother,' in *As You Like It*: Social Process and Comic Form," *Shakespeare Quarterly*, vol. 32, no. 1 (Spring 1981), 28–54; Zouheir Jamoussi, *Primogeniture and Entail in England*, 137–149.

251   "My elder brother forsooth must be": Thomas Wilson, *The State of England Anno Dom. 1600*, quoted in Montrose, 32.

251   brotherly conflict would recur: Thirlwell, 150.

251   back on the estate...though his family remains: RNHB 1, ff. 67, 104v.

252   "I must confess": Wilson, quoted in Montrose, 53.

253   Elizabeth stepped in: Leicester to Burghley, October 17, 1578, *CSP Domestic*.

253   acted out a masque: John Tucker Murray, *English Dramatic Companies*, 305, citing Peter Cunningham, *Extracts from the Accounts of the Revels at Court*, 143.

253   "Roger North's half-sister": Richard Bradshaw, "Edward White, Bookseller of London, His Associates, and the First Printing of Arden of the Play, *Arden of Faversham*," in Patricia Hyde, *Thomas Arden in Faversham*, 518–519.

254   replaced as master of revels: Bradshaw, 520; Richard Dutton, *Shakespeare, Court Dramatist*, 46.

254   living away from Kirtling: Roger was certainly in an angry mood those years. His wife, Winifred, died in the fall of 1578, and in addition to his conflict with Sussex, the following year found him feuding again with Richard Cox, the Bishop of Ely, who sent Burghley a letter complaining about "Lord North's vexatious dealings with him" as well as with the University of Cambridge, which was fighting with the town over control of the Sturbridge Fair. John Craig, "North, Roger, second Baron North," *ODNB*; Bishop of Ely to Burghley, BL Lansdowne MS 28/77; "Minute of a conference," February 15, 1579, *CSP Domestic*.

255   splitting the Privy Council: Susan Doran, *Monarchy and Matrimony*, 153.

255   quickly forbidden by Elizabeth: Doran, 160.

255   Simier now told the queen...Alençon to visit: Doran, 161–162.

255   "Monsieur came to court": JND, 66.

256   Sidney was playing tennis: Doran, 161; Alan Stewart, *Philip Sidney: A Double Life*, 215–218.

256   Roger North records a payment: RNHB 1, f. 85v.

256   "in the room of my uncle": JND, 56v.

256   Roger twice sent: RNHB 1, ff. 106, 109.

256   notice in the Stationers' Register: Stationers' Company, *Transcript of the Registers of the Company of the Stationers of London*, vol. 2, 159.

256   rubbing elbows with the literati: Anton Francesco Doni, Donald Beecher, John A. Butler, and Carmine Di Biase, eds., *The Moral Philosophy of Doni*, 72.

257   protégés continued to try to influence: Doran, 164.

257   Stubbs published a pamphlet: Rui Carvalho Homem and Fátima Vieira, *Gloriana's Rule: Literature, Religion, and Power in the Age of Elizabeth*, 184; Doran, 166.

257   commentary on Alençon: Edwin Greenlaw, "Spenser and the Earl of Leicester," *PMLA*, vol. 25, no. 3 (1910), 535–561.

257   open letter written to the queen: Philip Sidney, "Letter to Queen Elizabeth, 1580," from *The Miscellaneous Works of Sir Philip Sidney, Knt.*, William Gray, ed. Boston: TOHP Burnham, 1860, 289–303, reprinted online by Luminarium Editions.

258   Revels Accounts...a history": Murray, 38.

258   unveiled his greatest accomplishment: North's Plutarch is often characterized as being published in 1579. The dedication, however, was signed January 1579, and since the

Elizabethan calendar didn't start until March 25, that would make it January 1580 by modern terms, meaning the book was actually published in 1580.

259 Roger paid his brother: RNHB 1, f. 124v.

259 A few weeks later, Roger followed: RNHB 1, f. 126v.

260 soldiers on Ireland's Dingle Bay: William Palmer, *The Problem of Ireland in Tudor Foreign Policy, 1485–1603*, 108; Cyril Falls, *Elizabeth's Irish Wars*, 125–126.

260 died in a raid: Falls, 127–128.

260 "Leicester, finding himself in a tight place": Greenlaw, 557.

260 added a postscript about Thomas: Earl of Leicester to Lord Burghley, August 21, 1580, *Calendar of the Manuscripts of the Most Hon. the Marquis of Salisbury, Preserved at Hatfield House, Hertfordshire. Vol. 2: 1572–1582*, Entry 881, Page 339.

260 Burghley initially responded: Lord Burghley to Earl of Leicester, August 25, 1580, *CSP Domestic*, TNA SP 12/141 f.94.

261 Thomas captain of two hundred troops: Harold Davis, "The Military Career of Thomas North," *Huntington Library Quarterly*, vol. 12, no. 3 (May 1949), 315–321; APC October 3 and 4, 1580.

261 North wasn't poor: "Money to be paid to certain captains," October 3, 1580, TNA SP 63/77 ff. 13–14.

261 captain's salary: "Note of money ordered to be paid to divers persons and captains," October 10, 1580, *CSP Ireland*, TNA SP 63/77, f. 64.

261 arrived in Dublin: Ed. Waterhous to Walsyngham, November 11, 1580, *CSP Ireland*, TNA SP 63/78, ff. 52–53.

261 A new force... soldiers in any war: Falls, 142–144; Palmer, 109.

261 Spenser most likely witnessed: Hadfield, *Edmund Spenser's Irish Experience: Wilde Fruit and Salvage Soyl*, 18; Hadfield, *Spenser: A Life*, 163–170; Raymond Jenkins, "Spenser with Lord Grey in Ireland," *PMLA*, vol. 52, no. 2 (June 1937), 338–353, 341.

261 "cashing of some bands": Lord Deputy Grey to Walsingham, December 16, 1580, *CSP Ireland*, TNA SP 63/79 f.37.

261 North and three other captains: Note of the bands discharged, December 16, 1580, *CSP Ireland*, TNA SP 63/79 f.38.

261 presumably Grey himself: While Grey's title was "Lord Deputy," he is often referred to as Governor or Chief Governor; see, e.g., *CSP Ireland*, vol. 2, 330, 332, 336, 340, 355, 371, 372.

262 continuing work on the *The Fairie Queene*: Hadfield, *Spenser: A Life*, 185.

262 "original sin" that sparked the Wars of the Roses: Tony Tanner, *Prefaces to Shakespeare*, 386–387.

262 whether Richard "usurps himself": Tanner, 380–381, 393; David Bevington, *The Complete Works of Shakespeare*, 741.

262 "Antipodes"—the ends of the earth: Marjorie Garber, *Shakespeare After All*, 252.

262 living within his imagination: Garber, 244.

263 "In every aspect of the play": Garber, 316.

264 "a much nastier, meaner business": Tanner, 429

264 "woods and glens they came": Edmund Spenser, *A View of the Present State of Ireland*, quoted in Hadfield, *Spenser: A Life*, 163.

264 fighting raged on... executing the "guilty": Falls, 145–146; Jenkins, 349.

264 "one of the most disturbingly dramatic": Paul Jorgensen, "The 'Dastardly Treachery' of Prince John of Lancaster," *PMLA*, vol. 76, no. 5 (December 1961), 488–492, 488.

265 "busy giddy minds": Bevington, 827.

265   "is essentially ironic": Harold Bloom, *Shakespeare: The Invention of the Human*, 321.

265   "raise serious questions": Bevington, 875.

267   direct parody of *Plutarch's Lives*: Paul Cantor, *Shakespeare's Roman Trilogy*, 19; Christine Sukic, "His Bruised Helmet and his Bended Sword: The Politics of Criminality and Heroism in Henry V," in Line Cottegnies and Karen Britland, eds., *King Henry V: A Critical Reader*, 196; T. W. Craik, ed., *Henry V* (Arden), 312.

267   captain brought the head: Falls, 147; Jenkins, 350.

267   forcing Grey to discharge soldiers: Falls, 147; "Schedule of the captains to be discharged the last of Feb.," February 1582, *CSP Ireland*, TNA SP 63/89 f. 22.

267   "His estate will be hard": Loftus to Burghley, March 1, 1582, *CSP Ireland*, TNA SP 63/90, f. 3.

267   set sail from Dublin...North never repaid: Thomas M. Cranfill, "Thomas North at Chester," *Huntington Library Quarterly*, vol. 13, no. 1 (November 1949), 93–99; Barnaby Rich, *The True Report of a Late Practise Enterprised by a Papist, with a Yong maiden in Wales*, 1582, BL General Reference C.25.c.7.

268   last reference to Thomas's wife: RNHB 1, f. 141v.

268   in response to the opening preface: Marguerite Hearsey, "Sidney's *Defense of Poesy* and Amyot's *Preface* in North's *Plutarch*: A Relationship," *Studies in Philology*, vol. 30, no. 4 (October 1933), 535–550.

268   "purifying of the wit...mingling clowns and kings": Sir Philip Sidney, *The Defence of Poesy*, Poetry Foundation, 2009, http://www.poetryfoundation.org.

269   scholars have seen the chorus: Anne-Marie Miller-Blaise and Gisèle Venet, "Performance History," in Line Cottegnies and Karen Britland, eds., *Henry V* (Arden), 50–52; Craik, 32, 256.

CHAPTER THIRTEEN: TO BE, OR NOT TO BE

Quotations from *Romeo and Juliet* (*R&J*), *As You Like It* (*AYLI*); *Hamlet* (*H*), and other plays in this chapter are as follows: "To be, or not to be": *H* 3.1.57–61; "But soft, what light": *R&J* 2.2.2; "O, that she were an open-arse": *R&J* 2.1.38–39; "Two households, both alike": *R&J* 1.1.1–6; "With love's light wings": *R&J* 2.2.66–67; "My bounty is as boundless": *R&J* 2.2.133–134; "I would have thee gone...much cherishing": *R&J* 2.2.177–185; "It irks me the poor dappled fools": *AYLI* 2.1.22–25; "I myself must hunt this deer": *Henry VI, Part 2* 5.2.15; "How like a deer": *Julius Caesar* 3.1.211–212; "native dwelling place": *AYLI* 2.1.63; "Alas, Poor Yorick!...uses we may return": *H* 5.1.183–202; "was sick almost to doomsday": *H* 1.1.124; "Brevity is the soul of wit": *H* 2.2.90; "To thine own self be true": *H* 1.3.78; "Conscience does make cowards": *H* 3.1.91; "I am but mad north-north-west": *H* 2.2.378–379; "not above once": *H* 2.2.435–436; "Out, out, thou strumpet Fortune!": *H* 2.2.493; "The play's the thing": *H* 2.2.605–606; "story is extant": *H* 3.2.260–261; "grizzled...truncheon": *H* 1.2.201–247; "aerie of children...berattle the common stages": *H* 2.2.339–342; "abstract and brief chronicles": *H* 2.2.524–526; "To be, or not to be...undiscovered country": *H* 3.1.57–80; "a little patch of ground...nothing worth": *H* 4.4.19–67; "the soldiers' music": *H* 5.5.401–402.

Quotations from Thomas North's Journal (*TNJ*), *The Dial of Princes* (*Dial*), and *Plutarch's Lives* (*PL*) are as follows: "hacked and mangled among them": *PL* 794; "the wife of Gonzago": *TNJ* 85; "pikes and briars": *Dial* 533; "assaults of life": *Dial* 535–536; "pilgrimage uncertain": *Dial* 524.

Secondary historical sources for this chapter include: Sarah Gristwood, *Elizabeth and Leicester*; Anne Somerset, *Elizabeth I*; Alison Weir, *The Life of Elizabeth I*; Derek Wilson, *Sweet Robin* and *The Uncrowned Kings of England*.

271   had a real-life lady in mind: Alan Stewart, *Philip Sidney: A Double Life*, 238–240.
271   "Loving in truth, and fain in verse": Sir Philip Sidney, *Astrophil and Stella* 1, Poetry Foundation, https://www.poetryfoundation.com.
272   "Juliet Club": "About Us," The Juliet Club (website), www.julietclub.com. This phenomenon was background to the 2010 romantic comedy *Letters to Juliet*.
273   universally acknowledged...source: René Weis, ed., *Romeo and Juliet* (Arden), 2; Tony Tanner, *Prefaces to Shakespeare*, 95; David Bevington, *The Complete Works of Shakespeare*, 1005–1006.
273   "I saw the same argument": Arthur Brooke, *The Tragicall Historye of Romeus and Juliet*, 1562, Canadian Adaptations of Shakespeare Project, www.canadianshakespeares.ca /folio/Sources/romeusandjuliet.pdf; "Brooke's Romeus and Juliet," The British Library, www.bl.uk/collection-items/brookes-romeus-and-juliet; Bevington, 1005–1006.
273   "Old Free-town," the English translation: Richard Paul Roe, *The Shakespeare Guide to Italy*, 11–12.
275   press had published a book: David Ellis, *The Truth About William Shakespeare*.
277   suit for marriage—and more money: Mack Holt, *The French Wars of Religion*, 158.
277   arrived in London: Holt, 160.
278   Called the Queen's Men: Andrew Gurr, *The Shakespearean Playing Companies*, 198–200; John Tucker Murray, *English Dramatic Companies*, 7–11; E. K. Chambers, *Elizabethan Stage*, 104–107.
278   *Felix and Philomena*: Murray, 15; Gurr, 211.
278   *Three Ladies of London*: M. Lindsay Kaplan, ed., The Merchant of Venice: *Texts and Contexts*, 154.
279   set sail for Flushing: Leicester to Burghley, December 9, 1585, *CSP Foreign*.
279   Will Kemp: David Wiles, *Shakespeare's Clown*, 31–33.
280   Leicester's lavish Christmas entertainments: Sally-Beth MacLean, "Tracking Leicester's Men," in Paul Whitfield White and Suzanne R. Westfall, eds., *Shakespeare and Theatrical Patronage*, 264–266; Katherine Duncan-Jones, *Shakespeare: An Ungentle Life*, 37–40.
280   accepted the title of Governor-General: C. Aerssens to Davison, January 17/27, 1586, *CSP Foreign*.
280   dressed him down: The Queen to Leicester, March 30, 1586, *CSP Foreign*.
280   Roger North grumbled: Lord North to Burghley, January 28, 1586, and Lord North to Burghley, February 28, 1586, *CSP Foreign*.
280   made a goodwill tour: Leicester to Walsingham, September 12, 1586, in Robert Dudley, Earl of Leicester, *Correspondence of Robert Dudley, Earl of Leicester*, 410.
280   frenzied battle broke out: Stewart, 311–313.
280   Roger rose out of his bed: Leicester to Walsingham, September 28, 1586, in Leicester, 417.
280   "necessity is greater than mine": Stewart, 313.
280   Roger North and Essex knights banneret: *NPQ*, 335.
281   Sidney's wound festered: Gisbert Enterwit to Jan Wyer, October 16/26, 1586, *CSP Foreign*.
281   "the comfort of my life": Leicester to Walsingham, October 25, 1586, in Leicester, 445.

282 "fairest and handsomest companies": Leicester to Walsingham, July 4, 1586, *CSP Foreign (Holland and Flanders)*.

282 besieging the southeastern coastal town of Sluis...sixty miles from England: Preface, *CSP Foreign (Holland and Flanders)*, vol. 21, part 3.

282 Thomas was listed: "A note of the Muster of the garrison of Flushing," September 26/ October 6, 1587, *CSP Foreign (Holland and Flanders)*; TNA SP 84/18, f. 201.

283 During a raid...by a river: Richard Lloyd to Walsingham, August 28, 1587, *CSP Foreign (Holland and Flanders)*; TNA SP 84/17, f. 54.

284 *Armada Invencible*...Narrow Sea to attack: Robert Hutchinson, *The Spanish Armada: A History*, 89–91; Garrett Mattingly, *The Armada*, 24.

284 German mystic named Regiomontanus: Mattingly, 175–176.

284 delayed the Invincible Armada's passage: Hutchinson, 99–110; Mattingly, 250–253.

284 put in charge of a band: APC, June 24, 1588, vol. 16, 134.

284 recusants...brought to the Bishop's Palace: Samuel Purchas, *Hakluytus Posthumus Or, Purchas His Pilgrimes* (1624), 483; Francis Young, "The bishop's palace at Ely as a prison for recusants, 1577–1597," *British Catholic History*, vol. 32, no. 2 (2014), 195–216; Michael David Lane, "'Of Whims and Fancies': A Study of English Recusants under Elizabeth, 1570–1595," LSU Master's Thesis (2015).

285 Roger led a force of footmen and horsemen: Lord North to Walsingham, June 24, 1588, *CSP Domestic*; Lord North's certificate, July 1, 1588, *CSP Domestic*.

285 planned to land near Ipswich: Hutchinson, 99.

285 "We are now in peril of goods": Hutchinson, 136.

287 clan of Scottish border reivers: Derek James Stewart, *The Armstrongs: The History of a Riding Family, 1040–1650*, 16–18; George MacDonald Fraser, *The Steel Bonnets: The Story of the Anglo-Scottish Border Reivers*, 55–56, 101–102.

288 contemporary event...Armada in 1598: James Shapiro, *A Year in the Life of William Shakespeare*, 173–187.

288 closest...to a prolonged shared cultural experience: Marjorie Garber, *Shakespeare After All*, 466–467.

288 stretch all the way back...*Treatise of Melancholy*: Kenneth Muir, *The Sources of Shakespeare's Plays*, 166.

289 around spring of 1587: Alison Findlay in Emily Bartels and Emma Smith, eds., *Christopher Marlowe in Context*, 242; Harold Bloom, ed. *Christopher Marlowe*, 14.

290 based on the actual murder..."into the *Hamlet* play": Geoffrey Bullough, "The Murder of Gonzago," *The Modern Language Review*, vol. 30, no. 4 (October 1935), 433–444.

291 "mother's sister" could refer: Leanora Gonzaga was actually the sister of the Duke Guglielmo's father, Federico II Gonzaga, who died in 1540; since the Tudors used the terms "sister" and "sister-in-law" interchangeably, however, it would have made sense for North to refer to Leanora as the sister of the Duke's mother, Isabella d'Este, who was still living. Isabella did not have any other sisters. One other sister of the late Federico was still alive at the time, Ippolita Gonzaga, but she was living in a Dominican monastery.

293 tomb of black stone: "Memorials and Hatchments, All Saints Church, Kirtling," 2008, Cambridgeshire Archives P101/28/16, 3.

293 more garish memorial...crypt here, in 1965: "A Short Guide to All Saint's Church Kirtling, with some local history," E.G.M. Mann & Son, Fordham, Ely, 1979, Cambridgeshire Archives, P101/25/14, 6, "Memorials and Hatchments," 5–6; Ben Colburn & Mark Ynys-Mon, "All Saints, Kirtling," Cambridgeshire Churches (website), http://www.druidic.org/camchurch.

295 wishing her "all possible speed": James to Elizabeth, August 1, 1588, John Bruce, ed., *Letters of Queen Elizabeth and King James VI of Scotland*, 52.

295 Montague...volunteered: Hutchinson, 153.

295 "resolved, in the midst and heat": Weir, 394; "Timeline: Sources from History, Elizabeth's Tilbury Speech," British Library (website), http://www.bl.uk/learning/timeline /item102878.html.

CHAPTER FOURTEEN: FULL OF SOUND AND FURY

Quotations from *King Lear (KL)*, *Macbeth (M)*, and *Arden of Faversham (Arden)* in this chapter are as follows: "Out, out, brief candle!": *M* 5.5.23–28; "more sinned against than sinning": *KL* 3.2.60; "Why bastard?...lag of a brother?": *KL* 2.1.2–9; "little world of man...nothing of": *KL* 3.3.4–14; "philosopher...of thunder": *KL* 3.4.151–155; "Away, get thee away": *KL* 4.1.15–16; "expose thyself to feel what wretches feel": *KL* 3.4.34; "good years shall devour": *KL* 5.3.24–25; "Avaunt, you curs!": *KL* 3.6.63–70; "When priests are more in word...used with feet": *KL* 3.2.81–94; "Weird Sisters": *M* 1.3.32; "Out, damned spot!": *M* 5.1.34; "Her husband's to Aleppo...tempest-tossed": *M* 1.3.7–25; "I am in blood stepped": *M* 3.4.137– 139; "Thrice the brinded cat...boil and bubble": *M* 4.1.1–19; "With my nails, I'll scrape": *Arden* 14.253; "What, will these hands": *M* 5.1.43–44; "full o' th' milk": *M* 1.5.17; "Come to my woman's breasts": *M* 1.5.47–48; "while it was smiling": *M* 1.7.47–49; "My thanes and kinsmen": *M* 5.8.63–64; "hounds and greyhounds": *M* 3.1.94.

Quotations from Thomas North's Journal (*TNJ*), *The Dial of Princes (Dial)*, *The Moral Philosophy of Doni (Doni)*, and *Nepos's Lives (NL)* are as follows: "overtaken by some accident...that "cometh to nothing": *Doni* 12–13; "what that thunder meant": *NL* 8; "did love and embrace poverty...get thee away": *NL* 3; "We may aptly compare...to do worse": *Dial* 725; "a horse roasted": *Dial* 702; "heal infants": *Dial* 268; "tore in pieces a young child": *Dial* 258; "This worldly life representeth...cometh to nothing": *Doni* 12–13.

Secondary historical sources for this chapter include: John Guy, *Elizabeth: The Forgotten Years*; Anne Somerset, *Elizabeth I*; Alison Weir, *The Life of Elizabeth I*.

297 joined a troupe of players: Stephen Greenblatt, *Will in the World*, 161–164; Terence Schoone-Jongen, *Shakespeare's Companies*, 1–4; Lois Potter, *The Life of William Shakespeare*, 54.

297 the Rose: Glynne Wickham, Herbert Berry, and William Ingram, *English Professional Theatre*, 419–426.

298 company of players died with him: Andrew Gurr, *The Shakespearean Playing Companies*, 191.

298 Queen's Men faltered: Peter Ackroyd, *Shakespeare: The Biography*, 104; Gurr, 202–204.

298 Strange's Men: Ackroyd, 149–151; Gurr, 258–262; Potter, 55.

298 University Wits: Schoone-Jongen, 18; Greenblatt, *Will in the World*, 200–203; Potter, 73–80; Ackroyd, 139–148.

298 *Tamburlaine the Great*: Greenblatt, *Will in the World*, 189–190; Potter, 75; Ackroyd, 145–148.

299 *Spanish Tragedy*: Potter, 143–145; Siobhan Keenan, *Travelling Players in Shakespeare's England*, 64.

299 accompaniments to the Armada era: Gurr, 162.

299 with the Wits but not of them: Ackroyd, 144–145; Greenblatt, *Will in the World*, 200.

299 worked more closely with the Wits: Potter, 79

299 Queen's Men's plays..."coincidences": Ackroyd, 104, Potter, 55.

300 Richard Field: Greenblatt, *Will in the World*, 193.

300 waded into a "pamphlet war": Jason Scott-Warren, "Harvey, Gabriel," *ODNB*; Greenblatt, *Will in the World*, 206; Arul Kumaran, "Patronage, print, and an early modern 'pamphlet moment,'" *Explorations in Renaissance Culture*, vol. 31, issue 1 (Summer 2005); Maria Teresa Micaela Prendergast, *Railing, Reviling and Invective in English Literary Culture*, 81.

300 Greene had died that September: Greenblatt, *Will in the World*, 210–211; Schoone-Jongen, 18.

300 wasn't written by Greene at all: Potter, 99–100; Ackroyd, 189–190; D. Allen Caroll, ed., *Greene's Groatsworth of Wit*, 1–22; Schoone-Jongen, 24–26.

300 "memorably brilliant piece of writing": Katherine Duncan-Jones, *Shakespeare: An Ungentle Life*, 50.

301 "Why easily...if you will take the pains": *Groatsworth*, 68–70.

301 competing beast fables...bed for his wife: *Groatsworth*, 58–63.

301 "in the North parts": *Groatsworth*, 60.

301 numerous gifts and gambling debts: RNHB vol. 2, 104v, 109v, 140v-141, 141v-142, 147, 149v, 150.

302 Chettle issued an apology: Greenblatt, *Will in the World*, 214–215.

302 first appearing...*Fairie Queene*: David Bevington, *The Complete Works of Shakespeare*, 1201; Geoffrey Bullough, *Narrative and Dramatic Sources of Shakespeare*, vol. 7, 269–276; Kenneth Muir, *The Sources of Shakespeare's Plays*, 196–198.

302 *King Leir*:....source for Shakespeare's: Bullough, vol. 7, 276–277; Muir, 199–201; Schoone-Jongen, 99–100; Meredith Skura, "What Shakespeare Did with the Queen's Men's *King Leir* and When," *Shakespeare Survey*, vol. 63 (2010), 316–325.

303 "So great is the suffering": Barbara Mowat and Paul Werstine, eds., *King Lear* (Folger), ix.

303 "out-Iagos Iago": Harold Bloom, *Shakespeare: The Invention of the Human*, 499.

304 Father Edmunds...imprisoned at Wisbech: Greenblatt, *Shakespearean Negotiations*, 94.

305 married his widow, Judith: Tom Lockwood, "North, Sir Thomas," *ODNB*.

305 "special understanding of old age": Mowat, xvi.

307 symbol for the unification of Britain: Muir, 199; Marjorie Garber, *Shakespeare After All*, 651.

308 "eat me flesh and fell": Dennis McCarthy and June Schlueter, *"A Brief Discourse of Rebellion and Rebels."* 48; "drunkenness is taken for delight...treason esteemed": 35v; "our mouth with milk...heart doth bound": 46v.

310 in a seventeenth-century book: Thomas Pugh, *British and Outlandish Prophesies*, 1658.

311 "exceedingly weary": Weir, 404; Guy, 137–138.

311 "Captain North" appointed as lieutenant colonel: "The officers and captains of her Majesty's army in France," [1591], Cecil Papers, vol. 4, 169–170.

311 as Sir Thomas North: "North, Sir Thomas," *ODNB*.

312 creatures, in his estimation...fleeing into exile: Lawrence Normand and Gareth Roberts, *Witchcraft in Early Modern Scotland*, 31–49; Susan Dalgety, "The ladies not for burning," *Evening News* (Edinburgh), November 3, 2000; Neil Mackay, "The Scottish Witch Hunts: When Our Nation Went Mad," *The Herald*, October 27, 2019; Alison Campsie, "The Brutal Witch-Hunts of a Love-Struck Scottish King," *The Scotsman*, July 18, 2016.

313 liberties with history...that same year: Muir, 209–212.

314 there was a ship called the *Tiger*: Samuel Purchas, *Hakluytus Posthumus, Or Purchas His Pilgrimes*, 165.

315 Thomas North's own copy: *The Dial of Princes*, CUL, Adv.d.14.4; see Kelly Quinn, "Sir Thomas North's Marginalia in His *Dial of Princes*," *The Papers of the Bibliographical Society of America*, vol. 94, no. 2 (June 2000), 283–287.

315 "The condition of a wicked man": *Dial,* CUL, f. 450v; "lewd women compared to hedge-hogs": f. 432; "strange meats dressed and eaten": f. 436v; "women soothsayers": f. 172v.

319 had identified eight words: *Brief Discourse*, f. 45.

319 Paul McCartney had actually based his lyrics: "Golden Slumbers," The Beatles Bible (website), https://www.beatlesbible.com/songs/golden-slumbers.

322 "claim for North's *Discourse*...several generations–find": Michael Blanding, "Plagiarism Software Unveils a New Source for 11 of Shakespeare's Plays," *The New York Times*, February 7, 2018.

323 More positive coverage: Virginia Heffernan, "Shakespeare Stole from George North," *The Los Angeles Times*, February 9, 2018; Brigit Katz, "Software Points to Possible Inspiration for 11 Shakespeare Plays" *Smithsonian*, February 9, 2018; Thomas K. Grose, "Unmasking Shakespeare's Inspiration," *U.S. News & World Report*, April 2, 2018.

323 even carried across the ocean: "Inspiration for a Poet," *The Times* (London), February 9, 2018; Jacob Stolworthy, "Shakespeare May Have Plagiarized Long-Lost 1576 Manuscript," *The Independent*, February 10, 2018; Margi Murphy, "Anti-cheat Software Reveals Shakespeare 'Borrowed' Phrases," *The Telegraph*, February 9, 2018; Allison Flood, "Plagiarism Software Pins Down New Source for Shakespeare's Plays," *The Guardian*, February 9, 2018.

323 more courteous of the two: Laura Kolb, "Pretty Sprinkled Judgement," *Times Literary Supplement*, January 11, 2019.

324 more acid review: Rhodri Lewis, *The Library*, vol. 19, no. 4 (December 2018), 514–520.

CHAPTER FIFTEEN: OUR REVELS NOW ARE ENDED

Quotations from *Richard II* (*R2*) and *The Tempest* (*T*) in this chapter are as follows: "Our revels now are ended": *T* 4.1.148–150; "For sorrow's eyes": *R2* 2.2.16–17; "flatterer, a parasite": *R2* 2.2.69–72; "Though with their high wrongs": *T* 5.1.25–28; "For you, my most wicked": *T* 5.1.32–34; "Now my charms are all o'erthrown": *T* Ep.1–20.

Quotations from Thomas North's *Nepos's Lives* (*NL*) in this chapter are as follows: "to remedy the griefs...hope and confidence": *NL* 113–115.

Secondary historical sources for this chapter include: John Guy, *Elizabeth: The Forgotten Years*; Anne Somerset, *Elizabeth I*; Alison Weir, *The Life of Elizabeth I*.

326 University Wits: Stephen Greenblatt, *Will in the World*, 211–212.

326 1594 pamphlet..."whetstones and cods-heads": Thomas Nashe, *The Terrors of the Night*.

327 similar vein of attack..."writes or speaks": Thomas Lodge, *Wit's Misery*, 56–57.

327 Pembroke's Men collapsed...disappeared the same year: Terence Schoone-Jongen, *Shakespeare's Companies*, 120–121; Peter Ackroyd, *Shakespeare: The Biography*, 185–187, 201, 217.

327 Shakespeare jumped from company to company: Siobhan Keenan, *Travelling Players in Shakespeare's England*, 24.

327 *Venus and Adonis*: Ackroyd, 203–207; Lois Potter, *The Life of William Shakespeare*, 107–110; Greenblatt, 227, 240–241, 245.

328 two officially sanctioned companies: Andrew Gurr, *The Shakespeare Company*, 78; Greenblatt, 272–273; Keenan, 28–29; Ackroyd, 220–227.

328 dozens of different plays: Gurr, *Company*, 80, 84, 101.

328 Lord Chamberlain's Men performed Shakespeare: Ackroyd, 244–245.

328 tribute to Essex at court: Ackroyd, 284.

329 Earl of Tyrone…uneasy ceasefire: James O'Neill, *The Nine Years War*, 46–62; Cyril Falls, *Elizabeth's Irish Wars*, 186–192.

329 assumed duties as privy councilor: John Craig, "North, Roger, second Baron North," *ODNB*.

329 retained his position as lieutenant: BL Sloane 33, ff. 6–8b.

329 Tyrone rose again…rebel as well: Falls, 196–197.

329 lead one hundred troops: "1596. Troops for Ireland," *Calendar of the Manuscripts of the Most Hon. the Marquis of Salisbury, Preserved at Hatfield House, Hertfordshire*, vol. 6, 1596, APC, September 10, 1596, 2/21 f.396.

329 £250…to support himself: "Muster rolls of the companies," October 2–12, 1596, *CSP Ireland*, TNA SP 63/194 f.107.

329 Edward along as his lieutenant: William Russel to William Cecil, October 14, 1596, *CSP Ireland*, TNA SP 63/194 f.55.

329 armada limping back to its ports: O'Neill, 65.

329 "Of all the captains in Ireland": "Memorandum on the state of Ireland," [December] 1596, *CSP Domestic*, TNA SP 63/196 f. 116.

329 found himself in Carrickfergus: O'Neill, 217; Falls, 207–208; "Copy of a letter from Captains Charles Eggerton, Edward North…," November 6, 1597, *CSP Ireland*, TNA SP 63/201 f. 140; James Birt to ____, November 6, 1597, *CSP Ireland*, TNA SP 63/201 f. 146.

330 been killed in battle: D. J. B. Trim, "North, Sir John," *ODNB*.

331 five years after the quarto edition: "Richard II, first edition," Shakespeare Documented, https://shakespearedocumented.folger.edu/exhibition/document/richard-ii-first-edition.

331 *Isle of Dogs*: Potter, 232–233; Ackroyd, 327; Ian Donaldson, *Ben Jonson: A Life*, 116–122; David Riggs, *Ben Jonson: A Life*, 32–33.

332 personality types, or "humours": Donaldson, 129–131.

332 killed another actor in a duel: Ackroyd, 345; Riggs, 49–51; Donaldson, 133–135.

332 Burbage showed up: Glynne Wickham, Herbert Berry, and William Ingram, *English Professional Theatre*, 493–495; Greenblatt, 291–293; Ackroyd, 345–347.

332 publishing its plays: Greenblatt, 291; Ackroyd, 333.

333 opening in Bankside…*Julius Caesar*: Steve Sohmer, *Shakespeare's Mystery Play*; Greenblatt, 293.

333 full-scale replica: "The Third Globe," Shakespeare's Globe website, https://www.shakespearesglobe.com/discover/shakespeares-world/the-third-globe.

334 Ben Jonson began writing…mouths of babes: James Bednarz, *Shakespeare & the Poets' War*, 6–7.

334 the Poetomachia: Bednarz, 8–13; Andrew Gurr, *Playgoing in Shakespeare's London*, 185–191; Jay Simons, *Jonson, the Poetomachia, and the Purging of Renaissance Satire*, 10–12; Maria Teresa Micaela Prendergast, *Railing, Reviling, and Invective in English Literary Culture*, 104–105.

334 *Satiromastix*…Sir Adam Prickshaft: Jonathan Bate, *Soul of the Age*, 355–357; Gurr, *Company*, 143.

334   *Every Man Out*...\"Not Without Right": Bednarz, 113–114; Bate, 356; Greenblatt, 80.

334   *Cynthia's Revels*: Robert Cartwright also identifies Asotus with Shakespeare, see "Papers on Shakspere," in William Robson Arrowsmith, *Shakespeare's Editors and Commentators*, 1865, 29. Other scholars have come up with other identifications, for example, associating Asotus with Thomas Lodge and Amorphus with Barnabe Rich or Anthony Munday, though they admit the parallels are imperfect. See Roscoe Addison Small, *The Stage-Quarrel*, 48–52.

334   "an essence so sublimated": *Cynthia's Revels (CR)*, in Ben Jonson, *The Complete Plays*, Felix Schelling, ed., 159; "Give me your ears": *CR*, 190; *"Victus, victa, victum"*: *CR*, 205; "If you find none": *CR*, 175; "your merchant, your scholar": *CR*, 168; "somewhat a northerly face": *CR*, 169.

335   *Epicene*...John Daw: Dennis McCarthy, "Sir Thomas North as Sir John Daw," *Notes & Queries*, vol. 54, no. 3 (September 2007), 321–324.

336   massacred more than 1,200: Falls, 215–220.

336   massive army...made of the campaign: Falls, 232–247.

337   he died at his home: "North, Roger," *ODNB*.

337   Roger's will: TNA PROB 11/97/26; Zillah Dovey, *An Elizabethan Progress*, 118.

338   Privy Council recorded payments: "A letter to the Lord Treasurer," March 25, 1601, *APC 1600–1601*, 238.

339   appointed him to a new position: "A letter to Sir Thomas North," February 13, 1601, *APC 1600–1601*, 153.

340   pension of £40 a year: Tom Lockwood, "North, Sir Thomas," *ODNB*.

340   often read as a meta-commentary: Marjorie Garber, *Shakespeare After All*, 851–852; Grace Tiffany, ed., *The Tempest* (Evans), 29.

341   shipwreck of English...Duke of Milan in 1577: Kenneth Muir, *The Sources of Shakespeare's Plays*, 278–280; David Bevington, *The Complete Works of Shakespeare*, 1570.

342   early seventeenth-century book on horticulture: Sir Hugh Plat, *Floraes Paradise*, 18. Stuteville is referred to as "Mr. Stutfield, that married my L. Norths brothers daughter."

342   political allegory for the colonization of the New World: Garber, 853; Barbara Mowat, *"The Tempest*: A Modern Perspective," in Barbara Mowat and Paul Werstine, eds., *The Tempest* (Folger), 192–195.

342   essay "Of the Cannibals": Michel de Montaigne, *The Essays*, "either barbarous or savage," 101; "no name of magistrate," 103; Kenji Go, "Montaigne's 'Cannibals' and 'The Tempest' Revisited," *Studies in Philology*, vol. 109, no. 4 (Summer 2012), 455–473.

343   mystery why exactly Shakespeare titled: Harold Bloom, *Shakespeare: The Invention of the Human*, 667; John Paul Hampstead, "The Title of *The Tempest*," University of Tennessee Honors Thesis, 2007.

343   commissioned a painting...renunciation from the world: Michel de Montaigne, *The Autobiography of Michel de Montaigne*, Marvin Lowenthal, ed., xxxii–xxxiii; Jennifer Oliver, *Shipwreck in French Renaissance Writing*, 131–133.

343   obsessed with the idea of memory: Tony Tanner, *Prefaces to Shakespeare*, 809.

344   also stems from Montaigne: Montaigne, *The Essays*; "stung to the quick," vol. 1, 243; Eleanor Prosser, "Shakespeare, Montaigne, and the Rarer Action," *Shakespeare Studies*, vol 1, (January 1965), 261–264; Arthur Kirsch, "Virtue, Vice, and Compassion in Montaigne and The Tempest," *Studies in English Literature, 1500–1900*, vol. 37, no. 2, *Tudor and Stuart Drama* (Spring 2007), 337–352.

344   landing an armada...up for submission: Falls, 292–295, 304–312, 329–333.

345   new edition of *Plutarch's Lives*: Plutarch, *The Lives of the Noble Grecians and Romanes*, Sir Thomas North, trans. 1603.

345   lawsuit brought by a Sir Thomas North: Durham County Records Office, D/St/D12/46.

CHAPTER SIXTEEN: SUCH STUFF AS DREAMS ARE MADE ON

348   journal at the Huntington Library: Sir Thomas North, "The booke and diare of the ambassadors jorney to Rome": manuscript copy, nineteenth century, The Huntington Library, HM 81033.

348   Schlueter discovered...$43,750: "[Thirlby, Thomas] The Journey of the Queenes Ambassadours Unto Rome Anno 1555," Sotheby's (website), December 2–4, 2015, http://www.sothebys.com/en/auctions/ecatalogue/lot.798.html/2015/property-collection-robert-s-pirie-books-manuscripts-n09391. This copy is now at Lambeth Palace Library, MS 5076.

349   handwritten catalog of Phillipps's manuscripts: Bodl. MS. Phillipps-Robinson e. 466.

350   back to Ralph Starkey: Edwards traced the provenance of the journal to the Library of Sir Simonds D'Ewes. The catalog for that library indicated it had once been owned by Starkey. Andrew Watson, *The Library of Sir Simonds D'Ewes*, 322.

350   volume containing the manuscript: BL Harl, 252.

353   known as the First Folio: "What Is a Shakespeare First Folio?" Folger Shakespeare Library (website), https://www.folger.edu/what-shakespeare-first-folio; "Shakespeare's First Folio," British Library (website), https://www.bl.uk/collection-items/shakespeares-first-folio; Andrea Mays, *The Millionaire and the Bard*, 22, 35–43.

353   eulogy by Ben Jonson: Mays, 46–47.

360   commissioned by David Garrick: "The Shakespeare sculpture at the British Library," *English and Drama* (blog), British Library (website), November 11, 2013, https://blogs.bl.uk/english-and-drama/2013/11/the-shakespeare-sculpture-at-the-british-library.html.

360   bronze sculpture of Sir Isaac Newton: "Isaac Newton sculpture by Eduardo Paolozzi," British Library (website), http://www.bl.uk/about-us/our-story/explore-the-building/isaac-newton-sculpture.

EPILOGUE

Quotations from *The Winter's Tale* in this chapter are as follows: "Exit, pursued by a bear": *TWT* 3.3.57; "never saw the heavens so dim": *TWT* 3.3.54–56; "How the poor souls roared": 3.3.96–99.

Quotations from Thomas North's *The Dial of Princes* (*Dial*) are as follows: "huge monster...two bears behind"; "a marvelous dark cloud": *Dial* 728; "Judges are so greedy": *Dial* 381.

361   written a comment: *The Dial* CUL f. 483; "description of the Monster": *Dial* CUL f. 482.

INDEX